Sound Recording Handbook

A U D I O · L I B R A R Y

Audio Production Techniques for Video
David Miles Huber

Handbook for Sound Engineers: The New Audio Cyclopedia
Glen Ballou, Editor

Recording Demo Tapes at Home
Bruce Bartlett (John Woram Audio Series)

How to Build Speaker Enclosures
Alexis Badmaieff and Don Davis

Introduction to Professional Recording Techniques
Bruce Bartlett (John Woram Audio Series)

John D. Lenk's Troubleshooting & Repair of Audio Equipment
John D. Lenk

Modern Recording Techniques, Third Edition
David M. Huber and Robert E. Runstein

Musical Applications of Microprocessors, Second Edition
Hal Chamberlin

Sound System Engineering, Second Edition
Don and Carolyn Davis

Microphone Manual: Design & Application
David Miles Huber

Principles of Digital Audio, Second Edition
Ken Pohlmann

Audio Technology Fundamentals *(forthcoming)*
Alan A. Cohen

Sound Recording Handbook

John M. Woram

HOWARD W. SAMS & COMPANY

A Division of Macmillan, Inc.
4300 West 62nd Street
Indianapolis, Indiana 46268 USA

International Standard Book Number: 0-672-22583-2
Library of Congress Catalog Card Number: 89-61436

Acquisitions Editors: *Greg Michael, Scott Arant*
Development Editor: *James Rounds*
Manuscript and Production Editor: *Amy M. Perry*
Illustrators: *T.R. Emrick, Wm. D. Basham, Sally Copenhaver,
    K&S Graphics*
Production Assistant: *J. Stephen Noe*
Cover Photo: *Robert Wolsch, New York*
Indexer: *John M. Woram*
Technical Reviewers: *Ken C. Pohlmann, David Miles Huber*
Compositor: *Cromer Graphics*

Printed in the United States of America

Trademarks

To Christina Marie
for working all that overtime
(so I could stay home and write a book).

Overview

1   Basic Audio Theory   *1*

2   Music, Electronics, and Psychoacoustics   *39*

3   Microphones   *61*

4   Special Purpose Microphones   *109*

5   Monitor Systems   *157*

6   Delay and Reverberation Systems   *205*

7   Equalization   *247*

8   Dynamic Range   *299*

9   Magnetic Tape and Tape Heads   *331*

10   Tape Transport Systems   *379*

11   Noise Reduction   *423*

12   Recording Consoles   *461*

A   SMPTE Time Code   *521*

B   Glossary   *533*

C   Abbreviations, Acronyms, and Symbols   *559*

D   Bibliography and References   *563*

Contents

Foreword   *xix*

Preface   *xxi*

Acknowledgments   *xxv*

1 Basic Audio Theory   *1*

Logarithms   *1*
    Common Logarithms   *2*
    Natural Logarithms   *2*
Audio Applications of Logarithms   *2*
    Decibel Notation   *3*
Trigonometric Functions   *5*
    Sine, Cosine, and Tangent   *6*
    Sinusoidal Waveforms   *7*
    A Sine Wave Application   *8*
Phase and Phase Shift   *11*
    Polarity   *13*
    Coherence   *13*
Acoustic Waveform   *14*
    Sound Pressure Wave   *16*
    Ideal Sound Source   *18*
    Radian and Steradian Measure   *22*

The Speed of Sound   *22*
Wavelength   *24*
Sound Intensity and Sound Power   *25*
Sound Pressure   *26*
Threshold of Hearing   *26*
Threshold of Pain   *27*
Range of Hearing   *27*
Sound Pressure Level in dB   *27*
Reflection, Refraction, and Diffraction   *27*
Reflection   *28*
Refraction   *28*
Diffraction   *29*
Cumulative Effects of Reflection, Refraction,
and Diffraction   *31*
The Sound Field   *32*
Near Field   *32*
Far Field   *33*
Standing Waves   *34*
Room Modes   *34*

2 **Music, Electronics, and Psychoacoustics**   *39*

Music and Frequency Perception   *40*
The Harmonic Series   *40*
Harmonic Structure   *40*
The Just Diatonic Scale   *42*
The Equal-Tempered Scale   *43*
Music and Engineering Frequency Comparisons   *45*
Harmonics in Music and Electronics   *47*
Fourier Series   *47*
Square Wave Analysis   *47*
Harmonic Distortion   *51*
Psychoacoustics   *52*
Equal Loudness Contours   *52*
Definitions   *54*
Localization Parameters   *54*

3 **Microphones**   *61*

The Dynamic Microphone   *62*
The Moving-Coil Microphone   *62*
The Ribbon Microphone   *62*
The Capacitor Microphone   *64*
The Conventional Capacitor Microphone   *65*
The Electret Capacitor Microphone   *67*
Capacitor Microphone Power Supplies   *67*

External Power Supply   67
Phantom Power Supply System   70
Directional Characteristics   74
Polar Equations and Patterns   74
The Omnidirectional Microphone   78
The Bidirectional Microphone   80
The Unidirectional Microphone   83
Single-Element Unidirectional Microphone   85
Polar Response Comparisons   87
Three-Dimensional Polar Patterns   88
Microphone Response Parameters   88
Diffuse Field Response   88
Random-Energy Response (RER)   90
Random-Energy Efficiency (REE)   91
Directivity Factor (DRF)   92
Distance Factor (DSF)   93
Unidirectional Index (UDI)   93
Front-to-Total Ratio (FTR)   94
Variations on the Cardioid Response   94
The Subcardioid Microphone   94
The Supercardioid Microphone   95
The Hypercardioid Microphone   97
Review of Polar Patterns   97
Polar Patterns and Microphone Selection   99
Some Further Directional Characteristics   102
Proximity Effect   102
Off-Axis Coloration   103
Polar Pattern Tradeoff Considerations   104
Polar Patterns Expressed in dB Attenuation   106

4 Special Purpose Microphones 109

Microphone Response Patterns   110
Cartesian Coordinate System   110
Combining Microphone Outputs   112
Stereo Microphone Theory   113
The M-S Microphone   115
Sum and Difference Patterns   119
Working Backward: Sum-and-Difference to M-S   122
Mono and Stereo Pickup Angles   123
M-S Summary   129
Other Stereo Microphone Systems   130
X-Y Pair   131
The Blumlein Pair   132
ORTF System   133
NOS System   133
Spaced Microphones, A-B Pair   133

Binaural System   *133*
Multimicrophone Systems   *136*
Stereo Microphone Cable Requirements   *137*
Other Microphone Combinations   *137*
Creating a Pure Cardioid Pattern   *137*
Two Undirectional Microphones Placed
Back to Back   *139*
Multipattern Microphones   *140*
Two Unidirectional Microphones Oriented at Less than
180 Degrees   *141*
The Soundfield Microphone   *143*
Boundary Layer Recording   *145*
Transformer Interface   *153*

5 Monitor Systems *157*

Energy Conversion   *158*
Speaker Design Categories   *159*
The Dynamic Loudspeaker   *159*
The Capacitor, or Electrostatic, Loudspeaker   *160*
Some Useful Loudspeaker Parameters   *161*
Resonance Frequency   *161*
Cutoff Frequency   *162*
Directivity   *162*
Coverage Angle   *164*
Room Boundaries and the Ideal Sound Source   *165*
Full or Free Space   *165*
Half Space   *167*
One-Quarter Space   *167*
One-Eighth Space   *167*
Room Boundaries and the Practical Loudspeaker System   *167*
Speaker Directional Characteristics   *168*
The Direct Radiator   *170*
The Direct Radiator Enclosure   *171*
The Infinite Baffle   *172*
The Flat Baffle   *173*
The Open-Back Cabinet (Folded Baffle)   *175*
The Closed-Back Cabinet   *175*
The Vented Cabinet   *178*
The Indirect Radiator   *178*
Compression Drivers   *179*
The Indirect Radiator Horn   *180*
Nomenclature   *180*
Exponential Horn   *183*
Hyperbolic Horn   *185*
Conical Horn   *185*
Parabolic Horn   *186*

Horn Selection Criteria *187*
    Practical Horn Designs *188*
Loudspeaker Systems *191*
    Crossover Networks *192*
    Network Cutoff and Crossover Frequencies *195*
    Time Delay Considerations *198*

6 Delay and Reverberation Systems 205

The Sound Field *206*
    The Signal Paths in a Sound Field *206*
    The Sound Field in the Typical Room *210*
Delay and Equalization *218*
Distance Localization *218*
The Recorded Sound Field *219*
Direct Sound *220*
Echo *220*
    Delay Systems *221*
    The Haas Effect *223*
    Echo-Related Delay Applications *225*
Reverberation *225*
    The Acoustic Reverberation Chamber *226*
    Spring Reverberation Systems *228*
    Reverberation Plates *228*
    Digital Reverberation Systems *230*
    Stereo Reverberation *231*
    Recording and Mixdown with Reverberation *233*
Console Control of Echo and Reverberation *233*
Additional Delay Applications *235*
    Delaying Microphone Outputs *235*
    Flanging *236*
    Phasing *238*
    Doubling and Chorus Effects *238*
    Panning *239*
    Sound Reinforcement *241*
Echo, Reverberation, and Control Room Acoustics *242*
    LEDE Control Room Design *244*
    Close-Field Monitoring *244*

7 Equalization 247

Definitions *247*
Calculating Cutoff Frequencies *250*
Expressing Bandwidth in Octaves *251*
Equalizer Categories *251*
Filter Design *252*

First-Order Filters   *254*
  Lowpass Filter   *254*
  Highpass Filter   *258*
  Bandpass Filter   *259*
  Bandstop (Notch) Filter   *261*
  Shelving Filter   *261*
First-Order Filter Applications   *264*
  Tape Recorder Equalization   *264*
Second-Order Filters   *267*
  Second-Order Filter Amplitude Response   *267*
  The Effect of *Q* on Output Response   *268*
Symmetric and Nonsymmetric Filters   *268*
  Symmetric Filter   *268*
  Nonsymmetric Filter   *268*
  Series and Parallel Resonance   *272*
Phase Shift and Damping   *276*
  Phase Shift in Second-Order Filters   *276*
  Phase Response in a Recording-Studio Equalizer   *278*
  The Perception of Phase Shift   *283*
  Damping   *286*
Commercially Available Equalizers   *287*
  Rotary-Knob Equalizer   *287*
  Parametric Equalizer   *289*
  Graphic Equalizer   *289*
  Paragraphic Equalizer   *290*
  Digital Equalizer   *290*
Equalizer Applications   *293*
  Signal-Correction Equalization   *296*
  Signal-Enhancement Equalization   *297*
  A Few Concluding Words of Advice   *297*

8 Dynamic Range   *299*

Dynamic Range   *299*
  Signal-to-Noise Ratio   *300*
Room and Studio Gain Riding   *301*
Electronic Gain Riding   *302*
  The Compressor   *303*
  The Limiter   *310*
  The Expander   *311*
  The Noise Gate   *313*
  Combining Compression, Limiting, and Expansion   *316*
  Summary of Compression/Expansion Ratios   *317*
Output Level and Gain Calculations   *317*
Side-Chain Signal Processing   *319*
  Compression   *319*
  Expansion Using Side-Chain Compression   *320*

Side-Chain Control of Gain   *321*
Keyable Expanders   *322*
Compressor and Expander Applications   *324*
Program Compression   *324*
Voice-Over Compression   *326*
Frequency-Dependent Compression   *326*

9 Magnetic Tape and Tape Heads   *331*

Physical Properties of Magnetic Tape   *332*
Base Material   *332*
Magnetic Coating   *333*
Back Coating   *334*
Slitting   *334*
The Recording Process   *334*
Domain Theory   *335*
Saturation   *335*
Terminology   *337*
Magnetization vs. Recording Field   *340*
Bias   *343*
DC Bias   *343*
AC Bias   *344*
Bias and Recorded Performance Specifications   *345*
Optimum Bias Setting   *347*
Tape Erasure   *350*
Print-Through   *354*
Print-Through Reduction   *355*
Low-Print Tapes   *355*
Record and Playback Head Characteristics   *355*
Gap Dimensions   *356*
Head Design Details   *358*
Head Block   *359*
Erase Head   *359*
Record Head   *359*
Bias Level and Gap Length   *360*
Record Head Response   *360*
Playback Head   *360*
Playback Losses   *361*
Playback Head Response   *364*
Record and Playback Equalization   *365*
High-Frequency Playback Equalization   *366*
NAB Standard Reproducing Characteristic   *366*
IEC Frequency Response Standard   *368*
CCIR Equalization   *369*
NAB-IEC Comparisons   *369*
AES Recommended Practice   *369*
Summary of Reproduce Characteristics   *370*

Tape Recorder Calibration   *370*
   Playback Calibration Tape   *371*
   Reference Fluxivity Section   *372*
   Azimuth and Phase Adjustment Section   *372*
   Frequency Response Section   *374*
Playback Calibration Procedure   *375*
Record Calibration Procedure   *375*
High Output Tapes   *376*
Elevated Level Calibration Tapes   *376*

10 Tape Transport Systems   *379*

The Tape Transport System   *379*
Tape Drive System   *380*
Capstan Drive Systems   *382*
   Hysteresis Synchronous Motors   *382*
   Servo Control Drive System   *383*
Alternate Tape Drive Systems   *385*
   Vacuum Bin Transport System   *386*
   Dual-Capstan Systems   *387*
   Pressure Rollerless Capstan System   *389*
   Closed Loop Systems   *389*
Tape Sensing Systems   *389*
Reel Motors   *390*
   Reel Braking System   *392*
Tape Transport Control Systems   *392*
   The Basic Transport Controls   *394*
   Additional Transport Controls   *394*
   Tape Motion Specifications   *398*
Remote Control of Tape Transport and Electronic Systems   *400*
   Ready/Safe Mode   *400*
   Monitor Mode   *401*
   Time Reading Functions   *404*
   Tape Search Functions   *407*
   Rehearse Mode   *408*
Tape Recorder Alignment Procedures   *409*
Mechanical System Alignment   *410*
   Cleaning Procedures   *410*
   Head Adjustments   *410*
Electronic System Alignment   *412*
   Alignment Controls   *413*
Digitally Controlled Alignment Systems   *414*
   Alignment Procedure   *414*
   Automatic Alignment   *417*
   Summary   *418*
Synchronous Recording Techniques   *418*
   Overdubbing   *418*

Synchronous Recording   *419*
Bouncing Tracks   *421*

11 Noise Reduction   *423*

Noise Characteristics of Magnetic Recording Tape   *423*
  Low-Level Noise   *423*
  High-Level Distortion   *424*
Noise Masking   *424*
Basic Noise Reduction Systems   *425*
  Dynamic and Static Signal Processing   *426*
  Single-Ended Signal Processing   *426*
  Complementary Signal Processing   *426*
  Dynamic Complementary Signal Processing   *427*
Single-Ended Noise Reduction Systems   *428*
  Mute Switch   *428*
  Gain Riding   *428*
  The Noise Gate   *428*
  Static Filtering   *428*
  Dynamic Noise Suppressor   *429*
  Burwen Dynamic Noise Filter   *429*
  Spectral Program Filter   *431*
  Tick and Pop Removers   *432*
  Summary   *433*
Double-Ended Noise Reduction Systems   *433*
  EMT NoisEx Recording System   *434*
  Dolby Noise Reduction Systems   *434*
  Noise Reduction on Film   *446*
  dbx Noise Reduction Systems   *446*
  Burwen Noise Eliminator System   *451*
  Telcom Noise Reduction System   *451*
Noise Reduction System Comparisons   *452*
  Linear and Nonlinear Companding   *454*
  Gain Errors in Companding Systems   *454*
  System Compatibility   *457*
Noise Reduction/Tape Recorder Interface Requirements   *457*

12 Recording Consoles   *461*

Recording Consoles   *461*
  Console Bus   *463*
  Console Operating Modes   *463*
Console Design Styles   *464*
Rotary Knob Console   *465*
Split-Section Console   *465*
  Signal Flow   *465*

Inline Console   *467*
    Inline Console Modules   *467*
    Other Variations from Split-Section Design   *471*
I/O (Input/Output) Module   *473*
    Channel and Monitor Paths   *473*
    Channel Path Controls   *478*
    Channel Path Feeds   *482*
    Echo (or Auxiliary) Path Controls   *488*
    Cue Path Controls   *490*
    Monitor Path Controls   *490*
    Additional I/O Module Functions   *492*
Master Module Section   *497*
Master Echo Module   *498*
    Echo Send Section   *498*
    Echo Return Section   *498*
Communication Module   *502*
    Master Cue Send Section   *502*
    Talkback System   *504*
    Signal Generator   *504*
Master Monitor Module   *506*
    Master Monitor Signal Monitoring   *506*
    Monitor Override Modes   *509*
Console Patch Points   *510*
Summary   *513*

A **SMPTE Time Code**   *521*

B **Glossary**   *533*

C **Abbreviations, Acronyms, and Symbols**   *559*
Abbreviations and Acronyms   *559*
Frequently Encountered Greek Letters   *562*
Mathematical Symbols   *562*
Mathematical Prefixes   *562*

D **Bibliography and References**   *563*

Index   *571*

Foreword

This book is about the foundations of audio technology. The concepts, mathematics, and techniques described here provide a launching pad to advanced applications in audio, acoustics, and media production.

Much has been learned about the science of sound in the past few years, especially as it relates to the industry. As discoveries have evolved into product designs and then grown to consumer acceptance, the industry has constantly had to reexamine itself and redefine its multilayered identity. The only thing that hasn't really changed is the challenge to use all of the tools available to create great sound reproduction.

Not too many years ago, all that was known about audio technology fit within a handful of books. Today, vast libraries of books, tapes, trade magazines, CD-ROMs, and whatnot are easily available on the subject. With all of that wisdom out there, what is the entry-level person to choose for introductory understanding?

The *Sound Recording Handbook* is one of those friendly classic books that is a great place to start for an educational foundation in audio. It's also a great place to come back to for the answers to so many common questions.

John Woram's roots are deep in education. As an author, John penned one of the industry's first best-sellers, *The Recording Studio Handbook,* which defined the contemporary recording environment and served as the principal text for many courses on the subject.

As an editor, Woram ran the editorial desk at *db Magazine* for many years, and brought to it a warmth and humor previously rare in industry magazines.

And as an educator, John directed the Music Engineering program at the University of Miami School of Music, the first program of its kind.

There are few recording industry professionals who haven't learned something important from John Woram at some point in their careers.

Keep reading,

David Schwartz

Editor-in-Chief
Mix Magazine

Preface

Read just about any interview and you'll soon come to the part where the interviewer asks the authority of the month something like "Where do you predict the (whatever it is) will go in the next xx years?" The answer is always something like "Well, the way I see it," followed by something terribly profound, or at least mildly awesome.

My very first employer, the late Major Alexander de Seversky, once wrote something to the effect that if you ask enough "experts" what's going to happen next, the odds are that the wild guess of one of them will turn out to be correct and the man will be called a genius (at least until his next guess). Some years later, Bob Newhart tried a variation on this theme by placing an infinite number of monkeys in front of an infinite number of typewriters. Eventually one of them actually typed something that was readable. Newhart went on to even greater things; history does not record what happened to the monkey. I learned a great lesson from all this: never predict what's going to happen next, or worse, type it out on paper. You may look clever for a moment or two, but eventually you'll be just another monkey. It's much safer to look backward and report about what has happened. For unless one lives in one of those countries where the history books are periodically "revised," this is a lot less risky than writing about things that are still to come.

This brings us (or at least me) to the professional recording industry, where a lot has happened over the past quarter-century or so. Without too much fear of being proved wrong later, I can say that some twenty-five years ago there actually were recording engineers alive who had recorded a complete album on something less than two inches wide. In those technologically simpler days, the studio newcomer needed little more than a good ear, an enthusiastic attitude, and a cheerful willingness to start at the bottom—the old apprentice system that worked for Michelangelo and Leonardo and for quite a few recording engineers.

But times change. Today the well-equipped studio is not the place to look for work with no credentials other than a great personality and the ability to tune one's own guitar. The modern studio is in fact now as far removed from its forebears as Kitty Hawk from Cape Canaveral. And as at the latter launch site, one now needs to have done some serious homework if one wishes to get off the ground in style.

And this brings us (that is, me again) to the subject of this book. It's chock full of all the dull stuff that may help some of its readers decide the recording industry is not really where they want to be after all. It contains very little (all right, none) of the glamorous aspects of life behind the big board. That comes later on from the reader's own personal experiences once safely arrived at higher ground. Meanwhile, the present text will help serve as a guidebook through the surrounding swamps. It may be one of the few books on the market that has not been written for everyone from the preadolescent to the postdoctoral candidate. That is, it does not contain a little something for everybody. Instead, it should be of interest only to the intelligent adult reader who is ready to put a little time into learning a little something about recording technology.

Does that mean math? Yes, there is some here, but it's kept within reason. Much of it can be skipped by the reader who would rather not cope with the various equations. However, others may find the math helpful in proving that the various facts presented here were not pulled out of a magic hat by the author. Another reason for the math is that most if not all of the many graphs found herein were first plotted on an IBM personal computer, using the accompanying equations. Therefore, the reader who wishes to dig a little deeper (and/or who has the proper lack of respect for the printed page) is encouraged to prove for him or herself that a filter really does fall off at n dB per octave, or whatever else it is that needs to be proved. Given a little familiarity with BASIC or some other computer language, the equations can be used to generate the necessary graphs. And for the reader who wishes more background information, there are ample references to the many sources from which much of the information presented here was derived.

This book bucks present wisdom by almost ignoring digital technology. In fact, it even comes reasonably close to ignoring analog technology too, although there is some method to this madness. To cover everything that needs to be covered, and then to describe both analog and digital implementations, would make this a very big book—much bigger than it already is. Therefore the treatment limits itself to the basic conceptual or operational aspects of the various links in the signal path, with little regard to the format in which the signal happens to be passing by. The notable exceptions are the chapters on magnetic tape (Chapter 9) and noise reduction (Chapter 11), in which the characteristics of the analog storage medium are examined in some detail.

Within reason the various links in the audio signal path, and the chapters in this book, may be studied in just about any order that suits the reader's interest (or the instructor's whim). The basic background information in the first two chapters may be skipped entirely by those who would rather get down to business first. Chapters 3 and 4, which are on microphones, should be read in sequence, since the latter is based on much information presented in the former. After that, most of the remaining chapters are reasonably independent units which don't depend on each other for support. However, the tape storage link presents a few organizational difficulties, since in order to discuss a tape recorder some knowledge of tape is required. Needless to say, in order to discuss tape, some knowledge of a tape recorder is required. To further complicate matters, noise reduction systems are a logical extension of compressors and expanders and no doubt should follow a chapter on such devices. But such systems are found at either end of a tape recorder, and without a basic understanding of the limitations of magnetic tape, a chapter on noise reduction might appear to be somewhat out of context. Therefore, it would seem that of all the chapters in which these topics are covered, each one should be read before the others. A neat trick if you can pull it off, but otherwise I suggest a quick scan of all of them, followed by a closer reading in the sequence in which they appear here. And then, go back and try those first two chapters.

John Woram

Rockville Centre
New York

Acknowledgments

I wonder how much of a deduction I could take if I donated my Rolodex card file to some charitable institution? I think it cost me about 25 bucks, not counting the 25 or so years it took to fill it with the names of all those who know all there is to know about all one wants to know about (provided one wants to know only about pro audio of course).

The old Rolodex really got a workout over the past year as this book began to take its shape. There was always some "minor detail" that needed to be clarified (or in a few cases, explained in its entirety). A quick turn of the wheel never failed to turn up the right source for just about any question I could imagine. Fortunately for the cover art—to say nothing of author ego—none of my entries demanded equal billing. And, depending on how the following pages are received by the public, some may even be uncomfortable to find their names listed below. Nevertheless, the many people who helped me to write this opus must be cited here, if only as testimony to their enduring patience and goodwill.

To list everyone who helped would make this section quite long, so I take the easy way out by thanking as a group all those manufacturers who generously contributed photographs and technical literature to back up the text. In each case, I hope the appropriate illustration credit serves as a proper "thank you" note.

But there are many others whose aid went far beyond the product shot, and I hope I have remembered all of them here (*and* spelled their names correctly). Listed more or less in the order in which their help appears are my thanks to the following people:

To Russ Hamm and Jerry Graham at Gotham Audio, for those endless discussions of stereo microphone techniques, and to Jerry Bruck at Posthorn Recordings for the information about subcardioid microphones. And again to Jerry Graham for becoming the default photo librarian/research assistant/ historian and general source of information on more than just microphones.

To Jeffrey Gusman and Michael Nicoletti at Yamaha Communication Center for their help, and for the use of the Yamaha Research Center in exploring some of the fine points of signal processing.

To Dennis Bohn at Rane Corporation, who volunteered to read the chapter on equalizers and whose help made the chapter a lot stronger than it otherwise might have been.

To John G. (Jay) McKnight at Magnetic Reference Laboratory, who cheerfully patched up some of my more "creative" attempts at explaining the unexplainable.

Kenneth Gundry at Dolby Laboratories served as an excellent guide to the finer points of noise reduction and spectral recording. Thanks also to Win Craft at Carillon Technology for help with the transfer equations that were required for the graphs of the dbx system.

At Sound Workshop, Michael Tapes helped with the chapter on consoles and allowed his console to be used as a model for some of the signal flow examples.

To Sherwin Becker at SMPTE, who granted permission to reproduce the SMPTE Time Code in its entirety as an appendix.

In addition to the above list, there are a few colleagues whose help cannot be easily linked to a specific topic. For example, thanks are due

To Al Grundy, Institute of Audio Research, for general counseling on many of the equations that were used here and there to generate a graph or two and to explain (and I hope not confuse) a point.

To Patricia Macdonald at the Audio Engineering Society, for finding many AES papers that were needed by yesterday please.

To Kenneth Pohlmann at the University of Miami, who read the whole manuscript and made enough comments in the margin to make me seriously consider going into some other line of work. All errors remaining in the text are of course his fault. (Pohlmann did not get the chance to check this page.)

To Brian Michael Seltzer, Esq., attorney, friend, and sometime literary critic, whose help long ago passed far beyond the contractual.

To Hal Keith at K & S Graphics, for his aid in beating the deadline by turning out all the graphs in record time. And, especially if the cover photo is what attracted the reader to this book in the first place, then photographer Robert Wolsch deserves a special note of thanks.

And last but not least, my thanks to all those at Howard W. Sams & Company who had a hand in this (and no doubt sometimes wished they hadn't). From Fred Amich to Scott Arant, Wendy Ford, Don Herrington, Jim Rounds—and especially to Amy Perry for her meticulous attention to detail—my thanks to all for putting up with the trials and tribulations of this "little project." And to Jim Hill, *now* can I get that 735i?

1 Basic Audio Theory

This chapter contains mostly the dull stuff needed to survive the rest of the book. Certainly not intended to be the definitive dissertation on basic audio concepts, it seeks rather to offer a quick background review for readers who need a little brush-up on the math and physics of audio. A good understanding of much of the following material is essential to what follows, although from time to time a little information is offered that may be of peripheral interest only.

Because some of the topics presented here have almost no relation to others which follow, no attempt has been made to invent transitions between subject headings. In the interest of getting done with the chapter and moving on, its contents should be viewed as a series of often unrelated topics, any of which may be skipped by the reader who is already familiar with the subject heading.

Logarithms

Anyone who has survived high school has surely encountered a number raised to a certain "power," as in, say, "x is equal to 10 to the 5th power," or simply, $x = 10^5$. Those whose calculator batteries have died find the value of x the hard way; multiply 10 by itself, five times ($10 \times 10 \times 10 \times 10 \times 10 = 100,000$). Therefore, $10^6 = 1,000,000$, and so on. But, what about $10^{5.371}$? How does one multiply 10 by itself 5.371 times?

One doesn't. Instead, we turn to logarithmic notation, in which the *logarithm* (log) of a number, x, is defined as the exponent to which a *base* (e.g., 10 in the decimal system) must be raised in order to equal that number. Thus,

$$x = B^L$$

where

  B = the *base*
  L = the *logarithm* (log)

In English, we may say that the base-B logarithm of x is L, or

$$L = \log_B x \qquad \text{("L is the log of x")}$$

Common Logarithms

In the familiar decimal (base 10) system, the log of a number is therefore the exponent to which 10 must be raised. The term *common logarithm* is used to describe a base-10 logarithm.

By observation, it should be clear that $10^{5.371}$ must be greater than 10^5 and less than 10^6. Fortunately, the mathematical process of finding the actual value of y need not concern us here. We may instead rely on a calculator or computer for assistance, either of which will show that $10^{5.371} = 234{,}963.282$

This may be verified on the calculator by entering the number and pressing the *log* button on the keypad. The display should indicate the common log of 5.371. However, the computer will not display the same number, since a system with a different base is used.

Natural Logarithms

The *natural logarithm* (ln) system uses a base of ϵ (*epsilon* = the logarithmic constant 2.71828), and is used by most personal computer systems. Therefore, the statement PRINT LOG(234963.282) will display 12.367 instead. In other words, the natural logarithm of 234,963.282 is 12.367, or $2.71828^{12.367} = 234{,}963.282$. To convert from natural to common logarithms, simply divide the displayed natural log by the natural log of 10, which is 2.303 (12.367/2.303 = 5.371).

Note: To avoid discrepancies with the results shown here, use the calculator's ϵ^x key (with $x = 1$) to enter the value for *epsilon*. Or enter 2.7182818254 by hand.

Audio Applications of Logarithms

The common logarithm system is widely used in plotting frequency response, where frequency is usually plotted along the horizontal (x) axis using a logarithmic scale. For example, the logarithms of a few audio frequencies are listed below.

Frequency (Hz)	Logarithm	Frequency (Hz)	Logarithm
10	1	20	1.301
100	2	200	2.301
1,000	3	2,000	3.301
10,000	4	20,000	4.301

Note that for every doubling of frequency, the logarithm increases by a constant (0.301), and that for a tenfold increase, the log is incremented by 1. Figure 1-1 shows a typical sheet of semi-log graph paper in which the *x* axis is plotted according to the log of a number. The graph is called *semi-log* because only one axis is plotted logarithmically; the other is a linear scale.

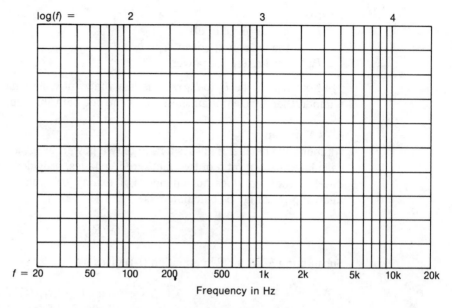

Figure 1-1. Semi-log graph paper. The *x* axis plots frequency on a logarithmic scale, while the *y* axis is linear.

The common logarithm is an important part of decibel notation, as explained in the section immediately below. And both common and natural logs will turn up in many other professional audio applications, several of which are to be found elsewhere in this book.

Decibel Notation

As the list above suggests, the logarithm may be used to reduce a wide ranging quantity to a more manageable notation. As noted, each tenfold increase simply raises the value of the log by 1, making the logarithm an ideal means to keep track of power changes that may occur over a range of some 10 million to one. As a further consideration, it is helpful to express a power level in terms of a ratio, P_1/P_0, where the numerator is the measured power, and the denominator is a known zero-reference power. By so doing, the following three conditions should be obvious:

Ratio of P_1/P_0	Significance
> 1	a power gain
= 1	no change in power
< 1	a power loss

To accomplish these goals, power level is measured in terms of the *decibel* (abbreviated dB), which is defined as ten times the logarithm of the power ratio just described. In other words,

$$L = 10 \log (P_1/P_0) \qquad \text{(1-1)}$$

where
  L = power level, in dB
  P_1 = the measured power
  P_0 = zero-reference power

Note that if the P_1-to-P_0 ratio is less than unity, its logarithm is a negative number, thereby clearly indicating that the decibel value represents a power loss.

dBV Notation

Although the decibel is always a ratio of two power levels, it may be conveniently calculated from a ratio of two measured voltages, provided the resistance of the device under test does not change. For example, if voltage and resistance are known, power may be calculated as

$$P = E^2/R$$

Substituting E^2/R for P in equation (1-1) gives us

$$\begin{aligned} L \quad &= 10 \log (E_1^2/R_1)/(E_0^2/R_0) \qquad \text{(1-2)} \\ &= 10 \log (E_1^2/E_0^2) \qquad \text{(since } R_1 = R_0\text{)} \\ &= 10 \log (E_1/E_0)^2 \\ &= 20 \log (E_1/E_0) \end{aligned}$$

where
  E_1 = measured voltage
  E_0 = zero-reference voltage

The notation *dBV* is used to specify that the zero-reference voltage is 1 volt.

dBu Notation

In pretransistor circuitry, most audio lines were terminated in a 600-ohm impedance. In such a circuit, a zero-decibel reference level at one milliwatt is reached when there is a 0.775-volt drop across 600 ohms, as seen here:

$$E = (PR)^{1/2} = (10^{-3} \cdot 600)^{1/2} = 0.775 \text{ volt}$$

Although the 600-ohm line is no longer in wide use, the notation *dBu* is still used to specify a zero-reference voltage of 0.775 volt. In some texts, *dBv* (note lowercase *v*) has been used, but this is easy to confuse with *dBV* and is rarely seen in modern usage.

dBm Notation

In circuit theory, the zero-reference level is usually one milliwatt (10^{-3} watt). However, since other reference levels are sometimes applied, the notation *dBm* is used to clearly indicate that one milliwatt is the zero-reference level.

The use of *dBm* to indicate a one-milliwatt reference level became widespread at a time when the 600-ohm line was practically an industry standard. As a consequence, the notation is often thought to be tied to both one milliwatt *and* 600 ohms. However, it is not, and the dBm may be correctly used with any convenient resistance or impedance.

Trigonometric Functions

In this and subsequent chapters, frequent reference is made to the sine (sin), cosine (cos), and tangent (tan) of an angle. Each of these *trigonometric functions* is nothing more than a ratio of the lengths of two sides of a right triangle. Assuming one side and one acute angle are already known, the appropriate functions may be used to calculate the values of the two other sides. Since one of the sides may often represent the amplitude of an audio signal or the sensitivity of a microphone, a basic understanding of all three functions is quite helpful.

It is customary to label each angle of a triangle with an uppercase letter and the side opposite that angle with the corresponding lowercase letter, as shown by the right triangles in Figure 1-2, both drawn with angles *A*, *B*, and *C* and sides *a*, *b*, and *c*. The *hypotenuse* is defined as the side opposite the right angle, and for any angle within such a triangle, its *opposite side* is the side that does not make contact with the angle, the *adjacent side* is the side (other than the hypotenuse) that does. Thus with respect to angle *A*, the opposite and adjacent sides of the triangle are sides *a* and *b*, respectively. If angle *B* were being considered, the opposite and adjacent sides would be *b* and *a*.

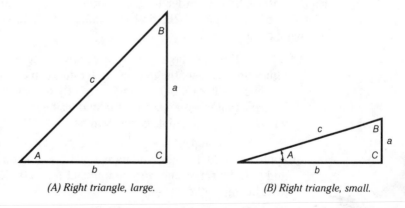

(A) Right triangle, large.   (B) Right triangle, small.

Figure 1-2. The component parts of two right triangles.

Sine, Cosine, and Tangent

The three trigonometric functions are defined as

$$\text{sin} = \text{opposite side} \div \text{hypotenuse}$$
$$\text{cos} = \text{adjacent side} \div \text{hypotenuse}$$
$$\text{tan} = \text{opposite side} \div \text{adjacent side}$$

and therefore, in Figure 1-2,

$$\sin A = a/c \text{ and } \sin B = b/c$$
$$\cos A = b/c \quad\quad \cos B = a/c$$
$$\tan A = a/b \quad\quad \tan B = b/a$$

In many problems which involve trigonometric functions, one angle and one side of the triangle are known, and it is necessary to find the value of one, or both, of the other sides. Therefore, the equations above may be rewritten as seen here, in order to find the value of an unknown side:

$$a = c \sin A, \quad \text{or } a = c \cos B$$
$$b = c \cos A, \quad \text{or } b = c \sin B$$
$$c = a / \sin A, \text{ or } c = b / \sin B$$

Range of Values for Trigonometric Functions

The value of a trigonometric function can certainly be found the hard way: construct a triangle with protractor and straightedge, measure the various sides, and then calculate the required function as described above. However, for our purposes it is far more efficient to consult a chart of trigonometric functions, or better yet, to use a calculator or computer.

However, before doing so it might be helpful to solve a few examples by simple observation, in order to get a better idea of what to expect. Using the triangle seen in Figure 1-2B, find the values of all three functions under the following conditions:

1. $A = 0°$. First, let the angle, A, be *almost* 0 degrees, as shown in the figure. In this case, the a/c and a/b ratios (sin and tan) are both almost 0, while the b/c ratio (cos) is almost 1. By observation it should therefore be clear that when angle A actually does become 0, its sine and tangent will both be zero and its cosine will be 1.

2. $B = 90°$. As angle A approaches 0, angle B in the same triangle approaches 90 degrees, and its sine, cosine, and tangent approach 1, 0 and ∞ (infinity) respectively, and in fact reach these values when angle B does become 90 degrees.

3. $A = 45°$. When A is 45 degrees, B is also 45 degrees and sides a and b are therefore equal to each other. This means that the hypotenuse, c, is equal to $1.414a$ (or $1.414b$). Therefore, the trigonometric functions are

$$\sin 45° \ = \ a/1.414a \ = \ 0.707$$
$$\cos 45° \ = \ b/1.414b \ = \ 0.707$$
$$\tan 45° \ = \ a/b \qquad \ = \ 1.000$$

When evaluating an angle that varies from 0 to 360 degrees, the angle is often identified by the letter θ (Greek *theta*). Therefore, we may say that as θ rotates from 0 to 360 degrees, sin θ increases from 0 to 1, then returns to 0, decreases to -1, and eventually returns to 0 again. At the same time, cos θ ranges from 1 to 0 to -1.

Table 1-1 lists the values of a few trigonometric functions as the angle increases from 0 to 360 degrees.

Table 1-1. Some Trigonometric Functions

Angle (°)	Sin	Cos	Tan
0	0	1	0
45	0.707	0.707	1
90	1	0	∞
135	0.707	-0.707	-1
180	0	-1	0
225	-0.707	-0.707	1
270	-1	0	∞
315	-0.707	0.707	-1
360	0	1	0

The Graph of a Trigonometric Function

When any trigonometric function is plotted on a linear scale, the resultant curve will be as shown in one of the parts of Figure 1-3, each of which shows three complete 0–360 degree cycles. Note that the sine and cosine (Figures 1-3A and 1-3B) functions differ only in the location at which each curve crosses the zero axis. The tangent (Figure 1-3C) function passes through infinity at 90 degrees, so only a portion of its curve can be shown in the illustration.

Sinusoidal Waveforms

Note that the only differences between the sine and cosine waves in Figure 1-3 are the horizontal location at which each one passes through the zero axis and the points at which maximum positive and negative amplitudes are reached. Due to their common characteristic shape, either one may be referred to as a *sinusoidal* waveform.

In the following sections, most descriptions of various properties of the sine wave apply as well to the cosine wave.

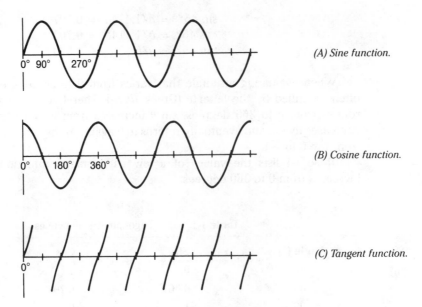

(A) Sine function.

(B) Cosine function.

(C) Tangent function.

Figure 1-3. A graph of the trigonometric functions.

A Sine Wave Application

An immediate application of the sine function is found in the calculation of the instantaneous amplitude of an audio frequency. To understand how the sine function is applied, first consider the simple electric generator shown in Figure 1-4A.

For ease of explanation, the illustration shows a single conductor passing through a magnetic field. An electric current is induced in the conductor as it cuts through the magnetic lines of force, which are shown as dashed lines in the illustration. If the conductor moves back and forth repeatedly, the current flow within it also alternates direction, and thus we have a rather primitive alternating-current generator. The generator may be improved by rotating the conductor through 360 degrees within the magnetic field, as shown in Figure 1-4B.

As the conductor rotates within the magnetic field, its direction with respect to the lines of force continuously alternates. Various points (p_1, p_2, etc.) show the conductor at 30-degree increments of rotation angle. When the conductor is either at point p_1 or p_7, it is at that instant moving vertically and therefore it cuts through no lines of force. By contrast, as it passes point p_4 or p_{10}, the conductor cuts through the maximum number of lines of force. As a result, the current induced in the conductor increases from zero at p_1 to a positive maximum at p_4, decreases to zero at p_7, continues to its negative maximum at p_{10} and then returns to zero when the conductor returns to p_1.

At any instant, the current is directly proportional to the conductor's vertical height above a horizontal reference line drawn through points p_1 and p_7. The greater the height, the more lines of force are being cut, and therefore, the higher the current flow through the conductor, and the higher the resultant voltage measured at the generator output. Although a plot of the generator's output current or voltage might be drawn by measuring and recording these heights at every angle from 0 to 360 degrees, there is an easier way.

Amplitude

Figure 1-4C is an enlarged view of the conditions at one instant during the rotation. Note that the illustration closely resembles the right triangles shown in Figure 1-2. Therefore, the vertical side of this triangle may be calculated simply by using the sine function.

$$e = E_m \sin A$$

where
$\quad e\quad$ = voltage when the conductor is at angle A

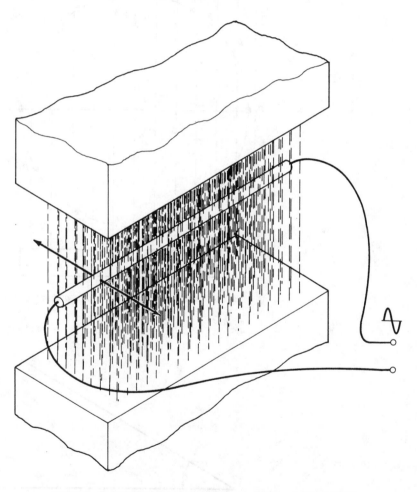

(A) A current is induced in the conductor as it moves back and forth within the magnetic field.

Figure 1-4. A simple electric generator.

E_m = magnitude of the maximum voltage

A = the instantaneous angle

For ease of calculation, E_m may be assumed to be equal to 1. Therefore, in the graph of $E_m \sin \theta$, the instantaneous voltage as the conductor—and consequently angle A—rotates from 0 to 360 degrees, is the familiar sine wave shown above in Figure 1-3A.

Frequency

To make a graph of the sine wave function more useful, it is convenient to mark

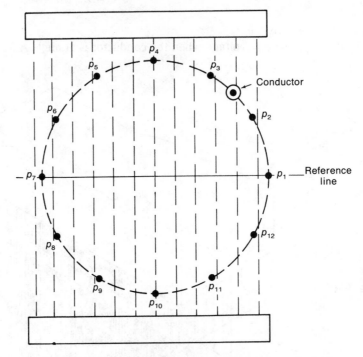

(B) The conductor may also be rotated within the magnetic field.

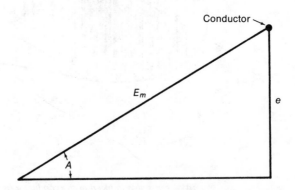

(C) A detail view of the conductor at one instant in its rotation within the field.

Figure 1-4 *(continued)*

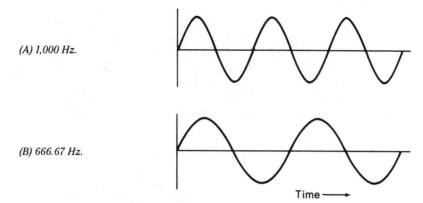

(A) 1,000 Hz.

(B) 666.67 Hz.

Time ⟶

Figure 1-5. The output waveforms from two devices
rotating at differing frequencies.

off the horizontal axis in units of time. For example, Figure 1-5 shows the output
waveforms of two devices measured over an interval of three milliseconds. Note
that within this time, one device makes three complete revolutions, while the
other completes only two revolutions. Although it's true that one device has
therefore rotated through 1080 degrees while the other has passed through 720
degrees, it's more informative to express such outputs in terms of *frequency*; that
is, the number of revolutions, or cycles, that each device passes through within
the same unit of time, which is typically one second. The preferred unit for
frequency is now the *hertz* (Hz), formerly stated as cycles-per-second (cps). Thus,
the output frequencies of the two devices under consideration are

$$\frac{3 \text{ rev}}{3 \text{ ms}} \cdot \frac{1,000 \text{ ms}}{1 \text{ sec}} = 1,000 \text{ rev/sec} = 1,000 \text{ Hz}$$

and

$$\frac{2 \text{ rev}}{3 \text{ ms}} \cdot \frac{1,000 \text{ ms}}{1 \text{ sec}} = 666.67 \text{ rev/sec} = 666.67 \text{ Hz}$$

Period
The *period* of a sine wave is the amount of time, t, it takes for the waveform
to pass through 360 degrees. It is simply the reciprocal of the frequency itself.
That is,

$$t = 1/f \text{ seconds (per cycle)}$$

Phase and Phase Shift

The *phase* at any point on a sine wave is a measure of that point's distance from
the most recent positive-going zero-crossing of the waveform. The *phase shift*

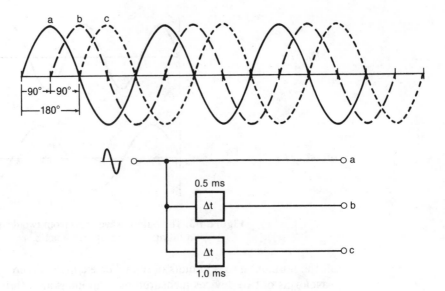

Figure 1-6. Three 500 Hz sine waves. Curve (b) lags (a) by 90 degrees; curve (c) lags (a) by 180 degrees. The time delay networks seen in the block diagram produce the required delays.

between two points on the same sine wave is simply the difference between their phases.

However, phase shift is more often used to describe the relationship between two sine waves. For example, when sine waves of identical frequency are compared, the phase shift between them is the distance between any point on one wave and the identical point on the other. The zero-crossing is the most convenient reference point. For example, Figure 1-6 shows three 500 Hz sine waves. The phase shift between curves (a) and (b) is 90 degrees. Curve (b) *lags* (a) by that amount, because it crosses the zero axis 90 degrees later than (a). Or, (a) *leads* (b) by 90 degrees, for the same reason. Curve (c) lags (a) by 180 degrees and lags (b) by 90 degrees.

It is important to remember that phase shift is caused by a time delay in the signal path, as indicated in the block diagram also shown in Figure 1-6. Each block marked with the symbol Δt indicates a fixed time delay in the signal path. In this example the delays are such that the blocks introduce phase shifts of 90 and 180 degrees at 500 Hz. If that frequency were slightly lower, the delays would create lesser phase shifts; if it were higher, the phase shifts would be greater. The following equation finds the phase shift, θ, at any frequency:

$$\theta = 2\pi ft \text{ in radians (radian measure is described later in the chapter)}$$
$$= 360ft \text{ in degrees}$$

where
$\qquad f$ = frequency, in Hz
$\qquad t$ = time delay, in seconds

For a fixed delay of 1 ms (0.001 sec), the phase shift at various frequencies is as shown below:

Frequency (Hz)	Phase Shift (°)	Frequency (Hz)	Phase Shift (°)
31.25	11.25	250	90
62.5	22.50	500	180
125	45.00	1,000	360

Phase Cancellations   When there is a 180-degree phase shift between two sine waves, the resultant output will be completely cancelled if the signals are combined. This may be visualized in Figure 1-6 by noting that curve (c) is a mirror image of curve (a); when one is positive the other is negative, and so their summation is always zero.

But as noted, at some other frequency there will be some other phase shift, so the cancellation will not be complete when the signals are combined. For example, Figure 1-7 shows the effect of a 1 ms time delay on all frequencies between 10 Hz and 20 kHz, as for example if outputs (a) and (b) in Figure 1-6 are combined.

Note that cancellations begin at 1,000 Hz and occur thereafter at fixed intervals of 2,000 Hz. The curve becomes compressed at progressively higher frequencies when these are plotted on a logarithmic scale. Therefore, each curve is also shown on a linear frequency scale to better illustrate the recurring pattern of cancellations.

Polarity

The *polarity* of a signal refers to its electric potential, with respect to a reference potential that may be either zero or the polarity of some other signal. Thus, a signal with an instantaneous amplitude of +4 volts has a positive polarity with respect to ground potential or to a −3 volt signal, but it has a negative polarity with respect to a +6-volt signal.

In measuring the instantaneous polarity of a single sinusoidal waveform, the x axis serves as the reference point: when the waveform is above the x axis, its polarity is positive; when below the x axis its polarity is negative.

If two audio signals are combined, the waveforms add when the signals are the same polarity (+ / + or − / −) and subtract when they are of opposite polarity (+ / − or − / +). It is therefore important to make sure that the polarity of every audio line is not accidentally reversed. Otherwise a signal common to two lines—one containing a polarity reversal—will cancel if the signals are combined.

Coherence

The term *coherence* describes the polarity relationship between two audio signals. While both signals are of the same polarity, they are said to be coherent. For example, two sine waves of the same frequency and zero phase shift are 100 percent coherent. Given a 90 degree phase shift the waveforms are 50 percent coherent, as may be seen by comparing the sine and cosine waveforms in Figure 1-3. And of course a 180-degree phase shift results in zero coherence; the polarities of the two waveforms are always opposite. Statistically, the coherence of

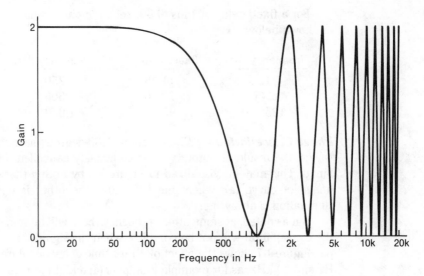

(A) Sensitivity vs. logarithmic frequency.

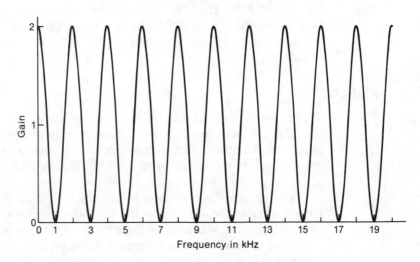

(B) Sensitivity vs. linear frequency.

Figure 1-7. The frequency response when a signal delayed

the typical stereo program is random; that is, the waveforms are of the same polarity about half of the time.

Acoustic Waveform

The effect of a vibrating mechanical device on the air particles surrounding it is analogous to the effect of a magnetic field on a conductor passing through that

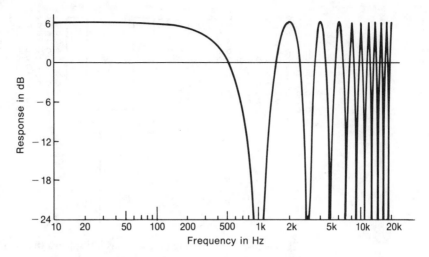

(C) Decibel attenuation vs. logarithmic frequency.

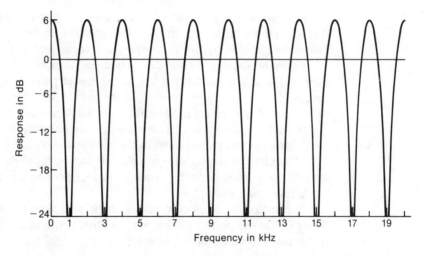

(D) Decibel attenuation vs. linear frequency.

by 0.5 ms is combined with the same signal with no delay.

field. This effect may be illustrated with the help of the tuning fork shown in Figure 1-8.

Assuming the fork is for the moment at rest, the air particles in the area surrounding it are evenly spaced, and the barometric (atmospheric) pressure is at some constant, or zero reference, level.

When the fork is in motion, both prongs simultaneously move outward, then reverse direction and move inward. To examine the effect of this motion, consider just a few of the air particles near one of the prongs, such as those in the horizontal line shown in the figure. As the righthand prong moves forward, it pushes against an adjacent air particle, displacing it from its position at rest. As

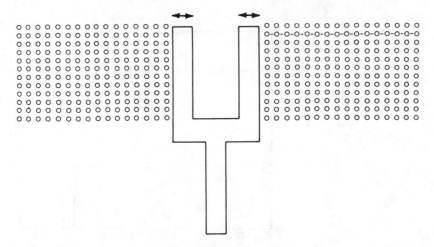

Figure 1-8. As the tuning fork vibrates it displaces the nearby air molecules.

the particle moves forward, it in turn displaces the next adjacent particle, and a chain reaction of particle displacements takes place.

Meanwhile, the prong reaches its maximum forward position, reverses direction and moves backward. In turn, the adjacent particle also reverses direction, followed soon after by the next-adjacent particle, and so on.

Figure 1-9 shows what happens as first one particle, and then the next, is set into motion. The figure examines a horizontal row of particles and plots the to-and-fro motion of each one as time passes. In the instant just after t_o, the first particle has moved closer to its neighbor, which has not yet itself moved. However, it soon does, and the disturbance is quickly passed along from one particle to the next. By time t_x, the disturbance has moved as far as the last particle seen in the figure.

As the illustration shows, each particle moves back and forth from its position at rest, and a trace of each particle's displacement versus time has the shape of the familiar sine wave.

A comparison of electric and acoustic sine waves leads us to the obvious; either one is the perfect analog for the other. (And this simple observation is all that it takes to make analog sound recording a reality).

Sound Pressure Wave

Figure 1-10 gives a closeup view of just a few air particles. Note that at time t_1, the particle represented by curve (b) is at the same position it occupies when at rest. However, at this same instant particles (a) and (c) are displaced from their respective rest positions, as indicated by the arrows pointing to their new positions. It can be seen that the distances between these three particles are therefore compressed, and as a result the air pressure in this region is greater than normal. Since t_1 in fact marks the point at which maximum compression occurs, this is the point of maximum air pressure.

In the time interval between t_1 and t_2, the spacing between particles expands, reaching a maximum at t_2, the point at which air pressure is therefore at a minimum. From t_2 to t_3, particle spacing again compresses until at t_3 the cycle begins again.

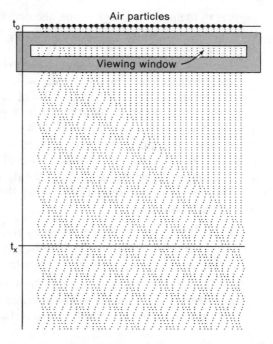

Figure 1-9. A closeup look at a row of air particles disturbed by a sound pressure wave. To simulate the effect of time, move a cut-out viewing window steadily downwards; within the window the condensations and rarefactions will appear to move from left to right, as explained in the section on Wave Motion.

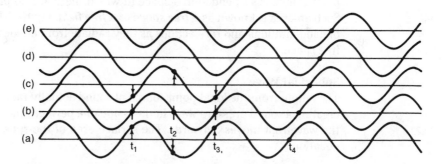

Figure 1-10. An even closer look at just a few air particles. The distance between particles is compressed at t_1, expanded at t_2, and compressed again at t_3. The series of condensations beginning at t_4 illustrates how the condensation/rarefaction effect moves outwards, away from the sound source.

The compression and expansion effects just described are respectively referred to as *condensations* and *rarefactions*.

Wave Motion
Beginning at t_4, the five highlighted particles mark the points at which a condensation occurs. Note that as time passes, this region moves outward, from one

particle to the next. In other words, the condensation moves steadily away from the sound source, with a rarefaction following close behind, then another condensation, and so on.

The movement of the pressure wave may be "seen" by examining the air particles through a narrow-slit viewing window (Wood 1975), as indicated by the cut-out rectangle shown in Figure 1-9. Cut the window into an index card and place it over the figure so that the t_0 axis appears in the window. Now slide the window downwards, or better yet, hold it steady and slide the figure upwards. In either case, the condensation regions seen in the window area should appear to move continuously from left to right, as would be the case if they were caused by a sound source at the left-hand side of the page.

This demonstration should help clarify the two degrees of motion associated with an acoustic wave:

1. Each air particle vibrates about its position at rest, at the same frequency as the device creating the disturbance. Regardless of the duration of the disturbance, each air particle remains near its position at rest.

2. The resultant pressure wave radiates away from the device creating the disturbance, and does so at a constant speed. As time passes, the initial pressure wave moves further and further away.

Ideal Sound Source

For the purpose of acoustic measurements, a convenient reference point is the so-called *ideal sound source*. This is understood to be an infinitely small sound-producing device, often called a *point source* because it has no dimension. The point source is suspended in a space in which there are no physical obstructions. Such an area is known as a *free space* or a *free field*. Figure 1-11 shows the pattern of condensations and rarefactions as they radiate from an ideal sound source into free space.

Spherical Wave
The output from the ideal point source of sound actually radiates in all directions, creating a sound pressure wave in the shape of a perfect sphere, which expands as the wavefront moves outwards. The surface area of the sphere is found from the equation

$$S = 4\pi r^2$$

where
    S = surface area of the sphere
    π = 3.14
    r = radius of the sphere

Inverse-Square Law
From the equation, note that for every doubling of the radius, there is a fourfold increase in the surface area of the sphere, as illustrated in Figure 1-12A. Therefore, the following observations hold for each doubling of distance:

- The radiated energy is spread over an area four times greater than it was before the doubling, and
- The energy per unit of area is one-quarter of its former value.

The term *inverse-square law* refers to any condition in which the magnitude of a physical quantity follows an *inverse* relationship to the *square* of the distance such as just described. A few important modifications to the inverse-square law are discussed later in this chapter, in the section on the Sound Field (page 32).

According to the inverse-square law, sound level is attenuated by 6 dB with each doubling of distance, as may be shown from the following equation.

$$L = 20 \log (r_1/r_2)$$

where
$\quad L$ = level, in dB
$\quad r_1$ = reference distance (see Figure 1-12A)
$\quad r_2$ = successive doublings of distance

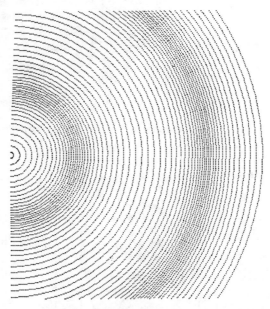

Figure 1-11. Condensations and rarefactions radiating from a point source into free space.

Plane Wave

By the time a spherical pressure wave reaches a microphone that is but a few feet from the sound source, the wave circumference is so large in comparison to the diameter of the diaphragm that the wavefront can be regarded as a *plane wave*; that is, a waveform whose condensations and rarefactions are represented as a series of parallel lines.

Figure 1-12B shows a spherical wave front striking the center of a microphone diaphragm placed one meter from the sound source. Assuming the diaphragm

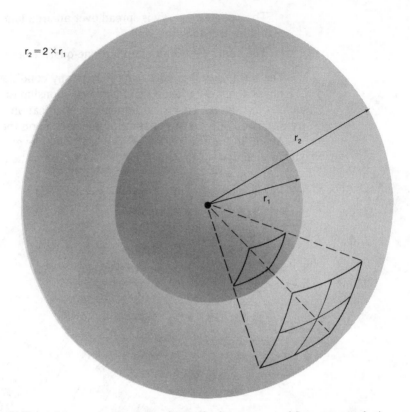

(A) The surface area increases according to the distance squared (inverse-square law).

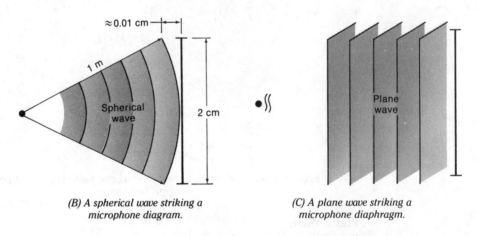

(B) A spherical wave striking a
microphone diagram.

(C) A plane wave striking a
microphone diaphragm.

Figure 1-12. A spherical wave, showing the effect of distance.

diameter is 2 cm, the additional time it takes for the wave to reach the outer edge
of the diaphragm is about 0.00000029 sec (0.29 μs). Such a minute delay has no
effect at all within the audio frequency range, and so may be completely ignored.
As a result, the wave may be drawn in the form of a plane wave, as shown in
Figure 1-12C.

As an acoustic wave travels through space, Figure 1-13 illustrates how a plane-wave pattern of compressions and rarefactions might appear at a given instant. The upper dotted-line segment (a) represents a small area in which vertical columns of air particles are shown at rest. The lower segment (b) shows the same area, with the particles horizontally displaced in response to a disturbance. The solid line linking the segments simply shows how far the particles have moved; it is the hypotenuse of a triangle whose base (not drawn) is the actual horizontal displacement of the particles. A graph of this displacement is redrawn in enlarged scale at the bottom of the figure (c), where each horizontal displacement is now represented by a vertical line. The length of the line indicates the amplitude of the displacement. Lines rising above the x axis represent particles moving away from the sound source; lines falling below the x axis represent particles moving back toward the sound source.

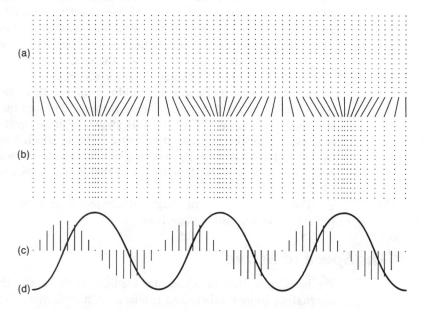

Figure 1-13. A plane-wave representation of air particles (a) at rest, and (b) displaced by a pressure disturbance. The amplitude of the displacement (c) and the sound pressure (d) are both represented by sine waves, separated by a 90-degree phase shift. The vertical scale of these waveforms has been expanded for clarity.

The overall wave shape is again the familiar sine wave. A comparison of the two parts of the figure shows that both condensations and rarefactions occur at points where there is zero displacement of the air particles; a plot of pressure (d) also appears in the figure. Note the 90-degree phase shift between displacement and pressure.

From this analysis of the plane wave we see again the direct analogy between electric and acoustic energy, from which it follows that if the input to the appropriate transducer is in one of these forms, its output will be in the other. In one case, the microphone converts the acoustic wave into its electric analog; in another, the loudspeaker converts the electric wave back to its acoustic analog.

Radian and Steradian Measure

When two radii of a circle are joined by an arc whose length is equal to the radius, the included angle is said to be one *radian*. A complete circle contains an included angle of 6.28, or 2π, radians. Therefore,

$$360° = 2\pi \text{ radians}$$
$$57.30° = 1 \text{ radian}$$
$$1° = 0.01745 \text{ radian}$$

In evaluating the characteristics of a sound pressure wave it is common practice to use a unit of measurement for solid angles. Unlike the familiar two-dimensional angle, a solid angle is defined in terms of surface area, not degrees. For example, consider the two small surfaces marked off on the sphere shown in Figure 1-14A. Although their areas are equal their shapes are different, so it cannot be said that a given area may be uniquely defined by just one set of angles between radii. Thus, the *steradian* is defined as any solid angle contained by a surface whose area equals the square of the sphere's radius. In practice, the solid angle itself is usually ignored and the steradian becomes a measure of the surface area.

The surface area of a sphere contains a solid angle of 4π steradians, and so it is often said that an ideal sound source suspended in free space radiates into a 4π steradian environment. Figure 1-14B shows a circle divided into 6.28, or 2π, radians. A hemisphere is shown in Figure 1-14C, in which a surface area described by one steradian is seen. By studying the illustration, it should be clear that the hemisphere contains 2π steradians, and therefore a complete sphere will contain 4π steradians.

The steradian will appear again in Chapter 5, in the discussion of loudspeaker radiation characteristics (page 165).

The Speed of Sound

We have seen that in an elastic medium such as air, the pressure wave of alternating condensations and rarefactions moves away from the source of the disturbance. In describing the rate at which the wave travels through the surrounding space, *speed* and *velocity* are often used almost interchangeably. However, there is a distinction to be made between the terms.

- *Speed* is the rate, per unit of time, at which an object moves, without regard to the direction of that movement.
- *Velocity* is the speed of an object, when measured with respect to direction. For complete accuracy, the direction should be stated.

From these definitions, we might say that a certain car has a top *speed* of 120 miles per hour, thus describing how fast it might go, but not limiting that capability to a specific direction. To be more specific, we could say that the vehicle is now moving northward at a *velocity* of 70 miles per hour. In some cases, the direction is assumed to be understood and is therefore not included in a statement of velocity.

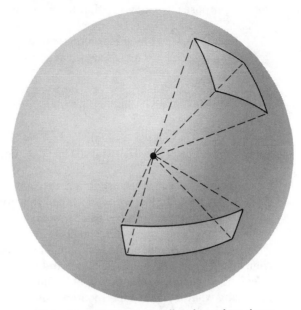

(A) A sphere showing two small surfaces of equal area.

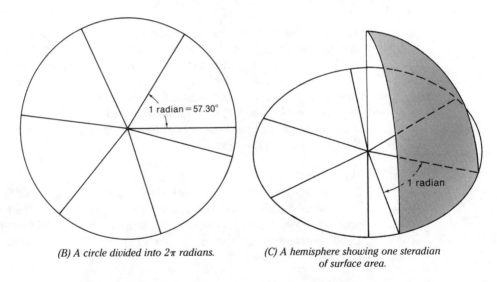

(B) A circle divided into 2π radians.

(C) A hemisphere showing one steradian of surface area.

Figure 1-14. Relationship between radian and steradian measure.

Since the movement of a sound wave is not confined to a specific direction, it should be referred to in terms of speed. The lowercase letter c is usually used as the specific abbreviation for the speed of sound in air, and its value is a function of several variables, including the density, elasticity, and temperature of the medium. In dry air at 0 degrees Celsius, the speed of sound, c, is given as

$$c = 331.45 \pm 0.05 \text{ meters/second}$$
$$= 1087.42 \pm 0.16 \text{ feet/second}$$

For our purposes, we may say that the speed of sound in air is

$$c = 344 \text{ meters/second, or}$$
$$c = 1130 \text{ feet/second (at about 71}^\circ \text{ Fahrenheit)}$$

The following equations may be used to find the speed of sound at other temperatures (Schomer 1985) within a range of about 20 degrees Celsius:

$$c = 331.45 + 0.607T_c \quad (T_c = \text{degrees Celsius})$$
$$= 1052.03 + 1.106T_f \quad (T_f = \text{degrees Fahrenheit})$$

In popular usage, the distinction between *speed* and *velocity* is more often than not ignored, and so we read of the "velocity of sound," and of "tape speed." Strictly speaking, the former phrase should be used only when a specific direction is also given, while the latter should be used not at all, since the direction in which that tape is speeding is presumably known, even if it is not stated. As a compromise between being accurate and being awkward, this book "follows the rules" in discussing the physics of sound and then follows popular usage in discussing what it is that tape recorders do.

Wavelength

Although the listener identifies a musical sound in terms of its frequency, a microphone in fact responds to the wavelength associated with that frequency. Furthermore, as a sound wave moves through space, its wavelength determines what effect various objects in its path will have on it, thus influencing the character of the sound we eventually hear.

The *wavelength*, λ (Greek *lambda*), of a frequency is simply the length of a single wave; that is, the longitudinal distance between any point in one cycle and the same point in the next cycle.

Wavelength in Air

To calculate wavelength, consider a fixed sound source from which a 1,000 Hz sound wave is radiating into the surrounding space at the speed of sound. As the pressure wave moves through space, it would require 344 meters to trace out 1,000 complete cycles, that is, 344 meters per 1,000 cycles. Therefore, the length of a single cycle would be

$$\lambda = \frac{344 \text{ meters}}{1 \text{ second}} \div \frac{1,000 \text{ cycles}}{1 \text{ second}}$$

$$= \frac{344 \text{ meters}}{1 \text{ second}} \cdot \frac{1 \text{ second}}{1,000 \text{ cycles}}$$

$$= \frac{344 \text{ meters}}{1,000 \text{ cycles}}$$

$$= 0.344 \text{ meters/cycle}$$

In other words, the wavelength, λ, of any frequency may be found simply by dividing the speed of sound, c, by the frequency, f. That is,

$$\lambda = c/f$$

or

$$\lambda = S/f$$

where
λ = wavelength, in meters
c = speed of sound in air, 344 meters/second
S = speed of sound in some medium other than air
f = frequency, in hertz

Note that the wavelength associated with a frequency is directly proportional to the speed of sound. Therefore, if the speed of sound changes (for example, as a function of temperature), the wavelength for a given frequency also changes.

Wavelength Recorded on Magnetic Tape
In analog magnetic recording, the variable, S, is the tape speed at the time the recording is made. For example, if a 1,000 Hz tone is recorded at 15 in/sec (38 cm/sec), the recorded wavelength is

English	Metric
$\lambda = S/f$	$\lambda = S/f$
$= 15/1,000$	$= 38/1,000$
$= 0.015$ in	$= 0.038$ cm

If the playback is at a different speed than the recording, the fixed wavelength on tape produces a different frequency than the one that was recorded. Of course, the listener should have no trouble recognizing a music recording played back at double or half-speed. However, in the absence of the obvious pitch/tempo cues in music, there is no way to detect an off-speed test tone, other than to know what its frequency is supposed to be.

Sound Intensity and Sound Power

Sound intensity is a measure of the rate at which acoustic energy radiates through an area of known dimension. In SI units (*Système International d'unités*), this area is one square meter.

Sound power is the total sound energy radiated by a sound source, per unit of time (one second in SI units).

The relationship between intensity and power is given by the equations

$$I = P/S = P/4\pi r^2$$

or

$$P = (I)S = (I)4\pi r^2$$

where
  I = intensity, in watts per square meter (W/m^2)
  P = power, in watts
  S = surface area, in square meters

Note that sound intensity follows the inverse-square law; if intensity is first measured at a certain distance from the sound source, and then that distance is doubled, the second intensity will be one-quarter of the first.

Sound power is the acoustic analog of electric power.

Sound Pressure

In the earlier discussion of the acoustic waveform, it was shown that a vibrating device creates a pressure disturbance in the surrounding area. Needless to say, the more power radiated by the device, the greater the change in pressure. The direct cause-and-effect relationship between sound intensity or power and sound pressure is significant, because the ear reacts to sound pressure (Brüel & Kjaer 1986).

In the following equation, we may assume that all terms except the distance, r, will remain constant. Therefore, we may quickly dispense with them by substituting a single constant, k, as seen here.

$$\begin{aligned}
p_a &= [I\beta c]^{1/2} \\
&= [(W/4\pi r^2)\beta c]^{1/2} \\
&= (1/r)[(W/4\pi)\beta c]^{1/2} \\
&= k/r
\end{aligned}$$

where
  p_a = sound pressure, in dynes/cm^2
  β = density of the medium
  c = speed of sound
  k = a constant, representing $[(W/4\pi)\beta c]^{1/2}$

From the simplified equation, $p_a = k/r$, it is easily seen that sound pressure is inversely proportional to distance, r. Therefore, if sound pressure is measured under the same conditions described above for sound intensity, the pressure will be halved (not quartered) at every doubling of the distance.

Sound pressure is the acoustic analog of electric voltage.

Threshold of Hearing

As sound pressure decreases, there comes a point at which the typical listener can no longer hear the sound. Although this point, called the *threshold of hearing*, varies from one listener to another, for the purpose of definition it is understood to occur when the sound pressure is 20×10^{-6} pascals, or $20\ \mu$Pa.

Threshold of Pain

At the opposite extreme, the point at which sound pressure begins to cause physical discomfort is called the *threshold of pain*. This is understood to occur when the sound pressure reaches $200,000,000 \times 10^{-6}$ pascals. As above, the actual threshold will of course vary from one listener to another.

Range of Hearing

If we take the thresholds of hearing and of pain to represent the lower and upper limits of hearing, we see that the human ear responds to sound pressure over a $10,000,000:1$ (10^7) range; the square of this value (10^{14}) represents the equivalent power range. It therefore follows that if an amplifier with an ouput of 100 (10^2) watts creates a sound at the threshold of pain, the same amplifier could (in theory, at least) create a sound at the threshold of hearing by reducing its output power to 0.000000000001 (10^{-12}) watts, or one pico-watt.

The actual response of the ear between the thresholds of hearing and of pain is discussed in detail in the next chapter (page 52).

Sound Pressure Level in dB

Since sound pressure (described above) is analogous to voltage, equation (1-2) (page 4) may be used to calculate the decibel relationship between a measured sound pressure and the pressure at the threshold of hearing. As the analog to resistance, the acoustic impedance of the sound source is assumed to remain constant, and is ignored in the calculation. Therefore,

$$L_p = 20 \log (P_1/P_0)$$

where
L_p = Sound pressure level, in dB
P_1 = measured sound pressure, in μPa (micropascals)
P_0 = zero reference pressure, 20 μPa

Static and Dynamic Pressure

In the case of the acoustic waveform, the zero-reference level is the ambient barometric pressure in the absence of a sound wave. Although this pressure may slowly fluctuate during the day, it is often referred to as *static pressure*, to distinguish it from *dynamic pressure*, which refers to the rapid fluctuations that occur as the sound wave moves through the area.

Reflection, Refraction, and Diffraction

Although it is convenient to discuss sound-transmission theory in terms of a free-space environment, in practice the sound pressure wave encounters all sorts of obstacles in its path. In addition to the regular room surfaces—walls, floor, and ceiling—there may be any number of additional acoustic barriers placed between a sound source and either the listener or a microphone.

Each of these surfaces has an effect on the sound that is eventually heard, and as we shall soon discover, the effect usually varies considerably over the audio frequency range.

In the following discussion, the terms *incidence* and *incident sound* refer to a sound pressure wave striking a surface. The *angle of incidence* is the angle between an arriving wave and a line drawn perpendicular to the surface.

Reflection

When a pressure wave reaches a surface barrier, the wave is reflected back into the room, as shown in Figure 1-15 The angle of incidence and the angle of reflection are both shown in the figure, and are found to be identical. (As a quick demonstration/proof, a mirror will reflect a light wave—say, a flashlight beam— in the same way.)

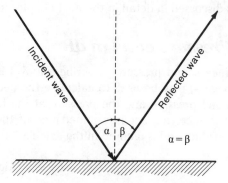

Figure 1-15. A sound wave reflected off a surface. The angle of incidence, α, and angle of reflection, β, are identical.

Absorption Coefficient

However, it is important to remember that no surface is a perfect reflector of incident sound. Some energy is absorbed by the surface, and the amount of this absorption varies according to both the construction materials and the wavelength of the incident sound wave. The *absorption coefficient* of a surface is its ratio of absorbed to incident energy. A perfect absorber (an open window, for example) has an absorption coefficient of $1:1 = 1$, and a perfect reflector has an absorption coefficient of $0:1 = 0$.

In practice, the absorption coefficient of most surfaces varies over the audio frequency range, as shown in Table 1-2.

Refraction

Refraction is the bending of a waveform as it passes from one medium to another, or as it experiences some change (e.g., in temperature) within the medium. The angle of refraction is a function of the speed at which sound travels in the medium. Since the

Table 1-2. Absorption Coefficients for Some Typical Construction Materials.*

Materials	Absorption Coefficients					
	125 Hz	*250 Hz*	*500 Hz*	*1,000 Hz*	*2,000 Hz*	*4,000 Hz*
Absorber, perfect	1.00	1.00	1.00	1.00	1.00	1.00
Brick, unglazed	0.03	0.03	0.03	0.04	0.05	0.07
Carpet, heavy, on concrete	0.02	0.06	0.14	0.37	0.60	0.65
Fabric, heavy velour	0.14	0.35	0.55	0.72	0.70	0.65
Glass plate, heavy	0.18	0.06	0.04	0.03	0.02	0.02
Plywood paneling, ³/₈″	0.28	0.22	0.17	0.09	0.10	0.11
Reflector, perfect	0.00	0.00	0.00	0.00	0.00	0.00

*materials list excerpted from Ballou, G., ed., *Handbook for Sound Engineers: The New Audio Cyclopedia.*

speed of sound in air is a function of temperature, a sound wave will bend upwards if the air above a surface is cooler than the air nearer the surface, as may be the case outdoors in the early morning. Later in the day, the upper air may become warmer than at the surface, and the sound wave will be refracted downwards.

Diffraction

In order to hear a sound, it is of course unnecessary to maintain a straight-line path between the source and the listener for, as is well known, a sound wave will bend around most obstacles placed in its path. The term *diffraction* describes any change in direction brought about by such an obstacle.

The angle of diffraction depends on the ratio of wavelength to barrier size, and is therefore inversely proportional to frequency. In other words, the higher the frequency, the smaller the angle of diffraction. Furthermore, the larger the barrier, the greater its overall effect. In practical terms this means that as a complex waveform passes over the edge of a barrier surface, the low-frequency components bend around the barrier while the high-frequency components do not. The result is a falling high frequency response.

Although the mathematics of the diffraction phenomenon are not simple (Rettinger 1977b), the illustration shown in Figure 1-16 and the following brief explanation may help to illustrate the effect of placing a partial barrier between a sound source and a listener (or microphone).

The following equations are used to calculate the sound-level reduction caused by diffraction effects.

$$SLR = -3 + 10 \log [(0.5 - x)^2 + (0.5 - y)^2]$$

where
$$x = \int_0^v \cos (\pi v^2/2) dv$$
$$y = \int_0^v \sin (\pi v^2/2) dv$$

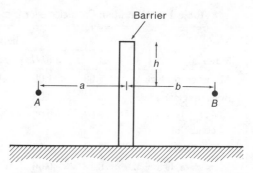

Figure 1-16. A barrier placed between a sound source, *A*, and a listener or a
microphone, *B*. The effect of diffraction varies according to the relative
distances, *a* and *b*, and the height of the barrier, *h*.

$v = h[^2\!/\!\lambda(1/a + 1/b)]^{1/2}$
a = distance; sound source, *A*, to barrier
b = distance; barrier to listener, *B*
h = height of barrier

The variables *x* and *y* are known as *Fresnel integrals,* and using them to
calculate frequency response based on the SLR equation is a tedious process best
left to a computer. Figure 1-17 shows one such computer solution, in which the
sound source and the listener are both 3 feet away from a barrier that is 1½ feet
high. Note that the response falls off at about 3 dB per octave.

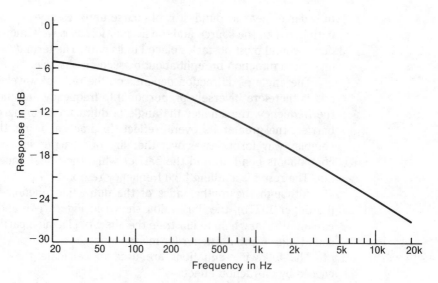

Figure 1-17. A computer calculation of frequency response measured at the
listener's position, *B*, in Figure 1-16. The source-to-barrier and listener-to-barrier
distances and barrier height are 3, 3, and 1½ feet, respectively.

Although the diffraction equations seen above do not lend themselves to easy
interpretation, a few conclusions can be applied based on some simple observations. First, raising the barrier height, *h*, will surely increase the amount of

attenuation, and from the last equation above, we see that as *h* increases, so does *v*. So we may conclude that attenuation is directly proportional to *v*. That being so, we may increase its value, and therefore gain more attenuation by doing one or more of the following:

- raise the barrier height
- decrease the wavelength
- increase the distance, *a*
- increase the distance, *b*

There is one more procedure that is not as immediately obvious as these steps, and that is to make sure that the distances, *a* and *b*, are unequal. For example, if the total source-to-microphone distance shown in Figure 1-16 is $a + b$, the sum $1/a + 1/b$ reaches its minimum when $a = b$. To increase this sum, and therefore the value of *v*, all that needs to be done is to move the barrier closer to either the source or to the microphone—thereby making *a* and *b* unequal; the greater the inequality, the greater the sum of the fractions and therefore, the greater the attenuation. To illustrate, Figure 1-18 shows the attenuation at 1,000 Hz when a two-foot barrier is placed between a source and a microphone that are ten feet apart. Note that when the barrier is placed somewhere between 3 and 7 feet from *either* the source or the microphone, the attenuation remains at about 15 dB. As the barrier is moved closer to either device, attenuation falls off rapidly. Of course it should be remembered that this theoretical curve is based on diffraction effects only, and that actual studio conditions rarely have much respect for textbook-type response curves.

Cumulative Effects of Reflection, Refraction, and Diffraction

Although it's just about impossible to isolate any one of the effects just described from the others, it is worth keeping in mind that the sound reaching a microphone is a complex mix of these elements, as summarized here.

- *Reflection*. Sound reflected from a nearby surface will be a frequency-distorted version of the direct sound, as determined by the absorption coefficients listed in Table 1-2.
- *Refraction*. Given a reasonably solid acoustic barrier, refraction of a sound wave passing through it is probably unnoticeable. Outdoors, however, the practical effect of temperature-induced refraction may result in a variation in coverage distance.
- *Diffraction*. A sound wave measured from behind an acoustic barrier will exhibit a falling frequency response.

It's a good idea to keep these cumulative effects in mind whenever an acoustic barrier, or *gobo*, is considered as a means to cut down on sound transmission. The desired attenuation may be more than offset by the frequency distortions introduced by the gobo. In fact, the frequency response shown in Figure 1-17 makes the unlikely assumption that the barrier is infinitely long,

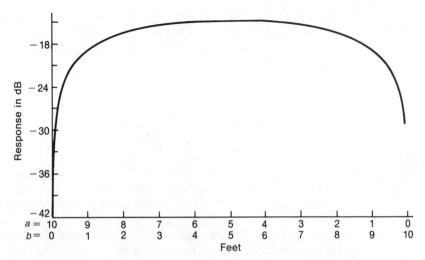

Figure 1-18. Attenuation at 1,000 Hz when a two-foot barrier is placed between a sound source and a microphone (a = source-to-barrier distance; b = barrier-to-microphone distance).

completely sealed at the floor, and a perfect absorber. The practical gobo falls far short of all these parameters and so the frequency response is probably even worse than that shown in the figure.

The final arbiter is, of course, the ear: listen to the unwanted sound with, and without, the gobo in place. If the gobo creates more frequency distortion than attenuation, remove it.

The Sound Field

A *sound field* is simply any space in which sound waves are present. The term is often used to describe the ambient sound perceived at a certain location, as opposed to just the sound of a specific nearby source.

When a microphone is placed very close to a sound source, it generally picks up only the direct sound from that source, while ignoring all other sounds from the surrounding space. A microphone placed farther away from a source will of course hear more of the entire sound field.

The sound field itself is subdivided as shown in Figure 1-19 and as described immediately below.

Near Field

Earlier in this chapter (page 18), the inverse-square law illustrated how sound level falls off 6 dB for each doubling of distance. The law, however, does not apply within the *near field*, which is a small area in the immediate vicinity of the source. Authorities do not seem to agree on the extent of the near field, and its boundary distance has been given variously as

- about the dimension of the radiator (speaker diameter) (Eargle 1986),
- less than the wavelength of the lowest frequency,

  or

  twice the dimension of the source, whichever is greater (Brüel & Kjaer 1984),
- within a few wavelengths of the source,

  or

  a few diameters of the source, whichever is larger (Minnix 1978),
- "not straightforward" (to find it) (Kinsler et al. 1982)

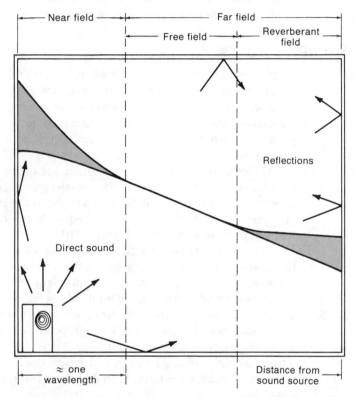

Figure 1-19. The sound field within a listening room (after Brüel & Kjaer 1984).

For the purposes of this discussion, we may say that the near field is simply an area quite close to a transducer. For a speaker this is probably within a few feet of the diaphragm; for a microphone, it is whatever it takes to eliminate the effects of the sound field—perhaps just a few inches.

The near field should not be confused with *close-field* monitoring, which is described in Chapter 6 (page 244).

Far Field

The *far field* is simply the area beyond the near field boundary. However, the far field is itself divided into two sub-fields, described here.

Free Field

The *free field* is the field in which the inverse square law applies. It begins at the near field boundary and ends wherever the sound pressure level no longer falls off at 6 dB per doubling of distance.

Reverberant Field

The *reverberant field* is that area of a listening environment in which the contribution of the source itself is no longer the strongest component in the sound field. Therefore, although the source level may continue to fall off at the 6 dB rate described above, the many reflections of that source maintain the level at a more or less constant, or slowly diminishing, level.

Reverberation and the reverberant field are discussed at length in Chapter 6.

Standing Waves

When a sound pressure wave travels to a wall and reflects back upon itself, as shown in Figure 1-20, the interaction between the incident and the reflected waveforms sets up a series of pressure nodes and antinodes along the sound path. A *pressure node* is a point at which sound pressure is zero; a *pressure antinode* is a point at which pressure is maximum. Since both points are stationary, the phenomenon is known as a *standing wave*.

The location of the nodes and antinodes is a function of the wavelength of the sound source. For example, if the wavelength is equal to twice the distance between the walls, there will be a single node at the center of the room, as shown in Figure 1-21A. If the wavelength is equal to the distance between the walls, there will be two nodes, as in Figure 1-21B.

In both parts of Figure 1-21, the sound source is located near the left wall and the waveform is shown moving toward the right wall and then reflecting back into the room. The reflected wave is the equivalent of a waveform originating at the image location seen near the right side of the figure, beyond the room boundary. The dashed line traces the node/antinode pattern within the room.

At each node the frequency, $f = c/\lambda$, is not heard, while at each antinode the same frequency is reinforced. The frequencies at which the nodes appear are integer multiples of the frequency at which the single node appears; that is, if frequency f creates one node, then $2f$ creates two nodes, $3f$ creates 3 nodes, and so on.

Room Modes

In both parts of Figure 1-21, note that a standing wave produces sound pressure maxima at the room boundaries, and thus the room has an acoustic resonance frequency, or *normal mode* of vibration (Beranek 1954), at every frequency that creates a standing wave. This *normal frequency*, or *modal frequency*, is one of the infinite series f, $2f$, $3f$, ...

The modal frequencies just described are those occurring between a single pair of parallel walls. However, additional standing waves are set up between the other wall-pair as well as between the ceiling and floor. Still more modes are established by waves reflected between more than one pair of surfaces.

Figure 1-20. A standing wave is created when a sound wave is reflected back upon itself. The waves travelling to and from the wall alternately cancel and reinforce each other.

Depending on the number of surfaces involved, the mode name and relative level are as seen in the following chart (Everest 1987).

Number of Surface Pairs	Mode Name	Level (dB)
Single pair	Axial	0
Two pairs	Tangential	-3
Three pairs	Oblique	-6

In a well-designed room, the modal frequencies should be distributed so as not to excessively reinforce or attenuate any one section of the frequency spectrum. For example, if one surface-pair dimension is an integer multiple of another dimension, then some modes will be additionally reinforced by appearing twice—or, even worse, three times if the same mode appears between each surface pair. In either case there will probably be a noticeable resonance peak within the room at that frequency. Such peaks may be avoided by a careful choice of room dimensions.

In the following discussion the room dimensions are based on the "golden section" of ancient Greece (Rettinger 1977a), which gives the ratio of length-to-width-to-height as

$$(\sqrt{5} + 1):2:(\sqrt{5} - 1) = 3.23607:2:1.23607$$

To describe a large golden-section room the ratio is multiplied by 20 to give

Length	64.72136 feet
Width	40 feet
Height	24.72136 feet

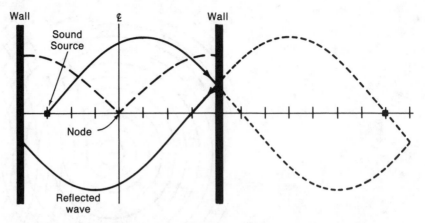

(A) A single node is created if the wavelength is twice the room dimension.

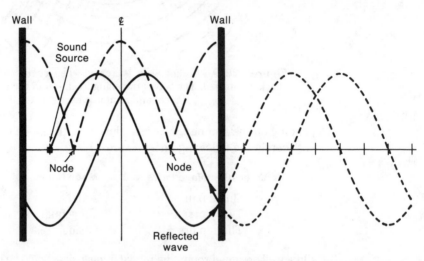

(B) Two nodes are established if the wavelength is equal to the room dimension.

Figure 1-21. Standing wave nodes and antinodes.

Computing Normal-Mode Frequencies

The following equation (Beranek 1954) may be used to calculate the modal frequencies in a rectangular room.

$$f_n = \frac{c}{2} \left[\left(\frac{p}{L}\right)^2 + \left(\frac{q}{W}\right)^2 + \left(\frac{r}{H}\right)^2 \right]^{1/2} \tag{1-3}$$

where

f_n	= *the n*th normal frequency
c	= velocity of sound
p,q,r	= a series of integers, 1, 2, 3, ...
L	= length of room
W	= width of room
H	= height of room

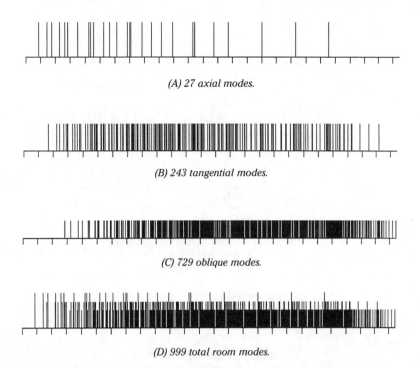

(A) 27 axial modes.

(B) 243 tangential modes.

(C) 729 oblique modes.

(D) 999 total room modes.

Figure 1-22. Modal frequencies for room with golden-section dimensions of 64.72136 (*L*) × 40 (*W*) × 24.72136 (*H*) feet, or 64,000.00 cubic feet. Displayed modal frequency range: 8.73–254.25 Hz. Integers: 0–9.

Figures 1-22 and 1-23 compare the modal frequencies computed for two rooms with volumes of 64,000 cubic feet. The linear scale is 10 Hz per division. The room in Figure 1-22 has golden-section dimensions of 64.72136 × 40 × 24.72136 feet. (The dimensions were entered with 5-point decimal accuracy simply to provide a convenient room volume of 64,000 cubic feet for use in the other example.) The room in Figure 1-23 has worst-case dimensions of 40 × 40 × 40 feet.

The figures are computer printouts of all modal frequencies for all integer combinations of *p, q, r* from 001 to 999. Because there are three axial dimensions and the integers 0 through 9 were used, 3 × 9, or 27 axial modes will be displayed if there are no frequency overlaps. In Figure 1-22 all 27 axial modes are indeed seen. By contrast, the worst case cubic room of Figure 1-23 shows only 9 visible modes. The missing 18 modes, however, are not missing at all; they are simply two superimposed sets of the same 9 modes seen in the figure. Therefore the axial mode-set provides a series of widely spaced and accentuated room resonances. Although the tangential and oblique modes are too densely spaced to allow an accurate count, some general observations may still be made.

In a well-designed room (Figure 1-22) the combination of all three mode-sets creates a dense sequence of resonance frequencies with minimal overlapping. Thus the room modes help to enhance the overall room response.

In a poorly designed room (Figure 1-23) of the same volume, there is much overlapping of modes and all three sets are much less dense. Thus there are modes of excessive reinforcement, separated by areas of no reinforcement.

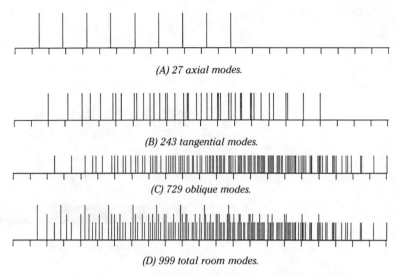

(A) 27 axial modes.

(B) 243 tangential modes.

(C) 729 oblique modes.

(D) 999 total room modes.

Figure 1-23. Modal frequencies for room with worst-case dimensions of 40 (*L*) × 40 (*W*) × 40 (*H*) feet, or 64,000.00 cubic feet. Displayed modal frequency range: 14.13–220.19 Hz. Integers: 0–9.

Although there are no cubic listening rooms in use today (one hopes), the comparison between the two figures should help point out at least one potential problem in a poorly designed room.

These modal-frequency displays also indicate why a small room may have a relatively weak low-frequency characteristic. In fact, even in the large golden-section room described here, the extreme low end (below about 70 Hz) exhibits visibly—and thus, audibly—less bass support from room modes. (The cubic room is even worse, of course.)

If the volume of any room is varied while maintaining the same ratio of dimensions, the mode sequence will not change. However, the lower and upper frequency limits and the horizontal frequency scale will vary according to the change in volume. For example, if the golden-section room dimensions described in Figure 1-22 are halved or doubled, the displayed frequency range and scale will shift up or down, as seen here:

Room Dimensions (ft.)			Modal Frequencies (Hz)		Frequency Scale (Hz per Division)
W	*H*	*L*	*Low*	*High*	
32.36068	20	12.36158	17.46	508.50	20
64.72136	40	24.72316	8.73	254.25	10
129.44272	80	49.44632	4.37	127.13	5

In any case, the lowest modal frequency is defined by the first axial model of the longest room dimension. The frequency may be found by substituting 1, 0, 0 for *p*, *q*, *r* in the equation on page 36.

2 Music, Electronics, and Psychoacoustics

Not too many years ago, the line between musician and engineer was clearly drawn, and the one often didn't quite understand the language of the other. But times change; the artist and the technician no longer dwell exclusively in their separate little environments, protectively shielded from each other by three layers of glass.

Today, the successful studio musician must know at least a little something about what goes on farther down the signal path, and the engineer must likewise have a basic understanding of what it is that goes on in front of a microphone. And an even better understanding may be required if there is no microphone.

Nevertheless, in a book about recording studio technology it might seem there is more than enough to cover without digressing into music theory, which requires—and has—many textbooks of its own. However, because without a little bit of the latter there isn't very much point to any of the former, the next few pages offer a reasonably brief overview of the technical side of music, for the benefit of those who have not been introduced to this aspect of the subject.

The cited references contain much more detailed explanations of the points presented here, and should be consulted by the reader in search of more information.

The chapter's mid-section offers a brief discussion of what happens to the music when it meets the electronics, and this is followed by an overview of psychoacoustics. Again, this is not the definitive word on the subject but perhaps enough to persuade the reader that there's more to localization than the pan pot (which is described in detail in Chapter 12).

Music and Frequency Perception

The ear's perception of the musical difference between any two frequencies does not follow a linear scale. For example, if listeners hear a tone that alternates between, say, 100 Hz and 200 Hz, they readily perceive the 100 Hz interval between these frequencies. If the tone now alternates between 1,000 Hz and 1,100 Hz, the same 100 Hz interval will make much less of a musical difference. From 10,000 Hz to 10,100 Hz, the interval may not even be perceptible.

In short, the ear's perception of frequency follows a logarithmic scale, in which the perceived musical interval is based on the *percentage*—not the absolute—interval between one frequency and another. For example, if two frequencies, f_1 and f_2, are 100 Hz and 200 Hz, then f_3 must be 400 Hz in order to create the sensation of the same musical interval. Succeeding intervals would end at 800 Hz, 1,600 Hz, 3,200 Hz, and so on.

To represent any frequency interval with a physical dimension that corresponds to the perceived musical interval, a graph of frequency response is drawn on a logarithmic scale, as was shown in Figure 1-1 in the previous chapter. Note that the distance between 100 Hz and 200 Hz is the same as the distance between 1,000 Hz and 2,000 Hz, and so on.

The Harmonic Series

Chapter 1 showed how a series of condensations and rarefactions radiates from a vibrating object at a certain frequency. In the case of a tuning fork, the resultant sound should be a pure tone; that is, a signal consisting of nothing but a *fundamental frequency*, which is the single frequency at which the fork vibrates. The waveform may be represented by one of the sine waves shown in the previous chapter.

In practice, most other vibrating objects produce a much more complex output signal, whose waveform is the sum of a *harmonic series*. Such a series consists of the fundamental frequency, f, and its harmonics. The upper harmonics are the integer multiples $2f$, $3f$, $4f$, and so on. The lower harmonics, or subharmonics, are the submultiples $f/2$, $f/3$, $f/4$, and so on. The fundamental itself is also called the first harmonic.

Harmonic Structure

An audio signal is recognized by its fundamental frequency, which is usually the frequency at which most of the energy is concentrated. The rest of the energy is spread in various proportions over the harmonics. The relative proportion of energy found at each harmonic varies from one vibrating object to another, and gives the resultant sound its *harmonic structure*. This structure is one of several variables that help us recognize the difference between the same fundamental frequency produced by, say, a violin and an oboe, and to tell either one from the pure tone of a tuning fork.

The specific frequencies that evolved into the European musical scale were firmly rooted in the harmonic series, as described immediately below. For the sake of brevity, the discussion confines itself to a basic overview of the subject, in which a simple vibrating string can serve as a model. The more complex relationships that exist in some instruments (low and high notes on a piano, percussion tone clusters, etc.) do not always "follow the rules" given here.

The Octave
In musical terms, the interval between a fundamental frequency and its second harmonic is the *octave*, which may be defined as the interval between any two frequencies, f_1 and f_2, when $f_2 = 2f_1$.

The upper frequency, f_2, is closely related to f_1 through the harmonic series, and in fact if a device vibrates at a fundamental frequency of f_1, it often has a significant energy component present at f_2 as well.

Consonance and Dissonance
Within any octave there are of course an infinity of frequencies which might be selected to form a sequence of notes, or a scale, leading from the fundamental to the octave. If music were to be restricted to a single melodic line, there would be little reason to restrict these notes to a limited set of specified frequencies. However, when two or more notes are heard simultaneously, some combinations seem to blend well while others don't.

Acoustically, *consonance* is defined as the degree of blending and fusion between two or more such notes (M. Bauer 1956). Since the days of Pythagoras (c. 500 B.C.), it has been known that frequencies bearing low-number, simple integer relationships (1:1, 2:1, 3:2, and so on) generally sound well blended, or consonant.

By contrast, the term *dissonance* defines frequency combinations bearing higher-number ratios (9:5, 9:8, and so on). When such tones are heard simultaneously, the listener generally senses a lack of musical blending, or a certain degree of discord.

The Major Scale
If the frequencies selected to form a scale are harmonically related to the fundamental frequency through simple integer relationships, there should be a certain amount of consonance when two or more such notes are heard simultaneously. Assuming that some relationships are harmonically simpler than others, there will be varying degrees of consonance, depending on the frequencies that are selected.

One example of consonance is the *major triad*, an important part of Western music for many years (Backus 1977). The first and second notes of the major triad have a frequency ratio of 4:5; for the first and third notes the frequency ratio is 4:6 (= 2:3). Therefore, the three notes are 4:4, 4:5, 4:6, or simply 4:5:6. Figure 2-1 shows how a major scale may be constructed using this triad as its foundation. The scale construction actually begins with the second set of frequencies shown in the table; 440, 550, and 660 Hz, to which the octave (880 Hz) is added. The next step is to construct one more triad working down from 440 Hz, and another upwards from 660 Hz. This gives us eight different frequencies, three of which (293.33, 333.67, 990 Hz) lie outside the octave. These frequencies are now doubled, or halved, to bring them within the octave, as indicated in the figure.

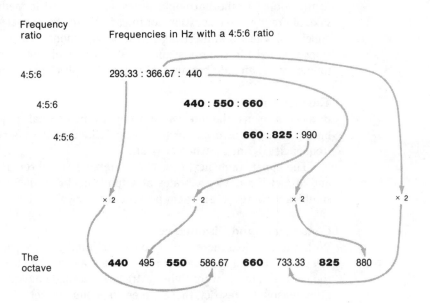

Figure 2-1. The frequencies in a just diatonic scale, based on three 4:5:6 triads. The frequencies that do not have to be changed to fall within the octave are shown in bold type. The others must be halved or doubled, as shown by regular type. In any octave, the highest frequency is twice the lowest frequency.

The Just Diatonic Scale

These as well as other musical frequencies within the octave are related to the fundamental through a ratio of two integers. The numerator is a harmonic of the fundamental, and the denominator is that subharmonic required to place the frequency within the octave that starts at the fundamental. Since this frequency series is firmly based on natural harmonics, it is known as a "pure" or "just" scale. Table 2-1 lists the ratios and interval names, as well as the notes and frequencies found in a *just diatonic scale* in the key of A. The column labeled "Consonance Index" ranks the intervals that are considered to be consonant (Plomp & Levelt 1965). However, the sequence seen in the table is by no means a universal standard: the ranking of the so-called imperfect consonances (the sixths and thirds) may vary according to the listener's musical training, especially in evaluating the minor intervals (Rossing 1983). But in any case, the intervals not ranked in the table are considered to be dissonances.

A problem now arises if another just diatonic scale is based on one of the frequencies given above. For example, using the given ratios and taking the B (= 495 Hz) from the table as our new fundamental, the next five frequencies would be 515.63 Hz, 556.88 Hz, 594 Hz, 618.75 Hz, and 660 Hz.

Note that only 495 Hz and 660 Hz coincide with frequencies already found in the table—all the other frequencies are new. In fact, there are only four frequencies common to both scales. This means that a keyboard tuned to A Major requires extra keys for the additional frequencies within the octave that are

Table 2-1. Frequency Ratios in a Just Diatonic Scale

Ratio	Interval Name	Note	Frequency (Hz)	Consonance Index
1:1	unison	A	440	1
25:24	semitone	A#	458.33	
9:8	major second	B	495	
6:5	minor third	C	528	7
5:4	major third	C#	550	6
4:3	perfect fourth	D	586.67	4
25:18	augmented fourth	D#	611.11	
3:2	perfect fifth	E	660	3
8:5	minor sixth	F	704	8
5:3	major sixth	F#	733.33	5
9:5	minor seventh	G	792	
15:8	major seventh	G#	825	
2:1	octave	A	880	2

required to play in the key of B Major. As Table 2-2A shows, several other scales also introduce frequencies not encountered previously. Each of the scales, from A# through G#, takes its fundamental from the appropriate note in the first column, as indicated by the frequency found in parentheses at the top of—and again, within—each column. A frequency appearing for the first time is printed in boldface type; the high number of these appearances shows that most instruments would need an unmanageable number of keys in order to modulate freely between all these scales.

As a further complication not shown in the table, sharps and flats are not identical; for example, the frequency of A# is slightly below that of B♭, and so on. Thus, while a system of just intonation is mathematically pure, it is not practical for sophisticated music making.

The Equal-Tempered Scale

As a practical solution to the problems of just intonation, the *equal-tempered* scale offers a compromise tuning system, in which the frequency of each note is slightly adjusted, or "tempered," so that a single frequency may be assigned to every note, regardless of the key in which it appears.

The equal-tempered scale divides the octave into twelve semitone intervals, each of which is based on the twelfth root of 2, as shown here:

$$f_n = f_0 2^{n/12}$$

where
f_n = the frequency of a note within the octave
n = the number of semitones above the fundamental
f_0 = the fundamental frequency

Table 2-2. Comparison of Just Diatonic and Equal-Tempered Scales

(A) Just Diatonic Scales*

	A (440.00)	A# (458.33)	B (495.00)	C (528.00)	C# (550.00)	D (586.67)	D# (611.11)	E (660.00)	F (704.00)	F# (733.33)	G (792.00)	G# (825.00)
A	(440.00)	429.69	445.50	440.00	440.00	440.00	424.39	440.00	440.00	440.00	445.50	429.69
A#	458.33	(458.33)	464.07	475.20	458.33	469.34	458.33	458.33	469.34	458.33	475.20	464.07
B	495.00	477.43	(495.00)	495.00	495.00	488.89	488.89	495.00	488.89	488.89	495.00	495.00
C	528.00	515.63	515.63	(528.00)	515.63	528.00	509.26	528.00	528.00	509.26	528.00	515.63
C#	550.00	550.00	556.88	550.00	(550.00)	550.00	550.00	550.00	563.20	550.00	550.00	550.00
D	586.67	572.92	594.00	594.00	572.92	(586.67)	572.92	594.00	586.67	586.67	594.00	572.92
D#	611.11	611.11	618.75	633.60	618.75	611.11	(611.11)	618.75	633.60	611.11	633.60	618.75
E	660.00	636.57	660.00	660.00	660.00	660.00	636.57	(660.00)	660.00	660.00	660.00	660.00
F	704.00	687.50	687.50	704.00	687.50	704.00	687.50	687.50	(704.00)	687.50	712.80	687.50
F#	733.33	733.33	742.50	733.33	733.33	733.33	733.33	742.50	733.33	(733.33)	742.50	742.50
G	792.00	763.89	792.00	792.00	763.89	782.22	763.89	792.00	792.00	763.89	(792.00)	773.44
G#	825.00	825.00	825.00	844.80	825.00	814.81	814.81	825.00	844.80	825.00	825.00	(825.00)
A	880.00	859.38	891.00	880.00	880.00	880.00	848.77	880.00	880.00	880.00	891.00	859.38
A#		916.67	928.13	950.40	916.67	938.67	916.67	916.67	938.67	916.67	950.40	928.13
B			990.00	990.00	990.00	977.78	977.78	990.00	977.78	977.78	990.00	990.00
C				1056.00	1031.25	1056.00	1018.52	1056.00	1056.00	1018.52	1056.00	1031.25
C#					1100.00	1100.00	1100.00	1100.00	1126.40	1100.00	1100.00	1100.00
D						1173.33	1145.83	1188.00	1173.33	1173.33	1188.00	1145.83
D#							1222.22	1237.50	1267.20	1222.22	1267.20	1237.50
E								1320.00	1320.00	1320.00	1320.00	1320.00
F									1408.00	1375.00	1425.60	1375.00
F#										1466.67	1485.00	1485.00
G											1584.00	1546.88
G#												1650.00

****Boldface** type indicates the first appearance of a frequency.

Table 2-2B lists the frequencies found in one octave of the twelve equal-tempered scales. At any frequency/note, f_n, the next-highest semitone is always $f_n 2^{1/12} = f_n(1.059)$.

One-Third and One-Half Octaves

The equal-tempered system may also be used to find various intervals within the octave that are not part of the equal-tempered scale itself. As a typical example, reference is often made to one-half or one-third octave intervals. Keep in mind that neither interval may be found by dividing the octave interval by 2 or by 3. Instead, multiply by $2^{1/2}$ (= 1.414, not 1.5) or by $2^{1/3}$, as seen here:

One-Half Octave Intervals	One-Third Octave Intervals
440.00 fundamental	440.00 fundamental
$440.00(2^{1/2}) = 622.25$	$440.00(2^{1/3}) = 554.37$
$622.25(2^{1/2}) = 880.00$	$554.37(2^{1/3}) = 698.46$
	$698.46(2^{1/3}) = 880.00$

Table 2-2. *(continued)*

(B) Equal-Tempered Scales**

	A (440.00)	A# (458.33)	B (495.00)	C (528.00)	C# (550.00)	D (586.67)	D# (611.11)	E (660.00)	F (704.00)	F# (733.33)	G (792.00)	G# (825.00)
A	440.00											
A#	466.16	466.16										
B	493.88	493.88	493.88									
C	523.25	523.25	523.25	523.25								
C#	554.37	554.37	554.37	554.37	554.37							
D	587.33	587.33	587.33	587.33	587.33	587.33						
D#	622.25	622.25	622.25	622.25	622.25	622.25	622.25					
E	659.26	659.26	659.26	659.26	659.26	659.26	659.26	659.26				
F	698.46	698.46	698.46	698.46	698.46	698.46	698.46	698.46	698.46			
F#	739.99	739.99	739.99	739.99	739.99	739.99	739.99	739.99	739.99	739.99		
G	783.99	783.99	783.99	783.99	783.99	783.99	783.99	783.99	783.99	783.99	783.99	
G#	830.61	830.61	830.61	830.61	830.61	830.61	830.61	830.61	830.61	830.61	830.61	830.61
A	880.00	880.00	880.00	880.00	880.00	880.00	880.00	880.00	880.00	880.00	880.00	880.00
		932.33	932.33	932.33	932.33	932.33	932.33	932.33	932.33	932.33	932.33	932.33
			987.77	987.77	987.77	987.77	987.77	987.77	987.77	987.77	987.77	987.77
				1046.50	1046.50	1046.50	1046.50	1046.50	1046.50	1046.50	1046.50	1046.50
					1108.73	1108.73	1108.73	1108.73	1108.73	1108.73	1108.73	1108.73
						1174.66	1174.66	1174.66	1174.66	1174.66	1174.66	1174.66
							1244.51	1244.51	1244.51	1244.51	1244.51	1244.51
								1318.51	1318.51	1318.51	1318.51	1318.51
									1396.91	1396.91	1396.91	1396.91
										1479.98	1479.98	1479.98
											1587.98	1587.98
												1661.22

**Every frequency is $2^{1/12}$ (1.059) times higher than the previous frequency, and A# = B♭, G# = A♭, etc.

Music and Engineering Frequency Comparisons

The frequencies commonly used in audio engineering rarely coincide with frequencies found within any musical scale. As an obvious example, just about any graph of frequency response shows numbers such as 20, 100, 1,000 Hz, and so on. Even the frequencies found on equalizer front panels rarely coincide with the music frequencies listed in Tables 2-1 and 2-2. Instead, such frequencies are usually based on a list of preferred frequencies defined and published by various standards organizations (e. g., ISO 266-1975, ANSI S1.6-1984). The purpose of using a standard frequency list is to reduce an infinity of frequencies to some manageable number that will permit easier comparisons between systems. In sound recording work, such a list offers the engineer a reasonable chance of duplicating, say, an equalization setting scribbled on a tape box from another studio.

A table of preferred frequencies may be calculated starting at a preferred reference frequency of 1 Hz and spanning an interval of one decade; that is, from *f* to 10*f*, or 1 Hz to 10 Hz. Higher frequencies may then be found by multiplying any frequency by 10, 100, and so on.

Although the frequencies thus found do not coincide with the notes in any musical scale, the musical interval of one-third of an octave is very close to the interval of one-tenth of a decade. Table 2-3 compares the preferred and musical frequencies that lie within an interval of one decade. The frequencies were found from the following equations:

$$f_p = 10^{n/10}$$
$$f_m = 2^{y/6}$$

where

f_p = preferred frequency
n = any integer between 0 and 10 (for one-tenth decade intervals)
f_m = musical frequency
y = any integer between 0 and 6 (for one-sixth octave intervals)

Table 2-3. ISO and Music Frequency Interval Comparison Chart

ISO Interval		Music Interval		Error**
n^*	f_p	y	f_m	(%)
0.0	1.000	0	1.000	0.000
0.5	1.122	1	1.122	0.044
1.0	1.259 (1.25)***	2	1.260	0.079
1.5	1.413	3	1.414	0.119
2.0	1.585 (1.6)	4	1.587	0.158
2.5	1.778	5	1.782	0.197
3.0	1.995 (2)	6	2.000	0.237
3.5	2.239	1	2.245	0.276
4.0	2.512 (2.5)	2	2.520	0.316
4.5	2.818	3	2.828	0.355
5.0	3.162 (3.15)	4	3.175	0.394
5.5	3.548	5	3.564	0.434
6.0	3.981 (4)	6	4.000	0.473
6.5	4.467	1	4.490	0.513
7.0	5.012 (5)	2	5.040	0.552
7.5	5.623	3	5.567	0.591
8.0	6.310 (6.3)	4	6.350	0.630
8.5	7.079	5	7.127	0.670
9.0	7.943 (8)	6	8.000	0.709
9.5	8.913	1	8.980	0.748
10.0	10.000 (10)	2	10.079	0.787

*Decade divided in 20 parts for comparison with 1/6 octave music intervals.
**Error is between music and ISO interval.
***Interval in parentheses is as rounded off in ANSI S1.6-1984.

ISO frequencies will again be encountered in Chapter 7 in the discussion of graphic equalizer center frequencies (page 290).

Harmonics in Music and Electronics

If it were not for the harmonic series, musical instruments would all sound pretty much the same and—even worse—would all sound more or less like a collection of tuning forks or sine wave generators. It's the rich harmonic series that gives each instrument much of its character and that makes it all worth listening to.

One way of analyzing harmonic structure is via Fourier analysis, which is briefly described below.

Fourier Series

A periodic waveform is any waveform that repeats itself, such as a simple sine or cosine function. A more complex, but still periodic, waveform may be constructed by simply combining two or more sine or cosine functions. The period of the composite waveform will be the least common multiple of each of the periods, as seen here:

The Periods of Several Sine Waves (ms)	The Period of the Composite Waveform (ms)
4 and 6	12
3 and 5	15
2, 9.5, and 17	323
8, 32, 48, and 96	96

Fourier analysis (after Jean Baptiste Joseph Fourier, 1768–1830) shows that any periodic waveform can be expressed as a series of sine and cosine functions. As obvious examples, we already know that each composite waveform produced by the combinations just listed is by definition the sum of several sine waves. As another example, a piano or guitar string produces a fundamental frequency and a series of harmonics—each of which is a sine wave. Figure 2-2 shows a simple example of such a periodic wave created by the summation of a fundamental and two harmonics. A simplified equation for each waveform is given in the figure, and it follows that the equation for the resultant waveform is therefore the summation of the three individual equations, as also shown in the figure.

Although the sinusoidal origins of the complex waveform shown in Figure 2-2D are still apparent, there will be little or no resemblance to the familiar sine (or cosine) wave in the actual waveforms generated by most musical instruments whose harmonic structure is far more complex than that shown in the figure.

Square Wave Analysis

A perfect square wave is likewise a periodic waveform, and Fourier analysis shows that it is comprised of a sine wave of some fundamental frequency, f, and a series

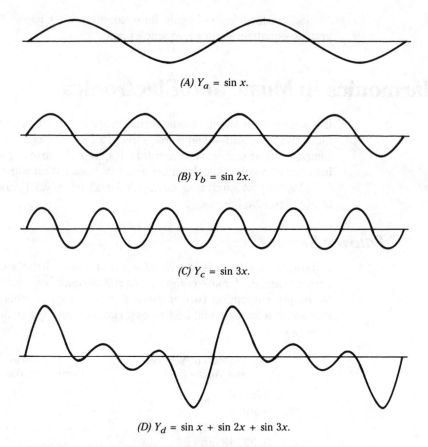

(A) $Y_a = \sin x.$

(B) $Y_b = \sin 2x.$

(C) $Y_c = \sin 3x.$

(D) $Y_d = \sin x + \sin 2x + \sin 3x.$

Figure 2-2. A complex periodic waveform may be expressed as a series
of sine and cosine functions, as seen here. In this example, the sine
waves in parts A, B, and C combine to form the waveform in
part D. It follows that any other complex periodic waveform also
comprises a similar series of sine and/or cosine functions.

of odd harmonics, $3f$, $5f$, $7f$, and so on. The amplitudes of these harmonics are $\frac{1}{3}$, $\frac{1}{5}$, $\frac{1}{7}$, ... that of the fundamental. The equation for a square wave may be written as the Fourier series

$$y = (4/\pi)\left[\frac{1}{1}\sin x + \frac{1}{3}\sin 3x + \frac{1}{5}\sin 5x + \cdots\right]$$

where
$$x = 2\pi ft$$

Figure 2-3 shows four waveforms, each constructed from a fundamental sine wave and a series of odd harmonics. As the figure illustrates, the more harmonics, the better the appearance of the square wave. Note that the ideal square wave is comprised of a fundamental frequency and an infinite series of odd harmonics. Such a waveform may be generated by an electronic switching system that simply alternates between a positive and negative DC voltage, as is in fact done in signal generators that provide a square wave output.

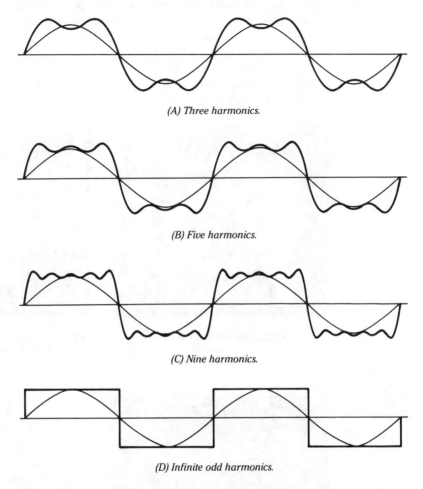

(A) Three harmonics.

(B) Five harmonics.

(C) Nine harmonics.

(D) Infinite odd harmonics.

Figure 2-3. A series of square waves, comprised of fundamental and differing numbers of harmonics. Note that the fewer the harmonics, the closer the waveform is to a sine wave.

However, since any audio signal processing system has a finite frequency response, it follows that when a perfect square wave is applied to its input, the system output will be something less than perfect. For example, consider a square wave whose fundamental frequency is 5 kHz. The odd-harmonic frequencies are at 15, 25, 35, 45 (and so on) kHz. Assuming the device is perfectly flat to 50 kHz and then falls off rapidly, its square wave output will closely resemble the waveform shown in Figure 2-3B. Given a device with a more realistic frequency response, the waveform will look even worse.

The square wave is therefore a useful tool for examining an audio system's bandwidth. For example, when the input is a low-frequency square wave, many upper harmonics will lie within the range of the system under test, and its output waveform should closely resemble the input. But as the input frequency is slowly raised, the output waveform deteriorates as more and more harmonics fall outside the system's upper limit. Eventually the output resembles a pure sine wave, once all the harmonics of the applied input signal are beyond the range of the system under test.

Figure 2-3 showed how the squareness of the waveform improves as a function of the number of harmonics present. In practice however, phase shifts and other factors are also introduced, and the "square wave" output of a device under test may bear little or no resemblance to the applied input signal, as shown by the examples in Figure 2-4.

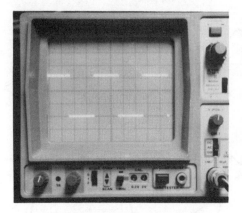

(A) Input waveform. (Courtesy Len Feldman)

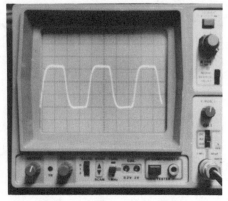

(B) Output waveform showing moderate waveform distortion. (Courtesy Len Feldman)

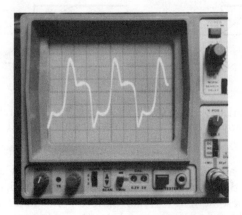

(C) Output waveform showing severe waveform distortion. (Courtesy Len Feldman)

Figure 2-4. Square wave tests.

It should be kept in mind that the square wave is not a reliable test signal for mechanical systems. For example, if a perfect square wave were applied to a loudspeaker, the diaphragm would have to follow the waveform contour in order to reproduce it with accuracy. For each complete cycle this would mean a four-step process; an instantaneous forward excursion, no motion at all for a half cycle, an instantaneous rearward excursion, and again no motion for the next half cycle. Such performance is still quite a bit beyond the capabilities of most mechanical systems, including the loudspeaker.

But, given a theoretically ideal loudspeaker—at least on paper—the next problem would be to get the surrounding air molecules to follow the same sort of stop/go motion. However, air is an elastic medium, and the perfect square wave would soon deteriorate as the molecules would fail to keep pace with the force disturbing them.

So with a practical loudspeaker operating on an elastic medium, there's not much chance of producing and then transmitting a square wave through the air, nor for that matter of finding a microphone that could faithfully convert it back to electric energy. The microphone would have the same problem as does the speaker, that of accurately tracking a square wave input signal.

Harmonic Distortion

When a signal—square wave or otherwise—passes through a transducer, amplifier, or other signal processing device, the output waveform should of course be a faithful replica of the input. However, in addition to the high-frequency filtering effects illustrated in the square wave examples above, most circuits also introduce harmonic components that are a distortion of the input signal frequency. The harmonics appear at integer multiples of the fundamental.

This *harmonic distortion* is usually expressed as a percentage. For example, if the input to a device is a 1-volt sine wave at frequency f, and the output contains a 0.1-volt component at $2f$, the output is said to contain 10 percent second-harmonic distortion.

Since second- and fourth-harmonic distortion components correspond to one- and two-octave intervals, they are (or should be) almost imperceptible. In fact, a bit of even-harmonic distortion is often perceived as adding a certain amount of "richness" to a musical signal; at least a few early vacuum tube devices were widely admired for the generous supply of upper octaves that they added.

Even third-harmonic distortion is not necessarily unpleasant. In musical terms, the third harmonic, $3f$, is one octave plus a perfect fifth (that is, a twelfth) above the fundamental, and so may add a little "color" to the sound. In fact, it's common practice for some organ stops to add this multiple for just this purpose. However, the equivalent equal-tempered interval, which is 19 semitones above the fundamental, is slightly out of tune with the natural third harmonic, as shown here.

$$440(3) = 1,320 \text{ Hz} \qquad \text{natural third harmonic}$$
$$440(2^{19/12}) = 1,318.51 \text{ Hz} \qquad \text{equal-tempered interval}$$

Although some even harmonics correspond to equal-tempered intervals ($2f$, $4f$, $8f$, and so on), all the other harmonics fall at just-intonation intervals. Therefore, the naturally occurring third harmonic of, say, a piano string is slightly out of tune with the equivalent note on the equal-tempered keyboard. However, the discrepancy between an equal-tempered interval and one of these harmonics is probably far below the general limits of pitch perception.

In the presence of a musical instrument whose entire character comes from a rich harmonic series (that is, from a lot of harmonic "distortion"), it may seem like nit-picking to quibble over some mere fraction of a percent distortion added by an amplifier or other signal-processing device. Nevertheless, a very little of the latter goes a long way toward deteriorating the sound of the former.

Psychoacoustics

The term *psychoacoustics* may be broadly defined as a study of the complex reactions of the listener to the sound field. Those reactions are a function of many variables, some of which are discussed in the remaining sections of this chapter.

Equal Loudness Contours

The threshold of hearing described in Chapter 1 is the point at which the average listener can just barely hear a sound. In 1933, Fletcher and Munson conducted a series of tests which demonstrated that this threshold is very much a function of frequency. The tests showed that the ear is quite sensitive to a low-level test tone in the vicinity of 4,000 Hz, but it becomes progressively less sensitive as the frequency is decreased. To a lesser degree, the ear also becomes less sensitive as the frequency rises above 4,000 Hz. In other words, as the test frequency falls below 4,000 Hz it must be made progressively louder in order to be heard. And as it rises above 4,000 Hz, it must also be increased in level, but not by as much as at low frequencies.

If the test is repeated with the 4,000 Hz reference tone somewhat higher in level, the same phenomenon appears. However, the extreme low and high frequencies do not require as much boost as previously. At each higher-level repetition of the test, the required boost at low and high frequencies diminishes. A set of response curves taken at various perceived listening levels is shown in Figure 2-4. Such curves are usually referred to as *equal loudness contours*, since each curve represents the variation in actual level required in order for the typical listener to perceive that all test tones are of equal loudness. Although the names of Fletcher and Munson are still widely used in association with the equal-loudness contours, their original contours have been slightly modified by later tests (Robinson & Dadson 1956). The revised curves shown in Figure 2-5 have been published as a standard by the International Organization for Standardization (ISO 226: 1987 Acoustics—Normal Equal-Loudness Level Contours).

In the figure, the contour at the threshold of hearing is indicated by the dashed line labeled MAF, meaning *minimum audible field*. At each frequency, the minimum audible field indicates the minimum sound pressure level that a person with normal hearing can perceive. The MAF contour shows that for a 31.5 Hz test tone (7 octaves below 4,000 Hz) to be just perceptible, its level must be about 60 dB greater than that of the 4,000 Hz tone. At 8,000 Hz (1 octave above 4,000 Hz), the level must be about 20 dB greater.

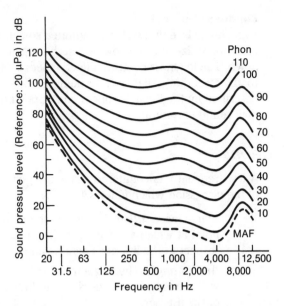

Figure 2-5. Normal equal-loudness level contours for pure tones. MAF =
Minimum audible field, 4.2 phon. *(From ISO 226: 1987 standard)*

The Phon

Each equal-loudness contour is given a value in phons. The *phon* is defined as the
sound pressure level for the contour when the test frequency is 1,000 Hz. Thus,
each phon contour defines a range of sound pressure levels across the frequency
spectrum of 20 Hz to 12.5 kHz. When the sound pressure level across this range is
continuously adjusted to follow a phon contour, the typical listener perceives all
frequencies to be equal in loudness to the 1,000 Hz reference tone.

Note that the equal loudness contours are a natural characteristic of human
hearing, and each contour merely illustrates the natural response of our ear/
brain mechanism at a certain listening level. No attempt should ever be made to
compensate for the shape of these contours (with the possible exception of the
loudness control discussed below).

The practical consequence of the equal loudness contours is that as the
overall listening level is decreased, the listener perceives a falling-off of bass
response, and to a lesser extent, of high frequency response. Therefore, a master
tape that was balanced at a high listening level will sound weaker in bass and
high end later on, when played back at a lower level. Conversely, a program
mixed at a low listening level will seem to have more bass and treble when played
back at a louder level.

Given these facts of auditory life, there's something to be said for keeping the
listening level within reason during a mixdown session. If that level gets too loud
(as often happens), the final product will probably suffer as a result, when heard
by the record buyer at a "normal" listening level. In contrast, if the mix is
acceptable at a low level, it will probably sound even better at higher levels. This
applies especially to contemporary popular music, where there's almost no such
thing as "too much bass."

Loudness Control

Some home listening systems contain a so-called *loudness* control, whose purpose is to emphasize extreme low and high frequencies as the volume control is turned down. The loudness control's effectiveness is often marginal, since it is an attempt to fix something that isn't broken; we are used to the natural phenomenon described by the equal loudness contours, and an attempt to reverse the process may sound unnatural.

Definitions

A few frequently encountered terms are given brief definitions here, for the sake of the discussion which follows.

- *Image localization.* The term *localization* refers to the perception of the point at which a sound source, or image, seems to be situated with respect to the listener's own position.
- *Arrival angle.* The angle from which an original sound source arrives, with zero degrees understood to indicate a source that is directly in front of the listener.
- *Interaural.* Refers to any comparison between an audio signal measured at one ear, and the same signal measured at the other ear.
- *Original source.* Any unrecorded sound that travels from its origin via a straight-line path directly to the listener.
- *Reproduced source.* Any sound recorded earlier and now played back over one or two speakers.

Localization Parameters

Using the listener's own position as a reference point, the location of a sound source may be conveniently described by two parameters: distance and arrival angle. For this discussion, height is ignored; it is assumed that all arriving sounds originate more or less at ear level.

Although a fair amount of localization information is often lost in the recording process, modern production techniques can go a long way toward restoring the missing information, provided the engineer has the basic tools available and understands their significance. As we shall soon see, the ubiquitous pan pot is not always the last word in determining where a signal is supposed to be coming from.

Distance Cues

The perception of the distance from which a sound arrives is itself a function of four variables, each of which is discussed below. The variables are

1. Loudness
2. Ratio of direct to reflected sound
3. Frequency response (high frequency attenuation)
4. Time delay

Loudness   All else being equal, obviously the closer the sound the louder it will be. However, all else is rarely if ever equal, and loudness by itself is relatively uninformative. For example, turning a volume control up and down does nothing to vary the impression of distance, unless the level change is accompanied by one or more other important distance cues.

Direct-to-Reflected Sound   A far more important distance cue is the ratio of direct to reflected sound that reaches the listener. (This subject is discussed in much greater detail in Chapter 6.) As an obvious example, consider a sound very close to the listener, and another at a great distance. In either case there is one direct path to the listener and many reflected paths, as the sound bounces off various surfaces in the listening area. However, the close-up source is heard almost entirely as direct sound; little or no reflected sound is perceived, because the direct path is so short and all the reflected paths are very much longer. Given the inverse-square law (Chapter 1, page 18), the amplitude of the arriving reflections is far below that of the direct sound.

By contrast, sound arriving from a distant source is accompanied by many reflections of itself, some of which arrive just after the direct sound. Again, the inverse-square law is at work: with little difference in path lengths there is less of a difference between the amplitude of the direct and reflected sounds. There still are, however, significant differences due to absorption of each reflected sound as it strikes the various surfaces in the room. But in any case, the relative locations of a loud sound from far away and a quiet sound nearby will never be confused.

Figure 2-6 illustrates typical direct and reflected paths for nearby and distant sound sources.

High-Frequency Attenuation   As a pressure wave travels through the surrounding air, there is a gradual loss of high-frequency information due to atmospheric absorption. For example, at a temperature of 68 degrees Fahrenheit, a 10 kHz signal is attenuated some 0.15 to 0.3 dB per meter, depending on the relative humidity (Davis 1987). This high-frequency attenuation may help convey a feeling of distance, provided the listener already has some frame of reference; that is, the same source has recently been heard close up, or is so familiar that the listener knows from experience what it is supposed to sound like when nearby.

Time Delay   As a final distance cue, it takes a certain amount of time for any sound to reach the listener. For example, the sound produced by a musician in the last row of a large ensemble may arrive some 20 or more milliseconds later than the sound of a front-and-center placed soloist. With the earlier sound serving as a frame of reference, the later arrival of a more distant source becomes a subtle yet powerful distance cue.

Angle of Arrival Cues
The listener's perception of the angle from which a sound arrives is determined by subtle differences between the way each ear hears the same signal. As with distance cues, there are several variables to be considered. These are

1. Relative loudness

2. Frequency response

3. Time of arrival difference

Relative Loudness   In theory, there will be an interaural level difference when an original sound source arrives from an off-center location. In practice, however, that difference is sometimes so slight as to be imperceptible. For example, consider a sound source originating 90 degrees off axis, but located only 2 meters away, as shown in Figure 2-7A. Given an ear spacing of, say, 21 cm, the ratio of the distances to each ear is 2/2.21 = 0.90. This means the interaural level difference attributable to distance alone is 20 log (0.90), or only -0.87 dB. (For the moment, we ignore the effect of head itself as a barrier between the source and the distant ear.)

In the more normal listening environment shown in Figure 2-7B, the arrival angle is 30 degrees, and the source distance is 4 meters. Under these conditions, the additional path length to the distant ear is only 0.1 meter, so the interaural level difference is reduced to 20 log (4/4.1) = -0.2 dB.

From these examples, it can be seen that under normal listening conditions, the interaural level difference from a slight additional path length to the more distant ear is not of much use as a localization cue.

Frequency Response   However, when a signal does arrive from some off-axis location, the effect of the listener's own head cannot be ignored; it becomes an acoustic obstacle in the path to the distant ear. At low frequencies, the resultant attenuation is minimal, due to the diffraction effects described in Chapter 1.

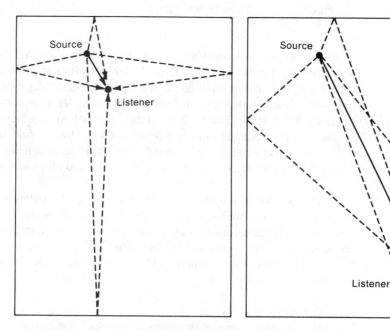

(A) Paths from a nearby sound source.   *(B) Paths from a distant sound source.*

Figure 2-6. Between the sound source and the listener there is always one
direct path and many reflected paths.

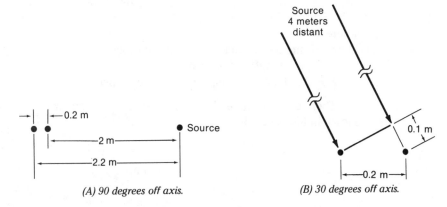

(A) 90 degrees off axis.   *(B) 30 degrees off axis.*

Figure 2-7. The interaural path-length differences for a sound arriving from 90 and 30 degrees off axis. In either case, the attenuation due to additional distance to the more distant ear is negligible.

However, as the frequency of the source signal increases, its wavelength decreases, and the head becomes more of a barrier to the arriving sound. Therefore, there is apt to be considerable high-frequency attenuation at the distant ear as the sound source moves farther off center.

Time of Arrival Difference   Within a certain frequency band, time becomes a very important localization cue. For example, consider a plane pressure waveform arriving from some off-center location. As noted above, if the sound pressure were measured at each ear, there would be almost no difference in level. However, the sound would arrive a bit later at the ear that is more distant from the sound source. In the following examples, a distance of 21 cm is used as the spacing between the ears. The actual spacing will of course vary from one listener to another, and this value was selected for the sake of other calculations that will follow.

To determine the additional time it will take for a sound to reach the more distant ear, refer to Figure 2-8. In the figure,

$$d = x \sin \theta$$

where
 d = path-length difference
 x = 21 cm (spacing between ears)
 θ = 55° (in this example)

and therefore,

$$d = 21(0.819)$$
$$= 17.20 \text{ cm}$$

At the speed of sound, the time delay is

$$t = d/c$$

where

t = time delay (time-of-arrival difference)
d = path-length difference
c = 34,400 cm/sec (speed of sound in air)

Therefore, the time delay for a signal arriving from the off-center source shown in Figure 2-8 is

$$t = 17.20/34,400$$
$$= 0.5 \text{ ms}$$

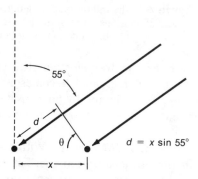

Figure 2-8. An example of interaural time delay when a sound originates at some off-axis angle.

A delay of only 0.5 ms may seem insignificant as a localization cue. In fact, at an ear spacing of 21 cm, the total extent of interaural time delay only ranges from 0 ms (sound source straight ahead) to 0.61 ms (source at 90 degrees). In other words, the longest path length delay is just a bit more than one-half of one-thousandth of one second—a very small delay indeed.

To get a better idea of how such a slight delay may influence the ear's localization mechanism, we first will examine the effect of the 0.5 ms delay on a 2,000 Hz sine wave. Since the period of 2,000 Hz is 0.5 ms, the signal arrives exactly one cycle, or 360 degrees, late at the distant ear. Of course the 0.5 ms delay will vary with different ear spacings, and the significant variable should be understood to be the ratio of wavelength to path length.

A comparison of the waveforms at each ear reveals the following characteristics:

arrival time difference	slight (0.5 ms)
amplitude difference	slight, perhaps none
phase shift	no measurable difference (since $360° = 0°$)

So far, there doesn't seem to be anything here to help the listener localize the sound source. But now let's look at what happens at frequencies lower than 2,000 Hz. Obviously, the arrival time doesn't change, since the speed of sound is not frequency-dependent. And if there was any amplitude difference at all at 2,000 Hz, that difference will be even less at lower frequencies, due to the diffraction effects described in Chapter 1 (page 29).

Phase Shift   This leaves phase shift to be considered. The following chart tabulates the interaural phase shift for various frequencies below 2,000 Hz when such a signal arrives 0.5 ms late at one ear.

Frequency (Hz)	Wavelength (cm)	Phase Shift (°)
125	265.160	22.5
250	132.580	45
500	66.290	90
1,000	33.145	180
2,000	16.573	360

As the table clearly indicates, a seemingly insignificant path length/time delay difference produces significant phase shifts for frequencies below 2,000 Hz. In the absence of any other differences between the sounds heard at each ear, we may assume that this phase shift is used by the ear/brain mechanism as a localization mechanism.

Now consider what happens when the arriving frequency is higher than 2,000 Hz: its wavelength is shorter than the path length difference between the ears, and therefore the interaural phase shift is greater than 360 degrees. If the waveform is only observable at each ear, as is indeed the case, there is no way to determine whether the phase is shifted by, say, 10, 370, or 730 degrees. Given this ambiguity, we may assume that as the frequency rises above 2,000 Hz the resultant interaural phase shift is no longer an effective localization cue.

However, as the frequency rises, the listener's head becomes more of an acoustic obstacle to the signal arriving at the distant ear, and this results in a measurable interaural level difference. This difference in interaural frequency response takes the place of phase shift as the variable which helps the listener determine the angle at which the sound originates.

The following summarizes the effect of a 0.5 ms time delay on various frequency ranges. Again, remember that 2,000 Hz was simply chosen as the frequency whose wavelength provides a 1:1 ratio with the path length found above.

Frequency (Hz)	Ratio of Wavelength to Path Length	Interaural Phase Shift (°)	Interaural Level Difference	Dominant Localization Cue
< 2,000	> 1:1	< 360	none	phase shift
2,000	1:1	360	slight	transition zone
> 2,000	< 1:1	> 360	increases with frequency	level difference

3 Microphones

Whether on stage or in the recording studio, the microphone of choice is rarely selected after a careful reading of its specification sheet. Instead, the engineer makes a decision based on a mixture of previous experiences, what's available at the moment, and—sometimes—on the wishes of an artist who has discovered a favorite microphone.

The recording-studio beginner often wastes time searching out the definitive list of preferred microphones, in the hopes that somewhere, someone actually has such a list. Of course, every seasoned engineer does indeed have a list of his own; but although it is a preferred list, it is certainly not the definitive list. And in the wrong hands, it is a useless list—or worse.

In short, and notwithstanding the occasional overly enthusiastic ad copywriter, there is no "correct" microphone for any application. Microphone choice is mostly a matter of taste, and as in choosing just about everything else in the world, we don't all share the same taste buds. That's why restaurants have menus, and why microphone manufacturers make more than one model.

Nevertheless, a basic understanding of how a microphone works will go a long way toward helping the user select the microphone that will best complement his or her personal taste. It may even help the engineer persuade an artist that a favorite microphone in one venue does not always work well in another, or even in the same one on a different occasion.

Figure 1-4 in Chapter 1 showed how a voltage can be generated by moving a conductor through a magnetic field. The generator which does this might be thought of as a *transducer*, that is, a device that converts energy from one form into another. A microphone is a transducer, in that it converts acoustic energy first into mechanical energy and then into electric energy.

Of the many methods that have been tried over the years to convert audio into electricity, today most practical studio-quality microphones may be classified under one of two major categories, the dynamic microphone and the capacitor microphone, both of which are described below.

The Dynamic Microphone

Conceptually, the dynamic microphone is a rather simple device, in which an electric conductor is suspended in a magnetic field. The variation in air pressure created by any sound in the immediate area forces the conductor to vibrate within the field. The current induced in the conductor is the electric analog of the acoustic pressure wave.

Dynamic microphones may be subdivided into two classes, moving-coil and ribbon, depending on the particular construction technique used in the manufacture of the microphone.

Nomenclature

Although the term *dynamic* properly refers to both the moving-coil and ribbon designs described below, in the jargon of the recording studio the dynamic moving-coil microphone is popularly known as, simply, a dynamic microphone. By contrast, the dynamic ribbon microphone is usually referred to as a ribbon microphone. Because of this popular but ambiguous use of terminology, this book uses *dynamic* only in conjunction with those characteristics that apply to the moving-coil *and* to the ribbon microphone.

The Moving-Coil Microphone

In the most widely used implementation of the dynamic microphone, a coil of wire is attached to the back of a thin circular membrane, or diaphragm, that is suspended in a magnetic field. As the diaphragm vibrates in response to an impinging sound wave, the coil moves back and forth within the magnetic field and an output current is induced in the coiled wire. Hence the name moving-coil microphone.

Figure 3-1 illustrates the principle of moving-coil design, and Figure 3-2 shows a few popular studio microphones in which the moving-coil mechanism is used.

The Ribbon Microphone

In contrast to the moving-coil design, some dynamic microphones use a metallic membrane which functions as both the diaphragm and as the moving conductor. In a typical design, a thin electrically conductive foil is suspended in the magnetic field. Wires attached to each end of the foil bring the induced voltage to a transformer mounted in the microphone housing. The transformer serves two purposes: to step up the voltage and to raise the microphone's output impedance to approximate that of the moving-coil microphone.

Because the diaphragm is usually formed in the shape of a thin ribbon of metallic foil, the microphone is referred to as a ribbon microphone. Figure 3-3

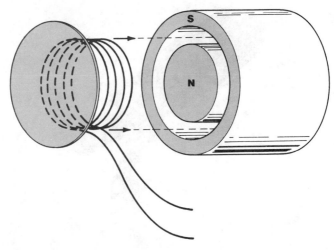

(A) A coil of wire attached to the diaphragm is suspended in a magnetic field. As the diaphragm moves back and forth, a current is induced in the coil.

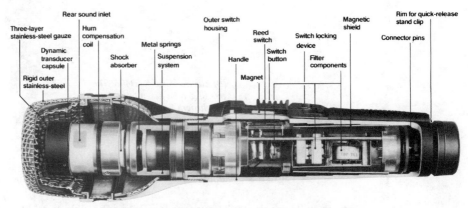

(B) Cutaway view of a modern dynamic moving-coil microphone, the Sennheiser MD 431. (Courtesy Sennheiser Electronic Corp.)

Figure 3-1. The dynamic moving-coil microphone.

illustrates the principle of ribbon microphone design, and Figure 3-4 shows a few popular studio dynamic ribbon microphones.

The earliest ribbon microphones were rather bulky devices with a delicate ribbon structure. Such microphones do not stand up well against the demands of contemporary recording; a misplaced puff of air is all it takes to put one out of commission. As a result, the older ribbon microphone could not compete with the much more robust moving-coil design and generally fell out of favor as a studio tool.

However, the extremely low mass of a ribbon diaphragm does offer a potentially excellent transient response. That, coupled with recent design improvements, has brought the ribbon microphone back into serious consideration. In terms of durability, the latest-model ribbon microphone will take about as much

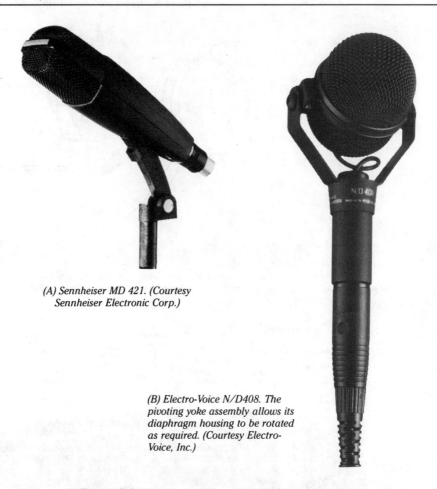

*(A) Sennheiser MD 421. (Courtesy
Sennheiser Electronic Corp.)*

*(B) Electro-Voice N/D408. The
pivoting yoke assembly allows its
diaphragm housing to be rotated
as required. (Courtesy Electro-
Voice, Inc.)*

Figure 3-2. Representative examples of moving-coil microphones.

abuse as its moving-coil counterpart. But as the ribbon design makes its way back
to popular acceptance, remember ruggedness is not retroactive; when using a
vintage ribbon microphone, treat it with extra care and avoid subjecting it to the
rigors of close-up placement.

The Capacitor Microphone

In contrast to the microphones with dynamic design principles briefly described
above, a microphone may also be designed in which the diaphragm is one of the
plates of a capacitor. As the diaphragm vibrates, the distance between it and the
other plate of the capacitor varies, and therefore so does the device's capacitance.

In order to function, the capacitor/diaphragm must be biased with a polarizing DC voltage across its plates. And, unlike the dynamic moving-coil microphone, the circuit output voltage and impedance are both high. Consequently, a
special preamplifier must be inserted between the diaphragm and the console or

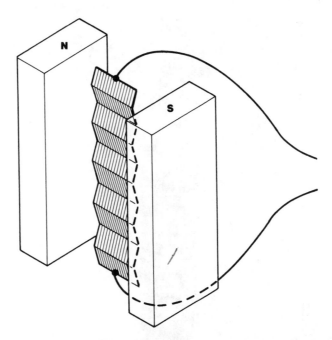

Figure 3-3. The dynamic ribbon microphone. A very thin corrugated metallic foil is suspended in a magnetic field and a current is induced within the foil as it moves back and forth.

tape recorder input. It should be noted that this preamplifier is part of the microphone system itself, and is an addition to—not a substitute for—the microphone preamplifier found in the console. The latter device is described in more detail in Chapter 12 (page 473).

Nomenclature
Some years ago, the term *condenser* was used to describe the circuit element now called a capacitor, and a microphone designed around this element was known as a condenser microphone. Although the term *capacitor* is today used almost universally in circuit design descriptions, either term may be found in descriptions of microphone design. For the sake of consistency, *capacitor* is used throughout this book.

The Conventional Capacitor Microphone

Figure 3-5 illustrates the basic design principles of the conventional capacitor microphone, so called here to distinguish it from the electret capacitor microphone described in the next section of this chapter. Figure 3-6 shows representative capacitor microphones suitable for studio use.

It should be clear that this type of transducer is electronically more complex than a dynamic microphone. As noted, a polarizing voltage and a preamplifier are required, and of course the preamplifier also requires its own source of power. Power supplies for capacitor microphones are described later on in this chapter.

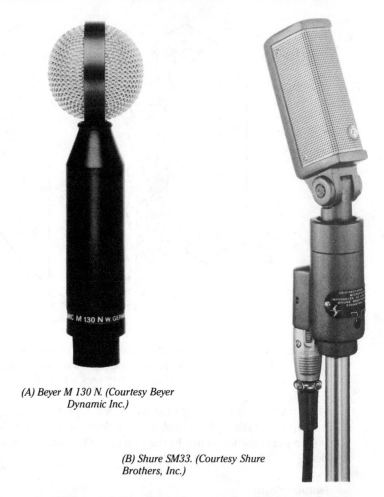

(A) Beyer M 130 N. (Courtesy Beyer
Dynamic Inc.)

(B) Shure SM33. (Courtesy Shure
Brothers, Inc.)

Figure 3-4. Representative examples of ribbon microphones.

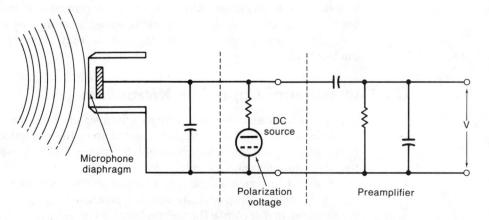

Figure 3-5. The capacitor microphone. The diaphragm is one of the plates of a
capacitor. Circuit capacitance varies according to the motion
of the capacitor/diaphragm.

The Electret Capacitor Microphone

The term *electret* describes a dielectric substance that exhibits a continuing polarization after an electric field is applied and then withdrawn (Bevan, Schulein & Seeler 1978). The electret polarization, or bias, is analogous to the magnetic retention of a permanent magnet.

In an electret capacitor microphone, the surface of one of the capacitor plates is covered with an electret material. A thin air gap separates the electret surface from the capacitor's other plate. Although either plate may be designed to function as the microphone's diaphragm, many recent designs attach the electret to the backplate. Such a microphone is often referred to as a *back-electret* microphone.

From the viewpoint of the microphone designer, a significant advantage of the electret principle is that it obviates the need to supply the capacitor/diaphragm with a bias voltage, although power is still required for the pre-amplifier built into the microphone housing. Compared to the conventional capacitor microphone, the electret offers a potentially higher signal-to-noise ratio and is also less susceptible to humidity-induced arcing.

In the representative example of a back-electret microphone shown in Figure 3-7A, the diaphragm is a gold-covered Mylar membrane. The backplate consists of a Teflon electret layer affixed to a stationary gold-covered plate.

Capacitor Microphone Power Supplies

As already noted, the capacitor microphone requires a DC voltage source for its preamplifier, and, in the case of the conventional capacitor microphone, for bias voltage as well. In the pretransistor age, the vacuum-tube microphone required a fairly substantial power supply to supply these voltages.

External Power Supply

Because the requisite supply was inevitably as big as—or bigger than—the microphone itself, it was built into its own chassis, which then had to be inserted in the microphone line. Although a standard microphone cable could be used between the power supply and the console, the line leading from the supply to the microphone required additional conductors for bias, B+ (plate), and filament voltages for the vacuum-tube preamplifier built into the microphone housing. Other conductors in the same cable accommodated the audio signal output from the microphone.

Needless to say, the power requirements of various capacitor microphones were rarely identical, and therefore each microphone required its own cable and its own power supply. As a further complication, the microphone's power supply required its own source of AC power, so it had to be placed reasonably near an electric outlet.

Figure 3-8 illustrates the cable requirements for a typical externally powered vacuum-tube capacitor microphone system, and also shows a typical power supply.

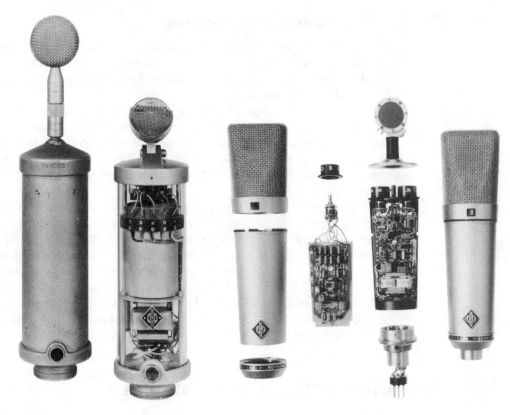

*(A) Neumann CMV 3. (Courtesy
Gotham Audio Corp.)*

*(B) Neumann U 89. (Courtesy Gotham
Audio Corp.)*

Figure 3-6. Representative examples of old and new capacitor
microphones.

(A) Shure SM81. (Courtesy Shure Brothers, Inc.)

Figure 3-7. Back-electret capacitor microphones.

(continued on next page)

(B) AKG C 1000 S. (Courtesy AKG Acoustics, Inc.)

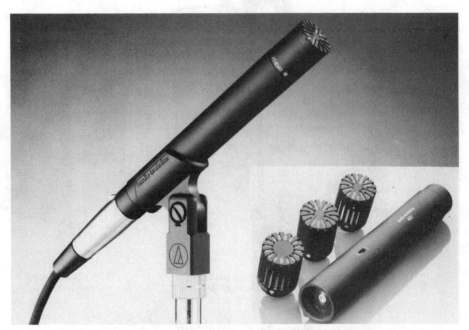

(C) Audio-Technica's AT4000 series modular studio microphone. Inset shows replaceable head (diaphragm) capsules. (Courtesy Audio-Technica U.S., Inc.)

Figure 3-7 *(continued)*

Although most such capacitor microphones have long since been superseded by more modern designs, a few have been accorded the status of collector's item and are jealously protected by their owners. In most cases, the microphone is admired for its distinctive sound, and its technological limitations are endured as a price well worth paying.

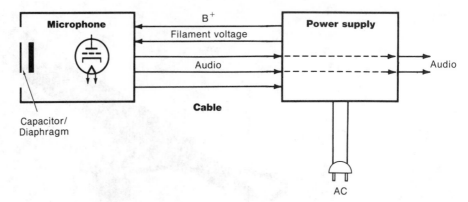

(A) The cable requirements for an externally powered capacitor microphone.

(B) Power supply for early capacitor microphone. (AKG N 24 Courtesy AKG Acoustics, Inc.)

(C) Power supply for early capacitor microphone. (Neumann NN24 Courtesy Gotham Audio Corp.)

Figure 3-8. Cable requirements and power supplies for early vacuum-tube capacitor microphones.

Phantom Power Supply System

Power supply requirements were greatly simplified with the introduction of the transistor, in that a single DC voltage could now handle both biasing and powering the microphone's built-in preamplifier.

An elegant method of supplying that power to the microphone is via a phantom power circuit, so called because the power is delivered to the microphone over the same conductors used for the audio signal. From the point of view of cable requirements, the phantom powered microphone is interchangeable with the dynamic microphone. On a suitably equipped microphone line, the phantom powered microphone receives the power it requires; any conventional dynamic microphone used in its place treats the power as if it weren't there. In short, the phantom power is there when it's needed and seems to vanish when no longer required.

Figure 3-9A illustrates the basic principle of phantom powering. The power supply's DC voltage is applied via a center-tapped transformer to both signal leads in the microphone line. When a microphone is plugged into the line, the identical voltage reaches both sides of the microphone's output transformer. But because a transformer does not pass direct current, the voltage applied at the center tap has no effect on either the microphone or the console; it's as if it weren't really there at all.

To recover the phantom voltage, the transformer in a suitably equipped capacitor microphone has a center tap on its output winding; the voltage appears at this point, from which it may be internally routed as required. The return path to the power supply is via the microphone cable's shield—making it important for all microphone cable shields to be connected to the plugs at both ends of the cable.

This method of phantom powering is sometimes referred to as *multiplex powering*, a term used in the DIN standard (DIN 45 596) describing its use.

Master Phantom Power Supply

The next logical step is to design a single master phantom power supply as an integral part of the console or as an external add-on system. Via multiple pairs of precision resistors, the phantom supply voltage is routed to each microphone line, as seen in Figure 3-9B. Many consoles supply a phantom power on/off switch on each input module, so that voltage may be removed from those microphone lines not requiring it. The switch is described in greater detail in Chapter 12.

Modulation Lead Powering Systems

Some capacitor microphones use a *modulation lead powering* system, also referred to as a *T* system (from the German *Tonader Speisung*, literally "sound artery powering"). The system follows an earlier DIN standard (DIN 45 595) in which only one of the audio signal leads supplies power to the microphone, with the other lead used as the return path (Boré 1970). It is one of several powering systems available in Nagra tape recorders, and several manufacturers supply microphones for use with this system. However, the DIN standard specifies that pin 2 is positive with respect to pin 3; in Nagra recorders the opposite polarity is observed. As a consequence, microphones using *T*-system powering may be found wired either to the DIN standard or to the Nagra convention. In most—but not all—cases, an identifying mark on the microphone indicates its wiring polarity. In some early systems, the voltage on each audio signal lead was different (Noble 1967), with the shield again used as the return path.

Whenever such systems are still found in use, it is important to make sure the power supply is disabled before another microphone is substituted on the same line. A microphone not designed to work with one of these powering systems may be damaged, or destroyed, if it is accidentally used. The risk is reduced by the fact that most such microphone systems use a distinctive set of cable connectors.

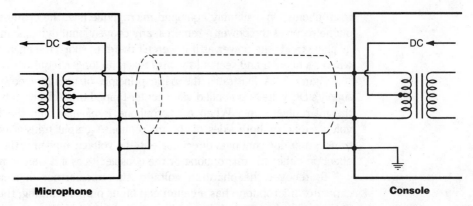

(A) Both audio leads in the mic line are used to supply voltage to the microphone. The voltage return path is via the cable shield.

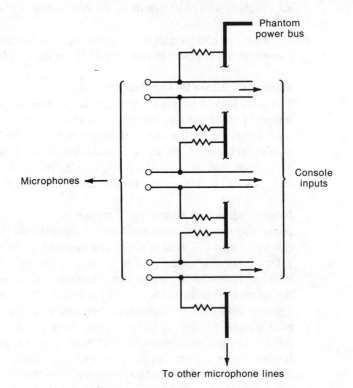

(B) In a master phantom power supply system, precision resistors deliver the voltage to each mic line.

Figure 3-9. A phantom power system.

Battery Power

Given the reduced power requirements of the modern capacitor microphone, it's often practical to supply it with power from a single battery. Depending on the size of the microphone housing, the battery may be placed either inside the housing or in an in-line chassis placed in the microphone line, as was done with the older style power supply described earlier in this section.

In many cases the use of the battery is optional; if it is not in place, the microphone picks up the phantom-supplied voltage from the microphone line, as described above. With the battery installed, the phantom supply is automatically disconnected. A representative example of a microphone which may use the optional battery is seen in Figure 3-10.

Figure 3-10. A capacitor microphone with an internal battery supply.
(Neumann U 87 Courtesy Gotham Audio Corp.)

There are advantages—and disadvantages—to using a battery in a capacitor microphone. The obvious advantage is to allow the use of the microphone in a system not equipped with phantom powering. Typical examples are the use of a single microphone directly feeding a microphone input on a tape recorder, or for use in the field in conjunction with other battery-powered devices.

A disadvantage is the battery's knack for failing at the wrong moment, say, in the middle of a live performance, or when the microphone is suspended over a large (and expensive) string section. In either case it is probably safer to remove the battery before the performance begins and rely on the phantom powering system. If there's a general power failure, the loss of the phantom supply will be the last thing to worry about.

Directional Characteristics

A microphone is often classified according to the manner in which it responds to the arrival of off-axis sound sources. To describe a microphone's directional characteristics, imagine that it is aimed directly at some distant fixed point, and that a straight line is drawn from that point to the microphone diaphragm. Any sound source originating on this line is said to be an on-axis sound, and the angle at which it arrives at the diaphragm is of course zero degrees. Sounds originating elsewhere are off-axis, and the microphone may or may not be as sensitive to them as it is to the on-axis signal.

Polar Equations and Patterns

For the purposes of the following discussion, a microphone's *sensitivity* to sounds arriving from various directions is defined as the ratio of its output level at any angle, θ, to its output level when θ is zero degrees, that is, when the sound arrives on-axis. Sensitivity may be measured by adjusting the level of a steady-state on-axis sound source until the microphone produces full-scale deflection on a meter calibrated from 0 to 1, thus indicating a reference sensitivity of unity. We now measure the output voltage as the source rotates through 360 degrees around the microphone, while maintaining a constant source-to-diaphragm distance for the duration of the test. The most practical way to conduct this test is to set up a fixed-location sound source and then rotate the microphone diaphragm instead, as shown in Figure 3-11.

A microphone is said to be *omnidirectional* if its output voltage remains constant (i.e., sensitivity = 1) regardless of the angle of the arriving sound source. By contrast, a *bidirectional* microphone is most sensitive to sounds which arrive from either the front or the rear, and is progressively less sensitive to sound arriving from the sides. In between these two extremes is the *unidirectional* microphone, which becomes progressively less sensitive as the angle of arrival increases to 180 degrees, at which point its sensitivity is at a minimum (theoretically, zero). As the arrival angle rotates from 180 to 360 degrees, the sensitivity again increases to the unity reference value.

Polar Equation
In practice, the directional sensitivity of any microphone may be measured as just described. However, in theory there is a single *polar equation* which may also be used to describe the directional sensitivity of the omnidirectional and bidirectional microphone, as well as that of any other microphone whose directional sensitivity falls somewhere in between. As we shall see, two variables within the equation determine the microphone's directional sensitivity.

Although it is probably not a good idea to think of a microphone in mathematical terms while under the pressure of a recording session, a basic understanding of the general and specific forms of the polar equation is useful when comparing one microphone type with another, and will also be the foundation for understanding many of the stereo microphone techniques to be described in the next chapter. Therefore, a little presession "mic math" may go a long way toward gaining a much better idea of what to expect when more than one microphone is in use. With that in mind, the following section should be read, and maybe even reread until it becomes clear.

To determine a microphone's output sensitivity to a sound arriving from a certain angle, the following polar equation may be used:

$$s = s_o[(1 - k) + k \cos \theta] \tag{3-1}$$

where

s = output sensitivity to sound arriving from angle θ
s_o = output sensitivity to sound arriving on axis $(0°)$
$1 - k$ = a component indicating pressure response
k = a component indicating pressure-gradient response
θ = the angle of the arriving sound

In order to compare one microphone with another, we may assume that each will have an output sensitivity of unity when a sound source arrives from a point directly in front of the diaphragm; that is, $s_o = 1$ at an angle of zero degrees. To further simplify the equation, we may substitute A and B for $k - 1$ and k, respectively. The polar equation may now be rewritten simply as

$$s = A + B \cos \theta = 1 \tag{3-2}$$

In this simplified form it is easy to see that the output sensitivity of any microphone is a function of two components: pressure, A, and pressure gradient, $B \cos \theta$. The latter is often referred to as the *cosine component* and is described in more detail later. By assuming that all microphones have a sensitivity of unity for a sound arriving on axis, we may say that $s = 1$ when $\theta = 0°$. Since the cosine of $0°$ is 1, the equation conveniently simplifies to

$$1 = A + B \cos \theta = A + B(1)$$

or

$$1 = A + B$$

Therefore,

$$A = 1 - B$$

and

$$B = 1 - A$$

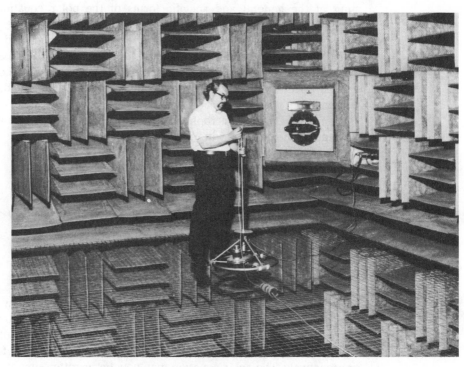

(A) The microphone is rotated through 360 degrees, with its diaphragm maintained at a constant distance from the sound source. (Courtesy Electro-Voice, Inc.)

Figure 3-11. Anechoic chamber test setup for

In other words, the sum of *A* and *B* is always, and quite simply, 1. As we shall soon discover, sometimes *A* or *B* (but not both) may be zero, in which case the other variable is 1. As each category of microphone is described below, the specific values for these components in its polar equation will be given.

Polar Pattern

The polar equation is also used to draw a *polar pattern*, that is, a graph of a microphone's directional sensitivity from zero to 360 degrees. The polar pattern is so called because it is a graph drawn in polar-coordinate format, in which each point on the curve defines the amplitude, or sensitivity, of the microphone output and the angle at which that amplitude occurs. The graph paper itself is nothing more than a series of concentric circles, as shown in Figure 3-12, where the outermost circle represents a sensitivity of unity, and each inner circle indicates a lesser sensitivity.

Although the polar pattern is a two-dimensional graph of directional sensitivity, the actual microphone of course operates in three-dimensional space, and so the pattern could represent either a vertical or a horizontal rotation about the microphone's diaphragm. A three-dimensional drawing might therefore seem more appropriate, and indeed it would offer us a better visual representation. However, the two-dimensional rendition is usually preferred for the sake of

(B) Detail view of speaker, microphone under test and calibration microphone.
(Courtesy Gotham Audio Corp.)

measuring the directional response of a microphone.

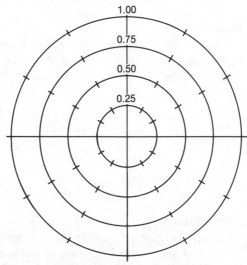

Figure 3-12. Graph paper drawn in a polar-coordinate format is used for plotting the polar response patterns described in this chapter. The concentric circles indicate sensitivity (as here) or dB attenuation (as in Figure 3-29).

simplicity. No information is lost, provided it is kept in mind that the actual pattern exists in three dimensions, as will be illustrated later in this chapter.

Note that each polar pattern is an indication of a microphone's output sensitivity, not of its decibel loss at various off-axis angles. However, because it is customary to evaluate a microphone in terms of decibel attenuation, we will convert the former to the latter later on in this chapter. For the sake of simplicity, however, we will first discuss sensitivity alone.

The following sections describe omnidirectional, bidirectional, and unidirectional microphones in some detail. In each case the specific polar equation is derived and then used to plot the directional sensitivity of the microphone. The graph so drawn will be that of the theoretically ideal microphone in each category. Knowing what it is supposed to look like helps when evaluating the performance of an actual microphone.

The Omnidirectional Microphone

About the simplest microphone that can be designed requires little more than a diaphragm stretched over a sealed cavity, as illustrated in Figure 3-13. A capillary (fine-bore) tube drilled through one of the cavity walls functions as a pressure equalization vent; that is, it allows air to slowly leak into—or out of—the cavity, which thus remains at the same static atmospheric pressure as the air outside the cavity. However, the vent is insensitive to acoustic pressure changes, which are by comparison too rapid to be equalized via the capillary opening.

When a varying acoustic pressure acts on the exposed surface of the diaphragm, the diaphragm vibrates accordingly and an output voltage is produced. This signal voltage is strictly a function of the varying acoustic pressure, for there is no way for the microphone to determine the angular direction from which this pressure wave arrived. Given the manner in which the microphone responds to sound, it is often referred to as a pressure microphone.

Polar Equation
Since the omnidirectional microphone is sensitive to pressure variations only, its cosine component ($B \cos \theta$) must always be zero. To meet this requirement, let $B = 0$; therefore, $A = 1$ and the omnidirectional polar equation simplifies to

$$s = 1 + 0 \cos \theta$$

or simply

$$s = 1$$

Polar Pattern
It's hardly necessary to go through the tedium of plotting 360 degrees' worth of values that are always 1 in order to discover that the polar pattern for the ideal omnidirectional microphone is simply a circle at unity sensitivity, as shown in Figure 3-14.

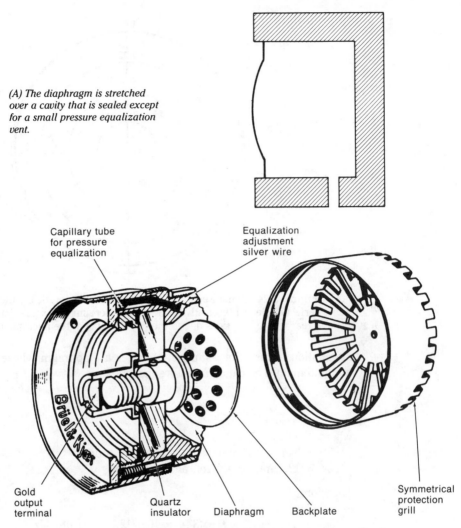

(A) The diaphragm is stretched over a cavity that is sealed except for a small pressure equalization vent.

(B) A detail view of an omnidirectional capacitor microphone capsule. (Courtesy Brüel & Kjaer)

Figure 3-13. Omnidirectional microphone assembly.

However, the actual omnidirectional microphone may differ from the ideal case, in that it is not infinitely small and as a consequence, it tends to get in its own way with respect to sounds arriving from the rear. This may cause a slight flattening of the response in the rear, as is also shown in Figure 3-14.

There may be a similar flattening of response if a high-frequency signal arrives at right angles to the microphone's main axis, a situation also illustrated in Figure 3-14. This attenuation reaches a maximum when the wavelength of the sound source matches the diameter of the diaphragm. As a consequence, the diaphragm is simultaneously acted upon by both a pressure condensation and a rarefaction, and the resultant output signal tends towards self-cancellation. Of course, the smaller the diaphragm, the higher the frequency at which maximum

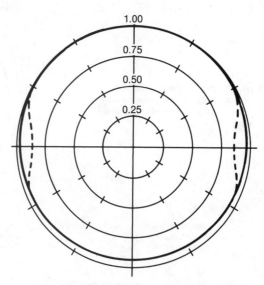

Figure 3-14. Omnidirectional polar response. Theoretically the pattern is a perfect circle at 1.0 sensitivity. However, there may be some flattening in the rear and/or the sides due to the physical size of the microphone housing.

attenuation occurs. For example, consider a diaphragm whose diameter is 12.7 mm (0.5 inch). The cancellation frequency is

$$f = c/\lambda$$

where

c = 344 × 10³ mm/sec, the speed of sound
λ = 12.7 mm, the diaphragm diameter

Therefore,

$$f = (344 × 10^3)/12.7 = 27{,}087 \text{ Hz}$$

The Bidirectional Microphone

Now consider what happens when both surfaces of the diaphragm are exposed to the surrounding sound field. As illustrated in Figure 3-15A, there is an additional path to travel before a sound reaches the rear of the diaphragm. By contrast, there is a zero path-length difference for a signal arriving at either side of the microphone. Both conditions are illustrated in the figure.

Pressure-Gradient Operation

Assuming for the moment that the sound source is reasonably distant, the slight additional path length has little or no practical effect on the amplitude of the signal arriving at the rear of the diaphragm. However, the path length does create a measurable phase shift, which increases with frequency. Because the

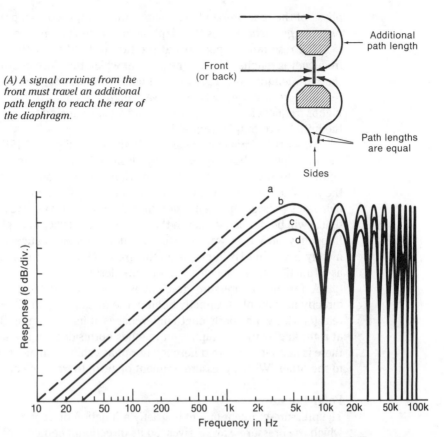

(A) A signal arriving from the front must travel an additional path length to reach the rear of the diaphragm.

(B) Due to pressure-gradient operation the frequency response rises at 6 dB per octave.

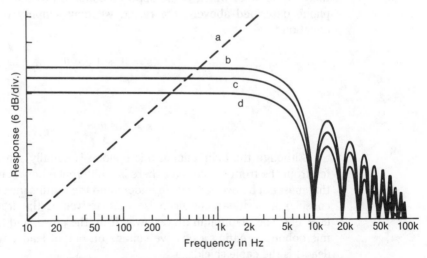

(C) A complementary rolloff results in the flat response seen here.

Figure 3-15. Bidirectional microphone response characteristics. In the two graphs, the four curves are (a) 6 dB per octave reference slope, (b) pure pressure-gradient response, (c) hypercardioid response, and (d) pure cardioid response.

phase of the rear pressure lags that at the front, there is a pressure difference, or *pressure gradient*, across the diaphragm, which is thereby set into motion.

The resultant output rises at the rate of 6 dB per octave until the *transition frequency* is reached. This is the point at which the wavelength of the signal is half the path length. At progressively higher frequencies the output falls off rapidly, reaching zero output when the wavelength is equal to the path length. At still higher frequencies the output rises and falls, returning to zero at each multiple of the initial zero-output frequency.

This rising frequency response is shown in Figure 3-15B. As compensation, the microphone housing is usually designed with a complementary 6 dB per octave roll-off characteristic, thus providing a flat response at frequencies below the transition frequency, as shown in Figure 3-15C. In each case, the upper curve illustrates pressure-gradient operation. The other two curves in each part of the figure will be discussed later in the chapter. For clarity of explanation a transition frequency of 5 kHz was selected so that complete cancellations would conveniently fall at 10 kHz intervals on the graph. Of course the actual values will vary as a function of the specific microphone design.

A maximum pressure gradient will be created by a signal arriving from directly in front of, or directly behind, the diaphragm. In either case, the front-to-rear (or vice versa) path length difference is at its maximum. But a signal arriving at right angles to the diaphragm reaches both sides via the same path length, so there is neither pressure difference nor phase shift from one side of the diaphragm to the other. With a pressure gradient of zero, there is of course no output at all.

Polar Equation

The pressure-gradient output is strictly a function of frequency and of the angle at which the pressure wave arrives. So its directional component, *B*, is always 1, and therefore $A = 0$, which is the opposite condition to the omnidirectional microphone described above. As a result, we may simplify the bidirectional polar equation to

$$s = 0 + 1 \cos \theta$$

or

$$s = \cos \theta$$

Although the bidirectional microphone is equally sensitive to sounds arriving from the front or the rear, there is a difference between the resultant signals that must not be overlooked. To understand the significance of the difference, first consider a positive acoustic pulse that arrives at the front of the diaphragm ($\theta = 0°$). The diaphragm moves away from the pulse, and toward the rear of the microphone, creating a positive voltage on output lead 2 with respect to lead 3 (lead 1 is the cable shield).

Now move the sound source to the rear of the microphone, so that the pulse arrives at the rear of the diaphragm ($\theta = 180°$). As before, the diaphragm moves away from the pulse, but now the direction of movement is toward the front of the microphone. Since the relative motion is the mirror image of the previous case, it creates a negative voltage on output lead 2—again with respect to lead 3.

This example shows that a signal arriving from the rear is equal in magnitude, but opposite in polarity, to the same signal arriving from the front. This observation is supported by the polar equation, since

$$\cos 0° = 1$$

and

$$\cos 180° = -1$$

Here, the negative value indicates the polarity reversal. As an obvious consequence, if the outputs of two bidirectional microphones are combined, the signals created by a pressure wave simultaneously arriving at the front of one and the rear of the other will cancel out, if the respective amplitudes are equal. Furthermore, the same effect will be noted whenever a pressure wave arrives at the rear of a bidirectional microphone and the front of any other microphone, regardless of the other microphone's directional characteristic.

Since the cancellation just described may be caused by any mixture of positive and negative voltages, it can be either a creative tool or a confusing variable, depending on whether the combination is intentional or accidental.

Polar Pattern

For obvious reasons, the bidirectional microphone is sometimes referred to as a *cosine* or *pressure-gradient* microphone. It is also called a *figure-8* microphone, after the distinctive shape of its polar pattern, which is seen in Figure 3-16. The pattern is simply a graph of the cosine of θ measured at all angles from 0 to 360 degrees. The negative cos θ (amplitude) calculated for angles between 90 and 270 degrees indicates that the output polarity is reversed when a sound source originates within this rear hemisphere.

The Unidirectional Microphone

Despite the conceptual simplicities of both the omnidirectional and the bidirectional microphones, the value of a unidirectional microphone has long been appreciated. Simply stated, a unidirectional microphone is most sensitive to sounds coming from one direction: the front. It is—at least theoretically— completely insensitive to sounds originating in the rear. Although it is now very much overused, there are still many applications in which a unidirectional response is a powerful production tool.

Some of the earliest unidirectional microphones employ two elements—one bidirectional, the other nondirectional—mounted within the same housing and set for equal sensitivity. A signal arriving at the front of both diaphragms will generate output voltages that are equal in amplitude and polarity; if combined, the signals add.

If the signal arrives instead from the rear, the bidirectional output will again be equal in magnitude to the omnidirectional output, but opposite in polarity—in

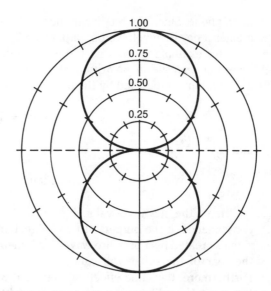

Figure 3-16. Bidirectional polar response. Due to the distinctive shape of its pattern, the bidirectional microphone is often referred to as a figure-8 microphone.

combination, the signals subtract. The result is a microphone with maximum sensitivity in front and zero sensitivity (again theoretically) in the rear. At angles between 0 and 180 degrees, the sensitivity of the omnidirectional component remains constant, while the bidirectional component varies from 1 to 0 to −1 as the signal angle moves from 0 to 90 to 180 degrees. Consequently, the combined sensitivity gradually varies from 2 (1 + 1) to 0 (1 − 1).

Polar Equation
Since the new microphone is nothing more than a combination of two previously introduced patterns, its polar equation is also nothing more than the combination of two previous equations, as seen here:

$$1 + 0 \cos \theta \text{ (the omnidirectional equation)}$$
$$\underline{0 + 1 \cos \theta \text{ (the bidirectional equation)}}$$
$$1 + 1 \cos \theta \text{ (the resultant unidirectional equation)}$$

Since the resultant sensitivity now varies between 2 and 0, all that needs to be done to restore an on-axis sensitivity of unity ($A + B = 1$) is to reduce both components by one-half; that is, let $A = 0.5$ and $B = 0.5$, so that the polar equation is

$$s = 0.5 + 0.5 \cos \theta$$

Polar Pattern
When s is calculated for all angles between 0 and 360 degrees, the resultant polar response is the cardioid pattern seen in Figure 3-17, so called for its heart-like shape.

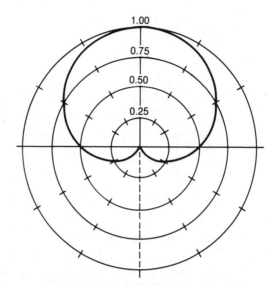

Figure 3-17. Unidirectional polar response. The pattern shown here is often referred to as a "pure" cardioid to distinguish it from the pattern variations that will be discussed later in the chapter (see Figure 3-22).

Single-Element Unidirectional Microphone

Most modern unidirectional microphones no longer use two unlike elements to create the cardioid polar pattern. Instead, a *uniphase* (from unidirectional/phase shift) system (Bauer 1941) permits a single element to produce the desired cardioid pattern.

To achieve the desired unidirectional polar response, a rear-entry port allows sound to reach the rear surface of the diaphragm. To do so, the sound must travel an additional path length, D_t. As shown in Figure 3-18A, this path is comprised of two elements:

D_e the external path length between the front of the diaphragm and the rear-entry port, and

D_i the internal distance between the rear-entry port and the rear of the diaphragm.

Note that the external path length, D_e, is a function of the physical distance, D, from the front of the diaphragm to the rear-entry port, and the angle, θ, of the arriving sound. Thus, $D_e = D \cos \theta$. By contrast, the internal distance, D_i, remains fixed.

The resultant pressure, P_t, acting on the diaphragm is now a function of two variables: the pressure at the front of the microphone, and the pressure gradient between the front, P_1, and the rear, P_3, of the diaphragm. Again considering the typical distance from the microphone to the sound source, the slight additional path length has little or no effect on the amplitude of P_3. However, P_3 does lag P_1 in phase, due to the additional time it takes for sound to travel the extra distance. The total phase shift is of course the sum of the shifts created by the external and internal paths, which are

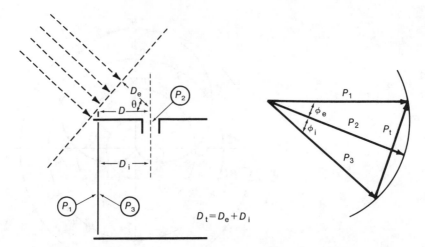

(A) Sound reaches the rear of the
diaphragm after traveling path length
$D_t = D_e + D_i$. The length of D_e is a function
of the angle θ of the arriving sound
$(D_e = D \cos \theta)$.

(B) A vector diagram of the forces acting
on the diaphragm. The phase of the
signal at the rear-entry port, P_2, lags P_1
due to the external path length, D_e. At
the rear of the diaphragm, P_3,
there is an additional phase lag due to
the internal path length, D_i. The resultant
pressure is shown as the vector P_t.

Figure 3-18. A single-element unidirectional microphone.

$$\phi_e = 2\pi fD_e/c$$
$$= kD_e = \text{external phase shift (in radians)}$$
$$\phi_i = 2\pi fD_i/c$$
$$= kD_i = \text{internal phase shift (in radians)}$$

where
$$k = 2\pi f/c$$

Now consider a microphone design in which the physical path lengths D and D_i are equal. For a sound arriving at 0 degrees, $D_e = D_i$, and therefore $\phi_e = \phi_i$. Figure 3-18B is a vector diagram of the various pressures acting within such a system and uses P_1 as its zero phase-shift reference. The illustration shows that

- The pressure at the rear-entry port, P_2, lags P_1 by the angle $\phi_e \, (= kD_e)$
- The pressure at the rear of the diaphragm, P_3, lags P_2 by the angle $\phi_i \, (= kD_i)$
- The pressure at the rear of the diaphragm therefore lags the pressure at the front by $\phi_e + \phi_i \, (= k[D_e + D_i])$
- Resultant pressure, P_t, acting on the diaphragm may be represented by a vector drawn between P_3 and P_1.

The following equation (Robertson 1963) may now be used to calculate the amplitude of the pressure acting on the diaphragm:

$$P_t = 2P_1 \sin k(D_e + D_i)/2$$

When the total path length is very small in comparison to the wavelength of the arriving sound, the equation may be simplified to

$$P_t = 2P_1 k(D_e + D_i)/2$$
$$= P_1 k(D_e + D_i)$$

We can now examine the performance of the single-element system for sounds arriving from various directions, several of which are given here. We arbitrarily set the total path length to unity, and therefore $D = D_i = 0.5$. Finally, remember that $D_e = D \cos \theta$.

θ	D_e	D_i	$D_e + D_i$
0°	0.5	0.5	1.0
45°	0.354	0.5	0.854
90°	0	0.5	0.5
180°	−0.5	0.5	0

The values for the sum of D_e and D_i are a precise match for those that are to be found using the cardioid polar equation seen earlier, that is, $s = 0.5 + 0.5 \cos \theta$. So we may conclude that the polar response for the single-element microphone described here is the same as the equivalent dual-element system that was first used to create a cardioid pattern.

Polar Response Comparisons

So far, we have described three microphone types, and, we have seen that as the relative values of the pressure and pressure-gradient components A and B vary, so does the polar pattern, as listed here:

A	B	Microphone Type	Polar Pattern
1.0 +	0 cos θ	omnidirectional	circle
0.5 +	0.5 cos θ	unidirectional	cardioid
0.0 +	1.0 cos θ	bidirectional	figure-8

In the case of the omnidirectional and bidirectional microphones, the polar equations are usually written simply as 1, and as $\cos \theta$, respectively. When either equation shows some other value (say, omnidirectional = 0.5 or bidirectional = 0.6 cos θ), it means that the microphone output has been attenuated to produce the lower sensitivity at zero degrees. Likewise, a cardioid equation written as $0.25 + 0.25 \cos \theta$ indicates its sensitivity has been reduced by one-half. Of course the A and B components must remain equal to preserve the cardioid pattern.

In addition to the A and B values seen above, other values are certainly possible; for example, A may range between 1 and 0, and therefore B will vary from 0 to 1. On some capacitor microphones, these values are continuously variable. Furthermore, various intermediate values will be of particular interest later in this chapter, and in the discussion of stereo microphone techniques in Chapter 4.

For the moment though, the unidirectional microphone's cardioid pattern may seem to make it the ideal tool for all occasions. It becomes most sensitive to the desired sound simply by pointing it directly at that sound, and by default, sounds in the rear (which presumably are unwanted) are attenuated the most. However, it should already be clear that a bidirectional microphone is far more effective at attenuating sounds that are 90 degrees off-axis—though of course at the expense of increased sensitivity at the rear. Therefore, its use may be worth considering when the unwanted sound is not at the rear, as in many typical recording studio applications.

Three-Dimensional Polar Patterns

As noted earlier in the chapter, a polar pattern is usually drawn as a two-dimensional curve in order to convey directionality information simply and accurately. However, it should be understood that the pattern actually exists in three dimensions around the microphone diaphragm. The pattern may be visualized as an imaginary *solid*, that is, an object with a specific volume and a characteristic surface shape. As an extension of the traditional polar pattern graph, the solid represents the microphone's relative sensitivity to sounds arriving from any point in the three-dimensional space surrounding it.

The obvious example is the omnidirectional pattern, in which the solid is a perfect sphere, indicating equal sensitivity regardless of the angle of the arriving sound wave. Figure 3-19 shows the three-dimensional solid representations for several polar patterns. In each case, if a constant-level sound source were moved to any point on one of the surfaces, the microphone output would remain constant.

Microphone Response Parameters

We can get a better idea of how each microphone responds to the sound field in which it is placed by comparing various response parameters to those of an omnidirectional microphone placed at the same location. This may be done by comparing the solid shapes seen in Figure 3-19, which shows that with respect to the spherical solid of the omnidirectional microphone, the others have less surface area, and thus the corresponding microphones are less sensitive to sounds arriving from various off-axis locations.

To be more specific, a few equations are given below to describe the performance of each microphone type. As we work through the math, two more microphone polar equations will suggest themselves. These lie between the conventional unidirectional and bidirectional types, as we shall discover.

Much of the following section is derived from the work of Glover (1940) and Bauer (1954), whose papers should be consulted for further details.

Diffuse Field Response

For the purpose of comparing one microphone to another, a *diffuse field* is understood to describe an environment in which sounds arrive at the diaphragm

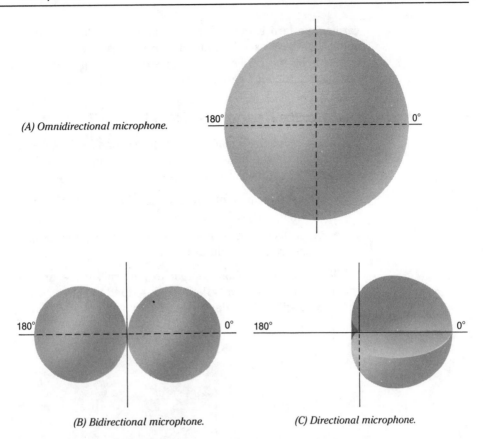

(A) Omnidirectional microphone.

(B) Bidirectional microphone.   *(C) Directional microphone.*

Figure 3-19. Three-dimensional polar patterns for omnidirectional, bidirectional, and directional microphones. A section has been removed from the latter to show the null at 180 degrees.

from every direction. It can be seen from the three-dimensional polar patterns that an omnidirectional microphone is the most efficient device for recording the diffuse field; at any given sensitivity, its spherical pattern presents the greatest possible surface area to the arriving sounds. Any other microphone will be less efficient to sounds arriving from off-axis directions, in proportion to the diminished surface area of its polar pattern.

In the typical recording environment, the microphone is not necessarily surrounded by a completely diffuse field. In fact, with the wanted sound source presumably located directly on axis, unwanted sounds may be found to originate from one of the following areas:

- The diffuse field, as described above
- The front hemisphere (the broad area from 0 degrees to ±90 degrees)
- The rear hemisphere (the broad area beyond ±90 degrees)
- A narrow area, defined by a specific off-axis angle

Depending on which of these conditions best describes the recording environment, one or another specific polar pattern will suggest itself. In fact, the cardioid pattern is the best choice *only* when all unwanted sound originates at about 180 degrees—a condition which does not really occur that often. In a diffuse field, the cardioid is no better than a bidirectional pattern, and in other fields anything *but* a cardioid may do a better job.

Random-Energy Response (RER)

When a microphone is placed in a diffuse sound field, its voltage output is directly proportional to the total surface area of its three-dimensional polar pattern. In studying these surface areas, note that

- The surface area of any directional pattern is always less than that of an omnidirectional pattern
- As surface area decreases, the pattern becomes progressively less responsive to the diffuse field

To equate microphone output to pattern surface area, we need a general equation to find the area of the solid described by the polar equation $A + B \cos \theta$. Figure 3-20 will help us derive the required equation.

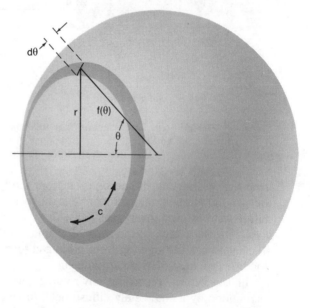

Figure 3-20. To find the surface area of a three-dimensional polar pattern, first find the surface of an incremental area. The total surface is the sum of all such areas. An omnidirectional sphere is seen here, but the procedure applies as well to any other pattern.

To make the following explanation as straightforward as possible, the solid in Figure 3-20 is the perfect sphere of the omnidirectional polar pattern, and the polar equation is simplified to $f(\theta)$; that is, "a function of theta." Once the derivation is complete, $f(\theta)$ may be replaced by any of the polar equations found in this chapter.

We begin by finding the area of a very small slice of the solid. The complete area is of course the sum of all such slices. The circumference of any slice is

$$c = 2\pi r$$
$$= 2\pi f(\theta) \sin \theta \qquad \text{(since } r = f(\theta) \sin \theta)$$

The width of the slice, $d\theta$, is assumed to be infinitely small, and therefore we may visualize the slice as a rectangle whose sides are c and $d\theta$. Therefore, its area is

$$a = c \cdot d\theta$$
$$= 2\pi f(\theta) \sin \theta \ d\theta$$

The following integral represents the sum of all such small surface areas (and may be safely ignored by all those who would rather not tangle with the calculus):

$$\int a = 2\pi \int_0^\pi f(\theta) \sin \theta \ d\theta$$

As seen here, the integral finds the surface area of any polar pattern described in this chapter, and the voltage response of that microphone is therefore directly proportional to this equation. But because energy is expressed in terms of power, not voltage, and power is proportional to voltage squared, we can now express the *random-energy response* of any microphone by substituting $f^2(\theta)$ for $f(\theta)$ in the above equation. Thus,

$$RER = 2\pi \int_0^\pi f^2(\theta) \sin \theta \ d\theta \qquad \text{(3-3)}$$

For an omnidirectional microphone, the equation simplifies to

$$RER_o = 4\pi$$

Random-Energy Efficiency (REE)

With all this as background, we can at last compare the efficiency of any microphone in a diffuse field to that of an omnidirectional microphone. We define a microphone's *random-energy efficiency* as the ratio of its own random-energy response to that of an omnidirectional microphone placed at the same location. In other words,

$$REE = RER/RER_o \qquad \text{(3-4)}$$
$$= \frac{1}{2} \int_o^\pi f^2(\theta) \sin \theta \ d\theta$$

where
    RER = the random-energy response of the microphone under test, and
    RER_o = the random-energy response of an omnidirectional microphone.

For the purposes of the discussion following, the integral in equation (3-4) may be simplified and rewritten as

$$REE = 1 - 2B + 1.333B^2 \qquad \text{(3-5)}$$

$$REE = 1 - 2B + 1.333B^2 \qquad \text{(3-5)}$$

Note that the REE of an omnidirectional microphone is 1, since $B = 0$. Although elsewhere efficiency is usually stated as a percentage, in this application it remains in the decimal-fraction form.

Presumably, an ideal directional microphone will have a very small random-energy efficiency, since it is expected to be as insensitive to off-axis energy as is possible. For example, curve (a) in Figure 3-21 plots the random-energy efficiency of all microphones as polar response varies between omnidirectional ($B = 0$) and bidirectional ($B = 1$). Note, however, that the pure cardioid and the bidirectional patterns have the same random-energy efficiency, and that the actual minimum point lies somewhere between them. In other words, neither one may be the ideal for all applications in which unwanted off-axis sounds are present.

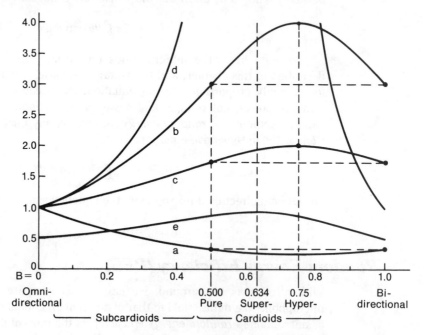

Figure 3-21. Microphone response parameters. Curve (a) represents REE, or Random-Energy Efficiency; curve (b): DRF, or Directivity Factor; curve (c): DSF, or Distance Factor; curve (d): UDI, or Unidirectional index; curve (e): FTR, or Front-to-Total Ratio.

Directivity Factor (DRF)

A microphone's directivity factor may be stated as the ratio of its response to two identical intensity levels, created under different conditions.

$$DRF = P_1/P_2$$

where

  P_1 = the response to a diffuse sound field
  P_2 = the response to a signal of the same average intensity, but created by an on-axis sound source

Since a microphone's directivity factor is the reciprocal of its random-energy efficiency, its value may be calculated as

$$DRF = 1/REE \qquad \text{(3-6)}$$

Curve (b) in Figure 3-21 plots the directivity factor for all microphones between omnidirectional and bidirectional. Again, the cardioid and bidirectional values are the same, and in this case the maximum value also lies somewhere in between the two.

Distance Factor (DSF)

As we have seen, as a microphone's random-energy efficiency decreases, it becomes less sensitive to the diffuse sound field which surrounds it. Therefore, it may be moved further away from a direct sound source, yet still maintain the same ratio of direct-to-diffuse sound as an omnidirectional microphone. The relative increase in working distance is known as the microphone's *distance factor*, and is calculated as

$$DSF = (DRF)^{1/2} \qquad \text{(3-7)}$$

For example, a cardioid microphone—with a random-energy efficiency of 0.333—has a directivity factor of

$$1/0.333 = 3.003$$

and a distance factor of

$$DSF = (3.003)^{1/2} = 1.733$$

Therefore, when placed at a working distance of 1.733 meters, the ratio of direct-to-diffuse sound energy is the same as that of the omnidirectional microphone placed at 1 meter.

Curve (c) in Figure 3-21 plots the distance factor for microphones whose polar response falls between omnidirectional and bidirectional. Once again, the maximum value lies somewhere between the cardioid and bidirectional patterns.

Unidirectional Index (UDI)

Another useful tool is a microphone's *unidirectional index*, which is an indication of a microphone's relative ability to accept sounds arriving from the front hemisphere while rejecting those arriving from the back hemisphere.

To separately calculate the front- and back-hemisphere random-energy efficiencies, REF and REB, the following equations are used:

$$REF = 0.5 - 0.5B + 0.167B^2 \qquad \textbf{(3-8)}$$

and

$$REB = 0.5 - 1.5B + 1.167B^2 \qquad \textbf{(3-9)}$$

The unidirectional index may now be found by dividing equation (3-8) by equation (3-9).

$$UDI = REF/REB \qquad \textbf{(3-10)}$$

The sum of REF and REB is of course equal to the total random-energy efficiency shown in equation (3-5). Curve (d) in Figure 3-21 plots the unidirectional index for all microphones whose polar patterns fall between omnidirectional and bidirectional. Although the pure cardioid UDI is greater than that of the bidirectional pattern, the maximum possible value again lies elsewhere.

Front-to-Total Ratio (FTR)

As a final measurement, the *front-to-total ratio* is a measure of a microphone's ability to favor sounds originating in front of it. It may be calculated by dividing equation (3-8) by equation (3-5).

$$FTR = REF/REE \qquad \textbf{(3-11)}$$

Curve (e) in Figure 3-21 plots the front-to-total random-energy efficiency; its maximum value occurs at the same point as the unidirectional index, somewhat beyond that of the pure cardioid.

Variations on the Cardioid Response

As the collection of curves in Figure 3-21 should suggest, neither the pure cardioid nor the bidirectional microphone is the ideal transducer for all occasions in which omnidirectional response is not desired. And now, using the various curves shown in the figure, three variations on the conventional unidirectional response may at last be considered. The polar equations and patterns are given below, followed by brief application notes later in the chapter (page 98).

The Subcardioid Microphone

Any microphone whose polar equation places it somewhere between an omnidirectional and a pure cardioid pattern may be classified as a subcardioid microphone. In other words, its pressure and pressure-gradient (cosine) components may fall within the following range:

$$1 > A > 0.5 \qquad (A \text{ is less than 1 and greater than 0.5})$$
$$0 < B < 0.5 \qquad (B \text{ is greater than 0 and less than 0.5})$$

Polar Equation

Unlike the other microphones discussed in this chapter, no single pair of values is used to define the subcardioid polar equation. Therefore, any microphone whose characteristics place it to the left of the pure cardioid line in Figure 3-21 may be considered as a subcardioid. One of many subcardioid equations might be written as, say

$$s = 0.75 + 0.25 \cos \theta$$

These specific values are given here for comparison with the hypercardioid pattern discussed below. In practice many microphones described as cardioid actually fall within the general subcardioid area.

Polar Pattern

A typical subcardioid polar pattern is shown in Figure 3-22A, plotted from the values given above. The pattern is sometimes referred to as a broad, wide, or wide-angle cardioid. However, relatively few manufacturers list a subcardioid microphone as such in their catalog. A notable exception is the Schoeps MK-21 subcardioid capsule, designed to follow the polar equation

$$s = 0.68 + 0.32 \cos \theta$$

This microphone is also referred to as having a *forward-biased omnidirectional* polar response (Bruck 1987).

The Supercardioid Microphone

If a subcardioid polar equation is any whose cosine component is less than that of a pure cardioid, then a supercardioid should be any in which the same component is greater than the pure cardioid (i.e., $B > 0.5$). However, the term has come to be identified with the specific cosine component at which the unidirectional index curve (such as that shown in Figure 3-21D) reaches maximum. Accordingly, a microphone that offers this characteristic is popularly called a supercardioid microphone.

Polar Equation

Although the math is not given here, it will be found that the highest point on the curve occurs when $B = 0.634$, and therefore, $A = 1 - 0.634 = 0.366$, and so the supercardioid polar equation is written as

$$s = 0.366 + 0.634 \cos \theta$$

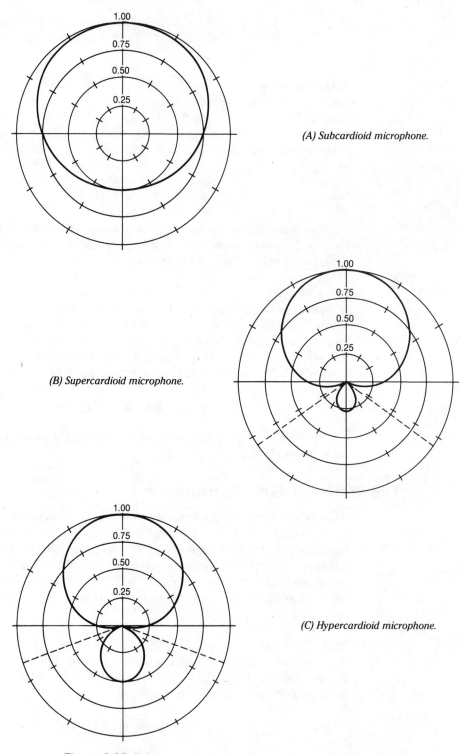

(A) Subcardioid microphone.

(B) Supercardioid microphone.

(C) Hypercardioid microphone.

Figure 3-22. Polar response pattern for the three types of cardioid microphones. In (B) and (C) the dashed lines indicate the null angles.

The unidirectional index itself may now be found by solving equation (3-9), and is 13.832.

Polar Pattern
The polar pattern drawn from the supercardioid equation is shown in Figure 3-22B.

The Hypercardioid Microphone

In the random-energy efficiency curve shown in Figure 3-21, curve (a), the minimum value occurs above the supercardioid pattern, at a point that seems to lie about midway between the conventional cardioid and the bidirectional responses. Such a characteristic is referred to as *hypercardioid*. Since the slope of the REE curve is zero at this point, equation (3-5) may be easily differentiated to find the actual minimum possible value for B.

$$dy/dB = -2 + 2.667B = 0 \qquad\qquad \text{(3-12)}$$
$$B = 0.750$$

and therefore

$$A = 0.250$$

Polar Equation
When the values just found are inserted in the general polar equation, the hypercardioid polar equation may be written as

$$s = 0.25 + 0.75 \cos \theta$$

Polar Pattern
Since the A and B components of the equation lie midway between those of the pure cardioid and the bidirectional microphones, the hypercardioid pattern itself lies midway between these two patterns, as shown in Figure 3-22C. Note that the maximum sensitivity of the rear lobe is half that of the bidirectional pattern shown in Figure 3-16.

Review of Polar Patterns

In any equation of the form $s = A + B \cos \theta$, the following relationships hold when $\cos \theta$ is negative:

$$
\begin{array}{ll}
\text{if } A > B \cos \theta & s \text{ is positive} \\
A = B \cos \theta & s = 0 \\
A < B \cos \theta & s \text{ is negative}
\end{array}
$$

As discussed earlier in this chapter (page 83), negative sensitivity simply indicates a polarity reversal. This condition is possible only in the family of patterns above pure cardioid, in which A is less than B, and therefore the condition $A < B \cos \theta$ can be satisfied at some values of θ. In these microphones the negative-sensitivity portion of the polar pattern is seen as a rear lobe between two nulls, that is, between the two angles at which s equals zero. These angles may be found by rewriting the basic polar equation and solving it for θ. If a solution is possible, the reverse-polarity rear lobe falls within the area indicated below, immediately following the values for A and B.

Polar Pattern	A	B	Rear Lobe Is Between*
omni	1	0	(no solution) none
subcardioid	0.75	0.25	(no solution) none
cardioid	0.5	0.5	$\theta = \pm 180°$ none
supercardioid	0.366	0.634	$\theta = \pm 125.26°$
hypercardioid	0.250	0.750	$\theta = \pm 109.47°$

$*\theta = \pm \arccos (A/-B)$

Since omnidirectional and subcardioid patterns do not have a rear lobe as described here, there is never a polarity reversal in their output sensitivity. As an example, compare the 180-degree sensitivity of the subcardioid whose polar equation is the inverse of a hypercardioid. Solving both equations, we find that

$$s = 0.75 + 0.25 \cos (180) = 0.75 + 0.25(-1) = +0.5 \,(\text{subcardioid})$$
$$s = 0.25 + 0.75 \cos (180) = 0.25 + 0.75(-1) = -0.5 \,(\text{hypercardioid})$$

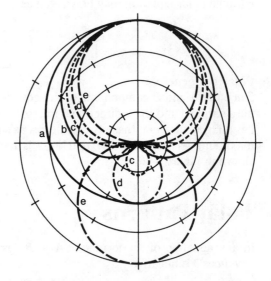

Figure 3-23. A comparison of the bidirectional and unidirectional polar patterns described in this chapter. Curve (a): subcardioid; curve (b): cardioid; curve (c): supercardioid; curve (d): hypercardioid; and curve (e): bidirectional.

In other words, at 180 degrees the microphone outputs are equal in sensitivity but opposite in polarity. This may be verified by comparing the polar patterns seen in Figures 3-22A and 3-22C.

Figure 3-23 graphically compares the uni- and bidirectional polar patterns described above. Note that as the pattern shape progresses from pure cardioid to figure-8, the size of the front lobe decreases and the rear lobe increases, and that the figure-8 pattern has the smallest possible front lobe. Although an infinite number of polar responses can be obtained by continuously varying the pressure and pressure-gradient components, most practical microphones are of a fixed-pattern design, with polar characteristics that may only approximate the values given in this chapter. Table 3-1 tabulates these characteristics and Table 3-2 lists a few representative microphones in each general category, some of which are shown in Figure 3-24.

Polar Patterns and Microphone Selection

By carefully studying the data presented in the illustrations it's possible to make some general conclusions to help narrow the choice of microphones for a given application. In the section following, the data is used to evaluate all five polar patterns in terms of their ability to attenuate sounds coming from various directions.

Omnidirectional Microphone

A microphone with an omnidirectional pattern obviously has no direction-sensing abilities. But since its design and construction are relatively simple, a high-quality omnidirectional microphone usually costs far less than an equivalent-grade directional microphone. It is of course the ideal choice when attenuation of off-axis sounds is not necessary.

Subcardioid Microphone

The subcardioid microphone offers a greater working distance than the omnidirectional pattern and less susceptibility to proximity effect and off-axis coloration (see page 103) than the cardioid.

Cardioid Microphone

The obvious characteristic of the pure cardioid pattern is maximum attenuation at 180 degrees. It is of course the ideal choice if all unwanted sounds originate directly behind the microphone. However, the microphone's random-energy response is no better than that of a figure-8 pattern, and neither distance factor, unidirectional index, nor front-to-total ratio are at a maximum. These parameters may argue against the cardioid pattern when—as is usually the case—unwanted sounds are not confined to the area near 180 degrees.

Supercardioid Microphone

This microphone has the highest possible unidirectional index and front-to-total (and front-to-rear) ratio. Therefore, the supercardioid pattern makes the greatest

Table 3-1. Microphone Characteristics

Microphone Type	Pattern Shape	See Figure	Polar Equation ($s = A + B\cos\theta$) A	B	Random Energy Efficiency (a)*	Direct- ivity Factor (b)*	Distance Factor (c)*	Uni- direct. Index (d)*	Front-to- Total Ratio (e)*
omni	circle	3-14	1.000	0.000	1.000	1.000	1.000	1.000	0.500
uni	subcardioid	3-22A	values may lie anywhere between omni and pure cardioid						
uni	subcardioid**	3-22A	0.667	0.334					
uni	cardioid	3-17	0.500	0.500	0.333	3.000	1.732	7.000	0.875
uni	supercardioid	3-22B	0.366	0.634	0.268	3.732	1.932	13.928	0.933
uni	hypercardioid	3-22C	0.250	0.750	0.250	4.000	2.000	7.000	0.875
bi	figure-8	3-16	0.000	1.000	0.333	3.000	1.732	1.000	0.500

*Cross-reference to curves in Figure 3-21 (a) through (e).
**Soundfield microphone; see Chapter 4 for further details.

differentiation between sounds originating in the front hemisphere and those coming from the back hemisphere. When unwanted sound comes mostly from behind—but not just from 180 degrees—the supercardioid pattern may be the most effective choice.

Hypercardioid Microphone
Here the distinguishing characteristics are minimum random-energy response and maximum distance factor. The pattern is therefore most effective in picking

Table 3-2. Representative Model Numbers for Various Polar Pattern Types

Manufacturer	Omni	Sub- cardioid	Regular Cardioid	Super- cardioid	Hyper- cardioid	Figure-8
AKG	D-130E		D-224E		D95S	C-414B/ULS*
Audio-Technica	AT4049		AT4051	none	AT4053	AT4055
Beyer	M 101		M 300	M 400	M 69	M 130
Brüel & Kjaer	4006		4011			
Electro-Voice	635A		RE20	RE15	N/D457	
Fostex			M11RP		M110	M88RP
Milab	VIP-50*	VIP-50*	VIP-50*		VIP-50*	VIP-50*
Neumann	KM 83i	TLM 170i*	KM 84i		TLM 170i*	TLM 170i*
Sennheiser	MKH 20		MKH 40	MD 431		MKH 30
Schoeps	MK 2	MK 21	MK 4	MK 41**	MK 41**	MK 8
Shure	SM80		SM81	SM87	SM89***	SM300
Yamaha	MZ series, all identified as "unidirectional," polar pattern not specified					

*The indicated pattern is one of several that are switch-selectable. See Chapter 4 for further details.
**Schoeps MK 41 is about midway between super- and hypercardioid.
***Shure SM 89 is hypercardioid below 1 kHz.

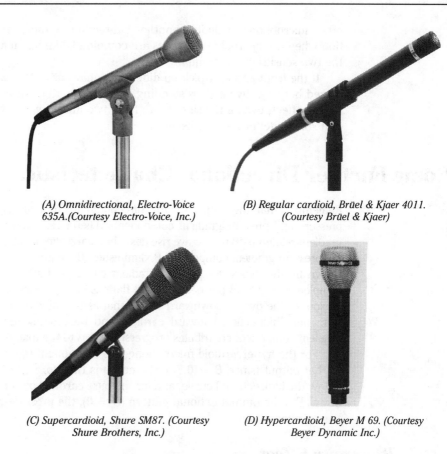

(A) Omnidirectional, Electro-Voice 635A.(Courtesy Electro-Voice, Inc.)

(B) Regular cardioid, Brüel & Kjaer 4011. (Courtesy Brüel & Kjaer)

(C) Supercardioid, Shure SM87. (Courtesy Shure Brothers, Inc.)

(D) Hypercardioid, Beyer M 69. (Courtesy Beyer Dynamic Inc.)

(E) Bidirectional, Sennheiser MKH 30. (Courtesy Sennheiser Electronic Corp.)

Figure 3-24. Representative examples of microphones listed in Table 3-1.

up a sound source in a diffuse sound field, with unwanted sounds coming from all directions.

Bidirectional Microphone
Note that the random-energy response and distance factor are identical to the cardioid pattern. But of course the figure-8 pattern is quite effective at attenuating unwanted sounds originating at the sides.

When a bidirectional microphone is used in conjunction with any other type of microphone, it is important to make sure that it faces in the right direction. Remember that although its front and rear sensitivities are equal in amplitude, they are opposite in polarity. Therefore, in the presence of a common signal picked up at the rear of the bidirectional microphone and at the front of some other microphone (including another bidirectional), there will be some attenuation when the microphone outputs are combined. Maximum attenuation occurs if the two sensitivities are equal.

If the front and rear pick up different signals, as in the case of a microphone placed between two groups standing face to face, the rear-axis polarity reversal has no effect, even if the signals are from two unison voices or from instruments that sound identical to the listener.

Some Further Directional Characteristics

Remember that the output of any directional microphone is a function of both pressure and pressure-gradient components. Therefore, it too exhibits the pressure-gradient-related 6 dB per octave rise described earlier in the chapter (page 82). But as the pressure-gradient component, B, diminishes, the entire curve shifts downward, as shown by the two lower pressure-gradient curves in Figure 3-15B. In each case a complementary 6 dB per octave rolloff flattens out the response (Figure 3-15C). The reason for the overall downward shift is that as the microphone design moves away from pure bidirectional toward cardioid and then omnidirectional, the pressure-gradient component contributes progressively less to the total output.

For the hypercardioid microphone, the component represents three-quarters of that output (since $B = 0.75$); the curve is therefore 2.5 dB (i.e., 20 log 0.75) below the bidirectional curve, and for the pure cardioid pattern ($B = 0.5$) it is 6 dB down. For the omnidirectional pattern ($B = 0$), the pressure-gradient component has no effect at all.

Proximity Effect

In the preceding discussion of bidirectional and unidirectional microphones, it was assumed that the pressures at the front and rear of the diaphragm were for all practical purposes equal in amplitude. As explained above, this is because the source-to-diaphragm distance is large compared to the diaphragm's own front-to-rear path length. Therefore, the pressure-gradient force acting on the diaphragm is strictly a function of the phase shift created over the additional path length.

However, when the microphone is placed quite near the sound source, the same front-to-rear dimension is no longer insignificant with respect to pressure amplitude. For example, consider a microphone with a 1 cm front-to-rear path length, first placed at a distance of 1 meter, and later at 10 cm, from a sound source. The pressures acting on the diaphragm at each distance are inversely proportional to the distance, as shown below.

	Source-to-Microphone Distance	
Pressure	*At 1 meter*	*At 0.1 meter (10 cm)*
At front, $1/d =$	$1/1.0 = 1.00$	$1/0.1 = 10.00$
At rear, $1/d =$	$1/1.1 = 0.91$	$1/0.2 = 5.00$
Rear-to-front ratio	0.91	0.5
Expressed in dB	-0.83 dB	-6.02 dB

In this example there is a 6 dB pressure difference across the diaphragm at a 10 cm working distance. The difference, which is independent of frequency/phase shift, must be added to all the pressure-gradient slopes shown in Figure 3-15B above, which now resemble those shown in Figure 3-25A.

As a practical consequence, remember that the microphone's physical design presents a complementary 6 dB per octave rolloff as compensation for the pressure-gradient effect. Since this rolloff is built into the microphone design, its effect on the curves in Figure 3-25A is no different than it was before; as in Figure 3-15B the curves flatten out nicely in the midsection. But low frequencies are now considerably boosted, giving us the *proximity effect* shown in Figure 3-25B. Like the pressure-gradient slope itself, the effect is most noticeable on the pure pressure-gradient microphone, but it is still significant for all versions of the cardioid pattern.

As working distance increases the effect diminishes and the curves in Figures 3-25A and B return to the contours of Figures 3-15B and C, respectively. Figure 3-26 summarizes proximity effect by retracing the four curves that apply to the pressure-gradient microphone.

Bass Rolloff Switch

Many directional microphones contain a built-in switchable highpass filter, which may be used at close working distances to minimize proximity effect.

Off-Axis Coloration

The polar response of a directional microphone may vary considerably over the frequency spectrum. In many cases such a microphone is quite directional at high frequencies but less so at low frequencies. As a consequence its output exhibits *off-axis coloration*, that is, a distortion of frequency response that gets progressively worse as the arrival angle increases. Since high frequencies usually deteriorate fastest, the resultant output is often described as "muddy."

Off-axis coloration is a function of the wavelength of the arriving signal and of the practical difficulties of designing a microphone to discriminate against sounds according to their angle of arrival. Generally, the better the off-axis response, the more complex the microphone and, therefore, the greater its cost. A high-quality unidirectional microphone usually requires an elaborate built-in acoustic network and multiple rear-entry ports, such as those shown in Figure 3-27.

The rear-entry ports must be kept clear of obstructions in order to function properly, and an acoustic barrier placed near the microphone often does more harm than good. The microphone ports are designed to allow all rear sounds to reach the diaphragm. Due to diffraction effects (page 29), the barrier prevents high frequency energy from doing so, thus aggravating the low-frequency problem.

In addition to a general tendency toward high-frequency attenuation, many directional microphones exhibit an off-axis frequency "bump," that is, a slightly higher sensitivity in a comparatively narrow frequency band. As a result, arriving off-axis frequencies within that band are favored. In sound reinforcement applications, it is no problem at all to set up an acoustic feedback loop which quickly identifies the frequency at which the microphone is most sensitive.

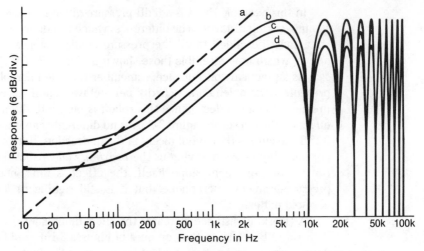

(A) At very close working distances, the lower frequencies are affected by both pressure and pressure-gradient operation.

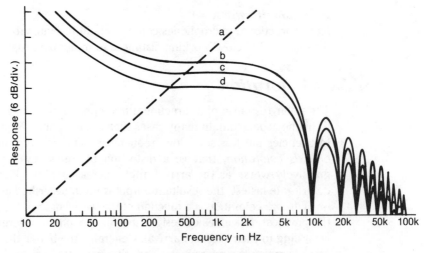

(B) The lower frequencies then are boosted due to the complementary rolloff built into the microphone.

Figure 3-25. Proximity effect.

Polar Pattern Tradeoff Considerations

Although a good unidirectional microphone is certainly a valuable production tool, it is perhaps the most abused tool in the studio workshop. In at least a few cases a microphone with an omnidirectional pattern would do a much better job, yet such microphones are often dismissed without thinking through all the problems that come along with the quest for directionality.

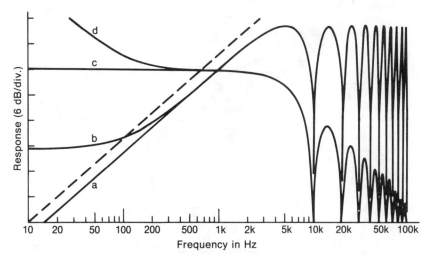

Figure 3-26. Proximity effect for a pressure-gradient microphone.
Curve (a) represents the 6 dB per octave rising frequency response.
In curve (b) the rising response is modified by the low-frequency
proximity effect. A complementary 6 dB per octave rolloff,
shown in curve (c), flattens out the overall
response, and in doing so boosts the low
frequencies, as shown in curve (d).

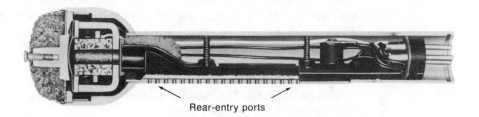

Figure 3-27. The open grille in the RE15 microphone body consists of
multiple rear-entry ports designed to optimize the microphone's off-axis
response. *(Courtesy Electro-Voice, Inc.)*

On many multitrack sessions each microphone is placed as close as possible to
an instrument, in order to pick it up while discriminating against all other nearby
sounds. Working distances of one foot or less are certainly not uncommon,
although such close-up placement brings with it the problem of proximity effect.
On one hand, a closer positioning may be desirable; on the other, bass build-up
requires the microphone to be backed off. Even if a workable distance can be
found, the slightest movement of the instrument produces a change in the
microphone's frequency response. Of course the latter problem doesn't exist when
the microphone is in front of a guitar amp, but in front of an acoustic instrument,
or even worse a vocalist, the problem just won't go away—unless one tries an
omnidirectional microphone.

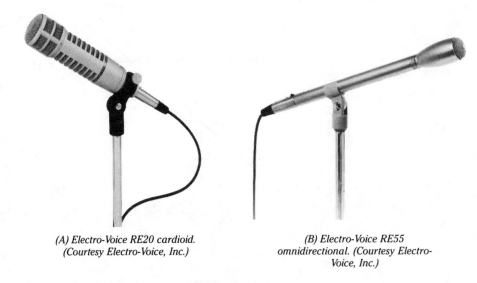

(A) Electro-Voice RE20 cardioid.
(Courtesy Electro-Voice, Inc.)

(B) Electro-Voice RE55
omnidirectional. (Courtesy Electro-
Voice, Inc.)

Figure 3-28. Equivalent-quality dynamic cardioid and
omnidirectional microphones.

An omnidirectional microphone may be placed as close as desired without
having its frequency response vary. And although it is certainly more sensitive to
off-axis sounds, this sensitivity is more than offset by the up-close working
distance. In fact, many experienced stage performers learn to rest such a microphone gently against the chin. There's no particular reason to sing into the front
of it, and the microphone may be forgotten (almost), without fear of proximity
effect, off-axis sound, wandering off mike, or of depriving the audience of a good
view of the artist's face. Not all of this matters in the recording studio, but enough
of it does to make the omnidirectional microphone worthy of a little more
consideration than it usually gets.

Figure 3-28 offers a comparison of two high-quality studio microphones; one
cardioid, the other omnidirectional. Note that the cardioid design is far more
complex than the equivalent omnidirectional microphone, although the microphones are about equal in on-axis performance. If the cardioid's excellent directional characteristics are not really needed, the operational simplicity of the
omnidirectional may make it the better choice for many studio applications.

Polar Patterns Expressed in dB Attenuation

In this chapter and the next, each polar pattern is drawn as a graph of sensitivity
versus angle. This makes it reasonably easy to compare each pattern to its polar
equation, and to derive a combined pattern from the sum or difference of two
polar equations, as we shall do in more detail in Chapter 4.

However, on a microphone specification sheet it is common practice to use a
decibel attenuation scale instead of sensitivity, making it far easier to answer the
"How many dB down?" question at a glance. If the concentric circles in this

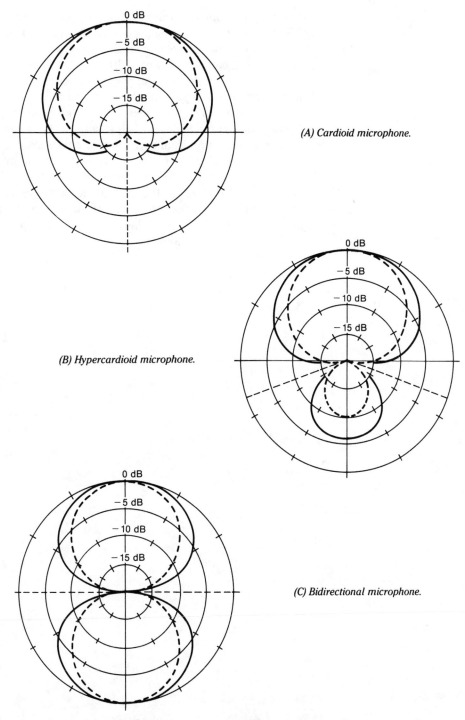

(A) Cardioid microphone.

(B) Hypercardioid microphone.

(C) Bidirectional microphone.

Figure 3-29. Polar response patterns drawn as dB attenuation vs. angle, for three types of microphones. For comparison purposes, the dotted line shows each microphone's equivalent sensitivity plot.

chapter were simply relabeled to show the equivalent dB attenuation (i.e., 0, 2.5, 6, and 12 dB), then no further change to each pattern should be needed. But since the decibel is a logarithmic expression, it is common practice to use a logarithmic scale in which each increment of, say, 5 dB, has the same linear dimension. For example, the circles in this chapter's figures might instead be labeled 0, 5, 10, and 15 dB. But the scale now suggests that the origin of the circle represents only 20 dB of attenuation, and it also precludes showing attenuation greater than that amount. Adding another circle or two helps, but still the origin never represents infinite attenuation, unless an infinite number of circles are drawn first.

To get around the problem, a polar pattern expressed in dB is often truncated at the inner circle, as shown in the solid-line curves in the three parts of Figure 3-29. In each part of the figure the dotted-line curve repeats the sensitivity pattern seen in earlier illustrations. Note that the decibel and sensitivity contours differ slightly, but their respective values do of course agree; for example 0.5 sensitivity = 6 dB attenuation, and so on.

4 Special Purpose Microphones

From the point of view of the recording engineer, a microphone's polar response is one of its most important characteristics. However, the published polar response of a microphone is valid only if the microphone is used by itself; that is, the output of no other nearby microphone will be fed to the same channel, or even to a different channel on the tape.

Remember that a polar response is just a graph of system output sensitivity with respect to the angle of arriving sound. So far, that system has been a single microphone, but it might just as well be the overall sensitivities of two microphones whose outputs are combined. In this case, the outputs combine to form a single new pattern which represents the overall sensitivity of the microphone combination. This has no practical significance if the microphones pick up entirely unique sources which share no common information. However, if two microphones are very close to each other, much information is shared between them, and thus is affected by the new polar pattern. To cite one obvious but often overlooked example, when any two directional microphones are placed back to back, their combined output is an almost perfect omnidirectional pattern, which is probably not what the user expected.

An entirely new pattern may make its appearance when microphone outputs are combined at any of the following times:

- Recording session: when more than one microphone output is fed to a single console bus, tape channel, or monitor speaker
- Mixdown session: when microphone outputs recorded on two or more tape channels are combined
- Mono playback: when a listener hears a stereo program over a mono playback system

If a combination of microphones produces an undesirable effect during a recording session, the time to take corrective action is, of course, immediately. However, if the effect is not discovered until after the session, there may still be some chance of "fixing it in the mix." But if the problem is not discovered until even later than that, then there's nothing whatever to do about it, other than make some feeble excuse about why the mono version sounds so strange. Remember that even in this day of the compact disc, there's still a mono version every time a listener turns on a mono radio.

Microphone Response Patterns

To get a better idea of what to expect when microphone outputs are combined, this chapter describes some procedures in which two or more microphone outputs are deliberately combined. In the following discussion it is assumed that the microphone diaphragms are placed as close together as is possible. That being so, the resultant polar pattern may be found by combining the two individual patterns. Doing so graphically is a tedious procedure, and of course there is a better way. However, for the sake of getting a better idea of what to expect, we begin with a graphical analysis.

In Chapter 3, each polar pattern was drawn in the polar coordinate system, to give an accurate representation of microphone sensitivity through 360 degrees. If two such patterns are drawn on the same piece of graph paper, a combined pattern could be laboriously constructed by measuring the radius of one pattern at any angle, then adding the radius of the other pattern at that same angle. The procedure would have to be repeated at many increments between 0 and 360 degrees.

Cartesian Coordinate System

For the purposes of the following discussion it may be easier to visualize various microphone combinations by redrawing the polar response in a two-dimensional *cartesian coordinate system*, which plots two variables along the y (vertical) and x (horizontal) axes. The vertical axis indicates sensitivity, the horizontal axis represents the angle of the arriving sound. In effect the cartesian system cuts each polar pattern at zero degrees, and then "unwinds" it along a horizontal axis, as shown in Figure 4-1, which compares three cartesian patterns with their polar equivalents.

When directional sensitivity is plotted in the cartesian system, some interesting pattern comparisons become a little easier to see. For example, Figure 4-2 shows a family of directional sensitivity patterns, plotted in the cartesian coordinate system. Note the following characteristics.

- Each pattern is nothing more than a cosine waveform.
- The sensitivity at ± 90 degrees is equal to the A component in the microphone's polar equation (since $B \cos \pm 90° = 0$).
- The points at which each pattern crosses the zero-sensitivity axis vary.

- The peak-to-peak amplitude of the pattern varies from zero (omni) to 2 (bidirectional).
- The portion of the curve below the $y = 0$ axis indicates the rear-lobe sensitivity.

Before continuing, make sure that the comparison between any polar response and its cartesian equivalent is well understood. And keep in mind that a negative sensitivity simply indicates a polarity reversal in the output signal.

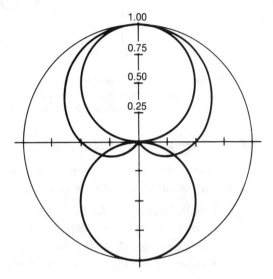

(A) Polar coordinate system.

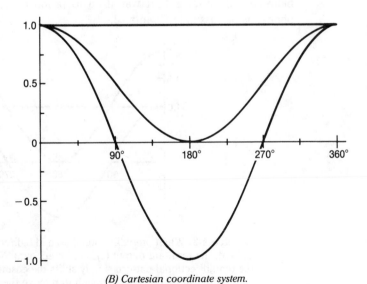

(B) Cartesian coordinate system.

Figure 4-1. The directional sensitivity of omnidirectional, unidirectional, and bidirectional microphones, drawn in a polar and a cartesian coordinate system.

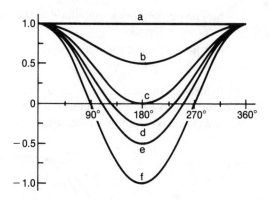

Figure 4-2. A family of directional patterns drawn in a cartesian coordinate system: (a) omnidirectional, (b) subcardioid, (c) cardioid, (d) supercardioid, (e) hypercardioid, and (f) figure-8.

Combining Microphone Outputs

Now let's see what happens when the outputs of two dissimilar microphones, M_1 and M_2, are combined. There are two ways in which this can be done:

- By addition $(M_1 + M_2)$: the outputs are combined without a polarity reversal in one of the microphone lines.

- By subtraction $(M_1 - M_2)$: the polarity of the second microphone is reversed before the outputs are combined.

The first example, in Figure 4-3, shows the addition of omnidirectional and bidirectional patterns that was used to produce the first unidirectional microphone, as discussed in Chapter 3.

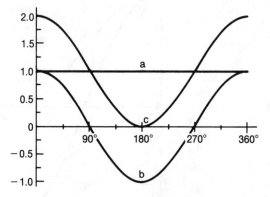

Figure 4-3. When omnidirectional (a) and bidirectional (b) outputs are combined, the resultant output (c) is unidirectional. Note that the sensitivity of the omnidirectional pattern simply shifts the cosine component upwards, in this case just enough to remove the rear lobe.

Note that the effect of adding the omnidirectional and bidirectional patterns appears to do nothing more than shift the latter pattern upwards. But in so doing, the resultant pattern reaches zero sensitivity at only one point: 180 degrees. A comparison with Figures 4-1 and 4-2 reveals that the combined pattern is the familiar unidirectional—or to put it in polar terms, cardioid—pattern.

Although the curves in Figure 4-3 show what happens if the outputs of an omnidirectional and a bidirectional microphone are added, the same three curves actually illustrate three possible combinations:

- Omni + bidirectional = unidirectional
- Uni − omnidirectional = bidirectional
- Uni − bidirectional = omnidirectional

Here a minus sign indicates the polarity of the second microphone output is reversed prior to combining it with the first microphone. Figure 4-3 thus illustrates that any microphone pattern may be realized by a simple combination of any other two patterns. And, of course, still other combinations are possible simply by reversing the plus and minus signs used here.

Stereo Microphone Theory

Perhaps the most useful implementation of combining the outputs of two dissimilar microphones is the stereophonic microphone system, which in its simplest form may be created with one unidirectional and one bidirectional microphone. In the following discussion, the unidirectional microphone will be a pure cardioid type. The unidirectional microphone is aimed straight ahead and the bidirectional microphone is oriented at 90 degrees. We might say that the former is pointed due north, and the latter is pointed due west (and therefore its rear end is pointed due east).

In curve (a) of Figure 4-4A the outputs of both microphones are plotted in the cartesian coordinate system. The sensitivity of the figure-8 microphone is set at 0.5, or one-half that of the cardioid. Note that since this microphone is shifted by 90 degrees, its pattern is now a sine wave, since $\cos(\theta - 90) = \sin\theta$.

Figure 4-4B shows the two curves representing the sum and the difference patterns; that is, the outputs when the cardioid and figure-8 patterns are either added or subtracted. The matrix device that produces these sum-and-difference outputs is described later in this chapter.

The curves in Figures 4-4 and 4-5 show that the sum and difference patterns are mirror images; the angular orientation of each pattern can be determined by noting the angle at which the curve reaches maximum positive sensitivity. The sensitivity itself is found by measuring the height of the curve above the x axis.

For the sum pattern, peak sensitivity of about 1.2 appears to be at 45 degrees, and for the difference pattern the same sensitivity falls at 315 (or −45) degrees. For a quick comparison, Figure 4-5 shows the same cardioid, figure-8, sum, and difference patterns as usually represented in the familiar polar-coordinate system. The polar pattern format may make it easier to see that the sum and difference patterns seem to have contours somewhere between cardioid and supercardioid.

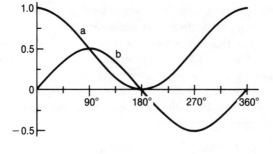

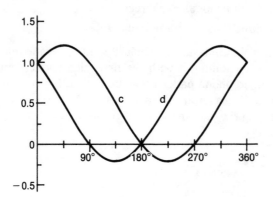

(A) A cardioid microphone pointing straight ahead (a), and a figure-8 microphone oriented at 90 degrees (b). Its output sensitivity has been reduced to 0.5.

(B) The resultant sum (c) and difference (d) sensitivities when the unidirectional and bidirectional outputs are combined.

Figure 4-4. The directional sensitivities of two microphones and their sum and difference outputs.

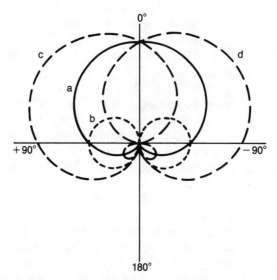

Figure 4-5. A polar response plot of (a) a cardioid and (b) a figure-8 microphone, along with their (c) sum and (d) difference patterns. The information presented is the same as that used in Figure 4-4.

So from the graphs we can determine that sum-and-difference combinations of a unidirectional and a bidirectional microphone will create two cardioid-like outputs, one pointing left of center, the other right of center, with each having a sensitivity slightly higher than that of the cardioid.

Of course, all of our conclusions so far are approximations, based on some observations of the curves seen in Figures 4-4 and 4-5. Later in this chapter we'll see how to determine the precise angle and sensitivity without resorting to graph work. But before doing so, we'll take a closer look at an actual microphone specifically designed for the sum-and-difference combinations just described, and also try to answer a few questions about why such microphones are valuable production tools.

The M-S *Microphone*

Figure 4-6 shows two implementations of a stereo microphone system, one using two microphones, the other a single microphone body containing two separate capsules. In each case, one capsule is a unidirectional element pointed straight ahead, the other a bidirectional element oriented at 90 degrees with respect to the unidirectional capsule. Both diaphragms are carefully aligned along a common vertical axis, and the complete system is referred to as an *M-S* microphone system, with two definitions given for *M-S*:

- *Middle-Side*, based on the assumption that the unidirectional (*M*) element is oriented toward the middle of the musical group, and the bidirectional (*S*) element points to the side.

- *Mono-Stereo*, since the unidirectional element picks up a mono (*M*) signal from the group, and the bidirectional element adds the stereo (*S*) component, as will be discussed later.

The first definition is the one most often encountered. In the following discussion the outputs of the two microphones will be combined to produce two new polar patterns, and the nomenclature will be as follows.

Microphone	Designation	Orientation	Pattern
M (middle)	M_M	0°	unidirectional
S (side)	M_S	90°	bidirectional
Sum	M_+	left-of-center	unidirectional
Difference	M_-	right-of-center	unidirectional

Note that although the *S* microphone is bidirectional by definition, the *M* microphone may actually have any pattern oriented at zero degrees. For the sake of keeping the explanation within reason, the *M* pattern will be limited here to the cardioid family (sub- through hyper-). The shapes of the sum and difference patterns will vary, depending on the actual *M* pattern and the relative sensitivity of the *S* microphone.

Since the polar equation for a bidirectional microphone is $B_S \cos \theta$, its on-axis sensitivity, S_S, is simply B_S.

(A) A two-microphone system: a hypercardioid with figure-8 below. (M 160 & M 130 courtesy Beyer Dynamic Inc.)

(B) Two capsules only: figure-8 with hypercardioid below. The cables lead to external housings containing preamplifier sections. (Schoeps MK 8g & MK 41g courtesy Posthorn Recordings)

(D) Cutaway view of the M (unidirectional) and S (bidirectional) capsules in a single microphone housing. (Neumann SM 69 fet courtesy Gotham Audio Corp.)

(C) Single microphone system: two capsules with continuously variable polar patterns. (Neumann USM 69i courtesy Gotham Audio Corp.)

Figure 4-6. *M-S* stereo microphone systems.

M-S Matrix Systems

The M and S microphone outputs may be routed to an external matrix system or directly to three console faders, as shown in Figure 4-7. In the matrix system, the polarity reversal shown in one of the transformer windings provides the difference signal. In an active matrix system the transformers may be replaced by amplifier sections, one of which contains the required inversion. In either case, post-matrix gain controls are provided in each output line.

When a dedicated *M-S* matrix is not available, the sum and difference signals may be derived by routing the M output to a single fader, panned to the center. The S output is fed to two faders, panned left and right respectively, with a polarity reversal in one of the lines.

The exercise of combining two microphones simply to produce two new polar responses may still seem like going to a lot of bother to create something that might be handled just as well by setting up two unidirectional microphones pointing in the desired directions. However, the whole *M-S* system is worth a lot more than just the sum (and difference, of course) of its parts. As we shall see, it is a production tool that is often far more useful than a matched pair of unidirectional microphones.

To illustrate the power of the *M-S* system, consider what we have learned so far: a pure cardioid M pattern combined with a figure-8 S pattern will produce sum and difference outputs oriented at ± 45 degrees if the sensitivity of the S pattern is one-half that of the M pattern. Obviously it's possible to turn one or the other microphone element off completely (that is, zero sensitivity), thus giving us these three possibilities:

Sensitivity of		Orientation of		
M	*S*	*Sum*	*Difference*	**Pattern Shapes**
1	0	$0°$	$0°$	cardioids
1	0.5	$+45°$	$-45°$	supercardioids (approx.)
0	1	$+90°$	$-90°$	figure-8s

From this we can form some general "what if" conclusions about how sum and difference patterns change as the *M*-to-*S* ratio varies between 1:0 and 0:1. At first (*M:S* = 1:0), we have nothing but two forward-pointing mono patterns. And at the opposite extreme (*M:S* = 0:1), the result is two back-to-back figure-8 patterns. So it's reasonable (*and* accurate) to assume that as the sensitivity moves between these impractical extremes, the following three things happen to the sum and the difference outputs:

- The patterns range from perfect cardioid to supercardioid, then to hypercardioid, and finally to figure-8.

- The orientation continuously varies from zero to ± 90 degrees; the sum pattern is oriented left of center, the difference pattern is right of center.

- The overall sound field varies from mono to stereo to a vague, perhaps overly reverberant image which cancels completely if the two ouputs are monitored in mono.

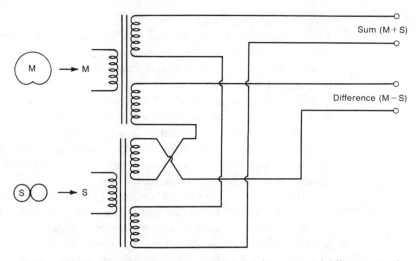

(A) The M *and* S *microphone outputs are combined to form sum and difference signals.*

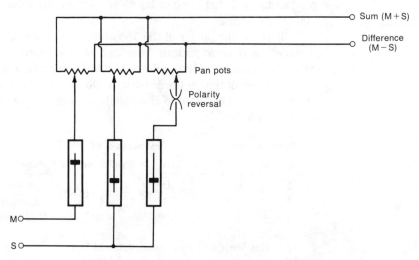

(B) The use of three faders as an alternative to the matrix.

(C) A battery-operated system combining 48V phantom powering, an M-S matrix and line-level (BNC connnectors) M, S, sum, and difference outputs. (Schoeps VMC 52 UB courtesy Posthorn Recordings)

Figure 4-7. *M-S* matrix systems.

In short, by varying the *M:S* ratio we can adjust the stereo image over a very wide range, and eventually find the ideal mix of *M* and *S* to create the desired effect. As a further consideration, the final blend need not be locked in during recording; the *M* and *S* outputs may be separately recorded on session, and matrixed to left and right signals later on during a tape-to-tape transfer. This is especially useful on remote recordings made under nonideal listening conditions. And as one more benefit, the *M* signal alone may be used as a mono version of the same recording.

Sum and Difference Patterns

When evaluating any recording, *M-S* stereo or otherwise, there's not much point in probing into the math behind the theory; if it sounds right, it *is* right, and it doesn't much matter whether the resultant patterns are super-, hyper-, or whatever-cardioid. However, a little more immersion in "mike math" can actually go a long way towards getting a better understanding of what to expect when various microphone ouputs are combined, either intentionally as an *M-S* configuration or by accident as an interaction between two closely placed microphones. A good grasp on the math may also make it possible to make an on-the-spot modification to a microphone pickup when nothing else seems to work.

In the following sections, we'll analyze the characteristics of the left- and right-oriented patterns that are created when *M* and *S* outputs are combined. From the graphs shown earlier in Figures 4-4B and 4-5, we estimated that the sum pattern peaks at about 45 degrees, and the difference pattern at 315 (-45) degrees. In each case, the maximum sensitivity is about 1.2, and the pattern looks like it might be close to a supercardioid contour. With a minimum of pain, we can verify each of these three parameters, not only for this particular combination, but for any other combination that may turn up, accidentally or on purpose. Each parameter is discussed separately in the next section.

Orientation Angle

Using the sum pattern as an example, curve (c) in Figures 4-4B and 4-5 is a plot of the polar equations for the two microphones, $M_M + M_S$. To make a general statement that covers this specific example as well as any other combination of two microphones, we may say that there is an included angle, α, measured clockwise from microphone M_S to M_M. The polar equations are then, respectively,

$$M_M = A_M + B_M \cos \theta$$

and

$$M_S = A_S + B_S \cos(\theta - \alpha)$$

and the curve of their sum is therefore defined by the equation

$$\begin{aligned} y &= M_M + M_S \\ &= A_M + B_M \cos \theta + A_S + B_S \cos(\theta - \alpha) \end{aligned}$$

From curve (c) in Figure 4-4B, we can see that the slope of this curve varies continuously as angle θ moves counterclockwise from 0 to 360 degrees. However, at the point at which sensitivity is maximum, the slope $(dy/d\theta)$ is zero. We can therefore calculate the angle at which this point occurs with a little more math. The procedure is given here, but need not be followed step by step by readers who have little patience with calculus. Fortunately, the final answer eventually reduces to a reasonably simple equation, as seen here:

$$y = A_M + B_M \cos \theta + A_S + B_S \cos (\theta - \alpha)$$
$$= A_M + B_M \cos \theta + A_S + B_S(\cos \theta \cos \alpha - \sin \theta \sin \alpha)$$
$$dy/d\theta = -B_M \sin \theta - B_S \sin \theta \cos \alpha - B_S \cos \theta \sin \alpha = 0 \text{ (i.e., slope} = 0)$$
$$= -B_M \tan \theta - B_S \tan \theta \cos \alpha - B_S \sin \alpha = 0 \quad \text{(divide both sides by cos } \theta)$$

Rearranging terms,

$$B_M \tan \theta + B_S \tan \theta \cos \alpha = -B_S \sin \alpha$$
$$\tan \theta(B_M + B_S \cos \alpha) = -B_S \sin \alpha$$

and therefore,

$$\tan \theta = -B_S \sin \alpha/(B_M + B_S \cos \alpha) \qquad \qquad \text{(4-1)}$$
$$= B_S/B_M \quad \text{(since } \alpha = -90°, \sin \alpha = -1, \cos \alpha = 0)$$

Finally (!),

$$\theta = \arctan(B_S/B_M)$$

To put this in English, when *any* coincident pair is set up with an included angle of 90 degrees, and the outputs are summed, the angle (θ) at which maximum sensitivity occurs is simply the angle whose tangent is the quotient of the B components of the microphones.

In the specific case of the unidirectional and bidirectional pair we have been discussing, the equations are

$$M_M = 0.5 + 0.5 \cos \theta,$$

and

$$M_S = \frac{1}{2}[0 + 1.0 \cos(\theta - 90°)] \quad \text{(i.e., half sensitivity)}$$
$$= 0 + 0.5 \cos(\theta - 90°)$$

Therefore, $\tan \theta = B_S/B_M = 0.5/0.5 = 1$, and so $\theta = 45°$, which fortunately confirms the value found earlier by direct observation of the graphs in Figures 4-4B and 4-5.

Sensitivity

To calculate the maximum output sensitivity of two microphones whose outputs are added, all that needs to be done is to add their outputs at the angle where that maximum occurs. Therefore,

$$
\begin{aligned}
s_M &= A_M + B_M \cos(45) &&= 0.5 + 0.5(0.707) \\
+ \; s_S &= A_S + B_S \cos(45 - 90) && \underline{\;0 \quad + 0.5(0.707)\;} \\
& && s_+ = 0.5 + 0.707 = 1.207
\end{aligned}
$$

To find the sensitivity when the outputs are subtracted, reverse the signs of A_S, B_S, and θ:

$$
\begin{aligned}
s_M &= A_M + B_M \cos(-45) &&= 0.5 + 0.5(0.707) \\
- \; s_S &= -A_S - B_S \cos(-45 - 90) && \underline{\;0 \quad - 0.5(-0.707)\;} \\
& && s_- = 0.5 + 0.707 = 1.207
\end{aligned}
$$

Note that the resultant sensitivity is the same as that of the sum pattern and agrees with the graphs in Figures 4-4 and 4-5.

Polar Equation

The polar equation of either pattern might be left at $s = 0.5 + 0.707 \cos\theta$, thus giving a maximum sensitivity of 1.207, as just shown above. However, to better compare the new pattern with other patterns, it is convenient to rewrite the equation so that it too will have a maximum sensitivity of unity. To do so, simply divide each term above by the maximum sensitivity. Thus,

$$
\frac{0.500}{1.207} + \frac{0.707}{1.207} = \frac{1.207}{1.207} = 0.414 + 0.586 = 1
$$

Therefore, the polar equation of the sum or difference pattern may be written as

$$
s = 0.414 + 0.586 \cos\theta
$$

In Chapter 3, Table 3-1 lists the A and B components for various microphone patterns, and it can be seen that the values just found lie about midway between those for the cardioid and the supercardioid microphone.

Sample Problem 1

As a quick example of *M-S* theory, what M and S combination will produce two hypercardioid patterns at ± 30 degrees? To find M_M,

$$
\begin{aligned}
& 0.25 + 0.75 \cos(+30°) && \text{(the hypercardioid equation)} \\
+ \; & \underline{0.25 + 0.75 \cos(-30°)} \\
& 0.50 + 1.5(0.866) && = 0.50 + 1.299 = 1.799
\end{aligned}
$$

Divide all three terms by 1.799 to find that

$$M_M = 0.278 + 0.722 \cos \theta$$

To find the sensitivity of the bidirectional microphone, S, remember that $\tan \theta = B_S/B_M$ and so

$$B_S = B_M \tan(30°) = 0.722(0.866) = 0.417$$

Therefore the polar equation for the bidirectional microphone is

$$M_S = 0.417 \cos \theta$$

Working Backward: Sum-and-Difference to M-S

Survivors of the preceding sections above have seen how the combination of two actual microphones, M_M and M_S, created the two new patterns M_+ and M_-. Looking at these patterns out of context, they might just as well have been created by two actual microphones. If this had actually been the case, then a combination of their outputs would create the M and S patterns instead. In other words, an M-S matrix works both ways; in Figure 4-7A the inputs and outputs can be on either side of the circuit, and therefore if

$$M_M + M_S = M_+$$

and

$$M_M - M_S = M_-$$

then

$$M_+ + M_- = M_M + M_S + M_M - M_S = 2M_M$$

and

$$M_+ - M_- = M_M + M_S - M_M + M_S = 2M_S$$

Sample Problem 2

To illustrate this aspect of M-S matrixing, consider the following problem: Given two microphones with pure cardioid patterns oriented at 45 degrees left and right of center, what is the resultant M pattern, and what is the sensitivity of the resultant S pattern?

To begin, add the two cardioid outputs to find the resultant M pattern, as follows:

$$\begin{aligned} M_M = M_+ \quad &= 0.5 + 0.5 \cos (+45°) \quad &&= 0.5 + 0.5(0.707) \\ + M_- \quad &+ 0.5 + 0.5 \cos (-45°) \quad &&+ \underline{0.5 + 0.5(0.707)} \\ & && \quad 1.0 + 0.707 \end{aligned}$$

Therefore, the polar equation of the M pattern may be written as

$$M_M = A_M + B_M$$
$$= 1.000 + 0.707 \cos \theta = 1.707 \text{ (when } \theta = 0°)$$
$$= 0.586 + 0.414 \cos \theta = 1 \quad \text{(divide all terms by 1.707)}$$

Earlier it was shown that the angle of orientation for the sum pattern is the angle whose tangent is B_S/B_M. Since we have specified that $\theta = 45°$, we know that B_S/B_M must be equal to 1, and therefore, $B_S = B_M$. We also know that M_S is a bidirectional pattern, and so $A_S = 0$. We may now write the polar equation of the S pattern as

$$M_S = 0.414 \cos \theta$$

In other words, when two microphones with pure cardioid patterns are oriented at ± 45 degrees and the outputs are combined, the resultant sum is a subcardioid pattern ($0.586 + 0.414 \cos \theta$) and the difference is a conventional side-oriented figure-8 pattern whose sensitivity is attenuated to 0.414.

Mono and Stereo Pickup Angles

When either an M-S or some other stereo microphone pair is used, two important variables to be considered are

1. The resultant mono signal when (and if) the stereo signal is heard in that mode, and
2. The stereo image width that results from the combination.

In either case, the signal may be analyzed in terms of a mono or stereo pickup angle; as we shall see, the first consideration is quite straightforward, the second is not.

Mono Pickup Angle

Since any microphone combination produces a polar pattern that is the equivalent of a single microphone, the pattern may be thought of as that of a mono microphone. As with an actual single microphone, there are two points on the pattern—one on either side of its zero-degree axis—at which the output level is down by 3 dB.

The *mono pickup angle* is defined as the included angle between these two points (Peus 1988), and it identifies an arc that might be considered as an arbitrary reference working range, as far as the efficient pickup of front-originating sound is concerned.

Regardless of whether the pattern is that of an actual M microphone or is the result of combining two (or more) other microphones, the mono pickup angle may be calculated from the appropriate polar equation; when the output is 3 dB down, the resultant sensitivity must be $10^{-3/20} = 0.708$. Therefore, the polar equation may be used to determine the angle at which the output sensitivity will be 0.708. The equation, and the values for a pure cardioid pattern, are given here.

General Form	Pure Cardioid Equation
$s = A + B \cos \theta = 0.708$	$= 0.5 + 0.5 \cos \theta = 0.708$

and so

$$\arccos \theta = (0.708 - A)/B \qquad = (0.708 - 0.5)/0.5 = 0.416$$
$$\theta \qquad = 65.418° \text{ at the } -3 \text{ dB point}$$

Therefore, the included mono pickup angle for a pure cardioid pattern is $\pm\theta$, or 130.835 degrees. In the following discussion the angle will be left in its $\pm\theta$ form.

In an actual *M-S* microphone, the mono pickup angle is simply a function of the *M* pattern alone. Even though the stereo outputs of the *M-S* matrix are the left- and right-oriented patterns described in detail in the preceding, when the program is heard later over a mono reproduction system, the *S* components in both sides of the stereo signal cancel and the listener hears only the original *M* microphone. Therefore, whether one listens to the direct (prematrix) *M* output alone, or hears a mono version of the stereo matrix output, the result is the same.

The mono pickup angle for a hypercardioid microphone is shown in Figure 4-8A, and Table 4-1 lists the mono pickup angle for this and other mono polar patterns. Note that the minimum possible mono pickup angle is ±45 degrees, since the figure-8 pattern at which this angle occurs has the smallest possible front lobe. (See Figure 3-23 for pattern comparison.) If a lobe is smaller than this (and therefore, so is its pickup angle), then it is the rear lobe of one of the cardioid family of patterns.

The other data in the table are described in the next section.

Table 4-1. Mono and Stereo Pickup Angles for Various *M-S* Combinations*

Polar Pattern	Mono Pickup Angle $\pm\theta_M$	Stereo Pickup Angle $\pm\theta_S$ When $M_S =$					$\theta_M = \theta_S$ when $M_S =$
		0.25	*0.36*	*0.50*	*0.75*	*1.00*	
Subcardioid	99.67				90	60.73	
Cardioid	65.42	126.80	107.52	90	67.39	53.14	0.78
Supercardioid	57.36	100.89	90	78.71	62.10	50.39	0.84
Hypercardioid	52.36	90	81.43	72.43	58.64	48.42	0.89
Figure-8	45	75.98	69.91	63.45	53.14	45	1.00

*Each included pickup angle is double the value listed in the table.

Stereo Pickup Angle

When listening to a stereo program recorded with an *M-S* microphone, it will be found that images within a certain range on either side of the zero axis are well placed, but that the location of images outside that range may be ambiguous or even worse, reversed. As an extreme example, consider an application in which a moving sound source follows a circular path around the microphone. When the

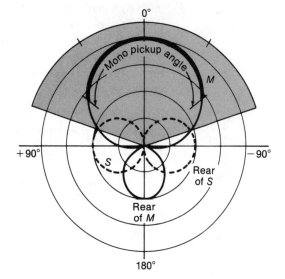

(A) The M *pattern, with mono pickup angle indicated, and the* S *pattern.*

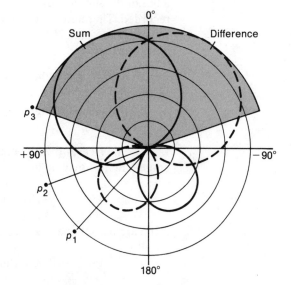

(B) The sum and difference patterns.

Figure 4-8. An *M-S* combination showing the mono pickup angle. In each part of the drawing, the semicircular wedge indicates the stereo pickup angle and the short line segments mark the fronts of the sum and difference patterns.

source is in the left-rear, it will seem to originate in the right-front. As the source moves in a clockwise direction around the microphone, the right-oriented image first becomes ambiguous, then resolves itself into a good left-oriented image. The image passes from left to center to right, then the problem reappears in reverse.

To understand the cause of the problem, Figure 4-8 shows the four polar responses of an *M-S* microphone. Note that the rear lobes of the sum and difference patterns in Figure 4-8B are oriented in the opposite left-to-right directions to the corresponding front lobes. Therefore, with respect to left-to-right imaging, any sound in the rear is picked up by the wrong microphone. Keeping in mind that the rear-lobe polarity of any directional microphone is reversed with respect to the front, follow a sound source from points p_1 to p_2 (Figure 4-8B), as listed here.

Source Is Located at	Sound Is Picked Up by	Apparent Location of Sound Source Is
p_1	rear lobe of right pattern only	right (incorrect)
p_1–p_2	both patterns, but with opposing polarities	right, but ill-defined
p_2	same, but now equal in amplitude, still opposite in polarity	ambiguous
p_2–p_3	both patterns, with diminishing effect of polarity reversal	left, but ill-defined
p_3	front lobe of left pattern only	left (correct)

Once beyond point p_3, the sound source is picked up entirely by the front lobes of the sum and difference patterns, and its actual position should be reliably recorded. Therefore, in order to maintain a reliable left-to-right stereo image, the sound source should be kept within this *stereo pickup angle*, which is defined (Peus 1988) as

1. The included angle between the forward intersections of the M and S patterns, or
2. The included angle between the forward nulls of the sum and difference patterns.

In either case, the angle is identical and—for readers who have *still* not had enough math—may be found from the following solution to a quadratic equation:

$$\tan \theta = [-B_1B_2 \pm A_1(B_1{}^2 - A_1{}^2 + B_2{}^2)^{1/2}]/(A_1{}^2 - B_2{}^2)$$

If the M microphone is a pure cardioid, the equation simplifies to

$$\tan \theta = 0 \text{ (and therefore, } \theta = 180°)$$

and

$$\tan \theta = -2B_1B_2/(B_1{}^2 - B_2{}^2)$$

In either case, two values of $\tan \theta$ are found; the stereo pickup angle is twice the smallest angle thus given, and it is shown in both parts of Figure 4-8. In addition, Table 4-1 lists the stereo pickup angles for various combinations of M and S microphones.

As a final note, it is important to remember what the stereo pickup angle is, and what it is not. It is an indication of the working area in front of an M-S pair in which there will be no directional ambiguities due to the polarity reversal between the front lobe of one pattern and the rear lobe of another. In other words, as long as sound sources remain within the stereo pickup angle, there will be no phase-related localization problems.

But despite its name, the stereo pickup angle is *not* an indication of the stereo image width of an *M-S* recording; in fact, this width is inversely proportional to the stereo pickup angle. To illustrate this apparent contradiction, consider two extreme cases. In the first, gradually reduce the sensitivity of the *S* microphone to zero (off). Using Figure 4-8A as a reference, note that if the bidirectional pattern were made progressively smaller, its intersection with the *M* pattern would move rearwards, and the stereo pickup angle would become greater. Yet at the same time the angle between the sum and difference patterns would decrease as both of them move closer to a zero-degree orientation. When the *S* microphone is completely removed, the sum and difference patterns are both simply the *M* microphone alone, or two identical mono patterns pointing straight ahead. With absolutely no phase-related cancellations possible, we have on the one hand a stereo pickup angle of ±180 degrees, but on the other, no stereo, hardly an ideal case.

At the other extreme, turn the *S* microphone on again and now gradually reduce the sensitivity of the *M* microphone. The situation reverses itself; as the stereo pickup angle gets smaller the sum and difference patterns rotate outwards and the entire program eventually becomes an ambiguous stereo directional blur due to two back-to-back polarity-reversed bidirectional patterns. Perhaps this qualifies as someone's version of total stereo, but as before it's no ideal case for the rest of us.

In a few cases, the ideal mixture of *M* and *S* microphone outputs is dictated by the requirement to provide a specific pickup angle, as described immediately below.

Matching Sound to Picture

In applications where the audio image accompanies video, the *M-S* pattern may be adjusted so that its included stereo pickup angle agrees with the picture angle. For example, given a certain picture angle, adjust the *M* and *S* microphone outputs to provide the appropriate stereo pickup angle.

Since we want the patterns to intersect (i.e., to be equal) at a known angle, we can write the *M* and *S* equations as

$$A_1 + B_1 \cos \theta = B_2 \cos (\theta - 90°) = B_2 \sin \theta$$

Assuming the *M* pattern equation is known, solve for B_2 as follows:

$$B_2 = (A_1 + B_1 \cos \theta)/\sin \theta \qquad \text{(4-2)}$$

Now, given a hypercardioid *M* microphone and a picture angle of ±60 degrees, the required setting for the *S* microphone is

$$B_2 = (0.25 + 0.75 \cos 60°)/\sin 60°$$
$$= 0.72 \text{ (or, about } -2.83 \text{ dB)}$$

The same general procedure can be followed to adjust the stereo pickup angle to encompass any stage width. For example, Figure 4-9 shows an *M-S* microphone positioned in front of a stage. The microphone-to-stage distance and the stage width are both known, so the required stereo pickup angle is found from the equation

$$\theta = \pm \arctan(0.5w/d) = \pm \arctan(w/2d)$$

where
    w = stage width
    d = microphone-to-stage distance

Once the value of θ is known, use equation (4-2) above to find the required *S*-pattern sensitivity for any given *M* pattern.

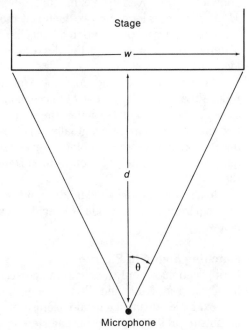

Figure 4-9. Setup for finding the required stereo pickup angle when an *M-S* microphone is located at distance d from a stage of width w. The stereo pickup angle is $\pm\theta$, or 2θ.

Matching Mono and Stereo Pickup Angles

Note that in the example shown in Figure 4-8, the mono and stereo pickup angles differ by about 20 degrees. For the ultimate in mono-stereo compatibility, the *S* microphone sensitivity can be adjusted so that the patterns intersect at the −3 dB points on the *M* pattern, thus making the mono and stereo pickup angles identical.

    Assuming the equation for the *M* pattern is known, the sensitivity required for the *S* pattern is

$$s_S = 0.708/\sin k \qquad\qquad\qquad (4\text{-}3)$$

where

$k = \arccos x$, or

$k = \pi/2 - \arctan [x/(1 - x^2)^{1/2}]$ (for personal computer programs lacking arccos function)

$x = (0.708 - A_1)B_1$

For example, if the M microphone has the hypercardioid pattern shown in Figure 4-8 and the S microphone sensitivity, s_S, is set at 0.894 (i.e., about -0.97 dB), the patterns will intersect at the -3 dB points, as shown in Figure 4-10. In Table 4-1, the last column gives the S microphone sensitivity that yields equal mono and stereo pickup angles for the listed M microphones.

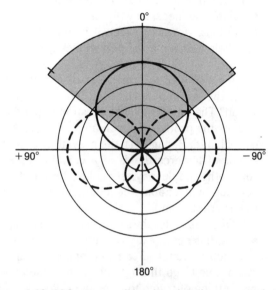

Figure 4-10. *M-S* pattern adjusted so that the mono and stereo pickup angles are equal.

With the stereo/mono pickup angle thus determined, the microphone will have to be physically moved so that the angle encompasses the stage, or a different M pattern may be selected and s_S recalculated. The procedure is to simply select the M-pattern equation that provides -3 dB points at either side of the stage, then use equation (4-3) to find the required sensitivity for the S pattern.

M-S *Summary*

From the foregoing, we may make some general conclusions about what happens when the outputs of any *M-S* pair are combined. The sum and difference outputs show the following characteristics:

- The output sensitivities are identical.
- The polar patterns are also identical.

- The orientation angles are mirror images; that is, if the sum pattern is oriented at *n* degrees left of center, the difference pattern is *n* degrees right of center.
- The orientation angle is that angle whose tangent is equal to B_S/B_M. In mathematical terms, this is often written as:

$$\arctan \theta \ (\text{or, } \tan^{-1} \theta) = B_S/B_1M$$

As we have seen, a little mathematical manipulation will help discover the combination of *M* and *S* patterns that will yield just about any desired effect. Of course, a little math does go a very long way, so in laboring though the preceding explanations some relief may be found by remembering that recording is really a musical, not mathematical, pursuit; once all the equations are digested, it shouldn't be necessary to bring them up again for many routine recording operations. However, when it is important to match sound to picture the math may help find, if not the perfect pickup, then at least a point at which to begin the search.

It's also well to remember that in many situations it really doesn't matter what the polar patterns look like on paper; what counts is, how does it all sound? The answer to that question depends largely on the skill of the engineer and/or the producer. Given a basic understanding of random energy efficiency (see Chapter 3, page 91), the prevailing conditions may suggest starting out with a pair of hypercardioids at a certain angle; elsewhere, a pair of cardioids at some other angle may seem like a better choice. In either case, making the right decision will enable the engineer to capture the ideal blend of direct and reverberant sound.

Of course, Murphy's Law instructs us that whatever pair is first chosen will be almost, but never exactly, right. But even in the unlikely event that a limitless selection of matched-pair microphones were available, it would simply take too much time to go through all the possible choices searching for the right one, to say nothing of trying to remember whether the last choice was better than some other one, and so on. Since all the choices are almost instantly available through a single *M-S* microphone, there's a strong argument to be made for learning how to creatively manipulate this powerful production tool.

This little excursion through the woods of *M-S* math does not end in a clearing where the ideal combination is at last revealed. Fortunately, that mixture is in the ear of the beholder, and despite all this math, *M-S* microphone usage remains an art form. Figure 4-11 shows a few additional examples of studio-quality *M-S* microphones.

Other Stereo Microphone Systems

In addition to the *M-S* microphone system, there are several other stereo techniques that utilize various microphone-pair combinations. A few examples are given here. For the sake of keeping this chapter within reasonable length, the mathematical aspects of each system are not covered here.

(A) 9-pattern capsules.
(C 422 courtesy AKG
Acoustics, Inc.)

(B) 3-pattern (omni,
cardioid, figure-8)
capsules. (Schoeps CMTS
501 courtesy Posthorn
Recordings)

(C) Fixed hypercardioid
and figure-8 capsules.
(Neumann RSM 190i
courtesy Gotham Audio
Corp.)

Figure 4-11. Studio-quality *M-S* microphones with two capsules
within a single housing.

X-Y *Pair*

When a coincident microphone pair is used in any non-*M-S* configuration, the two
microphones are generally identified as an *X-Y* pair. The designation is also
sometimes used to describe the matrixed sum and difference outputs of an *M-S*
microphone system.

In Figure 4-12A, two unidirectional microphones are placed in an *X-Y* configuration using a specially designed bracket. The figure also shows a microphone in
which two cardioid capsules are fixed at a 90-degree included angle within a
single housing.

Note that by definition, the mono summation of an *X-Y* pair is the *M* pattern
of an *M-S* pair. It follows therefore that any *X-Y* pair can be matrixed to *M-S* and
then rematrixed to recreate the original or any other *X-Y* pair.

(A) Two microphones on a bracket. (Schoeps CMS 541 U microphones and UMS 20 bracket courtesy Posthorn Recordings)

(B) Two cardioid capsules oriented at a fixed 90-degree angle (±45 degrees) within the microphone housing. (C 522 ENG courtesy AKG Acoustics, Inc.)

Figure 4-12. *X-Y* stereo microphone systems.

The Blumlein Pair

Much of the groundwork in stereo microphone technique is derived from the research of Alan Dower Blumlein in the 1930s, and from his patent (1931) covering various aspects of sound transmission, recording, and reproduction. The patent illustrates the matrix system now used in *M-S* recording, and describes the performance of various transducers in which a pair of elements is placed at right angles.

The use of a pair of bidirectional microphones with a 90-degree included angle is usually referred to as a *Blumlein Pair*; when the microphones are at ±45 degrees with respect to a zero-degree axis they are sometimes called a *Stereosonic* system (Ceoen 1972).

In the *M-S* mode described above, the matrixed outputs of a Blumlein pair are also bidirectional. The orientation angle is again found using equation (4-1), as described earlier in the chapter (page 120).

ORTF System

The ORTF system employs a pair of cardioid microphones spaced at 17 cm and with an included angle of 110 degrees, as shown in Figure 4-13A. The system derives its name from its early use by the ORTF (*Office de Radiodiffusion Télévision Française*—French National Broadcasting Organization).

NOS System

The NOS system uses a pair of cardioid microphones spaced at 30 cm and with an included angle of 90 degrees, based on an NOS recommendation (*Nederlandsche Omroep Stichting*—Dutch Broadcasting Organization).

Spaced Microphones, A-B Pair

In the 1930s, engineers at Bell Telephone Laboratories experimented with the concept of a "curtain of microphones" arrayed in a line in front of the performers, each to be connected to a separate loudspeaker similarly placed in front of the listener (Lipshitz 1986). As a practical alternative to an infinity of transducers, experiments were conducted with a practical limit of two or three channels.

In the intervening years, recording engineers have used two or three spaced microphones—often omnidirectional—as an alternative to the coincident techniques described above. In any such system, both amplitude and time differences are picked up by each microphone and transmitted to the stereo loudspeaker system.

When the microphones are spaced much farther apart than the listener's ears, the spaced microphone array records a sound field quite different from that which the listener would hear if present at the recording. In some cases, an acoustic "hole in the middle" will be noted, with instruments apparently clustered in the immediate vicinity of the two loudspeakers. The addition of a center blend microphone may help fill in the hole, but at the cost of a less spacious sound (Griesinger 1985).

In any case, some critics argue for, and some against, a spaced microphone technique, stating that it is better/worse than any coincident system. Both sides have presented rather convincing arguments (on paper of course) that the other side is wrong. Since there are as many variations on technique as there are microphones and distances between them, the best analysis remains as before, in the ear of the beholder.

A pair of spaced microphones used for a stereo pickup is often referred to as an *A-B* pair, and when the microphones are closely spaced, as a *near-coincident* pair. A typical example is shown in Figure 4-13B.

Binaural System

The term *binaural* refers to any sound field heard by two ears and has come to be associated with a recording system in which two microphones are set up to simulate the characteristics of the head and the interaural spacing of the ears. As shown in Figure 4-14, the binaural system consists of dummy head with a

(A) Microphone capsules placed in the ORTF configuration. (Neumann STH 100 stereo clamp courtesy Gotham Audio Corp.)

(B) A pair of spaced omnidirectional microphones. (MKH 20's courtesy Sennheiser Electronic Corp.)

Figure 4-13. Microphone placement.

(A) Dummy head used for binaural recording.

(B) Head assembly interior view, showing microphone capsules at ear positions. (Neumann KU 81i courtesy Gotham Audio Corp.)

(C) Binaural headset containing two omnidirectional capsules located at either ear, to be placed on a human or dummy head as shown. (MKE 2002 courtesy Sennheiser Electronic Corp.)

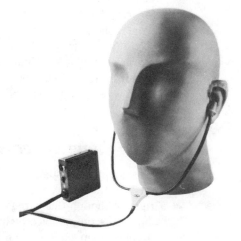

Figure 4-14. The binaural system.

microphone mounted at each ear. Binaural recording provides a startlingly realistic impression when the program is monitored over headphones, since in effect it places the listener at the location of the dummy head.

Unfortunately, the system may not be very effective when heard over loud-speakers. As with the spaced-microphone technique described before, binaural recording does not preserve the distance relationships between the recording and the playback system. When the sound field recorded by near-coincident binaural microphones is reproduced over widely spaced speakers, most of the subtle time-of-arrival and head-shading cues picked up by the dummy head are lost.

For example, the signal recorded by the microphone at, say, the left dummy-head ear should only be heard by the left ear of the listener. But when reproduced by a loudspeaker, the listener hears the signal in question in both ears, with a slight delay at the right ear. As compensation, a secondary delayed signal with polarity reversal may be fed to the right speaker. The delay is selected so that this signal reaches the right ear in time to cancel the primary signal from the left loudspeaker. But now the secondary signal is heard by the left ear, and so another compensating signal is required at the left speaker, and so on. Experi-mental systems with digital delay and filtering have been developed to accom-plish this, with very effective results (Griesinger 1989a & b, Møller 1989). In addition there have been many other new developments in *transaural stereo*, in which the listener's ears and not the loudspeakers are regarded as the end point in the recording/reproduction chain (Cooper & Bauck 1989). With the appropriate compensating circuitry, excellent reproduction of binaural recordings over loud-speakers can be expected, and binaural techniques may even be applied to multitrack production.

As a further complication of binaural recording, headphone listening can be disorienting if the listener moves slightly while wearing the headphones. In a normal listening environment, slight—and often unconscious—head movements help us to localize images in the surrounding, and presumably stationary, sound field. But when one listens over headphones, the entire sound field follows the listener's head movements, creating the sonic impression that the room is in motion too.

As a final point, the obvious physical constraints imposed by wearing a pair of headphones have worked against the binaural system becoming a very popular recording technique. However, as transaural stereo technology progresses, and the listener can anticipate good-to-excellent speaker reproduction rivaling the binaural effect heard over headphones, then binaural recording may become more widespread. For further details on the subject, the cited references should be consulted.

Multimicrophone Systems

This chapter has spent a lot of time ignoring the obvious technique of using many microphones and panning each output to the desired position between left and right. Although this is regarded as the high-tech answer to true stereo by some, and is the only choice available for many multitrack productions, it has not for nothing been dubbed "multitrack mono," since it loses most of the feelings of space that are captured by the various stereo systems described earlier.

Given the realities of contemporary popular music production and budget restrictions that don't allow much time for experimentation, multiple microphones and lots of pan pots are the only practical choice for many recording sessions. Nevertheless, the careful use of one of the simpler (in concept if not in execution) techniques described above should be tried, when and where conditions permit. And when conditions don't permit, the engineer should still be aware of the effects of combining two or more microphones.

Stereo Microphone Cable Requirements

The various *M-S* microphones require a special multiconductor cable as the interface between the microphone's dual outputs and the input to the external matrix system used to derive the *X-Y* signals. The matrix system outputs use conventional 3-pin plugs and may be treated as any other conventional microphone lines. If the *M-S* outputs are not maxtrixed prior to recording, then the matrix system routes these signals directly to its output plugs.

In the case of an *X-Y* system built into a single microphone housing, the microphone is usually supplied with a connector cable terminated in two standard 3-pin microphone plugs.

Table 4-2 lists selected stereo and binaural microphones and accessories available from various manufacturers.

The following section describes a few of the nonstereo effects of combining a pair of microphones, as may happen either intentionally while recording, or later on when the tracks are combined.

Other Microphone Combinations

The earlier discussion of polar combinations confined itself to the *M-S* pair, a forward-oriented unidirectional microphone and a side-oriented bidirectional microphone. However, the same general principles may be applied to any combination of two microphone outputs. For those readers who have survived the mathematics seen above, these examples should be no problem at all.

Some of the following examples are more practical than others. However, a careful review of each combination will help to get a better understanding of what happens when two coincident microphone outputs are combined under a variety of circumstances.

Creating a Pure Cardioid Pattern

Most unidirectional microphones have a polar pattern that is not a perfect cardioid shape. To create a perfect cardioid pattern, place any two identical directional microphones back to back and subtract their outputs. Adjust the level of the forward-oriented microphone, M_F, as required. Now bring up the level of the rear-oriented microphone, M_R, until sounds at the rear are completely attenuated. To see what's happening on paper, arbitrarily assign any convenient values to the A and B components. Then calculate the sensitivity, s, required for the

Table 4-2. Stereo and Binaural Microphones and Accessories*

Manufacturer	Model No.	Comments
AKG	C 34	9 patterns, remote control
	C 422	9 patterns, remote control
	C 522 ENG	*X-Y* only, 2 cardioids at 90°
Audio Developments	AD 066-11	Stereo microphone amplifier with *M-S* decoder
Audio Engineering Associates	MS-38	Active *M-S* matrix decoder
	MS-380	Mic/line amplifier with active *M-S* matrix decoder
Bang & Olufsen	BM5	dual bidirectional ribbons (discontinued)
Fostex	M22RP	*M-S* only, dynamic
MB-Electronic	Stereo-Q	uses four interchangeable capsules, remote control
Milab	XY-82	*X-Y* only, dual cardioid
Neumann	KU 81i	dummy head for binaural recording
	RSM 190i	*M* fixed hypercardioid, *S* variable figure-8, remote control
	SM 69 fet	9 patterns, remote control
	USM 69i	9 patterns, switches on microphone body
Schoeps	MSTC	2 interchangeable capsules, ORTF (17 cm, 110°)
	CMTS 301	Omni/cardioid/figure-8, switches on microphone body, 12 V phantom power (discontinued)
	CMTS 501	omni/cardioid/figure-8, switches on microphone body, 48 V phantom power
Sennheiser	MKE 2002	headset with two omnidirectional capsules for binaural recording.
Speiden	SF-12	dual bidirectional ribbons

*Microphones are all *M-S* and *X-Y*, unless otherwise noted.

rear-oriented microphone to cause complete attenuation at 180 degrees when its output is subtracted from the front-oriented microphone.

$$M_F = \quad 0.60 + 0.40 \cos 0° \quad = \quad 0.60 + 0.40$$
$$-M_R \quad -s(0.60 + 0.40 \cos 180°) \quad \underline{-0.60s + 0.40s}$$
$$A + B$$

In other words,

$$A = 0.60 - 0.60s$$
$$B = 0.40 + 0.40s$$

Since we want a perfect cardioid pattern, we know that A must be equal to B, and so

$$0.60 - 0.60s = 0.40 + 0.40s$$

and therefore

$$0.20 = 1.00s, \text{ or } s = 0.20$$

To prove the validity of this answer, note the sensitivity of the combination to a sound source arriving at the rear of M_F, and therefore at the front of M_R.

$$
\begin{array}{r}
0.60 + 0.40 \cos 180° = \quad 0.60 - 0.40 = \quad 0.20 \\
-0.12 - 0.08 \cos 0° \quad \underline{-0.12 - 0.08} \quad \underline{-0.20} \\
0.48 - 0.48 \quad\quad 0
\end{array}
$$

As expected, the sensitivity is zero. The combination's polar equation and sensitivity may now be written as

$$s = 0.48 + 0.48 \cos \theta = 0.96$$

Note that the polar pattern is indeed a perfect cardioid, achieved at the cost of a slight attenuation in overall sensitivity.

In a real-world situation, the actual values of the A and B components are probably unknown. However, as long as the two microphones are identical, it doesn't matter anyway; just adjust the levels until sounds from the rear are cancelled, or at least sharply attenuated.

Two Unidirectional Microphones Placed Back to Back

If a small musical group is placed as shown in Figure 4-15, it's worth considering what will happen when the microphone outputs are combined, either during recording or later on during mixdown. We'll assume that the two microphones are identical, but that the actual polar equation is unknown; a pretty safe bet in most circumstances. Therefore, we'll simply identify the pressure and pressure-gradient components as A and B and see what happens when they are combined.

First, let's add them:

$$
\begin{array}{r}
A + B \cos 0° \quad = \quad A + B(+1) \\
+A + B \cos 180° \quad \underline{+ A + B(-1)} \\
2A + 0
\end{array}
$$

Now, subtract them:

$$
\begin{array}{r}
A + B \cos 0° \quad = \quad A + B(+1) \\
-A - B \cos 180° \quad \underline{- A - B(-1)} \\
0 + 2B
\end{array}
$$

With almost no effort at all, we've discovered two important points about a back-to-back combination of *any* two unidirectional microphones:

- When the outputs are added, the resultant pattern is that of a perfect omnidirectional microphone.
- When the outputs are subtracted, the pattern is that of a perfect bidirectional microphone.

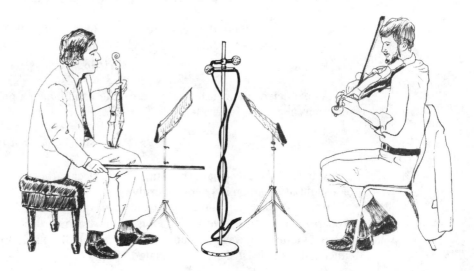

Figure 4-15. The use of back-to-back microphones to record a small ensemble.

Chances are, an omnidirectional pattern is not what is wanted, especially if there are other sound sources in the immediate area that are not supposed to be heard by these microphones. It's probably worth reversing the polarity of one of the microphones so that the combination combines subtractively. That way, the result is a bidirectional pattern that greatly attenuates the unwanted off-axis sound sources.

Multipattern Microphones

Some capacitor microphones employ a dual capsule system to provide pattern selection by means of a multiposition switch on the microphone housing, as shown in Figure 4-16. In a typical implemention, the capsules are placed in a back-to-back configuration, and each one alone provides a pure cardioid output response. With the selector switch in the cardioid position, only the forward-oriented system is active. In the omnidirectional mode, the outputs of both capsules are combined, and in the bidirectional mode, the outputs are again combined, but with a polarity reversal in the leads from the rear-oriented capsule. Intermediate patterns in the subcardioid, supercardioid, and hypercardioid ranges are possible by varying the sensitivity and polarity settings of the rear capsule, usually by additional switch positions.

(A) AKG C 414B. (Courtesy AKG Acoustics, Inc.)

(B) Milab VIP-50. (Courtesy Milab International AB)

Figure 4-16. Multipattern microphones. The dual-diaphragm outputs are combined in the desired mode via a multiposition switch on the microphone housing.

Two Unidirectional Microphones Oriented at Less than 180 Degrees

In preparation for the discussion of the Soundfield microphone that follows, it is important to understand the effect of combining two microphones at some angle other than 90 degrees.

Earlier in this chapter (page 120), we were able to simplify equation (4-1), since at that time the angle of orientation between the two microphones was 90 degrees. However, when this angle is some other value, its sine and cosine are not equal to 1 and 0, respectively. Consequently, the equation to find the angle at which the sum pattern, M_+, is oriented must remain as it was seen in equation (4-1) and as repeated here. Also shown, but without its derivation, is the equation for the orientation of the difference pattern, M_-.

For M_+

$$\tan \alpha = -B_2 \sin \theta / (B_1 + B_2 \cos \theta)$$
$$= -\sin \theta / (1 + \cos \theta) \qquad \text{(assuming } B_1 = B_2)$$

For M_-

$$\tan \beta = +B_2 \sin \theta / (B_1 - B_2 \cos \theta)$$
$$= +\sin \theta / (1 - \cos \theta) \qquad \text{(assuming } B_1 = B_2)$$

As seen here, if the two microphones are identical, all that we need to know in order to find the orientation of the sum and difference patterns is the angle between the two microphones. We also know that the difference pattern will be a perfect bidirectonal pattern, since the A components cancel out, as shown in the previous example.

Let's assume the two microphones are oriented 25 degrees left and right of center. Arbitrarily selecting M_1 as our reference, it is oriented at $+50$ degrees with respect to M_2. Therefore,

For M_+

$$\tan \alpha = -0.766/1.643$$

so

$$\alpha = -25°$$

For M_-

$$\tan \beta = +0.766/0.357$$

so

$$\beta = +65°$$

The orientation of all four output patterns is shown in Figure 4-17.

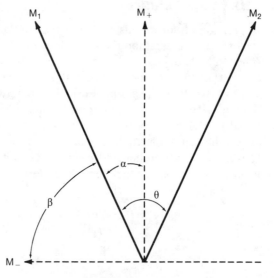

Figure 4-17. The result of combining any two identical microphones at an included angle, θ. The vectors illustrate the orientation of the microphones (M_1 and M_2) and the sum (M_+) and difference (M_-) patterns.

From Figure 4-17, we may draw the following important conclusions about the orientation of the sum and difference patterns when any two microphones are combined at the same sensitivity:

- The unidirectional sum pattern is oriented midway between the two microphones.
- The bidirectional difference pattern is oriented at 90 degrees with respect to the sum pattern; that is, normal (at right angles) to an axis drawn between the two microphones.

The observant reader may notice that these conclusions reinforce the *M-S* theory discussed earlier; the sum and difference patterns found here could just as well be an *M-S* microphone pair, in which case the two unidirectional microphones that we have oriented at ±25 degrees would be the resultant sum-and-difference matched pair. But more importantly, the present observations form a foundation on which to build a basic understanding of the Soundfield microphone theory which follows.

The Soundfield Microphone

Although the sensitivity of a single directional microphone varies as a function of the angle of the arriving sound, that sensitivity may of course represent a signal arriving from the left or right, or from above or below the zero-degree axis. The stereo microphone systems represent a significant improvement by providing a good left-to-right reproduction of the sound field, at the obvious cost of requiring two signal channels. To further improve the recording and reproduction of the complete spherical sound field, it might be argued that an infinity of channels are required, were it not for the obvious physical—to say nothing of financial—constraints.

As an alternative to an unrealistic number of signal channels, the Soundfield Microphone System utilizes four separate-but-identical unidirectional capsules placed within a single housing. The microphone is part of the Ambisonic Surround Sound System developed in the United Kingdom under the auspices of the NRDC (National Research Development Corporation). Although a fully implemented Ambisonic system requires four loudspeakers, the system is also used to great advantage with nothing more than a traditional two-channel reproduction system, as described here.

The orientation of the four capsules might best be illustrated by visualizing a geometric construction in which a small regular tetrahedron—a three-sided pyramid—is placed inside an imaginary cube, as shown in Figure 4-18. Note that the vertices of the tetrahedron touch the even-numbered corners of the cube. If a microphone capsule is placed at the center of each surface on the tetrahedron, it therefore points to one of the odd-numbered corners of the cube. In the illustration, these are

1. Left-front up
3. Right-back up

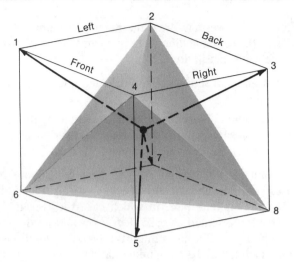

(A) The four subcardioid microphone capsules mounted on the four surfaces of a regular tetrahedron, pointing into four corners of a room.

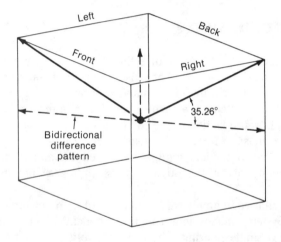

(B) Detail view of the orientation of the two upward-oriented capsules. The figure-8 difference pattern points front-left to back-right.

Figure 4-18. The Soundfield microphone layout.

5. Right-front down
7. Left-back down

If the tetrahedron is now suspended at the center of a square room, it follows that each microphone will point to a corner of that room, as also shown in Figure 4-18.

A-Format Outputs
By itself, each capsule produces a subcardioid output; that is, a pattern that lies somewhere between a perfect cardioid and an omnidirectional pattern. These four outputs are referred to as the system's *A-format* outputs. The polar equation is $0.667 + 0.334 \cos \theta$ (Farrar 1977), and for comparison purposes it was included in Table 3-1 in the previous chapter. However, the power of the Soundfield

microphone is not in the individual output of a single capsule, but in the infinite variety of outputs made possible by various capsule combinations.

So far, we have learned that

- When any two unidirectional patterns are combined, the resultant difference pattern is oriented at 90 degrees to the axis of the sum pattern (see Figure 4-17).
- When any two unidirectional patterns are subtracted, the resultant pattern is always bidirectional (see page 140).
- When any two unidirectional microphones are placed back to back and their patterns are summed, the result is always omnidirectional (see page 140).

With these points in mind, consider the two subcardioid capsules pointed at the left-front and right-back upper corners. Their figure-8 difference pattern is horizontally oriented on a diagonal between the left-front and right-back of the room, as shown in the detail view in Figure 4-18B. It follows that other subcardioid combinations will produce still other bidirectional patterns at other orientations. Table 4-3A lists four such orientations when *A*-format outputs are combined.

B-Format Outputs

If the combinations seen in Table 4-3A are again combined, the resultant signals are the *B-format* outputs listed in Table 4-3B, which are identified by the letters *W*, *X*, *Y*, and *Z*.

If the derivation of the omnidirectional pattern is unclear, just note that the summation of *any* two *A*-format patterns produces a unidirectional pattern; the summation of the other two produces the same pattern but oriented 180 degrees to the first one; and the summation of any two identical back-to-back patterns is always an omnidirectional pattern. Further combinations of the four *B*-format signals will create just about any polar pattern and orientation required, with a few typical examples listed in Table 4-3C.

The Soundfield microphone system is seen in Figure 4-19, along with the control unit used to process the outputs. By varying the relationship between the *W* signal and the other three, any polar pattern between omnidirectional and bidirectional may be selected, and the resultant pattern may be oriented left, right, up, or down. Two such patterns may be fed to the control unit's stereo output jacks, or all four *B*-format signals may be routed directly to a four-channel tape recorder for stereo processing after the recording session.

Boundary Layer Recording

In Chapter 1, Figure 1-7 showed the effect of combining two sinusoidal signals when one of them was slightly delayed. Since the signals were of equal amplitude, the combined output ranged from a 6-dB boost to complete cancellation, as the delayed signal alternately reinforced and then attenuated the direct-path signal.

Although the delay in that illustration was intentionally introduced by a delay line, a similar phenomenon may be experienced if a signal reaches a microphone

Table 4-3. Soundfield Microphone Outputs

(A) Subtraction of A-Format Outputs

A-Format Combinations	Resultant Output Is a Bidirectional Pattern Oriented	
	From	*To*
1–3	left-front center	right-back center
5–7	right-front center	left-back center
1–7	center-front up	center-back down
3–5	center-back up	center-front down

(B) B-Format Signals

Capsule Combinations	Polar Pattern	Pattern Orientation	B-Format Signal
(1 + 3) + (5 + 7)	omnidirectional		*W*
(1 − 3) + (5 − 7)	bidirectional	front-to-back	*X*
(1 − 3) − (5 − 7)	bidirectional	left-to-right	*Y*
(1 − 7) + (3 − 5)	bidirectional	up-to-down	*Z*

(C) A Few B-Format Combinations

B-Format Combinations	Polar Pattern	Pattern Orientation
W + X	cardioid	forward
W − X	cardioid	rearward
W + X + Y	cardioid	45° left-of-center
W + X − Y	cardioid	45° right-of-center

via the direct path and also after being reflected from a nearby floor or wall surface—or for that matter, from a nearby gobo.

For example, Figure 4-20A shows a vocalist standing in front of a microphone. Each part of the illustration shows the direct source-to-microphone path, P_D, and the path containing a single reflection, P_R. The sound waves travelling along each path are combined at the microphone and, because of the differing path lengths, some cancellations due to phase shift are to be expected. However, since the reflected path is longer, the late-arriving signal will also be attenuated and therefore the cancellations will not be complete.

The family of curves shown in Figure 4-20B–G demonstrates the effect of the reflected-path signal for various microphone-to-floor heights. In the first curve, the microphone is at the same height as the vocalist (5 feet in this example) and the ratio of reflected-to-direct paths is about 2.24:1. As a result, the output response fluctuates within a 4 dB range over most of the audio spectrum.

In each succeeding part of the illustration, the microphone is moved closer to the floor and the path length difference is thereby lessened. As a result, the

(A) Microphone.
(Courtesy AMS/Calrec, USA)

(B) Detail view of its four-capsule
assembly. (Courtesy AMS/Calrec, USA)

Figure 4-19. The Soundfield Microphone System. *(continued on next page)*

severity of the fluctuations increases, but the point of the first response dip moves higher in frequency and the level of the reinforced segments rises. Finally, in Figure 4-20G, the microphone diaphragm is 0.085 inches off the floor and the response is up 6 dB over most of the audio-frequency spectrum, with a 3 dB rolloff at 20 kHz.

We can summarize the information presented by the graphs as follows:

1. The output of a microphone placed in the vicinity of a reflective surface is subject to response fluctuations due to interaction between the direct and reflected sound waves reaching its diaphragm.

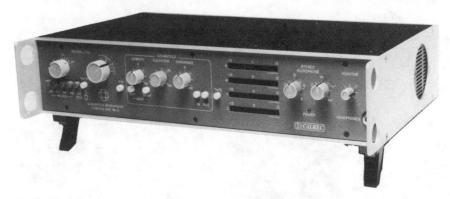

(C) Control unit used to process the A-format outputs received from the microphone.
(Courtesy AMS/Calrec, USA)

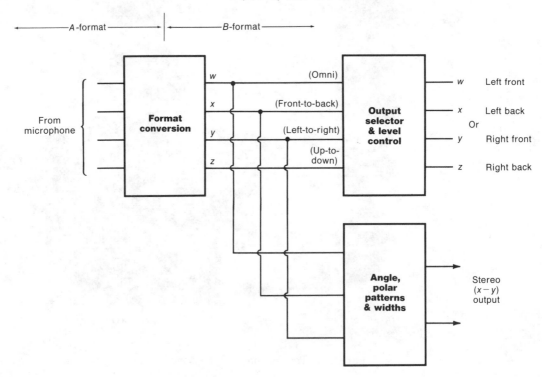

(D) Simplified block diagram of the Soundfield control system.

Figure 4-19 *(continued)*

2. The severity of the effect increases as the microphone is brought closer to the surface.

3. However, when the microphone is extremely close to the surface, the direct and reflected-path signals reinforce each other over most of the audio-frequency spectrum, resulting in a 6 dB level increase.

The advantages of placing a microphone close to a reflective surface have been well-known for years (Burroughs 1973), and many manufacturers marketed accessories made expressly for this purpose, two of which are shown in Figure 4-21. However, it was not until the introduction of the pressure zone microphone that this interesting production technique gained wide acceptance.

The Boundary Layer Microphone

The surface at which the sound wave is reflected is commonly referred to as a *boundary* and the *boundary layer* is the region in the immediate vicinity of the boundary, in which all paths from the source combine at the diaphragm with negligible phase cancellation within the audio-frequency range of interest. For example, the following table gives the boundary layer dimension required for flat response with various amounts of high-frequency attenuation at 20 kHz (Crown 1983).

Attenuation at 20 kHz	Boundary Layer	Corresponds to
6 dB	0.110"	$\frac{1}{6}$ wavelength
3 dB*	0.085"	$\frac{1}{8}$ wavelength
1 dB	0.052"	$\frac{1}{13}$ wavelength

*See Figure 4-20G.

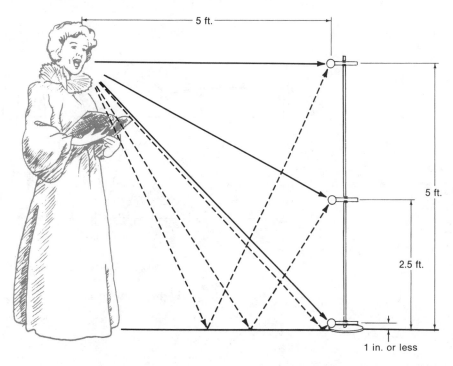

(A) Setup with microphone placed five feet from vocalist.

Figure 4-20. Effect of reflections on microphone output response. *(continued on next page)*

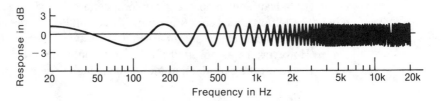

(B) Floor-to-diaphragm distance is 5 feet.

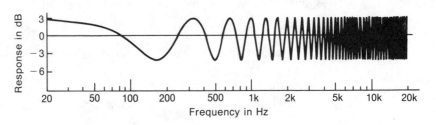

(C) Floor-to-diaphragm distance is 2.5 feet.

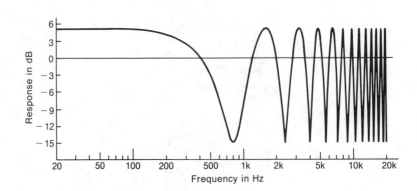

(D) Floor-to-diaphragm distance is 6 inches.

Figure 4-20 *(continued)*

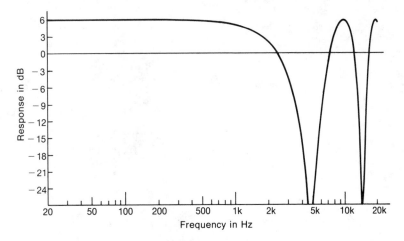

(E) Floor-to-diaphragm distance is 1 inch.

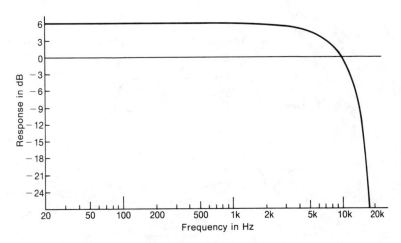

(F) Floor-to-diaphragm distance is ¼ inch.

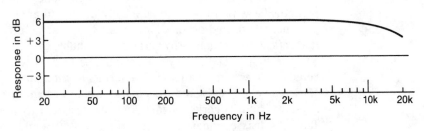

(G) Floor-to-diaphragm distance is 0.085 inch.

Figure 4-20 (continued)

(A) Shure S55P low-profile microphone stand. (Courtesy Shure Brothers, Inc.)

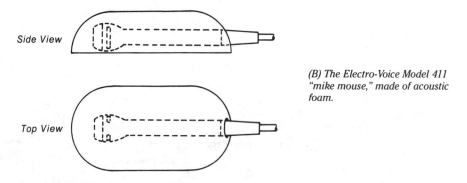

(B) The Electro-Voice Model 411 "mike mouse," made of acoustic foam.

Figure 4-21. Accessories for placing a microphone close to the floor.

Figures 4-22 and 4-23 show two microphones designed so that their diaphragms lie within the boundary layer described above. In either case, the flat base plate is placed on the floor or affixed to some other large surface area so that reflections from nearby surfaces are unable to reach the diaphragm.

The first boundary layer microphones to gain wide acceptance were marketed by Crown International. The terms *pressure zone*, *PZM*, and *Pressure Zone Microphone* are registered trademarks which Crown uses to describe the boundary layer and its series of microphones designed to work as described above. Table 4-4 lists boundary layer microphones currently manufactured by various manufacturers, along with the terminology each uses to describe its product.

Transformer Interface

The final "microphone" to be discussed here is in fact not a microphone at all, but simply a matching transformer placed between the output of an instrument amplifier and a microphone line to the console. Such devices have been popular since the days when the guitar amplifier was about the only electronic device to be found on the studio side of the glass. Although the guitar amp fed its own speaker, there was usually an amplifier-output jack available as well. By means of a plug-in transformer, this high-impedance output could be fed to a low-impedance microphone line, and then treated at the console as though it were a signal from a conventional microphone.

There are both advantages and disadvantages to the device, often referred to as a *direct box,* and to the technique of "going direct." Among the former, a direct

(A) PZM-6 microphone. (Courtesy Crown International, Inc.)

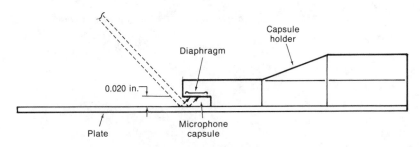

(B) Detail view of the microphone in (A).

Figure 4-22. A boundary layer microphone whose diaphragm is at the top of the boundary layer.

feed from an instrument amplifier bypasses any distortion produced by the system's own speaker. Furthermore, eliminating the use of a microphone prevents leakage from nearby instruments from being a problem. The result is a very clean signal (assuming of course that a high-quality instrument amplifier is in use). But the same properties can also be a disadvantage if the instrument speaker characteristics contribute to the musician's distinctive sound, in which case a microphone must be used.

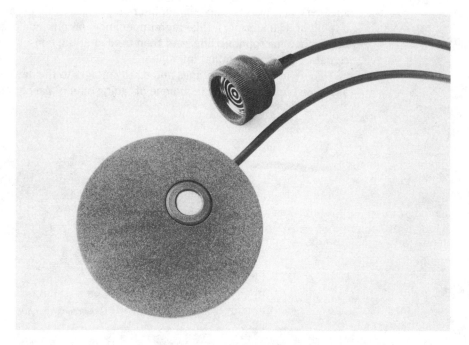

(A) Schoeps BLM 03 C microphone. (Courtesy Posthorn Recordings)

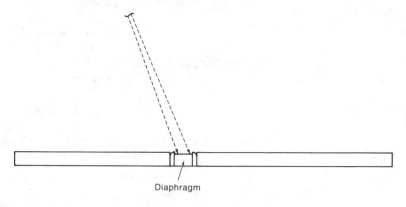

Diaphragm

(B) Detail view of the microphone in (A).

Figure 4-23. A boundary layer microphone whose diaphragm is flush mounted at the boundary.

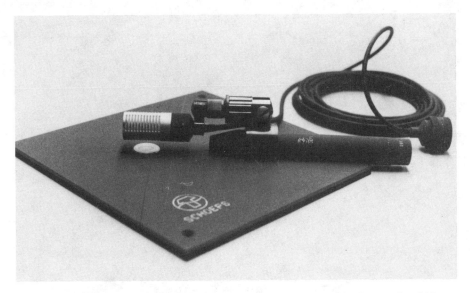

(C) Boundary layer microphone with bidirectional capsule immediately above, to form M-S *system. (Schoeps BLM 3 boundary layer and MK 8 figure-8 capsule courtesy Posthorn Recordings)*

Figure 4-23 *(continued)*

Table 4-4. Boundary Layer Microphones

Manufacturer and Model	Terminology and Polar Pattern
AKG	Boundary Layer
C-562	hemispherical
Beyer	Acoustical Boundary
MPC 40	hemispherical
MPC 50 N(C)	hemispherical
MPC 60/1	hemispherical
MPC 60/3	half cardiod
Crown	Pressure Zone
PZM-2.5	unidirectional
PZM-6	hemispherical
PZM-20RG	hemispherical
PZM-30	hemispherical
PZM-180	hemispherical
MB Electronic	Boundary
C-611	hemispherical
C-621	hemispherical
C-622	stereo
Milab	Pressure Zone, Acoustical Boundary
MP-30	hemispherical
Schoeps	Boundary Layer
BLM 03 C	hemispherical
BLM 3	hemispherical
Sennheiser	Boundary
MKE 212-3	hemispherical

5 Monitor Systems

A facetious question might occur to the outsider who observes a recording engineer endlessly switching microphones in search of "the" sound: why not switch loudspeakers instead? After all it *does* make a difference, as anyone who has visited a hi-fi showroom will agree. And in recognition of that difference it is not unusual for a studio control room to have two or more sets of speakers available for monitoring. Pair 'A' are of course the ultimate in accuracy (at least according to the person who installed them). Pair 'B' approximate what the rest of the world is expected to use when listening to the present sonic masterpiece later on. Needless to say, an A/B comparison between 'A' and 'B' is not even close.

Although further probing along these lines may be dangerous to anyone who spends too much time searching for the definitive sound, there are obvious practical advantages to swapping microphones instead of speakers. And so the microphone has come to be regarded as the variable in everyone's equation for finding the right sound. At the other end of the equation the speaker is more or less a constant. Therefore, this chapter looks at speakers from a somewhat different perspective than was found in the preceding two chapters.

The information presented here will give the reader a general understanding of the various components that are to be found in a typical studio monitoring system.

Unlike "microphone," there is no general agreement on the definition of "loudspeaker" (Small 1972). To some it is the transducer within an enclosure; to others it is that transducer and the cabinet in which it is enclosed. For the purpose of the following discussion, the loudspeaker is understood to be the transducer itself which, unless otherwise noted, is being examined without the cabinet in which it will eventually be enclosed. Once installed in its enclosure, the loudspeaker becomes part of a loudspeaker *system*.

Energy Conversion

In terms of energy conversion, the loudspeaker is the mirror image of the microphone; the electric signal applied to the loudspeaker input is first converted to magnetic energy, then to mechanical energy and finally to acoustic energy. These conversions are listed here and shown in Figure 5-1 in order to compare them to the energy-conversion sequence of the microphone.

Transducer	Input	1st stage	2nd stage	Output
loudspeaker	electric	magnetic	mechanical	acoustic
microphone	acoustic	mechanical	magnetic	electric

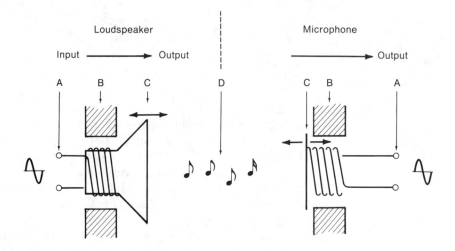

Energy is:

A. Electric
B. Magnetic
C. Mechanical
D. Acoustic

Figure 5-1. A comparison of the energy conversions that take place in a loudspeaker and in a microphone.

To further illustrate this mirror-image relationship between microphone and loudspeaker—and for demonstration purposes *only*—a reasonably sturdy moving-coil microphone may even double as a loudspeaker simply by plugging it into the earphone output on a cassette recorder. The recorder's low-level output should not damage the microphone, yet be sufficient to drive the microphone diaphragm as if it were a miniature speaker.

The experiment may also be tried in reverse, using a small loudspeaker in place of a microphone. Although neither transducer delivers optimum results when used at the wrong end of the signal path, these demonstrations help illustrate the similarity in concept, if not in design, between the microphone and the loudspeaker.

Speaker Design Categories

As with microphones, loudspeakers may be classified under two major design categories. For the sake of completeness, both ribbon and capacitor (or electrostatic) loudspeakers are given brief descriptions here, although for all practical purposes the dynamic moving-coil loudspeaker is the type found in almost exclusive use in recording and sound reinforcement applications.

The Dynamic Loudspeaker

To briefly describe the dynamic loudspeaker, almost all that's needed is to modify the description of the dynamic microphone given in Chapter 3 (page 62). As before, an electric conductor is suspended in a permanent magnetic field. An alternating current applied to the conductor sets up an alternating magnetic field. The interaction between the alternating and permanent fields produces a mechanical force (Knowles 1977) which moves the conductor back and forth. The speaker diaphragm, attached to the conductor, moves accordingly and in so doing displaces the air particles in the surrounding area. The resultant sound pressure wave is the acoustic analog of the applied electric signal.

A speaker operating according to the principles just described is often referred to as an electrodynamic loudspeaker. Again making a comparison to the microphone, such a speaker may be subdivided into two classes, as described here.

The Moving-Coil Loudspeaker

The dynamic moving-coil loudspeaker is comprised of two subsystems, consisting of a driver mechanism and a means of coupling that mechanism with the surrounding air mass. The driver is described here; the coupling system is described later in the sections on direct and indirect radiators (pages 170 and 178).

The dynamic moving-coil driver consists of a voice coil affixed to a diaphragm, as shown in Figure 5-2. The voice coil is suspended in a permanent magnetic field; when an audio signal is applied to the voice coil the interaction between the alternating electric and the permanent magnetic fields forces the diaphragm to move back and forth. For the purposes of the following discussion, the term *diaphragm* is confined to the dome-shaped membrane seen in the illustration, although the speaker cone—if any—is sometimes described as part of the diaphragm system. However, since the cone is not always present in a moving coil driver, it is described separately later in this chapter, in the section on direct radiators.

The Ribbon Loudspeaker

Not unlike its microphone counterpart, the diaphragm of a dynamic ribbon loudspeaker is a thin metal foil suspended between the poles of a permanent magnet, as shown in Figure 5-3. The ribbon is sometimes used as a high-frequency speaker in a consumer speaker system, but has not yet found its way into professional monitor systems.

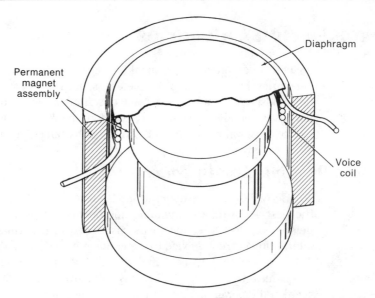

Figure 5-2. The driver assembly in a dynamic moving-coil loudspeaker.

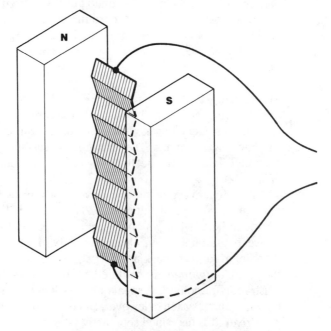

Figure 5-3. The ribbon loudspeaker.

The Capacitor, or Electrostatic, Loudspeaker

An *electrostatic* loudspeaker is one in which the diaphragm is one of the plates of a very large capacitor. A DC bias voltage applied across the plates sets up an electrostatic field between them. The AC signal voltage is also applied across the plates, and the interaction between the resultant alternating magnetic field and the electrostatic field forces the plate/diaphragm to move back and forth.

As shown in Figure 5-4, the diaphragm in an electrostatic loudspeaker is often curved in the horizontal plane to allow greater dispersion of high frequencies (Henricksen 1987).

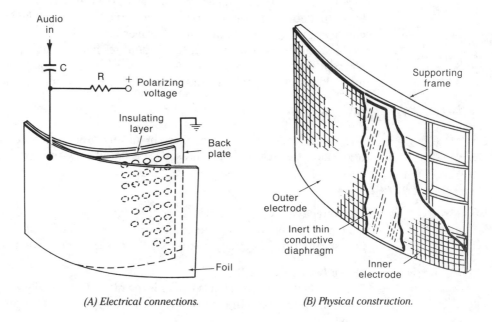

(A) Electrical connections.   *(B) Physical construction.*

Figure 5-4. The electrostatic loudspeaker.

Some Useful Loudspeaker Parameters

The following section introduces a few frequently encountered parameters used to describe a loudspeaker system.

Resonance Frequency

When a disturbing force is momentarily applied to a mechanical device, the device goes into free oscillation at a natural frequency determined by its mass and stiffness. But, in the case of a continuous disturbance, the device oscillates instead at the frequency of the applied force. As this forced oscillation approaches the device's own natural frequency, the amplitude of the resultant motion reaches a maximum and the device is said to be in a state of resonance. The frequency at which this occurs is referred to as the *resonance frequency* of the device, and it is the point at which the mechanical efficiency of the device is at its maximum.

Although it might appear that the acoustic power output of a speaker should be greatest at its resonance frequency, this is not always the case (Cohen 1968). For example, consider the electric impedance of the speaker; when at rest the impedance is simply the DC resistance of the voice coil. However, when the voice coil is set in motion it acts as a generator; the back-EMF (electromotive force) so produced raises the speaker impedance. At resonance the back-EMF—and, therefore, the impedance—is at maximum. Consequently, if the applied voltage remains constant the power delivered to the speaker reaches its minimum at the resonance frequency (since $P = E^2/R$). On the other hand, if the voltage rises due to a lighter load at the higher impedance, the power may rise slightly. Therefore, the actual power-handling performance of the speaker will be influenced by the characteristics of the amplifier which drives it.

As a further consideration, the natural resonance frequency of the speaker plays an important role in determining the speaker's output response when it is installed within an enclosure, as discussed in the following section.

Cutoff Frequency

The cutoff frequency of a speaker—or of any other audio component—is that frequency at which the system response is 3 dB below the maximum response.

Directivity

The directivity of a loudspeaker refers to its output at a certain angle, as compared to an omnidirectional loudspeaker radiating the same amount of acoustic energy. Directivity is expressed in one of the following ways.

Directivity Index (DI)

The *directivity index* of a loudspeaker is the ratio of its sound pressure level to that of an omnidirectional loudspeaker, and may be found from the following equation:

$$DI = 10 \log (I/I_{ref})$$

where

DI = directivity index, in dB
I = intensity at a certain angular distance from the speaker
I_{ref} = intensity at the same point, from an omnidirectional speaker

The directivity index of a directional loudspeaker would be greater than zero on axis, and would decrease as the angle increases. For example, Figure 5-5 shows the ideal polar patterns for an omnidirectional and a unidirectional (cardioid pattern) speaker. Since these patterns are analogous to those of the microphone described in Chapter 3, the radius of the omnidirectional pattern may be set so that its three-dimensional surface area ($4\pi r^2$) is equal to that of the cardioid (the two-dimensional areas in the illustration are not). The required value is the square root of the cardioid's random energy efficiency, or $\sqrt{0.333} = 0.577$.

Since the patterns represent sound pressure (not intensity), the directivity index can be written as

$$DI = 20 \log (r/r_{ref}) \qquad \text{(5-1)}$$
$$= 20 \log (1/0.577)$$
$$= 20 (0.239)$$
$$= 4.776 \text{ dB}$$

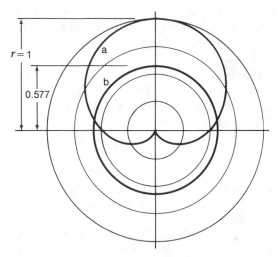

Figure 5-5. Cardioid (a) and omnidirectional (b) polar patterns
of equal surface area.

Since the cardioid and omnidirectional indexes are equal at the intersection of the patterns, the angle θ at which this occurs may be found by solving the cardioid equation for the value of θ which gives a sensitivity of 0.577. Thus,

$$r = 0.5 + 0.5 \cos \theta = 0.577 \qquad\qquad \textbf{(5-2)}$$

Therefore,

$$\theta = 81.14 \text{ degrees}$$

The directivity index at this angle is zero, as it is for the omnidirectional speaker at all angles. To find the directivity index at some other angle, solve equation (5-2) for r and then use this value in the numerator of equation (5-1). For example, the directivity index at 120 degrees is found as follows:

$$r = 0.5 + 0.5 \cos 120° = 0.250$$

and therefore,

$$\begin{aligned} \text{DI} &= 20 \log (0.250/0.577) \\ &= -7.265 \text{ dB} \end{aligned}$$

When the directivity factor, Q (described immediately below), is known, the directivity index may also be found from the equation

$$\text{DI} = 10 \log Q$$

Directivity Factor (Q)

Loudspeaker directivity is more often expressed as a dimensionless *directivity factor, Q,* defined as the ratio of sound pressure squared, at some fixed distance and specified direction, to the mean-squared pressure at the same distance, but averaged over all directions from the speaker (based on ANSI S1.1—1960).

The directivity factor given in a speaker specification is usually calculated by finding two values for Q—one in the horizontal and another in the vertical plane. The mean directivity factor, Q, is the square root of the product of these two values. In the case of a theoretically ideal speaker whose polar pattern may be calculated from a single equation, $A + B \cos \theta$, the directivity factor may be calculated as follows:

$$Q = 1/REE$$

where REE is found from equation (3-4) in Chapter 3. Since the directivity factor often varies considerably with frequency, an average value taken over a specified frequency range is sometimes given.

When the directivity index at a specific angle is known, the directivity factor at the same angle may be found from the following equation:

$$Q = 10^{DI/10} \qquad\qquad (5\text{-}3)$$

In equation (5-3), the directivity factor is valid only for the angle at which the directivity index was calculated. But in any case, the higher the value of Q, the more directional is the speaker, either at a specified single frequency or over a wide range of frequencies. A cross-reference between directivity factor and directivity index is given in Table 5-1.

Table 5-1. Q-to-DI Cross-Reference Guide

Q	DI	Q	DI	Q	DI
90	19.54	9	9.54	0.9	− 0.46
80	19.03	8	9.03	0.8	− 0.97
70	18.45	7	8.45	0.7	− 1.55
60	17.78	6	7.78	0.6	− 2.22
50	16.99	5	6.99	0.5	− 3.01
40	16.02	4	6.02	0.4	− 3.98
30	14.77	3	4.77	0.3	− 5.23
20	13.01	2	3.01	0.2	− 6.99
10	10.00	1	0.00	0.1	− 10.00

$Q = 10^{DI/10}$ Directivity Factor
DI $= 10 \log Q$ Directivity Index

Coverage Angle

The *coverage angle*, $C_\angle$, is the included angle between the points on either side of the speaker axis at which the polar response is attenuated by 6 dB, with respect to the on-axis (0 degrees) level. Figure 5-6 shows two speaker polar patterns in which the coverage angle is 100 degrees.

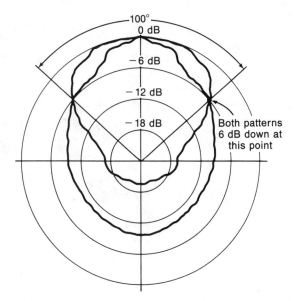

Figure 5-6. Two speaker polar patterns in which the coverage angle
is 100 degrees.

Room Boundaries and the Ideal Sound Source

In Chapter 1 (page 18) the *ideal sound source* was defined as a dimensionless (i.e., infinitely small) point suspended in space, from which sound energy may radiate spherically. In order for any sound source—ideal or otherwise—to freely radiate energy in every direction, there cannot be any barriers in the immediate vicinity.

Full or Free Space

If this condition is met then the sound source is said to be located in *full space*, or *free space*, as shown in Figure 5-7A. Since the surface area of a sphere such as the one in the figure is 4π steradians, as described in Chapter 1 (page 22), it is common practice to describe a sound source in full space as radiating into 4π steradians.

Due to the practical realities of transducer design, the actual loudspeaker is neither infinitely small nor is it suspended in free space. However, the ideal model does serve well as a reference condition against which to compare any actual monitor system.

As a first step in equating the ideal sound source to the practical loudspeaker system, we will now consider the effect of moving the source from full space into an environment in which one or more barriers interfere with the free radiation of energy.

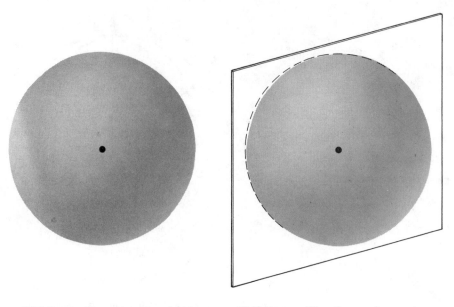

(A) Full space. Since there are no barriers near the sound source, its energy radiates in all directions—that is, spherically— from the point source.

(B) Half space. When the sound source is placed against a single surface (e.g., a wall), the available radiation space is halved.

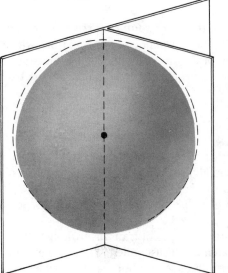

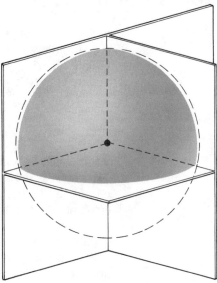

(C) One-quarter space. A source placed at the intersection of two such surfaces.

(D) One-eighth space. A sound source placed at the intersection of three surfaces (e.g., two walls and the floor or ceiling).

Figure 5-7. An ideal sound source, located in various environments.

Half Space

If the point source of sound is placed directly against a solid barrier, it is no longer able to radiate into full space. As shown in Figure 5-7B, the same amount of energy is now radiated into the space on one side of the barrier only; in short, into *half space*, or 2π steradians. This doubles the amount of energy in the half-space environment, giving a 3 dB increase in sound power level.

One-Quarter Space

If the sound source is now placed at the intersection of two barriers whose included angle is 90 degrees (Figure 5-7C), the available radiation space is again halved, resulting in a *one-quarter space* (π steradians) and another 3 dB increase in sound power level.

One-Eighth Space

As a final example of how various barriers affect a point source of sound, now consider what happens when the speaker is placed at the intersection of three surfaces, as shown in Figure 5-7D. The radiation space is again halved, resulting in a *one-eighth space* ($\pi/2$ steradians) and a further 3 dB increase in sound level within this space.

The following table briefly summarizes the effect of each barrier on the environment into which the sound source is able to radiate its energy.

Number of Barriers	Radiation Space	Radiation Angle (Steradians)	Reference Level
None	Full	4π	0 dB
One	One-half	2π	3 dB
Two	One-quarter	π	6 dB
Three	One-eighth	$\pi/2$	9 dB

Room Boundaries and the Practical Loudspeaker System

In the preceding theoretical examples, the environment into which the ideal sound source radiates its energy was progressively diminished from full space to one-eighth space, and at each step the sound level increased by 3 dB. However, when an actual loudspeaker is moved from full space to one-eighth space, the listener may note a significant increase in low frequency response at each step, while high frequencies show little or no increase in level. The reason for this apparent change in frequency response may be traced to the speaker's directional characteristics and the influence of nearby room surfaces on these characteristics.

Speaker Directional Characteristics

Assuming a speaker has a perfectly flat circular diaphragm (another ideal approximation of reality), the speaker's directional characteristic will vary considerably with frequency. At low frequencies, the energy radiates into all the available space; as the frequency is raised, the output becomes progressively more directional. It has been shown (Olson 1967) that the directional characteristic, or polar pattern, is a function of wavelength and speaker diameter. As a theoretical model, the equation given here may be used to find the directional characteristics of a loudspeaker whose diaphragm resembles a flat piston.

$$R = \frac{2J_1(x)}{x}$$

where
R = pressure ratio at angle α (compared to $0°$)
J_1 = Bessel function of the first order
x = $(\pi D/\lambda) \sin \alpha$
D = speaker diameter
α = angle
λ = wavelength

Figure 5-8 shows a set of computer-generated curves based on this equation. The curves illustrate directional characteristics as a function of speaker diameter and wavelength, and may be assigned to specific frequencies if the speaker diameter is known. Table 5-2 shows that for each doubling of diameter, the transition towards a highly directional response begins one octave lower.

Table 5-2. Speaker Diameter-Frequency Cross-Reference

Speaker Diameter (cm)	Frequency (Hz) of Directional Characteristic in Figure 5-8				
	(A)	(B)	(C)	(D)	(E)
8.60	1,000	2,000	4,000	8,000	16,000
17.20	500	1,000	2,000	4,000	8,000
34.40	250	500	1,000	2,000	4,000
$\lambda{:}D$ =	4	2	1	0.5	0.25

The curves show that the practical loudspeaker with a piston-like diaphragm has a tendency towards increased directionality, or "beaming," as the frequency increases. As seen in the curves of Figure 5-8, high-frequency output is focused into one or more narrow lobes.

As a result of this high-frequency phenomenon, the speaker's frequency response may change according to its physical placement within the room. To explain the influence of room surfaces on speaker response, it is first necessary to return to the ideal sound source described in the first chapter.

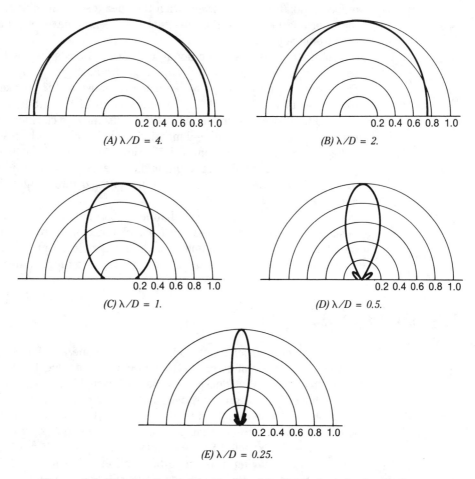

(A) $\lambda/D = 4$.

(B) $\lambda/D = 2$.

(C) $\lambda/D = 1$.

(D) $\lambda/D = 0.5$.

(E) $\lambda/D = 0.25$.

Figure 5-8. The directional characteristics of a flat-surface circular diaphragm, as a function of wavelength and diameter (after Olson 1967).

To demonstrate these effects, first place the speaker against a single wall at a position well away from the ceiling, floor, and other adjoining wall surfaces. The speaker radiates its energy into the room according to the illustrations shown in Figure 5-7. At the lowest frequencies the radiation pattern resembles the wide lobe shown in Figure 5-8A or, in three dimensions, the hemisphere of Figure 5-7B. However, at higher frequencies the speaker becomes progressively more directional, with the output concentrated into progressively narrower lobes. Although the actual directional characteristic will vary from the theoretical examples of the illustrations, there will still be a tendency toward increased directionality as the frequency rises.

When the speaker is moved from the half-space environment of a single wall to an intersection of two walls, the nondirectional long-wavelength energy is concentrated into one-quarter space and so the low frequencies become louder. However the shorter-wavelength (high frequency) energy does not increase since its directional characteristic is already sufficiently narrow to be unaffected by the reduced radiation space. Even when the speaker is placed at the intersection of the floor and two walls, the one-eighth space may have very little effect on the high frequency lobes.

In other words, each additional wall surface boosts the low-frequency energy while having little or no effect on high frequencies. As a result the listener perceives a steadily rising low-frequency response as the speaker is moved from the center of a single wall to the intersection of two walls, and again as it is lowered to a corner position on the floor. This may be clarified by visualizing the curves in Figure 5-8 as three-dimensional solids, any of which will fit within the half-space hemisphere of Figure 5-7B. However, as the available radiation space gets smaller and smaller, only the highest-frequency lobes still fit without modification. The lower-frequency lobes are pressed into progressively less space, and, therefore, sound louder.

In the early days of multichannel recording it was common practice to position four speakers across the front of the control room, creating potential monitoring problems if the outer speakers were close to the side walls. The bass response of a sound source might seem to vary as a function of speaker selection.

The Direct Radiator

As pointed out earlier (page 158), the microphone and loudspeaker are mirror images in concept if not in actual practice. But, due to the nature of their respective tasks, the loudspeaker has a practical problem not shared by the microphone. It is no great problem for a small device to sample and record the large phenomenon of a sound pressure wave. But it is quite another matter for a small device to recreate that pressure wave later on. Yet that is just what the loudspeaker is expected to do; in relation to its size, it must get an enormous amount of air moving in order to be at all useful. This consideration may have been demonstrated by the transducer-substitution experiment described earlier; the small loudspeaker does quite well as a temporary microphone, while the microphone is a very weak substitute loudspeaker.

In the case of the moving-coil driver described previously, the device is still quite small compared to the air mass which must be set in motion. Therefore, a system must be devised to more efficiently couple the driver and the air mass. Two such systems are described here.

As its name suggests, the *direct radiator* is designed so that the driver mechanism of voice coil and diaphragm is in direct contact with the air mass of the surrounding environment. In other words, the driver directly radiates its energy into the listening area. But, of course, the driver is quite small compared to the large amount of air that must be set in motion. In terms of impedance, the high mechanical impedance of the driver is directly coupled to the low acoustic impedance of the air, resulting in an inefficient transfer of power.

In order to increase the physical size of the moving system, and thus move more air, the diaphragm of a direct radiator is usually surrounded by a speaker cone, as shown in Figure 5-9. The combination is more efficient than the driver alone, although its size is still quite small compared to the surrounding air mass.

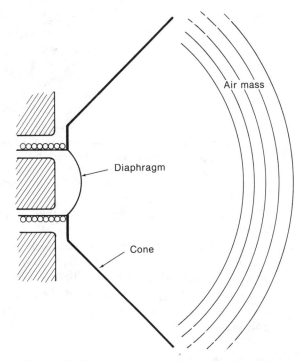

Figure 5-9. In the direct radiator the diaphragm is in direct contact with the air mass.

The Direct Radiator Enclosure

Beyond offering some obvious physical protection, the direct radiator's output performance is greatly influenced by the enclosure in which it is placed. To get a better idea of the interaction between the radiator and its enclosure, we must first take a closer look at how the radiator functions alone.

When an input signal is applied to the piston-like diaphragm of a direct-radiator loudspeaker, a pressure condensation at the front of the diaphragm occurs simultaneously with a rarefaction at the rear, and vice versa. Such a system is often referred to as a *dipole* or *doublet*—a device that exhibits opposite polarities at two points. In other words, there is a 180-degree phase shift between the pressure waves radiating from the device's front and rear.

Any speaker placed in free space is quite small compared to the longer wavelengths which radiate spherically away from it. In effect, it resembles a doublet with zero distance between two point sources, as shown in Figure 5-10. Since the sources are equal in amplitude but opposite in phase, the net result is that low-frequency output level is almost nonexistent.

As frequency is increased, the speaker itself becomes a greater physical obstacle separating its front and rear outputs. Furthermore, there is a tendency towards the "beaming" effects described earlier. As a result there is less cancellation and so, a rising output and a tendency towards a bidirectional characteristic.

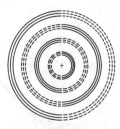

Figure 5-10. At low frequencies a speaker located in full space resembles a point source of sound. As a result, the simultaneous condensations (solid lines) and rarefactions (dashed lines) cause almost complete cancellation of the output.

These effects are often referred to as the speaker's *doublet action* or as a *dipole effect*.

The cancellation effects of doublet action may be greatly minimized by the use of a *baffle*, a structure that is both a physical support for the speaker and a means to lengthen the signal path between the front and the rear of the speaker. Depending on the type of baffle used, the rear output may be isolated completely, or suitably modified to reinforce the pressure wave radiating from the front of the speaker.

The Infinite Baffle

The *infinite baffle* is a barrier that creates a path length of infinity, as is the case when a speaker is mounted in the wall of a room, as shown in Figure 5-11. With no connecting path at all between front and rear outputs, there can be no doublet action and therefore no interaction between the two pressure waves. However, as an obvious consequence, all rear-directed energy is wasted.

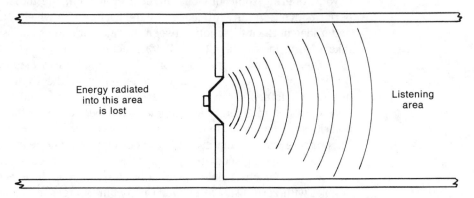

Energy radiated into this area is lost

Listening area

Figure 5-11. The infinite baffle. Since the rear-originating sound wave never reaches the front of the speaker there is no interaction, and half the speaker's output is wasted.

Frequency Response
The piston action of a direct radiator mounted on an infinite baffle produces a flat output response beginning at a cutoff frequency, f_c, whose wavelength is equal to

the piston circumference (Henricksen 1987). Therefore, since at the cutoff frequency

$$\lambda = c/f_c = \pi D = \text{circumference}$$

then

$$f_c = c/\pi D \qquad\qquad (5\text{-}4)$$

where
  λ = wavelength
  f_c = cutoff frequency
  c = speed of sound
  D = diameter of piston

Piston Band

From equation (5-4), it can be seen that the cutoff frequency is inversely proportional to the piston diameter; as diameter increases, cutoff frequency decreases. The flat response above the cutoff frequency is known as the *piston band* of the system. In practice this flat response will exhibit some rippling due to the effects of speaker resonance. Below the cutoff frequency the pressure response falls off at 12 dB per octave.

The term *piston band* is often used in reference to the frequency range in which a speaker is designed to operate.

The Flat Baffle

As its name suggests, the *flat baffle* is nothing more than a flat panel of finite dimension with a cutout into which the speaker is placed. Given a certain output frequency, *f*, if the panel edge is located one-quarter wavelength from the speaker center, then a rear-originating signal at that frequency must travel an extra distance of one-half wavelength around the baffle, thereby shifting its phase by 180 degrees. But as noted above, there is already a 180-degree phase shift between the front and rear outputs, so the rear pressure wave now arrives in front shifted through 360 degrees (= 0 degrees) and will therefore reinforce, not cancel, the front pressure wave.

As frequency falls below *f*, output response drops because of increasing doublet action; the baffle has progressively less of an effect on the destructive interference caused by the phase shift between the front and rear pressure waves.

In the unlikely case of a flat baffle cut in the shape of a circle, all path lengths around the baffle would be the same length, as shown in Figure 5-12A. As a consequence the destructive interference between rear and front outputs would create a sharp notch in response at the frequency whose wavelength is equal to the path length around the baffle.

The square baffle shown in Figure 5-12B offers some improvement, since there is no longer a single path length around the baffle. If the speaker is mounted off-center on a square or rectangular baffle (Figure 5-12C) there are even more path lengths, which smooths out the response even further.

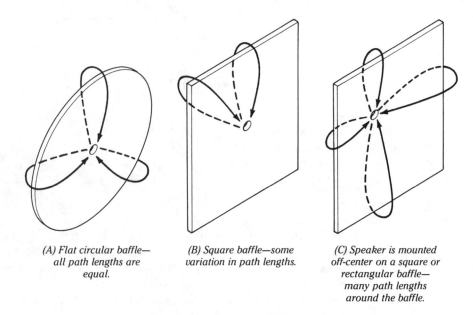

(A) Flat circular baffle—
all path lengths are
equal.

(B) Square baffle—some
variation in path lengths.

(C) Speaker is mounted
off-center on a square or
rectangular baffle—
many path lengths
around the baffle.

Figure 5-12. The paths around a flat baffle.

Frequency Response
Considering the effects of just the baffle on a doublet sound source, a single delay—as in the case of the circular baffle described in Figure 5-12A—would produce a series of output notches at multiples of the first notch frequency. As more and more signal delays are introduced by placing the doublet source off-center, the response smooths out considerably. The theoretical effects of various numbers of signal delays are shown by the family of curves in Figure 5-13.

Each curve in Figure 5-13 represents a composite of one direct-path output signal and one or more delayed replicas which are combined subtractively. Note that in each case the response rises at 6 dB per octave until a transition frequency is reached, with an output notch occurring one octave above the transition frequency. In practice subsequent notches are less severe than shown, due to the diminishing effects of doublet action.

For the purposes of the following discussion, the *transition frequency* is defined as the frequency whose wavelength is twice the effective path length of the complete baffle. The first notch occurs when the wavelength equals the path length. At this frequency, the path length simply delays the rear waveform by one complete cycle, so it remains shifted by 180 degrees.

Flat-Baffle System Response
When an actual speaker is mounted on the flat baffle, the combination forms an elementary speaker system, in which both the baffle and the speaker itself play a

part in shaping the frequency response. Depending on the relationship between the speaker and the baffle, one of three characteristics may be noted:

- If the baffle is quite large, the pressure response below the resonance frequency falls off at 12 dB per octave, as it did with the infinite baffle described before.
- On a smaller baffle, if the speaker's resonance frequency is lower than the baffle transition frequency, the response will fall off at 6 dB per octave below the transition frequency.
- If the resonance frequency is close to the transition frequency, the response below this point will fall off at 18 dB per octave.

As can be seen from these examples, the overall system performance is influenced by the interaction between the speaker and the panel on which it is mounted.

The Open-Back Cabinet (Folded Baffle)

A somewhat more practical speaker enclosure may be realized by folding over the sides of a flat baffle, as shown in Figure 5-14A. This decreases the back-to-front path length slightly, and creates a second resonance frequency based on the air column within the enclosure, which may be compared to a pipe closed at one end only. Accordingly, the wavelength of the cabinet resonance frequency is four times the length of the cabinet side, *L*.

Frequency Response
Since the open-back cabinet is simply a variation on the flat baffle, the pressure response acts in the same manner; below the transition frequency the response falls off at 6 dB per octave if the speaker's resonance frequency is lower than the baffle transition frequency, or at 18 dB per octave if the resonance frequency is close to the transition frequency.

The Closed-Back Cabinet

When a speaker is mounted on the front panel of an otherwise completely sealed cabinet (Figure 5-14B), the air inside the cabinet has no means of escaping and it therefore functions as an acoustic spring against which the speaker cone must now act. The practical result of this stiffened mechanical system is that the resonance frequency of the speaker rises beyond its natural resonance point in free air. The effect on the system frequency response is again a function of the relationship between the speaker and the enclosure.

Due to the characteristics just described, the closed-back cabinet is referred to as an *acoustic suspension system*.

Frequency Response
In the open-back cabinet the system transition frequency was defined by the cabinet itself, and a lower speaker-resonance frequency created a 6 dB per octave rolloff below the transition point. Sealing the cabinet eliminates doublet action

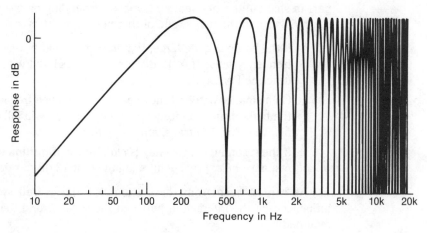

(A) One signal-delay path (e.g., a circular baffle).

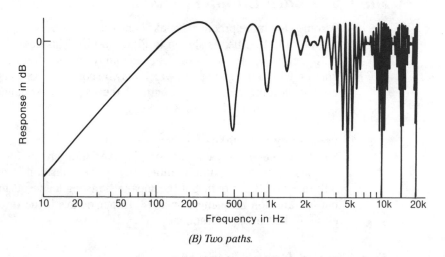

(B) Two paths.

Figure 5-13. Output response when one or more delayed signals combine destructively with a nondelayed signal, as in the theoretical model of a doublet sound source mounted on a flat baffle.

and raises the speaker resonance frequency. However, if this new resonance frequency is lower than the resonance removed by sealing the cabinet, the net effect is an improvement in overall low frequency performance; although speaker resonance is higher, the system resonance has been brought down. The response below resonance now falls off at 12 dB per octave instead of at 6 dB per octave.

If the speaker and the equivalent open-back cabinet have about the same resonance frequencies, sealing the cabinet raises the speaker resonance frequency as described before. But again the destructive interference of the doublet action is eliminated and therefore the low-frequency response falls off at the more gradual 12 dB per octave rate, although of course it does so beginning at the new (and higher) resonance frequency.

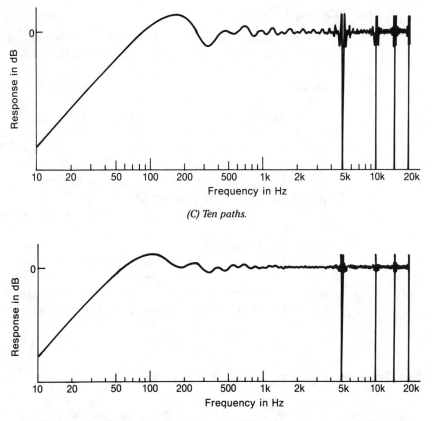

(C) Ten paths.

(D) 100 paths (approximation of a rectangular baffle with speaker mounted off-center).

Figure 5-13 *(continued)*

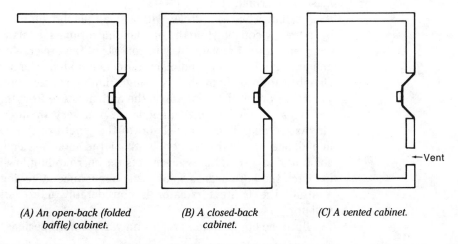

(A) An open-back (folded baffle) cabinet.

(B) A closed-back cabinet.

(C) A vented cabinet.

←Vent

Figure 5-14. Simple speaker enclosures.

The Vented Cabinet

Like the infinite baffle, the completely sealed enclosure is a relatively inefficient device, in that it does not permit energy from the rear of the speaker to radiate into the listening area. Efficiency is further reduced by the increased stiffness of the mechanical system brought about by the action of the air column trapped within the enclosure.

To make use of the energy lost within the sealed enclosure, a vent or port may be cut in the face of the enclosure, usually below the speaker cutout as shown in Figure 5-14C. The performance of such a vented enclosure may be studied by comparing the vent and the volume of air within the cabinet to their electronic equivalents—the inductor and the capacitor. As in any reactive device, the resonance frequency of this acoustic circuit may be tuned by adjusting the vent dimensions (inductance) and cabinet volume (capacitance) as required.

Frequency Response

By carefully selecting the cabinet and speaker resonance points, it is possible to extend the system low-frequency response beyond that found in the sealed enclosure. However, it should be noted that the extreme low frequencies will now roll off at 24 dB per octave, compared to the 12 dB rolloff of the sealed enclosure.

The Indirect Radiator

Earlier in this chapter it was shown that the pressure output of a piston-like diaphragm becomes more directional with increasing frequency (page 168). Since the piston's directionality is inversely proportional to its diameter, it follows that a small diaphragm will offer better high-frequency dispersion than a large one. However, this improvement comes at the cost of a much lower output level, since the small diaphragm simply aggravates the problem of trying to move a large air mass with a small piston.

The efficiency of a driver with a small diaphragm may be greatly improved by indirectly coupling it to the surrounding air mass, as shown in Figure 5-15. The complete indirect radiator system consists of the driver, a compression chamber, and a horn with an expanding cross-sectional area. The driver and compression chamber are usually treated as a single unit known as a compression driver.

At the driver/horn interface, the high pressure from the compression chamber faces the high acoustic impedance of a very small cross-sectional area of air. As the sound wave travels down the length of the horn, its pressure and impedance are both reduced, until at the mouth a comparatively large air column of low sound pressure meets the surrounding low-impedance air mass. In effect, the horn acts as an acoustic impedance-matching transformer and, as a result, the indirect radiator is considerably more efficient than a direct radiator.

Both the compression driver and various horn designs are described below.

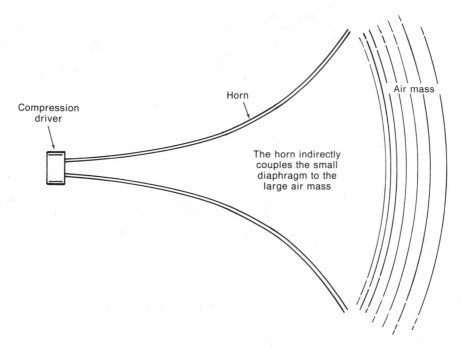

Figure 5-15. An indirect radiator. The complete system consists of the driver, compression chamber, and a horn with an expanding cross-sectional area. The compression chamber is usually an integral part of the driver assembly.

Compression Drivers

In a compression driver the *compression chamber* is a cavity with a large opening on one side and a small opening on the other. The driver's diaphragm is coupled to the large opening, and at the opposite side of the chamber the smaller opening is coupled to the horn throat, as shown in Figure 5-16A. As a result of the dissimilar openings, the moving diaphragm creates a high acoustic pressure within the chamber, and therefore at the throat of the horn. The horn itself is described in detail below.

Phase Plug

Since the area of the driver diaphragm is larger than the mouth of the compression chamber, there are many path lengths between the diaphragm and the mouth. There will therefore be some high-frequency phase cancellations at the driver mouth, where the paths converge as shown in Figure 5-16A.

To prevent this sort of cancellation, a phase plug is inserted between the diaphragm and the mouth of the compression driver. As the pressure wave radiates away from the diaphragm, it must travel through the phase plug in order to reach the chamber mouth. Since all paths through the plug are the same length, there is no phase cancellation when the paths combine at the mouth. Figure 5-16B shows a cutaway view of a typical phase plug.

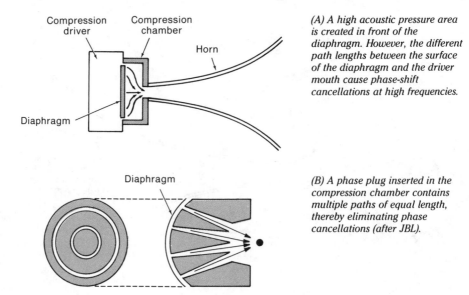

(A) A high acoustic pressure area is created in front of the diaphragm. However, the different path lengths between the surface of the diaphragm and the driver mouth cause phase-shift cancellations at high frequencies.

(B) A phase plug inserted in the compression chamber contains multiple paths of equal length, thereby eliminating phase cancellations (after JBL).

Figure 5-16. The compression driver.

The Indirect Radiator Horn

Figure 5-17 shows the compression driver, phase plug, and horn of a typical indirect radiator, and identifies the various components of the horn section. Readers who do not care to dive into the muddy waters of horn contour description may wish to skip ahead to the section on complete speaker systems (page 191).

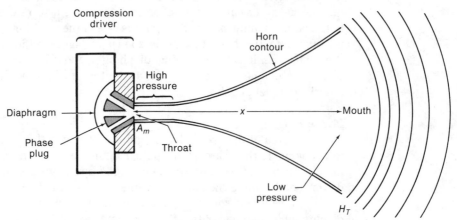

Figure 5-17. An indirect radiator system, consisting of compression driver, compression chamber with phase plug, and horn assembly.

Nomenclature

The equations in the following section help define the physical dimensions of various indirect-radiator horns. Although not essential to a basic understanding of the subject, they are presented here for the reader who wishes to take a closer look into the variations between one design and another. Also, a word that describes an equation (exponential, hyperbolic, etc.) is sometimes seen in the description of a horn style; hence, familiarity with the nomenclature may help explain the difference between one horn contour and another. However, the contour that follows nothing more than a single equation is probably found only in textbook examples.

Unless otherwise noted, the horns described in this chapter have a circular cross section in order to keep the calculations within reason. In practice, the actual cross-sectional area is more apt to be rectangular. However, the same general conclusions regarding length and horn mouth size still hold. As far as possible the nomenclature used here closely follows that found elsewhere in the literature, and consists of the variables and constants listed in Table 5-3.

Table 5-3. Indirect Radiator Variables and Constants

Variable or Constant	Definition
A_x or D_x	cross-sectional area or diameter, at distance x from horn throat
A_t or D_t	cross-sectional area or diameter at the horn throat
A_m or D_m	cross-sectional area or diameter at the horn mouth
c	the speed of sound
ϵ	2.718; the base of the natural logarithm (ln) system
f_c	cutoff frequency; the low-frequency limit of the horn
λ	c/f_c; wavelength of the frequency under discussion
m	flaring constant (described in text)
π	3.142
T	shape constant (described in text)
x	distance from throat at which the area is measured

Flaring Constant

The flaring constant, m, is often seen in equations as a simplification of the following expression.

$$m = 4\pi f_c / c \qquad \text{(5-5)}$$

or

$$m = 4\pi / \lambda$$

For any specified cutoff frequency, the numerical value of the flaring constant depends on whether the speed of sound is given in English or metric units. Therefore, care should be taken to make sure this constant is expressed in the same system of units used elsewhere in the equation in which it appears.

Shape Constant

The shape constant, T, in a horn-contour equation is a design constant used to adjust the length of the horn. Its value typically lies between 0 and 1, but may go as high as infinity; for a given cutoff frequency the lower the shape constant, the greater the horn length required to reach the specified mouth area.

Cutoff Frequency

As described earlier in this chapter (page 162), the cutoff frequency of a speaker is the speaker's practical lower frequency limit. In the case of a horn, the size of its mouth is analogous to the direct-radiator piston, and the greater the mouth area, the lower the cutoff frequency.

Horn Mouth

To find the required horn mouth dimension, equation (5-4) may be rewritten to calculate either the diameter or the area of the mouth, once the desired cutoff frequency is specified.

$$D_m = c/(\pi f_c), \text{ or } D = \lambda/\pi$$

or

$$A_m = c^2/(4\pi f_c^2)$$

which may be rewritten as

$$A_m = c/f_c \cdot c/(4\pi f_c) \tag{5-6}$$
$$= c/(f_c m)$$

Horn Contours

Once the size required for the mouth is known, there are several methods of designing the horn's transition contour from the throat to the mouth. For example, Figure 5-18 shows three possible contours. The relative merits of each of these are briefly discussed later in the chapter (page 187).

A single equation plots the family of contours that lies between the conical and hyperbolic horn.

$$A_m = A_t(\cosh mx/2 + T \sinh mx/2)^2 \tag{5-7}$$

Note: When solutions of the hyperbolic cosine (cosh) and sine (sinh) functions are not available (as in many personal computers and calculators), the functions themselves may be rewritten as follows:

$$\cosh k = (\epsilon^k + \epsilon^{-k})/2$$
$$\sin k = (\epsilon^k - \epsilon^{-k})/2$$

where
$$k = mx/2$$

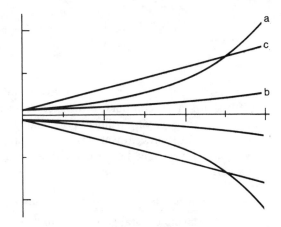

Figure 5-18. Three possible horn contours: (a) exponential, and (b) hyperbolic, and (c) conical. In this example the exponential and conical contours share a common intersection and thus either one may be used for a given horn length and mouth dimension.

In the description of an indirect radiator, equation (5-7) is often used to graph the cross-sectional area of a horn versus the axial distance from its throat. A family of such curves may be shown, all drawn above the x axis (for example, Figure 5-19A). In this case the y axis indicates the area in square inches or centimeters. Although the shape of the area curve sometimes resembles a horn contour, the actual contour may vary considerably, depending on whether the horn's cross section is square, rectangular, or circular.

Illustrations of actual horn contours in this chapter show mirror-image curves, with one set above and the other below the x axis, as in Figure 5-18. At any point along this axis, the vertical distance between similar contours represents the diameter of a horn of circular cross-sectional area. Each curve is drawn by finding the radius at a distance, x, from the throat and marking off this radius above and below the x axis. Therefore the illustration is, in effect, a template for a horn with a circular cross section.

For certain values of T, the horn contour equation describes a specific type of horn design, as listed here and described below. In two cases the equation may be simplified as shown in the appropriate section.

T	Horn Type
1	Exponential
< 1	Hyperbolic cosine
> 1	Hyperbolic sine
∞	Conical

Exponential Horn

In equation (5-7), if the shape constant $T = 1$, the equation may be written in simplified exponential form as shown here (and hence the name *exponential horn*).

$$A_m = A_t(\cosh mx/2 + T \sinh mx/2)^2 \qquad \text{(5-8)}$$
$$= A_t[(\epsilon^k + \epsilon^{-k})/2 + (\epsilon^k - \epsilon^{-k})/2]^2$$
$$= A_t\epsilon^k$$
$$= A_t\epsilon^{mx}$$

Figure 5-19A shows a family of exponential cross-sectional areas and Figure 5-19B shows horn contours, drawn for various values of flaring constant, m. In designing or specifying a horn, presumably the cutoff frequency and the throat area needed to physically match the driver are both known, and the following two parameters may be calculated from equations presented earlier in the chapter.

Parameter	Symbol	Equation
flaring constant	m	(5-5) (page 181)
mouth area	A_m	(5-6) (page 182)

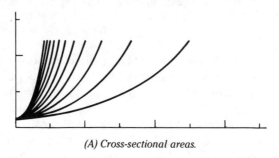

(A) Cross-sectional areas.

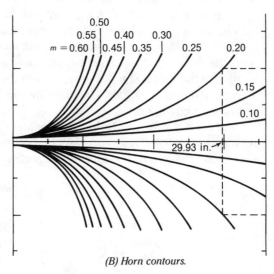

(B) Horn contours.

Figure 5-19. The exponential horn.

The following sample exercise is used to find the required horn length, x. To begin, rewrite equation (5-8) as follows:

$$x = \ln(A_m/A_t)/m \qquad (\ln = \text{natural logarithm; see Chapter 1, page 2})$$

For the sake of the calculations which follow, a throat area of 0.79 in^2 (i.e., a diameter of one inch) and a cutoff frequency of 215.81 Hz are used. To find the horn length, first calculate the flaring constant and mouth area:

$$
\begin{aligned}
m &= 4\pi f_c/c = (12.57 \cdot 215.81)/(1130 \cdot 12) = 0.2 \\
A_m &= c^2/(4\pi f_c^2) = c/(mf_c) \\
&= (1130 \cdot 12)/(0.2 \cdot 215.81) = 314.17 \text{ in}^2
\end{aligned}
$$

The horn length may now be found as

$$x = \ln(A_m/A_t)/m = \ln(314.17/0.79)/0.2 = 29.93 \text{ in}$$

Note that in Figure 5-19B this horn length is marked off by a vertical line crossing the x axis at 29.93 inches. The line describes the horn mouth, and the sides of the horn follow the contour of the 0.2 flaring constant. The illustration shows the horn mouth has a radius of 10 inches, which agrees with the mouth area calculated above.

Hyperbolic Horn

When the value of the shape constant T in equation (5-7) is less than infinity but not equal to 1, the equation may not be simplified as in equation (5-8) above. Therefore, the longer form is required to plot the family of hyperbolic contours shown in Figure 5-20. The curves were calculated with a flaring constant of 0.25 and various finite values of T.

In Figure 5-20A, the contours were drawn with a shape constant of 1 or less. Such contours are sometimes referred to as *hyperbolic cosine* because of the diminishing contribution of the sinh term in equation (5-7) as T approaches zero.

The horn contours in Figure 5-20B illustrate values of T between 1 and 25. These contours are described as *hyperbolic sine* because the sinh term in equation (5-7) becomes progressively more important as the value of T increases beyond 1. In either part of Figure 5-20, when the shape constant is unity, the contour is the same as would be found from the simpler exponential equation (5-8). Therefore, the $T = 1$ contour in either part of Figure 5-20 matches the $m = 0.25$ contour in Figure 5-19.

Conical Horn

The most straightforward horn design is simply an enclosure in the shape of a cone. In Figure 5-20 it can be seen that as the shape constant increases from 1 to 25, the horn contour flattens out considerably and at $T = 25$ it is almost a straight line, as it would be in a conical horn. When T eventually reaches infinity, the horn contour equation may be written as seen here (Plach 1953).

$$A_m = A_t(1 + mx/2)^2 \tag{5-9}$$

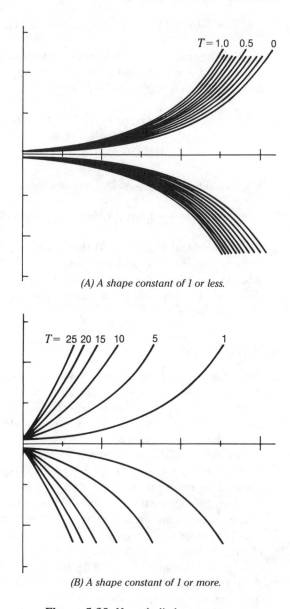

(A) A shape constant of 1 or less.

(B) A shape constant of 1 or more.

Figure 5-20. Hyperbolic horn contours.

Figure 5-21 shows a family of conical horns drawn with flaring constants between 0.5 and 2.5.

Parabolic Horn

The equation for a parabolic horn is perhaps the simplest example of all:

$$A_m = A_t x \tag{5-10}$$

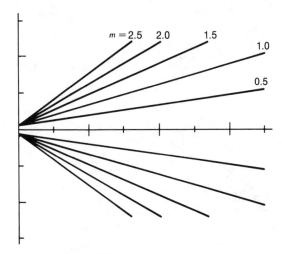

Figure 5-21. Conical horn contours.

The parabolic equation is included here for the sake of comparison with the other horns described earlier, although in practice this horn design is rarely if ever found. As equation (5-10) suggests, a graph of the cross-sectional area of a parabolic horn is nothing more than a straight line, as shown in Figure 5-22A. If such a horn were constructed with a circular cross-sectional area, its contour would be as shown in Figure 5-22B. An alternative parabolic horn might be designed as shown in Figure 5-22C. Note that the top and bottom surfaces of the horn are parallel and the sides expand at a uniform rate. The equation is therefore rewritten as

$$A_m = A_t kx \qquad \text{(5-11)}$$

where
k = included radian angle between the nonparallel sides.

Horn Selection Criteria

In addition to the obvious cutoff frequency, other variables affect the selection of the horn contour. For example, proper acoustic impedance matching suggests a throat-to-mouth contour that begins its expansion gradually, as in a hyperbolic horn. On the other hand, it has been pointed out that if a horn were designed in the shape of a long cylindrical pipe (as at the beginning of a gradual expansion), distortion would increase with the length of the pipe. Since the throat of a hyperbolic horn closely approximates a cylinder, a conical horn will minimize this type of distortion, at the cost of poorer impedance matching. The conical horn does provide uniform coverage, although with less output than an exponential horn in the lowest two octaves (Keele 1975).

Note that a parabolic horn with circular cross-sectional area (Figure 5-22B) combines the worst aspects of the conical and hyperbolic horn, and if designed as

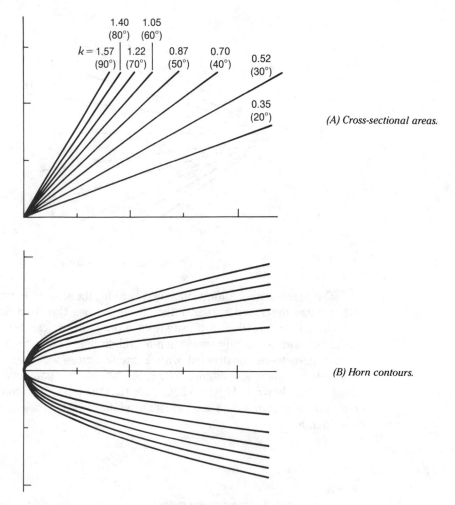

(A) Cross-sectional areas.

(B) Horn contours.

Figure 5-22. The parabolic horn.

shown in Figure 5-22C it would approach the distortion characteristics of a cylindrical pipe.

Practical Horn Designs

The exponential horn is perhaps the best compromise system (Beranek 1954), although in practice the horn of an indirect radiator is often a combination of exponential and other contours, a few of which are briefly described in the following.

The Radial Horn

The radial horn has straight vertical sides with an included angle determined by the desired horizontal coverage. The top and bottom horn surfaces flare outwards at whatever rate is required to achieve the correct mouth area. Figure 5-23A, B, and C shows a representative radial horn.

(C) A parabolic horn with constant-flare sides and parallel top and bottom.

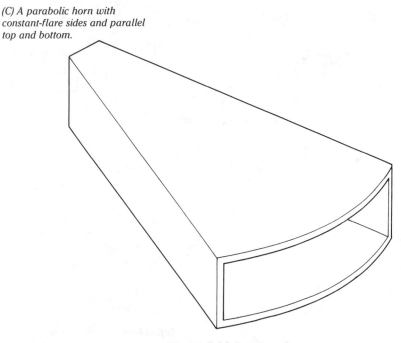

Figure 5-22 *(continued)*

The Biradial Horn

In the biradial horn both the vertical and horizontal surfaces flare outwards, though usually at different rates, as shown in Figure 5-23D, E, and F. This design provides different coverage angles in the horizontal and vertical planes.

The Multiflare Horn

As its name suggests, a multiflare horn combines two or more contours, as shown in Figure 5-24. In this illustration the horn contour is exponential at the throat and conical at the mouth, thus combining the impedance-matching characteristics of the former with the good coverage angle of the latter.

The Multicell Horn

A multicell horn is in effect a combination of two or more horns coupled to a single compression driver. The purpose is to extend the coverage angle beyond that of a single horn. However, at high frequencies each cell tends to function independently, resulting in a series of response peaks and dips at various off-axis angles. A typical multicell horn system is shown in Figure 5-25.

The Diffraction Horn

A diffraction horn has a long and narrow mouth opening which acts as a quasi-point source for any frequency whose wavelength is large compared to the narrow mouth dimension. As the sound wave leaves the horn mouth, it diffracts around the mouth edges; hence the term *diffraction horn* (Cohen 1968).

Figure 5-26 shows a diffraction horn, whose outer profile resembles the parabolic horn described earlier (page 186). However, the horn interior is in effect

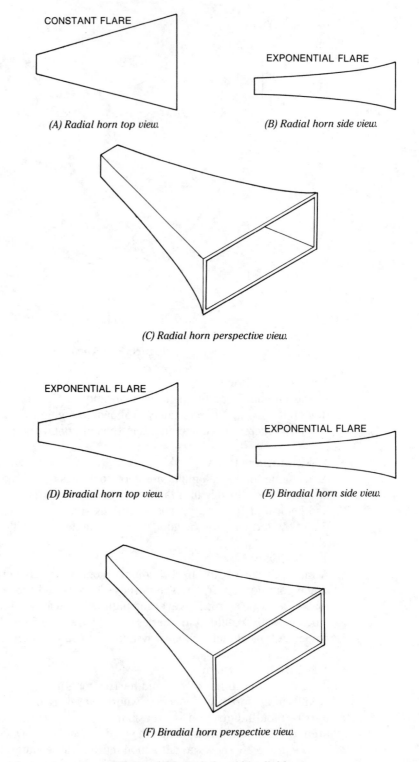

CONSTANT FLARE

(A) Radial horn top view.

EXPONENTIAL FLARE

(B) Radial horn side view.

(C) Radial horn perspective view.

EXPONENTIAL FLARE

(D) Biradial horn top view.

EXPONENTIAL FLARE

(E) Biradial horn side view.

(F) Biradial horn perspective view.

Figure 5-23. Radial and biradial horns.

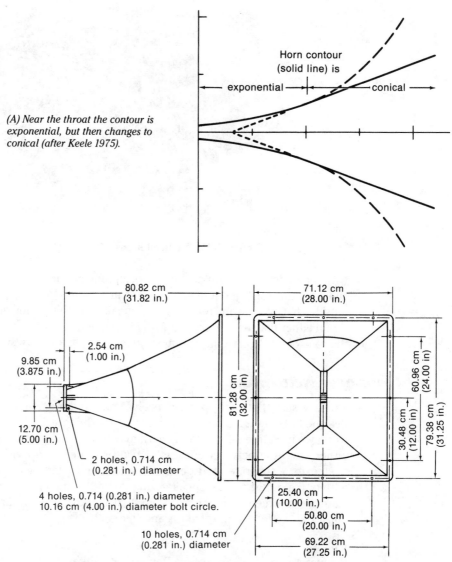

(A) Near the throat the contour is
exponential, but then changes to
conical (after Keele 1975).

(B) Dimension drawing for a high-frequency horn showing changing horn contours.
(Courtesy Electro-Voice, Inc.)

Figure 5-24. The multiflare horn.

an array of radial horns whose contours are defined by the series of spacers seen
in the figure.

Loudspeaker Systems

Since a good low-frequency speaker will not handle high frequencies well, and
vice versa, most professional monitor systems consist of two or more speakers

Figure 5-25. Multicell horns. *(Courtesy Altec Lansing Corp.)*

within an enclosure, with each speaker optimized for a segment of the complete audio bandwidth. Therefore some means must be provided to prevent frequencies outside that band from reaching the speaker. If this is not done the undesired signal either may be reproduced with distortion or may damage the speaker, as in the case of a high-level low-frequency signal applied to a tweeter.

Crossover Networks

To make sure that each speaker receives only the frequency band for which it is designed to operate, a crossover network may be inserted between the speakers, as shown in Figure 5-27. The network may be either a passive or active design. In either case, the network consists of two or more filters, with each output connected to a separate loudspeaker. Each filter is designed to pass frequencies within the range of its speaker and to attenuate all other frequencies. For example, a three-way monitor system such as the one shown in Figure 5-27 might consist of the following speakers and filters:

Speaker Popular Name	Frequency Range		Filter	Cutoff Frequency
woofer	Low	< 1 kHz	lowpass	1 kHz
squawker	Mid	1–4 kHz	bandpass	1 kHz & 4 kHz
tweeter	High	> 4 kHz	highpass	4 kHz

Passive Networks

A passive crossover network consists of a series of response shaping filters inserted at some point ahead of the speakers. Each filter comprises one or more inductors and capacitors whose values are determined by the desired crossover frequency and the impedance of the source (amplifier) and load (speaker), which are assumed to be equal. Such a network is often an integral part

(A) As part of a four-way monitor system (above the three direct radiators).
(SM-1 Studio Monitor courtesy Westlake Audio)

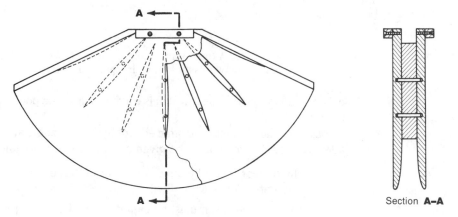

(B) Detail drawing of interior (after JBL 2397).

Figure 5-26. The diffraction horn.

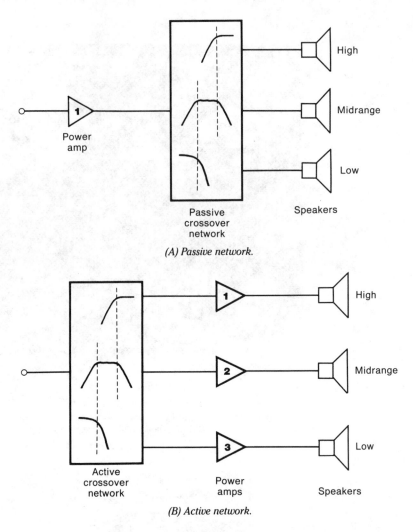

(A) Passive network.

(B) Active network.

Figure 5-27. A three-way monitor system, showing passive and active crossover networks for low, midrange, and high frequency speakers.

of the speaker system itself, which is driven by a single power amplifier as shown in Figure 5-27A.

Despite the obvious economic advantage of the single-amplifier system, it has a few drawbacks which must be given consideration. For example,

- The network must be built to withstand the full power of the amplifier, much of which is wasted within the network itself.

- The amplifier itself must be capable of delivering sufficient power to drive the complete speaker system.

- Low frequency response is especially prone to distortion brought about by the inductance coils in the lowpass network.

- Low-frequency distortion within the amplifier may produce upper harmonic components that damage one of the higher-frequency speakers.
- Attenuation may be required between the network and any speaker that is more efficient than the least efficient speaker within the system.
- Network design usually assumes a purely resistive load, while a speaker's impedance contains an inductive component as well.
- If a speaker is replaced by another with a different impedance, the network element values will have to be changed.

Active Networks

By contrast, the crossover network inserted ahead of the amplification stage may be designed to operate at line level rather than at speaker level. Although such a network might also be a passive system, it is more often designed in conjunction with active components. In either case its position within the monitor system is as shown in Figure 5-27B.

Some of the advantages of an active crossover network are listed here.

- Network components need not be specified with large power-handling capabilities.
- Amplifier power may be reduced to that required by a single speaker (although additional amplifiers will of course be required).
- There are no passive components within the speaker line.
- The sensitivity of each amplifier may be readily adjusted to suit the efficiency of the speaker it is driving.
- The amplifier acts as a buffer between the crossover network and the frequency-dependent impedance of the speaker.
- Speakers with different impedances may be interchanged without affecting network design.

Network Cutoff and Crossover Frequencies

In each filter within the crossover network, the *cutoff frequency* is that frequency at which the output level is attenuated by 3 dB. The *crossover frequency* is simply that frequency at which the curves of two such filters intersect. Unless otherwise noted, the low- and highpass filter sections are designed for a cutoff frequency at the crossover point. In other words, if a network filter is designed with a certain upper rolloff frequency, the same frequency is used as the lower rolloff frequency for the next filter in the network.

Beyond the cutoff frequency, response falls off at a uniform rate determined by the design of the filter. As a typical example, Figure 5-28 is a graph of frequency versus attenuation for a family of *n*-order lowpass filters. The curves were plotted using the following equation (Geffe 1966):

$$A = 10 \log (1 + 2\pi f^{2n})^{1/2}$$

where
    A = attenuation in dB
    f = frequency in Hz
    n = order number of filter

In this example each filter is designed with a 1 kHz cutoff frequency. Beyond that point the filter attenuates high frequencies at the rate of $6n$ dB per octave. That is, if n = 1, 2, or 3, then attenuation is 6, 12, or 18 dB per octave, and so on. Filter design is covered in greater detail in Chapter 6.

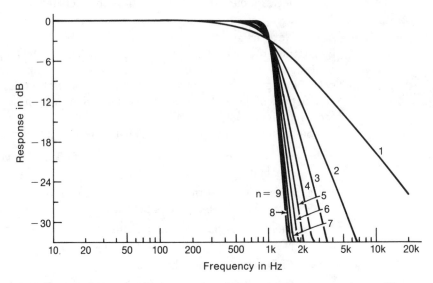

Figure 5-28. Output response for a family of n-order lowpass filters. The number of reactive elements in the filter defines its order number. As the order number increases, the rolloff slope falls off at a rate of $6n$ dB per octave.

Phase Shift

Since every reactive element introduces a phase shift, it follows that a crossover network will shift the phase of the signal passing through it, and that this shift will be related to the number of reactive elements within the network. For example, Table 5-4 lists the phase shift for various-order filters at their low- and high-frequency limits and at the cutoff frequency. In practice the phase shifts will be slightly less than those seen in the table since these extremes represent DC and infinity, respectively. The table also gives the attenuation in decibels-per-octave for signals in the stopband range.

Figure 5-29 shows the amplitude and phase response of a crossover network consisting of second-order low- and highpass filters, each with a cutoff frequency of 1,000 Hz.

Note that the low- and highpass phase shifts are mirror images, and that in the second-order filter the difference between them at crossover (−90, 90) is 180 degrees, as may also be seen by the phase-shift curves in Figure 5-29. This means that signals in the crossover region, which are reproduced by both speakers, are equal in amplitude but opposite in phase. Therefore their combination produces a

Table 5-4. Crossover Network Phase Shift and Attenuation Slope

Order Number	Attenuation (dB/octave)	Lowpass Filter			Highpass Filter			Highpass Filter*		
		Low	Cutoff	High	Low	Cutoff	High	Low	Cutoff	High
1	6	0	−45	−90	90	45	0	−90	−135	−180
2	12	0	−90	−180	180	90	0	0	−90	−180
3	18	0	−135	−270	270	135	0	90	−45	−180
4	36	0	−180	−360	360	180	0	180	0	−180

*Phase shifts when the polarity of the input signal is reversed (180 degree phase shift).

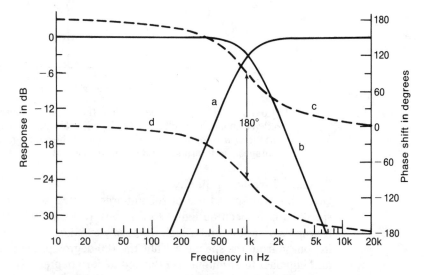

Figure 5-29. The amplitude and phase responses for both sections of a second-order crossover network with a crossover (cutoff) frequency of 1,000 Hz. Note the 180-degree phase shift at the crossover frequency. Curve (a) shows the highpass amplitude response and curve (b) the lowpass amplitude response. The highpass phase response is shown by curve (c) and the lowpass by curve (d).

sharp acoustic power notch at the crossover frequency, as shown by curve (c) in Figure 5-30. The amplitude responses from Figure 5-29 are also included for reference.

To correct this phenomenon the polarity of one of the filter sections may be reversed. For example, if the output polarity of the highpass filter is inverted at the speaker, the resultant phase shifts will be those listed in the last three columns in Table 5-4, where it can be seen that the second-order phase difference at the crossover frequency is now identical to the lowpass filter. In this case the combination of the two signals produces a 3 dB boost at crossover, as shown by curve (d) in Figure 5-30. The polarity reversal technique is not useful with filters other than second-order.

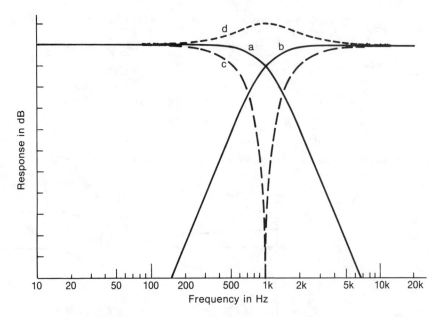

Figure 5-30. There is a power null at the crossover frequency when the voltages applied to each speaker are equal in amplitude but opposite in phase ($c = a - b$). If the polarity to one of the speakers is reversed, the voltages add to produce a 3 dB power gain at crossover ($d = a + b$).

Speaker Terminal Polarity

Given the widespread use of second-order filters, some—but by no means all—speakers have been designed so that positive-going signals applied to matching terminals on a low- and a high-frequency speaker will produce outputs of opposing phase from the speakers. Thus the 180-degree phase difference between low- and highpass filter outputs is returned to zero degrees. However, this convention is not followed by all speakers, and sometimes not even by all speakers within a single manufacturer's product line. As an additional variable, the relationship between speaker polarity and the black-and-red color coding on some speaker terminals is not always consistent. Therefore, network and speaker polarity should be checked carefully whenever there is any doubt about either a crossover output or a speaker input.

Time Delay Considerations

In a monitor system with two or more speakers, it follows that if a musical instrument produces a single complex tone whose fundamental frequency lies near the top of one speaker's piston band, the upper harmonics of the same tone will be reproduced by the next speaker within the system. An instrument whose frequency range stretches across a crossover area will likewise be reproduced by one or another speaker, depending on the note being played. And finally, a wide-range polyphonic instrument—the piano is an obvious example—will be heard over all the speakers within the complete monitor system.

If we think of the output of a single musical instrument or of an entire ensemble as one complex sound pressure wave, some attention must be given to the problem of reproducing that signal from a multipoint sound source. For example, if a tape track is played back over a monitor system containing three speakers, the single-track source is now a three-point source. If those three points are at different distances from the listener's ear, their respective outputs will arrive at different times, resulting in a certain amount of phase shift distortion.

For example, consider what might happen to a waveform if it were reproduced by a two-source system in which source *A* reproduces the fundamental, and is slightly ahead of source *B*, which reproduces the harmonics. Figure 5-31 shows a 1,000 Hz square wave when two such sources are separated by 0.5 inch. If the source of the fundamental were behind by the same distance instead, the waveform would be the inverse of that shown in the illustration. In either case the resultant waveform is a distorted replica of the square wave input.

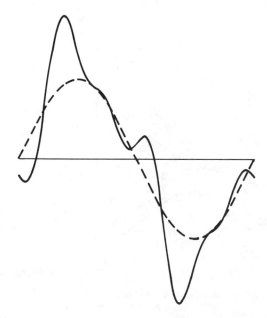

Figure 5-31. A reproduction of a 1,000 Hz square wave, in which the upper harmonics are delayed due to a 0.5 inch spacing difference between two point sources. One source reproduces the fundamental, the other the harmonics.

Although there may be no such thing as a perfect acoustic square wave anyway (see Chapter 2, page 50), the example in Figure 5-31 still shows how any complex waveform may be distorted by a speaker system with more than one path between the system and the listener.

Acoustic Center
The *acoustic center* of a speaker is that point from which its spherical sound waves appear to originate (based on ANSI S1.1-1960). To provide a single path length between the listener and each speaker within a monitor system, the speakers are

often physically aligned so that the acoustic center of each one lies in the same vertical plane, as shown in Figure 5-32. However, a speaker's acoustic center is not necessarily found at the physical center of its diaphragm, and in general lies behind this point by some inverse function of the speaker's high-frequency cutoff (Heyser 1969). The acoustic center may also vary with frequency over the speaker's piston band (Møller 1974), and as a function of phase-related time delay introduced by the crossover network.

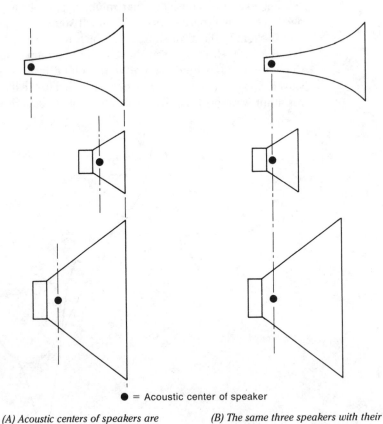

● = Acoustic center of speaker

(A) Acoustic centers of speakers are usually not in the same vertical plane.   *(B) The same three speakers with their acoustic centers vertically aligned.*

Figure 5-32. The effect when speaker mouths are mounted on a common front baffle.

As a good example (Uzzle, n.d.) of phase-related center shift, an 860-Hz sine wave has a wavelength of 40 cm (about 19.2 in.) and therefore a one-eighth wavelength of 5 cm (2.47 in.), which corresponds to a phase shift of 45 degrees. Therefore, at 860 Hz a 45-degree phase shift will create an acoustic center shift of 5 cm.

Although a displacement of the acoustic center related to frequency and/or crossover delay cannot be corrected by repositioning one of the speakers, the static centers can be physically aligned for some improvement in overall response. Due to obvious size differences between various speakers, each one's center lies at a different distance from the outer edge of its cone, or in the case of a horn, from the horn's mouth. Therefore, a simple mechanical alignment of speaker rims will not provide an alignment of acoustic centers. Either the speakers will have to be aligned in space or their crossover networks aligned in time in order to minimize the distance/time differences between them.

Various terms have been used to identify a speaker system in which speaker positions and/or network time delays have been adjusted to minimize time-related anomalies. Two such frequently encountered terms are briefly described here. In either case, the end result is the same.

Time Alignment

The term *time alignment* is a trademark of E. M. Long Associates, who describe it as a design method for a multispeaker system in which the physical and electric components are adjusted so that the fundamental and overtones of a complex signal arrive at the listener's ears with the same time relationship they had in the electronic signal (Long 1977). Figure 5-33 shows a few time-aligned professional monitors which use a two-way coaxial speaker. Since the coaxial construction precludes physical readjustment to align the acoustic centers, the alignment is accomplished by a delay line built into the crossover network.

Figure 5-33. Time-Align™ monitor systems. Since the relative position of the coaxial drivers is fixed by speaker construction, time-alignment is realized in the design of the crossover network. *(UREI "C" series Studio Monitors courtesy JBL Inc.)*

Linear Phase Speakers

In Figure 5-29 the graphs of phase shift through low- and high-pass filters were seen to vary nonlinearly over the 20 kHz displayed bandwidth. By contrast, *linear phase* is a phase shift which varies as a linear function of frequency. (It is not a fixed phase shift at all frequencies.) For example, if the output of a system with a fixed time delay is compared with its own input, the observed phase shift will vary linearly with frequency. If such a phase shift were plotted on linear graph paper, the curve would be the straight line shown at (a) in Figure 5-34. On the more familiar logarithmic scale the curve would be as shown at (b) in Figure 5-34.

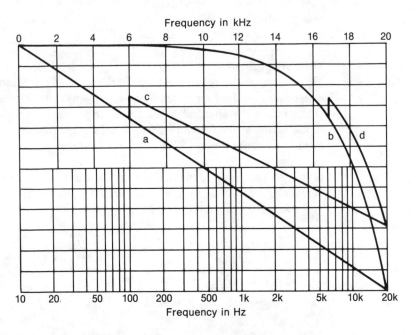

Figure 5-34. Two ways of plotting linear phase shift. The straight line (a) is plotted on the linear frequency scale seen in the upper half of the graph. The identical phase response (b) is plotted on the logarithmic frequency scale used in the lower half of the graph. The discontinuities (c and d) indicate a time shift at 6 kHz and beyond.

In either example, if all frequencies beyond a certain point were delayed by a different fixed interval, there would be a discontinuity at that frequency (6 kHz in Figure 5-34), and beyond it the phase response would follow curves (c) and (d). Such a break might occur in a two-speaker system if the speakers were not properly aligned with respect to time.

The term "linear phase" is used by some manufacturers to identify a monitor system in which the speakers are physically and/or electronically aligned to provide a linear phase response.

Absolute Polarity

It is well known that when two or more monitors are used—as for example in a stereo playback system—the signal polarity to each system should be the same. Thus, when the same signal is fed to all speakers, each diaphragm moves in the same relative direction. In the case of a two-channel playback system, the signal should be clearly localized at a point midway between the speakers. However, if the polarity to one of the speakers is inverted, the origin of the source will not be so clearly defined. The sound may appear to originate at some indeterminate location that cannot be localized with certainty. A simple reversal of one pair of signal leads corrects the problem immediately.

Once the relative polarity of the system is correct, a subtle change may be noted if the polarity to both speakers is reversed. For example, consider what happens when a musical instrument plays a percussive sound. A pressure condensation radiates away from the instrument, followed immediately by a rarefaction (see Chapter 1, page 16). When the sound is eventually reproduced by a speaker, the speaker diaphragm should also produce a condensation first. However, the diaphragm might move outward or inward first, depending on the polarity of the speaker leads. In the case of an initial inward movement, a rarefaction comes before a condensation—just the opposite of the original event. A polarity reversal at *both* speaker system inputs will correct this condition.

The difference is at best a subtle one, and on nonpercussive signals is probably imperceptible. Furthermore, maintenance of absolute phase has not received wide attention throughout the industry, so there's about an even chance of noting an improvement when monitoring a tape or disc recorded elsewhere. Nevertheless, it's good engineering practice to check the entire audio signal path to make sure that absolute polarity is maintained from microphone input to speaker output.

6 Delay and Reverberation Systems

Not that many years ago sound recording was pretty much a matter of setting up a microphone or two to capture the sound field—the complete sound field—as it existed in the room at the moment the musicians were playing. To improvise on a current computer theme, WYHIWYG; What You Heard Is What You Got. The musicians were recorded as an ensemble, complete with the "room sound" and maybe a passing subway or two. At the time, this aspect of recording was perhaps more art than science.

Les Paul and Mary Ford changed all that (see page 419). The multitrack tape recorder was born and microphones moved down from their booms, ever closer to the instruments they captured on tape. The engineer enjoyed unprecedented control over the final balance and "We'll fix it in the mix" took its rightful place alongside "The check is in the mail" and a few other universal truths that can't be printed here.

Like most technological blessings, this one was itself a bit mixed. On the positive side, music was freed from the constraints of real-time performance. The traditionalists were of course appalled, despite there being no law that said music must be performed at once or not at all. But as the obvious production controls were gained, others were lost, or at least misplaced, and not a few multitrack productions sounded more like data collection than music. The greatest problem was, and perhaps still is, to find a means to restore the illusion that musicians, live or otherwise, are actually performing real music in real space.

This statement of the problem makes the assumption that reality is desirable. When it's not, the rules can—and should—be creatively bent to produce an effect that might not be possible during a real-time performance in a real room.

The Sound Field

The term *sound field* is used in this chapter and elsewhere to refer to the complex combination of direct and reflected energy that exists in any listening environment. With respect to the sound field itself, it's now possible to come close to reality or leave it far behind, as required. However, this signal processing power comes with its price tag; the engineer must have a much better understanding of echo and reverberation than was required in simpler days. Therefore, this chapter devotes much of its own space to a close examination of the various acoustic components that make up the sound field. Once these are better understood it's an easier task to create the desired effect, real or otherwise.

Although echo and reverberation are the main topics of this chapter, the digital delay line has many other applications than the simple creation of an echo or two. Therefore, several other delay-related applications are also discussed later in the chapter (page 235).

The chapter concludes with a very brief discussion of control room acoustics and speaker placement. Although much of this section is concerned with loud-speakers, it is presented in this chapter in order to relate it more closely to the general subject of echoes and reverberation.

The Signal Paths in a Sound Field

Like any other two points in space, the shortest distance between a sound source and a listener is the single straight-line path between them. Given the speed of sound and the length of that path, it is easy enough to calculate the time it takes for a sound to travel from the source to the listener. However, in any normal listening environment the straight line is but one of many paths taken by a sound pressure wave as it radiates away from its source.

In Chapter 1 (page 18) it was shown that a source radiates its energy in all directions, so that if a pressure wave traveling along any path strikes a surface at an angle, it is reflected away from that surface at an equal angle, as shown in Figure 1-14 (page 23). All else being equal, each such reflected signal that eventually reaches the listener is simply a delayed and attenuated version of the direct signal. Both the delay and the attenuation are a function of the additional distance along each reflected path.

But of course all else *isn't* equal, and so each reflection sounds just a bit different than the direct-path signal. The differences are attributable to the manner in which each surface reflects energy. In Chapter 1, Table 1-2 listed the absorption coefficients of a few building materials. Since these coefficients vary with frequency, the sound of a reflected signal depends on the surface from which it is reflected. In a typical listening environment there are many surface materials and therefore many response variations in the reflected signals reaching the listener. In combination with the single direct-path sound, these variations give the listener a sense of the size and character of the listening room, and also of the distance that he or she is from the source of the sound. For example, in Chapter 2 (page 55) it was pointed out that if the listener is very close to the sound source, all reflected paths will be quite long by comparison to the direct path. Therefore the listener will hear mostly the direct sound, and the frequency responses and other characteristics of the reflected sounds won't matter much anyway, since they will be an insignificant part of the total sound.

By contrast, when the sound source is at some distance from the listener, some of the reflected paths are not that much longer than the direct path. Therefore the direct path itself is but one of many paths reaching the listener, and the overall sound is a complex mixture of direct and reflected information.

The Components of the Sound Field

To get a better idea of how reflected energy influences the listener's perception of a sound source, consider the sound field at a center-front seat in a good concert hall in which a large orchestra and chorus are performing. Some of the variables affecting the listener's perception of the sound source are listed here.

Signal Characteristic	Is a Function of
Time delay	The additional path length from source to listener.
Direct-to-reflected energy ratio	The relative distances from the source to the listener, along the direct and reflected paths.
Sound level	The inverse square law along the path length.
Frequency response	The frequency-dependent absorption coefficient of the surface from which the signal is reflected, plus additional high-frequency attenuation over long distances.
Visual cues	Observation. Although the visual cue is not an "official" component of the sound field, the eye is a very important influence on the ear.

Each of these variables is briefly described in the following sections.

Time Delay As shown in Figure 6-1, there are variations in distance between the listener and various parts of the orchestra, soloists, and chorus. Assuming that the group is well rehearsed and that all entrances are made on time, the listener will still hear the soloists first, followed a few milliseconds later by the strings. The percussion sounds will arrive just a little bit later, and the chorus will be heard even later.

In a normal concert hall environment the listener should not be consciously aware of these time-of-arrival differences. Nevertheless the minute variations give the ear/brain combination the information needed to determine the relative distance of each sound source, with respect to other sources heard at the same time. Taken alone, these time-delay cues provide a sense of the spatial depth of the ensemble. However, additional cues are needed to determine the distance of the entire ensemble from the listener.

Direct-to-Reflected Energy Ratio The ratio of direct to reflected energy also varies from one part of the ensemble to another; the musicians closest to the listener sound closest—not because they are louder (in fact, they may not be), but

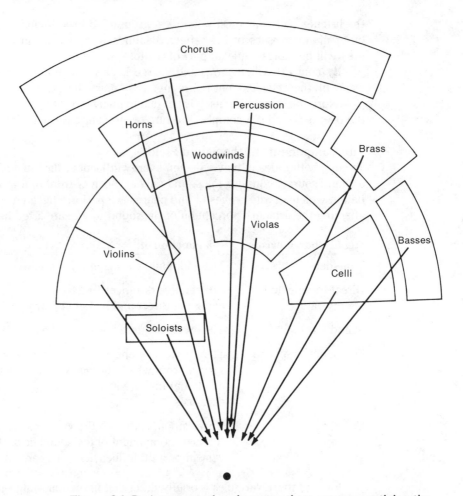

Figure 6-1. During an actual performance there are many path lengths
between the listener and the sections of the performing ensemble.
The sounds from the more distant sections take a little longer
to reach the listener.

because their ratio of direct-to-reflected energy is higher than that from the musicians
at stage rear. The higher the ratio, the closer the sound source seems to be.

Sound Level   As an obvious example of the relative unimportance of level
alone, consider what happens as the dynamic range of a single instrument or
orchestral section varies. The listener is certainly not fooled into thinking there is
a variation in distance taking place. By contrast, a singer maintaining a constant
output level while moving all over the stage does not seem immobilized; the
shifting time and distance cues give the listener a very good idea of where the
singer actually is.

Frequency Response   Since high-frequency response falls off slightly with distance (page 55), a close-up source will usually sound a bit brighter than the same

source heard over a greater distance. In addition, the reflected energy reaching the listener is usually weak in high frequencies; thus the overall sound from a distant instrument lacks the high-frequency content of a closer source.

Visual Cues   The role of the eye in the perception of acoustic space is frequently overlooked or poorly understood. Often, it just doesn't seem possible that the eye can influence the listener's perception of where a sound originates, but this phenomenon has been demonstrated countless times.

From simple observation, every listener accepts the fact that a single speaker creates the illusion that a sound source is physically present at the location of the speaker. From experience, most listeners also acknowledge that a sound source may appear to be positioned somewhere on a line between two speakers, even though they know very well that no such source actually exists at that point. However, few listeners will agree that a speaker pair is capable of reproducing a sound that seems to originate on that line but outside the segment between the two speakers. And even fewer accept the fact that two speakers in front of a listener can create the illusion that a sound source is off to the side, or even behind that listener.

But, taking the latter example first, what is the difference between two sound sources, one directly in front of, the other directly behind, the listener? Consider an actual source in the room and in full view of the listener. If echo and reverberation cues are at a minimum, as in a moderately dead room, the only difference comes from the filtering action of the ears; that is, a sound in the rear has a slight attenuation of high frequency content, compared to the same sound originating up front. If the source begins up front and then moves around to the rear, there is the obvious "moving around to the rear" cue as the source passes closer to one ear. This is followed by the very slight spectrum difference once the sound is in the rear. The listener has the previous frontal sound as a subconscious frame of reference, and also the very powerful visual cue of watching the source change its position, accompanied by the shifting aural sensations during the period of movement. By the time the source is in place at the rear, the listener has been sufficiently prompted to expect to hear a rear-originating sound.

In the absence of the visual and aural conditioning cues just described, it is by no means so easy to distinguish front from rear. For example, if a loudspeaker or other source is not in plain view in front of the listener, there may be some momentary confusion when a sound is suddenly heard. A slight—often unconscious—movement of the head, is usually all it takes to resolve the confusion. However, if a listener does see speakers in front, and thinks there are none in the rear, then a sound that actually does originate in the rear is often reported as coming from up front; the listener "knows" that a rear-originating sound is impossible, and the brain does the rest.

During the mid 1970s, several quadraphonic matrix encoding systems were proposed. As part of the ensuing experimentation it was shown that within limits, a two-channel system could convey the illusion of sounds originating not only from the area between the two front loudspeakers, but from locations to the side and even behind the listener. However, when demonstrated to an audience of test subjects, the demonstration often did not work. The demonstrator, who knew how the system worked, could hear the side- and rear-originating sounds; the audience, who did not know about the system, did not experience the desired effect.

The dilemma was eventually resolved by placing dummy speakers in the rear. The same audience, now knowing that sounds in the rear were possible, heard them. In fact it was often difficult to persuade the listeners that the rear speakers were not connected to a power source. If nothing else was proven, the power of the visual cue was made clear.

The point of this little excursion into the visual side of psychoacoustics is to remind the reader that the eyes are a very important part of the hearing mechanism, especially when it comes to location perception. When there is nothing to look at, as in an audio-only recording, there is a double burden on that medium to do the best it can to compensate for the missing visual image.

In some audio demonstrations, location perception is helped along by a recorded narrator who says "I'm moving around to the left-rear, and now I'm standing behind you," and so on. The listener is carefully prompted about what is going to happen, and that makes it a lot easier to hear the sound at the location where it's supposed to be. However, a demonstration full of such advance warnings is rarely effective when the narration is in a foreign language.

The Sound Field in the Typical Room

To illustrate the sound field in a typical room, Figures 6-2 and 6-3 show some of the many reflected paths that can exist between a sound source and a listener. Assuming the room length and width and the positions of the source and listener are known, the length of each path may be calculated. In each illustration uppercase letters indicate the known dimensions, while lowercase letters indicate path lengths that may be calculated from the known information. With that calculation done, the time of arrival and attenuation along each path may also be found. For the purposes of the following discussion, reflections from the floor and ceiling are not considered.

Figure 6-2 shows the direct path and the only four paths that each contain a single reflection from one wall surface. Note that the path segments to and from each wall are hypotenuses of similar triangles, as illustrated by the two shaded areas in the illustration. Similar-triangle pairs also exist between the path segments to every other wall surface, although of course no pair is necessarily similar to any other pair within the room. Triangles are defined as similar if their angles are equal and their sides are therefore proportional. An understanding of this relationship is particularly helpful in visualizing paths that contain two or more reflections.

In all parts of Figure 6-3 the area between the source and the front wall is omitted, and in Figure 6-3A only the reflection from the left wall is shown. To find the length of this reflected path, the unknown sides of the two shaded triangles must first be found. Since the triangles are similar, the ratios of their sides are

$$A/(C - y) = B/y$$

and therefore

$$y = BC/(A + B)$$

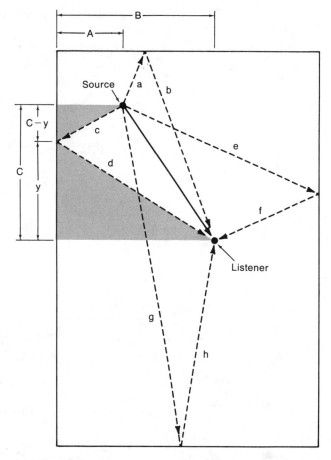

Figure 6-2. The direct path and the first four reflected paths between a sound source and a listener.

The following equations now find the length of the reflected path, $p_1 = p_a + p_b$, and of the direct path, p.

$$p_a = [(C - y)^2 + A^2]^{1/2}$$
$$p_b = [y^2 + B^2]^{1/2}$$
$$p_1 = p_a + p_b$$
$$p = [(B - A)^2 + C^2]^{1/2}$$

Since the reflected path is longer than the direct path, the sound reaching the listener along this path will be attenuated. Assuming the direct-path signal creates a 0 dB reference level at the listener's position, the attenuation of the reflected-path signal is found from the following equation.

$$L = 20 \log (p/p_1) \text{ dB}$$

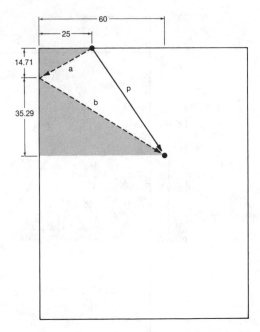

(A) The single direct path, p, and one path containing a single reflection.

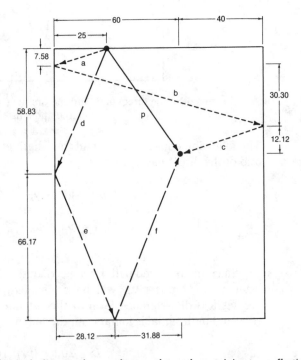

(B) The single direct path, p, and two paths, each containing two reflections.

Figure 6-3. Direct and reflected

Although not shown here, the above equations may be rewritten to find the path length and attenuation for each of the other single-reflection paths that were shown in Figure 6-2.

Next we examine a few paths containing two or more reflections. Again using the left wall as the site of the first reflection, Figure 6-3B shows two possible paths for a sound wave with two reflections, and Figure 6-3C shows three possible paths containing three reflections. The distances listed along the outside of the illustrations are calculated from the known room dimensions and positions of source and listener and may in turn be used to find the length of each path.

In each illustration a similar set of paths might be drawn using one of the other room surfaces as the site of the first reflection. And of course many more paths might be drawn for sound waves with progressively more reflections within their total length.

To relate all these reflected-path signals to a real room, Table 6-1 lists the calculated path length, time delay, and sound level for a series of paths leading to a point 50 feet from the stage in an auditorium 100 feet wide and 125 feet long. The sound source and the listener are respectively 25 feet and 60 feet from the left wall. These dimensions were used in the calculation of the paths shown in Figures 6-2 and 6-3.

Figures 6-4A and B are graphs of amplitude versus time for each of the reflections seen in Figures 6-2 and 6-3, using the data listed in Table 6-1. For purposes of clarity, the direct signal is an impulse of very short duration.

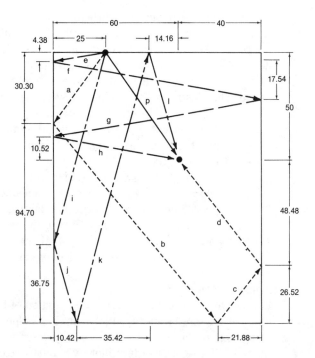

(C) The single direct path, p, and three paths, each containing three reflections.

paths in a typical rectangular room.

Table 6-1. Path Lengths and Attenuation at a Single Point in an Auditorium*

Figure	Path Labels	Path Lengths				Total (ft.)	Arrival Time (ms)**	Attenuation (dB)
		1	*2*	*3*	*4*			
6-2 & 6-3	p	61.03				61.03	0.00	0.00
6-2								
	ab	21.46 +	75.11 =			96.57	31.45	3.99
	cd	29.00 +	69.61 =			98.61	33.26	4.17
	ef	81.78 +	43.62 =			125.40	56.96	6.26
	gh	126.90 +	76.14 =			203.04	125.67	10.44
6-3B								
	abc	26.12 +	128.62 +	41.80 =		196.54	119.92	10.16
	def	63.92 +	71.90 +	81.49 =		217.31	138.30	11.13
6-3C								
	abcd	39.28 +	122.76 +	34.38 +	62.85 =	259.27	175.43	12.56
	efgh	25.38 +	101.53 +	101.53 +	60.92 =	289.36	202.06	13.52
	ijkl	91.71 +	38.20 +	129.92 +	51.97 =	311.80	221.92	14.17

*Room dimensions: width—100 feet, length—120 feet.
  Distances: source to left wall—25 feet, listener to left wall—60 feet, listener to stage—50 feet.
**Arrival time is given with respect to the direct signal.

In Figure 6-4A the first vertical line represents this impulse at the instant it reaches the listener via the direct path. The impulse is shown at a convenient zero reference level, and each succeeding line gives the amplitude and arrival time of a delayed reflection of the impulse. The dotted lines represent a few additional paths reflected from the front, back, and right walls, but not shown or calculated above. The illustration shows but a few of the many reflections that make up the sound field in any room.

In Figure 6-4A it is assumed that all wall surfaces are perfect reflectors. Consequently the amplitude of each reflection is strictly a function of the distance travelled to reach the listener. However, since most surfaces absorb a certain amount of incident energy, each reflection will in practice be further attenuated, as shown by Figure 6-4B. In practice, the amount of attenuation varies with frequency, according to the absorption characteristics of the surface.

Although the order and amplitude of the reflection patterns vary from room to room, and from one location to another within the same room, every enclosed sound field consists of a series of reflections such as those seen in the figure.

Nomenclature

In order to better understand the composition of the sound field, or to simulate the effect of a desired sound field later on, it is helpful to break the field down into its component parts, each of which is briefly described here. A few definitions based on the ANSI USA Acoustical Terminology Standard ANSI S1.1960 (R 1976) are also given. Each of these is prefaced by its ANSI section number within the standard.

The terms defined here are all indicated in Figure 6-4A.

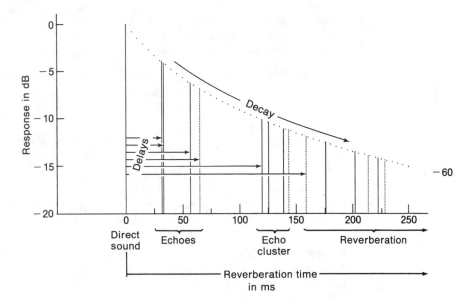

(A) The series of reflections in the ideal room seen in Figures 6-2 and 6-3.

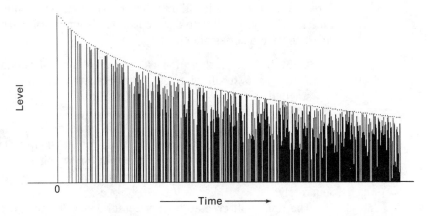

*(B) The reflection pattern in a typical room, with further amplitude variations
due to each surface's absorption characteristics.*

Figure 6-4. Graphs of amplitude versus time delay for a direct sound
followed by a series of reflections. The height of each line indicates
the sound level, and each line's horizontal position shows
the arrival time of one of the reflections.

Direct Sound   The direct sound is comprised of just the sound wave that travels
along the straight-line path between the source and the listener. Although it takes
a certain amount of time for it to reach the listener, for obvious reasons it is
usually convenient to begin timing at the arrival of the direct sound.

Echoes   An *echo* is a single repetition of a signal, which arrives at the listener's location some time after the direct sound is heard. Depending on the listening environment, one or more discrete echoes may be heard.

> **ANSI 1.30:** An echo is a wave that has been reflected with sufficient magnitude and delay to be detected as a wave distinct from that directly transmitted.

Early Reflections   In a typical room, the direct sound is usually followed shortly by a few closely spaced echoes, and then there is a further delay before additional echoes arrive. These first few echoes are often identified as *early reflections*, to distinguish them from what follows. The early reflections are usually limited to those signal paths containing a single reflection, as shown in Figure 6-2.

Echo Cluster   The early reflections just described are followed by a longer delay, and then another sequence of closely spaced reflections, often referred to as an *echo cluster*. The cluster may comprise those signal paths with just a few reflections, as shown in Figures 6-3B and C.

Reverberation   As the sound field continues to develop, more and more echoes arrive at the listener's location. However, the echoes are now so closely spaced in time that it is impossible to distinguish one from another. The term *reverberation* refers to such a series of echoes.

> **ANSI 1.39:** Reverberation is the persistence of sound in an enclosed space, as a result of multiple reflections after the sound source has stopped.

Delay   Although every echo arrives after the direct sound, *delay* is generally understood to refer to the time it takes for each discrete echo in the early-reflection series to arrive, or to the time at which reverberation begins. The closely spaced delays within the reverberant field are usually not considered separately.

The time shift created by any signal-delay device is often labeled with a Δt ("delta-tee") symbol.

Decay   Because reflections arrive at progressively lower sound levels, *decay* refers to the gradual attenuation of the sound field over time.

Reverberation Time   A room's *reverberation time* is defined as the time it takes, when a steady-state sound source is stopped, for the sound pressure level to decrease by 60 dB. Reverberation time varies with frequency, and such variations may be a function of several factors, such as

- The natural attenuation of high frequencies within the room over distance (see page 55).
- Absorption characteristics of the various room surfaces from which the direct sound is reflected back into the room.

• Frequency spectrum of the music.

To better understand how the sound field gradually decays when a sound source is removed, it may help to visualize a theoretical acoustic model, in which the field is created not by a single source arriving via many paths, but by a primary source and a multitude of identical images, each representing a single reflection. Each image originates at a different angle and distance from the listener (Eyring 1930). Figure 6-5 shows the actual location of the primary source and the apparent locations of several such sources. Note that all the image sources appear to be outside the room's boundaries.

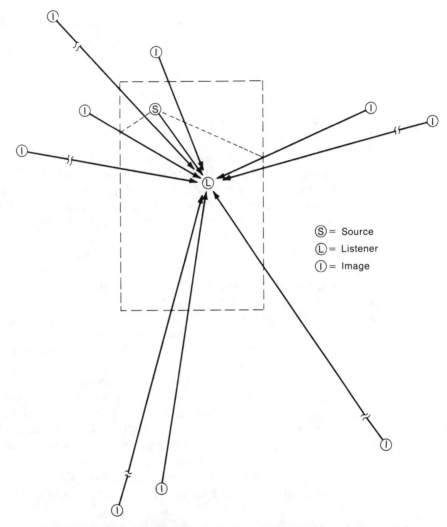

Figure 6-5. The reflected paths from Figures 6-2 and 6-3 are here treated as though created by a group of separate images originating at distant points outside the room boundaries. The two dashed lines each indicate an actual path simulated by an external image.

The primary source and all image sources begin at the same instant. But due to the relatively slow speed of sound in air, it takes some time until all the image sounds arrive at the listener's location. The listener first hears the primary source alone, followed shortly by the arrival of one—and, eventually, all—of these sources.

When the primary source stops, there is a brief interval until the listener no longer hears it. And although the image sources ceased at the same instant, it takes a little bit longer until the nearest images are no longer heard, and still longer until all the images are lost. Consequently, the sound pressure level does not collapse instantly when the primary source is turned off. Instead, it decays gradually as the sound wave from each image removes itself from the sound field.

Channel and Channel Path   The terms *channel* and *channel path* refer to the normal signal path from a single console input (for example, from a microphone line) to the point where that signal is combined with others to feed a single *track* on a tape recorder. The channel path is described in greater detail in Chapter 12.

Delay and Equalization

As noted earlier, the absorption characteristic of each room surface influences the response of sound waves reflected from that surface. As a result most natural reflections do not have the same frequency spectrum as the direct signal, which arrives with no modification other than perhaps a slight high-frequency loss over distance. To better simulate the effect of natural reflections, some equalization may therefore be required in the signal path at one or more points before the delayed signals are combined with the direct signal.

Since it is obviously impractical to insert a separate equalizer in each delay line, a reasonable approximation may be realized by placing a single equalizer ahead of the delay system. Although this imposes the same equalization settings on all delays, the effect is probably more natural than equalizing only one of the available delays. Hardware budget permitting, it may be possible to separately equalize at least the first couple of reflections and then equalize those remaining with a single overall setting.

Some delay lines incorporate low-frequency and/or high-frequency filters which may be used to help simulate a more realistic reflection sound. In general, reflections in a small space will have less low-frequency content than is found in a large concert hall. And in any room, the more glass and other hard reflective surfaces, the greater will be the high-frequency content. By keeping these typical characteristics in mind, a little equalization may go a long way toward creating a more natural room sound—or a less natural one if that is what's required.

Chapter 7 describes equalization in much greater detail.

Distance Localization

The variables described above give the listener a sense of the environment in which he or she and the sound source are situated. As may be seen from Figure

6-6, the size of the room influences both the time it takes for each reflection to reach the listener, and the amplitude of that reflection, while having no effect on the direct sound itself. Therefore, the intervals between the direct sound and the early reflections help the listener to determine the distance of the sound source.

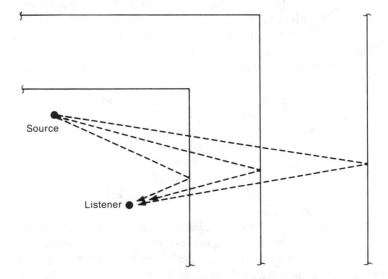

Figure 6-6. The time it takes for reflected signals to reach the listener varies with the size of the room.

When some or all of the variables just described are absent, it is often difficult to impossible to determine the distance between the sound source and the listener. For example, in a series of tests conducted in an anechoic chamber, a listener was seated three feet in front of a loudspeaker (Gardner 1968). Four more speakers were positioned in a straight line behind the reference speaker, with the last one 30 feet distant from the listener, who was asked to identify the speaker from which a recorded speech was heard. Although none of the speakers was ever active except the most distant one, every listener thought the sound originated at the closest speaker. In the complete absence of normal echo and reverberation cues, the listener was left with only the visual cue—the sight of the nearby speaker. Without exception, distance recognition was immediate, unambiguous, and wrong.

The lesson to be learned here is that in the absence of good aural localization cues, all reproduced sounds seem to originate at whatever distance the speaker is, rather than at various distances from the listener, as would be the case in a normal listening environment. This leads us to a consideration of the difference between the sound field picked up by a microphone in a recording studio, and the sound field heard by a listener in a good seat at a good concert in a good concert hall.

The Recorded Sound Field

When a microphone is placed very close to a sound source, reflections from even the closest room surfaces are received at a comparatively low level. For example, if the microphone working distance is one foot and the shortest reflected-path length is 10 feet, the reflected signal reaching the microphone will be 20 log (1/10) = −20 dB with respect to the direct signal. If the microphone is closer and/or the reflected-path length is longer, this attenuation will be even greater. Consequently, the microphone's sound field is almost entirely made up of direct sound, with little or no echo or reverberation added.

Now consider what happens when a large musical ensemble—say, the orchestra and chorus shown earlier in Figure 6-1—is recorded on a multitrack tape recorder, with each orchestral section close-miked to minimize leakage from nearby sections. If all the microphones are at about the same working distance, all the sections are recorded at the same instant. As a result, all the space and distance cues described earlier are lost; the only thing on the tape is the direct-path sound of each instrument, or group of instruments.

When the tape is played back over a stereo monitor system, each track may be panned to any position on a straight line between the two speakers. (Panning is described in detail in Chapter 12, page 484) However, all tracks will seem to originate on this straight line; in other words, at the same distance from the listener.

To restore the missing sense of depth, various signal processing devices may be used. For the purposes of simulating the effect of instruments playing in a natural environment, the three component parts of the sound field are treated separately, as described below.

Sound Field Component	Consists of	Simulated by
Direct Sound	Output of instrument	—
Echo	Early Reflections	Time Delay System
Reverberation	Later Reflections	Reverberation System

Direct Sound

The direct sound is simply the output of the microphone, as recorded on tape. Assuming the microphone is quite close to the instrument being recorded, the recorded signal is mostly the sound arriving along the straight-line direct path, as just described above.

Of course the ultimate in direct sound is the output signal from any electronic device routed directly to the tape recorder. In this case there is no intervening microphone, and so the recorded signal is nothing but the direct sound.

Echo

Although every reflection is an echo, for the purposes of this discussion only the earliest reflections are considered as discrete echoes.

Delay Systems

Since an echo is nothing more than a delayed replica of a direct signal, an echo may be simulated via any medium capable of storing a signal and reproducing it after a suitable delay. Magnetic tape comes immediately to mind, and indeed it was the only practical delay medium prior to the introduction of digital technology. Both magnetic and digital delay systems are described here.

Magnetic Delay Systems

The earliest electronic echo device was the tape recorder itself. On any machine with separate record and playback heads, it takes a certain amount of time for a recorded signal to travel the distance to the playback head. The interval is of course a function of head spacing and tape speed, and may be calculated as:

$$t = D/S$$

where

t = time, in seconds
D = distance between heads, in inches (or cm)
S = tape speed, in in/s (or cm/sec)

An auxiliary tape recorder may be used as a tape delay system, as shown in Figure 6-7. Although a spare track on a multitrack tape may also be used for tape delay, this is of course limited to the delay produced at the playback speed required by the tape.

Table 6-2 lists several of the delays available at various head spacings for three different tape speeds.

Table 6-2. Delay Versus Tape Speed and Head Spacing

Tape Speed (in/s)	Distance Between Record and Playback Heads (in.)				
	1	*2*	*3*	*4*	*5*
7.5	133.33*	266.67	400.00	533.33	666.67
15.00	66.67	133.33	200.00	266.67	333.33
30.00	33.33	66.67	100.00	133.33	166.67

*Delays are given in milliseconds.

As shown in Figure 6-7, it's possible to create a long sequence of echoes by feeding one of the playback-head outputs back to a record-head input. Doing so, however, reveals the basic weaknesses of the tape recorder as a delay system:

- All delays are at integer multiples of the first delay.
- The level of the delayed outputs decreases linearly over time.

The delay is of course strictly a function of tape speed and head spacing, as shown in Table 6-2. And because attenuation is determined by the proportion of output signal fed back to the input, it lacks the logarithmic falloff that is a function of the inverse square law described earlier in the chapter (page 207). The resultant pattern of echoes is shown in Figure 6-7B.

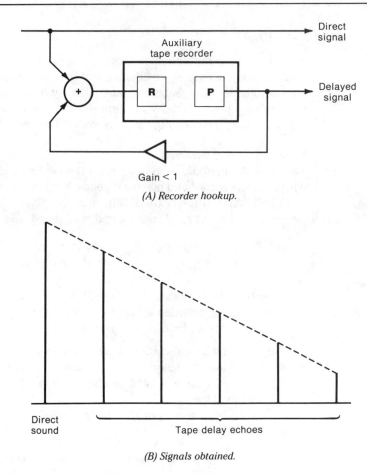

(A) Recorder hookup.

(B) Signals obtained.

Figure 6-7. An auxiliary tape recorder used as a tape delay system.
When an attenuated output signal is fed back to an input,
a series of evenly spaced and attenuated
echoes is produced.

To provide somewhat more delay flexibility than offered by the tape recorder, several early magnetic delay systems employed either an endless loop of tape passing over multiple playback heads, a magnetically coated rotating drum surrounded by multiple heads (Crane & Brookes 1961), or a magnetic platter. Most such devices have long since been replaced by electronic echo systems, as described in the following section.

Digital Delay Systems
A digital audio delay system has the advantage of providing a range of delay times considerably greater than the tape recorder, with the further advantage of not being dependent on a reel of tape that usually runs off the supply reel at the worst possible moment. A typical system may have one or two inputs and several outputs, each with a separately variable delay. Although the input and output signals may be analog, processing within the system is in the digital mode, as shown in the block diagram in Figure 6-8A.

The delay available at the outputs often may be increased by expanding the system's memory, just as is done in any personal computer by adding more RAM (Random Access Memory). In some systems the delay may be distributed between two channels up to the capacity of the system. Thus in a two-channel (*A/B*) system with a one-second delay maximum, the delays may range from *A/B* = 1/0 sec to 500/500 ms to 0/1 sec, etc. Various delay configurations often may be programmed, stored, and recalled for later use as required. Figure 6-8B shows the front panel of a representative digital delay system.

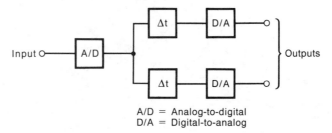

A/D = Analog-to-digital
D/A = Digital-to-analog

(A) The block diagram shows the analog inputs converted to digital format for processing, and then converted back to analog just before the output.

(B) The front panel of a digital audio delay system. The desired delay time for each of three outputs may be entered via the front-panel push buttons. (DN 716 courtesy Klark-Teknik Electronics, Inc.)

Figure 6-8. The digital delay system.

The Haas Effect

A very important aspect of delay is its influence on the localization of a sound source. For example, consider a signal routed to two speakers, as shown in Figure 6-9A. One of the speakers is identified as the primary speaker and the other as the echo speaker. If both reproduce the signal at the same level, the sound seems to originate at a position midway between them. However, if a delay line is inserted in the echo speaker line, the apparent source shifts away from the echo speaker and towards the primary speaker.

It has been reported (Haas 1949) that when the delay reaches only 10 milliseconds, the echo speaker is no longer heard, despite its output level matching the primary speaker. Figure 6-9B shows a graph of the *Haas Effect*, as it has come to be known since Helmut Haas first published his observations on the subject. The graph shows several significant delay-related phenomena, each of which is described here.

- *0–10 ms delay:* As the delay is increased from 0 to 10 ms, the sound source appears to move to the location of the primary speaker. To restore the center image, the echo speaker level must be raised about 10 dB.

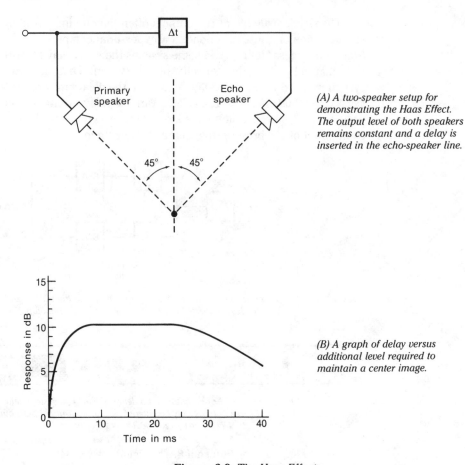

(A) A two-speaker setup for demonstrating the Haas Effect. The output level of both speakers remains constant and a delay is inserted in the echo-speaker line.

(B) A graph of delay versus additional level required to maintain a center image.

Figure 6-9. The Haas Effect.

- *10–30 ms delay:* As long as the delay stays within this range, the apparent location of the signal remains exclusively at the primary speaker. However, the echo speaker contributes a sense of "liveliness" or "body" and, as might be expected, additional volume. In a concert environment, echoes of 10 to 30 ms would be heard but not "seen," that is, the listener would sense the presence of the reflected energy, but not the locations from which it arrives.

- *30–50 ms delay:* In this range the listener becomes aware that the echo speaker is on, although the apparent sound source remains at the primary speaker.

- *50 ms or more (not shown on graph):* Although a discrete echo is now heard at the echo speaker location, the original source is still situated at the primary speaker.

The delay ranges given above are all approximate and will vary slightly according to the content of the reproduced signal. For example, echoes from a percussive sound will be apparent sooner; echoes from a sustained source, later.

The Haas Effect explains why the perceived location of a sound source is never confused by the arrival of echoes. In fact, even if the echoes are louder than the direct signal (not possible in nature, but easy in the control room), the apparent source remains at the location from which it first arrives. This is an important point and it will be brought up again later in this chapter, in the section on sound reinforcement (page 241).

Echo-Related Delay Applications

Given the flexibility of digital technology, electronic delay is now used to create a wide variety of effects in addition to its use in echo and reverberation systems. A few echo-related applications of delay are described here, with additional applications described later in this chapter (page 238).

Early Reflections

The obvious use of a delay system, digital or otherwise, is to create the first few echoes—the early reflections—of the sound field. As with tape delay, the outputs may be routed back to the input, often via a front-panel feedback control. Compared to a natural series of echoes occurring at uneven intervals and with varying degrees of attenuation, these echoes are not a very convincing simulation of a natural sound field. However, one or two delay outputs might be combined with the direct signal to simulate a few early reflections, and they might be fed back at a very low level to help supplement the effect of a reverberation system.

Reverberation Delay

A delay line output might also be used to feed an electronic reverberation system, if such a system does not have its own built-in delay line. Doing so gives a better simulation of natural reverberation, which by definition does not begin until after the early reflections.

Some modern electronic reverberation systems may be programmed to produce one or more discrete echoes before the onset of reverberation. Such systems are described later in this chapter, in the section on digital reverberation systems (page 230).

Slap Echo

As a special effect, a series of feedback echoes might be used to simulate the sound field between parallel reflective walls on either side of the listener. In this case the multiple reflections, or *slap echoes*, that reach the listener are almost equally spaced, as shown in Figure 6-10.

Reverberation

After the early reflections and echo cluster, the remaining echoes in a natural reverberant field become so closely spaced that they are not perceived as discrete echoes. And so to recreate such a field one echo at a time is not only complex and costly, but somewhat counterproductive as well. Therefore, reverberation is usually simulated by devices other than the echo systems described above.

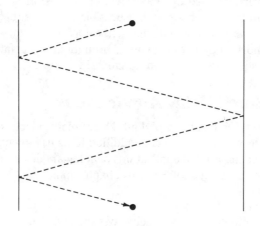

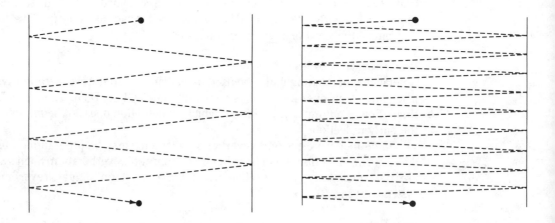

Figure 6-10. A delay system can be used to simulate the slap echo effect of reflections between nearby parallel walls. Since all transits across the room are about equal in length, the echo series is regularly spaced in time.

The Acoustic Reverberation Chamber

One of the most convincing ways to create a natural reverberant field is to do it the hard way, by constructing an acoustic *reverberation chamber*, that is, an actual room in which all surfaces are highly reflective. To create the most natural effect, the walls are usually built at irregular angles and coated with hard plaster or tile.

Figure 6-11 shows a typical reverberation chamber; a direct signal recorded elsewhere is routed to a loudspeaker in the chamber, where one or more microphones pick up the sound field created by the chamber's reflective surfaces. The microphone outputs are combined with the direct signal to create the illusion that the direct signal was actually recorded in a large room along with the natural reverberant field of that room.

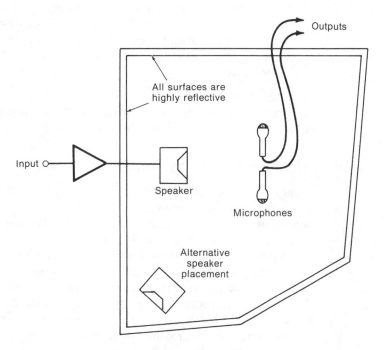

Figure 6-11. An acoustic reverberation chamber. Sound is fed to the speaker
in the chamber and picked up by one or more microphones. The
highly reflective surfaces create a diffuse and reverberant
sound field within the chamber. The speaker may be
aimed into a corner for even greater diffusion
of sound within the chamber.

Before the introduction of electronic reverberation systems, the use of a highly reflective room was about the only means available for adding reverberation to a recording. And although such a room remains a very effective way to simulate the sound field in a good concert hall, there are certain practical matters to be considered before building an acoustic reverberation chamber. A few of these are listed here.

- Construction. A good reverberation chamber is not cheap. In addition to the surface treatment itself, the room must be sufficiently isolated so that noises outside the chamber are not picked up by its microphones.

- Hardware. Optimum performance requires a wide-range speaker system within the chamber, plus two high-quality microphones with good off-axis response.

- Real Estate. To be effective a reverberation chamber requires a lot of space, and it may also require that nearby areas be restricted to quiet-zone applications. Given the cost of real estate, a reverberation chamber may not be able to pay its own rent.

- Flexibility. Once construction is finished, it is difficult to modify the characteristics of a reverberation chamber, especially on a moment's notice. Movable drapes or acoustic barriers may be effective but they also may be difficult to adjust within the time constraints of a recording or mixdown session. Remote control of such devices is desirable, but expensive.

These drawbacks notwithstanding, a well-designed and built reverberation chamber produces results which often justify its expense, particularly when the required space does not have to be rented at a big-city price.

Spring Reverberation Systems

A very inexpensive reverberation device may be built around a coil spring, as shown in Figure 6-12A. In fact, such systems were often found in early electronic organs, using an electromechanical (spring) delay line developed by the Hammond Organ Company (Dow & Swift 1961).

In concept, the operation of a spring reverberation system is quite simple: the spring is suspended between two transducers, as illustrated in the figure. A signal sent to the system transmitter drives the spring in a torsional (twisting) mode. The applied signal travels the length of the spring and is reflected back and forth, until it eventually falls below the residual noise level. At the opposite end of the spring, the receiving transducer converts the resultant mechanical energy back into an electrical signal. The complete system is analogous to a loudspeaker and a microphone, linked by a spring transmission line instead of by air molecules.

In practice, early spring reverberation systems didn't come very close to simulating natural reverberation, and in fact many were well known as "boing boxes" due to their very obvious "springy" sound. Nevertheless, the spring reverberation device is still used in a few guitar amplifiers, where it contributes an often used decay sound, if not the sense of a guitar lost in a cathedral.

Reverberation Plates

Perhaps the most popular predigital reverberation device was developed in 1957 by Dr. Walter Kuhl of the *Rundfunktechnisches Institut* (Institute of Broadcasting Technology) in Hamburg, Germany. Dr. Kuhl proposed suspending a large rectangular steel plate at all four corners and exciting it with an audio signal via a suitably designed transducer (EMT-Franz 1985). At the edges of the plate the bending waves thus created are reflected in a similar manner to sound waves striking the reflective surfaces in a room.

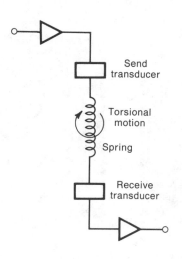

(A) Block diagram.

(B) Interior view. (Courtesy AKG Acoustics, Inc.)

(C) Exterior view. (Courtesy AKG Acoustics, Inc.)

Figure 6-12. The spring reverberation system. The photographs show interior and exterior views of a much improved torsion transmission line, the BX25E Reverberation Unit developed by AKG (Fidi c. 1971).

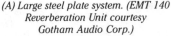

(A) Large steel plate system. (EMT 140
Reverberation Unit courtesy
Gotham Audio Corp.)

(B) Smaller gold foil system. (EMT 240
Reverb Foil courtesy
Gotham Audio Corp.)

Figure 6-13. The reverberation plate. Bending waves travelling through a
large steel plate or a 30 × 30 cm gold foil simulate the natural
reverberant field of a large room.

As a result of Dr. Kuhl's work, the famous EMT 140 Reverberation Unit
became a very popular studio device, with more than 4,000 units installed
worldwide. The EMT 140 was eventually supplanted in 1971 by the smaller EMT
240 Reverb Foil system, in which the large steel plate was replaced by a much
smaller gold foil. Both are shown in Figure 6-13.

On the earliest reverberation plates a single receiving transducer picked up
the bending waves, delivering an output that closely approximated the reverberant sound field of a large room. Later systems—models of the steel plate
produced beginning in 1961 and all gold foil systems—employed two pickup
transducers for stereophonic applications. In either device a damping system can
be used to adjust the reverberation time.

Digital Reverberation Systems

The various delay and reverberation systems described above have been largely
supplanted by devices made possible by digital technology and its constant
companion, the computer.

In the predigital era, the best simulation that could be obtained of the
multiplicity of reflections in any sound field was with a relative handful of discrete
echoes from a delay system, followed by the output(s) of a reverberation system,
as previously described. But with the introduction of the computer, it is—
conceptually, at least—a simple task to calculate the delays and amplitudes of the
hundreds, if not thousands, of echoes heard at any location in any room of known
dimension. Given a set of dimensions such as those seen above in Figure 6-3, a

computer can quickly calculate (almost) all the delays that will reach the listener, along with the amplitude of each one.

In a typical digital reverberation system, the user may be able to program one or more of the following echo and reverberation parameters:

Early reflections
> Arrival time for one or more early reflections
> Direction from which each reflection arrives
> Amplitude of each early reflection
> Frequency response

Echo cluster
> Arrival time of first cluster reflection
> Direction from which cluster arrives (usually, distributed left-center-right)
> Amplitude of first cluster reflection
> Decay of amplitude within cluster
> Frequency response

Reverberation
> Delay before onset
> Arrival direction (usually, of two returns)
> Amplitude at start of reverberation
> Frequency response
> Reverberation time (may be separately adjustable for low, mid, and high frequencies).
> Density (i.e., number and spacing of reflections making up the reverberation program)

A signal flow chart for a typical echo-reverberation system is illustrated in Figure 6-14, and Figure 6-15 shows the control panels of representative systems which allow control of some of the parameters listed above.

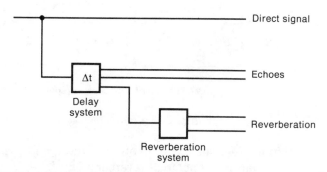

Figure 6-14. Complete echo-reverberation system signal flow chart.

Stereo Reverberation

Often overlooked is the fact that during an actual performance each direct signal comes from a single location, while the resultant echoes and reverberation come

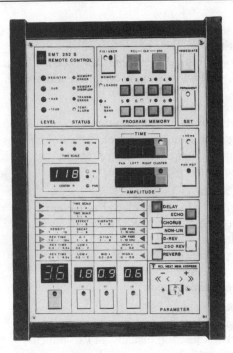

(A) EMT 252 Digital Reverberation
System. (Courtesy Gotham
Audio Corp.)

(B) DN 780 Digital Reverberator/Processor. (Courtesy Klark-Teknik Electronics, Inc.)

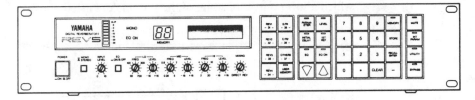

(C) REV5 Digital Reverberator. (Courtesy Yamaha Music Corp., USA)

Figure 6-15. Control panels for digital reverberation systems.

from everywhere else. In other words, the listener should be able to point to an
instrument but not to its reverberation.

Therefore when an instrument is panned to, say, the extreme left, its reverberation return should *not* be panned to the extreme right. Instead, a two-channel
stereo reverberation return should be used, with one return panned left and the
other right. The same technique should be used on any discrete echoes that are
being returned. The direct signal from the instrument itself may be panned as
desired and will partially mask the reverberant information returning from the

same general area. Follow this procedure whenever a reasonably natural effect is wanted; ignore it when something a little less natural is needed.

Recording and Mixdown with Reverberation

The reverberation that sounds right when monitoring or recording a single instrument is rarely right once all the other instruments are added. Although usually a little more reverberation is needed during mixdown, this is not always the case, and it should be remembered that any effect added during recording cannot be removed later on if it no longer seems to work. (For a possible exception, see the section on expanders in Chapter 8, page 311.) Therefore, recording-session reverberation must be applied with some caution. On most modern consoles it's possible to send the reverberation returns to the monitor system only, so that each instrument is recorded *"dry"* (without reverberation) but heard *"wet"* (with reverberation) in the control room. This allows the engineer to hear the effect without being stuck with it later on.

Needless to say, if two or more instruments are combined on a single track, one of them cannot have reverberation applied separately later on. For example, several microphones are usually used on a drum set, with their outputs combined to one or two tape tracks. In this case a little reverberation added just to the snare drum signal may enhance the overall drum sound; the same reverberation added to the entire set later on will probably not work well at all.

Console Control of Echo and Reverberation

Most consoles provide auxiliary controls for sending signals to and from various effects devices, including an echo and/or reverberation system. Although the function of these controls as a console subsystem is described in detail in Chapter 12, their use in echo and reverberation applications is described here.

On most consoles the controls described below are labeled in one of several ways, such as

- Echo send
- Echo return

- Effects send
- Effects return

- Aux[iliary]send
- Aux return

For the sake of consistency, this book uses the *echo* nomenclature, because this is the application for which the controls are most frequently used, as well as the label appearing on many console modules. It should be understood, however, that there is nothing in the control system that limits its use to this application, and that the same set of controls may certainly be used with devices other than echo and reverberation systems.

Pre/Post Echo-Send Controls

On early recording consoles, the pre/post switch described below was permanently associated with the slide fader used to control the level of each incoming signal. It was therefore designated as a pre/postfader switch. However, the modern console usually provides facilities to route an echo-send signal to this switch from one of two locations. Therefore, the switch is usually labeled simply as pre/post, and this book follows that convention. Chapter 12 describes the alternate feeds to the switch in detail (page 489).

Practically every console uses the familiar slide fader to separately adjust the level of each signal before it is combined with other signals. But it is unlikely that the user will want to route all such signals in the same proportion to the same external device. Therefore some additional control is needed to separately adjust each signal prior to sending it to, say, a delay or reverberation system. The control is often a rotary potentiometer, located as shown in Figure 6-16A.

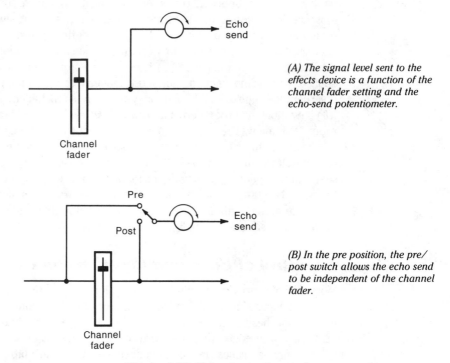

(A) The signal level sent to the effects device is a function of the channel fader setting and the echo-send potentiometer.

(B) In the pre position, the pre/ post switch allows the echo send to be independent of the channel fader.

Figure 6-16. The echo-send control.

Note that the signal sent to the effects device is now a function of two controls: the regular slide fader and the additional echo-send potentiometer. As the potentiometer is turned from full-off to full-on, the echo-send signal varies from zero to whatever maximum is defined by the position of the slide fader. Once a reference position is set, the actual send level will of course vary according to the position of the slide fader.

From Figure 6-16A it should be clear that when the signal passing through the regular signal path is faded out, the effects send also fades out. During the course of a mixdown this is probably desirable, especially if a recorded track is faded down or completely out and then back in again later in the mix; no doubt that track's echo and reverberation should fade out and then in again too. However, a signal fade as just described—and as heard at the tail of practically every hit single that has no real ending—usually sounds as though someone is simply turning down the volume control, which of course is just exactly what is happening.

A more pleasing effect often can be accomplished by fading the direct signal but not the echo-send. When you do so the proportion of direct-to-reflected sound changes, and the instrument or ensemble seems to recede into the distance, leaving just its reverberation behind. Of course this requires a little extra time, because the reverberation must now be faded out as well, but it does create a more interesting fadeout.

The effect may be realized by feeding the echo-send line from a point before the channel fader. Figure 6-16B shows the switching system that permits either a pre- or a postfader send to the effects system. As the figure indicates, the echo-send signal is independent of the channel fader when the switch is in the *pre* position.

The *pre* position also allows the level of the echo-send signal to exceed the channel signal during an entire mixdown, as might be required to simulate the effect of a distant instrument.

Echo-Return Controls

With the exception of a few very early systems, most delay lines and reverberation devices have at least two outputs, and some have more than one input as well. To accommodate such systems most well-equipped consoles provide a pair of echo-return controls for each echo-send line. This allows a signal to be routed to, say, a one-input/two-output delay line or reverberation system. Each output may be separately returned and adjusted at the console as required. The echo-return controls on the console typically are those listed here.

Return Control	Purpose
Level	To mix the returned signal with the direct signal in the desired proportion.
Pan pot	To pan the returned signal between two locations, either two console channels or, more often, the left and right side of a stereo monitor or mixdown system.
Channel select	To select the two channels used by the pan pot.

Note that to create a convincing stereo reverberation effect as described above, one return line should be panned to the extreme left, and the other to the extreme right. If either return is panned to the center position and thereby fed equally to both left and right, the effect will be that of a mono return signal.

Additional Delay Applications

In addition to its role in the modern echo-reverberation system, the ready availability of digital delay makes it useful in many other applications, some of which are described here.

Delaying Microphone Outputs

When a large ensemble is recorded with a stereo microphone or other two-microphone setup, it is often necessary to supplement the overall pickup with one or more accent microphones, to bring out an instrument or a section that is otherwise too low in level.

Compared to the main microphone position, each accent microphone is usually placed at a considerably closer working distance; therefore it picks up its section of the ensemble a bit sooner. As a result, the section is recorded first by the accent microphone and a few milliseconds later by the main pair. There is apt to be some image blurring when the two outputs are combined. Or, each accented section may seem to "leap out" of the ensemble due to the arrival-time differences.

To alleviate this problem, a single delay line may be inserted in the signal path from each accent microphone. The delay is adjusted so that the output is recorded at the same instant the airborne sound reaches the main pair, as shown in Figure 6-17.

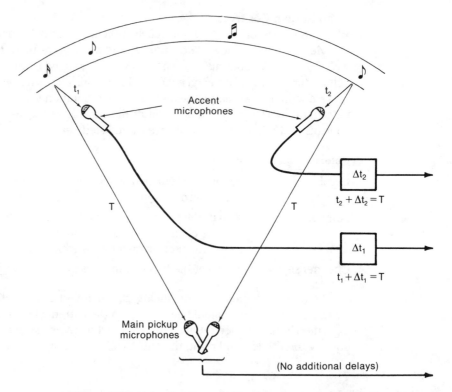

Figure 6-17. Delay lines inserted in the accent microphone lines. The delays are adjusted to coincide with the transit time to the main pickup microphone pair.

Flanging

As described in Chapter 1 (page 13), when a signal is combined with a delayed replica of itself, some frequencies are reinforced and others are cancelled as a result of the time (phase) shift between the direct and the delayed signals. The comb-filter frequency response is shown in Figures 6-18A and B, the difference being whether the signals are combined with the same or opposite polarity, as indicated in the following equations:

Positive Flanging	Negative Flanging
$e = 1 + \cos{(2\pi ft)}$	$e = 1 - \cos{(2\pi ft)}$

The output response plots shown in the figure were made at a fixed delay, *t*, of 0.5 ms, giving the positive and negative notch sequences seen in the illustration. However, when the time shift is continuously varied, these notches will

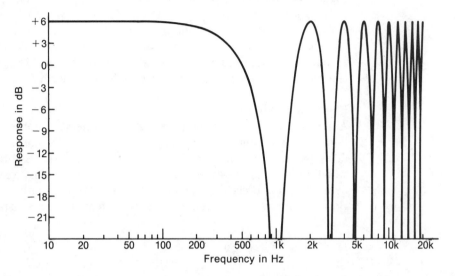

(A) Positive flanging. The delayed output is added to the main signal.

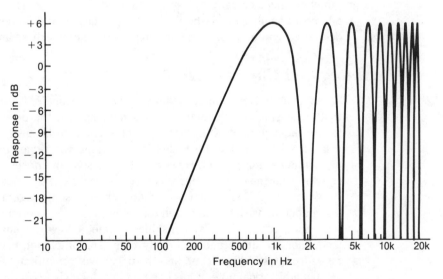

(B) Negative flanging. The delayed output is subtracted from the main signal.

Figure 6-18. The comb-filter effects of flanging. The output notches are moved up and down the frequency spectrum by continuously varying a delay line and combining its output with the nondelayed signal.

sweep up and down the frequency spectrum, producing a very distinctive effect. The effect, which came to be known as flanging, enjoyed brief popularity (some say not brief enough) for a few years beginning in the late 1960s.

The earliest implementation of flanging may be credited to recording engineer George Chkiantz, who fed the same signal to two tape recorders whose outputs were combined. By keeping the speed of one machine constant and slightly varying the speed of the other, the frequency notches swept back and forth as just described. The effect soon found its way to *Itchycoo Park*, a 1967 release by the Small Faces, and from there to a legion of imitators.

Those who lacked other means to vary tape speed found that they could accomplish the desired effect by slowing one of the machines, which they did by leaning on the flange of its supply reel—hence the term *flanging*.

Electronic Flanging

Although modern servo-controlled tape recorders do not tolerate the abuse of flanging (see Chapter 10, page 395), the effect is now available via many electronic delay systems, provided the delay is continuously variable. If the delay is instead varied in increments—even as short as 1 ms—the flanging may be accompanied by a background clicking sound as the delay steps from one value to the next. However, many such incremental delay systems have a separate flanging mode available.

Phasing

Due to the practical difficulties of tape flanging, attempts were made to duplicate the effect electronically by using a phase-shift network. This procedure came to be known as phasing. Although the terms phasing and flanging have sometimes been used synonymously, the phasing effect is not nearly so apparent as flanging.

Doubling and Chorus Effects

When a signal is combined with a *fixed*-delay replica of itself, the effect may be that of hearing two versions of the same signal. If the delay is long enough to isolate the signals in time, but not long enough to be perceived as an obvious echo, the listener may be fooled into thinking the singer or instrumentalist is performing a unison duet. However, this *doubling* or *chorus* effect is not entirely convincing if the delayed signal is an exact replica of the direct signal.

In the case of an actual duet, there is always some slight but continuous time and amplitude variation between the signals. To offer a better simulation of a real-time duet, some delay systems incorporate a low-frequency oscillator which modulates the amplitude and delay time. The amplitude may be varied over a range from 0 to 100 percent, and the delay over several milliseconds.

On a historical note, it has been reported (Lewis 1978) that the term *flanging* may date back to an early application of doubling. Producer George Martin, looking for an alternative to doing actual vocal double-tracking, asked engineer Ken Townsend to come up with something. Townsend fed the sync head output of one machine to the record head of another and mixed the playback outputs of both machines, with the second machine running slightly behind the first one.

Impressed, Beatle John Lennon inquired about this ADT (artificial double track-ing) system, and Townsend explained it as "a double bifurcated sploshing flange." For some time thereafter, ADT was known as flanging, until the term eventually found its way elsewhere, as described in the section on flanging above.

Panning

The time-honored means of moving a signal source from left to right is the ubiquitous pan pot, which is described in detail in Chapter 12 (page 484). Briefly stated, the pan pot achieves its purpose by routing a common signal to two outputs in whatever proportion is required. At the risk of stating the obvious, when the signal is routed to a single speaker the source appears to originate at the location of that speaker—presumably, extreme left or right. The same signal panned to the center (routed equally to both speakers) creates the illusion of a well-centered image, since the listener hears the signal at equal level at each ear.

What may not be so obvious is the solution to the problem of how to create the illusion that a sound source is at some other location, such as left of center, as shown in Figure 6-19A. To understand the potential difficulty, consider an actual sound source present at that location. A single sound wave radiates toward the listener, arriving at the left ear first, and a few milliseconds later at the right ear. However, the sound level difference between left and right ears is, for all practical purposes, zero.

Now consider a signal panned left-of-center. As shown in Figure 6-19B, the signal is simultaneously reproduced by both speakers, with a significant level difference between them. In addition, both speakers are heard by both ears, in the two-step sequence of arrivals given in Table 6-3A.

Table 6-3. Pan Pot/Delay Line Comparisons

(A) Arrival Sequence: Signal Panned Left of Center

1. Left speaker to left ear and right speaker to right ear
2. Left Speaker to right ear and right speaker to left ear

(B) Arrival Sequence: Signal Delayed to Right Speaker*

	or	
1. Left signal to left ear		1. Left signal to left ear
2. Left signal to right ear		2. Right signal to right ear
3. Right signal to right ear		3. Left signal to right ear
4. Right signal to left ear		4. Right signal to left ear

(C) Some Differences Between Actual and Panned Signals

Source Is	Number of Sources	Interaural Level Difference	Interaural Delay
Actual	1	Insignificant	Slight delay at distant ear
Panned	2	Varies according to panpot setting	Delays at both ears from opposing speakers

*The sequence depends on the amount of delay introduced to the right-speaker signal.

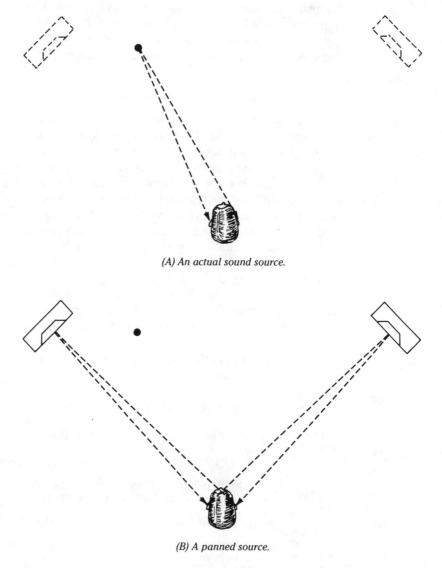

(A) An actual sound source.

(B) A panned source.

Figure 6-19. The signal paths between the listener and two kinds of sources.

Note that at the right ear, the right-speaker signal arrives *before* the left-speaker signal does. So the slight but very important time delay associated with the left-speaker signal is masked, or at least confused, by this earlier arrival. To further confuse things, the interaural delay will be slightly different due to the difference in angle between the speaker and the apparent or actual source, both measured with respect to the listener and indicated in Figure 6-19. Table 6-3C summarizes these differences.

By now it should be apparent that there are differences between an actual off-center source and a panned image of that source, and that a delay line may be a viable alternative to that pan pot. By delaying (but not attenuating) the signal to the right speaker, the two-step arrival sequence given in Table 6-3 becomes one of the four-step sequences also listed in the table. The sequence seen in the left-hand column applies whenever the introduced delay is longer than the interaural delay, as would be the case in most circumstances. Although this setup also does not duplicate reality, it often allows a little more latitude in positioning sources at off-center locations. It should at least be tried a few times to reinforce the power of the Haas Effect described earlier in the chapter (page 223).

Sound Reinforcement

Due to the Haas effect, the ear/brain combination tends to localize a sound source at the location from which it arrives first. For example, if the listener is closer to a loudspeaker than to the actual sound source, as shown in Figure 6-20, the source will seem to originate at the loudspeaker and not at its actual location.

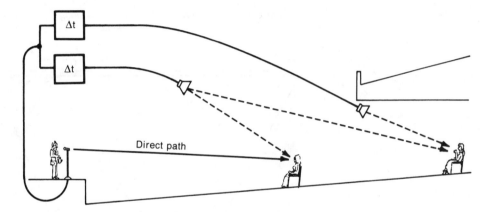

Figure 6-20. The paths between a listener and the actual and reproduced sound source. To maintain the illusion that all sound originates at the actual source, the amplified signals must be delayed so that they reach the listener after the direct signal.

To remedy the problem, the speaker feed may be delayed by whatever it takes to allow the direct sound to reach the listener first. Practical experience has shown that 30 milliseconds is a useful limit for the difference in time of arrival for speech signals (Klepper 1975). Provided the reinforced sound arrives within that limit, the direct and delayed signals will reinforce each other, and the signal will seem to originate at the site of the actual sound source. Once the delay between direct and amplified signal exceeds about 30 milliseconds, intelligibility deteriorates.

Additional delay lines may be needed if there is an area in which listeners are in a path from two or more speakers, as also shown in Figure 6-20.

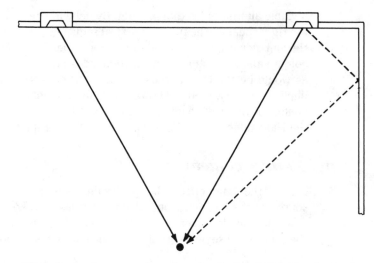

(A) A reflection from a nearby wall reaches the listening position shortly after the direct sound.

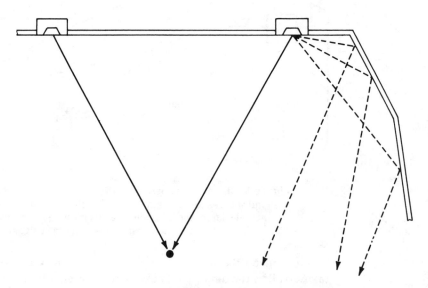

(B) Corner detail showing wall surfaces angled so that early reflected-path signals do not reach the listening position.

Figure 6-21. Control room reflections.

Echo, Reverberation, and Control Room Acoustics

In the ideal environment one judges the quality of the recording without being influenced by the quality of the listening room. Presumably, the desired mix of

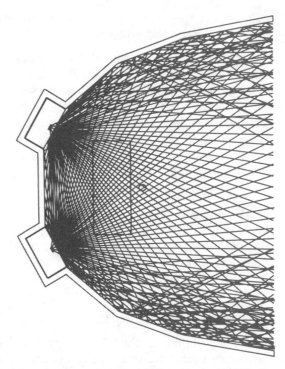

(C) Plan view of control room using principle shown in detail in (B). (Courtesy Mix Magazine)

Figure 6-21 *(continued)*

direct sound, echo, and reverberation is already on the master tape and this mix should not be modified by yet another set of variables, such as the walls, floor, and ceiling of a control room, to say nothing of the hardware arsenal scattered about that room.

Meanwhile, back in the real world of studio acoustics, there's no such thing as an ideal listening environment, especially in a control room. On one hand it's probably too small, and on the other too cluttered with sound-reflecting devices that would not be tolerated in anyone's serious listening room. We must therefore make do with the next best thing—a well-designed control room whose acoustic influence on reproduced sound is kept to a reasonable minimum.

There is no universal agreement on how such a room should be designed, and there are several conflicting theories on the ideal location for reflective and absorptive surfaces within the room. This section will acquaint the reader with a few potential problems, but will stop short of adding still more confusion by proposing another ideal solution to add to those already in circulation.

As discussed earlier in the chapter, a sound source creates a complex mixture of direct sound, early reflections, echo cluster, and reverberation within the room. The perceptions of a listener in the same room are influenced by the resultant sound field. But when that sound field is instead recorded and played back in another location, yet another set of echoes and reverberation is created. Since the typical control room space is much smaller than the recording space, the new set imposes a conflicting sound field on the recording. Given the relatively shorter distances to the nearby surfaces in the control room, these new echoes may create two problems:

- Each echo creates a comb-filter effect such as shown above in Figure 6-18 when it combines with the direct signal at the engineer's position. Although the filter effect does not sweep up and down, it does change from one position to another due to the different direct-to-reflected distance ratios at each incremental listening position.

- The echoes reach the listener much sooner than do those that are recorded on tape. As an understanding of the Haas Effect (page 223) might suggest, the recording may therefore sound like it was recorded in a much smaller space.

Figure 6-21A shows a potential reflection problem created by a nearby reflective wall surface, and Figure 6-21B offers the solution of orienting the wall so that reflections from it pass behind the engineer's listening position. Figure 6-21C shows a plan view of a control room in which all nearby surfaces are splayed for the same reason (Morrison 1988).

LEDE Control Room Design

As another alternative, the LEDE™ (Live End, Dead End™) system specifies that the front surfaces be acoustically absorbent, while the rear of the room is reflective (Davis 1979). The LEDE design goal (Davis 1980) is to create the following sequence of arrivals at the engineer's position:

1. The direct sound from the studio
2. The first studio reflection
3. The first control room reflection

If the rear wall is, say, 10 feet behind the engineer, then the first control-room reflection arrives at the engineer's position about 18 milliseconds after the direct sound from the speaker. The LEDE design makes the assumption that during that interval the first reflection from within the studio will have been heard over the monitor system. Therefore, the later-arriving first control-room reflection does not detract from the acoustics of the studio (once again, evidence of the power of the Haas Effect).

Close-Field Monitoring

A *close-field* monitor system is simply a pair of speakers mounted close to the engineer's position—often directly above the console meter panel, as shown in Figure 6-22. The technique is often used to minimize the influence of the control room on the sound field at the engineer's position. By placing the speakers so close to the listener, the ratio of direct-to-reflected energy is much greater.

Since close-field speakers are usually much smaller than the regular studio monitors, there are both advantages and disadvantages to their use. Perhaps the greatest advantage is that the visiting engineer or producer can easily bring in a pair of familiar speakers to use as a convenient frame of reference and by placing

Figure 6-22. A close-field monitoring system at Record Plant Studio 1, Los Angeles, showing two USCO Audio Engineering DTM-3 speakers on a Neve Series V console. Control room and main monitor system designed by Tom Hidley. *(Courtesy Record Plant)*

them so close "tune out" the effects of an unfamiliar environment. Such speakers are also a little closer than the studio super system to what the typical listener may have at home. However, the small size of the close-field speakers means that their bass response is not equal to the studio monitors, which are much larger.

In popular usage the term *near field* is sometimes seen in this context. However, the near field is actually a much smaller area in the immediate vicinity of a loudspeaker, as described in Chapter 1 (page 32).

7 Equalization

The term *equalizer* describes any signal processing device whose primary function is to modify the frequency response of the signal passing through it. The first such devices were introduced in the early days of telephony and film, to compensate for the low- and high-frequency losses incurred during transmission or recording. The devices were designed to make the output response the equal of the original input; hence, *equalizer* for the device, *equalization* for what it did.

Today's control-room equalizer goes far beyond its original function, and in fact might be better called an *un*equalizer. For with the exception of those built into a tape recorder, most if not all equalizers today are used to modify a signal so that it is anything but the equal of some input signal. A little closer to the original concept is the sound reinforcement equalizer, whose purpose is to compensate for any system and/or room anomalies so that the system delivers a reasonable replica of the system input.

Equalizers may be classified as either passive or active, with several design variations found within each category.

Definitions

A few terms to be encountered in this chapter are given brief definitions here. In most cases further details are provided later on, in the appropriate section.

Passive Equalizer.   A *passive* element is any circuit component that is not a source of energy, such as a resistor, a capacitor, or an inductor. A *passive equalizer* is an equalizer whose circuit consists entirely of such passive elements. Therefore it may be used only to attenuate certain frequencies or frequency ranges.

Active Equalizer.   An *active* element is any component capable of producing a signal gain. Active components include the transistor and vacuum tube. Thus, an *active equalizer* is an equalizer capable of boosting and/or attenuating certain frequencies or frequency ranges.

Filter.   A *filter* is any network that attenuates a portion of the audio frequency spectrum. An equalizer contains one or more filter sections and is often referred to as a filter itself, especially when describing its attenuation characteristics.

First- and Second-Order Filters.   The order number of a filter refers to the number of reactive elements in its circuit. Thus, a first-order filter contains one capacitor (or inductor), a second-order filter has two, or one of each, and so on.

Lowpass Filter.   This is an equalizer in which attenuation increases with frequency. As the name suggests, a *lowpass filter* passes low frequencies with little or no attenuation.

Highpass Filter.   In contrast to the lowpass filter, the attenuation in a *highpass filter* decreases with frequency, thereby passing high frequencies with little or no attenuation.

Bandpass Filter.   A *bandpass filter* attenuates low and high frequencies, while a contiguous band of midrange frequencies is passed without attenuation.

Bandstop Filter.   This type of filter attenuates a contiguous band of midrange frequencies, while passing frequencies on either side of this band without attenuation.

Shelving Filter.   In some filters a rising (or falling) response eventually levels off at a fixed gain or attenuation shelf; hence the term *shelving filter.*

Pass Band.   In any of the filters described above, a *pass band* is any contiguous band of frequencies passed with 3 dB or less attenuation.

Stop Band.   A *stop band* is any contiguous band of frequencies attenuated by a specified amount (not necessarily 3 dB). For example, a 6 dB stop band is the range that is attenuated by 6 dB or more.

Cutoff Frequency (f_1, f_2).   The frequency at which a filter output reaches a point 3 dB below its maximum output is known as its *cutoff frequency,* or *cutoff point.* In the case of a bandpass or bandstop filter, there are two cutoff frequencies; one at either end of the pass band or stop band. The lower cutoff is usually identified as f_1, the higher as f_2. The cutoff frequency was previously introduced in Chapter 5 (page 162).

Center Frequency (f_c).   This refers to the geometric mean between cutoff frequencies. The center frequency between cutoff frequencies of $f_1 = 100$ and $f_2 = 1,000$ Hz is

$$f_c = [f_1(f_2)]^{1/2} = [100(1,000)]^{1/2} = 316.23 \text{ Hz} \tag{7-1}$$

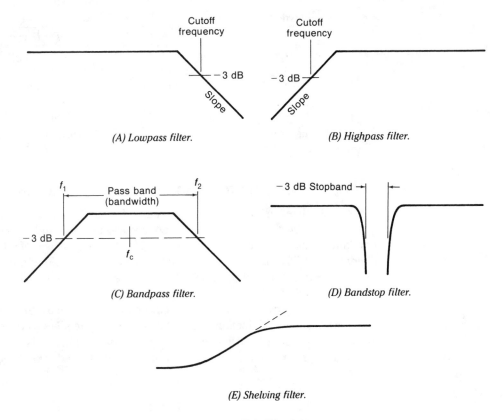

(A) Lowpass filter.

(B) Highpass filter.

(C) Bandpass filter.

(D) Bandstop filter.

(E) Shelving filter.

Figure 7-1. Filter types.

Bandwidth (B). This is the difference between the lower and the upper cutoff frequencies. Thus, the bandwidth, B, of an equalizer with cutoff frequencies of 200 and 2,000 Hz is

$$B = f_2 - f_1 = 2,000 - 200 = 1,800 \text{ Hz} \qquad (7\text{-}2)$$

Quality Factor (Q). The *quality factor* of a bandpass or bandstop equalizer is not a measure of the device's excellence. Instead, Q is the ratio of the center frequency to the bandwidth. Thus,

$$Q = f_c/B = f_c/(f_2 - f_1) \qquad (7\text{-}3)$$

Thus, the narrower the bandwidth, the higher the Q.

Slope. Beyond cutoff, the *slope* of a high- or lowpass response curve defines the rate at which attenuation rises or falls with frequency. The slope is $6n$ dB per octave, where n is the filter's order number (actually, it is $6.02n$ dB, but it's usually rounded off as shown). The slope is sometimes expressed in dB per decade. Since the decade is an interval of 3.322 octaves, the former may be converted to the latter by multiplying by 3.322, as shown here.

Order	Slope	
n	Per Octave	Per Decade
1	6 dB	20 dB
2	12	40
3	18	60

Figure 7-1 briefly summarizes much of the information presented above; further details and additional definitions are found throughout the rest of this chapter.

Calculating Cutoff Frequencies

It should be kept in mind that if the center frequency and bandwidth are both known, the lower and upper cutoff frequencies are *not* found by simple subtraction and addition. For example, given a center frequency of 500 Hz and a bandwidth of 250 Hz, f_1 and f_2 are not 375 Hz (500 − 125) and 625 Hz (500 + 125), respectively, although these values may be close enough to the actual values (390.388 and 640.388 Hz) for most applications.

When accuracy is required, the cutoff frequencies may be found from the following procedure (which may be safely ignored by readers who would prefer to avoid another bout of mathematics). Assuming the bandwidth is known, equation (7-2) may be rewritten as $f_2 = f_1 + B$, and then substituted for f_2 in equation (7-1). Thus,

$$f_c = [f_1(f_1 + B)]^{1/2} = [f_1^2 + Bf_1]^{1/2}$$

Therefore,

$$f_c^2 = f_1^2 + Bf_1$$

and so,

$$f_1^2 + Bf_1 - f_c^2 = 0$$

or, in quadratic form,

$$f_1 = \frac{-B \pm [B^2 - 4f_c^2]^{1/2}}{2} = \frac{-250 \pm [250^2 - 4(500^2)]^{1/2}}{2} \qquad \text{(7-4)}$$

Solving for the positive root,

$$f_1 = 390.388 \text{ Hz}$$

and

$$f_2 = f_1 + 250 = 640.388 \text{ Hz}$$

Expressing Bandwidth in Octaves

The next procedure (Bohn 1983) is useful for expressing the bandwidth, in octaves, when Q is known. First, find the positive root of an intermediate value, y, and then the octave interval, N. From these two values, the cutoff frequencies for any center frequency may also be found. The necessary equations are given below, along with a worked-out example in the right-hand column based on $Q = 2$ and $f_c = 500$ Hz. As above, the exercise may be skipped until needed.

$$Q = 2 \tag{7-5}$$

$$y = \frac{2Q^2 + 1}{2Q^2} \pm \left[\frac{(2Q^2 + 1)/Q^2)^2}{4} - 1\right]^{1/2} = 1.6404 \text{ (positive root)}$$

$$N = \log(y)/\log(2) = 0.714$$

Therefore, for any bandpass filter with a Q of 2, the bandwidth is 0.714 octave, and the cutoff frequencies are 0.357 octave on either side of the center frequency, or

$$f_2 = f_c \times 2^{N/2} = 500(2^{0.357}) = 640.388 \text{ Hz}$$
$$f_1 = f_c \times 2^{-N/2} = 500(2^{-0.357}) = 390.388 \text{ Hz}$$

To verify the octave interval between these frequencies,

$$B = \frac{\log(640.388/390.388)}{\log(2)}$$

$$= 0.714 \text{ octave}$$

For more details about the relationship between frequency and octave intervals, see the section on One-Third and One-Half Octaves in Chapter 2 (p. 44).

Equalizer Categories

The following sections cover the circuit building blocks that are used in most professional equalizers. To keep components to a minimum and explanations reasonably brief, the equalizer circuits described here comprise one or two simple first-order filters. Although the actual professional-quality equalizer is considerably more complex than many of these examples, the basic principles of operation are nevertheless the same.

For the sake of some explanations an inductor (coil) is used as a high-frequency attenuator. However, modern circuit design often replaces the inductor with a *gyrator filter*, that is, an *RC* network that synthesizes the characteristics of an inductor (Bohn 1988).

In some equalizer texts, attenuation is plotted on a rising vertical scale; the greater the attenuation, the higher the curve. Because this convention seems contrary to an understanding of what an equalizer actually does, this book follows the more conventional amplitude tradition, in which up is more, and down is less. Putting it another way, a rising curve indicates increasing gain—or, in a passive equalizer, decreasing attenuation.

> **NOTE:** For comparison purposes most graphs in the following section are plotted with either a cutoff frequency or a center frequency of 500 Hz, as appropriate. Since 20 Hz (at the left-hand edge of each graph) is 4.64 octaves below 500 Hz, on some graphs a vertical line is placed 4.64 octaves *above* 500 Hz, at 12,467 Hz. This makes it easier to compare the lower and upper halves of graphs that are symmetrical about the center-frequency axis.

The vertical scale for most graphs is either 3 dB or 10 degrees per division, as appropriate. In Figures 7-6 through 7-9, three sets of contours are plotted for each filter type. Again for the sake of making comparisons, the cutoff frequencies are always as listed below.

Figures 7-6 Through 7-9	High Frequency (Hz)	Low Frequency (Hz)
Part (A)	500	500
Part (B)	125	2,000
Part (C)	2,000	125

Filter Design

Although a detailed discussion of network theory and filter design is well beyond the scope of this book, a few points are presented here to give the reader a general understanding of how a filter network operates. The information is based on a second-order lowpass Butterworth filter. Butterworth, Tchebycheff, and other names refer to specific filter designs that are covered in greater detail elsewhere (Shepherd 1985).

It is common practice in filter design to begin with one of the simple reference circuits shown in Figure 7-2. The reference component values are given in Table 7-1.

Table 7-1. Filter Network Reference Circuit Components

Circuit Component		Matched Load*	Bridged Load**
Source impedance	R_i	1 ohm	1 ohm
Load impedance	R_o	1 ohm	open circuit
Inductance	L_1	1.414 henries	0.707 henries
Capacitance	C_2	1.414 farads	1.414 farads
Cutoff frequency	f_c	1 radian per second	1 radian per second

*As shown in Figure 7-2A.
**As shown in Figure 7-2B.

The inductance and capacitance values are generally taken from one of many readily available tables of element values for filters (for example, Geffe 1966,

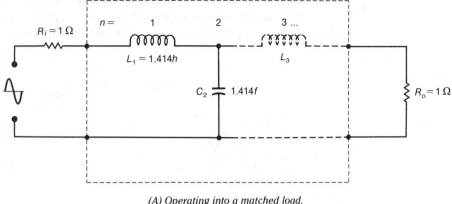

(A) Operating into a matched load.

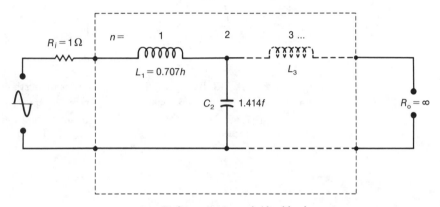

(B) Operating into a bridged load.

Figure 7-2. Reference design circuits for a second-order lowpass filter.

Shepherd 1985). Additional values are usually given for higher order filters as well. The second-order lowpass Butterworth filter for which values are given here has 3 dB attenuation at the cutoff frequency. Higher values for L_1 and C_2 would provide greater attenuation at the cutoff point, and vice versa. A complementary highpass filter may be designed by simply swapping the positions of all capacitors and inductors and using the reciprocals of the values seen above. Thus, $L_1 = 1/C_2$, $C_2 = 1/L_1$, etc.

To find the inductance and capacitance values required for a practical circuit, simply replace the 1-ohm impedance and 1-radian frequency with the desired values and then multiply the inductance and capacitance values given above by

$$L = L_1 R_i / 2\pi f_c$$
$$C = C_2 / 2\pi f_c R_i$$

where
R_i = source impedance, in ohms
f_c = cutoff frequency, in hertz

Figure 7-3 shows a family of response curves for first-order through fourth-order bandpass filters, each with cutoff frequencies of 125 and 2,000 Hz. Then the following sections provide more details about first- and second-order filters.

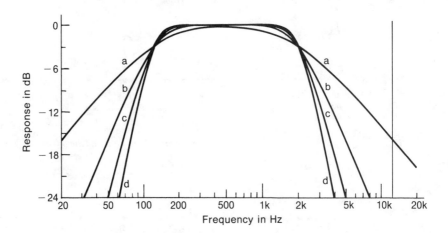

Figure 7-3. Bandpass filters of first-order to fourth-order.

Curve	Order	dB/Octave	Curve	Order	dB/Octave
(a)	First	6	(c)	Third	18
(b)	Second	12	(d)	Fourth	24

First-Order Filters

The simplest equalizer is nothing more than a single reactive component placed in series or parallel with the load. The addition of a variable series resistor allows a family of response curves to be drawn, as shown in the following examples.

The bandpass and bandstop filters described later in this section are considered—again for the sake of keeping things simple—as combinations of two first-order filters.

For readers who would like a closer look at how a simple filter works, the lowpass filter section concludes with a brief analysis of a few circuit details; the general principles apply as well to a highpass filter. However, the analysis is not essential to the rest of the chapter and may be skipped if so desired.

Lowpass Filter

The *lowpass filter* shown in Figure 7-4A passes frequencies below cutoff with minimum attenuation due to the negligible effect of the shunt capacitor seen in the figure. In other words, the shunt impedance is quite high compared to the series resistance, R_1. At the cutoff frequency the ratio of shunt-to-total impedance has decreased to 1:1.414, so the output level is 20 log(1/1.414) = − 3 dB. Beyond cutoff the shunt impedance continues to decrease, so response falls off at a constant per-octave rate over the remainder of the audio spectrum. The schematic in the figure is that of a first-order lowpass filter, and its output response is shown in Figure 7-4C.

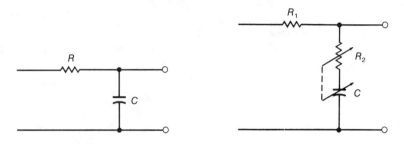

(A) A simple first-order lowpass filter.

(B) The addition of a potentiometer allows various high-frequency attenuation shelves to be introduced. To maintain a fixed cutoff frequency, a ganged variable capacitor must be used.

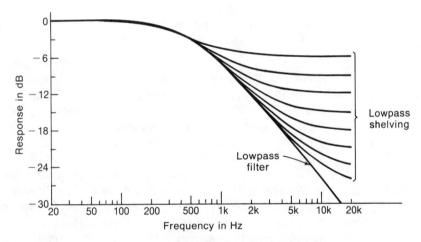

(C) A family of lowpass filter curves. The bottom curve is from the filter shown in (A) and the other curves are from the lowpass shelving filter shown in (B).

Figure 7-4. Two first-order lowpass filters and their output responses.

Lowpass Shelving Filter

In a *lowpass shelving filter* (Figure 7-4B), response beyond the cutoff frequency starts to fall off as just described, but only within a transition zone where the capacitive reactance is still considerably greater than R_2. As the reactance continues to diminish, the response flattens out to an attenuation "shelf" defined by the ratio of $R_2/(R_1 + R_2)$.

A family of lowpass shelving curves is also shown in Figure 7-4. As shown, the crossover point is maintained at the same frequency for all curves—500 Hz in this illustration. However, this complicates the circuit design, since the capacitor must now also be variable and ganged with the potentiometer. If a fixed capacitor is used, the crossover frequency drops as the shelf level increases.

Since the effect of every lowpass filter is the attenuation of high frequencies, it is often referred to by a term that better describes what it actually does, such as high-frequency rolloff, high-end cut, etc.

Lowpass Circuit Analysis

For the filter in Figure 7-4A, the attenuation across the capacitor may be found as follows:

$$Z_c = X_c$$
$$Z_t = (1 + X_c^2)^{1/2}$$
$$E = Z_c/Z_t$$
$$N = 20 \log E$$

where
Z_t = total impedance
X_c = capacitance or inductance
Z_c = shunt impedance (= X_c)
Z_t = total impedance
E = voltage across the shunt impedance
N = attenuation, in dB

Since the reactive element is a capacitor, the reactance, X_c, and shunt impedance, Z_c, are very high at low frequencies. Therefore the ratio of $Z_c{:}Z_t$ (= E) is very close to unity, and there is almost no attenuation across the capacitor. However, for each doubling of frequency, capacitive reactance is halved, so the $Z_c{:}Z_t$ ratio decreases and attenuation increases.

Table 7-2A shows how all these values vary with frequency. In addition, the slope of the response curve is also given. Note that the slope eventually reaches -6 dB per octave, as it should for a simple first-order filter.

Remember that the frequency column actually lists multipliers to be used with whatever cutoff frequency is required. Therefore the values for Z_c and Z_t will change according to the selected frequency. However, the ratio, attenuation, and slope will remain as shown in the table. For example, at a cutoff frequency of 1 (= 500 Hz), the attenuation values and slope agree with the lowpass contour shown in Figure 7-4C (bottom curve).

To conclude the circuit review, it was noted earlier that when a variable resistance, R_2, is inserted (Figure 7-4B) to create a family of shelving contours, the capacitance must also vary if the cutoff frequency is to be held constant. This is because the shunt impedance, Z_c, is now a function of both R_2 and C. So if R_2 varies, so also must C in order to maintain the correct shunt impedance. To find R_2, we first assume that at the upper end of the frequency spectrum the capacitive reactance will be zero. Therefore, high-frequency attenuation is strictly a function of R_1 and R_2. Assuming that $R_1 = 1$ ohm (our reference value),

$$k = 10^{-N/20}$$
$$R_2 = k/(1 - k)$$

Table 7-2. Lowpass Filter Values

(A) Lowpass Filter Frequency, Impedances, Attenuation, and Slope*					
	Impedances				
Frequency	Z_c	Z_t	Z_c/Z_t	**Attenuation**	**Slope**
0.004	256.000	256.002	1.0000	0.000	0.000
0.008	128.000	128.004	1.0000	0.000	0.000
0.016	64.000	64.008	0.9999	0.001	0.001
0.031	32.000	32.016	0.9995	0.004	0.003
0.063	16.000	16.031	0.9981	0.017	0.013
0.125	8.000	8.062	0.9923	0.067	0.050
0.250	4.000	4.123	0.9701	0.263	0.196
0.500	2.000	2.236	0.8944	0.969	0.706
1.000	1.000	1.414	0.7071	3.010	2.041
2.000	0.500	1.118	0.4472	6.988	3.979
4.000	0.250	1.031	0.2425	12.032	5.314
8.000	0.125	1.008	0.1240	18.126	5.824
16.000	0.063	1.002	0.0624	24.095	5.969
32.000	0.031	1.000	0.0312	30.102	6.007
64.000	0.016	1.000	0.0156	36.118	6.016
128.000	0.008	1.000	0.0078	42.137	6.019
256.000	0.004	1.000	0.0039	48.156	6.019

(B) R and C for Various Shelving Levels**		
Level	R_2	**C**
−3	2.424	0.000
−6	1.005	0.705
−9	0.550	0.744
−12	0.335	0.799
−15	0.216	0.848
−18	0.144	0.886
−21	0.098	0.916
−24	0.067	0.939
−27	0.047	0.955

*As shown in Figure 7-4A.
**As shown in Figure 7-4B.

where

N = attenuation in dB.

The next task is to find the capacitance required for any value of resistance. From basic circuit theory,

$$Z_c = (R_2{}^2 + X_c{}^2)^{1/2}$$

and

$$Z_t = [(1 + R_2)^2 + X_c{}^2]^{1/2}$$

and for 3 dB attenuation at f_c,

$$-3/20 = -0.150 = \log(Z_c/Z_t)$$

Therefore,

$$Z_c/Z_t = 0.708$$

$$Z_c = 0.708Z_t$$

$$(R_2{}^2 + X_c{}^2)^{1/2} = 0.708[(1 + R_2)^2 + X_c{}^2]^{1/2}$$

$$X_c = \frac{[0.501(1 + R_2)^2 - R_2{}^2]^{1/2}}{0.499}$$

And finally,

$$C = 1/X_c = 0.499[0.501(1 + R_2)^2 - R_2{}^2]^{1/2} \tag{7-6}$$

Table 7-2B lists the resistance and capacitance required for the shelving attenuation contours shown in Figure 7-4C (all but the bottom curve). Note, however, that the response for a -3 dB shelf is not shown. In order for the response to be down 3 dB both at the cutoff and on the shelf, the capacitance would have to be zero; in other words, the lowpass filter response would now be just a flat line, 3 dB down across the entire frequency spectrum. This can be verified by first finding the resistance required for 3 dB of attenuation, which is 2.424 ohms. Inserting this value in equation (7-6) gives us $C = 0$.

With a bit of reverse engineering, the general principles discussed in this section may be applied as well to the highpass filter. However, this little project is left as an exercise for those readers who still have not had enough circuit analysis.

Highpass Filter

The output response of a *highpass filter* is the mirror image of the lowpass filter described above—frequencies above cutoff are passed with minimum attenuation. As frequency decreases below the cutoff, response falls at a constant per-octave rate. Figure 7-5A shows a first-order highpass filter schematic whose output response is seen in part (C) of the same figure.

Highpass Shelving Filter
In a *highpass shelving filter* frequencies below cutoff fall off until reaching a low-frequency attenuation shelf. Figure 7-5C shows a family of such curves, plotted

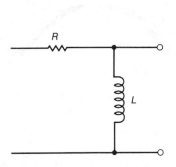

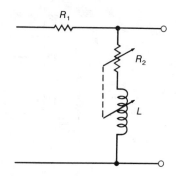

(A) A simple first-order highpass filter.

(B) The addition of a potentiometer allows various low-frequency attenuation shelves to be introduced. To maintain a fixed cutoff frequency, a ganged variable inductor must be used.

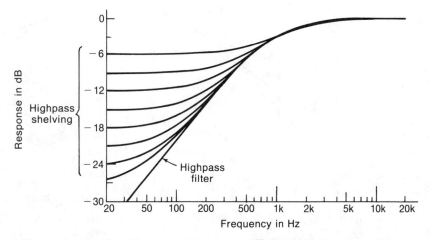

(C) A family of highpass filter curves. The bottom curve is from the filter shown in (A) and the other curves are from the highpass shelving filter shown in (B).

Figure 7-5. Two first-order highpass filters and their output responses.

with a 1,000 Hz cutoff to better illustrate the low-end shelving. The fixed cutoff frequency requires a ganged variable inductor, as shown in Figure 7-5B.

Like its lowpass counterpart, the highpass filter is often referred to by a more descriptive term, such as low-frequency rolloff or low-end cut.

Bandpass Filter

If the output of a lowpass filter is fed to the input of a highpass filter (or vice versa), frequencies on either side of the selected center frequency are attenuated, resulting in the family of response curves shown in Figure 7-6A. The filter is called a *bandpass filter* because it passes a band of frequencies, which in the figure is centered about 500 Hz.

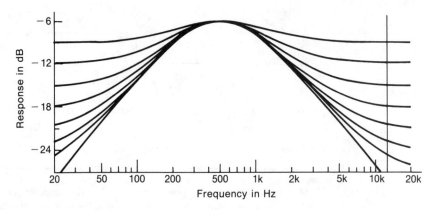

(A) Highpass, 500 Hz; lowpass, 500 Hz.

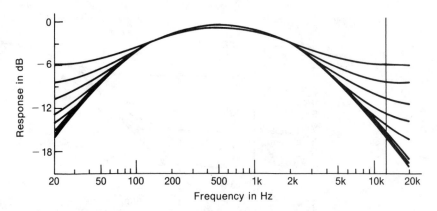

(B) Highpass 125 Hz; lowpass, 2,000 Hz.

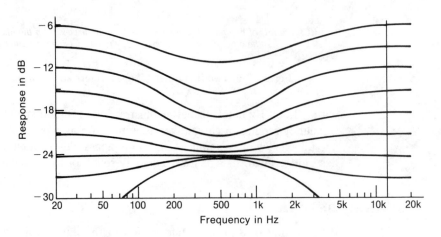

(C) Highpass, 2,000 Hz; lowpass, 125 Hz.

Figure 7-6. Bandpass filter response curves. Low- and highpass filter outputs are multiplied, and cutoff frequencies are given in the subcaptions.

Note that the minimum attenuation of the filter is now 6 dB, and that each curve reaches this level at 500 Hz. To check the validity of this, remember that both the low- and the highpass sections are by definition 3 dB down at cutoff, and therefore each section's output voltage is $0.707E_{max}$. When filters are combined in series their outputs are multiplied, so at the cutoff frequency the output voltage, e_o, is

$$
\begin{aligned}
e_o &= 20 \log [e_{HPF}e_{LPF}] \\
&= 20 \log [0.707(0.707)] \\
&= 20 \log 0.5 \\
&= -6 \text{ dB}
\end{aligned}
$$

Figure 7-6 also shows the effect of shifting the cutoff frequencies. In Figure 7-6B the highpass cutoff is lowered two octaves and the lowpass cutoff is raised two octaves, to 125 and 2,000 Hz respectively. These actions simultaneously expand the pass band downward and upward, thus giving a wider bandwidth than when both cutoffs were at 500 Hz. The bandwidth may be widened further by continuing to shift the cutoffs in these relative directions, until eventually all filtering action takes place outside the audio bandwidth and the filter is in effect out of the circuit.

Figure 7-6C shows the effect of moving each cutoff in the opposite direction, that is, of raising the highpass and lowering the lowpass cutoff. Note, however, that this action does not narrow the bandwidth (as compared to Figure 7-6A), but instead gives a new family of low- and high-frequency shelving curves centered about 500 Hz.

In either case the entire contour may now be shifted by moving both cutoffs downward or upward, as desired. For example, if both cutoffs are raised one octave (to 250 and 4,000 Hz), the contours will be centered about the geometric mean frequency of $[250(4,000)]^{1/2} = 1,000$ Hz.

Bandstop (Notch) Filter

A *bandstop filter* is a filter that sharply attenuates a narrow band of frequencies. It is often referred to as a *notch filter* due to its distinctive response contour, as shown in Figure 7-7. The curves were plotted by subtracting the outputs of the low- and highpass filters described above.

As in Figure 7-6, the figure also shows the effect of shifting each cutoff frequency by two octaves. Note, however, that shifts in either direction cause the stop band to widen, but by different amounts. In the first case (Figure 7-7B), the center band is attenuated by both filter sections. Next (Figure 7-7C), the center band is passed by both sections, but then cancelled when the section outputs are subtracted.

Shelving Filter

When high- and lowpass filter outputs are combined through a summing network their outputs are added, creating the family of shelving contours shown in Figure 7-8A. Since most frequencies are now passed with minimum attenuation by either

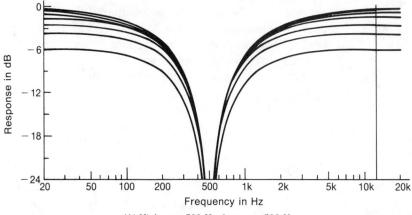

(A) Highpass, 500 Hz; lowpass, 500 Hz.

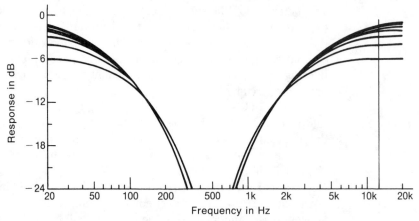

(B) Highpass, 125 Hz; lowpass, 2,000 Hz.

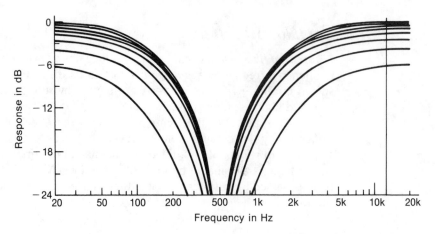

(C) Highpass, 2,000 Hz; lowpass, 125 Hz.

Figure 7-7. Bandstop (notch) filter response curves. Low- and highpass filter outputs are subtracted, and cutoff frequencies are given in the subcaptions.

the high- or the lowpass filter, the net effect of the summation is a slight shelving action on either side of the center frequency. The center frequency output is 20 log (0.707 + 0.707) = +3 dB.

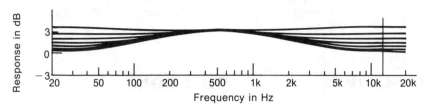

(A) Highpass, 500 Hz; lowpass, 500 Hz.

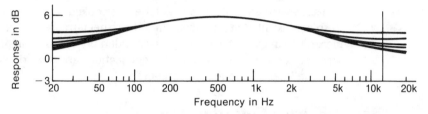

(B) Highpass, 125 Hz; lowpass, 2,000 Hz.

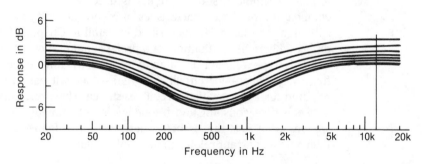

(C) Highpass, 2,000 Hz; lowpass, 125 Hz.

Figure 7-8. Shelving contours created by adding the outputs of a low- and a highpass filter. The cutoff frequencies are given in the subcaptions.

Again, the figure shows the effect of shifting the center frequencies. As the highpass cutoff is decreased and the lowpass cutoff is increased, the band surrounding the center frequency is boosted as shown in Figure 7-8B. The reason for the boost is that a comparatively wide band of frequencies is now passed with little attenuation by both filter sections. By contrast Figure 7-8C shows the opposite effect. Here, both filter sections attenuate the center-frequency area, resulting in a deeper falloff—again with shelving on either side.

Boost/Cut Shelving Filter
Since we have so far multiplied, subtracted, and added the outputs of highpass and lowpass filters, it follows that the same outputs might also be divided. This is generally accomplished by inserting the filter section in a negative feedback loop.

Figure 7-9 shows the family of contours that result when the output of a highpass filter is divided by the output of a lowpass filter (E_L/E_C). The response begins on a boosted low-frequency shelf, is then attenuated through cutoff, and eventually levels off on a high-frequency shelf. In each case, if the division were reversed (E_C/E_L), the response curves would be a mirror image of those seen in the figure.

First-Order Filter Applications

Since the slope of the n-order filter networks described above is $6n$ dB per octave, the basic first-order filter is probably not adequate for many equalization applications. Nevertheless it should not be overlooked when a slight modification of response is all that's needed. In a few special cases—such as the notch filter described above—the slope gets considerably steeper, approaching 12 dB per octave. This is because two first-order sections are at work within the same band and the filter is, in effect, second-order.

Tape Recorder Equalization

A pair of simple first-order filters is used in analog tape recorder circuits to compensate for the characteristics of record and playback head characteristics. Although tape heads are described in detail in Chapter 9, the filter sections are discussed here as an example of a professional first-order filter application.

This type of filter is often described by time constant instead of cutoff frequency, which—for circuit designers—makes it easy to find the capacitance required for any specified circuit resistance. However, because the relationship between time constant and frequency is not immediately obvious, others may wonder what it is that is being described. The following section shows how a filter's time constant relates to its cutoff frequency.

Time Constant (*t*)
The *time constant*, in seconds, of a simple first-order filter is the product of circuit resistance and capacitance, in ohms and farads, respectively. To find one from the other,

$$f = 1/2\pi t$$

or

$$t = 1/2\pi f = RC$$

Thus, if the cutoff frequency is 500 Hz, the time constant is
$$t = 1/(2\pi 500)$$
$$= 1/3142$$
$$= 318 \times 10^{-6} \text{ s} = 318 \ \mu s \text{ (microseconds)}$$

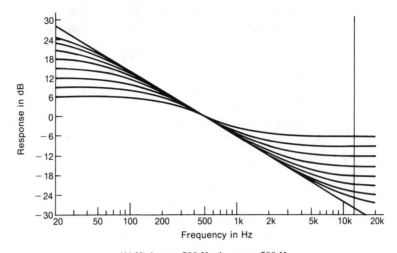

(A) Highpass, 500 Hz; lowpass, 500 Hz.

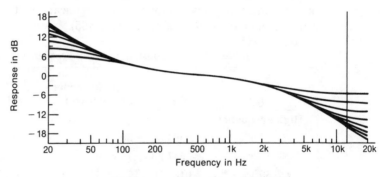

(B) Highpass, 125 Hz; lowpass, 2,000 Hz.

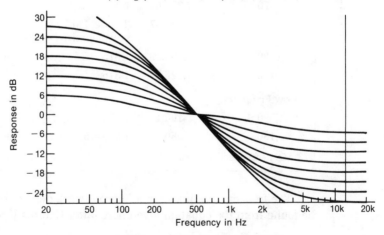

(C) Highpass, 2,000 Hz; lowpass, 125 Hz.

Figure 7-9. Boost/cut shelving contours created by division. The cutoff frequencies are given in the subcaptions.

As noted, the advantage of describing a filter by its time constant is that the capacitance may be easily found for any value of resistance. For example, if the circuit resistance is 100 ohms and the time constant is 318 μs, the capacitance is

$$C = t/R = (318 \times 10^{-6})/100$$
$$= 3.18 \times 10^{-6} \text{ F}$$
$$= 3.18 \ \mu\text{F (microfarads)}$$

Since at the cutoff frequency, capacitive reactance is equal to resistance, the capacitance should provide a reactance of 100 ohms, which may be verified as follows:

$$X_c = 1/2\pi fC$$
$$= 1/(6.28 \times 500 \times 3.18 \times 10^{-6})$$
$$= 1/.01$$
$$= 100 \ \Omega \text{ (ohms)}$$

Table 7-3 lists some of the time constants frequently encountered in filter descriptions, especially in tape recorder applications. Tape recorder equalization is discussed in detail in Chapter 9 (page 365).

Table 7-3. Time Constant-to-Cutoff Frequency Cross-Reference

t (μs)	f (Hz)	Tape Recorder Speed (in/s)	Standard Speed NAB	Standard Speed IEC
High Frequency				
17.5	9,094.57	30		1981*
35	4,547.28	15 & 30		1971
50	3,183.10	7½ & 15	1965	
70	2,273.64	7½		1971
75	2,122.07	(lp disc, FM preemphasis)		
90	1,768.39	1.875, 3.75	1965	1971 (3.75 only)
120	1,326.29	1.875		1971 (1.875 only)
Low Frequency				
1,590	100.10	1.875		1971
3,180	50.05	1.875–15	1965	1971 (3.75 only)

*AES Recommended Practice, 1971.

The frequency response of a filter network defined by its time constants may be found from the equation given here (after Camras 1988).

$$y = 10 \log (A/B) \tag{7-7}$$

where
y = output level, in dB
A = $1 + 1/(2\pi ft_L)^2$
B = $1 + (2\pi ft_H)^2$
f = frequency, in hertz
t_L = low-frequency time constant, in microseconds
t_H = high-frequency time constant, in microseconds

For a network with only one time constant, set either A or B equal to 1, depending on which element is *not* needed.

Figure 7-10 plots a family of filter response curves using the tape-recorder time constants listed in Table 7-3. Equation (7-7) will appear again in Chapter 9, in the section on the IEC frequency response standard (page 368).

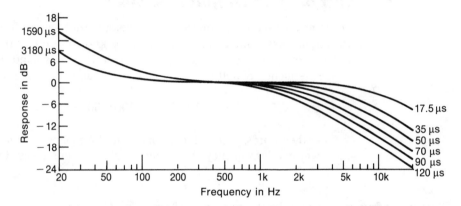

Figure 7-10. Filter response curves as a function of time constants.

Second-Order Filters

A second-order filter contains two reactive elements, therefore offering a slope of up to 12 dB per octave. However, the slope is often modified to suit the needs of the application, notably by varying the circuit Q, as described below.

Second-Order Filter Amplitude Response

Most of the curves seen in the second-order bandpass and bandstop illustrations were plotted from one of the two equations given below. Both equations were derived from the appropriate second-order filter transfer functions (Tedeschi 1979). As before, the equations may be safely ignored by readers with mathematical allergies.

For a bandpass filter,

$$e = \frac{-kB\omega}{[(B\omega)^2 + (\omega^2 - 1)^2]^{1/2}} \tag{7-8}$$

For a bandstop filter,

$$e = \frac{k(\omega^2 - 1)}{[(B\omega)^2 + (\omega^2 - 1)^2]^{1/2}} \qquad (7\text{-}9)$$

where
e = filter output voltage
k = gain
B = $1/Q$
ω = f/f_c
f_c = center frequency

The Effect of Q on Output Response

On some bandpass and bandstop equalizers, a front panel control varies the Q of the circuit. Assuming a center frequency is known, it might therefore seem that this control could be used to achieve the desired pass band. For example, at a center frequency of 500 Hz and a pass band (bandwidth) of 250 Hz,

$$Q = f_c/B = 500/250 = 2$$

In other words, if $Q = 2$, the upper cutoff frequency *should* be 250 Hz above the lower cutoff frequency. As we shall see, this is not always the case.

Symmetric and Nonsymmetric Filters

The filters to be described below may be classified as either symmetric or nonsymmetric, according to the relationship between the filter's bandpass and bandstop contours. Both categories are described in the following sections.

Symmetric Filter

A *symmetric filter* is one in which the bandstop contours are mirror images of the bandpass curves. In Figure 7-11, the bandpass contours at the top of the figure were plotted using equation (7-8) above. A simple inversion of the equation (i.e., $1/e$, as in a negative feedback loop) plots the bandstop contours seen in the same figure. Such a circuit design is often referred to as a *reciprocal filter* due to the $1/e$ function just mentioned.

Nonsymmetric Filter

In a *nonsymmetric* filter the contours are not mirror images. While the bandpass response rises and falls at up to 12 dB per octave, the bandstop response is usually quite flat over most of the audio spectrum, with a sharp dip, or notch, at the center frequency. Examples of passive and active nonsymmetric filters are given below.

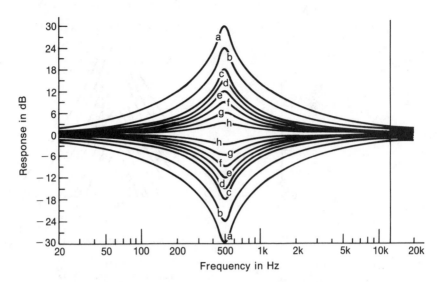

Figure 7-11. Output response for a variable gain/variable Q symmetric bandpass/bandstop filter.

Curve	k	Q	Curve	k	Q
(a)	30.62	5	(e)	2.98	3
(b)	14.84	4.5	(f)	1.818	2.5
(c)	6.94	4	(g)	0.99	2
(d)	4.62	3.5	(h)	0.414	1.5

Passive Filters

In Figure 7-12, Q is held constant and the pre- or postfilter gain is varied in 3 dB increments between unity and -18 dB. Therefore each curve is identical, except for its downward displacement. In both parts of the figure the bandwidth is marked off by vertical lines at 390.39 and 640.39 Hz, as calculated earlier in the chapter (equation (7-4), page 250).

Although the bandstop slopes are also proportional to Q, the two sets of curves obviously are not mirror images. However, for any given value of Q, the pass bands are the same. To verify this, simply note that the bandpass and its equivalent bandstop curve both cross their respective -3 dB points at the same frequency. It should be kept in mind that in either case, the system gain is unity or less. In other words, the passband output level is 0 dB at the center frequency and falls off on both sides as indicated. System gain must be inserted before or after the filter section. For example, the purpose of the illustrated bandstop filter is to sharply attenuate a narrow frequency notch, and not to attenuate the entire pass band by 3 or more dB as the curves in Figure 7-12B have done. Therefore, this loss will probably require some postfilter amplification.

Figure 7-13A again shows a family of response contours for a passive second-order bandpass equalizer, but calculated for 0 dB insertion loss and values of Q between 0.25 and 8. Since the slope of the response curve is proportional to Q, the higher the Q, the narrower the pass band. Figure 7-13B shows a family of second-order bandstop contours drawn for the same values of Q. As in Figure 7-12, both sets of curves pass through their respective -3 dB points at the same frequency.

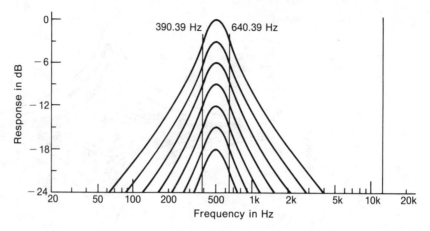

(A) Bandpass filter response.

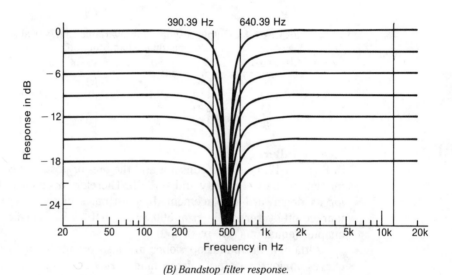

(B) Bandstop filter response.

Figure 7-12. Second-order passive bandpass and bandstop filter response.
In each part of the figure, $Q = 2$, bandwidth $= 250$ Hz, $f_1 = 390.39$ Hz,
and $f_2 = 640.39$ Hz.

Active Filters

Figure 7-14 shows the family of active bandpass and bandstop response curves when the gain is held constant and Q is varied. In this and the following two examples the filter is designed to provide 30 dB of gain at the center frequency.

At the center frequency, all bandpass curves peak at 30 dB, and again Q may be verified by dividing the center frequency by the observed bandwidth at the 27 dB line (3 dB down). From the preceding discussion we already know that when $Q = 2$ the bandwidth is 250 Hz and the lower and upper cutoff frequencies should be 390.39 and 640.39 Hz; these conditions are all met by the $Q = 2$ contours in Figure 7-14.

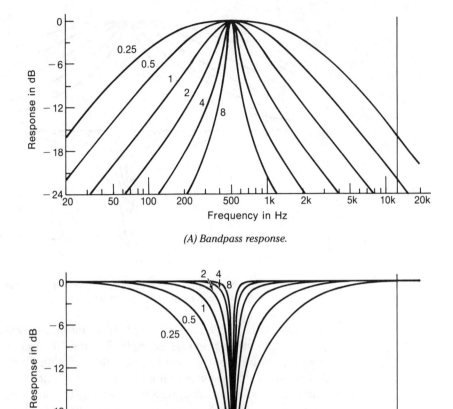

(A) Bandpass response.

(B) Bandstop response.

Figure 7-13. Second-order passive filter response curves for values of Q indicated on the graph.

In Figure 7-15, both Q and gain are varied, and here we find that Q may not be measured from the graph. For example, the actual and apparent values are

Gain (dB)	Actual Q	Apparent Q
30	4.00	4.00
24	2.00	2.00
18	1.00	0.96
12	0.50	0.38
6	0.25	0.13

Note that the accuracy of the Q observed on the graph diminishes as gain decreases. This condition may show up in an active equalizer if the system gain

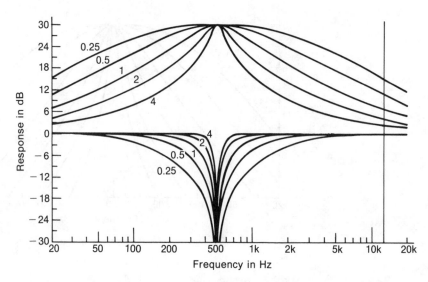

Figure 7-14. Second-order active filter responses for fixed gain (30 dB) and values of Q indicated on the graph.

control is built into the filter section itself. To maintain the expected Q-bandwidth relationship seen in the previous example (Figures 7-13 and 7-14), the equalizer's gain stages must be kept separate from the filter section (Bohn 1985).

A discrepancy between actual and apparent Q is not necessarily a problem, since there is no inherent advantage in being able to read system Q from a graph. Furthermore, equalizer settings should really be judged by ear, not by eye. However, in trying to anticipate what settings might work best, it does help to understand why every now and then, what you see is not quite what you hear.

As a final example of Q versus gain, Figure 7-16 shows a family of bandpass curves for a constant Q (= 2) and various amounts of gain within the filter section. In this example the decreasing accuracy is even more apparent. For example, the 6 dB gain curve has a bandwidth of approximately $850 - 300 = 550$ Hz, and therefore an apparent Q of $500/550 = 0.909$.

Figure 7-16 shows only one bandstop curve for all gain settings, instead of a family of contours such as those seen in the previous illustration. The reason is that system gain has been held constant at 0 dB, assuming as before that the filter should only attenuate the notch frequencies. Furthermore, there are only three variables in the equation for a second-order equalizer: gain, bandwidth, and frequency (see equations (7-8) and (7-9), above). Since both gain and bandwidth are held constant in this example, only the frequency varies, and this variation is of course identical for each of the plotted bandstop curves; hence each one follows the identical contour.

Series and Parallel Resonance

The *resonance frequency* of a circuit is that frequency at which the inductive and capacitive reactances are equal (i.e., $X_L = X_C$). Depending on the specific circuit configuration within an equalizer, one of several families of response contours

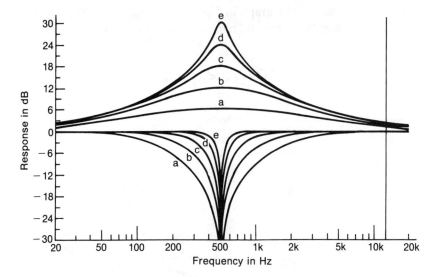

Figure 7-15. Second-order active filter responses for various values of *Q* and dB gain.

Curve	Q	Gain (dB)	Curve	Q	Gain (dB)
(a)	4	30	(d)	0.5	12
(b)	2	24	(e)	0.25	6
(c)	1	18			

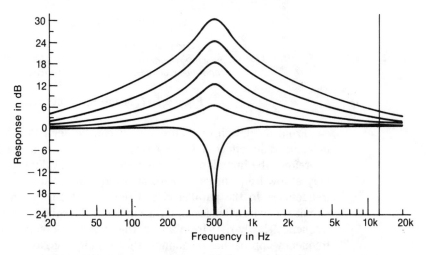

Figure 7-16. Second-order active filter responses for fixed $Q = 2$ and various gain settings.

occurs when this condition is met. To get a better idea of how resonance and frequency response are related, it may be helpful to review how the impedance of an *LC* (inductance and capacitance) circuit varies with frequency. Figure 7-17A shows a simple series resonant circuit; Figure 7-17B shows a parallel resonant circuit. The graph in Figure 7-17C shows the reactance of both circuit elements and the series and parallel impedance versus frequency for both circuits.

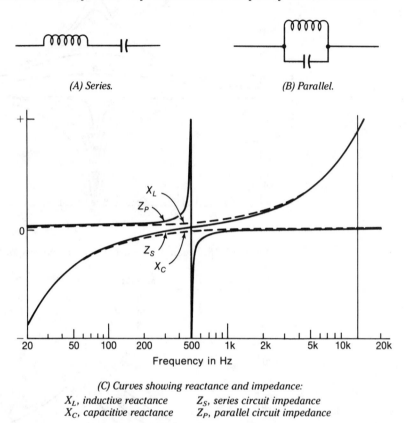

(A) Series.   (B) Parallel.

(C) Curves showing reactance and impedance:

X_L, inductive reactance Z_S, series circuit impedance
X_C, capacitive reactance Z_P, parallel circuit impedance

Figure 7-17. Simple resonant circuits.

From the graph in Figure 7-17 it can be seen that at low frequencies the inductor is in effect a short circuit, as is the capacitor at high frequencies. Therefore, the impedance of the series LC circuit (Figure 7-17A) varies from X_C only at low frequencies, to zero at the resonance frequency, to X_L only at high frequencies. In the parallel circuit (Figure 7-17B), the inductor creates a short circuit at low frequencies, and the capacitor does the same at high frequencies. As frequency slowly rises from 20 Hz, the impedance remains close to zero until the frequency approaches resonance, then rapidly increases to infinity at resonance, and finally as rapidly falls back to zero just beyond resonance.

This brief summary of resonance should lead to a better understanding of how the amplitude and phase response contours in the following examples are created. In the first set of examples (Figures 7-18 to 7-21), a family of amplitude response curves is plotted for various values of R. This is followed (Figures 7-22 to 7-25) by the phase response for the same set of filter networks.

The filter itself is assumed to be part of an active network with maximum gain of unity at the center frequency. Therefore, given a one-volt input signal, its output ranges from zero to a unity-gain reference of one volt. The filter section output is added to that of an unequalized unity-gain section, thus creating a system output that varies between $1 + 0 = 1$, and $1 + 1 = 2$. This gives a decibel range of 20 log 1 to 20 log 2 = 0 to 6 dB.

The response contours in the next four illustrations therefore show a maximum gain of 6 dB. Presumably, an additional amplification stage following the filter section would be used for additional gain as required. However, the contour shapes seen here remain the same, regardless of the system gain. Again for the sake of simplicity, each network is described in terms of a simple *LC* combination, and the position of the filter within the active circuit is not shown.

Note that the bandpass and bandstop networks are identified as *series* or *parallel*, according to the position of the *LC* combination with respect to the source resistance and the load. In either case the inductor and capacitor may also be arranged either in series or parallel with each other. But so readers will not have to put up with awkward "series/parallel" or "parallel/parallel" constructions, the configuration of *L* and *C* will simply be described according to where it is (series or parallel) and what it does (bandpass or bandstop).

Bandpass Circuits

Series Bandpass Circuit   In Figure 7-18A, a series *LC* combination is placed in series with the output. At low and high frequencies the circuit reactance is high, resulting in minimum gain. As frequency is gradually increased towards resonance, reactance approaches zero, and at resonance the circuit is comprised of just the resistance, *R*, and the load, R_L. Therefore, if $R = 0$ the circuit has maximum (unity) gain at resonance, as shown in Figure 7-18B by the $R = 0$ contour on the upper half of the chart. As *R* is increased, the output response at resonance falls off as shown by the other contours.

In each case, the mirror-image contours in the lower half of the figure are achieved by inverting the filter section of the equalizer.

Parallel Bandpass Circuit   As another example of a bandpass circuit, Figure 7-19 places a parallel *LC* combination in parallel with the load. In this configuration the impedance of the parallel branch is always highest at resonance, in effect removing the branch from the circuit at that frequency. As before, response on either side of resonance is a function of resistance, *R*, and the mirror image contours in the lower half of the figure are again achieved by an inversion of the filter network.

Bandstop Circuits

Series Bandstop Circuit   In the next example, a parallel *LC* combination is placed in series with the output, as shown in Figure 7-20A. In this case, the impedance across the *LC* network is very low at both ends of the frequency spectrum and therefore the *R-LC* branch is equal to *R* alone. However, at all values of *R*, the very high impedance of the *LC* combination at resonance creates the very sharp notch response in the upper half of Figure 7-20B. As *R* is increased, the attenuation on either side of the notch changes as shown by the other bandstop curves in the figure.

As before, the mirror-image contours are realized by inverting the filter section.

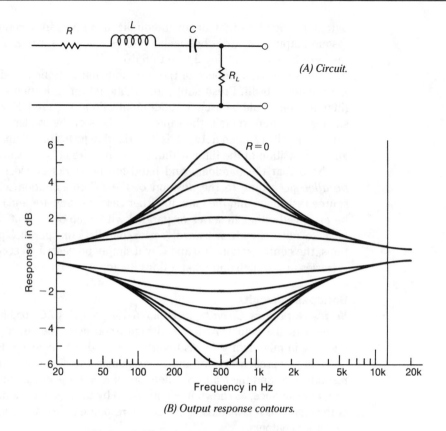

(A) Circuit.

(B) Output response contours.

Figure 7-18. A series bandpass resonant circuit and its
output response contours.

Parallel Bandstop Circuit   In the final example, if a series inductor and
capacitor are placed in parallel with the load, the internal impedance of the
equalizer is zero at resonance, as shown by the family of notch response contours
in Figure 7-21B. Here, the depth of the notch is a function of R. Note, however,
that as the notch depth is reduced, the overall gain also drops.

Phase Shift and Damping

Phase Shift in Second-Order Filters

In each of the preceding four illustrations, the filter output level was seen to vary
as a function of frequency and the source resistance, R. In the next set of
illustrations, the phase response is plotted for various values of R.

Bandpass Circuits
Bandpass Circuit Phase Response   Figure 7-22 illustrates the phase response
for the series bandpass filter shown in Figure 7-18A. If the resistance, R, is zero,
then at very low frequencies the network impedance is due entirely to circuit

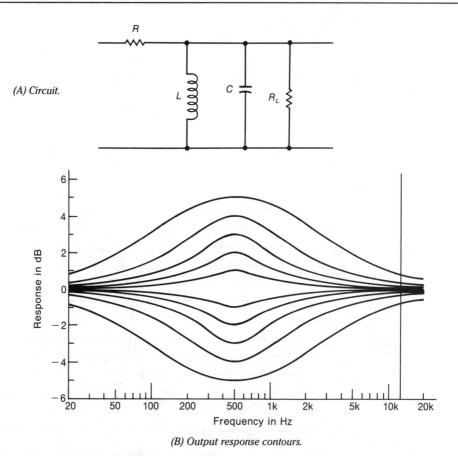

(A) Circuit.

(B) Output response contours.

Figure 7-19. A parallel bandpass resonant circuit and its output response contours.

capacitance, resulting in a phase shift of close to + 90 degrees. As frequency increases, the capacitive reactance decreases and the inductive reactance increases, until at the center frequency the two reactances are equal and opposite, thus canceling out. With no reactance, the phase shift is zero.

As frequency continues to increase, the opposite effect is noted as the phase shift approaches – 90 degrees at the high end of the spectrum.

In Figure 7-23, the phase response for the parallel bandpass filter shown in Figure 7-19A is shown. In this case, the parallel inductance places a low impedance across the network at very low frequencies and the phase shift is again almost zero. As frequency rises, the impedance of the parallel *LC* combination slowly increases and phase shift rises towards + 90 degrees. The rate of increase rapidly accelerates as the signal approaches the center frequency. At the center frequency itself the two reactive forces are again equal and opposite and there is an instantaneous zero phase shift, followed by an equally rapid falloff beyond the center frequency. The phase response again approaches zero as a low impedance is once more placed across the network—this time by the capacitor.

Bandstop Circuit Phase Response
The phase relationships in bandstop filter circuits are not unlike those described for bandpass filters, although the contours themselves are somewhat different, as

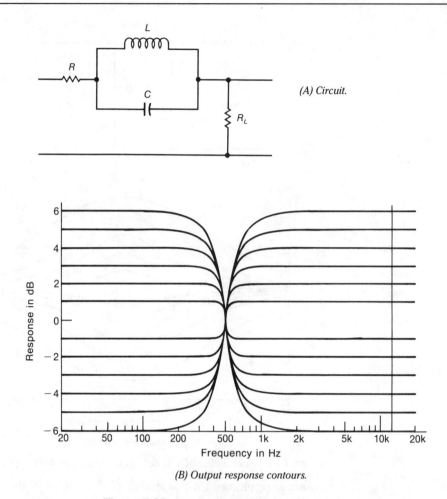

(A) Circuit.

(B) Output response contours.

Figure 7-20. A series bandstop resonant circuit and its
output response contours.

shown in Figures 7-24 and 7-25. Particularly with respect to the transition
through the center frequency, Figure 7-23 may be compared to Figure 7-24 and
Figure 7-22 to Figure 7-25. In either case, it is the series or parallel configuration
of inductor and capacitor that influences the shape of the response contour.

Phase Response in a Recording-Studio Equalizer

The response contours shown above were plotted by calculating the phase shift
across the load resistance seen in the appropriate circuit diagram, and are valid
for a simple network consisting of nothing more than an *LC* combination and a
few resistors. However, the studio-grade equalizer is a far more complex device,
and the filter section is more apt to be inserted in the feedback loop of an active
network.   In this case, the system phase responses for bandpass and bandstop
filters are as shown in Figure 7-26.

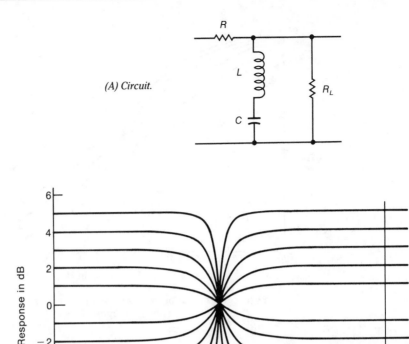

(A) Circuit.

(B) Output response contours.

Figure 7-21. A parallel bandstop resonant circuit and its
output response contours.

Note that with the exception of the discontinuity through zero degrees in the
bandstop filter, the shapes of the two contour families are otherwise identical.
The contours shown in the figure were calculated from the following phase
response equations (after Tedeschi 1979).

Bandpass Filter (Figure 7-26A):

$$\phi = -\tan^{-1}[(\omega^2 - 1)/B\omega]$$

Bandstop Filter (Figure 7-26B):

$$\phi = \pm 90° - \tan^{-1}[(\omega^2 - 1)/B\omega]$$

where
ϕ = phase shift at frequency, f
ω = $2\pi f$
B = bandwidth (= $1/Q$)

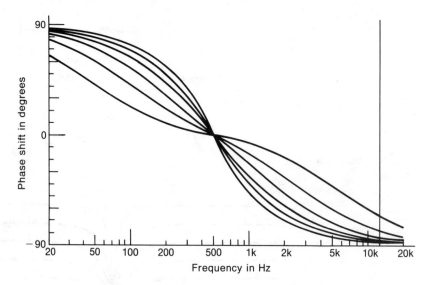

Figure 7-22. The phase response of the series bandpass filter
shown in Figure 7-18A.

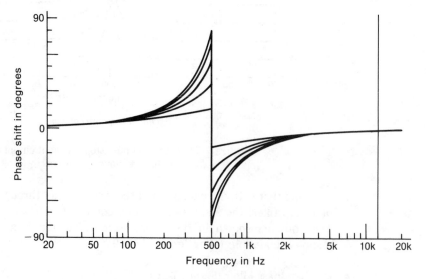

Figure 7-23. The phase response of the parallel bandpass filter
shown in Figure 7-19A.

Note: In the bandstop equation above, use $+90°$ when the total network reactance is inductive, $-90°$ when it is capacitive. The change occurs at the center frequency.

As the final example of equalizer phase shift, Figure 7-27 (pages 284–285) shows the contours that are seen in many commercially available equalizers. Note that in this example, both the bandpass and bandstop responses start and

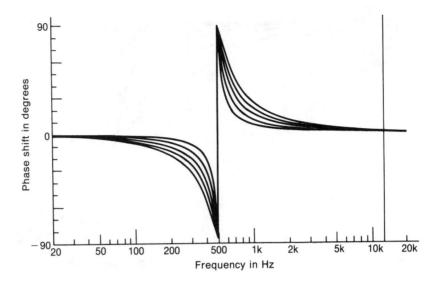

Figure 7-24. The phase response of the series bandstop filter shown in Figure 7-20A.

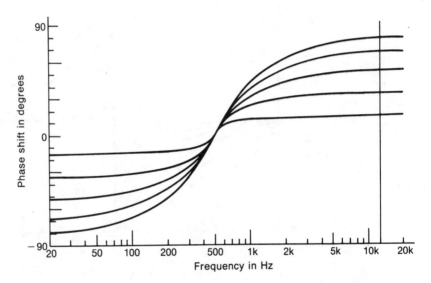

Figure 7-25. The phase response of the parallel bandstop filter shown in Figure 7-21A.

end near zero degrees. This is because the equalizer section is combined with a unity gain amplifier. Doing so allows the bandpass equalizer to boost frequencies within its passband, rather than attenuate those outside the band; in the bandstop configuration, frequencies within the stop band are attenuated, while the rest of the audio spectrum is passed at or close to unity gain.

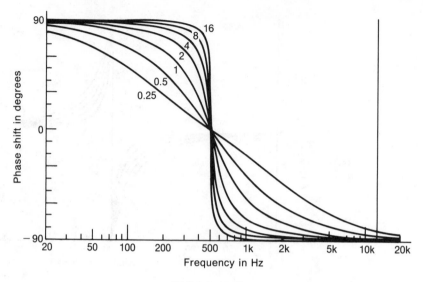

(A) Bandpass filter.

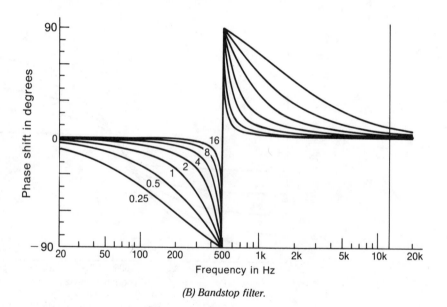

(B) Bandstop filter.

Figure 7-26. Phase responses for the indicated values of Q in
two typical second-order active filters.

Therefore, in the frequency areas outside the pass (or stop) band, the equalizer is simply a unity-gain amplifier, presumably with zero phase shift. As the input frequency moves into the area affected by the filter, the combined phase shift is as shown in the figure. The phase characteristics of such a circuit may be plotted by subtracting the phase response across the filter section alone from the phase response across the filter and its load.

The amplitude and phase responses may also be calculated from the following equations (after Waldman 1988).

$$E = [(A^2 + B^2)/(A_1{}^2 + B^2)]^{1/2}$$
$$\phi = \text{atn}(B/A) - \text{atn}(B/A_1)$$

where

E = amplitude at frequency, f
ϕ = phase shift at frequency, f
A = k/Q
A_1 = k/Q_1
B = $k^2 - 1$
k = f/f_c
Q_1 = $Q(10^{n/20})$
n = desired boost or cut, in dB

Although the phase response contours shown in the various illustrations above are not all alike, they do share one common characteristic: the phase angle is a function of the rate of gain change with frequency (Bode 1945). For example, in any of the bandpass frequency response curves seen in this chapter, system gain rises slowly at first, then more rapidly as the center frequency is approached. At the center frequency the slope of the amplitude curve is instantaneously zero, indicating a momentary zero-gain change. Therefore, the slope of the bandpass phase characteristic should grow steeper as the center frequency is approached and should pass through zero degrees at the center frequency. This condition is satisfied by every phase contour shown above.

The Perception of Phase Shift

Much has been written about whether phase shift is or is not audible. In the face of claims that it cannot be heard at all, the late Richard C. Heyser would ask (perhaps with tongue in cheek), if a woofer and tweeter are, say, a mile apart wouldn't the phase shift from the more distant speaker be perceptible—even to an untrained listener? In fact, Lipshitz, Pocock, and Vanderkooy (1982) point out that if one portion of an audio spectrum were delayed by only one second with respect to the remainder, the time (i.e., phase) distortion would surely be audible to anyone; so, they reason, "It is clear that phase distortion of sufficient magnitude *must* be audible." The authors describe a reasonably simple test to demonstrate phase perception.

Tune a high-quality sine-wave generator to a frequency, f_1, in the 200–300 Hz range, and a second generator to the second harmonic, $2f_1$. Feed the summed output in phase to both ears via a good pair of high-quality headphones. Adjust one of the generators so that the relative phase slips 360 degrees (one cycle) every few seconds. It will be found that the timbral quality of the tone varies at the slip rate.

If a phase-locked oscillator pair is available, an additional test may be tried.

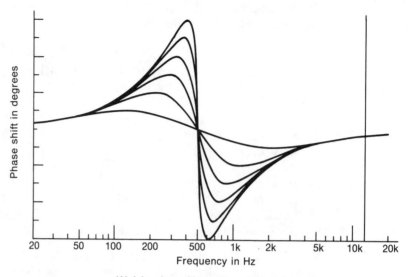

(A) A bandpass filter with variable gain.

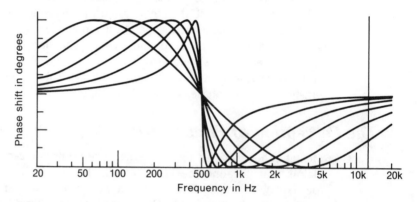

(B) A bandpass filter with constant gain and variable bandwidth.

Figure 7-27. Phase shift in a

Using an oscilloscope, adjust the phase difference between the selected frequency and its second harmonic for a stationary pattern which is markedly asymmetrical (positive-to-negative). Compare the sound quality as the absolute polarity is reversed. Again, a timbral change should be noted.

The authors caution that the differences noted in these and other tests are subtle and should not be applied out of context. Furthermore, tests at a higher frequency did not yield the same result (Lipshitz et al. 1983). It's also important to note that these and other phase-perception debates are usually related to multi-way speaker systems and not to crossover networks and other equalizers used elsewhere.

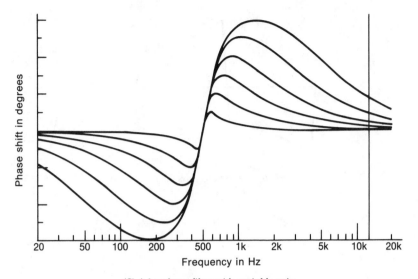

(C) A bandstop filter with variable gain.

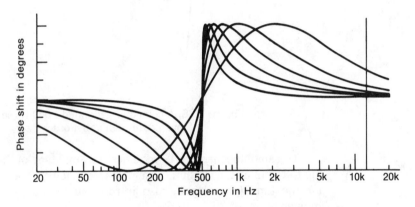

(D) A bandstop filter with constant gain and variable bandwidth.

typical active equalizer system.

When an equalizer is used in a signal-processing application, phase-related subtleties may be even harder to pin down, because the phase shift is a secondary function of the equalizer. The primary function—to change the frequency response—may make it difficult or impossible to isolate any phase effects that are also present. But phase shift, if not always audible, is certainly visible; Figure 7-28 shows a few examples of a 1,000 Hz square wave passed through various first-order filters. The curves were calculated from the equation for a square wave given in Chapter 2 (page 48) which is expanded here with the addition of an amplitude and time factor for each member of the series.

$$y = (4/\pi)[A_1 \sin (2\pi f(t + t_1)) + A_3 \sin (2\pi \times 3f(t + t_3))/3$$
$$+ A_5 \sin (2\pi \times 5f(t + t_5))/5 + \cdots]$$

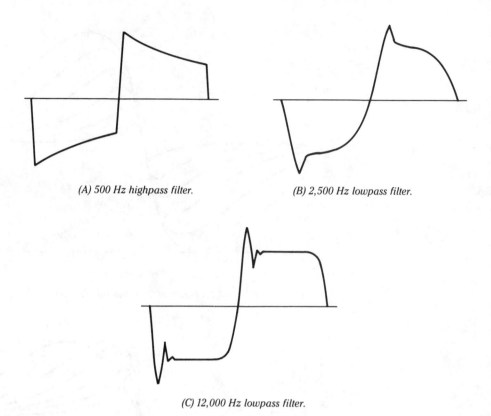

(A) 500 Hz highpass filter.   *(B) 2,500 Hz lowpass filter.*

(C) 12,000 Hz lowpass filter.

Figure 7-28. A computer-generated 1,000 Hz square wave
passed through a first-order filter.

The amplitude factor, A_n, modifies the amplitude of the nth harmonic according to the filter attenuation present at frequency f_n. The time factor, t_n, accounts for the time (phase) shift also introduced by the filter action at the same frequency.

The curves seen in Figure 7-28 are computer generated, and assume that the load is purely resistive. There will be considerable variation under real-world conditions, where the reactive characteristics of the load also vary with frequency. Nevertheless, most such curves will be difficult to recognize as originating from square waves.

Damping

The components in an equalizer are of course selected to provide whatever output response is required, as seen in any of the illustrations above. When all circuit components are the correct value for the specific design, the output response follows the expected contour, and the filter is said to be critically damped.

However, if the value of one circuit component is changed without making the necessary adjustments to the other components, the output response will no longer follow the same contour. For example, Figure 7-29 shows the response contours of a simple lowpass filter in which R, L, and C are separately varied from one-tenth to ten times their intended design value. The contours with a response peak just before cutoff are caused by an underdamped condition; those contours that fall off well before the normal cutoff are the result of an overdamped condition.

Commercially Available Equalizers

Practically every recording and sound reinforcement console contains an equalizer within each input channel, with capabilities ranging from rudimentary to awesome, according to need (and budget). Although the convenience of an equalizer at every possible location cannot be denied, the luxury does represent a certain amount of overkill, for chances are that not every input signal requires extensive equalization (unless something is very wrong somewhere). Also, given the knob factor on the typical sophisticated console, there is a very good chance of equalizing something that doesn't really need it—perhaps because of a setting not cleared at the end of someone else's session, or after a previous take on the present session.

There's also the very real possibility of encountering the console equalizer that meets every possible need—except the present one. As a result, most studios have on hand a selection of outboard equalizers to be patched in as required and quickly removed when no longer needed. In most cases, such equalizers are built in rack-mount format, with controls a bit easier to read and manipulate than those in a console module where space is at a premium. A few representative examples of such outboard equalizers are described below. In each case the same general comments should apply to a similar equalizer found within a console module.

Rotary-Knob Equalizer

Regardless of the type of equalization offered, the rotary-knob equalizer's control mechanism is as the name suggests: simply a rotary knob. The famous Pultec (Pulse Techniques, Inc.) equalizer of the vacuum tube era is still in demand today and is a good example of the classic rotary knob design. Rotary potentiometers vary the amount of boost or cut, while rotary switches are usually used for frequency selection.

The rotary level controls may or may not be calibrated in dB of boost or cut. For example, the Pultec EQP-1A3 Program Equalizer provides up to 18 dB of boost or cut, but the face plate surrounding the knob is printed with a 0 to 10 scale. Therefore, the amount of attenuation at the selected frequency is not directly readable from the front panel.

Representative rotary-knob equalizers are shown in Figure 7-30. In Chapter 12, Figures 12-7A and C show rotary-knob equalizers built into console modules (page 480).

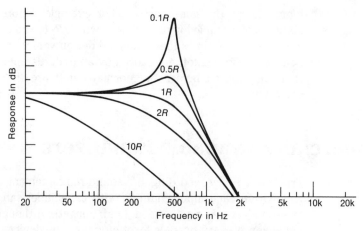

(A) Varied component is resistance.

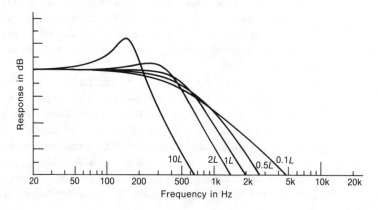

(B) Varied component is inductance.

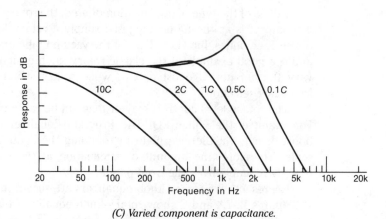

(C) Varied component is capacitance.

Figure 7-29. Response contours for a lowpass filter in which
one circuit component is varied.

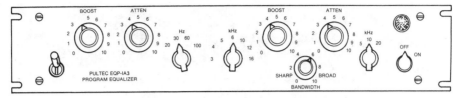

(A) The face plate of the Pultec EQP-1A3 Program Equalizer.

(B) A modern rotary knob equalizer. (Model 4400 one-third octave LC Active Equalizer courtesy White Instruments, Inc.)

Figure 7-30. Rotary-knob equalizers.

Parametric Equalizer

The *parametric* equalizer is so called because it offers separate controls of all three parameters for each filter section; center frequency, bandwidth/Q, and the amount of boost or cut. In the case of a lowpass or highpass equalizer, the bandwidth/Q control may instead determine the amount of shelving equalization that takes effect beyond the cutoff frequency. Figure 7-31 shows a few commercially available parametric equalizers.

Graphic Equalizer

The graphic equalizer uses a series of slide potentiometers to achieve the desired amount of boost or attenuation. As shown in Figures 7-32A and B, the relative positions of the faders provide a graphic depiction of the output response, hence the name *graphic equalizer*.

The graphic equalizer typically comprises a set of bandpass or bandstop filters designed to function at the fixed center frequencies marked near each fader. However, some equalizer outputs are more graphic than others; in other words, the correlation between what you see on the front panel and what you get at the output may be marginal at best, especially when adjacent bands are at quite different gain/loss settings. The actual relationship between fader position and frequency response is a complex function of various design parameters which vary from one system to another. Therefore, before assuming that the output response is a replica of the front panel display, it's a good idea to run a frequency sweep test.

Some graphic equalizers intended for sound reinforcement applications offer attenuation only. In this case the sound system is designed for as flat a response as

(A) Orban 642B Parametric Equalizer/Notch Filter. (Courtesy Orban Associates)

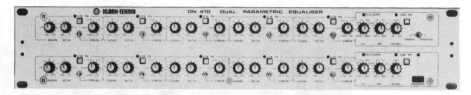

(B) Klark-Teknik DN 410 Dual Parametric Equalizer.
(Courtesy Klark-Teknik Electronics, Inc.)

Figure 7-31. The parametric equalizer allows separate control of bandwidth, gain, and center frequency.

possible, and the equalizer is then used to attenuate those frequency bands at which a response peak is noted. The equalizer is usually set up via instrumentation and then protected against knob twiddlers by a security cover over the front panel.

Graphic Equalizer Center Frequencies

The graphic equalizer is often further identified by the interval between center frequencies, which may be one-sixth, one-third, one-half, two-thirds or one full octave. Table 7-4A lists these intervals, which on many graphic equalizers are rounded to the nearest ISO values, as shown in Table 7-4B.

Paragraphic Equalizer

The term *paragraphic* (*para*metric/*graphic*) is sometimes used to describe a graphic equalizer in which the parameters of bandwidth and/or center frequency are adjustable for each filter section. The controls for varying these parameters are usually rotary potentiometers, as shown in Figure 7-33.

Digital Equalizer

As an outboard signal-processing device, the digital equalizer is often equipped with both analog and digital signal inputs and outputs, with a representative two-channel equalizer like the one shown in Figure 7-34 (pages 294–295). In the block diagram, note that each analog signal passes through A/D (Analog/Digital) and D/A (Digital/Analog) converters at either side of the signal-processing chain, and is also converted from parallel to serial (P/S) and then back to parallel (S/P) format. The serial-mode signals are alternately fed through a single digital processor (DEQ × 7 and DSP). In the event of a digital signal input, these signal-

(A) Rane GE 27 and GE 14 graphic equalizers with one-third octave and two-channel two-thirds octave center frequencies. (Courtesy Rane Corp.)

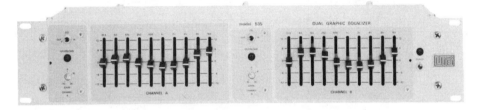

(B) UREI 535 two-channel graphic equalizer with one-octave center frequencies. (Courtesy UREI)

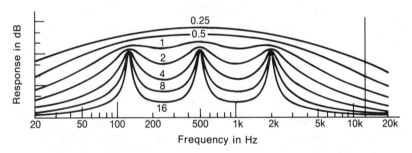

(C) Representative graphic equalizer response contours for various values of Q, with three slide faders (125, 500, 2,000 Hz) set to +18 dB.

Figure 7-32. Graphic equalizers and representative response contours.

processing steps are of course not needed, and the input therefore passes directly to the signal processing system, as also shown in the block diagram.

The typical digital equalizer offers the production advantage of being programmable: once a set of desirable parameters are found, they may be stored in memory for recall later. In addition, parameter changes may be made often, either by toggling a foot switch or by MIDI (Musical Instrument Digital Interface) control. This allows the user to make complex equalization changes instan-

Table 7-4. Comparison of Graphic Equalizer Center Frequency Intervals

(A) Center Frequency Intervals (Hz)

		Octave Interval		
1/6	*1/3*	*1/2*	*2/3*	*1*
40.00	40.00	40.00	40.00	40.00
44.90				
50.40	50.40			
56.57		56.57		
63.50	63.50		63.50	
71.27				
80.00	80.00	80.00		80.00
89.80				
100.79	100.79		100.79	
113.14		113.14		
126.99	126.99			
142.54				
160.00	160.00	160.00	160.00	160.00
179.59				
201.59	201.59			
226.27		226.27		
253.98	253.98		253.98	
285.09				
320.00	320.00	320.00		320.00
359.19				
403.17	403.17		403.17	
452.55		452.55		
507.97	507.97			
570.17				
640.00	640.00	640.00	640.00	640.00

Figure 7-33. A graphic equalizer with rotary-knob control of center frequency (top) and bandwidth (bottom) for each section.
(672A Equalizer courtesy Orban Associates)

Table 7-4 *(continued)*

(B) ISO Center Frequency Intervals (Hz)

1/6	1/3	1/2	2/3	1
40	40	40	40	40
44.90				
50	50			
56.57		56.57		
63	63		63	
71.27				
80	80	80		80
89.80				
100	100		100	
113.14		113.14		
125	125			
142.54				
160	160	160	160	160
179.59				
200	200			
226.27		226.27		
250	250		250	
285.09				
315	315	315		315
359.19				
400	400		400	
452.55		452.55		
500	500			
570.17				
630	630	630	630	630

taneously, or to recall a set of parameters stored during a previous session. A possible disadvantage is that the front panel controls are often simply a set of push buttons, so the long-familiar visual correlation between knob position and effect is no longer there.

Equalizer Applications

Equalizers are generally used in one of two ways, both of which are described below.

*(A) Front panel controls of the Yamaha DEQ7 Digital Equalizer.
(Courtesy Yamaha Music Corp., USA)*

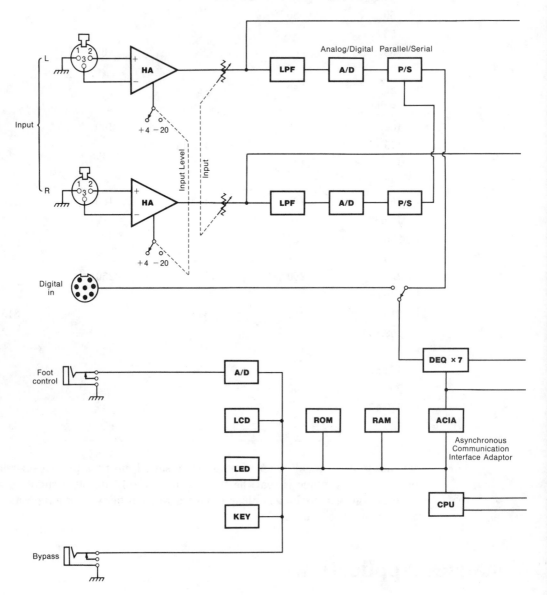

(B) Block diagram of the DEQ7. (Courtesy Yamaha Music Corp., USA)

Figure 7-34.

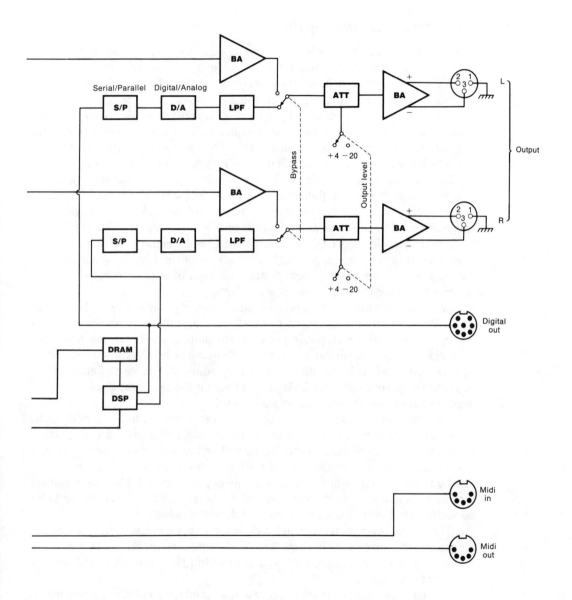

A digital equalizer.

- *Correction:* to compensate for some deficiency in the transmission medium
- *Enhancement:* to modify the response of a sound source to provide a more pleasing effect.

Signal-Correction Equalization

This chapter began with a reference to early equalizer applications in telephone and film work, to which we might now compare tape recorder equalization. Due to various tape and tape head characteristics, neither the record nor playback response of an analog tape recorder will be flat, unless some equalization is applied during both recording and playback. Although this application of equalization is described in more detail in Chapter 9, it is cited here as a modern application of the traditional role of the equalizer: to normalize (or "equalize") a signal to bring it as close to the sound of the original source as possible.

Equalization may also be used as a simple form of noise reduction. For example, assuming that high-frequency information will be partially masked by transmission noise, high frequencies may be boosted just before transmission and then attenuated by the same amount at the receiver. The high-end boost will raise the high frequencies above the noise level; the complementary cut at the receiver "equalizes" the high frequency response back to normal, while simultaneously lowering the accompanying noise signal. This type of boost/cut equalization is commonly referred to as *pre-* and *postemphasis*.

In sound reinforcement applications, various room characteristics may emphasize some frequency bands while attenuating others. Here, the equalizer may be used to trim a response peak by attenuating the frequency band that produces the peak. A similar dip in response may not be as easily corrected by equalization though. If the dip is caused by some sort of cancellation effect, boosting the output will have little or no effect on the problem, since equal and opposite forces cancel regardless of signal level.

The notch filter is often used to good effect to remove a noise from an audio signal, provided the noise is sufficiently narrow-band to be filtered out without removing too much of the surrounding audio band as well. Sometimes it is easier to filter out a noise component by first applying a boost and sweeping through the nearby frequency range until the noise frequency is localized. Then the equalizer may be switched over to the cut position. If possible, adjust the equalizer Q for minimum effect on frequencies on either side of the noise.

The loudspeaker crossover network is also an equalizer, although in this application the purpose of the equalizer is strictly to deemphasize, that is, make sure that frequencies outside each speaker's piston band (see page 173) are not received at the voice coil.

In digital audio, the sampling process may produce spurious artifacts within the audio-frequency range. To prevent these alias frequencies from occurring, a lowpass anti-aliasing filter must be used. Again, the purpose is simply to prevent interference from distortion-producing signals outside the system's pass band.

Signal-Enhancement Equalization

It's obvious that one must *listen* to whatever it is that is being equalized. However, the instrument should be monitored in the context in which it will be heard later on; beyond making sure that everything is working properly, there's not too much point to equalizing while listening to an instrument in the solo mode (that is, with all other signal sources muted). Unless the instrument is in fact playing a solo, it doesn't really matter what it sounds like all alone, since no one will ever hear it that way. What does matter is how it sounds along with everything else. And once that sound is achieved, it may be surprising to find that in solo mode the same equalizer settings no longer sound right. Conversely, when the solo mode does sound good, the effect on the ensemble may suffer.

For the same general reasons, when recording tracks sequentially it's a good idea not to spend too much time making heavy equalization decisions that won't be appropriate later on anyway. However, if two or more instruments are to be combined on the same track, then separate equalization may need to be applied prior to recording. For example, if the instruments are similar in timbre, introducing some differences via equalization may help to better distinguish one source from the other. But if the instruments are at opposite ends of the spectrum (say, bass and tambourine), then high- or low-end equalization may be used later on to change the sound of one, with minimal effect on the other.

A Few Concluding Words of Advice

Remember that an equalization boost only brings that portion of the audio spectrum a little closer to overloading the system, as for example with tape saturation. Therefore, when a large amount of boost is required it may be necessary to drop the overall level of the signal being recorded.

And a brief application note: when recording drums with multiple microphones, there's often a tendency to use a separate track for each microphone, sometimes suggesting the engineer is better at balancing the drums than is the drummer. Assuming however that this is not the case, it's usually possible to get a much better drum sound with fewer microphones and a drummer who does the balancing work out in the studio. In fact a two channel (left/right) pickup, with bass drum split to both tracks, should at least be tried by anyone with imagination enough to do a little experimenting. In this case, the bass drum can (within reason) be boosted or attenuated later on by applying the same low-frequency equalization to both tracks.

This chapter has been long on theory, and short on practice. This is because—as with most recording tools—there are few equalization rules and no regulations that must be followed. Like microphone placement, equalization is mostly a matter of personal preference. So we might very well conclude by borrowing a page—actually, just a sentence—from a cookbook:

When all is done, equalize to taste (and hold the salt).

8 Dynamic Range

This chapter describes the various devices that are used to vary the dynamic range of a program; specifically, the compressor, limiter, and expander. Most well-equipped studios have a generous sprinkling of each, often mounted in an equipment rack near the console, with each device accessible via the console patch bay (which is described in Chapter 12).

Until recently, most consoles did not have such devices built in. However, miniaturization now permits each module (again, Chapter 12) to contain its own compressor, limiter, and/or expander. The section in which they are found is referred to as the dynamics section.

Dynamic Range

The *dynamic range*, in decibels, of an audio system or transmission medium is the difference between the lowest and highest level the system is capable of handling. The lower limit is usually the residual noise level of the system; the upper limit, the point at which the system begins to distort the signal passing through it. Thus,

$$N = 20 \log (e_2/e_1)$$

where

e_1 = minimum (noise) voltage
e_2 = maximum voltage
N = dynamic range, in dB

Dynamic range is often defined as the *ratio* of output to input voltage (as in e_2/e_1) or power. However, since $\log (e_2/e_1)$ is the same as $\log e_2 - \log e_1$, the term *difference* is preferred here as being more informative of what dynamic range really describes. Within a system's dynamic range, there is (or should be) a linear relationship between input and output.

Dynamic range may be used to describe the level-handling capability of both a transmitter and a receiver of an audio signal. Thus, the human ear also has a dynamic range. In terms of sound pressure level, its lower limit is of course at the threshold of hearing, or 0 dB. The upper limit is generally put at about 130 + dB, provided that daily exposure is for an extremely short duration.

For the purposes of this chapter, we may put the maximum signal level for the ear at about 120 dB, which is the threshold of feeling—the point at which the sound begins to cause physical discomfort. (Aesthetic discomfort is beyond the scope of this discussion.)

Signal-to-Noise Ratio

In expressing the useful dynamic range of any transmitter or receiver of audio information, the system's *signal-to-noise ratio* is defined as the ratio of the amplitude of a signal to the amplitude of the noise measured at the same point in the system. Since the level of a musical signal obviously varies continuously over time, the signal voltage is usually understood to be the voltage that creates some criterion distortion level such as 1 percent. And since noise is usually masked by the signal itself, the noise level is measured in the absence of the signal (Blesser & Ives 1972).

To determine the signal-to-noise ratio that the ear is capable of resolving, the residual noise level of the listening room itself may be used as the noise level. Since this is about 30 dB in a very quiet room, we may say that the useable signal-to-noise ratio for the ear is about 90 dB.

Table 8-1 lists the dynamic range and signal-to-noise ratio of the ear and the signal-to-noise ratios of various other systems.

Table 8-1. Dynamic Range of Various Audio Systems

System	Dynamic Range (dB)	Signal-to-Noise Ratio (dB)
Human ear	120	90
Symphony orchestra	100	65
Compact disc	—	100
Digital tape recorder	—	>90
High-quality microphone	—	75
LP record	—	70–80
Analog tape recorder	—	65–70
	—	60–65 (c. 1955)
Magnetic tape (analog)	—	60–70
FM transmission	—	60
Telephone line (class A)	—	60
AM transmission	—	50
Telephone line (normal)	—	45

As Table 8-1 shows, the signal-to-noise ratio of most audio systems is less than that of the ear, and, in fact, is often not even sufficient to record or transmit the dynamic range of an orchestra. Even if the system does approach, or even exceeds, the capabilities of the ear, extremely low-level signals will probably not be heard due to the residual noise level present in even the quietest of listening rooms. Therefore, the dynamic range of the message must be compressed until it fits within the limitations imposed by the medium.

Figure 8-1 introduces a graph that will be seen repeatedly in this chapter. The x (horizontal) axis shows input level and the y (vertical) axis is output level. Horizontal lines at -12 and $+12$ dB mark off the lower (system noise level) and upper (system overload) limits of the system, though not of the signal applied to it. The limits were chosen for the purposes of the following discussion and do not (one hopes) represent the actual dynamic range of a real system.

The horizontal line below the graph represents an input signal whose level fluctuates between -15 and $+15$ dB. The system amplitude response may be plotted by a *transfer characteristic*, $y = f(x)$ (i.e., y is a function of x). In the simplest case, the diagonal line (a) is the response of a unity-gain amplifier ($y = x$). The corresponding vertical line (a) at the right of the graph shows that an input signal below -12 dB will be lost in the system noise, while an input above $+12$ dB will be distorted due to overload.

Figure 8-1 also illustrates the limitations of simply making a static gain change. Diagonal line (b) plots the transfer characteristic for an amplifier with 10 dB of gain ($y = x + 10$). Note that a -15 dB input is now raised to a -5 dB output level, which is 7 dB above the system noise level. However, any input level above $+2$ dB now causes system overload. As diagonal line (c) shows, attenuation of 10 dB ($y = x - 10$) is no improvement; the problem is merely transferred to the opposite end of the amplitude spectrum. In either case, the vertical lines (b) and (c) at the right of the graph show the output in relation to the upper and lower limits of the system.

Figure 8-1 not only shows the problem of a dynamic range that exceeds system capabilities, it also points toward a solution. At the risk of stating the obvious, all we need to do is compress the dynamic range of the input signal so that it fits within the limits imposed by the system.

Control Room and Studio Gain Riding

The earliest form of such dynamic-range compression was, and still is, known as *gain riding*, in which the engineer makes continuous level adjustments, riding the gain to bring low-level signals up above the noise floor, and high-level signals down below the distortion point of the recording tape (or transmission line). Given a program in which the overall gain changes are gradual with no sudden surprises (Ravel's *Bolero* comes to mind), gain riding can be a reasonably effective way to compress dynamic range.

Unfortunately, it does not always work; the probability of accurately changing gain on either side of a momentary peak is low at best, and zero when the peak comes without warning. The problem is even greater when the engineer is

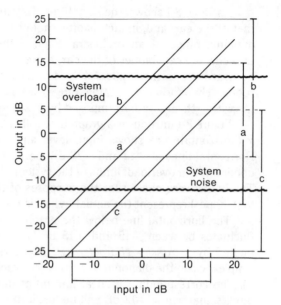

Figure 8-1. Amplifier gain transfer characteristics. The vertical lines at the right are keyed to the following diagonal-line transfer characteristics: (a) unity gain, (b) 10 dB gain, and (c) 10 dB attenuation.

trying to keep an ear on many input signals at once and has no idea which one will cause trouble next.

Some relief can be expected when working with musicians familiar with the limitations of the recording medium. Up to a point, musical gain riding—a little more *pp* and a bit less *ff*—can help, but again it's a solution that is not always complete. If the musicians modify their playing by compressing the expression of dynamics, the program comes out sounding about the way one might expect—musically lifeless due to a lack of dynamic expression.

When either of the above forms of gain riding isn't satisfactory, a purist technique might be tried; simply set the level controls so that the highest peaks don't distort, and let the rest of the program fall where it may. The problem is again that shown by curve (c) in Figure 8-1; too much of the signal will be recorded at a very low level, near or below the system noise level.

Electronic Gain Riding

As one more solution to various problems associated with dynamic range, a variable-gain amplifier may be used. In such a device, the gain is varied not by a human operator at the input level control, but by an electronic circuit whose gain varies automatically as a function of input signal level. Three such devices are in wide use, and each is described in detail immediately following.

The Compressor

A *compressor* is a variable-gain amplifier in which the dynamic range of the output signal is less than that of the applied input signal. A typical transfer characteristic for such a device is shown in Figure 8-2. Note that low level signals are boosted above the noise level, high level signals are dropped below system overload and, in this example, the output dynamic range is half that of the input.

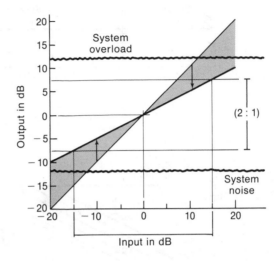

Figure 8-2. The transfer characteristic of a compressor with a 2:1 compression ratio. The shaded areas indicate low and high level signals raised and lowered from the unity gain transfer characteristic.

The following sections describe the controls that are found on most compressors.

Compression Ratio

The ratio of input to output dynamic range is known as the *compression ratio* of the device, and in Figure 8-2 the compression ratio is 2:1. On most if not all compressors the ratio may be varied by the user, either over a continuous range beginning at unity gain (1:1 compression ratio), or in a few incremental steps. For example, Figure 8-3A shows a family of compression ratios. Note that a ratio of 30:24, or 1.25 to 1, might have been used instead of 2:1 without exceeding either of the level limits imposed by the system. A 1.67:1 ratio would permit the entire 40 dB input range to be accommodated. Higher compression ratios would of course allow even-greater dynamic ranges to pass through the system.

Rotation Point

The point at which the transfer characteristic passes through unity gain is known as the compressor's *rotation point*, since the transfer characteristic rotates about this point as the compression ratio is varied. In Figure 8-3A, the rotation point for each curve was set at 0 dB. However, the rotation point is often variable as well,

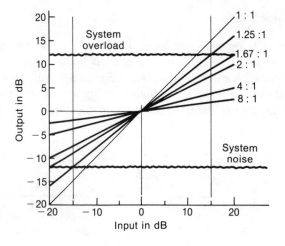

(A) Various compression ratios.

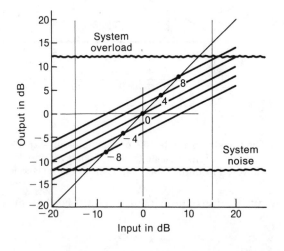

(B) A family of 2:1 compression ratios passing through unity gain at various rotation points.

Figure 8.3. Compressor transfer characteristics.

as shown in Figure 8-3B. For example, this illustration shows that with a rotation point of − 4 dB and a compression ratio of 2:1, input levels of − 20 dB or higher will be above the noise level.

Threshold

In the examples given above, the compressor's transfer characteristic was applied across the entire input range. However, a compressor may also be set so that compression does not begin until the input signal rises above a certain level. This compression *threshold* is therefore defined as the level at which compression begins. Below threshold the device functions as a conventional linear amplifier with manually adjustable gain.

Gain Before Threshold

The *gain before threshold* is simply the amount that low-level input signals are boosted before compression begins. In Figure 8-4 the gain before threshold is 10 dB, and the compression ratios have been selected so that in each case a + 20 dB input signal provides a + 12 dB output. Thus, every transfer characteristic shown in the illustration reduces the dynamic range from 40 dB to 22 dB, for an effective overall compression ratio of 40:22, or 1.82:1. In each case, the threshold is the point at which the transfer characteristic departs from the 10 dB gain line.

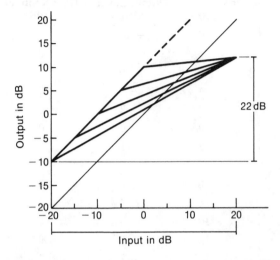

Figure 8-4. Compressor transfer characteristics showing 10 dB gain before threshold, followed by a family of compression ratios that deliver a + 12 dB output level when the input level is + 20 dB.

Finishing Point

In most routine applications of compression, the compression characteristic starts at threshold and is continuous as the input level rises beyond that point. However, if compression action were to cease at some higher level, that point might be thought of as the *finishing point* for the 2:1 compression ratio. For example, if any of the compression slopes seen in Figures 8-3 or 8-4 reverted to unity gain at the rotation point, or to some other constant gain elsewhere on the slope, that point would be the compressor's finishing point. Although the term is not often encountered in routine descriptions of compression action, it will be found again in Chapter 11 in the discussion of Dolby noise reduction (page 434).

Bilinear Characteristic

The transfer characteristic of a compressor with gain before threshold and unity or other gain beyond a finishing point may be referred to as a *bilinear characteristic*, since it contains two separate segments of constant gain (Dolby 1983).

System Gain

For most applications, an understanding of compression ratios should be sufficient to allow the user to select the appropriate setting. However, a closer look at compressor gain may be helpful in explaining a few of the side effects of compression.

Table 8-2 lists the input and output characteristics of a compressor with a threshold of 0 dB and a compression ratio of 2:1. The final column illustrates how the system gain drops as the input level increases.

Table 8-2. Input/Output Characteristics of a Compressor
with 2:1 Compression Ratio

Input Level (dB)	Output Level (dB)	Gain Reduction (dB)	E_{in} (V)	E_{out} (V)	System Gain
− 10	− 10	0	0.32	0.32	1.00
− 8	− 8	0	0.40	0.40	1.00
− 6	− 6	0	0.56	0.56	1.00
− 4	− 4	0	0.71	0.71	1.00
− 2	− 2	0	0.89	0.89	1.00
0	0	0	1.00	1.00	1.00
2	1	1	1.26	1.12	0.89
4	2	2	1.58	1.26	0.79
6	3	3	2.00	1.41	0.71
8	4	4	2.51	1.58	0.63
10	5	5	3.16	1.78	0.56
12	6	6	3.98	2.00	0.50
14	7	7	5.01	2.24	0.45
16	8	8	6.31	2.51	0.40
18	9	9	7.94	2.82	0.35
20	10	10	10.00	3.16	0.32
22	11	11	12.59	3.55	0.28
24	12	12	15.85	3.98	0.25
26	13	13	19.95	4.47	0.22
28	14	14	25.12	5.01	0.20
30	15	15	31.62	5.62	0.18

The system gain figures given in the table are used in Figure 8-5 to show system gain versus input level. Figure 8-5 also shows system gain for several other compression ratios. In each example, the threshold is set at 0 dB, with unity gain before threshold. Therefore, the system gain is unity before threshold, and less than unity for input signals above threshold.

"Breathing" or "Pumping"

Figure 8-5 draws attention to an important characteristic of any compressor: in the presence of a wide-range program, the gain of the compressor varies considerably, with the greatest gain change taking place just above threshold. Therefore, if the input signal fluctuates in this general vicinity, the system gain rides up

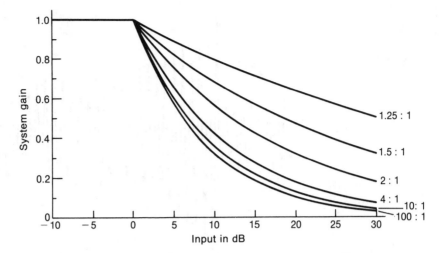

Figure 8-5. Compressor gain vs. input level for several compression ratios.

and down. As it does, the rise and fall of low-level background noise may create an audible "breathing" effect (also called "pumping"). Within reason, this side effect may be masked by other signals that are not passing through the same compressor. As usual, it's a good idea to listen to the compressed signal in context to make sure the compressor action is not doing more harm than good. The breathing effect may be minimized by selecting a lesser compression ratio or, as described later, a longer release time.

Attack Time

Once the input signal rises above threshold, the compressor's *attack time* is that interval during which the output moves from its prethreshold gain, to whatever gain is dictated by the compression ratio setting. The interval is often adjustable over a range from less than 1 ms to 20 ms or greater.

Figure 8-6 illustrates the effect of attack time on a sustained sine-wave signal. Eight cycles are shown at a below-threshold level, after which the input signal suddenly jumps to a new level requiring compression. At first (Figure 8-6A), the attack time is about 12 ms; long enough for about 25 cycles (at 2,000 Hz) to pass through the system before it stabilizes at its new gain setting. During this transition period there is some waveform distortion since the positive and negative halves of each cycle are not of equal amplitude. In Figure 8-6B, the attack time is reduced to about 3.5 ms. Finally in Figure 8-6C, it is set at zero and the waveform reaches the compressed gain setting instantaneously.

Although an attack time close to zero certainly offers maximum protection against high-level transients, it often gives the compressed signal a rather dull "lifeless" sound, since the sonic impacts of sharp musical attacks are lost. A longer attack time will allow at least some of each peak to pass through the system, thus preserving the sense of a percussive attack. In fact, the attack may sound even more percussive than usual, since the level is quickly pulled down immediately after the onset of the attack. Without the compression, the attack may decay at a slower rate, and therefore give a more sustained effect.

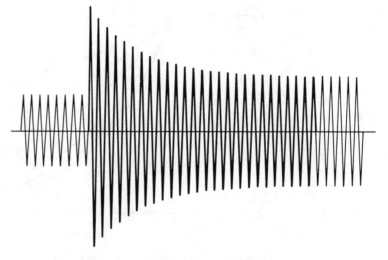

(A) Long attack time.

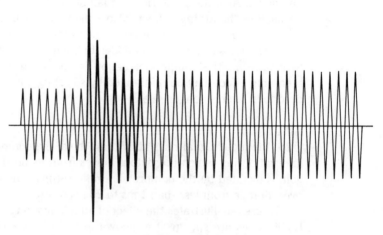

(B) Short attack time.

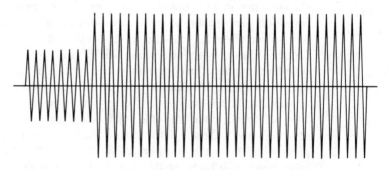

(C) Zero attack time.

Figure 8-6. The effect of attack time on a sustained sine wave.

Release Time

When the signal level falls below threshold, it again takes the compressor some time to restore itself to its gain-before-threshold level. Thus, when the signal causing the compression is removed, the *release time* is the interval required for normal system gain to be reached. Figure 8-7 illustrates the effect of various release times on a sine wave when compression is suddenly turned off. In this set of examples, the signal level drops at the end of eight complete cycles and the system then takes the indicated interval to restore itself to normal (no compression) gain.

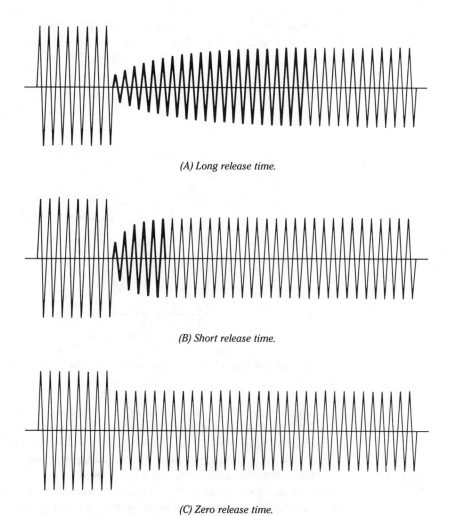

(A) Long release time.

(B) Short release time.

(C) Zero release time.

Figure 8-7. The effect of release time on a sustained sine wave.

If the input signal is heavily compressed and a short release time is selected, the breathing effect described earlier may be quite audible whenever compression is removed and the gain rises quickly, thus bringing up the sound of system and background noise, tape hiss, etc. In this case, a longer release time may help minimize the distraction of the fluctuating noise level.

Release time is often given in decibels-per-second.

The Limiter

The term *limiter* describes a compressor whose compression ratio is 10:1 or greater. At such high ratios the output remains for all practical purposes at a fixed level. In other words, the output signal above threshold is limited to a very narrow dynamic range; hence the term.

Figure 8-8 shows the transfer characteristics for a limiter with compression ratios of 10:1 and 20:1. In either case, the variation in level for input signals above threshold is negligible, and for even higher ratios it would be almost unmeasurable.

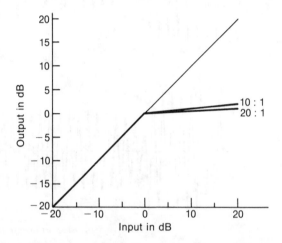

Figure 8-8. Transfer characteristics for a limiter, showing compression ratios of 10:1 and 20:1.

Some compressors allow the user to select two compression ratios, each of which takes effect at a different threshold. In a typical application, a moderate compression ratio—say 2:1 or 4:1—may be used over most of the input signal range. However, if an input peak comes along that would cause trouble at the selected compression ratio, the device goes into a limiting mode, with a compression ratio of 10:1 or greater. This feature allows the user to select a compression ratio appropriate for most of the program, and yet have protection against the occasional peak that needs even more compression. A representative transfer characteristic for such a combination compressor/limiter is shown in Figure 8-9.

The front panels of representative single-channel compressor/limiters are shown in Figure 8-10.

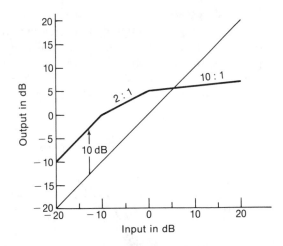

Figure 8-9. Transfer characteristic for a combination compressor and limiter, showing 10-dB gain before threshold, followed by compression ratios of 2:1 and 10:1. The compression threshold is −10 dB; the limiting threshold is 0 dB.

(A) Continuously variable control of compression ratio from 2:1 to infinity. (Orban 412A Compressor/Limiter courtesy Orban Associates)

(B) Switch-selectable compression ratios of 4:1, 8:1, 12:1, and 20:1. (UREI 1176 LN Peak Limiter courtesy UREI)

Figure 8-10. Two single-channel compressor/limiters. In both examples, the input and output potentiometers adjust gain before threshold and post-compression output level.

The Expander

In contrast to the compressor, an *expander* is a variable-gain amplifier in which the dynamic range of the output signal is greater than that of the applied input signal. Therefore, it has the opposite effect of a compressor; low level signals are attenuated, and high level signals are boosted.

The following sections compare the controls found on most expanders to the equivalent controls on a compressor.

Expansion Ratio

The ratio of input to output dynamic range is known as the *expansion ratio* of the device, and Figure 8-11A shows a family of expansion ratios. For comparison purposes, the ratios are the inverse of the ratios shown earlier in Figure 8-3A. Note that as the slope of the expansion characteristic is increased, the dynamic range at the expander output is decreased.

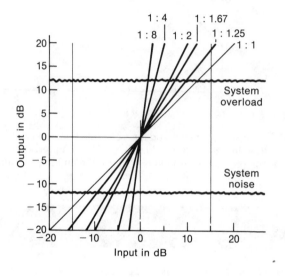

(A) Various expansion ratios.

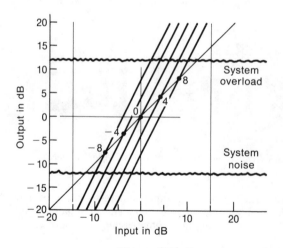

(B) A family of 1:2 expansion ratios passing through unity gain at various rotation points.

Figure 8-11. Expander transfer characteristics.

Rotation Point

The point at which the transfer characteristic passes through unity gain is—as before—the expander's *rotation point*. In Figure 8-11B, the rotation points used earlier in Figure 8-3B are used along with an expansion ratio of 1:2.

Threshold

In contrast to the compressor, the expander's *threshold* is the point below which expansion begins. Above threshold the expander functions as a conventional linear amplifier. Figure 8-12 shows a transfer characteristic with a 1:2 expansion ratio and a threshold of − 5 dB.

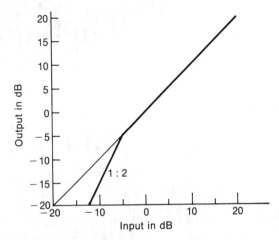

Figure 8-12. An expander transfer characteristic with a 1:2 expansion ratio and an expansion threshold of − 5 dB.

Attack Time

In the presence of a very low-level input signal, expander gain is at a minimum, since the input level is far below the system threshold. For example, with an expansion ratio of only 1:2, a − 20 dB input would create a − 40 dB output. When the input signal rises above threshold, the *attack time* is the interval required for the system to reach unity gain. By contrast to the compressor, it is the time it takes for the system to *stop* working.

As shown in Figure 8-13, the shape of an expander's attack-time envelope is similar to a compressor's release-time envelope, as seen earlier in Figure 8-7.

Release Time

Once the input level falls below threshold, the expander's *release time* is the interval required for the system gain to fall to the level determined by the transfer characteristic. Figure 8-14 shows three release-time envelopes, which may be compared to the attack-time envelopes of a compressor that were shown in Figure 8-6.

The Noise Gate

On many multimicrophone and/or multichannel sessions, the overall noise level may often be reduced by muting any microphone input or tape channel that is for the moment inactive. However, given several microphones feeding several tape channels, it's hard enough to keep track of what's going on, without also trying to find and remove whatever is *not* going on at the same time. In this case, an

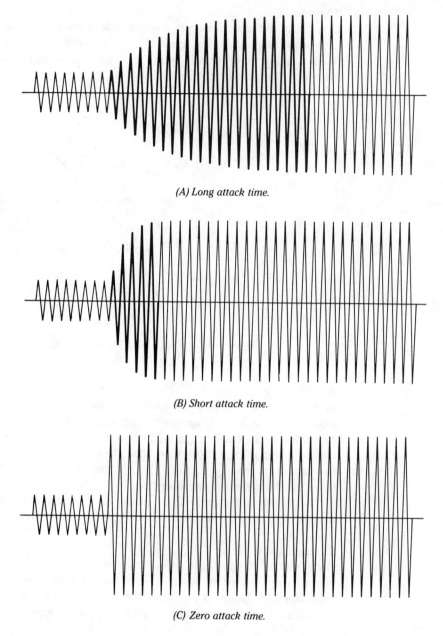

(A) Long attack time.

(B) Short attack time.

(C) Zero attack time.

Figure 8-13. The effect of varying the attack time of an expander
on a continuous sine wave.

expander used as a noise gate may be used to turn channels on and off as required.

A *noise gate* is simply an expander whose parameters are set to sharply attenuate an input channel whenever its level falls below threshold. The noise gate works on the assumption that the channel noise level is somewhat lower

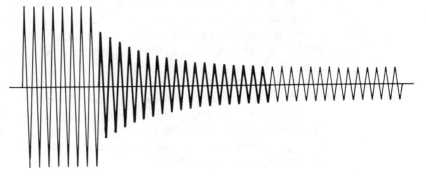

(A) Long release time.

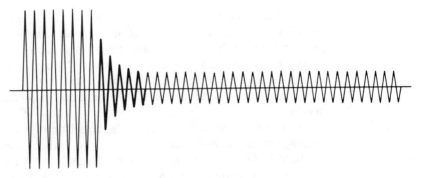

(B) Short release time.

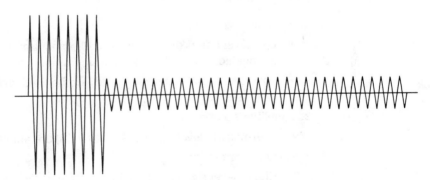

(C) Zero release time.

Figure 8-14. The effect on a continuous sine wave of varying the release time of an expander.

than the lowest signal level of interest. Therefore, if the threshold is set just below this minimum signal level, the expander's output level will be attenuated whenever the signal is absent, as for example during a musical pause. With a steep expansion ratio setting, the channel will be effectively turned off whenever the input level to the expander falls below threshold.

The noise gate may be used not only to clean up noisy channels, but to create a wide variety of special effects. For example, any percussive signal (a snare drum, for example) has a very short attack time, followed by a minimum sustain and then a rather fast decay. If the expander attack time is very short, and the threshold is set just below the peak level of the attack transient, then the percussive attack will pass through the system. But as soon as the instrument's own decay falls below threshold, the expander drops the level at a rate determined by its release-time setting. If the expander decay is faster than the normal decay of the instrument itself, the effect will be to "tighten" the sound, making it more percussive. In addition, background noise will be reduced during the intervals between each attack.

Combining Compression, Limiting, and Expansion

It's quite possible that the use of just one of the dynamic-range modifications described in this chapter will not be suitable, and may in fact create more problems than solutions. For example, compression alone may raise low-level signals too much, limiting may excessively "squash" the dynamic range, and expansion may cause severe distortion in the case of an unexpected transient peak. In short, a combination of two or more gain-changing devices may be needed.

Figure 8-15A shows a transfer characteristic of a comprehensive dynamics system that combines expansion, linear amplification, compression, and limiting.

Note in Figure 8-15A that all input levels lying between the expander and compressor rotation points are raised in level, while signals falling beyond these points are reduced in level. The characteristics of each part of the graph are summarized here.

1. Expander section
   - Low level noises (below the − 13 dB expansion threshold) are attenuated, due to the 1:4 expansion ratio.
   - Low level signals (above − 13 dB) are boosted, due to the same expansion ratio.
2. Amplifier section
   - Intermediate level signals (− 10 to 0 dB) are amplified by 10 dB.
3. Compressor section
   - Higher level signals (0 to + 10 dB) are compressed by the 2:1 compression ratio.
4. Limiter section
   - Very high level signals (above + 10 dB) are limited by the 10:1 compression ratio.

Given the flexibility of a dynamics system such as that described here, the program dynamic range may be adjusted so that background noise is attenuated, dynamic range is reduced, and only the occasional high-level peak is subjected to heavy limiting.

Summary of Compression/Expansion Ratios

As described in the preceding, the ratio of input to output dynamic range determines the mode of dynamic range modification. These ratios are listed in Table 8-3.

Table 8-3. Dynamic Range Modification Modes

I/O Ratio	Function
< 1:1	Expansion
= 1:1	Unity gain
> 1:1	Compression
= > 10:1	Limiting

Output Level and Gain Calculations

This section describes the equations used to plot the transfer characteristics seen in the preceding illustrations, and may be skipped by readers who are not interested in the math behind each graph.

The output level of a compressor or expander may be found by dividing the input level by the compression (or expansion) ratio. Thus,

$$dB_{out} = dB_{in}/CR \qquad \text{(8-1)}$$

where
    dB_{out} = output level, in dB
    dB_{in} = input level, in dB
    CR   = compression ratio

Equation 8-1 calculates the output for a transfer characteristic whose rotation point is 0 dB. Thus, it may be used to plot any of the slopes seen in Figures 8-3A or 8-11A, in addition to the compression and expansion segments of Figures 8-4 and 8-12.

To find the gain of the device, remember that decibel level is equal to $20 \log E$ (assuming a 1-V reference). Therefore, equation 8-1 may be rewritten as

$$20 \log E_{out} = 20 \log E_{in}/CR$$

and so

$$E_{out} = 10^a \qquad \text{(8-2)}$$

where
    $a = \log E_{in}/CR$

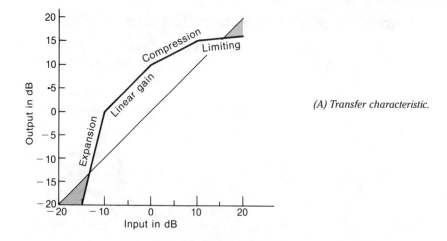

(A) Transfer characteristic.

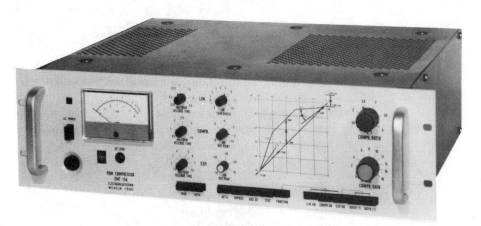

(B) The front panel controls of a combination system. Note the similarity between the engraved front-panel graph and the transfer characteristic in (A). The limiter ratio is fixed (>> 10:1) and does not appear on the front-panel graph (EMT 156 Stereo Compressor + Limiter courtesy Gotham Audio Corp.)

Figure 8-15. A combination expander, linear amplifier, compressor, and limiter.

When the rotation point is not 0 dB, the equation takes the following longer form:

$$E_{out} = 10^{a + b} \tag{8-3}$$

where
$b = [1 - (1/\text{CR})] \log E_{th}$
$E_{th} = \text{threshold voltage}$

In either case, the gain of the compressor or expander is

$$G = E_{out}/E_{in} \qquad \text{(8-4)}$$

Equation 8-4 was used to plot the gain characteristics seen in Figure 8-5.

Side-Chain Signal Processing

Like most other signal processors, the compressor or expander is usually inserted directly in the signal path. The signal enters the system, is compressed or expanded, and the processed signal appears at the device's output terminals. There is no other input/output path than the one through the gain-changing circuit.

However, it is sometimes desirable to combine the compressed/expanded signal with a nonprocessed version of itself. Therefore, there must be two signal paths available; a straight-line path with no compression, and a second path, or side chain, in which the signal passes through the compressor section. At the output of this section, the main channel and the side-chain signals are combined and then routed to the system output.

Several variations on this type of signal processing are described below.

Compression

The undesirable effects of compression are usually most audible at low and high levels. At low levels, the pumping and breathing described earlier is noticeable; at high levels, the output tends to sound "squashed" due to severe gain reduction.

Both effects may be minimized by confining the compression action to intermediate-level input signals. To do so, low-level signals are boosted, without compression, by a linear amplifier. Beyond threshold, the compressor takes effect, but compression is gradually reduced as the input level rises. This may be accomplished by placing an amplifier and a compressor in a side-chain path, as shown by the block diagram in Figure 8-16. For a gain before threshold of 10 dB, the side-chain amplifier gain is set at 2.16. Since the below-threshold gain of the compressor itself is unity, the side-chain gain is for the moment 2.16 × 1 = 2.16. When the side chain signal is summed with the main-path signal, the total below-threshold gain is therefore 20 log (2.16 × 1 + 1.00) = 10 dB.

When the input signal level rises above threshold, the compressor begins to function and its gain is reduced. For example, given a 2:1 compression ratio and a threshold of − 10 dB, the compressor output in the presence of a + 10 dB input may be found from equation (8-3), as shown below. Two examples are given in the following. Those in the first column are for a 1-V (dBV) zero reference and those in the second column are for a 0.775-V (dBu) zero reference.

$$E_{in} = 3.162 \text{ V } (+10 \text{ dBV}) \qquad\qquad E_{in} = 2.451 \text{ V } (+10 \text{ dBu})$$

The gain is therefore,

$$G = \frac{E_{out}}{E_{in}} = \frac{10^{a+b}}{3.162}$$

$$= \frac{10^{\log (0.3162)/2 + \log (3.162)/2}}{3.162}$$

$$= 1/3.162 = 0.316$$

$$G = \frac{E_{out}}{E_{in}} = \frac{10^{a+b}}{2.451}$$

$$= \frac{10^{\log (0.2451)/2 + \log (2.451)/2}}{2.451}$$

$$= 0.775/2.451 = 0.316$$

The side-chain gain is

$$2.162(0.316) = 0.684 \qquad\qquad 2.162(0.316) = 0.684$$

and the system gain (main channel plus side chain) is 1.684. The output voltage is the product of input voltage and gain, or

$$3.162(1.684) = 5.325 \text{ V} \qquad\qquad 2.451(1.684) = 4.127 \text{ V}$$

Therefore, the ouput level should be

$$20 \log (5.325) = 14.526 \text{ dB} \qquad 20 \log (4.127/0.775) = 14.526 \text{ dB}$$

Figure 8-16B plots input vs. output level through a side-chain compressor for several compression ratios, and it can be seen that as the input level rises beyond threshold, the action of the compressor moves the transfer characteristic gradually closer to the unity gain curve. In other words, as the input level increases, the contribution of the compressor—and therefore, the audibility of any of its side effects—decreases. Note that for a +10 dB input, the output level on the 2:1 compression curve agrees with the value found above.

By following the 2:1 compression ratio used before, it can be seen that the output is indeed about 14.52 dB for a +10 dB input. Also note that the effective compression ratio is less than that of an equivalent compressor acting alone. For example, over a −10 to +15 dB input range, the 2:1 output range is actually 0 to about +18.5 dB, for an effective compression ratio of 25:18.5, or 1.35:1.

Side-chain compression is also used in some noise reduction systems, as will be explained in greater detail in Chapter 9.

Expansion Using Side-Chain Compression

If the gain of the side-chain amplifier is set to unity, and the polarity of its output signal is reversed, there will be a below-threshold cancellation when this signal is combined with the main-channel signal. However, as the input signal rises in level there will be progressively less cancellation of the combined signals, since the diminishing gain in the side chain path effectively removes the cause of the cancellation. The technique may be useful when an expander is needed but not otherwise available.

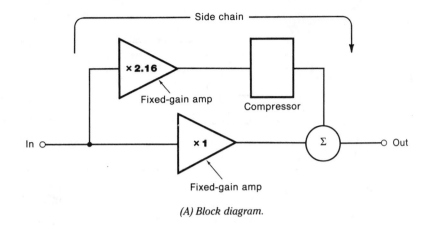

(A) Block diagram.

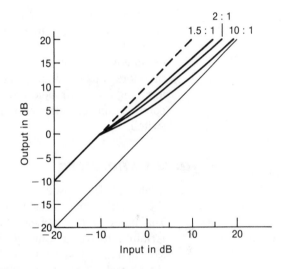

(B) Transfer characteristics for various compression ratios.

Figure 8-16. A side-chain compressor. The amplifier before the compressor has a gain of 2.16, for a total system gain of 3.16 (10 dB) below threshold.

Side-Chain Control of Gain

In the side-chain systems described before, the audio signal followed two paths through the signal processor, and these were combined before the system output.

Another important side chain is the one used to regulate the gain of a compressor or an expander. This is illustrated by the simple block diagram in Figure 8-17. Here, the side-chain signal is a DC control voltage proportional to the audio input signal amplitude. As the input signal changes level, so does this control voltage, which is used to vary the gain of a VCA (voltage-controlled amplifier) in the audio signal path. The diagram also shows a user-adjustable sensitivity control in the side chain which may be used to vary the amount of gain change that occurs for any fluctuation in input signal level.

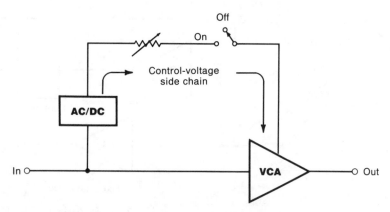

Figure 8-17. Block diagram showing the side-chain gain-sensing circuit in a compressor or expander.

The diagram also shows a two-position switch in the side chain. When the switch is in the *off* position the audio input signal will have no influence on system gain. In the case of an expander, the absence of a control voltage implies an extremely low-level signal (that is, none at all), and the expander attenuation is therefore at its maximum. For a compressor, the same condition would suggest an input signal so far below threshold that it cannot be sensed at all; hence, no compression. In either case, normal operation is restored simply by closing the switch.

Keyable Expanders

In about 1970, Allison Research, Inc. introduced the "KEPEX," (KEyable Program EXpander), which carried the gain-sensing mechanism one creative step further. The input to the gain-sensing circuit was brought out to an auxiliary input terminal, to which some *other* audio signal could be applied. Therefore, expansion action would be regulated by the gain of this externally applied keying signal, and not by the audio signal passing through the normal signal path.

Today many expanders provide this sort of flexibility, either by means of a front-panel *key* switch and auxiliary input jack, or via a pair of jacks labeled *detector out/in* (or similarly). For normal operation a jumper connects the two jacks, but this may be removed in order to route an external signal to the detector input. Figure 8-18 shows block diagrams and front panel controls for a typical expander.

To create a unique sound, a percussive instrument (e.g., drums) may be fed to the auxiliary or detector input, while a more sustained sound (organ, strings, etc.) is routed along the normal audio signal path. As the drum peaks drive the system gain up and down, the percussive envelope is applied to the organ or string output, as shown in Figure 8-19. The result sounds like an organ or string section being "played" by a drummer. The effect may be interesting or merely annoying, depending on the creativity of the engineer or producer.

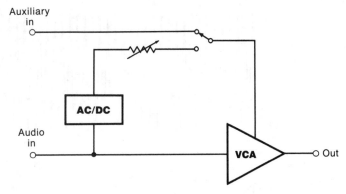

(A) Block diagram of key switch and auxiliary input.

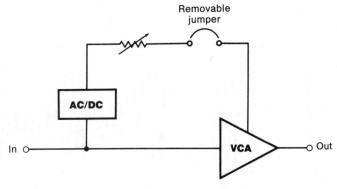

(B) Block diagram of detector out/in jacks with jumper.

(C) Front panel controls for dbx 904 Noise Gate. (Courtesy dbx, Inc.)

(D) Front panel controls for Valley International KEPEX II. (Courtesy Valley International)

Figure 8-18. A keyable expander.

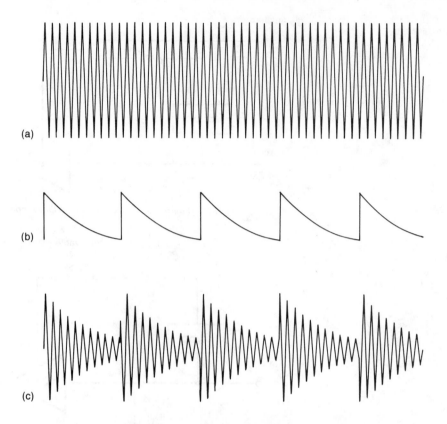

Figure 8-19. Keyed expander operation. A sustained audio signal (a) is fed to
the normal system input, with a percussive signal fed to the auxiliary input,
producing a DC control voltage (b) that regulates system gain.
The output waveform (c) is the same frequency as the input,
but its envelope follows the percussive input.

Compressor and Expander Applications

Although compressors and expanders are most often used to modify the sound of
a single instrument or channel to create a desired effect, there are several other
important applications to be considered. These include processing of the entire
program and protection against various undesired effects. A few such applications
are described in this section.

Program Compression

When mixing multiple sources to either one or two new channels, it's quite possible
that the combined signal(s) will need some compression that cannot be handled by
compressing the individual sources. For example, in a mono mix of, say, bass, piano,
and drums, there may be an occasional moment when the bass, together with the
other two instruments, produces a mixed output level that is excessive. Yet the bass

alone does not need compression, nor do the other instruments. In this case, *program compression* is recommended; that is, compression applied to the composite program, rather than to each of its component parts.

Program compression presents a potential problem to a center image in a stereo mixdown. For example, consider a vocal solo in the center with instrumental backup on either side. If either composite track requires compression, the soloist will drift toward the opposite track every time the compressor drives down the gain. As first one track and then the other is compressed, the soloist wanders back and forth across the stereo stage. The effect may be interesting, but not for long.

To resolve the problem, a variation on the external auxiliary input circuit may be used, as follows. Identical compressors are inserted in both the left and the right channel outputs. Their control voltages are combined and the common voltage is then fed to the VCAs in both compressors. Accordingly, if either track requires compression, the other track is compressed by the same amount. As a result, the center image does not shift back and forth between the two stereo channels.

Delay-Line Compression

As described earlier in this chapter, a compressor or expander needs a finite length of time in which to respond to the audio signal passing through it. This means that the leading edge of a transient peak may pass with little or no attenuation. Although such peaks may be too brief to be heard anyway, they may not be too brief to cause system trouble, especially in broadcast or satellite transmission lines.

To protect against this sort of distortion, some compressors include a delay line in the program signal path. The side chain path feeds the signal directly to the gain-control circuit, which drops the system gain as required. Meanwhile, due to the delay line the system gain is adjusted downwards *before* the audio signal arrives at the VCA. This delay before compression is often referred to as *predelay*.

Predelay has the advantage of allowing gain to be adjusted in anticipation of a peak, rather than waiting until the peak has already reached the VCA. As a result, waveform distortion caused by overshoots is eliminated. In order that the delayed signal is not time shifted with respect to other signals, the predelay gain-changing function is best applied within a program compressor, not in the compression of an individual instrument or audio channel.

Compression and Loudness Perception

As anyone who has sat through the interminable "but first, this important message" break already knows, radio and television commercials are always "louder" than the program they interrupt. People outside the audio industry generally assume there's someone at the station in charge of turning up the volume so the commercial may be heard from one end of the house to the other. Not much sympathy can be expected from assuring such listeners that the peak level is no higher than it was during the program.

In fact, commercials are often heavily compressed so that low-level information is considerably raised in gain, thereby narrowing the range between the lowest and highest level signals. Since the ear/brain mechanism bases its perception of loudness on average level over time, the heavily compressed program seems louder, even if a lightly compressed program on either side of it has higher-level transient peaks from time to time.

Similar compression is often applied to all programming on some radio stations in an effort to sound "louder" than competing stations. The practice is perhaps effective in attracting listeners who choose their programming by density instead of content.

In a more reasonable application of loudness by compression, some inherently quiet instruments may be given a little help in being heard via low-level compression. For example, with a little compression a small string section may better hold its own against louder instruments playing in the same room. This is often effective on those sessions where the producer expects the engineer to squeeze the sound of twenty violins out of half that number, or less. The same technique won't be approved for more traditional music where, presumably, the conductor gets the number of musicians that the score demands.

Voice-Over Compression

As a variation in program compression, a voice-over compressor, or "ducker," may be used whenever it is necessary to temporarily drop the level of a music program so that an announcement may be heard. A compressor in the line from the voice microphone generates a control voltage. However, this voltage is routed to VCAs in the musical or other program line(s), but not back to the vocal line itself, as shown in Figure 8-20. Therefore, whenever the voice microphone is active, the level of everything else is reduced.

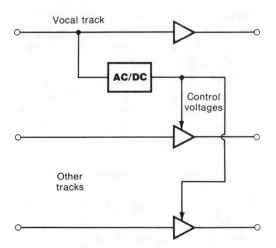

Figure 8-20. Block diagram for a voice-over compressor, or "ducker."

Frequency-Dependent Compression

It is sometimes desirable for compressor action to be made dependent on the frequency content of the program. This may be accomplished by inserting an equalizer in the control-voltage side chain. For example, in order to add extra compression at high frequencies, a high-frequency boost is applied in the side chain. Thus, in the presence of high frequencies the control voltage increases and the system gain is accordingly brought down.

In most cases the signal is treated by a single compressor, so of course the level of the entire frequency spectrum is brought down by the extra compression. However, a few multiband compressors are also available in which the input signal is divided into several frequency bands, each of which is processed separately and then recombined after compression.

Multiband compression is often found in noise reduction systems, and this application will be described in greater detail in Chapter 11 (pages 435 and 451).

A few applications of frequency-dependent compression are described in the following.

De-Esser

In the case of an overly sibilant vocal track, it's often desirable to compress just those sounds contributing to the sibilance problem. In this case the side-chain equalizer is set for a peak boost in the frequency range containing the sibilants. This drops the gain whenever a spitty "s," "sh," or similar sound occurs.

Figure 8-21 shows a de-esser with a front-panel frequency potentiometer for tuning the compression to the desired sibilance band.

Figure 8-21. Front-panel detail of a compressor with built-in de-esser function.
(Model 902 De-Esser courtesy dbx, Inc.)

Broadcast Compression

In broadcast transmission, a 50- or 75-μs time constant is used to boost high frequencies for a better signal-to-noise ratio. Therefore, it should be kept in mind that sibilants and other high-frequency information may cause adjacent-channel interference or other distortion effects. This may be a particular problem during a live broadcast, when the control-room engineer does not hear what is actually being transmitted. As with the de-esser just described, a high-frequency boost in the side chain will bring down the high-frequency level.

Figure 8-22 shows a 50-μs preemphasis characteristic and the resultant compression threshold when this equalization is applied in the side chain. In Chapter 7, a family of other time constants was shown in Figure 7-10 (page 267).

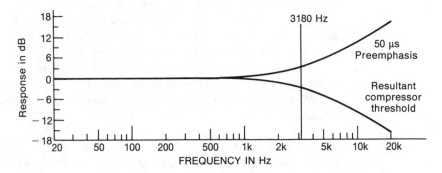

(A) A 50-μs preemphasis will lower the high-frequency compression threshold as shown here.

(B) The front-panel "EQUAL" switch on the EMT 257 Compact Limiter inserts the preemphasis network into the side chain. The time constant may be altered by changing the components on a plug-in module. (Courtesy Gotham Audio Corp.)

(C) The front-panel "BASS" switch on the EMT 256 Compact Compressor inserts a high-pass filter into the side chain to lessen the effect of low frequencies. (Courtesy Gotham Audio Corp.)

Figure 8-22. Compressors with high- and low-frequency controls.

Low-Frequency Compression

In Chapter 2, the equal-loudness contours shown in Figure 2-5 (page 53) illustrated that the ear is relatively insensitive to low-frequency energy. Therefore, a low-frequency instrument playing at high level may drive the overall program into compression, even though the instrument itself does not sound that loud to the listener. In fact, the compression may cause the "pumping" effect described earlier, as the program level rides up and down in rhythm with the bass instrument.

To minimize undesirable low-frequency effects such as this, some compressors incorporate a high-pass filter in the control-voltage side chain. When required, the filter may be switched in to minimize the effect of low frequencies on the overall compression.

9 Magnetic Tape and Tape Heads

More than 100 years have passed since Oberlin Smith of Cincinnati, Ohio, introduced magnetic recording to the world. Writing in the September 8th, 1888 edition of *The Electrical World*, Smith's article on "Some Possible Forms of Phonograph" proposed using a ferromagnetic wire as the recording medium. Within ten years, Valdemar Poulsen had developed his *Telegraphon*, whose storage medium was a steel wire wound around a cylinder, perhaps the first helical-scan magnetic recorder in history.

Recording on tape followed soon after. In 1928, a paper-based tape was patented by Fritz Pfleumer. One year later a steel tape was introduced by Dr. Curt Stille, and the Marconi-Stille steel tape recorder was built in the early 1930s. Unfortunately for the unwary operator, the machine exhibited some of the properties of a band saw (Thiele 1988).

In the intervening years, wire—and, fortunately, steel tape—have given way to more practical and certainly less dangerous recording media. And although the magnetic recording tape of today may face competition tomorrow from optical or other storage media, it remains—at least for the foreseeable future—the medium of choice for recording, storage, and reproduction of sound.

In any description of magnetic recording principles, it's difficult—perhaps almost impossible—to separate a discussion of tapes from a discussion of tape heads. Accordingly, this chapter doesn't even try. Here, the tape and the tape head are treated as two component parts of a complete magnetic recording system. However, the mechanism required to drag the former past the latter is treated separately, in the following chapter.

The present chapter begins with a brief overview of the complete system, followed by a discussion of magnetic tape fundamentals, then moves on to tape heads, and eventually concludes with a look at the interaction between the heads and the tape. The optimization of the record and playback sections of the tape recorder is described here in general terms, with specific system adjustments given more attention in the following chapter.

Figure 9-1 shows a simplified block diagram of the recording and reproduction system, including the tape and tape heads. During recording the tape passes through a field of varying magnetic strength, which emanates from a record head on the tape transport. Driven by the record amplifier, the record head functions as an electromagnetic transducer which converts the electric signal it receives into a magnetic field whose strength is proportional to that signal. As each segment of tape leaves the field, it is left with a permanent magnetic charge. If all goes well, the tape therefore contains an accurate magnetic replica of the electric signal that was applied to the head during the recording process.

When the recorded tape is played back later on, its magnetic field is sensed by the playback head and converted back into an electric signal which matches the original signal that was applied earlier to the record head.

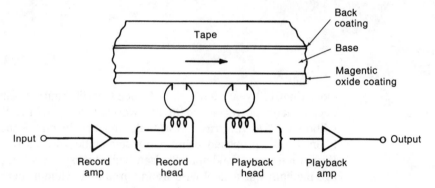

Figure 9-1. Detail view of magnetic tape and record and playback heads and amplifiers.

Physical Properties of Magnetic Tape

As Figure 9-1 illustrates, magnetic tape consists of a base material and magnetic coating, both of which are given brief descriptions here. This overview is based largely on the work of Müller (1988), an excellent resource which should be consulted for further details.

A back coating is also applied to many tapes, and this is also briefly described below.

Base Material

The purpose of the base material is to provide a robust yet flexible surface upon which the comparatively fragile magnetic coating can be applied so it can be transported past the tape heads. The base must be strong enough to stand up to the physical abuse of tape motion, which was no small consideration in the very early days, long before sophisticated tape-handling mechanisms had been developed. In addition, the tape itself must be able to withstand at least a little physical abuse during a razor-blade editing session.

Over the years various materials have been used as a tape base, as listed below (after Müller 1988).

Year	Base Material
1928	paper
1930	steel
1933, 1948	paper-impregnated
1936–1963	AC (cellulose acetate)
1943–1954	PVC (polyvinyl chloride)
since 1957	polyester
currently	polyester almost exclusively

In the event of a tape transport malfunction, tape with a paper or cellulose acetate base had the advantage of snapping cleanly instead of becoming deformed by stretching. Unfortunately, poor flexibility led to tape breaks under the slightest amount of pressure. But although repeated tape breaks were certainly a nuisance on early machines, such tapes could at least be spliced back together again with little or no lasting evidence of the fault.

By contrast, PVC-based tape was quite a bit stronger and more flexible, and a considerable amount of force was needed to break it. However, such tapes were prone to stretching under tension, so that information recorded on the deformed section could not be recovered. Given a choice, most engineers preferred to stick with the acetate-base tapes.

The more recent polyester base combines the best of both worlds; such tapes are flexible, physically robust, and quite resistant to stretching. Although polyester will stretch more than cellulose acetate, it will withstand about 20 percent more force before permanent deformation (Eilers 1969).

The physical advantages of a polyester base may be easily demonstrated by cutting off a short length of tape and then trying to break it by pulling on both ends. The tape will of course be grossly deformed, but a fair amount of strength is required before any permanent harm is done. Needless to say the experiment should be tried with either a tape scrap or someone else's master.

Magnetic Coating

The base material described above must be coated with a magnetic substance that is both physically flexible and magnetically consistent. This coating is obviously not a solid length of iron, but is instead a collection of individual magnetic particles (Müller 1988). By comparison to a solid bar, the isolated particles are not nearly as efficient as a magnetic surface, and it is therefore important to pack the particles as closely as possible in order to achieve at least a reasonable performance specification.

By just about any standard, the development of a successful recipe for this magnetic "soup" is an impressive accomplishment. Briefly, *acicular* (that is, needle-like) magnetic particles are suspended in a nonmagnetic liquid binder, to form a *slurry* which is then applied to one surface of the base material. For greatest packing density (i.e., particles per unit volume), the particles must be physically aligned along the direction of tape travel. This is accomplished by passing the slurry through a strong magnetic field prior to the drying process. Then as the solvent in the liquid binder evaporates, the particles remain fixed in the resulting plastic coating which becomes permanently bonded to the base.

Back Coating

The reverse side of some magnetic tapes is often given a special coating both to improve the tape's winding characteristics and to reduce static electricity. The highly conductive back coating usually contains fine particles of carbon, and typically displays an opaque black surface finish (Simmons 1979a).

A tape's winding characteristics may be easily demonstrated by fast-winding a complete reel of tape on a smoothly functioning tape transport. To avoid learning about tape adhesion the hard way, make sure the tape winds onto a reel, *not* to an open hub. If the wind is as even as a spool of unplayed tape, the back coating surface has sufficient texture to adhere naturally to the adjacent tape layer. However, if the rewound tape shows many protruding edges, the coating is probably quite slick and such tape should never be trusted to high-speed operation on an open hub.

Either characteristic is simply an indication of the back-coating treatment, and provides no useful indication of the tape's other performance specifications.

Slitting

Magnetic tape is manufactured in wide rolls which are then slit to produce the desired tape widths. Although such techniques are beyond the scope of this book, slitting is briefly mentioned here because it too has an effect on tape winding performance. If the slitting is not done with great precision, there can be a slight physical "wobble" in the tape which also leads to a poor wind.

Table 9-1 lists the physical dimensions of various magnetic tapes. Since tape manufacturers are inconsistent in choice of units, all thicknesses have been converted into micrometers (μm). The earlier term *microns* (μ) represents the same dimension and is still seen on some specification sheets. Note that in some cases, the only difference between tapes with adjacent catalog numbers is in the base thickness (e.g., Ampex 406/407, 3M 206/207, etc.). The higher number generally indicates the thinner base, thus permitting more tape on the reel for greater playing time.

For comparison purposes a few very early tapes are also included in the listing.

The Recording Process

The study of magnetic tape is made considerably more complex by the fact that tape does not have a linear transfer characteristic. Therefore, in the absence of any corrective system, a program with a wide dynamic range will display the following characteristics when played back.

Recorded Program Level	Playback Response
very low	missing
low	nonlinear compression
medium	linear transfer
high	nonlinear compression
very high	limiting

To understand the reason for the nonlinear transfer characteristic, the action of magnetic particles is briefly described here. However, the reader should keep in mind that the following is at best an overview of a very complex subject, and one that is still not completely understood. Since the first days of magnetic recording, it has not been unusual to stumble upon some new characteristic that seems to work, after which the experts spend no small amount of time trying to explain what's going on. Over the years, it has been observed that some explanations border on the magical (McKnight 1967b). Others are simply incomprehensible. In an effort to avoid the former and sidestep the latter, this chapter briefly summarizes some of the more plausible theories that have been proposed, and refers the reader to the cited references for greater details.

Domain Theory

In magnetic theory, a *domain* is considered to be the smallest particle that can sustain permanent magnetization (Camras 1988). Such particles are separated from each other by a nonmagnetic matrix, and in the absence of an externally applied magnetic force, the net magnetization of the domain field is close to zero, since the orientation of the permanent magnetic domains is random. The domain field should not be confused with the magnetic particles suspended in a binder solution and physically oriented as described earlier in the chapter (page 334). In fact, each such magnetic particle contains more than one domain.

When a slight magnetic force is applied, some of the domains are magnetically reoriented into alignment with that force. However, when the force is withdrawn, most of these domains return to their original orientation. Thus the tape is left with a poor magnetic record of the applied force.

At progressively higher levels of applied force, more domains are brought into alignment, and more of them will retain that alignment when the force is removed. In fact, within a certain range the magnetism left on tape will be a linear representation of the applied force.

Saturation

As the magnitude of the external force is progressively increased, still more domains are forced into alignment with it, until such time when all the domains are in the same magnetic alignment. At this point, the material has reached magnetic *saturation*, the condition in which further increase in the applied magnetic force has no additional effect on the domains. Saturation is analogous to

Table 9-1. Physical Dimensions of Magnetic Tapes

Manufacturer and Catalog No.	Year	Base Type*	Thickness, in Micrometers**			
			Magnetic Oxide	*Base*	*Back Coating*	*Total*
Agfa						
F 875	1948	AC	16	37	none	56
PEM 291D (digital)	1987	PE	5	20.5	1.5	27
PEM 297D (digital)	1981	PE	4	19	2	25
PEM 428	1976	PE	15.24	20.07	2.03	37.34
PEM 468	1974	PE	17.02	29.97	2.03	49.02
PEM 469	1984	PE	15.49	33.02	1.52	50.03
PEM 526 (bin mastering)	1977	PE	16.00	35.91	1.02	52.93
PER 528	1981	PE	16	29	none	45
Ampex						
406 (on NAB reel)	1972	PE	12.70	36.07	1.27	50.04
407 (on NAB reel)	1972	PE	12.70	22.35	1.27	36.32
456 (Grand Master)	1974	PE	13.97	36.07	1.27	51.31
467 (digital)	1978	PE	5.1	21.1	1.0	27.2
478 (low print)	1988	PE	13.2	36.07	1.52	50.79
615 (cassette C-60)	1965	PE	4.6	11.6	none	16.2
616 (cassette C-90)	1965	PE	4.6	6.6	none	11.2
619 (chrome C-60)	1965	PE	4.8	11.2	none	16.0
620 (chrome C-90)	1965	PE	4.8	7.1	none	11.9
621 (extended play)	1965	AC	10.16	23.37	none	33.53
631 (open reel dupl)	1965	PE	10.67	25.40	none	36.07
641 (double play)	1965	PE	10.14	12.67	none	22.81
642 (same, ext. play)	1965	PE	10.67	11.68	none	22.35
BASF						
Lextra	1949	***	55	–	–	55
LGH	1950	PVC	35	20	none	55
911 (on NAB reel)	1987	PE	17	33	3	53
920 (bin mastering)	1987	PE	12	30	none	42
930 (digital)	1989	PE	4	20	4	28
I.G. Farben						
C	1936	AC	28	37	none	65
Sony						
D-1/4, D-1/2 (digital)	1986	PE	5.5	20	2.0	27.5

Table 9-1 *(continued)*

Manufacturer and Catalog No.	Year	Base Type*	Thickness, in Micrometers** Magnetic Oxide	Base	Back Coating	Total
3M						
111	1948	AC	11.18	36.07	none	47.25
201	1962	AC	12.95	36.07	none	49.02
202 (early PE base tape)	1962	PE	12.95	36.07	none	49.02
206	1969	PE	14.2	36	2.0	52.2
207	1969	PE	14.2	21.6	2.0	37.8
226	1980	PE	14.2	33.0	2.0	49.2
227	1980	PE	14.2	20.1	2.0	36.3
250	1974	PE	17.3	33.0	2.0	52.3
265 (digital)	1977	PE	4.1	20.0	2.5	26.6
275 (digital)	1984	PE	6	21	none	27
806	1985	PE	10.2	36.0	2.0	48.2
807	1985	PE	10.2	23.4	2.0	35.6

*AC = cellulose acetate, PE = polyester, PVC = polyvinyl chloride
**1 micron (μ) = 1 micrometer (1 μm) = 10^{-6} meter (= .04 mil)
 1 mil = 25.40 μm (used above if mfrs. specification is in mils only)
***Entire tape thickness contained magnetic powder mixed with PVC

the action of a limiter with an infinite compression ratio. The saturation may be either positive or negative, depending on the direction of the applied magnetic force.

Saturation Recording

Since the analog signal recorded on tape must be a faithful replica of the applied audio signal, saturation must be avoided. In digital recording, however, the signal to be recorded is a data stream of ones and zeroes, and these are recorded by alternately saturating the tape in one magnetic direction for a digital one and in the other direction for a zero. The process is therefore often referred to as *saturation recording*.

Terminology

The following section introduces some additional terms that will be encountered when reading a magnetic tape specification sheet or a description of the magnetic properties of a tape head.

Until recently, most such literature for the U. S. market used a mix of customary English (mils, inches, feet) and cgs (centimeter-gram-second) units to describe various physical and magnetic properties. Due to an increase in metric awareness, SI units (formerly mks) are gradually taking the place of English/cgs units. However, the transition is by no means complete; some specification sheets still use English/cgs, some use SI, others supply both, and still others meander between them. In some of the literature, English/cgs units are referred to as "customary" units.

In subsequent descriptions of magnetic properties, both cgs and SI units are given, along with the means to convert from one to the other. When only one such unit is given, the equivalent unit is no longer, or has never been, in wide use.

Recording Field

A *recording field* is the magnetic field set up at the record head by an applied input signal.

SI Symbol	H	
SI unit	A/m	ampere-per-meter
cgs unit	Oe	oersted (after the Danish physicist Hans Christian Oersted, 1777–1851)

$$1 \text{ A/m} = 4\pi(10^{-3}) \text{ Oe}$$

Remanent Tape Magnetization

When a magnetic tape passes through the recording field just described, the amount of that field that is permanently stored on the tape is referred to as the *remanent tape magnetization*. To compare the tape's stored magnetic field with the applied recording field, both may be expressed in the same units—typically, kA/m.

SI symbol	M_r	
SI unit	A/m	ampere-per-meter
cgs unit	Oe	oersted

Flux

In Chapter 1, Figure 1-3 showed the magnetic field that exists within a generator. The imaginary lines shown in that illustration are referred to as magnetic lines of force, or *magnetic flux*. Since a recorded tape is in effect a permanent magnet, the strength of its stored magnetism is often referred to in terms of magnetic flux.

SI symbol	ϕ	
SI unit	Wb	weber (after the German physicist Wilhelm Eduard Weber, 1804–1891)
cgs unit	Mx	maxwells (after the Scottish physicist James Clerk Maxwell, 1831–1879)

$$1 \text{ Wb} = 10^8 \text{ Mx}$$

Flux Density

Within a permanent magnet such as the oxide coating on recording tape, *flux density* is a measure of the flux per unit of area. Flux density is a function of magnetic field strength, H, and magnetization, M, which are related by the formula $B = \mu_0(H + M)$ where μ_0 is the magnetic constant 1.28 μH/m. Magnetic field strength is due to electric current flow and magnetization is the contribution from a magnetic material such as iron. Thus the flux density from a solenoid is entirely from its magnetic field strength, and the flux density of a permanent magnet is entirely that of its magnetization. In other words, a tape head exhibits magnetic field strength, while magnetic tape exhibits magnetization.

SI symbol	B	
SI unit	T	tesla (after the American/ Yugoslavian inventor Nikola Tesla, 1856–1943), or
	Wb/m²	webers-per-meter²
cgs unit	G	gauss (after the German mathematician Karl Friedrich Gauss, 1777-1855)

$$1 \text{ T (Wb/m}^2) = 10^4 \text{ G}$$

Retentivity

As a measure of the actual performance of magnetic tape under dynamic operating conditions, it is convenient to refer to the tape's ability to retain an image of the applied magnetic force, once that force is withdrawn. *Retentivity* is a measure of the flux density remaining after the external magnetic force has been removed.

Note that a material's flux density may be quite high in the presence of an applied magnetic field, but its retentivity low once the field is withdrawn.

The symbol and units for retentivity are the same as those given for flux density.

Coercivity

Once a magnetic material has been driven into saturation, *coercivity* is a measure of the magnetic field strength required to return the material to a state of zero magnetization.

SI symbol	H	
SI unit	A/m	ampere-per-meter
cgs unit	Oe	oersted

$$1 \text{ A/m} = 4\pi(10^{-3}) \text{ Oe}$$

Permeability

The *permeability* of a magnetic material is a ratio of magnetic flux density, B, to the applied magnetic field strength, H.

SI symbol	μ	
SI unit	H/m	henries per meter (after the American physicist Joseph Henry, 1797–1878)

Relative permeability is a ratio of a material's own permeability to that of air.

SI symbol	μ_r	
SI unit	none (dimensionless ratio)	

For example, a few relative permeability figures are given here.

A vacuum	1.28
Magnetic recording tape	1.5–2
Magnetic head core	2,000–20,000

Operating Level

For magnetic tape applications, it is convenient to measure magnetic strength in terms of the width of a recorded tape track, without regard for the entire magnetic area of the tape (that is, tape width-times-depth of the oxide coating). For example, a single track on a playback head senses the flux of a small portion of the total tape width. From an operational point of view, it is important to know the effect the stored magnetic flux will have on the tape head.

Accordingly, a tape's *operating level* is an indication of the recorded flux required to deflect a meter to its zero reference mark.

SI symbol	ϕ/w	(w = width of track)
SI unit	Wb/m	webers per meter
cgs unit	mMx/mm	millimaxwells per millimeter

Operating level is also referred to as *reference level* or *reference fluxivity*, and is described in greater detail later in this chapter, in the section on test tapes (page 376).

Remanent Saturation Fluxivity

The *remanent saturation fluxivity* is a measure of the flux per unit of track width after a saturating magnetic field has been withdrawn. The units are those just given for operating level and, again, Wb/m is the common unit.

Since tape track widths are considerably narrower than the reference one-meter width, operating level and remanent saturation flux are usually expressed in nanowebers-per-meter (nWb/m, 1 nWb = 10^{-9} weber).

Magnetization vs. Recording Field

If magnetic tape were an ideal medium, there might be some nice linear relationship between tape magnetization, M_r, and the applied recording field strength, H; say, $M_r = kH$, where k is a constant. Of course there is no such convenient relationship, as illustrated by Figure 9-2A, which plots recorded magnetization versus applied magnetizing field. Note that as the applied field strength is gradually increased from zero to a positive maximum, and then returned to zero, the stored magnetization increases to the positive saturation point of the tape and then falls off again, but does not return to zero as the field strength diminishes. Instead, some residual magnetism, or retentivity, is left on the tape, and a further applied force, $-H$, is required to bring the tape back to zero magnetization. As noted above, the tape's coercivity is the amount of force required to completely demagnetize the tape.

In Figure 9-2B, the applied force continues its increase in the negative direction, until the tape eventually reaches negative saturation. Then the force is once more reduced to zero, again leaving the tape with some residual magnetism on it.

Hysteresis Loop

If the magnetizing force is now increased in the positive direction, the curve eventually reaches the positive saturation point again. Now, if the applied force continues to swing between positive and negative maxima, alternately driving the tape into positive and negative saturation, the curve will follow the completed loop shown in Figure 9-2C, which is referred to as a *hysteresis loop*; derived from the Greek *hystérēsis*, signifying a delayed state. Here, the delay refers to the lag in reacting to a changing magnetic force.

The shape of the hysteresis loop will vary from one magnetic tape to another, depending on the tape's coercivity and retentivity, both of which are published on a tape's specification sheet.

The performance of a magnetic material is sometimes evaluated in terms of the squareness of its hysteresis loop. For example, Figure 9-3 shows hysteresis loops for temporary and permanent magnets. In the ideal case, a temporary magnet should retain no magnetization when the applied magnetic force is removed. In other words it should have zero retentivity. Figure 9-3A shows the loop for a material with a very low retentivity, and therefore a low coercivity as well (since it should not take much force to remove the slight residual magnetization). Such material would make a good temporary magnet, but would not be of much use in a magnetic tape. By contrast, Figure 9-3B shows a material with a very high retentivity and likewise a high coercivity. The tape retains most of the magnetic force applied to it, and as a consequence may require a comparatively large force to return the tape to zero magnetization. This material would be more suited to magnetic tape than the first example.

M-H Curve

Although the hysteresis loop is of value in showing the coercivity and retentivity of a magnetic tape, some additional information is required to help understand how the tape will react to something a little more useful than a saturating magnetic field (page 337). For example, we really need to know how much magnetism will remain on the tape for various intermediate levels of applied force. In other words, if the horizontal axis represents input level, and the vertical axis is the magnetization left on the tape for various input levels, what does the transfer characteristic really look like?

To find out, the applied magnetic force is increased to some intermediate level, then returned to zero. The magnetization is noted, and the procedure is repeated for all input levels between zero and saturation. The resultant *M-H* curve shown in Figure 9-4A (page 346) represents the transfer characteristic of the tape. Note that the curve has two linear segments, but is nonlinear at low and high input levels.

In Figure 9-4B (page 347), the transfer characteristic is used to plot the output waveform when a sine wave is recorded on tape, and it is seen that the output is a distorted replica of the input waveform.

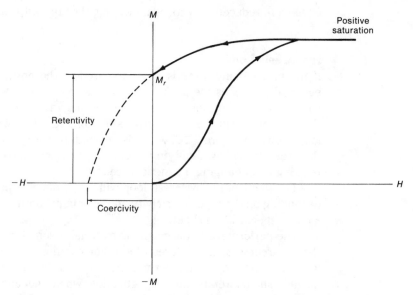

(A) If a positive force is applied and then withdrawn, the tape is left with some residual
magnetism, or retentivity. Coercivity is the opposing force required to return the tape
to a state of zero magnetization.

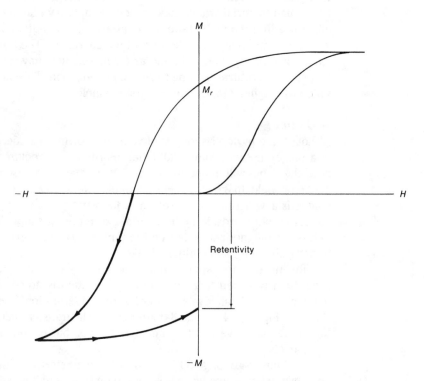

(B) If the opposing force continues to increase and is then withdrawn, the tape is driven
into negative saturation, and again left with some residual magnetization.

Figure 9-2. Magnetic tape magnetization, *M*, versus magnetizing field, *H*.

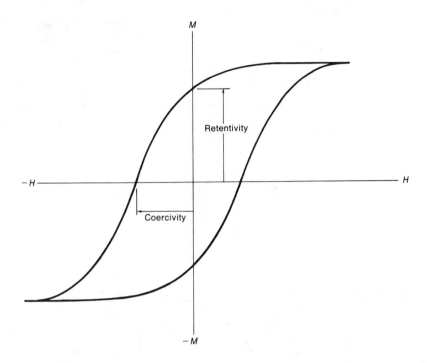

(C) The hysteresis loop shows the reaction lag between applied force and residual magnetization.

Figure 9-2 *(continued)*

Bias

The nonlinearity of the tape transfer characteristic was at first minimized by applying a direct-current offset, or DC bias, to the applied input signal. Although the system accomplished its task, there were certain limitations which were eventually overcome by AC bias. Both systems are described below.

DC Bias

A nonlinearity cure of sorts was incorporated in Poulsen's first Telegraphon. As shown in Figure 9-5 (page 348), a DC bias voltage was used to offset the input signal to a midpoint on one of the linear segments of the transfer characteristic. The audio input signal would then alternate above and below the bias point.

The DC bias system had the disadvantage of restricting the input signal to the rather narrow dynamic range represented by just one of the linear segments of the transfer characteristic. And as the illustration shows, the system utilized less than half of the tape's available magnetization. Nevertheless, DC biasing remained a standard practice through the early 1940s (Camras 1988).

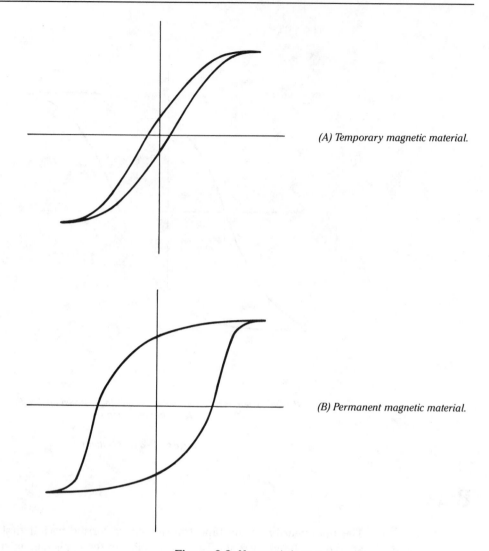

(A) Temporary magnetic material.

(B) Permanent magnetic material.

Figure 9-3. Hysteresis loops.

AC Bias

AC biasing was discovered almost by accident during experiments by Carlson and Carpenter in 1921, and later on by Von Braunmühl and Weber in 1940 (Tall 1958). In each case, an oscillating audio amplifier applied a very high-frequency current to the record head, and the observers noted an improvement in the recorded quality of the applied audio signal. The latter research team subsequently developed the Braunmühl-Weber AC-bias theory, and are generally given credit for the introduction of AC bias in commercial tape recorders. However, as a historical note it should be pointed out that AC bias was also under independent development by researchers in other parts of the world at about the same time (Nagai, Sasaki, Endo 1938, Camras 1941).

To help illustrate the basic principle of AC bias, Figure 9-6 (page 349) shows three waveforms: an audio signal, a bias signal (a high-level, ultrahigh fixed frequency), and a combination of the two. In practice the relative amplitude of the bias signal would be considerably higher than that shown in the illustration. For comparison purposes an amplitude-modulated waveform is also shown; however, it is *not* used for biasing.

In Figure 9-7 (page 350), the amplitude of the bias frequency has been adjusted so that its positive and negative peaks each fall at the midpoint of one of the linear sections of the transfer characteristic. As a result, the audio waveform is confined to the two linear segments, and the average amplitude is recorded linearly on the tape (Camras 1988).

To take another view of AC bias (Camras 1949), the positive bias peaks may be considered to displace the *M-H* curve (Figure 9-4A) horizontally to the right, while the negative peaks displace an identical curve to the left, as shown respectively by the $M+$ and $M-$ characteristics in Figure 9-8 (page 351). The average of the two curves is the mostly linear characteristic also shown in the figure.

Bias and Recorded Performance Specifications

The applied bias current has an effect on all recorded parameters of magnetic tape: distortion, sensitivity, maximum output level, modulation noise, and frequency response. It must therefore be carefully set to achieve the best overall performance specifications. The influence of bias current on various recording parameters is described in the following sections and illustrated by the graphs in Figure 9-9 (pages 352–353).

Distortion
If the bias current is set too low, a portion of the input waveform falls on the nonlinear segment of the transfer characteristic separating the two linear segments, resulting in a distorted output waveform.

Assuming the bias current is gradually raised from an initially low setting, third-harmonic distortion diminishes until a minimum level is reached. If bias current is increased beyond this point, distortion again increases, although to a lesser degree. Beyond a certain point the distortion levels off, and may once again decrease if bias level continues to rise.

Sensitivity
Tape sensitivity is also a function of bias current. Again starting at a low bias setting, recorded sensitivity rises with increasing bias, then falls off again as bias continues to increase. The point at which output level begins to fall off varies with recorded wavelength, which for convenience is described here in terms of frequency at a reference tape speed of 15 in/s (38 cm/s). For example, if bias is increased from an initially low level while recording a series of test tones at a fixed input level, all frequencies will initially rise in level. At a certain bias setting, a 10-kHz input signal begins to fall off in level. Meanwhile, a 1-kHz signal continues to rise as bias is increased beyond this setting. In fact, the 10-kHz signal may fall by some 2–3 dB before the 1-kHz signal begins its own fall.

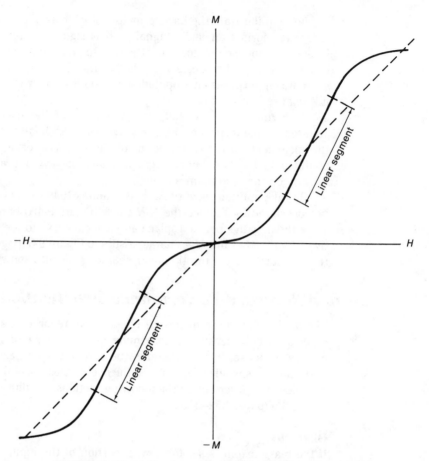

(A) M-H *curve illustrating the transfer characteristic for a magnetic tape.*

Figure 9-4. Magnetic tape transfer characteristics.

Maximum Output Level (MOL)

The *maximum output level* of a magnetic tape is the magnetization level at which a recorded 1-kHz sine wave reaches 3 percent third-harmonic distortion. This point is again a function of bias level; as bias is increased, the maximum output level quickly rises until it reaches a plateau, beyond which there may be a slight further increase. At 10 kHz, MOL falls off quite gradually as a function of increasing bias.

Modulation Noise

Modulation noise is a low-level noise signal that occurs on either side of a recorded tone, and is generally an artifact of the tape manufacturing process. To a certain extent modulation noise is masked by the signal causing it, but in extreme cases a "grainy" noise may be perceived, especially in the presence of a single recorded frequency.

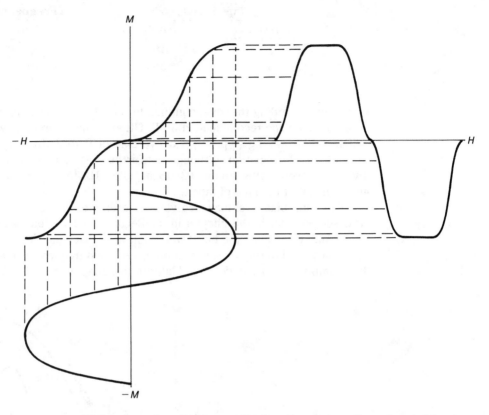

(B) Output waveform distortion resulting from the curve's nonlinear characteristic.

Figure 9-4 *(continued)*

As bias level is increased, the modulation noise level curve closely follows the distortion curve described above. However, the optimum bias settings for minimum distortion and minimum modulation noise may be slightly apart.

Optimum Bias Setting

As illustrated in Figure 9-9, it is common practice to express bias level in dB, usually as observed by metering the recorded tape output in the playback mode. Since the best bias setting for each of the parameters is slightly different, most tape manufacturers recommend an optimum setting that achieves a reasonable balance of frequency sensitivities and distortion levels. For example, in the graphs shown in Figure 9-9, Ampex recommends adjusting the bias for maximum high-frequency sensitivity, and then overbiasing by 3 dB. In other words, while recording a high frequency test tone, increase the bias level until the output level reaches a maximum. The frequency of the test tone varies according to tape speed, and should be as shown here.

Tape Speed		Frequency
(in/s)	*(cm/s)*	*(kHz)*
7.5	19	5
15	38	10
30	76	20

While recording the tone, continue to raise the bias level until the observed level drops by the recommended 3 dB. Other manufacturers may recommend a different bias setting (typically, an overbias of 0 to 3 dB), depending on the specific tape formulation. Although not further described here, another alternative is to overbias by about 0.2 dB at 1,000 Hz to achieve a setting that is independent of the kind of tape used.

Optimum bias level may also vary according to the record-head gap length, as described later in this chapter in the Record Head section (page 360).

In any case, once the bias level is set, level discrepancies between the high frequency used during biasing and other recorded frequencies may be corrected by equalization, as also described later in this chapter (page 376).

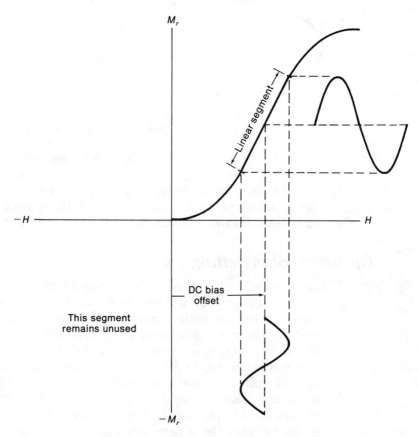

Figure 9-5. The DC bias system. The bias voltage offsets the applied audio signal into a linear segment of the transfer characteristic.

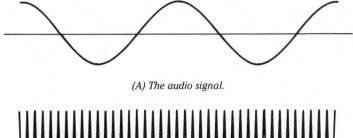

(A) The audio signal.

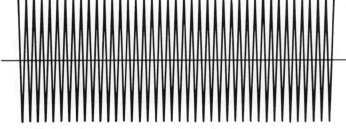

(B) The bias signal.

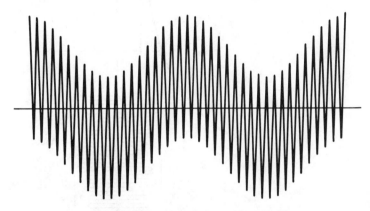

(C) Combination of the audio and bias signals.

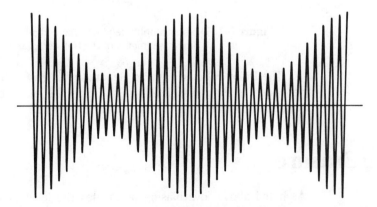

(D) An amplitude-modulated combination of audio and bias (for comparison purposes only; not used in bias systems).

Figure 9-6. The combination of audio and bias.

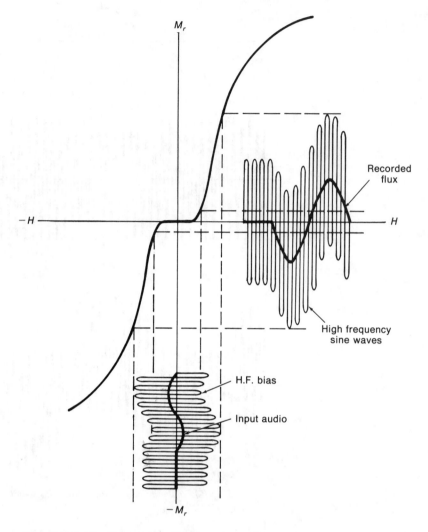

Figure 9-7. The bias amplitude places the audio-frequency signal within the
linear segments of the transfer characteristic.

The Dolby *HX* and *HX Pro* Headroom Extension Systems utilize a program-dependent sliding bias level to optimize the bias according to the dynamic content of the program.The systems are described in Chapter 11 (pages 438, 441).

Tape Erasure

As noted above, overbiasing attenuates the level of the recorded signal. The reason for this is that the bias signal begins to act as an erasing force, and actually erases part of the signal during the recording process. Although excessive bias

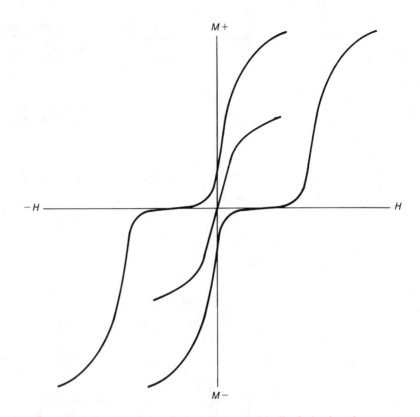

Figure 9-8. A linear transfer characteristic graphically derived as the average of two *M-H* curves (after Camras 1949).

defeats the purpose of trying to record in the first place, it does lead us to another important recording procedure, that of erasing a tape prior to use.

To get a better idea of how a tape is erased, consider a very high-level alternating-current bias signal fed to a tape head. A stationary segment of magnetic tape lying across the head will be alternately driven into positive and negative saturation. However, if the tape segment is moved slowly away from the applied magnetic force, each alternation will have slightly less effect on that segment. As a result, the hysteresis loop (Figure 9-2C) for the segment gets smaller and smaller; with each alternation the residual magnetism is less, and eventually the tape segment leaves the vicinity of the head in a completely demagnetized state.

The erasing force just described is so great that if an audio signal were actually present it would have little or no effect on the tape. From this we may deduce that if it were possible to increase the bias signal far beyond the optimum level suggested by the tape manufacturer, eventually nothing would be recorded on the tape, regardless of the actual presence of an audio signal. However, anything previously recorded would be erased. And that of course is the function of the erase head.

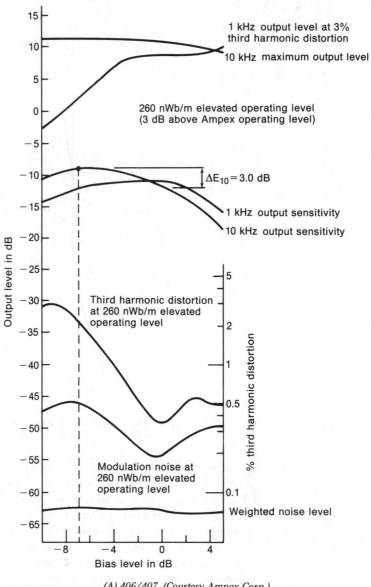

(A) 406/407. (Courtesy Ampex Corp.)

Figure 9-9. The effect of bias on recording parameters. The graphs are taken from the Ampex specification sheet for its 406/407 and Grand Master studio mastering tapes. The sharp dip in the third-harmonic distortion level may vary with recording level.

The block diagram in Figure 9-10 illustrates the conceptual relationship between a tape recorder's erase and record heads. A high-level high-frequency erase current is fed directly to the erase head. A similar current is also fed to the record head, where it is known as the bias current. However, before reaching the

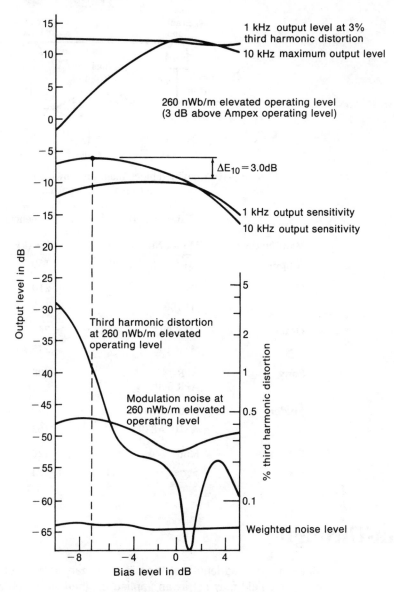

(B) Grand Master. (Courtesy Ampex Corp.)

Figure 9-9 *(continued)*

record head the current is reduced to the level required for biasing, and it is combined with the record signal as shown earlier in Figure 9-6.

In practice, the erase head requires considerably more power than the record head, but the frequency is relatively unimportant. Most modern tape recorders use an erase frequency that is one-third or one-half that of the bias frequency, as listed in Table 9-2.

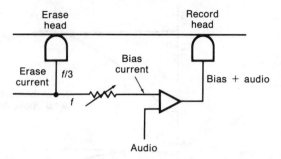

Figure 9-10. Simplified block diagram showing erase and record heads, plus bias level control.

Table 9-2. Bias and Erase Frequencies

Manufacturer	Model No.	Bias (kHz)	Erase (kHz)
Ampex	AG-440, MM-1100	150	150
MCI	JH-24	210	105
	JH-100	120	120
Otari	MTR-90	246	123
	MTR-100	245.76	81.92
Sony	APR-24, APR-5000	400	100
Studer	A80, A800	240	80
	A810, A820	153.6	153.6
3M	M56	120	120
	Series 79	234	234

Print-Through

Since a recorded length of tape is a permanent magnet, it follows that its own magnetic field may act as an applied magnetic force on any other piece of tape that comes in contact with it. As a practical consequence, a reference signal on any layer of tape tends to magnetize the layers immediately adjacent to it when the tape is wound on a reel. During playback, this *print-through* phenomenon is heard as low-level echoes of the reference signal, which are identified as

Preecho   one or more echoes heard before the reference signal

Postecho   one or more echoes heard after the reference signal

In extreme cases, such as a loud noise preceded and followed by periods of silence, the print-through may be clearly heard through several layers of tape on either side of the sound.

In music recording, preecho is often perceptible (and distracting) during the relative silence immediately before a musical entrance. By contrast, postecho may be masked by the level of the music which follows.

Print-Through Reduction

There are several techniques that may be used to reduce the effect of print-through, the first of which is to store all recorded tapes tails out; that is, do not rewind after recording or playing the tape. On a stored reel, print-through radiates outwards with greater efficiency. Therefore, the greatest print-through will be in the postecho direction where, as noted, it may be masked by the music itself.

It has also been found that fast-winding a tape a few times before playing it reduces the print-through already recorded.

High temperature storage accelerates print-through, as does storing the tape in a tightly wound condition. As a final, though obvious, prevention measure, remember that print-through is a function of the magnitude of the stored signal—the lower the level, the less the print-through. In other words, print-through is just one more reason to avoid recording at excessive tape operating levels.

Low-Print Tapes

Many manufacturers produce a low-print tape, in which the base material is somewhat thicker than on the standard-play tape and the oxide coating may be slightly thinner. By contrast, extended play tapes, which pack more tape on a reel by reducing the base thickness, are more prone to print-through.

A low-print tape is often preferred for voice recordings, where there is statistically little signal to mask print-through either before or after each word. In this case, a tape whose formulation has been optimized for minimum print-through (perhaps at the cost of other parameters) may be desirable (Bertram 1980).

Most magnetic tape specification sheets list a print-through figure, which is defined as the ratio of output level between a signal of 1 kHz recorded at reference level and the signal on the adjacent tape layer after 24 hour storage at a temperature of 20 degrees C (68 degrees F). Table 9-3 (page 357) lists the print-through specifications for various magnetic recording tapes and the standard (or other published details) under which the print-through was measured.

Record and Playback Head Characteristics

We next turn our attention to the other half of the magnetic recording system—the tape head. Figure 9-11A is a detail view of a typical magnetic tape head gap. The magnetic tape rides across the gap in the direction shown.

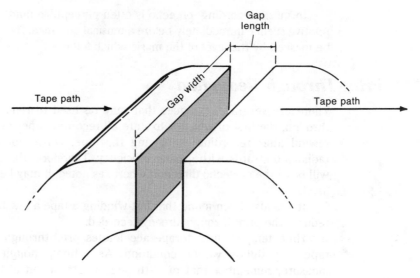

(A) Head gap and tape path across the head.

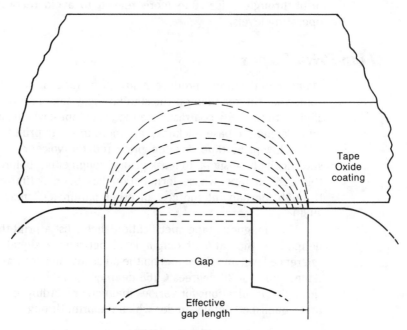

(B) Magnetic field across the gap.

Figure 9-11. Magnetic tape heads.

Gap Dimensions

In any discussion of the interaction between magnetic tape and tape heads, the critical dimension is the distance from one gap edge to the other. As pointed out in Figure 9-11A, this dimension is usually referred to as the *gap length*, while the

(C) Tape heads of various types: from left to right—2-track, ¼"; 8-track, 1"; 2-track, ½";
16-track, 2"; 24-track, 2"; 2-track, ¼"; 4-track, 1"; mono, ¼", 4-track, ½".
(Courtesy Studer Revox America, Inc.)

Figure 9-11 *(continued)*

Table 9-3. Print-Through Specifications

Manufacturer	Catalog No.	Print-Through (dB)	Measurement Standard
Agfa	PEM 428	56	DIN 45 519 Part 1
	PEM 468	58	DIN 45 519 Part 1
	PEM 469	53	DIN 45 519 Part 1
Ampex	406	58	1 kHz @ 15 in/s, stored 24 hrs. @ 70° F
	407	57	1 kHz @ 15 in/s, stored 24 hrs. @ 70° F
	456	55	1 kHz @ 15 in/s, stored 24 hrs. @ 70° F
	478	60	1 kHz @ 15 in/s, stored 24 hrs. @ 70° F
BASF	911	56.5	IEC/DIN (not specified)
3M	206	50	DIN 45 519 Part 1
	207	48	DIN 45 519 Part 1
	226	53	1 kHz @ 15 in/s, stored 24 hrs. @ 20° C, 50% R.H.
	227	50.5	1 kHz @ 15 in/s, stored 24 hrs. @ 20° C, 50% R.H.
	250	47	DIN 45 519 Part 1
	256	59	DIN 45 519 Part 1
	806	55	1 kHz @ 7.5 in/s, stored 24 hrs. @ 20° C, 50% R.H.
	807	52.5	1 kHz @ 7.5 in/s, stored 24 hrs. @ 20° C, 50% R.H.
	808	60	1 kHz @ 7.5 in/s, stored 24 hrs. @ 20° C, 50% R.H.
	809	58.5	1 kHz @ 7.5 in/s, stored 24 hrs. @ 20° C, 50% R.H.

longer gap *width* runs in the same direction as tape width. This departure from
traditional measurement practice is sometimes confused when this distance is
referred to as width, as happens now and then. However, the length/width

ambiguity notwithstanding, the dimension referred to is probably clear from the context in which it appears.

The gap is usually filled with a nonmagnetic material to provide mechanical support and prevent the gap from becoming contaminated with tape oxide. Table 9-4A lists the typical gap lengths that may be encountered on tape heads (after Camras 1988). The table also lists the record-head gap lengths actually found on several professional tape recorders (after Simmons 1979b). In each case, the gap width (not given) is whatever it takes to adequately cover the recorded track width.

Table 9-4. Typical Magnetic Tape Gap Lengths

(A) Tape Head Gap Lengths

Head	Gap Length				
	Micrometers			*Mils*	
	min.	*max.*		*min.*	*max.*
Erase	25	125		1	5
Record	2.5	12		0.1	0.5
Playback	1.5	6		0.06	0.25

(B) Record Head Gap Lengths

Manufacturer	Model No.	Gap Length	
		Micrometers	*Microinches*
Ampex	ATR-100	12.70	500
	AG-440	12.70	500
	MM-1200	6.35	250
MCI	JH series	7.62	300
Otari	MTR-100	n/a	n/a
Scully	280B	4.06–5.08	160–200
Sony	APR-24	7.62	300
Studer	A820	7	276
	others	7.19	283
3M	M79	6.35	250

Head Design Details

Although erase, record, and playback heads are similar in concept, each is optimized to suit its designated task, the most obvious difference being between the record and playback functions.

When a signal is applied to the coil of an erase or record head, a magnetic field is set up in the head core. However, in order to complete the magnetic path, the flux lines must bridge the gap in the head. In comparison to the core itself, the gap is a very poor magnetic path, and the flux lines tend to move out of the gap (Manquen 1987), as shown in Figure 9-11B. A tape passing over the gap provides a better magnetic path than the surrounding air, and in the process becomes magnetized in proportion to the applied magnetic force.

Head Block

On many modern tape recorders the heads are mounted within a *head block*, an integral assembly containing all the heads, which may be removed from the transport for replacement by a head block containing a different head format. Head preamplifiers are often contained within the head block assembly, and are thus automatically swapped along with the heads themselves.

Erase Head

The erase head is, in effect, a special-purpose record head. In the detail view seen in Figure 9-11B, note that the flux lines are straight within the gap, elliptical near the top of the head surface, and semicircular at greater distances from that surface. As might be expected, magnetic field strength decreases with vertical distance from the gap.

The gap length of the erase head is quite large, so that a strong alternating erase field—represented by the elliptical flux lines—saturates the oxide coating. The tape is exposed to multiple cycles of this high-level erase current while passing over the gap.

Despite an adequate initial erasure, the magnetic tape may display a partial recovery, in which a small fraction of the erased signal is restored to the tape. This may be attributed to the erase current acting as a bias current, partially recording the erased signal back onto the tape. To counteract this phenomenon, some erase heads place a double gap in the head. Since the recovery is almost instantaneous, the second gap erases the restored signal. The subsequent recovery level is too low to be of any practical consequence.

Record Head

As a general rule of thumb, the optimum record-head gap length is about equal to the required depth of penetration of the applied magnetic field (Dyer 1976). Therefore, in order to magnetize the entire oxide coating, the gap length should be equal to the coating thickness. In actual practice, gap lengths usually fall within the limits seen in Table 9-4, which shows a maximum gap length that is less than the oxide thickness of some presently available tapes (as was shown in Table 9-1). However, the *effective gap length* is greater than the actual gap size, as may be surmised from Figure 9-11B, in which the radiating flux lines appear to originate beyond the dimensions of the gap itself.

Bias Level and Gap Length

Some magnetic tape specification sheets recommend varying the amount of overbias according to the record-head gap length. For example, Ampex suggests the following modifications to the 3 dB overbias seen on its specification sheets.

Record Gap (mils)	Length (μm)	Overbias by (dB)
1.0	25.4	1.0
0.5	12.70	2.5
0.25	6.35	3.0

Record Head Response

If a constant-current signal is applied to a record head, a constant level of flux will be recorded on the tape. However, the nature of most recorded material is such that the energy levels at the extreme low frequencies are considerably lower than those within the midrange. Therefore, it has long been a practice to add a pre-emphasis network in the record amplifier. Its purpose is to function as a simple noise-reduction system; low frequencies are boosted in order to record them above the residual noise level of the tape and the system electronics. During playback a complementary postemphasis network restores the low-frequency signal to its proper level and in the process reduces the accompanying tape/system noise.

This low-frequency record boost was initiated long before the introduction of noise reduction systems and general improvements in record head technology. It has long been felt (McKnight 1962) that such compensation is no longer necessary, and indeed may work to the detriment of some forms of musical program, notably pipe organ recordings or any other music with a significant low-frequency content. Accordingly, standards published in recent years often omit low-frequency equalization.

The specific amount of low-frequency playback equalization defined by various standards is described later in this chapter (page 366).

Playback Head

When a recorded tape passes over the gap in a playback head, the tape's magnetic flux flows through the head core. The lines of force cut through the coil wrapped around the core, setting up an induced voltage across the coil. Such a system is known as a *differentiating head* (McKnight 1960), and its output may be expressed by the differential equation

$$e = -N\frac{d\phi}{dt}$$

where

e = output voltage

N = number of coil turns

$\dfrac{d\phi}{dt}$ = flux change per unit time

If a constant-flux frequency sweep was previously recorded on a tape passing over the playback head, a constant flux is produced within the head gap. Since the flux rate of change within the gap is directly proportional to that frequency, the head output level rises at a 6 dB/octave slope, subject to various wavelength-related losses that will be described in the next section.

Playback Losses

If a 6 dB/octave rise in playback head output were the only response consideration, a simple playback amplifier with a complementary integration network would be all that would be required to restore a flat frequency response. However, there are other factors that must be taken into account, and appropriate compensation methods must be devised in order to ensure that the playback output response is a faithful replica of the signal sent to the record head.

We begin by describing a few losses that are either a function of the playback head or that are first observed during playback. After describing the various losses, the resultant playback head response is illustrated, and the necessary corrective equalization is described.

Dropouts and Spacing Loss

A dropout is a momentary attenuation in signal level due either to a defect within the oxide formulation, a scratch on the oxide coating, or a speck of dust or loose oxide between the tape and the head. Regardless of the cause, the effect is to insert a space between the head and the tape oxide. The resultant spacing loss may be found from the following equation (after Mee & Daniel 1987).

$$L_d = 20 \log(1/\epsilon^{2\pi d/\lambda})$$

where

L_d = spacing loss, in dB

ϵ = 2.781

d = space between head and tape

λ = wavelength

As the recorded wavelength diminishes with rising frequency, attenuation increases exponentially. If the wavelength is ten times the length of the space, the output attenuation is 5.58 dB. But if the wavelength is equal to the length of the space, the output attenuation is 54.57 dB. In other words, the severity of the dropout is proportional to frequency; the higher the frequency, the worse the dropout.

During recording, the high-frequency dropout may be minimized by over-biasing. As the dropout momentarily lowers the sensitivity of the tape, the effective bias level is reduced. This increases the high frequency response for the duration of the dropout, thus minimizing its effect. Of course overbiasing has no effect on dropouts caused by dust particles on the playback head. And in the case of a gross oxide defect, the affected section of tape should be discarded.

In Figure 9-12, spacing loss is plotted as a function of the ratio of tape-to-head space and wavelength.

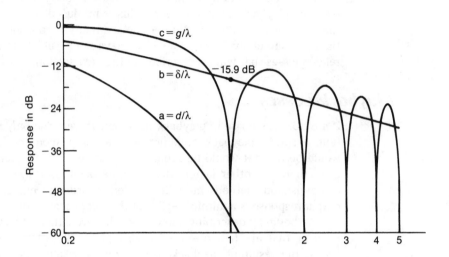

Figure 9-12. Various head and tape losses: (a): high frequency spacing loss as a function of tape-to-head space and recorded wavelength; (b): tape thickness loss as a function of oxide thickness and wavelength; (c): gap loss as a function of gap length and wavelength.

Tape Thickness Loss

The tape oxide itself imposes another form of spacing loss which must be taken into account. Since the oxide has a finite depth, it follows that there is an increase in spacing loss with respect to oxide particles that are not in direct contact with the head. For example, according to the spacing loss equation above, oxide that is one wavelength removed from the head suffers a 54.57 dB loss. Therefore, as frequency increases (that is, as wavelength decreases) progressively less of the oxide thickness is effectively used.

Tape thickness loss may be found from the following equation (after Camras 1988):

$$L_t = 20 \log \left[\frac{1 - 1/\epsilon^{2\pi\delta/\lambda}}{2\pi\delta/\lambda} \right]$$

where
L_t = tape thickness loss, in dB
ϵ = 2.781
δ = oxide thickness
λ = wavelength

Tape thickness loss is also shown in Figure 9-12, where it is plotted as a function of the ratio of oxide thickness to recorded wavelength. Note that the attenuation falls off at about 6 dB per octave.

Since oxide thickness is a published specification and wavelength may be easily calculated if tape speed is known, the tape thickness curve may be presented in a more informative format, as shown in Figure 9-13. Here, the oxide thicknesses for three commercially available tapes are used to plot the output response for a tape running at 38 cm/s (15 in/s).

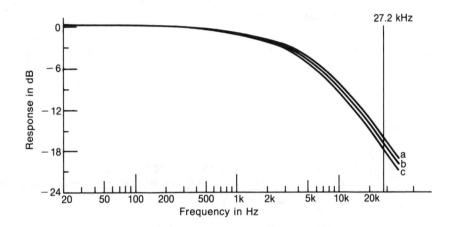

Figure 9-13. Tape thickness loss in dB at 38 cm/s (15 in/s)
for selected audio tapes. Curve (a) is for Ampex Type 456 tape with
an oxide coating of 13.97 μm (1 μm = 10^{-4} cm), curve (b) is for
Agfa PEM 428 with an oxide coating of 15.24 μm, and curve (c)
is for 3M 256 and BASF 911 with an
oxide coating of 17.00 μm.

To compare the thickness loss curves in Figures 9-12 and 9-13, note that in the former, when the oxide thickness is equal to the recorded wavelength ($\delta/\lambda = 1$), the attenuation appears to be slightly less than 16 dB (actually, 15.9 dB). Using Ampex 456 as an example, at a tape speed of 38 cm/s, the equivalent frequency at this point is

$$f = s/\delta$$
$$= 38/(13.97 \times 10^{-4})$$
$$= 27.20 \text{ kHz}$$

In Figure 9-13, 27.20 kHz is indicated by a vertical line on the graph. Note that the Ampex 456 loss curve (a) crosses the line at about -16 dB attenuation, as expected.

Note: This section has presented a much-simplified review of tape thickness loss, based on one of several possible explanations. For an alternative explanation of wavelength-related losses, the work of Bertram (1975) should be consulted.

Gap Loss

The *gap loss* of a playback head is an attenuation of output level as a function of gap length. As noted before, the head responds to the rate of flux change within the gap. This rate increases until the decreasing wavelength reaches one-half the gap length. Beyond that point it falls off rapidly, reaching a null when the wavelength is about equal to the gap length. At still shorter wavelengths (that is, higher frequencies) a series of diminishing peaks and nulls occurs, with a null at every upper harmonic of the first null frequency.

Figure 9-12 also includes a graph of gap loss in dB vs. the ratio of gap length to wavelength of the recorded signal. The curve is plotted from the following equation (after Mee & Daniel 1987):

$$L_g = 20 \log \sin(x)/x$$

where
  L_g = gap loss, in dB
  x = $\pi g/\lambda$
  g = gap length
  λ = wavelength

The graph is not very informative unless the gap length and tape speed are known, from which the first null frequency, f_1, may be determined. Since at f_1, $g/\lambda = 1$, and $\lambda = s/f_1$,

$$f_1 = s/g$$

where
  s = tape speed
  g = gap length

As a typical example, if $s = 38$ cm/s, and $g = 5$ μm (5×10^{-4} cm, approx. 0.2 mil) then $f_1 = 76$ kHz.

As the example shows, with a first null at 76 kHz, the 6 dB/octave slope continues to $\frac{1}{2}f_1 = 38$ kHz. Obviously, gap loss is no longer the concern it was in earlier days, when the gap length of a typical playback head was about 0.001 in (25.4 μm).

Playback Head Response

The only corrective factor for dropouts during playback is to make sure the head is clean and that there is good tape-to-head contact. And as just illustrated, gap loss is no longer a practical consideration. However, the record-mode thickness loss must be taken into account, since it begins to roll off the high frequency response well within the audio bandwidth (Figure 9-13).

The rolloff is of course a characteristic of the tape and not of the head. But since the playback head requires a constant recorded flux level in order to produce its rising 6 dB/octave slope, the diminishing flux level works against that slope. The resultant head output is plotted in Figure 9-14, which shows the characteristics for both 38 and 19 cm/s (15 and 7.5 in/s) tape speeds. Note that in either case, the response begins its departure from the 6 dB/octave slope below 1 kHz and eventually reaches a high-frequency shelf. Both curves were calculated for an oxide thickness of 15.5 μm, which is about midway between Ampex 456 and 3M 256 (13.97 and 17 μm, respectively).

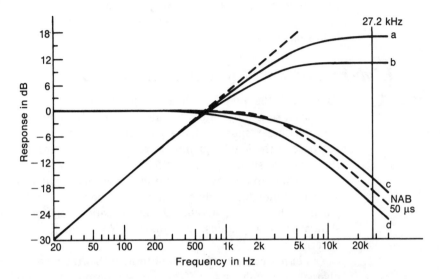

Figure 9-14. Playback response characteristics. The combination of a 6 dB/octave playback head slope and the tape thickness loss at (a) 38 cm/s (15 in/s) and (b) 19 cm/s (7.5 in/s). The same characteristics after a compensating attenuation at 6 dB/octave at (c) and (d). All curves calculated for oxide thickness of 15.5 μm.

Record and Playback Equalization

Given the present state of the art, it is routinely assumed that the frequency response at the output of any signal chain will not be altered by an electronic device inserted in the signal path. Although there may indeed be some response modification within the total system, the output is still expected to be a faithful replica of the input. The obvious exception is of course an equalizer used deliberately to alter response according to taste. However, even such a device is expected to be flat when its various filter sections are bypassed or otherwise zeroed. In any case, corrective equalization should not be required simply to maintain a flat system response.

We have seen that such assumptions cannot be made about magnetic systems such as the tape recorder, where a considerable amount of equalization is required to maintain a flat input-to-output relationship. As noted before, the frequency response of an audio signal is subjected to several frequency-related variables in the interval between the record head input and the playback head output. To briefly review;

- Overall playback voltage response rises by 6 dB per octave.

- High frequencies are rolled off due to tape thickness loss.
- Low frequencies may be boosted prior to recording (NAB standard, described later).

To restore the output signal to a flat response, the playback amplifier provides the required equalization network. For analysis, the complete equalization system may be divided into three sections, each of which is described in the following.

High-Frequency Playback Equalization

To correct the playback head response, the playback amplification system includes a simple op-amp integrator network to compensate for the basic 6 dB/octave rising response of the playback head itself. The network restores flat response in the low-frequency range, but the tape thickness loss is of course still there, as also shown in Figure 9-14.

The high-frequency equalizer just described is not a user-adjustable network, since it is intended solely to compensate for the fixed 6 dB/octave slope of the playback head. The additional compensation required is defined by various standards organizations, such as the NAB and IEC. Both standards will be described.

In either case, it is important to note that the standard defines the playback characteristic only. In fact, "The *only* standard for the record chain is that it must produce tapes which reproduce properly on a standard reproduce chain" (McKnight 1960, italics added). Specific details about record equalization are described later in this chapter (page 376).

NAB Standard Reproducing Characteristic

The NAB (National Association of Broadcasters) publishes a standard (NAB 1965) which specifies the response of a standard tape reproducer in both the low- and high-frequency ranges of the audio spectrum.

For high-frequency equalization the standard specifies a lowpass filter whose response is the *inverse* of a lowpass filter with a 50 μs time constant (90 μs for $3^3/_4$ and $1^7/_8$ in/s). The responses for such a filter were shown in Figure 7-10. The inverse responses prescribed by the NAB standard are shown here in Figure 9-15. Note that the 50 μs characteristic is approximately the inverse of the high-frequency attenuation shown in curves (c) and (d) in Figure 9-14. As a guide to comparison, the NAB 50 μs characteristic has been inverted and drawn in Figure 9-14 as the dashed line in between the curves.

In other words, when the NAB high-frequency reproduce characteristic is combined with a basic 6 dB-per-octave attenuation network in the playback amplifier, the resultant filter response is a mirror image of the ideal playback head voltage output response when playing a standard calibration tape. Therefore, the high-frequency system response is flat within the audio spectrum.

Earlier in this chapter it was noted that low frequencies are boosted prior to recording. To compensate for the boost, the NAB standard prescribes a 3,180 μs rolloff, as illustrated in Figure 9-15B, where this component is added to the high-

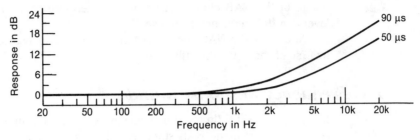

(A) High frequency section only.

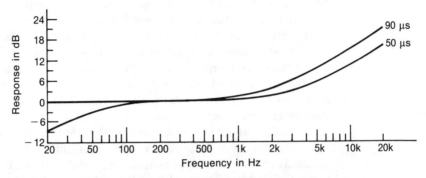

(B) Complete characteristic, showing low- and high-frequency compensation.

Figure 9-15. The NAB Standard Reproducing Characteristic.

frequency section to form the complete NAB reproduce characteristic. (Note that the 3,180 μs rolloff is specified for all four tape speeds included in the standard.)

The curves shown in the illustration were plotted from the following equation, which is part of the NAB standard.

$$N_{dB} = 20 \log A(B/C)^{1/2}$$

where

N_{dB} = dB level at frequency f
A = $2\pi f t_L$
B = $1 + (2\pi f t_H)^2$
C = $1 + (2\pi f t_L)^2$
t_L = low-frequency time constant (3,180 μs)
t_H = high-frequency time constant (50 or 90 μs)
f = frequency

Summary of NAB Characteristic

The reproduce characteristic is described in the NAB standard as the "reproducing amplifier output for constant flux in the core of an ideal reproducing head." As previously noted, however, low frequencies are boosted prior to recording, and there are high-frequency record losses on the tape due to thickness loss. Therefore, when a constant-*level* signal is applied to the input of a tape recorder, a constant flux is *not* recorded on tape. Instead, the recorded flux is the mirror image of the NAB characteristic, which therefore restores the playback output level to a flat frequency response.

Note that the NAB reproduce characteristics in Figure 9-15 are indeed the inverse of the equivalent filter responses shown in Figure 7-10.

IEC Frequency Response Standard

In Europe, the IEC (International Electrotechnical Commission) standard is similar in concept to the NAB standard, although it prescribes different time constants, and the curve itself is defined as a "recording characteristic." In Figure 9-16, the curve with a flat low-frequency characteristic followed by high-frequency attenuation is now identified as IEC 1. It specifies *no* low-frequency correction, taking into account the fact that modern recording technology has made low-frequency compensation unnecessary. The absence of low-frequency compensation is usually noted by a time constant of infinity.

The IEC 2 standard, specifying a rising low-frequency characteristic, was added later to conform to the NAB standard cited before and to the AES recommended practice described later.

The IEC 1 and 2 curves are sometimes referred to as the IEC European and American standards, respectively. It is important to realize that—differing time constants notwithstanding—the IEC and NAB documents both describe the same thing: the standard recorded tape flux required during playback. The IEC standard describes the curves as "the characteristic of the (recorded) short-circuit magnetic tape flux versus frequency" in the presence of an applied constant-amplitude sine wave signal. In other words, the curve shows the flux level on the tape. As in the NAB standard, the playback amplifier must supply the equalization required to restore flat frequency response.

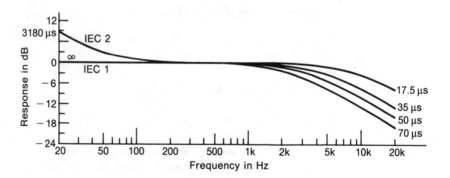

Figure 9-16. The IEC Recording Characteristic.

The curves shown in Figure 9-16 were plotted from the following equation, based on a similar one in the IEC standard, but presented here in simplified form. This equation was introduced previously in Chapter 7 (equation 7-7, page 266).

$$N_{dB} = 10 \log(A/B)$$

where

N_{dB} = dB level at frequency f
A = $1 + 1/(2\pi f t_L)^2$
B = $1 + (2\pi f t_H)^2$
t_L = low-frequency time constant (3,180 μs or ∞)
t_H = high-frequency time constant (17.5, 35, 50, or 70 μs)
f = frequency

CCIR Equalization

Some tape recorders offer record and playback equalization controls which are labeled CCIR (*Comité Consultatif International des Radiocommunications*). Despite the difference in identification, CCIR and IEC record and reproduce standards are identical.

NAB-IEC Comparisons

As published, the NAB standard identifies the low- and high-frequency time constants as t_1 and t_2 respectively, while the IEC standard reverses the sequence. For the sake of consistency, both equations in this chapter used t_L and t_H. As a further note, despite the quite different forms in which the NAB and IEC equations are published, the two are in fact identical, except that one is the inverse of the other. In fact, if the same time constants were applied to each equation, the resultant curves would be mirror images.

But since identical time constants are *not* used, there will be some response errors if an IEC program is reproduced on a tape recorder equalized to the NAB standard, and vice versa. Figure 9-17 illustrates both conditions at a tape speed of 38 cm/s (15 in/s). Note that the NAB playback characteristic assumes low frequencies need attenuation and high frequencies must be boosted according to the 50 μs time constant. Therefore, if an IEC tape (flat low-frequency response and 35 μs time constant) is played back on an NAB system, it will exhibit a low-frequency rolloff and a + 3 dB high frequency shelving response, as shown in the graph. The opposite condition is noted if an NAB tape is reproduced on an IEC playback system.

AES Recommended Practice

For 76 cm/s (30 in/s) operation, an engineering group meeting under the auspices of the Audio Engineering Society drafted a "Proposed AES Recommended Practice No. 1" (AES 1971). This is sometimes popularly referred to as the "AES 30 in/s standard," but in fact it is not. Since the same conditions are now satisfied by the IEC 2 standard, the AES engineering group has not formally proposed a standard of its own, which would in any case be redundant. The point is made here for the benefit of readers who might otherwise have trouble searching for an AES standard which does not exist.

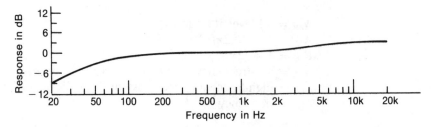

(A) When an IEC tape is played back on an NAB system.

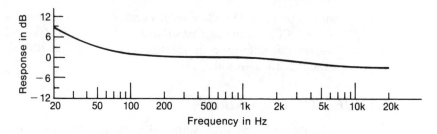

(B) When an NAB tape is reproduced on an IEC system.

Figure 9-17. Playback frequency response errors. Tape speed is
38 cm/s (15 in/s).

Summary of Reproduce Characteristics

Table 9-5 lists the various time constants, t, and resultant 3-dB frequencies, f, for the standards described in this chapter. The frequencies seen in the table are calculated from the equation $f = 1/2\pi t$. Elsewhere the values are more often rounded off to the nearest ISO preferred frequency, or to the nearest 10, or sometimes 100, hertz (for example, 3,183.10 to 3,180 Hz, 1,768.39 to 1,760 or 1,800 Hz, and so on). However, the practice often creates some initial confusion, especially over the coincidental relationships of 3,180 μs = 50 Hz, and 3,180 Hz = 50 μs.

Tape Recorder Calibration

If the output frequency response of tape recorder does not match its input response, it is not immediately clear whether the error is in the record section, the playback section, or both. For example, if a 5-kHz signal is applied to the input and the output level is down by, say, 3 dB, the problem could be caused by one or both of the following conditions.

- Playback level is down 3 dB at 5 kHz.
- Record level is down 3 dB at 5 kHz.

It would be easy enough to "fix" the problem by simply adjusting the playback equalization for a flat response. However, if the fault were actually in the record section, the cure would only be good for as long as the tape were played

Table 9-5. Tape Speed and Time Constant/Frequency Summary

Standard	Tape Speed		Low Frequency		High Frequency		Notes
	cm/s	*in/s*	*t (μs)*	*f (Hz)*	*t (μs)*	*f (Hz)*	
NAB	38	15	3,180	50.05	50	3,183.10	
	19	7.5	3,180	50.05	50	3,183.10	
	9.5	3.75	3,180	50.05	90	1,768.39	
	4.75	1.875	3,180	50.05	90	1,768.39	
IEC	76	30	∞	none	35	4,547.28	IEC 1
			∞	none	17.5	9,094.57	IEC 2
	38	15	∞	none	35	4,547.28	IEC 1*
			3,180	50.05	50	3,183.10	IEC 2
	19	7.5	∞	none	70	2,273.64	IEC 1
			3,180	50.05	50	3,183.10	IEC 2
AES	76	30	∞	none	17.5	9,094.57	Recommended Practice

$t = 1/2\pi f$ in a first-order *RC* filter
$f = 1/2\pi t$ in a first-order *RC* filter

IEC 1 = European standard
IEC 2 = American standard, to match NAB or AES
*IEC 1 @ 38 cm/s, 15 in/s no longer in use

on the present machine. When played elsewhere, the playback level would again be off by 3 dB at 5 kHz.

Therefore the correct tape recorder calibration procedure consists of the following two steps.

1. Adjust the playback section while playing the appropriate NAB or IEC standard calibration tape.

2. While recording test tones on a fresh piece of tape (*not* on the calibration tape please!), adjust the record section while monitoring the playback section.

The indicated sequence is important, since once the playback section is properly adjusted, any errors observed during recording are thereby localized to the record section.

Playback Calibration Tape

To make sure that the playback section of the tape recorder is properly aligned, a calibration tape is required. The tape contains a series of discrete sine wave frequencies recorded at a known operating level under laboratory conditions. Furthermore, the frequencies have been recorded according to the NAB (or IEC, as appropriate) standard. Therefore, when the calibration tape is played back, the observed output response should be flat across the entire audio spectrum. If it is not, then the machine's playback system must be adjusted until the response is correct. (The actual physical adjustments are described in detail in the next chapter (page 412).

The calibration tape usually consists of the following sections.

1. Reference fluxivity
2. Azimuth and phase adjustment
3. Frequency response

The sections are used in the sequence in which they appear above. Each section, and its use, is described here.

Reference Fluxivity Section

The calibration procedure begins by making sure the machine is in the safe mode, then playing a 700- or 1,000-Hz tone at the head of the test tape, which is known to have been recorded at a certain reference fluxivity, or operating level. While playing the tone, the playback level is adjusted until a zero dB reading is observed.

Over the years, calibration tapes have been prepared at various flux levels. The practical differences between one such tape and another will be discussed later on in this chapter, in the section on elevated level calibration tapes (page 376).

Azimuth and Phase Adjustment Section

In tape recorder terminology, *azimuth* refers to the angle measured between any tape head and the tape passing across its gap. Assuming the tape passes horizontally across the heads, the *azimuth angle* is the deflection from the vertical of a center line drawn through the head gap, as shown in Figure 9-18A.

To illustrate the importance of correct azimuth alignment, Figure 9-18B shows two tracks with a common signal correctly recorded on both of them. If the azimuth of the playback head is out of alignment, then there is a slight shift between the times at which each section of the head reproduces the signal. When the outputs of each head section are combined there will be some phase cancellation as a result. The cancellation will be most severe at high frequencies.

For example, consider a two-channel ¼-inch tape with a distance between track centers of 3.96 mm (0.156 in). If tape speed is 38 cm/s (15 in/s), the recorded wavelength of a 10,000 Hz signal is $38/10,000 = 0.004$ cm. If the playback head azimuth is slightly out of alignment, as shown in Figure 9-18A, there is a 180-degree phase shift between the two outputs (1 & 2). To determine the azimuth angle at which this occurs,

$$\tan \theta = 0.004/0.396 = 0.010$$
$$\theta = 0.579°$$

In other words, an error in *azimuth angle* of only 0.579 degrees causes a *phase angle* (i.e., phase shift) error of 180 degrees at 10 kHz. Since the azimuth angle is fixed, the phase angle will vary with wavelength of the recorded signal. And of course if the azimuth error is some other amount, the 180-degree phase shift will occur elsewhere within the audio bandwidth.

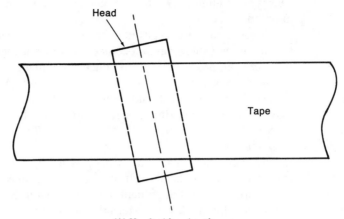

(A) Head with azimuth error.

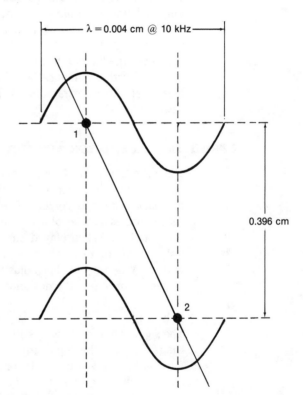

(B) High-frequency signal common to two tracks picked up by off-azimuth head.

Figure 9-18. Azimuth error and its effect.

Azimuth Correction

It can be seen that proper azimuth alignment is critical to the performance of the record/playback system. For azimuth alignment, a series of tones at progressively higher frequencies (500 Hz, 8 kHz, 16 kHz, for example), are reproduced. To verify the azimuth between any two tracks, their outputs are summed and the combined output level is observed. Since a phase shift between the two signals causes an attenuation of the combined signal, the azimuth error is noted by a dip in output level.

Gross errors are checked first, using the lowest frequency in the azimuth section of the calibration tape. Since higher frequencies (shorter wavelengths) are more critical, progressively finer checks are made as the test frequency rises.

The physical correction of azimuth errors is described in the next chapter (page 411). However, it should be noted that gap scatter within a multitrack head may create internal azimuth errors that cannot be corrected.

Gap Scatter

In any multitrack head, *gap scatter* is a physical misalignment of track gaps encased within the head itself. For example, it may be noted that, say, tracks 10 and 11 are in perfect alignment, but tracks 9 and 10 are not. When the latter two are aligned by making an external adjustment, the former two are now found to be out of alignment, and so on. Although no single adjustment can be made to align all tracks within the head, it may be worthwhile to periodically check various track pairs to at least become aware of combinations that may cause phase-shift problems if their outputs are combined. The degree of gap scatter will vary over the life of a head, as a function of head wear.

As a further complication, the apparent gap scatter will vary as a function of bias level (after Bertram 1974). Therefore, gap scatter should be checked after setting bias.

Frequency Response Section

Once the tape recorder's playback level has been properly set and the azimuth adjusted, the final step is to verify that the overall frequency response of the playback section is correct. The frequency response section of the calibration tape contains a series of test tones recorded according to the appropriate NAB or IEC standard. When played back, a flat frequency response should be noted. If not, the recorder's playback equalization must be adjusted until the response is correct. When no further adjustments are required, the system is properly calibrated according to the designated reproduce characteristic.

Fringing

The signal on almost every calibration tape is recorded across the entire width of the tape, thus allowing a single tape to be used for any track configuration that falls within its width. As an obvious consequence, the width of the recorded signal is always greater than the gap width of the playback head.

At short wavelengths, the playback head is sensitive only to the recorded signal lying directly in the gap path, so the additional flux on either side of the gap has no effect. However, as the wavelength of the recorded signal increases, the head begins to pick up additional flux from the fringe areas on either side of the gap. This *fringing effect* results in a rising output level as frequency is decreased.

The amount of fringing rise depends on various factors related to head geometry, and so a fixed correction cannot be applied to, for example, a one-quarter inch calibration tape. Such a tape might be used on a machine with one, two, or more tracks; each of these formats implies a different gap width, and therefore a different fringing compensation is required (McKnight 1967a). In this case, a table is usually supplied with the calibration tape, indicating the amount of correction required for each track format.

If a calibration tape has been made with fringing compensation, this fact is usually made clear in the accompanying documentation.

Note that the low-frequency rise attributed to fringing is simply an artifact of reading a wide recorded track with a narrow playback head. Therefore no compensation is required, for when the machine's own record head is used, the fringing effect will not be present.

Playback Calibration Procedure

To briefly review the various sections of the calibration tape, the following procedure outlines the steps in calibrating the playback section of the tape recorder.

1. Preliminary. Demagnetize the tape heads and metal guides. Clean the tape heads and make sure they are perfectly dry. Turn the machine on and make sure it is in the safe mode. Then thread the calibration tape on the transport and rewind to the head of the tape.

2. Playback level. While playing the tape, set the playback level control(s) so that the tone(s) in the reference fluxivity section of the calibration tape read zero on the tape recorder's meters.

3. Playback head azimuth (if adjustable). Play the azimuth section of the tape while monitoring the combined output of two tracks on a single meter. Watch for peaks and dips in the output response at high frequencies. If present, adjust the *playback* head azimuth until a smooth response is noted. If necessary, repeat the procedure for other track pairs.

4. Frequency response. Adjust the high frequency equalizer control(s) so that high frequency tones on the calibration tape read zero on the tape recorder's meters.

5. Verify that the 700 or 1,000 Hz tone reads zero. If not, repeat steps 2 and 4 as required.

Record Calibration Procedure

Once the playback calibration is complete, it may be assumed that the frequency response of a properly recorded tape will be flat when it is observed on a meter which monitors the playback section. Therefore, the record calibration procedure may now begin. In the following procedure, all adjustments are made to the record section of the tape recorder, while maintaining a constant output level from the signal generator being used to supply the test tones.

1. Preliminary. Remove the calibration tape and load the machine with the type of tape that will be used during the actual recording session. While recording, feed a 1,000-Hz sine wave signal at 0 dB to the tape recorder input, and adjust the record level for a convenient meter reading.

2. Coarse bias. Adjust the bias level for a maximum reading on the output meter.

3. Fine bias. Switch the input signal to the correct high frequency (e.g., 10,000 Hz @ 15 in/s, 38 cm/s) and overbias as described earlier in this chapter (page 360).

4. Record head azimuth (if adjustable). Record a test signal on two tracks while monitoring their combined output on a single meter. Vary the input frequency and watch for peaks and dips in the output response at high frequencies. If present, adjust the *record* head azimuth until a smooth response is noted. The record head azimuth is now in alignment with the playback head. If necessary, repeat the procedure for other track pairs.

5. Record level. Repeat Step 1, but adjust the record level for a zero reading on the output meter.

6. Frequency response. Record a series of frequencies, or a frequency sweep, and adjust the record section equalizer for flat response. In case of gross errors, Steps 5 and 6 may have to be repeated.

Note again the absence of a record equalization standard. As mentioned earlier, record equalization is simply whatever it takes to align the record section so that recorded flux on the tape will conform to the standard curve and therefore the frequency response of a recorded tape will be flat when played back on a machine whose playback section is properly aligned.

High Output Tapes

As noted earlier in the chapter, a tape's MOL (maximum output level) is the level at which three percent third-harmonic distortion is reached. By contrast with previous tape products, more recent formulations can tolerate higher input levels before reaching that point, and a higher MOL rating is generally accompanied by an increase in retentivity and in some cases by a higher coercivity. Table 9-6 lists these specifications for several tape formulations.

Elevated Level Calibration Tapes

Early calibration tapes (c. 1950) were recorded at a level that produced about one percent third-harmonic distortion, which was subsequently determined to represent an operating level of 185 nWb/m at 700 Hz (Eargle 1986). With NAB equalization at 7.5 or 15 in/s, this corresponds to 180 nWb/m at 1,000 Hz. But as magnetic tape technology made it possible to record higher program levels without distortion, *elevated level* calibration tapes were also introduced. As the

Table 9-6. Maximum Output Level for Selected Tapes

Manufacturer	Catalog No.	Output Level	MOL (dB)	Coercivity (Oe)	Retentivity (G)
Agfa	PEM 428	standard	+9	380	1,060
	PEM 468	high	+11.5	380	1,060
	PEM 469	high	+12.5	340	1,350
Ampex	406, 407	standard	+8.8	290	1,150
	456	high	+12.3	295	1,400
BASF	911	high	+12	325	1,440
3M	206, 207	standard	+8	320	1,050
	226, 227	high	+11.5	360	1,400
	250	high	+11	365	1,200
	256	high	+10	380	1,000

name suggests, the elevated level tape has been recorded at an operating level higher than 185 nWb/m, and is used to calibrate a tape recorder to take advantage of high output tapes such as those listed in Table 9-6.

The difference between any two operating levels may be found from the following equation.

$$N_{dB} = 20 \log(A/B)$$

where

N_{dB} = level difference between operating levels, in dB
A = new operating level, in nWb/m
B = a reference level (e.g., 185 nWb/m)

For example, if the operating levels of two tapes are 260 and 185 nWb/m, the difference between them is 20 log(260/185) = 3 dB.

For a better understanding of the practical difference between these or any other two operating levels, carefully review the following four-step procedure.

1. Using a calibration tape with an operating level of 185 nWb/m, adjust the recorder's *playback* level for a zero reading on the output meter.

2. Place a blank reel of tape on the machine and record a 1-kHz tone at any convenient input level. Adjust the *record* level until the playback meter again reads zero. The tape is now being recorded at a flux level of 185 nWb/m.

3. Place a test tape with a 260 nWb/m operating level on the machine and observe the output level. It should be 3 dB above the former zero reference level. Turn the *playback* level down until the meter again reads zero.

4. Place a blank reel of tape on the machine and begin recording without making any other changes. Although the tape is once again being recorded as in Step 2, the playback meter reads 3 dB too low, due to the

adjustment made in Step 3. Raise the machine's *record* level until the meter once again reads zero.

As this procedure illustrates, when the playback level is readjusted to accommodate a higher operating level, the recorder (that is, the tape) requires a higher-level input signal in order to produce a zero reading on the output meter. Assuming the tape is capable of accepting the higher level without distortion, the result is a recorded program whose relative noise level is improved by (in this example) 3 dB.

Table 9-7 lists a few operating levels that have been used in the preparation of calibration tapes.

Table 9-7. Reference Fluxivity of Several Calibration Tapes

Fluxivity (nWb/m)	Frequency* (Hz)	Level** (dB)	Comments
150	400	−2	NAB 1965***
180	1,000	0	
185	700	0	early Ampex and 3M
200	1,000	+1	general purpose
250	1,000	+3	elevated level
260	700	+3	
290	1,000	+4	****
320	1,000	+5	DIN 45 513

*Frequency at which fluxivity was measured.
**Level is with respect to 185 nWb/m @ 700 Hz, or 180 nWb/m at 1,000 Hz, as appropriate. Level rounded to nearest unit.
***Reference fluxivity is approximate.
****When a DIN 320 nWb/m tape is measured according to U. S. standards, its fluxivity is 290 nWb/m.

10 Tape Transport Systems

The modern tape transport system contains such a wealth of operational features that it's easy enough to lose sight of its primary function—to move a length of magnetic tape past a head stack at a reasonably consistent speed while recording or reproducing an audio signal on the tape.

In the previous chapter the tape itself was described in some detail, and the requirements for recording and playing it back with a flat frequency response were also described. In the present chapter, the actual details of moving that tape across the heads and the alignment procedures for various tape recorders will be described. We begin with a description of the tape transport system, followed by a look at how the electronics system on a representative modern transport is aligned.

The Tape Transport System

At first glance, the function of the complete transport system appears to be a simple task that can be divided into three separate functions, as seen here.

Subsystem	Function
drive	to move the tape across the heads at the desired tape speed
supply	to feed the tape into the drive system
takeup	to accept and store the tape after it leaves the drive system

These simple functions become complicated when we consider the interaction required between the three subsystems; while the drive system is moving the tape past the head stack, the supply system must make tape available at a rate precisely matched to the drive requirements. If tape is supplied faster than needed, there will soon be too much slack tape between the supply reel and the tape heads. But if the supply rate is not fast enough, then as the drive system tries to pull tape past the heads, one of the following will happen; the tape will be stretched as the drive system overcomes the resistance of the supply system, or the tape speed will slow down due to resistance from the supply system.

Similar constraints apply to the takeup system; it must wind the tape smoothly onto the takeup reel, yet must not exert such force as to pull the tape from the grip of the actual drive system.

As a further complication, the rotational speed of both reel motors must vary continuously as the tape moves from the supply side to the takeup side. For example, on a full 10.5-inch supply reel, a single layer of tape at the outer circumference is about 31 inches in length; by contrast, the first layer to wrap around the NAB hub (4.5 in. diameter) on the takeup side is only some 14 inches long. Therefore, at the start of the play or record mode, the takeup reel must make slightly more that two rotations for every one rotation of the supply reel. As the tape continues to play, this 2:1 ratio of rotational speeds gradually moves toward 1:1 when half the tape is on each reel, and then approaches 1:2 as the quantity of tape on the supply reel continues to diminish. In other words, as one reel slows down, the other speeds up—a task which must be accomplished without upsetting the linear speed of the tape past the heads.

Therefore, there must be a certain amount of coordination between the subsystems, so that the drive system is not forced to work against the supply and takeup reel systems. If all goes well, the tape should move smoothly from one side of the transport to the other without being destroyed in the process.

Tape Drive System

The first task to be considered is that of moving the tape past the heads. Figure 10-1 shows the tape path and the capstan drive system found on three professional open-reel transports. Immediately beyond the head stack, the tape passes between a fixed-position rotating shaft, or *capstan*, and a movable *pressure roller*, also known as a *pinch roller* or *capstan idler*. In the play or record mode, the roller moves against the capstan and is held there under pressure. The capstan rotation forces the pressure roller to likewise rotate, and as a result the tape is pulled across the heads. On earlier-generation transport systems, the capstan motor continued to rotate in the stop mode provided tape was properly threaded between the supply and takeup reels. But with the pinch roller disengaged, the tape of course remained stationary. The continuously rotating capstan allowed the system to reach operating speed with minimal delay when the play button was pressed. Modern DC capstan motors are able to accelerate from full stop to play speed almost instantaneously (e.g., in about 0.1 s) and usually do not continue to rotate when the transport is stopped.

The force under which the pinch roller is held against the capstan must be carefully set so that the tape neither is damaged by excessive capstan/roller pressure nor is able to slip due to insufficient pressure. On many professional tape recorders the capstan is now made of a ceramic (nonmetallic mineral) substance, which generally provides an excellent nonslip surface contact with both the tape and the pinch roller. On some pinch rollerless systems (described later in this chapter), the capstan is rubber coated for the same reason.

(A) Ampex 351 in portable cabinet. (Courtesy Ampex Corp.)

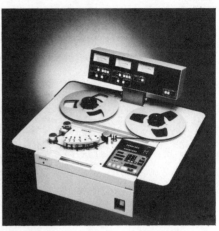

(B) Sony APR-5003V. (Courtesy Sony Professional Products Company)

(C) Studer A820-24. (Courtesy Studer Revox America, Inc.)

(D) Detail view of 24-track head assembly and capstan/pressure roller. (Courtesy Studer Revox America, Inc.)

Figure 10-1. Tape paths, showing capstan/pressure roller drive systems on early and modern professional tape recorders.

In one early variation on the tape drive system, the capstan was located on the supply side of the head stack, so that it pushed the tape across the heads. The system proved too difficult to keep in operation and was soon retired from production.

A few other significant drive-system variations will be described later in this chapter, in the section entitled Alternate Tape Drive Systems (page 385).

Capstan Drive Systems

On some early-generation tape recorders the capstan and its motor were separate components, linked by a belt drive. And in at least one case, the motor and capstan were coupled by a friction-wheel drive system (3M Isoloop series, c. 1970). However, on most modern machines the capstan is now an integral part of the drive motor, as shown in Figure 10-2.

Figure 10-2. Detail view of a capstan drive motor on a modern tape recorder.
(Courtesy Studer Revox America, Inc.)

The two types of motors that have been widely used as capstan drives in professional tape recorders are briefly described in the next section.

Hysteresis Synchronous Motors

For many years, the *hysteresis synchronous* motor was widely used as a capstan drive. Although motor design details are well beyond the scope of this discussion, such motors operated well at a fixed *synchronous speed*, which was a function of line frequency and the number of poles in the motor. The synchronous speed of such a motor is found from the equation

$$S = 2f/n$$

where

S = motor speed, in revolutions-per-second
f = line frequency, in hertz
n = number of poles

The speed of a hysteresis synchronous motor may be changed by varying the number of active pole windings, easily accomplished via a front-panel speed-selector switch. However, design considerations usually limit such motors to two-speed operation only.

Since the speed of a hysteresis synchronous motor is defined by line frequency and number of poles, the capstan diameter is therefore also defined as

$$D = S_T/(\pi S_M)$$

where

D = capstan diameter, in cm (or in.)
S_T = tape speed, in cm/s (or in/s)
S_M = motor speed, in revolutions-per-second

On some early machines (e.g., Ampex 300 series, c. 1955) an oversize sleeve could be placed over the capstan to increase its effective diameter. The sleeve was designed to double the capstan circumference and therefore double the tape speed.

To otherwise operate a hysteresis synchronous motor at any speed other than the two (typically) for which it is designed, it is necessary to vary the frequency of the line voltage to the motor. Numerous varispeed systems were devised, often consisting of nothing more than a borrowed sine wave generator feeding an amplifier with sufficient power to drive a coil wound in a capstan motor instead of in a speaker driver.

Needless to say, most such varispeed systems were inconvenient to use, and it was difficult to impossible to duplicate a speed setting with any sort of accuracy.

Servo Control Drive System

In most modern tape transport systems the hysteresis motor has been replaced by a DC servo-controlled motor drive system, as shown in Figure 10-3. A tachometer mounted on the capstan shaft creates a series of pulses whose frequency is a direct function of motor speed. The period of this signal is compared to that of a reference signal generated by a precision crystal oscillator in the recorder electronics system. An error signal is generated proportional to the difference between the periods of the reference and the tachometer frequencies, and this is used to vary the capstan drive speed as required.

To change tape speed, all that's required is to change the frequency of the reference signal, which is usually accomplished in one of three ways.

- Discrete speed changes (e.g., 30 to 15 in/s). The internal crystal oscillator reference frequency is divided, as required.

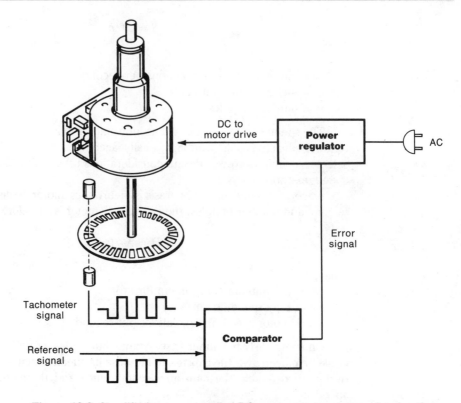

Figure 10-3. Simplified servo-controlled DC capstan motor system, showing the tachometer used for speed control.

- Variation above or below a selected speed. An internal variable-frequency generator supplies the reference.
- Speed controlled by an external device (such as another transport). The reference signal is provided by the external device.

On most modern servo-controlled systems, two or more fixed speeds are available, and each may be varied over the range shown in Table 10-1.

Bidirectional Operation

From time to time it is desirable to play a tape backwards, usually for the creation of a special effect such as a "backwards" echo or reverberation. On a hysteresis synchronous drive system, this is possible by carefully threading the tape around the capstan, as shown in Figure 10-4A. Although not the last word in hi-tech elegance, the technique works reasonably well provided the rest of the system is capable of handling the reverse operation.

Since a DC motor may be reversed simply by reversing the polarity of the applied power, it is an easy matter to run most servo-controlled systems backwards, and, in addition, to take advantage of all the control functions available in normal forward operation. The obvious method is to add one more switch to the control panel. A simple flip of polarity is all that is needed to provide forward/

Table 10-1. Tape Speeds of Representative Tape Recorders

Mfr.	Model No.	Speeds (in/s)*				Variation Percent	Semitones
MCI	JH-24			15	30	±20	+3.9, −3.2
	JH-110	3.75	7.5	15		±20	+3.9, −3.2
			7.5	15	30	±20	+3.9, −3.2
Otari	MTR-90			15	30	±20	+3.9, −3.2
	MTR-100A		7.5	15	30	±50	+7, −12
Sony	APR-24		7.5	15	30	±50	+7, −12
	APR-5000			15	30	±50	+7, −12
Studer	A800		7.5	15		+55, −35	±7.5
				15	30	+55, −35	±7.5
	A807	3.75	7.5	15		+55, −35	±7.5
			7.5	15	30	+55, −35	±7.5
	A810	3.75	7.5	15	30	+50, −33	±7
	A820	3.75	7.5	15	30	+50, −33	±7
3M	Series 79		7.5	15		+50, −33	±7
				15	30	+50, −33	±7

*Where two sets of tape speeds are listed for a model, the user must specify the desired set.

reverse play-mode operation (not to be confused with high-speed fast-forward or rewind modes). In this case, the tape need not be threaded in a different manner.

However, it is also desirable to provide some means for automatic direction sensing, as, for example, during a time code-directed search operation. In some systems, this direction sensing is accomplished by generating two tachometer signals with a 90-degree phase shift between them. Using one signal as reference, the relative phase shift of the other (leading or lagging) defines the direction in which the capstan is rotating, as shown in Figure 10-4B. The actual direction signal may now be compared with a desired direction signal, and a polarity-change command generated when required.

Alternate Tape Drive Systems

As previously noted, the capstan/pressure roller system shown in Figure 10-1 is found on many currently manufactured tape transport systems. However, various alternative transport systems have been designed, often incorporating some means to increase the physical isolation between the head stack area and the reel systems. The purpose of doing so is to shield the sensitive tape-to-head interface from the comparatively rough handling of supply and takeup reel motions. A few such designs are briefly described here.

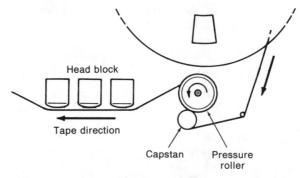

(A) Physical conditions permitting, the tape may be threaded around the capstan and pressure roller as shown.

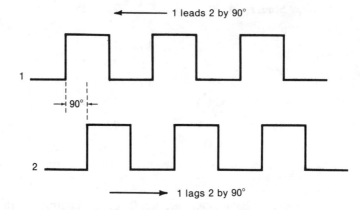

(B) Dual tachometer signals provide directional information for automatic reverse-mode operation. Arrows above and below tachometer signals indicate forward and reverse motor direction.

Figure 10-4. Reverse-play operation of a tape transport.

Vacuum Bin Transport System

In both computer and high-speed audio tape duplication systems, one or two storage bins hold a certain amount of slack tape on either side of the drive system. The slack tape may either form a continuous loop within a single bin, or a pair of bins may form intermediate links between the drive system and the two reels. In either case, the drive system need only pull slack tape out of, and back into, the bin(s), as shown in Figure 10-5. There is no need to overcome the inertia of the two reel systems which are—either actually, or in effect—removed from the system. The tape can move at very high speed across the heads, and in computer-drive systems, rapidly change direction with little fear of damage. In the latter application, either a dual-capstan or a closed-loop drive system is usually required for bidirectional operation.

Although effective for its intended applications, the bin system is not practical for use in the recording studio.

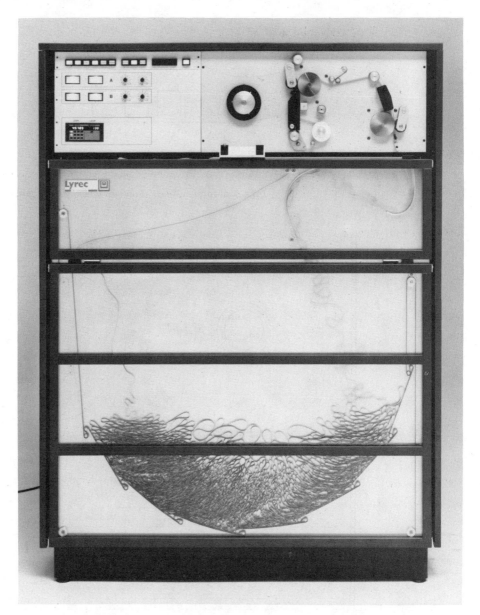

Figure 10-5. A vacuum bin transport system used for high-speed tape duplication work. *(Model P-4409 courtesy Lyrec Manufacturing Co.)*

Dual-Capstan Systems

As another form of isolation, a dual-capstan system places a capstan drive on either side of the head stack. In the case of the dual-capstan system shown in Figure 10-6A, tension across the heads is maintained by designing the capstan on the takeup side to run slightly faster than the supply-side capstan. The section of tape between the two drives is effectively isolated from both the supply and

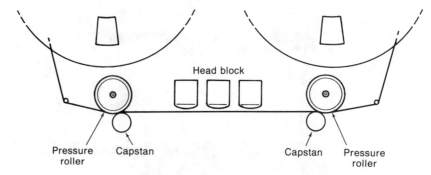

(A) A dual-capstan system using two motor-driven capstans.

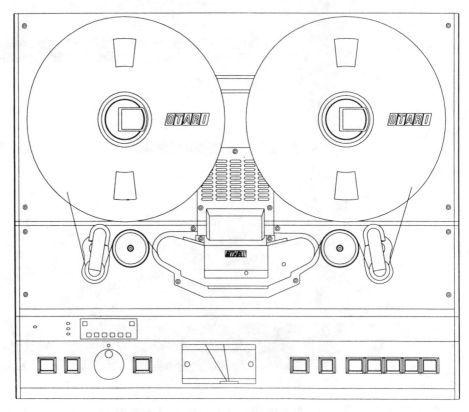

(B) A variation in the dual-capstan system, in which only the roller on the takeup side is motor-driven. Note the absence of the usual pressure roller. (Courtesy Otari Corp.)

Figure 10-6. Dual-capstan tape transport systems.

takeup reels by the dual capstan/pressure roller assemblies. However, the two drive speeds must be maintained with great care to keep the tape at the ideal tension. On one hand, excessive tension will stretch the tape while on the other, insufficient tension allows the tape to go slack, thus preventing it from making good contact with the heads.

Pressure Rollerless Capstan System

As just described, the complexity of the dual-capstan system does not warrant its use in audio recording systems. However, an effective variation has been employed, as shown in Figure 10-6B. When a DC motor is used as the capstan drive, capstan diameter is no longer restricted to the dimension dictated by line frequency and pole windings, as in the hysteresis synchronous motor described earlier in the chapter. Instead, the capstan diameter may be made considerably greater, and the tape path designed so that tape wraps around a large segment of the capstan circumference. The capstan itself may be rubber coated to provide positive traction, and the need for a pressure roller is obviated.

In Figure 10-6B a similar-sized roller is seen on the supply-reel side of the head stack. The combination of oversize capstan and auxiliary roller, both providing a large surface for tape wrap, effectively isolates the tape from both the supply and takeup reel systems. The lack of a pressure roller also reduces wear on the oxide coating of the tape, which is no longer pinched between the roller and the capstan.

As a further consideration, the tachometer may be mounted on the auxiliary roller instead of on the capstan motor shaft.

Closed Loop Systems

As another alternative to the dual-capstan system, Figure 10-7A shows how a single capstan may be used with two pressure rollers to isolate the tape in a closed loop around the head assembly. The tape passes through the first pressure roller/capstan pair, then around the heads, and finally back over the same capstan, where a second pressure roller closes the loop.

In one popular implementation of this type of closed-loop system (3M Iso-loop), the capstan and pressure roller profiles were indented as shown in Figure 10-7B. Note that the effective capstan diameter is slightly smaller on the supply side of the head stack. As a result, the takeup side of the capstan tries to pull tape across the heads faster than it can be supplied. The discrepancy is sufficient to keep the tape under tension, yet slight enough to prevent the tape from being damaged by stretching. Since a single capstan drives both ends of the tape loop, there is no danger of tape damage from capstan mistracking.

Tape Sensing Systems

Every tape transport system provides some means for sensing the presence of a properly threaded tape between the supply and takeup reels. As part of the tape-loading procedure, the tape must be passed over the sensing device, which is either a mechanical tension arm, a photoelectric cell, or some other device that will disable the transport system if the tape does not make proper contact. Without such a system, a tape might be loosely threaded between reels and, when the play button is pressed, the reel motors would attempt to wind the tape in opposite directions. Lacking an immediate holdback tension, both motors would accelerate, pulling the tape in opposite directions until the slack was taken up. In a worst-case situation, the tape would be stretched or otherwise damaged as the reel motors were forced into a sudden stop.

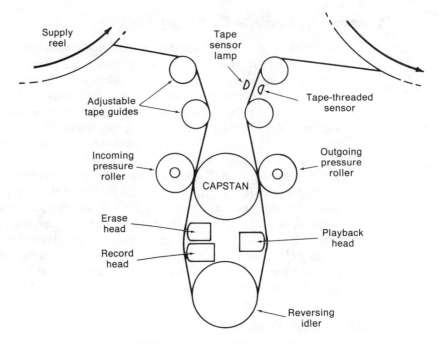

(A) Tape path on the 3M Isoloop *system.*

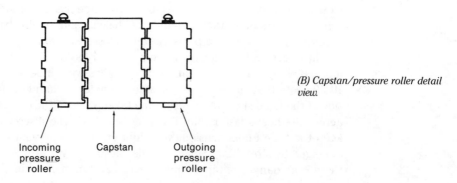

(B) Capstan/pressure roller detail view.

Figure 10-7. A closed-loop tape drive system.

Figure 10-8 shows a few of the tape sensing devices that have been used on studio tape transport systems.

Assuming the tape makes proper contact with the sensing device, the transport system will go into play, fast-forward, or rewind mode when the appropriate button is pressed.

Reel Motors

On all professional-grade tape transport systems, the supply and the takeup reel are driven by separate dedicated motors. Although both are usually taken for

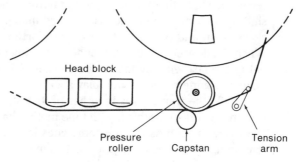

(A) Tension arm with properly threaded tape.

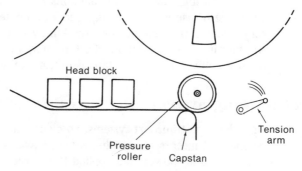

(B) Tension arm in relaxed position.

(C) Photoelectric cell senses presence of tape.

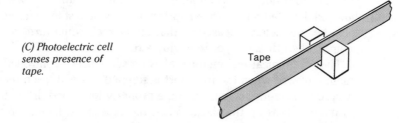

Figure 10-8. Tape sensing systems.

granted, their operation is by no means a simple task. For example, in the fast-forward mode the takeup motor must quickly pull tape onto the takeup reel, while the supply motor must provide sufficient holdback torque to prevent tape from spilling, yet the holdback force must not be so great as to work against the takeup motor. To further complicate matters, the required torque varies from one end of the reel to the other, and the entire relationship reverses itself when the tape is rewound or played in reverse.

Smooth operation becomes even more complex during a manual search for a particular tape segment. At such times it is common practice to alternately press the transport's fast-forward and rewind buttons while the tape is in motion. Unlike trying the same motion-control technique in a moving automobile (not recommended), there is no danger in putting the transport into reverse and then shifting back again into the fast-forward mode. The forward-moving tape simply slows down and then shuttles back and forth in response to the button pushing. When the desired location is reached, pressing the play button takes the transport out of the fast winding mode; the capstan drive system takes over and the tape begins running at the desired play speed.

While the transport is in either of its fast-winding modes, the capstan drive system is in effect disabled, with tape motion handled entirely by the reel motors. However, as soon as the transport goes into the play or record mode, the tape tensioning system must adjust itself immediately, the capstan drive takes over, and the tape is once again isolated from the same reel motors that were controlling it an instant earlier.

The various mechanical functions just described are much the same even when the transport is operating under computer control. On a cautionary note, some older transports do not take kindly to entering the play mode while fast winding in either direction. The tape may be damaged if the capstan pressure roller is activated while the tape is in fast motion.

Reel Braking System

On older tape transport systems, an electromechanical braking system was used on the reel motors. When the transport was stopped, the brakes were relaxed slightly and no power was applied to the reel motors; the slight brake pressure prevented the reels from accidentally spilling tape while the system was stopped. However, the capstan motor usually remained spinning as long as tape was threaded from one reel to another. If the tape tension arm was relaxed, or the photocell detected no tape, the capstan motor would stop spinning and the brakes would be completely released so that either reel would turn freely, as would be required when threading or removing a reel.

The mechanical reel-motor brakes on some servo-controlled systems do not remain engaged when the transport is stopped. Instead, each reel motor may be powered sufficiently to keep the tape properly tensioned. If the tape is cut, each reel motor winds up the slack. When the tape is no longer properly threaded, both reels cease rotation.

On some early servo-system transports, there was apt to be a certain amount of tape "creeping" in the stop mode if the reel motor torques were not properly balanced.

Tape Transport Control Systems

Figure 10-9 shows the typical tape transport controls found on an early professional tape recorder, where each button or switch performed but one function. There was no need to guess what might happen when a button was pushed or a switch was flipped; its one and only purpose was clearly marked on the surrounding panel.

By contrast, the modern tape transport system operates largely under software control. Although the basic start/stop/fast-mode functions remain intact, various other functions are regulated by *soft keys*, each of which is not hard-wired to perform a single task. Instead, its immediate function is software controlled (hence the name), and it may perform various tasks, depending on the mode in which the transport happens to be in at the time the key is pressed.

Figure 10-9. The tape transport controls on an early-generation professional tape recorder. *(Model 351 courtesy Ampex Corp.)*

For readers who have not yet encountered the soft key in audio applications, a hallway lighting system serves as a simple example. A single switch at either end of the hall turns the light on if it is off, or off if it is on. The up/down positions on the switch cannot be labeled *on* and *off*, since either position may represent either mode, depending on the present condition of the light itself. If the switch requires a label, it will have to be *hallway* or something equally descriptive. The label is more ambiguous than *on/off* but with luck the operator should have little difficulty figuring out what it does.

In the case of a soft key on a tape transport system, the key may enable many context-specific functions that are unrelated to each other. Therefore, even a simple label (like *hallway*) cannot be used. However, most such systems place the soft keys immediately next to an LED (light-emitting diode) or LCD (liquid crystal display) readout device. The readout shows the current functions of the soft keys, and as each key is pressed, the display changes as required to indicate the new functions of the keys. If the purpose of the key is not immediately clear, there should be a user's manual handy. Or if not, push the key and see what happens.

The following section begins with a brief overview of the basic transport controls, then continues with a detailed description of the more complex transport functions found on late-model tape recorders. It should be noted that nomenclature and operation of the latter functions vary significantly from one transport to another, and of course not all transports support all the functions described. Nor is it possible to describe all functions found on all tape recorders.

The Basic Transport Controls

For anyone who has grown up in the electronics age, the basic transport controls are *so* basic they hardly need explanation here. These are the handful of controls found on all transports, from those costing less than this book to others whose price tags would look good on an annual income statement.

The four push buttons seen in Figure 10-9 are rewind, fast forward, stop, and play; they are physically arranged for one-handed operation and all are self-explanatory. On either side of the push buttons, toggle switches select tape tension and tape speed. The former control was necessary to optimize the tension system for either reels with NAB hubs or smaller-hubbed plastic reels which could not operate properly under the same amount of holdback tension. The record button was located on the front panel of the electronic assembly.

The same four push buttons are still found on more modern transport systems, though often placed in a different sequence and surrounded by many more controls, most of which will be explained later in this chapter.

Additional Transport Controls

Practically every modern tape transport system now offers additional transport control beyond the basic functions just described. A few of the additional controls often found on the transport front panel are described in the following.

Tape Editing Control
On early-generation tape transports, such as the one shown in Figure 10-9A, no additional controls were needed for tape-editing purposes. The basic technique for razor-blade editing a tape was, and still is,

1. Play the tape until the approximate editing point is heard,

2. Stop the transport,

3. Rock the tape back and forth across the playback head until the exact edit point is found.

The time-honored method to accomplish Step 3 was to simply grasp the supply and takeup reel hold-downs and twist them one way, then the other until the edit point was directly over the playback head gap. The reel brakes on nonservo-controlled machines permitted the reels to be hand turned, yet enough force remained to keep the reels from spinning freely.

As tape transport systems grew ever more sophisticated, some systems would no longer permit the user to hand-turn the tape reels while the transport was stopped. To do so would be to contradict the servo system, which in the stop mode was programmed to supply the necessary signal to each reel motor to prevent the tape from moving. Any external force applied to a reel would be immediately counteracted by an equal and opposite internal force acting upon the same reel.

In this case, new edit-mode circuitry was required to override some of the transport logic so that razor-blade editing could once again be done. The same edit mode could also be used to enhance the traditional way of disposing of unwanted tape (as for example, an ending so bad it's not worth keeping, but followed by a better retake).

For example, the addition of a front-panel *edit* button might permit one of two edit modes to be enabled. In the *edit/stop* mode, the reel servo system is disabled so that hand turning of the reels is again possible (this is not necessary on all modern systems).

In the *edit/play* mode, the play mode is initiated but the takeup reel remains in its parked position. As a result, the unwanted tape segment plays off the supply reel and onto the floor (provided the system uses a pressure roller to pull tape across the capstan). As the end of the discard segment approaches, the operator stops the tape. After cutting off the tail end of the segment to be discarded, the supply and takeup tape segments are rejoined, the tape rethreaded across the tension arm, and normal play mode is resumed.

On many systems employing an oversize capstan with no pressure roller, the capstan itself may be turned by hand without fear of demolishing either the tape or the servo system.

Cue Wheel

On either type of transport system, a cue wheel is often provided on the transport front panel or remote control unit (see Figures 10-11B and C later in this chapter). In a typical system, the wheel performs one of two functions, as described here. In the *shuttle* mode, when the wheel is hand-rotated clockwise or counterclockwise, the tape moves forward or backward, at a speed dictated by the degree to which the wheel is turned. A fractional rotation moves the tape slowly; at a few full turns the tape moves much faster. In the *jog* mode, the wheel becomes a tactile substitute for the capstan itself, or for reel twisting. That is, tape motion across the heads tracks the movement of the cue wheel, so the tape may be rocked back and forth across the playback head in ever-diminishing amounts until the precise edit point is found.

On some earlier-model transports (for example, MCI JH series), a joy stick performed much the same function as the cue wheel. And in each case, tape lift and muting (described below) are disabled so that the tape can be monitored while using the cue wheel or joy stick.

The cue wheel may also be used during electronic system alignment, as described later on in this chapter (page 417).

Tape Lift and Muting Systems

All transport systems provide some means to lift the tape off the heads during fast winding modes for two reasons: to reduce physical wear on the heads, and to prevent damage to the studio monitor system (to say nothing of the engineer's ears) from the high-level high-frequency signal that otherwise would be reproduced as the tape speeds across the playback head.

It is sometimes necessary to defeat the tape lift system so that the engineer can hear the program in order to find the desired tape segment. This was an absolute necessity before the days of time code systems and may still be required when searching for a section whose location is unknown.

On older tape transports, the tape lift mechanism was built into a hinged head cover, as shown in Figures 10-10A and B. When the cover was closed the tape made contact with the heads; when opened the tape was lifted off the heads. During either fast winding mode, the engineer could partially close the cover, allowing the tape to approach—but not touch—the playback head. By "gain riding" the head cover, the engineer could hear enough of the signal to identify the program content, yet not blow the monitor system's tweeters.

Later model systems "improved" this arrangement by incorporating electro-mechanical tape lifters which automatically lifted the tape from the heads in the fast-wind modes, as also shown in Figures 10-10C and D. Although the system precluded accidental high-speed tape-to-head contact, it also made it difficult to monitor the tape as before. However, it was usually possible to manually force the tape back towards the head by applying thumb pressure to the tape lifter. A further "improvement" allowed the tape lifters to be completely disabled, usually by pressing the *edit* button while the transport was in a fast winding mode. This would retract the lifters, the tape would make complete contact with the heads, and the speaker tweeters would be destroyed if the engineer forgot to turn down the monitor gain before pressing the *edit* button. The latest designs eliminate this little problem by automatically attenuating the output level and rolling off the high-frequency response if the edit mode is entered while the transport is in either of its fast-wind modes.

Alternate Function Modes

On a personal computer, the *alternate key* is a familiar feature; as long as this key is depressed, the normal functions of other keys are replaced with other functions. On a modern tape transport, depressing an *alternate*, or *second, function key* makes various nonstandard functions available via the regular transport motion controls. Representative examples are given here.

Reverse Play *or* Recording/Erasing *Modes*   To permit the bidirectional operation of the transport that was described earlier in the chapter (page 384), the alternate-function key is held down while pressing the play button; the tape now moves backwards, but at normal play speed. When the record button is pressed, either the record *or* the erase head is activated, according to a preselected switch setting. Since the reverse mode passes the tape over the erase head immediately after the record head, the erase head must be disabled in order to preserve the reverse-recorded program.

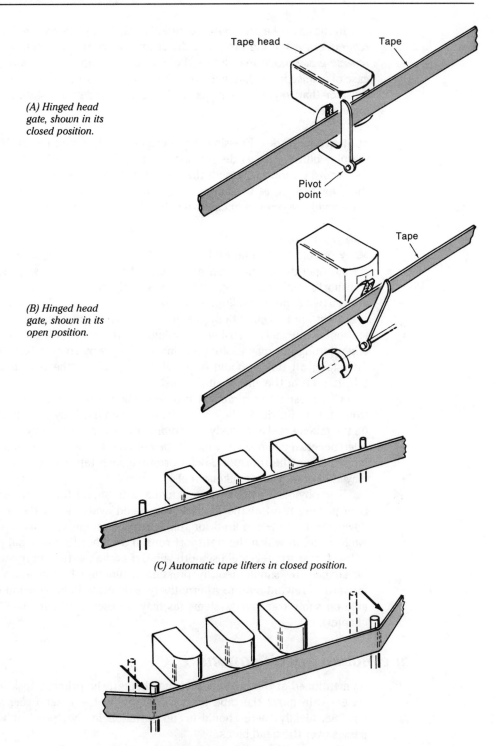

(A) Hinged head gate, shown in its closed position.

(B) Hinged head gate, shown in its open position.

(C) Automatic tape lifters in closed position.

(D) Automatic tape lifters in open position.

Figure 10-10. Tape lift systems.

In the case of a previously recorded track, two passes are required: the first to reverse erase the old program, the second to record the new material. Or, the *reverse erase* mode may be used alone to clean up a noisy tape section. In the case of a noise immediately before a musical entrance, the reverse procedure may be safer than trying to get out of the record mode an instant before the music begins.

Spot Erase *Mode*   Pressing the alternate function and record buttons (but not the play button) places the transport in a spot erase *ready* mode. The next time the record button is pressed, the system will enter the record mode and remain there for as long as the button is held down. This feature can be used to erase very small program segments while hand moving the tape across the erase head.

Library Winding

Many smooth-backed tapes do not wind evenly onto a reel during fast-forward or rewind operation. And even matte-backed tapes may not wind smoothly if the transport's reel tensioning system is slightly out of adjustment. Although an uneven wind poses no immediate problem, tapes should not be stored—even overnight—in this condition. The uneven wind is symptomatic of a tape in which tension is unevenly distributed throughout the reel and, in addition, the tape edges jutting out may easily be damaged simply by routine handling of the reel. Therefore, all tapes should be carefully wound, in the play mode, onto their takeup reels at the end of all sessions.

This presents no practical problem when simply playing/recording a tape from start to finish. At the end of the reel, the tape is by default properly wound on the takeup reel and ready for storage. However, during any typical session it is often necessary to quickly wind a tape onto a takeup reel so that another one can be placed on the transport. Before storage such tapes should be rewound, then played back onto their takeup reels.

The obvious post-session technique is to spend time rewinding each tape, then playing it off at the highest play speed available on the transport. To cut down on the time required for this operation, some systems provide a *library-wind* mode, in which the transport runs at a higher-than-normal play speed, yet not so fast as to preclude a smooth wind. If available, the library-wind mode may be enabled by simultaneously pressing a function button and either the fast-forward or rewind button. Alternatively, a dedicated library-wind button is available on some transport systems (as may be seen in Figure 10-13B later in this chapter).

Tape Motion Specifications

As mentioned at the beginning of the chapter, the primary task of the transport system is to move the tape from the supply to the takeup reel as smoothly as possible. Ideally there should be no variation in the speed at which the tape passes over the head block.

However, given the complexity of any mechanical system comprising three motors, a capstan, and assorted other rollers and tape guides, some minor (one hopes) fluctuations in speed are inevitable. Although all such fluctuations are known as *flutter* due to the nature of the resultant program distortion, the fluctuations may be further defined by a term that describes the listener's perception of that distortion (Manquen 1987).

Wow   Not an expression of amazement, *wow* is the low-frequency modulation of an audio signal caused by uneven motion of the tape during recording, playback, or both. It is typically caused by irregularities in various motor speeds and/or capstan or roller eccentricities.

Flutter   As the term implies, *flutter* is a higher-frequency modulation of the audio signal, which may also be caused by motor problems or by poor bearings within a roller or other tape guide.

Scrape Flutter   When a length of tape is suspended between two contact points, it acts more or less as a vibrating string. If there is excessive friction between the tape and the contact point, the vibration may become excessive as the tape is, in effect, scraped over the contact point. The audible effects of scrape flutter may be minimized by designing the transport system so that the unsupported tape path on either side of the head is very short. This places any flutter well above the audible frequency range. A flutter filter, in the form of a rotating bearing or fixed post, is often placed in the vicinity of the record and playback heads for this purpose. In Figure 10-1D, a flutter filter is seen between the 24-track playback head and the capstan/pressure roller system.

Wow and Flutter Measurements   Most transport specification sheets include a single specification for wow and flutter, as an error expressed in percent. Given the state of the tape transport art, the specification has shown much improvement over the years. For example, the following wow and flutter figures are taken from representative transport specification sheets issued in the years indicated.

	Wow and Flutter (%)			
Year	@ 7.5 in/s	@ 15 in/s	@ 30 in/s	Timing Accuracy (%)
1953	0.25	0.20	—	0.2
1970	0.10	0.08	0.04	0.2
1988	0.06	0.04	0.03	0.1

If a wow or flutter problem occurs while recording, it may not be noticed during simultaneous monitoring from the playback head. However, when the tape is played back later, the pitch fluctuation will be heard to a greater or lesser extent, depending on whether the playback wow and flutter is in or out of sync with that recorded on the tape.

A scrape flutter condition may be aggravated by a build-up of loose tape oxide or other dirt particles on various stationary guides along the tape path. Unless regularly cleaned, such sticky surfaces will quickly scrape even more oxide off the passing tape, and generally attract other dirt from the immediate area.

Remote Control of Tape Transport and Electronic Systems

On just about any tape recorder other than the simple mono system shown above in Figure 10-9, something more than the single record button shown in that illustration is required. For example, means must be provided to separately record on some tracks while simultaneously monitoring previously recorded program on other tracks. In addition, most systems now provide a wide variety of search features, which the user must be able to program and utilize conveniently. And, given the open-ended possibilities of any software-controlled electronic system, there are an infinite (well, almost) number of other functions that can be made available to the operator.

As is typical of many modern electronics systems, the space required for the operator interface (jargon for user-operated controls) far exceeds the space required for the corresponding electronics. And it also exceeds the amount of space conveniently available on the transport itself. As a further consideration, it is far more convenient to place these controls near the operator, with the transport itself located elsewhere, perhaps even in a different room. Therefore, most if not all modern multitrack tape recorders provide a separate remote control unit; representative examples are illustrated in Figure 10-11.

In each case, the remote control unit duplicates the basic functions found on the tape transport system front panel, and supplies the additional functions to be described below. As above, nomenclature and physical and operational characteristics vary from one transport to another. In most cases, the described (or similar) controls may be found on each of the remote control units seen in Figure 10-11. When necessary, the discussion will refer the reader to the specific control panel that best illustrates the function under discussion.

For the purposes of the following description, it is assumed the reader is already familiar with basic synchronous recording techniques, which are described later in the chapter (page 418). Readers who would prefer to review these techniques may want to read that section first and then return here for more information.

Ready/Safe Mode

As with the simplest mono tape recorder, the *record* mode is entered by pressing the single *record* button found on the transport front panel and duplicated on each remote control unit. But on almost any multitrack recording session, it's necessary to preselect the tracks that will be recorded when the button is pressed, and to guard against the accidental erasure of program material previously recorded on other tracks. Therefore, a separate *ready/safe* switch may be provided for each track (Figure 10-11C). In the ready position, the associated track will go into record the next time the record button is depressed; in the safe position it will not. To help prevent accidents from happening when playing back between takes, an *all safe* switch disables any switch left in the ready position. Therefore, an accidental press on the record button during a playback-only session will have no effect.

In most cases, a red *status light* indicates the selected mode for each track. Typically, the light is off in the safe mode, blinks to indicate record ready, and is steadily illuminated during actual recording.

Monitor Mode

During any recording session it is usually necessary to alternate between monitoring the output of the recording console and the output of the tape recorder. For example, during initial rehearsals the engineer will need to hear the console output in order to balance all the input signals. During recording the option is to either continue monitoring the console output, or to switch to the tape output to verify that the signal is indeed being recorded properly. And during playback, of course it's the tape output that is of interest.

Since the console output represents the same point in the signal path as the recorder input, the latter's monitor mode switch usually permits the user to monitor this point as well as the normal tape head outputs. Therefore, the tape recorder's own mode-select facility may be used as a single-point monitor mode selector, as shown in Figure 10-12A. The three monitor modes are also listed here.

Mode	Signal Is Monitored From
Input	Tape recorder inputs (i.e., console outputs)
Sync	Record (sync) head for previously recorded tracks; tape recorder input for tracks presently being recorded
Repro	Playback (repro) head

Since synchronous recording requires the record head to alternately function in the record and the playback modes, it is often labeled as the *sync* head, in reference to its potential double duty. In the same context, the playback head is referred to as a *repro* (reproduce) head. Thus, descriptions of playback from the *sync* or the *repro* head are less apt to be confused with each other.

For most routine sessions, monitoring is done in the sync mode during recording and in the repro mode during playback. Thus all previously recorded tracks are monitored from the sync (record) head during recording, and all tracks are monitored from the repro (playback) head during playback only. In this case, submaster switches select the appropriate mode. These are labelled *All Sel-Rep* (Selective Reproduce) and *All Repro* in Figure 10-11A.

An alternative *All Input* switch is also available. This mode may be used prior to actual recording, when the console is set up to monitor the output of the recorder. In the absence of a tape output, the all-input mode simply routes the recorder inputs (console outputs) back to the monitor system so that the engineer can hear what will be recorded, once the record button is pressed. The monitoring interaction between the tape recorder and the console is described in greater detail in Chapter 12 (page 506).

If it becomes necessary to change the monitor mode of one or more tracks, an *individual* mode is also switch selectable. When this mode is enabled, the monitor mode for each track may be independently varied via a set of 24 *Input/ Sel-Rep/Repro* switches.

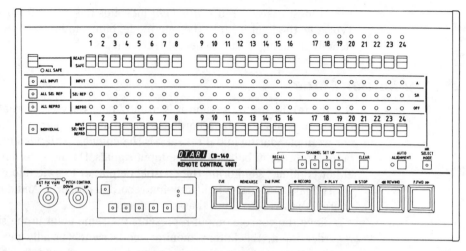

(A) Otari MTR-100A. (Courtesy Otari Corp.)

(B) Sony APR-24. (Courtesy Sony Professional Products Company)

Figure 10-11. Multitrack remote control units.

Monitor Mode with Noise Reduction Systems

A further monitoring consideration is the integration of a noise reduction system with the tape recorder. The noise reduction system itself is described in detail in Chapter 11, so here we consider just the monitoring requirements.

The complementary noise reduction systems described in the next chapter all process the signal immediately before and again immediately after it is recorded on tape. However, it is common practice to assign a single noise reduction system to each tape track. The module is switched between the input line during recording and the output line during playback, as shown in Figures 10-12B and C, obviating the need for (and the expense of) two noise reduction modules for each track. Therefore, a recorder's output signal will sound distorted if it is monitored while in the record mode, since at that time there is no noise reduction module in the output line.

(C) Studer A820. (Courtesy Studer Revox America, Inc.)

Figure 10-11 *(continued)*

To prevent this from happening, the noise reduction module provides the additional switching facility shown in Figure 10-12D. While in the record mode, the input signal is routed back to the console from a point immediately ahead of the noise reduction section. Therefore, all input signals to the recorder are correctly heard in their preprocessed state. Since the signal is routed back to the console before it reaches the tape recorder, the recorder's own monitor mode switch has no effect for those tracks currently being recorded. Tracks previously recorded are monitored through their respective noise reduction modules, as shown in the signal flow diagram in Figure 10-12C.

To accomplish this automatic switching within the noise reduction module, most multitrack tape recorders provide a multipin *noise reduction connector* on the rear panel of the transport. Its purpose is to supply the noise reduction system with the required switching logic signals so that as each recorder track switches in and out of record mode, the noise reduction module for that track switches modes automatically. In the case of tape recorders with built-in noise reduction modules, all switching takes place within the recorder itself.

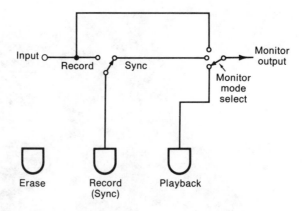

(A) Three-position mode select switch.

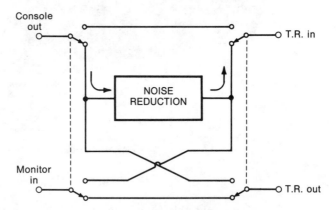

(B) The interface between tape recorder and noise reduction system during record mode.

Figure 10-12. Tape recorder monitor modes.

Time Reading Functions

On just about any recording or mixdown session, an accurate time-keeping system is essential. Although the clock on the wall is all that's needed to keep track of billing time, something more than that is needed to keep track of the recorded program. Such information is useful for tasks ranging from the simple to the complex—from logging the running time of a take, to identifying and then controlling the points at which one or more tracks enter and exit the record mode.

Figure 10-13 illustrates timing devices old and new. In the early example, the tape is passed over the roller seen in the figure and a mechanical linkage to an odometer-style gauge provides a readout of real time in hours, minutes, and seconds. Although certainly a useful tool, the generated time information travels no further than the five-wheel dial seen in the photo.

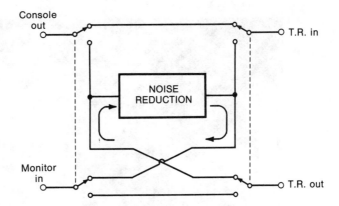

(C) The interface between tape recorder and noise reduction system during playback mode.

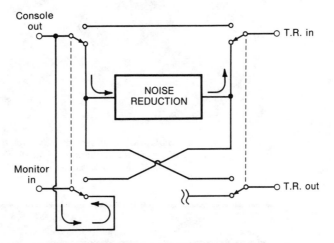

(D) Detail of monitor switching system during record mode.

Figure 10-12 *(continued)*

Figure 10-13B shows a more modern readout system, which may display time according to one of the following modes.

Tape Time. As on the early transport, tape motion is detected by a roller in the tape path. However, the mechanical linkage is replaced by an electronic system which displays hours, minutes, seconds and tenths of a second on a digital readout. If the time is set to zero at the beginning of the tape (or of a new take), then the readout displays the cumulative time as the tape passes over the roller.

Time Code. The display now reads a time code signal and provides a readout in hours, minutes, seconds, and frames. The code may be read from a time code track already recorded on the tape or from a time code generator.

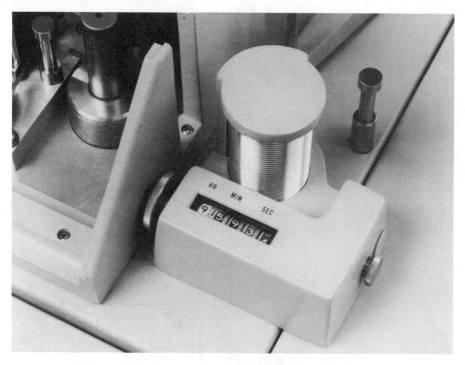

*(A) The simple mechanical system reads elapsed time based on rotations
of the metal drum seen immediately above the readout.
(MM-1000 tape recorder courtesy Ampex Corp.)*

*(B) An LED readout which displays either tape time or time code.
(A820 tape recorder courtesy Studer Revox America, Inc.)*

Figure 10-13. Tape recorder timing systems.

The selection of the *tape time* or *time code* mode may be accomplished by a
front-panel switch, such as the *TC Displ* (Time Code Display) switch seen in
Figure 10-14.

Tape Search Functions

The early readout system was a passive device; it simply informed the user of the elapsed time based on tape travel over the roller, but did nothing more. By contrast, more recent generations of timing systems may be programmed to read the present time from a time code track recorded on the tape and then to compare that time with some known reference, for example, the time at which a previously recorded segment begins, the end of the present take, the middle of take 3, etc. A few functions that take advantage of this facility are described here.

To help describe these functions, Figure 10-14 shows a detail view of the keypad and time display section of the remote control system seen in Figure 10-11B.

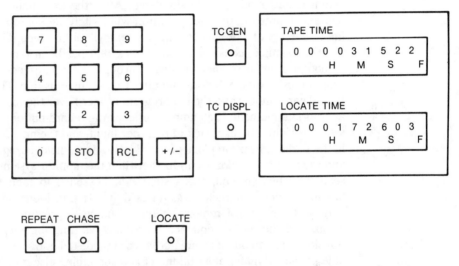

Figure 10-14. Detail of the numeric keypad and time display sections of the remote control panel on the Sony APR-24.

Locate

Assuming the time at which some event was previously recorded is known, the user may enter this time via the keypad and then enable a *locate* function. As shown in Figure 10-14, the *tape time* display indicates that the tape is presently at 3:15:22 (3 minutes, 15 seconds, 22 frames). The operator has used the keypad to enter a desired time of 17:26:03, which is seen on the *locate time* display. When the *locate* button is depressed, the tape fast winds from its present (*tape time*) position to the location (i.e., to the time) displayed by the *locate time* readout.

Memory Registers

The *locate time* readout displays the most recently entered keystrokes, and may be used to quickly locate the desired location on the tape. Once entered, the desired time data may also be stored in various memory registers for later recall. Some of these registers are reserved for special purpose information, as described in some of the following sections.

The general procedure is to key in a time, which is immediately displayed on the *locate time* readout. Next, press the *STO* (store) button followed by two digits to represent the desired storage register (00–99). To recall a register, press *RCL* (recall), followed by the two digits which define the desired register.

Rehearse Mode

Whenever an attempt is made to redo a segment of a previously recorded track, a certain amount of rehearsal is usually needed to make sure that the new material will fit in with the old, that entrance and exit cues are understood, and so on. Once the record button is pressed, all decisions become final; there is no such thing as an "unerase" mode. However, there is a rehearse mode, in which the actual record mode is only simulated. After the front-panel *rehearse* button is depressed, pressing the record button will switch the appropriate track monitoring to the input mode, but the input signal will not be recorded.

For example, consider a single track that has been recorded in its entirety. Although a small segment midway through the take needs to be redone, the program immediately before and after that segment is fine. The tape is played in the rehearse mode, and the old program is heard over the monitor system. At the appropriate moment, the engineer presses the record button; the monitor output switches from tape playback to recorder input, and the new program originating in the studio is heard in place of the old. However, the old program remains intact and the new material goes no further than the monitor system. At the end of the section to be replaced, the system switches back to tape playback, and the previously recorded track is again heard. If both transitions work well, the system may be taken out of rehearse mode, usually by pressing the rehearse button again, and the entire sequence repeated, this time for keeps. However, if the transitions in and out of (simulated) record mode did not go well during rehearsal, at least the old material is still intact and something else may be tried instead.

The points at which the system goes into, and out of, the record mode are popularly referred to as the *punch-in* and *punch-out* points, respectively. And of course the fine art of doing so is known as "punching in" and "punching out."

Programmed Rehearse Mode

To prevent the accidental erasure of program material due to punching in or out at the wrong time, the entire sequence may be programmed by entering and storing the following data in four dedicated registers.

Pre-Roll	The point prior to the punch-in at which the tape is to begin playing
Punch-In	The point at which recording is to begin
Punch-Out	The point at which recording is to end
Post-Roll	The point beyond punch-out at which the tape is to stop playing

Once the required data is stored in memory, the transport will fast wind to the pre-roll position, begin playing, go in and out of record at the punch-in and punch-out points, continue to the post-roll position, and then stop. The sequence may be initiated by depressing one of the following buttons, which modifies the procedure as described here.

Preview	The punch-in and punch-out are simulated only, as in the *rehearse* mode described before.
Edit	The punch-in section is actually recorded.
Review	The tape plays from the pre-roll to the post-roll positions and is monitored from the repro head.

Entry of Punch-In and Punch-Out Data

The best way to identify the initial punch-in and -out points is the old way: by ear (some things never change). However, listening to a tape while watching time pass on a digital readout is not the most reliable way of noting the desired points, especially when split-second or frame accuracy is sought. Instead, a data entry mode may be enabled by holding down an *entry* button and pressing an *in* button to mark the punch-in point and an *out* button to mark punch-out. In either case, the points are stored in their designated registers, but the punch-in/punch-out itself is not initiated.

The entry-mode controls just described are seen at the left in Figure 10-11B, but do not appear in the Figure 10-14 detail drawing.

Repeat

It is often desirable to play a segment of tape, then stop and rewind to the start of the segment and play it again, as for example during rehearsal of the punch-in/punch-out just described. To set up the system for this purpose, the two times are entered and stored in dedicated *start time* and *stop time* registers. Once this is done, the user presses the *repeat* button. The transport winds to the stored start time, plays to the stop time, rewinds, and repeats the process over and over again. The cycle continues until the *stop* button is pressed. In the case of punch-in/punch-out recording, the start and stop times may be transferred to the pre- and post-roll registers for use as described previously.

Chase

When the *chase* button is depressed, the transport becomes a *slave* system whose motion is synchronized via time code with the designated master transport (See Appendix A for the SMPTE Time Code Standard). For example, if the *repeat* mode is programmed on the master and the *chase* button is depressed on the slave, the latter will play and rewind according to the data stored in the master transport registers.

Tape Recorder Alignment Procedures

To ensure the proper operation of any magnetic tape recorder, a series of mechanical and electronic system checks should be carried out prior to doing any serious recording work. The following sections describe both sets of procedures.

Mechanical System Alignment

The presession alignment of a tape recorder's mechanical system consists primarily of routine cleaning of the various tape guides, rollers, and heads, and making sure all heads are in good physical alignment with the tape.

Cleaning Procedures

Routine cleaning of all tape guides, rollers, and heads is actually a prealignment procedure, and although short on glamour, should not be overlooked in favor of more rewarding work. A little contamination along the tape path will go a very long way towards degrading sound quality and, possibly, help degrade the next tape placed on the machine.

All metal surfaces along the tape path—including the tape heads themselves—should be cleaned with a cotton swab moistened in pure (97–99%) isopropyl alcohol, *not* rubbing alcohol. Do not use any other type of liquid cleaner, especially on the tape heads, where the laminations may be weakened by various unknown liquid substances.

Before cleaning any rubberlike surface, consult the manufacturer's instructions. Some rollers may be deformed by alcohol, others may absorb lint from the swab itself. In case of doubt, clean these surfaces with a dampened lint-free cloth.

Make sure that all such surfaces are completely dry by evaporation before threading the tape on the transport. Otherwise, the residual alcohol on the guides will nicely dissolve the oxide on the tape passing over them. The results will not be pleasing.

Head Demagnetization

As part of routine housekeeping procedures, the tape heads and metal guides in the tape path must be kept magnetically clean; although the heads are temporary magnets, some slight magnetic build-up over the passage of time is nevertheless inevitable, and may act as an unwanted magnetization of the tape passing over the head. The result is an increase in recorded noise level and some high-frequency erasure.

To remove this remanent contamination, the heads and other metal surfaces may be magnetically "cleaned" with a head demagnetizer: a wand-like device which produces a strong magnetic field, usually at the tip of a probe. The device is turned on and brought slowly near the tape head or other surface to be demagnetized, then slowly removed from the area. The procedure is repeated for each head and other metallic surface to be demagnetized.

Note: Before demagnetizing the heads, make sure the tape recorder is turned off; otherwise, the applied magnetic field will overload the recorder's electronic system.

Head Adjustments

Although the cleaning and demagnetization procedures just described should be carried out at regular intervals, head adjustments should not be required at the same time. However, it is a good idea to double check the following alignments every time the head block is swapped, to make sure the head block is properly seated on the transport and that the heads themselves have not gone out of alignment. Figure 10-15 shows the various head adjustments that should be routinely checked, with corrections made as required.

Azimuth Alignment

The difficulty of correcting the azimuth errors described in the previous chapter (page 372) is proportional to the number of tracks on the head. On a two-track head the alignment procedure is, given a little hands-on experience, reasonably simple. But as the number of tracks increases (4, 8, 16, 24, ...), the number of track combinations goes up quickly, as does the difficulty of bringing all tracks into alignment with all other tracks.

In any case, the azimuth alignment procedure begins at the repro head. Play the 700-Hz or 1,000-Hz tone on the alignment tape and feed the combined repro-head output from any two tracks to an external meter. Adjust the meter for a convenient midscale reading. Then play the azimuth section of the alignment tape and observe the meter reading. A conspicuous dip in output level signifies an azimuth error. If a dip is noted, carefully turn the azimuth-adjustment screw, which is located in the immediate vicinity of the repro head, while observing the combined output. Adjust for maximum output at the lowest frequency in the tape's azimuth section. Continue fine tuning the adjustment at the progressively higher frequencies in this section of the tape. Repeat the entire procedure for various other track pairs, keeping in mind that gap scatter (see page 374) may preclude optimizing all possible track combinations.

Once the azimuth of the repro head is properly aligned, repeat the entire procedure for the sync head by monitoring the alignment tape in the sync mode. For two-track or other recorders without a sync facility, record a series of sine wave signals onto a fresh piece of tape. While monitoring the playback head output, adjust the record head azimuth as just described. Assuming the playback head azimuth was previously aligned, the record head is now in proper alignment with respect to the playback head.

Zenith and Other Head Adjustments

In addition to an azimuth error, a tape head may also be out of alignment with respect to zenith, height, and/or rotation, all of which are illustrated in Figure 10-15.

To check all these variables, the head is first coated with a thin film of head-marking ink. After the ink has completely dried, a piece of scrap tape in good physical condition is played over the head(s), thus wiping off part of the inked coating. The head area wiped clean by the tape should be rectangular, centered about the head gap, and also centered between the undercut slots at the top and bottom of the head face (Otari 1989).

Figure 10-16 illustrates some of the wear patterns that will be seen if the head is out of physical alignment. If any such pattern is noted, the appropriate head adjustment should be made, after which the head is again coated with ink and the tape once again run over the heads. The entire procedure should be repeated until the proper wear pattern is seen.

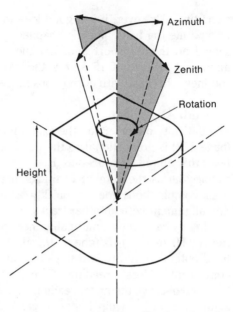

Figure 10-15. Proper tape-to-head contact is a function of azimuth, zenith, height, and rotation of the head.

Once the head is in good alignment, clean off the ink residue and discard the piece of tape that was used during the alignment process.

After making any azimuth, zenith or other head-moving adjustment, all of the physical alignments should be rechecked to make sure the specific adjustment has not affected any other parameter than the one for which it was intended.

Electronic System Alignment

In Chapter 9 the basic principles of tape recorder equalization were described in some detail. The alignment process may be briefly summarized as follows. A calibration tape recorded under laboratory conditions is played and the output level at various frequencies is noted. The overall level and frequency response are adjusted to bring the electronic system as close to a flat frequency response as is possible. Next, a series of sine wave signals is applied to the tape recorder inputs and recorded on tape. While observing the playback level, the level and frequency response of the record section are adjusted until the playback output response is again flat.

The controls on the tape recorder that are used for this alignment are discussed immediately below. Again, the basic principle is identical for all systems, although the actual procedures vary considerably from one system to another. As in the description of various transport functions, the examples given here are based on controls found on representative models of currently available multitrack tape recorders.

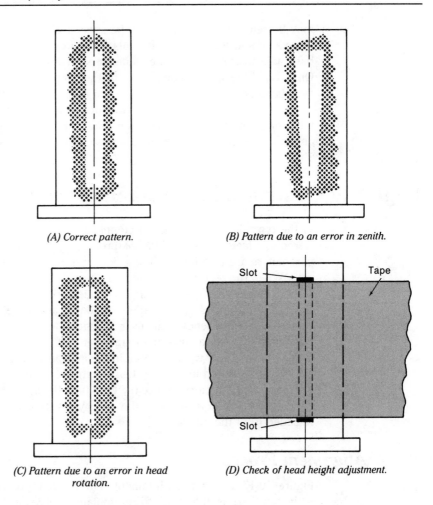

(A) Correct pattern.

(B) Pattern due to an error in zenith.

(C) Pattern due to an error in head rotation.

(D) Check of head height adjustment.

Figure 10-16. Wear patterns due to various head alignment errors.

Alignment Controls

On the early Ampex 351 tape recorder shown in Figure 10-1A, record and playback level controls were found on the front panel of the electronic system. All other changes (e.g., in bias, in equalization) were made via screwdriver adjustments at the rear of the amplifier chassis. On later systems, the controls were moved forward for more convenient adjustment through small access holes on the front panel, or they were accessed by removing a front panel cover (or by removing 24 front panels on an old Ampex MM-1000).

As the number of tracks expanded and multiple tape speeds became commonplace, to say nothing of multiple tape formulations, the number of screwdriver adjustments grew astronomically; the alignment of a modern 24-track tape recorder to meet all possible conditions is no longer the work of a few spare moments between sessions. For example, there are six basic adjustments to be made (playback level, low- and high-frequency playback equalization, bias, record level, high-frequency record equalization). A separate set of adjustments may be required for up to four tape speeds, (6 × 4), for NAB and IEC standards (6 × 4 × 2), and for two tape formulations (6 × 4 × 2 × 2). This means there are 96 basic adjustments that may be made for each track, or 2,304 on a 24-track system. Once this little task is completed, further adjustments may be required for the sync head output level and equalization and for the noise reduction system.

To prevent tape recorder alignment from turning into a career opportunity, most modern tape recorders offer some form of digital-control system for the automatic alignment of the audio system, as described next.

Digitally Controlled Alignment Systems

In the typical control system, a complete set of default alignment parameters is stored in a factory-installed PROM (programmable read-only memory). The same parameters are also loaded into a battery-protected RAM (random-access memory). When the recorder is turned on, the values are loaded into system registers for immediate use. The registers are loaded with values appropriate to the user-selected tape speed, equalization standard, and tape type. A different set of values is loaded whenever the user changes speed, equalization, or tape type.

When the user adjusts any parameter (e.g., high-frequency equalization of a single track), a new value is stored in the appropriate register and also overwrites the old value stored in RAM. When the machine is turned off, these new values are retained in memory for use the next time the system is turned on. If the RAM contents are subsequently lost, the factory-set standard values are automatically reloaded from the PROM.

Alignment Procedure

Figure 10-17 shows the alignment panels on representative tape recorders. Although there is little physical resemblance between them, the basic alignment procedures are quite similar. In each case, a single set of controls is used to adjust each track.

The following sections describe a few of the basic procedures used during system alignment.

Soft-Key Alignment

The control panel shown in Figure 10-17A consists of an alphanumeric keypad, an LCD readout with a set of five soft keys immediately below it, and a set of six dedicated keys to the right of the display. Figure 10-18 shows several displays that may be seen on the LCD screen during the course of an alignment. In each case, the upper line describes the present alignment mode, and the lower line lists the present function of the five soft keys immediately below the display. To get an idea of the general concept of soft-key alignment, a few procedures are described here. The alignment of other system parameters follows the same general pattern.

Before setting new values, it is good operating procedure to clear any previously changed parameters by restoring all system default settings for the type of tape in use. To do this, follow the sequence given here.

(A) Otari MTR-100A. (Courtesy Otari Corp.)

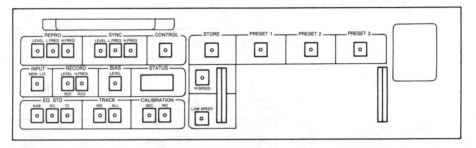

(B) Sony ATR-24. (Courtesy Sony Professional Products Company)

(C) Studer A820. (Courtesy Studer Revox America, Inc.)

Figure 10-17. Tape recorder alignment control panels.

Press	To Display	See Figure 10-18
STOP	Opening screen	(a)
INITIAL	Initial value set mode	(b)
DEFAULT	Recommended default value set mode	(c)
ALL	(to reset all parameters, or	(c)
FREQ.	to reset record frequencies only, or	(c)
LEVEL	to reset record level only)	(c)

After pressing the appropriate soft switch key at (c) in Figure 10-18, additional displays allow the changes to be stored for the present speed only, or for all speeds, and for the present tape type (displayed as [A]) or for all tape types.

To change to a different tape type prior to entering new settings, the following sequence would be used.

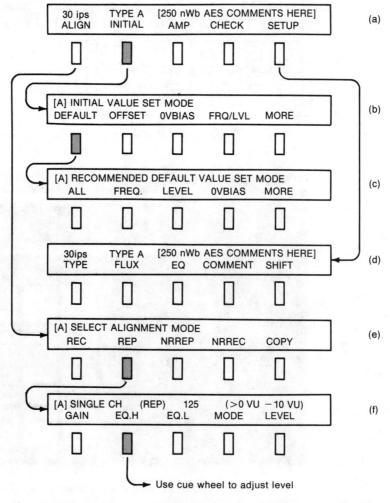

Figure 10-18. Selected alignment modes seen on the LCD screen of the alignment control panel shown in Figure 10-17A. Pressing a shaded soft key changes the alignment mode, as shown by the arrows.

Press	To Display	See Figure 10-18
STOP	Opening screen	(a)
SETUP	Tape setup mode	(d)
TYPE	(to toggle between tape types A–D)	(d)

The *STOP* key is one of the dedicated keys to the right of the LCD readout. At (d) in Figure 10-18, the LCD shows that tape type *A* is currently defined as 250 nWb/m fluxivity, with AES equalization. The "comments here" area may be used to store a 13-character message for informational purposes. To do so, the *COMMENT* soft key is pressed and the message entered via the alphanumeric keypad at the left-hand side of the alignment control panel, as shown in Figure 10-17A.

Soft-Key Level Changes

The soft keys are also used in conjunction with the *cue wheel* (to left of splicing block in Figure 10-6B) to make the continuously variable changes that are required when adjusting bias, equalization, and levels. For example, to manually align the high-frequency playback equalization on a single channel,

Press	To Display	See Figure 10-18
STOP	Opening screen	(a)
ALIGN	Select alignment mode	(e)
REP	Select alignment method	(not shown)
MANUAL	Select channel(s)	(not shown)
SINGLE	Single-channel reproduce mode	(f)
EQ.H	(to select high-frequency equalization)	(f)

Once manual high-frequency equalization has been selected, the number of the track to be equalized is entered on the alphanumeric keypad, and the cue wheel will now function as a high-frequency equalization potentiometer for that track. As the cue wheel is turned, the numeric readout (125) seen at (f) in Figure 10-18 will vary between 000 and 255 to indicate the relative position of the equivalent potentiometer. While playing the alignment tape, turn the cue wheel until the output meter reads the desired level. Then press the *STORE* button in the dedicated key section to store the equalization setting in memory.

After the reproduce mode is properly adjusted, pressing the *MODE* key at (f) in Figure 10-18 selects the output from the sync head in the sel-rep mode, which may now be similarly adjusted. The same adjustments for any other track may be made simply by selecting a new track via the keypad.

Also seen at (f) in Figure 10-18, the *LEVEL* key may be used to toggle back and forth between meter sensitivities of 0 and −10 VU. The greater-than symbol, >, acts as a cursor to indicate that 0 VU sensitivity is currently selected.

Automatic Alignment

As just described, the track-by-track alignment of a multitrack tape recorder requires just as many steps per track as does an older-generation machine with dedicated potentiometers for each parameter. With some practice, however, the manual alignment procedure may go somewhat faster because a single set of controls may be used to adjust every parameter within the entire electronics system.

However, an even greater time saver is the automatic alignment mode. Again, the soft-key panel is used to step through a series of displays in which the user specifies the operating level, desired alignment (e.g., record, repro, equalization), tape type, repro and/or sync output, etc. Once all this data is entered, the alignment tape is played and the system aligns itself automatically to the required specifications.

Summary

The procedures described in the preceding are unique to the tape recorder whose alignment control panel is shown in Figure 10-17A, and it must be remembered that the physical description of the various controls will not be the same on other systems. For example, the control panel shown in Figure 10-17B contains many more dedicated switches for enabling various alignment functions. Here, separate switch groups enable the desired equalization, repro and sync modes, etc.

In place of the cue wheel adjustment described previously, a *DEC* or *INC* (decrement or increment) button is pressed, as appropriate. In either case, the level changes in the desired direction at a rate of about 1 dB per second until the same button is pressed again, or the end of range is reached.

These and other important physical design differences notwithstanding, both systems provide the same type of control over the alignment process; the entire system may be adjusted from a single set of controls.

Synchronous Recording Techniques

The process of adding tracks to a basic recording has been an important production technique almost since the introduction of the tape recorder. However, the present method of doing so bears no resemblance to the way it was done in the days predating the multitrack tape recorder. The following section begins with a brief discussion of early methods, followed by a more detailed description of present-day technique.

Overdubbing

The term *overdub* was first used to describe the process of adding new program material to a previously recorded program by recording both new and old onto a new tape, as shown in Figure 10-19. In a typical session of the period, the entire orchestra would be recorded at once onto a one- or two-track master tape. Later on, the tape would be played back and the vocalist would sing along while monitoring the previously recorded program over headphones. The vocal track would be mixed with the orchestral track(s) and recorded on a second machine.

At the cost of a second tape generation, overdubbing allowed the obvious production advantage of not tying up a large (read, expensive) studio orchestra while the vocalist rehearsed the lead part. The procedure continued in widespread use as the number of tracks on the studio tape recorder increased, at first to three tracks on half-inch tape, and very soon after that, to four.

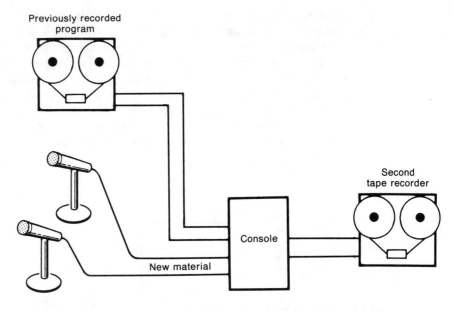

Figure 10-19. The original overdub process: combining and recording new and previously recorded program material on a second tape recorder.

Les Paul and Mary Ford took overdubbing about as far as it could be driven. Their "How High the Moon" and other hits of the day were made by overdubbing as many tracks as the medium could stand before the hiss level became completely unacceptable. The listening public was satisfied with the sound, but Les Paul wasn't. Working closely with the Ampex Corporation, he became responsible for the system that has subsequently done away with the original multigenerational overdubbing process.

Ampex dubbed the process Sel-Sync (selective synchronization) and since Sel-Sync is their trademark, the process is generically referred to as synchronous recording. With the original overdub process no longer in active use, the term *overdub* is now also used to describe synchronous recording. The following is a short list of terms commonly used to describe the synchronous recording technique.

Manufacturer	Term
Ampex	Sel-Sync (selective synchronization)
Otari	Sel-Rep (selective reproduction)
Scully	Sync
Sony	Overdub
Studer	Sync
3M	Cue

Synchronous Recording

On a multitrack tape recorder with separate control of the erase and record functions for each track, it is a comparatively easy matter to sequentially record on the available tracks, one or more at a time until all tracks are recorded. The practical difficulty comes in monitoring the previously recorded tracks while adding new material, as shown in Figure 10-20A. Given the distance between the sync and repro heads, there is a slight delay until the recorded program reaches the repro head for reproduction. Therefore, if musicians monitor the repro head output while recording new material on the same tape, the new material will be recorded out of sync with the old, and it will be heard that way on subsequent playback of the tape.

The solution is the synchronous recording technique shown in Figure 10-20B. While the sync head records new material on unused tracks, previously recorded tracks are monitored from the same sync head instead of from the repro head.

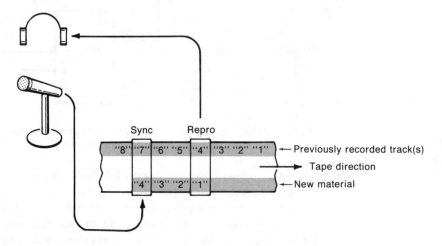

(A) Monitoring the repro head.

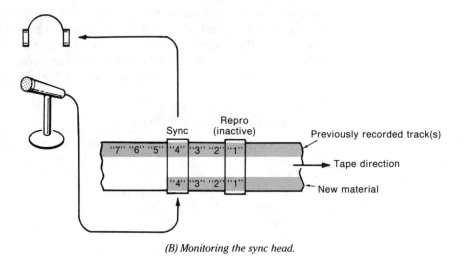

(B) Monitoring the sync head.

Figure 10-20. Recording new material while monitoring previously
recorded tracks.

Since the tape is now monitored from the same point at which the new program is recorded, both new and old tracks are in perfect synchronization.

When the selective synchronization process was first introduced, tape head technology imposed certain limitations on the quality of the signal reproduced by the sync head. But although frequency response and noise level specifications were considerably below acceptable levels, this was considered a small price to pay for the production advantages of the process. Of course the poor quality reproduction was only encountered during the actual recording session; later on, the completely recorded tape would be monitored and mixed down via the normal repro head, so the inconvenience was strictly a temporary matter.

More recently, the state of the tape head art has progressed to the point where sync head reproduction quality is almost indistinguishable from that of the repro head. Furthermore, most modern tape recorders provide separate reproduction alignment for both heads, so each may be optimized as required.

Bouncing Tracks

Given the reproduction quality of most sync heads, it's possible to exceed the usual limitations imposed by the number of tracks available on a single tape recorder. For example, consider a tape with one track open and three tracks worth of additional material to be recorded. As shown in Figure 10-21, the output from three previously recorded tracks may be combined and "bounced" over to

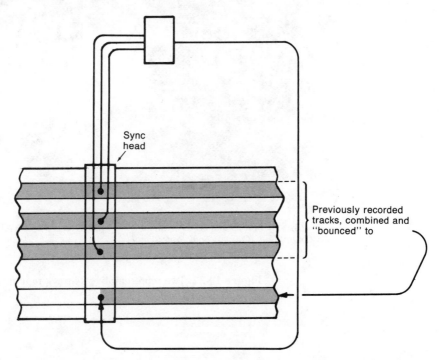

Figure 10-21. Track bouncing, as used to make room for recording additional tracks on a multitrack tape.

the one remaining open track. Once this is done, the three tracks may be reused for new material.

On some tape recorders, it may not be possible to bounce onto an open track immediately adjacent to one of the combined signals. This is because there is a certain amount of leakage within the head itself, and material recorded on one track may be sensed by adjacent sync head windings currently operating in the playback mode. If one of these head windings is supplying part of the signal being recorded on the open track, the resultant feedback loop will create a loud squeal. However, this is no longer the problem it was with earlier head technology. In case of doubt, try some before-the-fact experimental recording. Better yet, avoid adjacent-track bouncing entirely.

To conclude this discussion of tape transport systems, Figure 10-22 shows two representative 24-track analog tape recorders.

 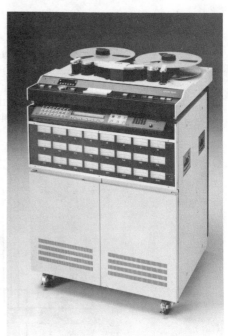

(A) Sony APR-24 and SU-224 Remote Control Unit. (Courtesy Sony Professional Products Company).   *(B) Otari ATR-100. (Courtesy Otari Corp.)*

Figure 10-22. Two representative 24-track tape recorders.

11 Noise Reduction

In Chapter 8 (page 300) it was pointed out that the dynamic ranges of most storage and transmission media are somewhat less than that of many musical performances, and considerably less than that of the ear. Since analog recording on magnetic tape remains an important storage device, this chapter begins by reviewing its limitations with respect to dynamic range, and then discusses various signal processing systems that are available to improve that range.

Since the signal-processing devices described later in this chapter all accomplish the same task, increasing the dynamic range of the recorded program by pushing back the noise barriers, they are referred to collectively as *noise reduction* systems.

Noise Characteristics of Magnetic Recording Tape

At extremes of listening level, either noise or distortion is the limiting factor; at low levels, tape hiss creates a "noise floor," with signals below this level masked by the hiss. At the opposite extreme, the distortion components introduced by tape saturation impose a ceiling on the maximum signal level. So it becomes imperative to keep the dynamic range of the recorded program well within the signal-to-noise limits imposed by the tape in order to avoid the effects of both low-level noise and high-level distortion.

Low-Level Noise

Every transmission medium introduces a certain amount of low-level noise to the signal it transmits. In the case of analog magnetic tape, the noise is, of course, the familiar tape hiss. Therefore, every time a recorded program is copied, three elements are stored on the new tape: a copy of the musical program, a copy of the hiss from the master tape, and an entirely new hiss from the tape copy itself.

Assuming the master and its various copies are all made on the same type of tape, the noise level will rise according to the equation

$$L = 10 \log n$$

where
L = noise level in dB
n = number of tape generations (or tracks, on a multitrack recorder)

In other words, each copy raises the noise level by 3 dB. The same equation finds the combined noise level for two or more tracks on a multitrack tape, compared to that of a single recorded track on the same tape. Thus with each additional recorded track the noise is seen to increase as follows:

Recorded Tracks	Noise Level (dB)	Recorded Tracks	Noise Level (dB)	Recorded Tracks	Noise Level (dB)
1	0.00	9	9.54	17	12.30
2	3.01	10	10.00	18	12.55
3	4.77	11	10.41	19	12.79
4	6.02	12	10.79	20	13.01
5	6.99	13	11.14	21	13.22
6	7.78	14	11.46	22	13.42
7	8.45	15	11.76	23	13.62
8	9.03	16	12.04	24	13.80

The table shows that for each doubling of tracks the noise level increases by 3 dB. Or to put it another way, the dynamic range of a 16- or 24-track tape is considerably less than that of a stereo program recorded directly to a 2-track master tape. However, if that 2-track master is mixed down from a multitrack tape, then two more tracks of noise are effectively added to the total. In other words, one of the disadvantages of adding more tracks is a reduction in dynamic range due to a steadily rising noise level.

High-Level Distortion

Fortunately the addition of more tracks does not lower the high level ceiling in addition to raising the noise floor. However, that ceiling may be reached sooner if the overall signal level is boosted in order to keep it above the noise floor.

Noise Masking

In the physical sciences it is a well-known phenomenon that a source of energy may be concealed in the presence of another source whose energy level is higher. The obvious example is the disappearance of the stars at dawn. Most of us don't doubt that they're really still up there, but the light from our own star, the sun, becomes so bright that those lesser lights can no longer be seen, despite their physical presence.

Meanwhile, back here on earth the sound of an outdoor concert may be momentarily blocked by a passing aircraft, or the sounds of quiet conversation concealed by a noisy construction crew. Both conditions are examples of *masking*, a process by which the threshold of audibility for one sound is raised by the presence of another (masking) sound (ANSI S1.1–1960 [R1976]).

Therefore, in the presence of a loud audio signal confined to a certain frequency band, lower-level background noise within that same band will be masked. As a result, for as long as the audio signal continues, it is not necessary to attempt to remove the nearby noise via signal processing. At least a few of the noise reduction systems described in this chapter take advantage of the masking phenomenon by minimizing their action, and therefore its audibility, during those intervals when the signal itself acts as a noise-masking device.

Basic Noise Reduction Systems

In Chapter 8 it was shown how dynamic range may be modified by a compressor or an expander. Although either device may be used for general signal enhancement or to create a special effect, they are also often used to improve the overall specifications of a signal, with respect to the low-level noise and high-level distortion described above. To a lesser extent, the equalizer may also be used for the same purpose.

The following list briefly summarizes these noise reduction functions of the compressor, expander, and equalizer.

Compression   To raise low-level signals above the residual noise level.
　　　　　　　　To drop high-level signals below the overload level of the transmission medium.

Expansion   To drop low-level noise to a less audible level (as a noise gate).
　　　　　　　To turn off inactive signal paths.

Equalization   To raise low and/or high frequencies above the residual noise level (preemphasis).
　　　　　　　　To restore low and/or high frequencies to their normal level (postemphasis).

As listed here, compression takes place prior to recording, in order to keep the signal within the limits of the tape. Expansion may also be applied before recording, so that low-level background noise is not recorded in the first place. Or, it may be applied during playback to attenuate both the recorded background noise and tape hiss. As noted, equalization is added during recording and removed during playback.

These then are the "building blocks" of the noise reduction systems to be described in this chapter. Depending on their selection and arrangement within the signal path, the noise reduction system may be categorized as dynamic or static, and as a single- or double-ended (complementary) system. Each category is described immediately below.

Dynamic and Static Signal Processing

Compression and expansion are examples of *dynamic signal processing*, which is a process that varies according to some characteristic of the device's input signal. In this case, the characteristic is the level of the audio signal, and the effect of the processing is an output level that varies dynamically with respect to the input signal level.

By contrast, the equalization described so far has been *static* in nature; the equalizer simply alters the gain of a certain frequency band, without regard for the momentary presence (or absence) of information within that band.

Single-Ended Signal Processing

In the applications of equalization, compression, and expansion discussed in previous chapters, the described device enhances the signal and no further processing is used later on to remove the effect. An exception may occur when the producer has second thoughts about the effect, but this is a special case not considered here (and is perhaps another reason for not making too many "final" decisions while recording a single track).

An equalizer, compressor, or other device used as described above is often referred to as a *single-ended* system, since processing takes place but once, that is, at only one end of the signal path. The single-ended system is commonly used to attenuate noise in a program that did not use a noise reduction system during recording. A typical application of a single-ended noise reduction system would be to minimize the Kellogg Effect ("snap, crackle, pop") when playing back an old 78-rpm disc. An expander used as a noise gate is another example of single-ended noise reduction.

Complementary Signal Processing

When equalization is applied in order to raise the signal above the noise during transmission, then an equal-but-opposite treatment is required during playback to return the signal to its original condition. Thus, *complementary signal processing* is a two-step, or double-ended, process in which whatever is added during recording is removed during playback. In the case of pre- and postemphasis equalization, the high-frequency attenuation that returns the frequency response to normal also drops the level of any low- and high-frequency noise added during transmission. (Tape recorder pre- and postemphasis were discussed in detail in Chapter 9, page 360).

Note that the playback half of a double-ended noise reduction system should not be used alone, for example to attenuate the 78-rpm ticks and pops mentioned in the previous section. The double-ended system works by expanding a compressed signal back to its normal state, and in the process it reduces noise that was not part of the original program. It does nothing for noise that *was* part of the original program. For example, studio air conditioner hum is not reduced, and in fact may be even more noticeable since it is no longer masked by tape hiss.

Dynamic Complementary Signal Processing

The next step in signal processing is to combine dynamic and complementary signal processing. For example, consider the problem of recording a program whose dynamic range exceeds that of the magnetic tape on which it is to be recorded. For the purposes of illustration, assume high-level peaks are causing tape saturation, and low-level signals are recorded below the residual hiss level of the tape.

The obvious solution is to compress the program prior to recording so that both level extremes are brought within the limits of the recording medium, as shown by the compressor section of Figure 11-1.

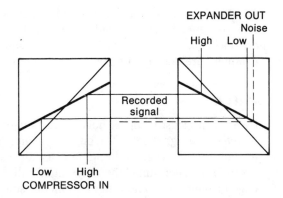

Figure 11-1. Dynamic complementary signal processing. The 2:1 compressor is followed by its complement, a 1:2 expander. Since both devices continuously react to the program, the process is dynamic.

Although the compressor solves one problem, it introduces another; the recorded program has a reduced dynamic range. However, complementary processing may now be applied as shown in the expander section of Figure 11-1. Here the compressed output from the tape recorder is routed to an expander whose ratio is the reciprocal of the compression ratio (in Figure 11-1, CR = 2:1 and ER = 1:2). Therefore, the dynamic range at the expander output matches that at the compressor input. Furthermore, as the expander drops low-level signals back to their original pre-compression level, it simultaneously drops the level of the tape hiss. Since the hiss component of the recorded signal was not compressed earlier, the net result is that as the musical program is restored to its original condition, there is a reduction in the hiss level from the tape.

The Compander

This example of dynamic complementary signal processing is the foundation of most commercially available noise reduction systems. A signal processor specifically designed for this application is often referred to as a *compander* (i.e., *com*pressor/ex*pander*), and the process itself as *companding* or, sometimes, *compansion*.

Like most other "simple" ideas, the successful noise reduction system requires far more sophistication than simply following a compressor with an expander. In most cases doing nothing more than that would result in an objectionable amount of "breathing" action, as described in Chapter 8 (page 306). Therefore, a considerable amount of thought has gone into noise reduction system design. The goal is, of course, to reduce the noise without introducing objectionable side effects, such as those heard as a byproduct of excessive compression or expansion.

The following sections describe the various noise reduction systems that have enjoyed popularity in the professional recording studio.

Single-Ended Noise Reduction Systems

To attenuate low-level background noise occurring simultaneously with the desired signal, a single-ended noise reduction system may be used. Such devices are available with varying degrees of complexity, and a few representative examples are described here.

Mute Switch

Perhaps the least complex noise reduction system is nothing more than a *mute switch* in the signal path. The engineer simply turns off (mutes) the channel when it contains no useful information, as for example during pauses in a vocal overdub. At such times the only "information" recorded is headphone leakage, page-turning noise, and other extraneous sounds, all of which can be eliminated by reaching for the mute switch. This form of noise reduction is certainly effective, if not the last word in elegance.

Most consoles provide a mute switch in each input channel, and in many the function may be automated.

Gain Riding

As a variation on muting, the gain of a noisy channel may of course be lowered during those times when it contains no useful information. Although not as effective as the mute switch, this sort of gain riding may be required when a sudden on/off change in background level would be audibly distracting.

The Noise Gate

The noise gate described in Chapter 8 (page 313) may of course be used to automatically drop the gain of a channel whenever the level falls below threshold. Its effectiveness as a noise-reduction device depends on the separation in level between signal and background noise, but in many cases at least a slight amount of noise-gate expansion may help reduce the noise while not interfering with the signal.

Static Filtering

Another simple (but rarely satisfying) noise reduction system is nothing more than a lowpass filter whose cutoff point is set at some compromise frequency intended to pass the signal and attenuate high-frequency noise. Unfortunately, there is no clear demarcation line between the two, and such a "noise filter" often removes a substantial portion of the signal along with the noise.

Some improvement in noise-reduction capability may be realized by using a dynamic filter, that is, a filter whose cutoff frequency varies according to the nature of the program passing through the filter. A few of these devices are briefly described here, and some of their operating principles will reappear in the double-ended systems described later on in this chapter.

Dynamic Noise Suppressor

The earliest attempts at more sophisticated noise reduction were made during the days of the shellac disc, when a single-ended "Dynamic Noise Suppressor" was proposed. This consisted of a system of dynamic high- and lowpass filters to be used during playback of the disc (Scott 1947). The system took advantage of the fact that high-level music masks low-level noise occupying the same general frequency band and hence there is no need for noise reduction.

When the signal level drops, the noise is no longer masked, and especially in the 78-rpm era, it could be quite objectionable. However, low-level music is usually concentrated within the midrange of the frequency spectrum, and therefore a certain amount of low- and high-frequency filtering can be introduced with minimal effect on the music itself.

Scott's Dynamic Noise Suppressor used dynamic filters at both ends of the frequency spectrum. Each filter cutoff frequency varied according to program level and frequency content, so that during high-level wide-range passages the filters were in effect removed from the signal path. As the level at either end of the frequency spectrum diminished, the appropriate filter closed in on the diminishing signal, thereby attenuating the background noise.

Burwen Dynamic Noise Filter

Although the Scott system was intended to address the deficiencies of shellac, it was later found that the device could provide acceptable results in other applications by varying the circuit time constants (Orban 1974). In fact, the 1970s saw the introduction of an improved "Dynamic Noise Filter" based on the principles of the earlier device (Burwen 1971a).

The Burwen Dynamic Noise Filter consisted of dual high- and lowpass filter networks in the audio signal path, as shown by the simplified block diagram in Figure 11-2A. We will use the highpass filter section to explain system operation. A lowpass filter in the control path generated a DC voltage proportional to the low-frequency content of the program. In the absence of significant low-frequency information, the cutoff frequency of the audio-path filter was set at 400 Hz. However, as low-frequency program content increased, so did the control voltage, thus driving the audio-path cutoff frequency down toward 12 Hz, at which point the highpass filter was in effect out of the audio circuit.

The complete highpass filter in the audio path consisted of a 6 dB/octave network followed by a 12 dB/octave network. Either section could be bypassed, thus providing a choice of 6, 12, or 18 dB/octave filter slopes. The lowpass section was constructed in the same manner, with a program-dependent cutoff frequency that varied between 1.2 and 37 kHz. Filter slopes of 6, 12, or 18 dB/octave could be selected independently of the highpass section's settings.

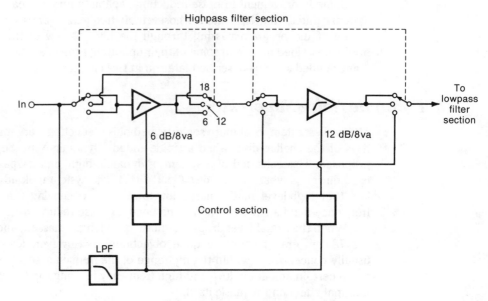

(A) Block diagram of dual highpass network only.

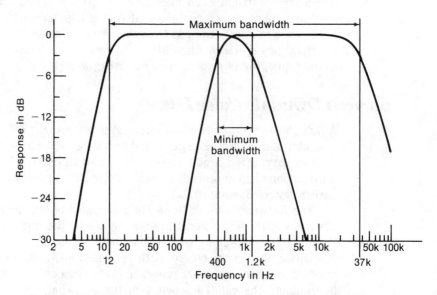

(B) Graph showing program-dependent cutoff frequencies (18 dB/octave highpass and 12 dB/octave lowpass filtering) in the model 1000 Dynamic Noise Filter.

Figure 11-2. The Burwen Dynamic Noise Filter.

In an actual production model for professional applications, the switchable slope feature was eliminated in favor of a fixed 6 dB/octave setting, and a set of notch filters (not described here) was eliminated. For applications that did not require low-frequency filtering, several lowpass-only models were also built.

Today, the primary application of the Burwen Dynamic Noise Filter is in consumer audio, where a DNF chip is manufactured under license by National Semiconductor, for use in car radios and also in some consumer audio and video hardware.

Spectral Program Filter

As just described, the control voltages in the Burwen filter are derived from the outputs of low- and highpass filters in its control section. It has been pointed out (Ives 1972) that these voltages may not be truly representative of the actual music spectrum. For example, the shaded areas in Figure 11-3 represent two frequency bands that would deliver identical control voltages to the highpass filter in the audio path. It's clear that the bands have greatly differing frequency spectra, and therefore require different degrees of high-frequency filtering. Therefore, Ives proposes a system whose control voltage is derived instead from the actual music spectrum, which in Figure 11-3 should result in two quite different voltages.

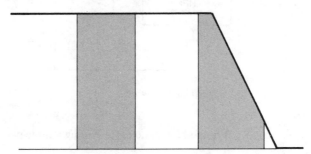

Figure 11-3. Two energy bands (shaded areas) that would deliver the same control voltage, despite their very different frequency spectra.

Figure 11-4A shows a block diagram implementation of a dynamic noise filter using a three-part network consisting of lowpass, bandpass, and highpass filters. The audio input signal is fed in parallel to all three filters. A common, but variable, cutoff frequency is used for the low- and highpass filters, and also as the center frequency of the bandpass filter. The audio output is taken only from the lowpass filter. The other two filters feed a comparator circuit, which compares their energy contents, as seen here:

Highpass Output with Respect to Bandpass Output	Cutoff Frequency Is
> bandpass	too low
= bandpass	correct
< bandpass	too high

If the energy at the highpass filter output is unequal to that at the bandpass output, the common cutoff/center frequency is adjusted until the two controls are equal. For example, consider an audio input signal whose high-frequency content has just increased, thereby raising the output from the highpass filter. This indicates there is more program energy in the highpass than in the bandpass filter and the cutoff frequency accordingly shifts upwards until the two are again equal. The cutoff frequency of the lowpass filter in the audio path likewise shifts upwards, thereby allowing the increased high-frequency program content to pass without attenuation. In a typical implementation, a front-panel calibration control lets the user vary the filter sensitivity as required.

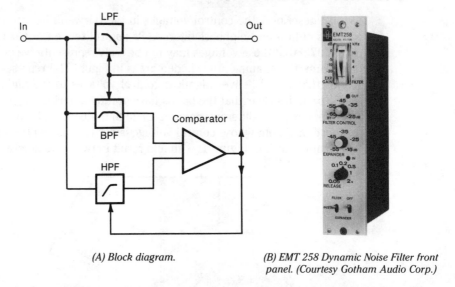

(A) Block diagram.   *(B) EMT 258 Dynamic Noise Filter front panel. (Courtesy Gotham Audio Corp.)*

Figure 11-4. A noise filter using a three-part dynamic filter network.

Note that the dynamic filter action described here is not level sensitive, since a simple change in overall level does not influence the ratio of bandpass to highpass output. Since the filtering action is instead a function of frequency spectrum, the device is described as a *spectral filter*. Such filters are widely used in film production and other applications in which high background noise levels are frequently encountered.

Tick and Pop Removers

The Scott Dynamic Noise Suppressor is but one of many single-ended systems used over the years to clean up noisy program sources. One reasonably effective "system" is to make a tape copy of the program and then do some razor-blade tick-editing; neither elegant nor sophisticated and certainly a tedious job, tick-editing nevertheless works, especially for tasks that require a little human perception to distinguish signal from noise.

Other techniques utilize equalization such as a notch filter or other frequency attenuator to reduce the output level in the vicinity of the noise spectrum.

As a more "high-tech" solution, various computer systems analyze the signal spectrum in an attempt to recognize various impulse noises. In the presence of such a noise, the system mutes itself and in some cases fills in the gap with a signal voltage extrapolated from the previous signal.

Summary

Depending on the nature of the program source and the sophistication of the signal processor, any of the single-ended noise reduction systems mentioned here may accomplish their task at the cost of being audible. Therefore, a compromise setting may be required as a tradeoff between removing all the noise and interfering with the program content. Nevertheless, the single-ended system offers the only means to deal with programs that did not employ noise reduction during the recording process.

Double-Ended Noise Reduction Systems

Although pre- and postemphasis equalization has been around since the earliest days of electric sound recording, the compander (compressor/expander) noise reduction system is a comparatively recent development. In each of the following systems, the dynamic range of the program is compressed just prior to recording, and expanded at playback, as shown by the block diagram in Figure 11-5. The expansion ratio is in each case the reciprocal of the compression ratio.

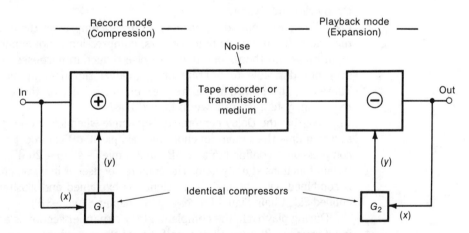

Figure 11-5. Block diagram of a dynamic double-ended noise reduction system (based on Dolby A- and B-type systems; see Figures 11-7A and 11-9A for detail of G_1 and G_2 blocks).

Since a tape recorded with a double-ended system must be played back through the same system to remove the record-mode processing, the record process is often referred to as *encoding*, the playback process as *decoding*.

EMT NoisEx Recording System

Perhaps the earliest practical dynamic double-ended processor was the NoisEx Recording System introduced in the mid-1960s by EMT (*Elektromesstechnik Wilhelm Franz KG*). Predating the introduction of the descriptive term "noise reduction," the system used a compressor with a 1.5:1 compression ratio during recording, followed by a 1:1.5 expander during playback. Although the NoisEx system enjoyed some popularity, it was soon eclipsed by the Dolby *A*-Type Noise Reduction System.

Dolby Noise Reduction Systems

In 1966 Dr. Ray Dolby introduced his Audio Noise Reduction system to a generally unenthusiastic recording industry which had seen—and worse, heard—enough other noise reduction schemes to expect that this one too would soon find its well-deserved place in oblivion. But as one perceptive early reviewer pointed out, "This one is really different. This one works" (Canby 1967). The Dolby model A301 S/N Stretcher eventually became known as the Dolby *A*-Type Noise Reduction System, to distinguish it from the *B*- and *C*-type systems which followed a few years later on. Although the later Dolby systems are limited to consumer audio applications, they are briefly described here since some of their basic principles have been applied to the professional *SR* (Spectral Recording) system.

In each case, the cited reference should be consulted for further information and a more rigorous explanation of system details.

Dolby A-Type System

Like all other companding systems, Dolby *A* compresses the audio signal prior to recording. But unlike its predecessors, compression is not applied over the entire input range, on the theory that for noise reduction purposes, it is neither necessary nor desirable to operate on high-level signal components (Dolby 1967). Therefore, the record-mode transfer characteristic for the Dolby *A*-type noise reduction system is as shown in Figure 11-6.

Note that the Dolby compressor is inactive when low-level signals are recorded, at which time the system functions as a simple 10-dB gain device. Above threshold, compression is confined to a 20-dB input range (-40 to -20 dB), beyond which the system functions at unity gain. The compressor itself is in a side chain, and its output is combined with the main path signal as explained and illustrated in the section entitled Side-Chain Signal Processing in Chapter 8 (page 319).

During playback, the complementary expander section is active over a 10-dB input range (-30 to -20 dB), half that of the record-mode compressor.

The companding action for a low-level signal may be followed in Figure 11-6 by noting that a -35 dB input signal (compressor in) is recorded at -27.5 dB (compressor out). During playback this compressed signal is fed into the expander (expander in) and it emerges at -35 dB (expander out). The signal is therefore restored to its original level.

Signals recorded below the compressor threshold are simply boosted by 10 dB, and accordingly cut 10 dB during playback, while signals above the compressor's finishing point are recorded and played back at unity gain.

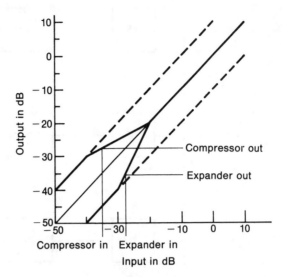

Figure 11-6. Transfer characteristics for the Dolby *A*-Type
Noise Reduction System.

	Compressor	Expander
gain below threshold	+ 10 dB	− 10 dB gain below finishing point
threshold	− 40 dB	− 20 dB
finishing point	− 20 dB	− 30 dB
ratio	2:1	1:2

Side-Chain Operation Prior to compression (and later, expansion), the side-chain signal is split into four filter bands, each of which is processed separately, as shown by the block diagram in Figure 11-7A. Note that the only difference between the Dolby compression and expansion modes is the manner in which the side chain signal combines with the main path signal. Therefore, the identical processor is used in both the record and the playback mode, in the positions G_1 and G_2 shown in Fig. 11-5.

The characteristics of the four bands are shown by the graph in Figure 11-7B, and are listed here.

Band	Filter Type	Cutoff Frequencies	Slope (dB/Octave)	Companding Occurs
1	lowpass	80 Hz	12	fairly often
2	bandpass	80 Hz, 3 kHz	12	almost all the time
3	highpass	3 kHz	12	fairly often
4	highpass	9 kHz	12	rarely

Since companding action takes place at fairly low levels, a single-band system would not conceal program-modulated noise. However, by splitting the side-chain signal into the four bands just described, action within one band has no effect on the others, and may in fact be masked by the noncompanded bands, or by bands in which the companding action lies elsewhere on the frequency spectrum.

Figure 11-8 shows representative Dolby *A*-Type Noise Reduction Systems.

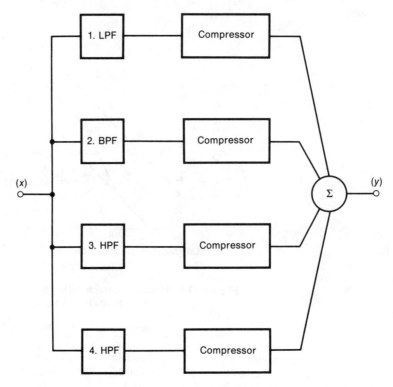

(A) Detail block diagram of variable-gain blocks G_1 and G_2 seen in Figure 11-5.

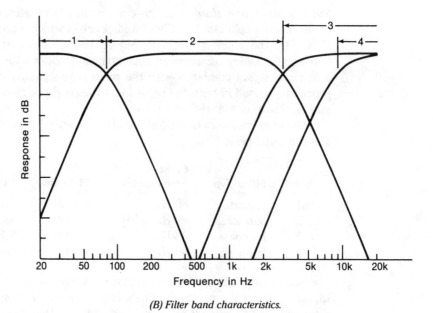

(B) Filter band characteristics.

Figure 11-7. The Dolby A-Type Noise Reduction System.

Identification Signal   Most noise reduction systems are sensitive to gain and/or equalization errors between the tape recorder's record and playback modes. As explained in the section on Gain Errors in Companding Systems later in this chapter (page 454), such errors are magnified by a noise reduction system. It is therefore particularly important to make sure the playback system matches the level used during recording. At the very least, a single test tone should be placed at the head of the tape for future level-setting use.

Many noise reduction systems contain an internal signal generator for recording a distinctive-sounding signal that accomplishes the dual purpose of providing a reference level and a positive verification of the type of noise reduction system that was used. For example, all Dolby *A*-type systems (except the early model A301 "S/N Stretcher") provide a front-panel control for recording a *Dolby Tone*: a constant-amplitude 850 Hz sine wave that is frequency-modulated by +10 percent for 30 ms. The modulation repetition rate is 0.75 second.

B-Type System
Within a few years, the Dolby *A* system became widely accepted by the recording industry, and the company was ready to bring noise reduction to the consumer marketplace as well. The much-simplified *B*-type system was designed for hiss-reduction in consumer tape recorders, and is now primarily found as a built-in option in cassette recorders.

Like the professional *A*-type system, Dolby *B* utilizes side-chain signal processing. However, the filter is a single fixed-gain, variable bandwidth device, as shown in the block diagram in Figure 11-9A. The side chain path begins with a 1.5-kHz highpass filter, and therefore low frequencies do not pass through the side chain. A second highpass filter has a program-dependent cutoff frequency which moves upwards as high-frequency program content increases. (The low-frequency program has no effect due to the fixed 1.5-kHz filter). The filter output is combined with the unprocessed audio in the main signal path (Dolby 1971).

During recording, as the high-frequency program content increases, the side-chain filter cutoff frequency rises, and it therefore contributes progressively less to the combined output. The result is that at low levels the *B*-type encoder displays a boosted high-frequency output response, which gradually flattens out as the high-frequency input level rises, as shown in Figure 11-9B. The playback characteristic is again complementary, thus restoring the signal to its correct frequency response and attenuating high-frequency hiss components in the process.

The *B*-type system was also used in FM broadcasting, but did not gain wide marketplace acceptance. Most FM stations have subsequently phased out their Dolby *B* transmissions.

Identification Signal   The *B*-type *Dolby Tone* is a constant-amplitude 400-Hz sine wave with the same modulation rate and duration (+10% and 30 ms) as the *A*-type tone, but with a repetition rate of 0.5 second. Facilities for applying this tone are usually found only on professional-grade tape duplication systems, and on a few high-end cassette recorders.

(A) The original Audio Noise Reduction System A301 S/N Stretcher.
(Courtesy Dolby Laboratories Inc.)

(B) The later model 361. (Courtesy Dolby Laboratories Inc.)

Figure 11-8. Dolby *A*-Type Noise Reduction Systems.

HX (Headroom Extension) System

In Chapter 9 the interaction between bias and high-frequency response was described (page 345). It was pointed out that as a recording tape is overbiased, the high-frequency response falls off but distortion also decreases. Therefore, some compromise setting is necessary in order to provide acceptable response and distortion performance for all types of musical program. But using that

(C) Model 372 portable two-channel system. (Courtesy Dolby Laboratories Inc.)

(D) Model 363 two-channel rack-mount system with switchable
(SR or A-type) Cat. No. 300 modules. (Courtesy Dolby Laboratories Inc.)

(E) Cat. No. 234 two-channel plug-in card for Sony BVH 2000 series videotape recorders.
(Courtesy Dolby Laboratories, Inc.)

Figure 11-8 *(continued)*

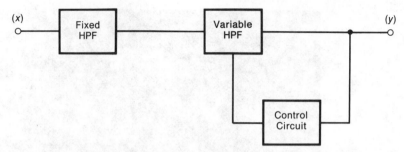

(A) Detail block diagram of variable-gain blocks G_1 and G_2 seen in Figure 11-5.

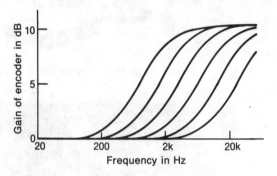

(B) Filter band characteristics.

Figure 11-9. The Dolby B-Type Noise Reduction System.

setting as a reference point, better performance might be achieved if the bias could be varied continuously according to the momentary high-frequency content of the program. For example, the following chart lists a few bias-related improvements that might be made (Gundry 1979).

High Frequency Spectrum	Bias Level	Result
low level	increase	lower distortion, lower modulation noise, fewer dropouts
high level	decrease	reduce tape saturation

However, since frequency response also varies as a function of bias, a compensating adjustment—especially at high frequencies—would have to be made in order to maintain a flat response with varying bias.

The Dolby *HX Headroom Extension System* combines a signal-dependent bias along with compensating variable high-frequency equalization, as shown in the block diagram in Figure 11-10A. However, it was found that an *HX* system optimized to a specific tape formulation did not always perform ideally when a different tape was used. An alternative technique was initially devised by Bang & Olufsen, with subsequent joint development of a practical system, now licensed by Dolby as the *HX Pro* system.

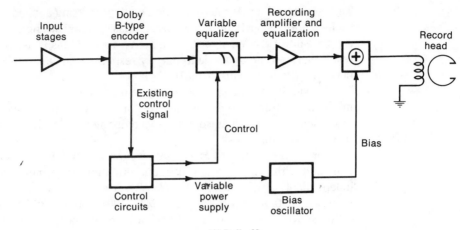

(A) Dolby Hx.

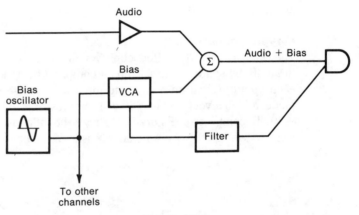

(B) Dolby HX Pro.

Figure 11-10. Block diagrams of the Dolby *HX* and *HX Pro* Systems.

HX Pro System

To briefly explain the *HX Pro* system, it helps to take a closer look at certain aspects of AC bias, which was itself described in Chapter 9 (page 344). Since an audio frequency, f, may be biased by a frequency $5f$ or greater, it follows that a 20-kHz bias should be adequate for a 4-kHz bandwidth, 40 kHz for an 8-kHz bandwidth, and so on (Jensen 1983). However, the actual applied bias frequency in a professional tape recorder is many times higher (see Table 9-2, page 354). Therefore, the *active bias* on a low-frequency signal is a combination of the applied static bias level and the biasing effect of any high-frequency audio that may be present. Since this latter component varies with program content, the result is that the applied static bias level becomes a varying bias level as the high-frequency program content varies.

The *HX Pro* system counteracts this effect by varying the applied bias level by means of a voltage-controlled amplifier, as shown in Figure 11-10B. The gain of the VCA is regulated by a filtered and rectified signal taken from the record head.

This control voltage is thus a function of all processing applied to the audio signal, such as noise reduction (if any), preemphasis, signal strength, and the bias itself. As the gain of the VCA varies, the active applied bias is held constant, and as a result there are no dynamic frequency response changes caused by a fluctuating bias level (Bang & Olufsen 1981).

Although not a noise reduction system in the usual sense of that term, *HX Pro* might be better thought of as a distortion reduction device. However, it is described here since it so often accompanies other Dolby circuitry in tape recorder systems.

For example, the *HX Pro* system is now widely found in consumer recorders equipped with *B*-type noise reduction, although the former system is completely independent of the latter. The *HX Pro* system alone is also built into some professional tape recorders (Otari MTR-100A, Studer 807 for example). Figure 11-10B shows a block diagram of a record circuit incorporating the *HX Pro* system.

Note that both the *HX* and *HX Pro* systems are a record-only function, with no complementary action required during playback. Neither system requires an identification signal.

C-Type System

The Dolby *C*-Type Noise Reduction System increases the maximum gain reduction to 20 dB, by splitting the side-chain companding action between two processors, each operating within a separate input level range (Dolby 1983). In the record mode, a high-level (− 30 to − 10 dB) compressor is followed by a low-level (− 50 to − 30 dB) compressor. Figure 11-11 shows the individual transfer characteristics for each, as well as the overall characteristic of the complete system.

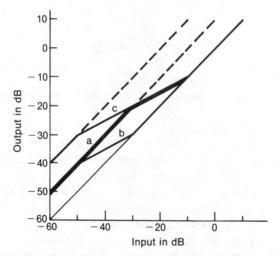

Figure 11-11. The record transfer characteristics of the Dolby *C*-type Noise Reduction system: (a), high-level; (b), low-level; (c), overall compression characteristic. The gain of each compressor is given in Table 11-1.

Table 11-1 lists the gain of each compressor, and the system gain, for various levels of input signal. Note that each compressor has a maximum gain of 3.16 (i.e., 10 dB) and dynamic action confined to a 20-dB range. Although the total action appears identical to that of a single 2:1 compressor operating over a 40-dB range, the system, which Dolby refers to as a *staggered action, dual-level* format, minimizes overshoot distortion, which would be considerably higher in a single-compressor/expander system.

Table 11-1. Dolby *C*-Type Noise Reduction System Gain Structure

dB$_{in}$	G_1 (a)*	G_2 (b)*	G_{total} (c)*	dB$_{out}$
− 60	3.16	3.16	10.00	− 40
− 55	3.16	3.16	10.00	− 35
− 50	3.16	3.16	10.00	− 30
− 45	3.16	**2.37**	7.48	− 27.5
− 40	3.16	**1.77**	5.61	− 25
− 35	3.16	**1.33**	4.21	− 22.5
− 30	3.16	1.00	3.16	− 20
− 25	**2.37**	1.00	2.37	− 17.5
− 20	**1.77**	1.00	1.77	− 15
− 15	**1.33**	1.00	1.33	− 12.5
− 10	1.00	1.00	1.00	− 10
− 5	1.00	1.00	1.00	− 5

*Cross-references to Figure 11-11. **Boldface** numbers indicate dynamic action (compression)

The sliding band filter network is similar in principle to that of the *B*-type system, except that the fixed-frequency cutoff is dropped two octaves, to 375 Hz.

As in all other Dolby noise reduction systems, the expander action during playback is complementary.

Identification Signal   The *C*-type *Dolby Tone* is a 400-Hz sine wave with the same modulation rate (+ 10%) as the *A*-type system, but with a duration of 5.5 ms and a repetition rate of 1.1 second. However, since the *C*-type system is limited to one-to-one consumer recording applications, the tone is rarely utilized.

SR (Spectral Recording) Process

The Dolby *spectral recording* process combines some of the characteristics found in the earlier *A*-, *B*-, and *C*-type systems. In brief, the system does the following:

- High-level signal components at both ends of the frequency spectrum are attenuated, to provide a better match to the overload characteristics of analog magnetic recording tape.
- Low-level signal components are greatly amplified, via a complex frequency-selective filter system.

As with its predecessors, the *SR* system uses complementary signal processing during playback to restore the signal to its original frequency spectrum. The *SR* system goal is to modify the level of all input signal components so that the recorded signal is optimized within limitations imposed by the recording medium (Dolby 1987a).

The staggered action principle introduced in the Dolby *C*-type noise reduction system is again applied, this time in a three-stage system with thresholds at -30, -48, and -62 dB with respect to a reference level about 20 dB below peak signal level.

The band-splitting found in the *A*-type system is likewise employed, though in a configuration far more complex than that of the earlier system. A series of ten filters is used; five are fixed-frequency, variable-gain networks, and five are fixed-gain, variable-frequency systems. For the high- and mid-level (-30 and -48 dB) stages, low- and high-frequency filters are employed with a crossover frequency of 800 Hz. The lowest-level stage (-80 dB) uses an 800-Hz highpass filter only.

Figure 11-12 shows the record and playback response in the absence of a signal. The contour of the playback response has been shaped so that low-level tape noise will be at or slightly below the threshold of hearing (see Figure 2-5). Note that upper midrange frequencies are boosted considerably. It is within this range that the ear is most sensitive at low levels, so as complementary playback attenuation restores the correct signal level, there is maximum attenuation of hiss within the region where the ear would be most apt to hear it.

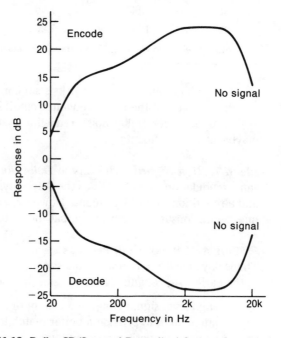

Figure 11-12. Dolby *SR* (Spectral Recording) System. Low-level record and playback characteristics. Note that the playback characteristic approximates the threshold of hearing (Figure 2-5).

However, in the presence of a moderate to high input signal level, the full encoder gain seen in Figure 11-12 would be excessive and cause tape overload. Accordingly, the gain is dropped in the vicinity of the input signal frequency, as shown by the curves in Figure 11-13. In the presence of any such signal, an *action*

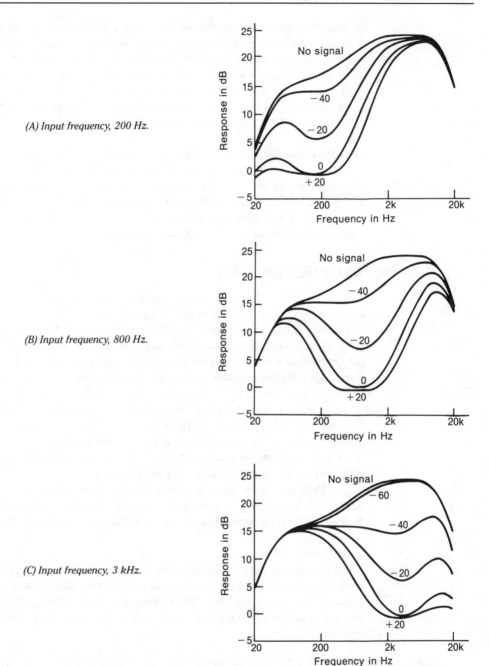

(A) Input frequency, 200 Hz.

(B) Input frequency, 800 Hz.

(C) Input frequency, 3 kHz.

Figure 11-13. Dolby *SR* record characteristic in the presence of a high-level input signal component. In the immediate vicinity of the input frequency the recording gain is reduced as required, to prevent tape overload. *NOTE: On many graphs of SR encode and decode characteristics, a sharp spike is seen at the input frequency. This is an artifact of the measuring system and does not represent an actual response peak.*

substitution system determines which filter set (fixed- or sliding-band) will predominate, and then sets the appropriate gain and cutoff frequency parameters to produce the optimum record characteristic. As the actual spectrum/level of the input signal varies, the system filter continuously adjusts itself to maintain the highest gain practical at every frequency (Dolby 1987b).

A noise reduction module that is switchable between the Dolby *A*-type noise reduction and *SR* systems was shown in Figure 11-8C.

Identification Signal   The Dolby *SR* system uses an internal *Dolby Noise* generator to record a pink-noise signal which is muted for 20 ms at two-second intervals. During playback the recorded signal is alternated in four-second intervals with an uninterrupted reference pink noise signal from the Dolby generator. The recorded and reference signals may be compared for level and/or spectral balance. (Pink noise is described on page 506.)

Noise Reduction on Film

The Dolby *A*-Type Noise Reduction System is used on both optical and magnetic Dolby Stereo film tracks. However, if a surround channel is matrix-encoded on a 2-channel 35-mm sound track, that channel is processed through a *B*-type system prior to matrixing/recording. Therefore, the theater playback system requires an *A*-type playback system, followed by a feed to a surround-sound decoder which in turn feeds a *B*-type decoder. If the surround channel is recorded separately, as on track 6 of a 70-mm film, the *A*-type system is used instead.

In theaters not equipped for Dolby playback, the sound system's high-frequency rolloff is usually sufficient to minimize the otherwise overly bright sound of a Dolby program played back without decoding.

Figure 11-14 shows a magnetic and optical film sound noise reduction system designed for 35- and 70-mm theater installations.

A VHS consumer videotape of a Dolby Stereo film is identified as "Dolby Surround" (*not* Dolby Stereo) and it is not encoded with the *A*-type system. Instead, the *B*-type system is used, with encoding applied to the linear tracks only.

Ultra Stereo System

The Ultra Stereo System (Ultra Stereo Laboratories) is a four-band process quite similar to the Dolby *A*-type system used in Dolby Stereo films. Although front-channel encoding is the same, the surround matrix is slightly different, and uses a straight 2.5-dB boost at 8 kHz instead of the *B*-type encoding used in Dolby Stereo production.

dbx Noise Reduction Systems

Figure 11-15 shows a block diagram of the dbx Noise Reduction System. Prior to compression, the encoder system provides a 12-dB high-frequency preemphasis network, whose purpose is to further boost high-frequency program content above the hiss level, as shown by the transfer characteristics in Figure 11-16.

Since the encoder preemphasis raises high frequencies even further above the tape hiss level, the action may cause tape saturation if the input signal is

Figure 11-14. A noise reduction system designed for cinema use. The system provides four channels of Dolby *A*-type noise reduction, a matrix decoder for derived center and surround channels, three channels of one-third-octave equalization, and other related signal processing. *(Dolby model CP200 Cinema Sound Processor courtesy Dolby Laboratories Inc.)*

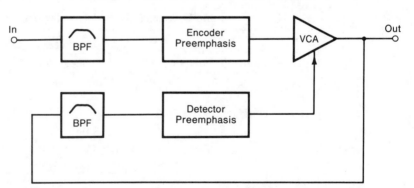

Figure 11-15. Block diagram of the dbx Noise Reduction System, showing encoder and detector bandpass filters and preemphasis networks.

already at a high level. Therefore, an additional preemphasis network is inserted in the control voltage (detector) signal path, where the extra boost further reduces the compressor gain, thereby keeping recorded high-frequency program content below the saturation point of the tape.

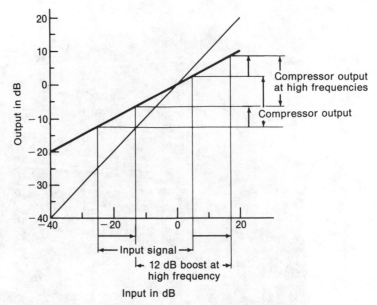

Figure 11-16. dbx system record-mode transfer characteristic, showing low-frequency input signal and high-frequency input with 12 dB boost.

Type *I* and Type *II* Systems

The dbx Type *I* system is intended for high-speed (15 in/s or greater) tape operation and for use with any other wide-band audio transmission system. The Type *II* system is designed for slower tape speeds and other restricted-bandwidth media (Tyler n. d.). The difference between the two systems is found in the level detection circuits, where the responses of the preemphasis networks are as shown in Figure 11-17. The bandpass filter cutoff frequencies and the 3-dB points for each curve shown in Figure 11-17 are listed in Table 11-2.

Table 11-2. dbx Noise Reduction System Parameters

Type	Bandpass Filter Cutoff Frequencies		Preemphasis Networks			
			Encoder Path*		Detector Path**	
			− 3 dB	+ 3 dB	− 3 dB	+ 3 dB
I	20 Hz & 27 kHz	f_a		370 Hz		1,750 Hz
		f_b	5 Hz		50 Hz	
		f_c	1,590 Hz		18,250 Hz	
		f_d	22,200 Hz			
II	30 Hz & 10 kHz	f_a		380 Hz		440 Hz
		f_b	16 Hz		44 Hz	
		f_c	1,600 Hz		5,330 Hz	
		f_d	22,300 Hz			

*See Figure 11-17A.
**See Figure 11-17B.

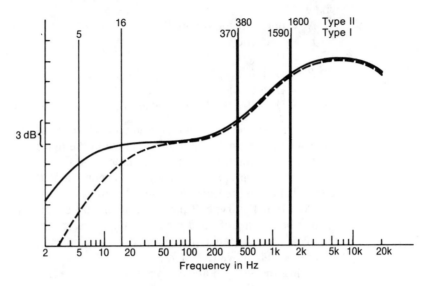

(A) High-frequency encoder-path response.

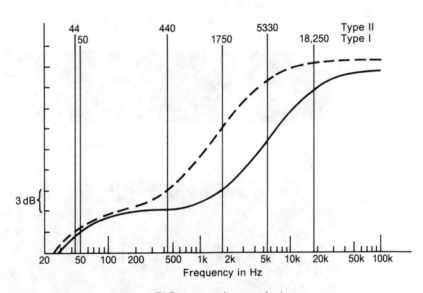

(B) Detector-path preemphasis.

Figure 11-17. dbx preemphasis network responses.

The preemphasis network amplitude response curves shown in Figure 11-17 are plotted from the equations

$$N = 20 \log(Af/BCD) \text{ for encoder-path response}$$
$$= 20 \log(Af/BC) \text{ for detector-path response}$$

where

N = output response, in dB

f = frequency, in Hz

$A = [1 + (f/f_a)^2]^{1/2}$

$B = [1 + (f/f_b)^2]^{1/2}$

$C = [1 + (f/f_c)^2]^{1/2}$

$D = [1 + (f/f_d)^2]^{1/2}$ (f_{a-d} taken from values listed above)

As written above, each equation plots the desired response *shape*, but does not place the flat region at 0 dB as shown in the figure. Accordingly, each curve has been attenuated by a constant (approx. 10 to 20 dB) so that its first -3-dB point is at the appropriate frequency f_b. Having done that, dthe other 3-dB points fall very close to the frequencies listed above.

Note that the Type *II* preemphasis in the encoder path begins about two octaves below that of the Type *I* system. Therefore there is more compression of the mid and upper range prior to recording or transmission, as would be required by a reduced-bandwidth system.

Unlike the Dolby *A* and *SR* systems, dbx uses a single-band compander with a compression ratio of 2:1 and an expansion ratio of 1:2. Furthermore, the companding action takes place across the entire dynamic range of the system. Figure 11-18 illustrates the dbx Noise Reduction System.

(A) Model 180A Type I system.

(B) F900A powered frame for nine noise reduction or other signal processing modules.

Figure 11-18. The dbx Noise Reduction System. *(Courtesy dbx, Inc.)*

Identification Signal   No identification signal has been proposed for dbx noise reduction systems, since these systems are not level sensitive. In the presence of a level error the entire dynamic range will of course be shifted up or down, but the total dynamic range will not change as a function of a level shift. Although the dbx system is sensitive to frequency-response errors, a single calibration tone will do nothing to point out such an error.

Burwen Noise Eliminator System

Like the dbx systems, the Burwen *Noise Eliminator* is a single-band compander (Burwen 1971b). However, its compression ratio is 3:1 and there are three switch-selectable characteristics (A, B, C) to optimize the system for various tape speeds, as listed here.

	High-Frequency Preemphasis	Gain-Before-Threshold (dB)	Compression Threshold (dB)	Tape Speed (in/s)
A	13 dB @ 20 kHz	44	−66	15
B	4.4 dB @ 20 kHz	24	−66	7.5
C	4.4 dB @ 20 kHz	24	−36	3.75

The figures seen here are approximations based on graphs appearing in Burwen product descriptions.

Although introduced at about the same time as the dbx system, the Burwen Noise Eliminator was not widely accepted within the industry and it is rarely encountered anymore.

Telcom Noise Reduction System

In comparing the professional noise reduction systems, the Dolby systems use multiband companding over a comparatively small range of input levels, while the dbx system employs a single-band compressor which operates over the entire range of input levels.

c4 System

The Telcom *c4* Noise Reduction System combines the four-band processing found in the Dolby system with the unrestricted operating range of dbx (Ford 1978). However, the filter bands and the compression ratios are different, as shown by the comparison chart in Table 11-3. In Bands 1 and 4, the extreme cutoff frequencies of 10 Hz and 25,000 Hz make these networks, in effect, highpass and lowpass filters. In some early-model *c4* systems, these cutoffs were placed at 20 or 30 Hz, and at 20,000 Hz.

The Telcom *c4* filter bands are also shown in the graph in Figure 11-19B. Note that there are slight departures from the expected 3-dB intersections, due to interaction between the lower and upper cutoff sections of each filter band.

In the block diagram (Figure 11-19A), note the presence of an additional filter in the control voltage line. Its cutoff frequencies match those of the equivalent program filter, but its slope is 12 dB per octave. Therefore, the signal from which the control voltage is derived is filtered at 18 dB per octave, while the program itself only passes through 6 dB-per-octave filters. The additional filtering provides higher control-voltage selectivity between filter bands, while the mild slopes within the program path minimize the effects of the filters within the crossover regions (Schneider 1988).

Table 11-3. Noise Reduction System Comparison Chart

Manufacturer and Filter Type	Cutoff Frequencies (Hz)	
	Lower	*Upper*
Telcom (6-dB/octave)		
Bandpass	10	215
Bandpass	215	1,450
Bandpass	1,450	4,800
Bandpass	4,800	25,000
Dolby (12-dB/octave)		
Lowpass		80
Bandpass	80	3,000
Highpass	3,000	
Highpass	9,000	
	Compression Ratio	**Expansion Ratio**
dbx	2:1	1:2
Dolby	2:1*	1:2*
Telcom	1.5:1	1:1.5

*Approximate

Figure 11-20 shows the Telcom noise reduction system. Identified on the front panel as a *c4* Compander System series e300, the frame shown in the illustration houses either an electronically or transformer-balanced system (e312 or e322, respectively).

Note: The first Telcom *c4* systems were sold by AEG-Telefunken. Following a 1983 corporate reorganization, the system has been marketed by a separate company, *ANT Nachrichtentechnik GmbH* (ANT Telecommunications in U. S. and England).

Identification Signal   As its identification signal, the Telcom *c4* system uses a constant-amplitude sine wave whose frequency alternates between 550 and 650 Hz at half-second intervals.

Noise Reduction System Comparisons

The following section does *not* render value judgments as to which of the various noise reduction systems is superior, for if any such judgment could be made this chapter would have been a lot shorter. However, the Dolby, dbx, and Telcom systems described here all continue to enjoy popularity, and any reasonably active recording engineer will probably encounter all three systems, though presumably not on the same session.

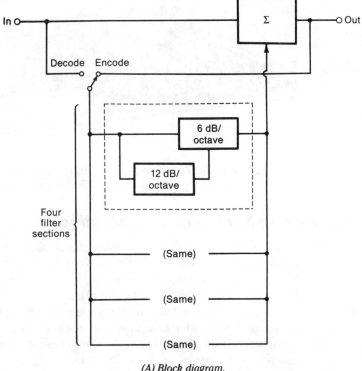

(A) Block diagram.

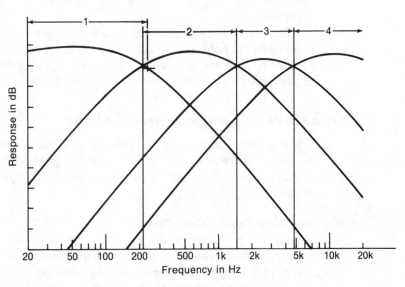

(B) Filter band characteristics.

Figure 11-19. The Telcom *c4* Noise Reduction System. Compare with the Dolby *A*-type characteristics seen in Figure 11-7B.

Figure 11-20. The Telcom noise reduction system. *(c4 Compander System series
e300 courtesy ANT Telecommunications, Inc.)*

Linear and Nonlinear Companding

A *linear compander* is one in which the companding ratio is constant—that is,
linear—across the entire input range of both the compressor and the expander.
By contrast, in a *nonlinear compander* one or more segments of the transfer
characteristic may follow a different ratio.

This use of the term *linear* should not be confused with a linear-gain
segment of a transfer characteristic, such as seen in the various Dolby noise
reduction systems. In other words, since these systems vary from linear gain, to
compression/expansion, to unity gain, they are nonlinear companders. By
contrast, the dbx system is a linear compander (always 2:1 and 1:2), and
therefore its gain is continuously variable (nonlinear) over the entire range of
input levels.

In this context, the linear compander is sometimes referred to as a *linear dB
compander*. To help confuse the issue, a Dolby compander is sometimes called a
bilinear compander, in reference to the two linear gain segments that exist on
either side (but obviously not within) the compander characteristic.

Gain Errors in Companding Systems

When a complementary noise reduction system is used, an error in gain or
frequency response between the record and playback modes will be magnified
during playback. The following sections describe the types of errors that may be
encountered.

Nonlinear System Gain Error

A nonlinear companding system will magnify any gain errors that exist between
the record and playback modes; to show the potential for a gain-related companding error, Figure 11-21 illustrates the compression/expansion process by tracing
a signal through a nonlinear companding system. The three diagonal lines in
the upper right-hand section are used to trace gain-shift errors of − 5, 0 (none),
and + 5 dB. These errors illustrate the effect of a simple gain error at the tape
recorder.

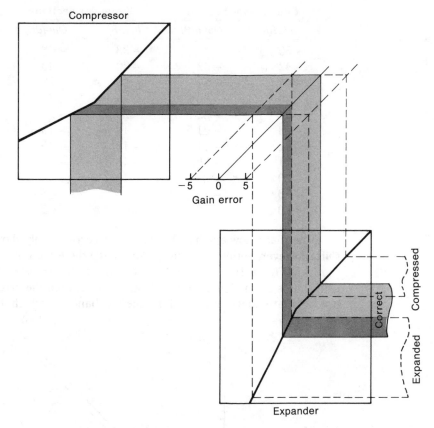

Figure 11-21. Gain error in a nonlinear compander system
(after Wermuth 1975).

The shaded portion of the drawing indicates a signal passing through a system with no gain error. For purposes of illustration, a 10-dB input range is seen compressed to 7.5 dB, then expanded back to 10 dB. The input program signal is placed so that only its lower half is compressed; the upper half passes through the compressor at unity gain. The compressed/expanded segment of the signal is identified by the darker shading.

If a postcompressor gain error shifts the signal by +5 dB, the entire compressed program falls along the unity-gain section of the expander, and so it remains in its compressed state, with a 7.5-dB dynamic range at the expander output. By contrast, if the gain error is −5 dB the entire recorded program is expanded and the output dynamic range is 15 dB.

As a practical example of gain-shift error, refer to the Dolby *A*-type transfer characteristics shown earlier in Figure 11-6 (page 435). Add, say, 2 dB to the expander-in level and then compare the expander output to the compressor input. The results are as given here.

Compressor Section		Expander Section		Error in dB
In (dB)	Out (dB)	In (dB)	Out (dB)	
− 50	− 40	− 38	− 48	2
− 42	− 32	− 30	− 40	2
− 41	− 31	− 29	− 38	3
− 40	− 30	− 28	− 36	4
− 24	− 22	− 20	− 20	4
− 23	− 21.5	− 19.5	− 19.5	3.5
− 22	− 21	− 19	− 19	3
− 21	− 20.5	− 18.5	− 18.5	2.5
− 20	− 20	− 18	− 18	2
− 10	− 10	− 8	− 8	2
0	0	+ 2	+ 2	2

Note that at low and high levels the 2-dB error simply shows up as a 2-dB gain shift. However, within the companding range the error ranges from 2 to 4 dB, as shown in Figure 11-22 by the discontinuities in the transfer characteristic. If the gain shift is a function of an equalization error, then the error at the output will boost or attenuate only that frequency band in which the equalization is incorrect.

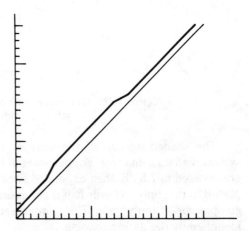

Figure 11-22. The transfer characteristic for a Dolby *A*-type system with a 2-dB gain error between the compressor and expander.

Linear System Frequency Response Error

If the noise reduction system's compander has a linear transfer characteristic, a gain shift between record and playback will simply move the entire playback response up or down in level. The shift will be double the gain error. But since the transfer characteristic is a straight line, the companding action across the program's dynamic range does not change.

If there is a frequency-response error somewhere in the system, then only a portion of the input signal is shifted in level, and therefore only those frequencies within the affected band will be played back at the wrong level. However, this equalization error is not confined to a segment of the input signal, but instead will be heard across the entire dynamic range of the program. Therefore, the linear compander is more sensitive to frequency-response errors than the nonlinear system is to gain-shift errors.

System Compatibility

Due to the widely disparate operating principles of the noise reduction systems described in this chapter, it is not possible to properly decode a tape using a noise reduction system other than the one that was used when the tape was recorded.

In the absence of the correct decoder, a tape recorded with a multiband system will sound overly bright. Some high-frequency attenuation may or may not help to achieve a (marginally) acceptable signal. A tape recorded with a linear compressor will probably sound too "squashed" to be usable. In a dire emergency, any convenient expander may be pressed into service, again with a marginal improvement to be expected.

Multitrack Noise Reduction Systems

For multitrack applications there are a number of rack-mount noise reduction units that accept plug-in cards manufactured by Dolby, dbx, and Telcom. Representative examples are shown in Figure 11-23. Some professional tape recorders also provide slots for plug-in noise reduction cards, as also shown in the same illustration. Currently available rack units and noise reduction cards are listed in Table 11-4.

Noise Reduction/Tape Recorder Interface Requirements

Figure 11-24 shows the correct position in the signal path for any complementary noise reduction system. Note that the encode section is placed immediately before, and the decode section immediately after, the tape recorder. Therefore, all other signal processing takes place before or after noise reduction.

Although Figure 11-24 shows two noise reduction systems per channel, in practice a single noise reduction module is usually switched between the record and the playback sections, as previously described in Chapter 10 (page 402).

If it is desired to tape-monitor the signal as it is being recorded, then a duplicate noise reduction system is required for each track, with one module in the record mode and another in the playback mode. This requirement is often encountered in recording classical music, where a single take may be relatively long—as, for example, a complete pass through an entire movement of a symphony. The same requirement may exist while recording a concert performance, when it is necessary to continually monitor the recording in progress. In either case, a complete retake is either very expensive, or completely out of the question.

(A) A rack-mount system that accepts plug-in noise reduction cards. (Courtesy ANT Telecommunications, Inc.)

(B) Dedicated 24-channel Dolby SR system. (Courtesy Dolby Laboratories Inc.)

(C) Multitrack tape recorder with provision for plug-in cards. (Studer A820 tape recorder with Telcom c4 and Dolby SR cards seen in drawers 2 and 3 courtesy Studer Revox America, Inc.)

Figure 11-23. Multitrack noise reduction systems.

Table 11-4. Noise Reduction Frame/Card Cross-Reference Guide

(A) Frames

Mfr.	Part No.	No. of Channels	Accepts dbx	Dolby Cat. No.	Telcom
dbx	140	2 (½-rack size)	Type *II* NR built-in		
	150	2 (½-rack size)	Type *I* NR built-in		
	180A	2	Type *I* NR built-in		
	F900A	9	911, 941A, 942A (& other dbx products)		
	FS900	2	911, 941A, 942A (& other dbx products)		
Dolby	330	2 (tape duplication)		66, 219B	
	334	2 (FM broadcast)		66	
	360	1	K9-22*	22, 280	c4 DM
	361	1 (auto change)	K9-22*	22, 280	c4 DM
	362	2	K9-22*	22	c4 DM
	363	2		300, 350, 450	
	364	1 (cinema)		22	
	365	2	K9-22*	22, 280	c4 DM
	372	2 (portable)		225	
	M-16, M-24	16, 24	K9-22*	22, 280	c4 DM
	SP	24	K9-22* + 230	22 + 230, 431	c4 DM + 230
	XP	24		331, 431	
	CP50	2 (cinema)		22, 280-T	
	CP55	2 (cinema)		222	
	CP100	3 (cinema)		22, 280-T	
	CP200	4 (cinema)		22, 280-T	
Fabac	TTM 202B	2	K9-22*	22	c4 DM
	TTM	24	K9-22*	22	c4 DM
Telcom	e111	1 record or playback			c4 E
	e112, e122**	2 record or playback			c4 E
	e114, e124**	4 2 record & 2 playback (fixed)			c4 E
	e232	2 auto change			c4 E
	e233	3 auto change			c4 E
	e312, e322**	2 auto or manual change			c4 E
	ESF 2-24	2, 4, 8, 16, 24			c4 E
	E413	24			c4 E

*discontinued
**e122, e124, e322 are transformer-balanced

Table 11-4 *(continued)*

(B) Noise Reduction Cards

Mfr.	System	Part No.	For Use in Frame
dbx	Type *I*	K9-22*	Dolby 360-362, 365, M
		911	F900A, FS900
	Type *II*	941A (2-ch encode)	F900A, FS900
		942A (2-ch decode)	F900A, FS900
Dolby	*A*-type	Cat. No. 22	360-365, M, SP, CP100, CP200
		Cat. No. 222	CP55
		Cat. No. 225	372
		Cat. No. 450	363
		Cat. No. 230	SP series carrier card for Cat. 22 (or equivalent)
		Cat. No. 331	XP
	B-type	Cat. No. 66	330, 334
	C-type	Cat. No. 219B	330
	A & SR	Cat. No. 300	363
	SR	Cat. No. 280	360-362, 365, M, SP
		Cat. No. 280-T	decode only for CP55, CP100, CP200
		Cat. No. 350	363
		Cat. No. 431	SP, XP
Telcom	*c4*	c4 DM	Dolby 360-362, 365, M, Fabac TTM
		c4 E	series e100, e200, e300, E413

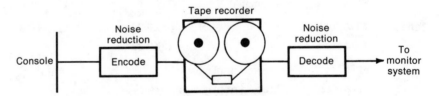

Figure 11-24. The noise reduction system in the signal path to and from the tape recorder.

12 Recording Consoles

In the earliest days of magnetic sound recording, the recording console was not at all unlike the broadcast console of the same period; in either application, the device provided the controls needed to route a few input signals to a single output line. The inputs were from a small handful of microphones and, in the broadcast studio, a turntable or two; a single output fed a monaural tape recorder or a transmitter. The recording application did require one additional feature—a play-back function allowed the engineer to hear the tape after it was recorded.

The two-channel tape recorder introduced one more requirement for the recording studio console—a track-select function. On some early consoles, a certain number of inputs were dedicated to each of the two available tracks. Track selection was accomplished by plugging the microphone into an input that fed the desired track.

Figure 12-1 shows an early (c. 1960) two-channel console and, for comparison purposes, something a little more recent. Regardless of complexity, the purpose of both consoles is to accept multiple input signals, each of which may be processed, balanced, and combined into one or more outgoing signal lines. Each incoming signal may now be from a microphone, from the direct output of an electronic instrument (e.g., guitar amp or synthesizer), or from a previously recorded tape track. The console outputs may be routed to a tape recorder, a broadcast transmitter, a telephone line, a sound reinforcement system, etc.

Recording Consoles

In the following discussion of the various knobs, buttons, and switches to be found on the recording studio console, some need more explanation than others. Some—pan pots for example—require a rather lengthy discussion; others—studio monitor level comes to mind—don't deserve much more space than it takes to list

(A) An early two-channel console used by RCA Victor Records at Webster Hall in New York City. (Courtesy RCA)

(B) A modern inline console with 60 inputs and 48 outputs (Neve V series Mk-3 courtesy of Sisapa Record Co., Inc., Columbus, Ohio)

Figure 12-1. Recording consoles.

them. For the sake of completeness however, each control mentioned is given the courtesy of at least a few words of explanation, even when that explanation may not seem needed. Readers are invited to skip over all functions that are so simple that they don't need to be described on paper.

Whenever possible, controls are introduced in the order in which they appear in the signal path. There is however no shortage of interaction here; many controls depend on the position of other controls, and each control must be fully explained before the other one. In these cases, the reader may want to read at least a few sections twice in order to get the most out of the descriptions.

As a final caveat, the reader is warned in advance that parts of this chapter may read more like a product description than a theoretical text. Unlike the dynamic microphone or the bandpass equalizer, there's almost no such thing as the generic console; although the basic signal paths are found in all consoles, each switching system is usually unique in form if not in function. Many signal path details are illustrated by a flow chart excerpt and a view of the controls as found on an actual console. In each case, the illustration is but one of several ways in which the same task might be accomplished.

Console Bus

Within the console each signal is processed as required and then routed to a combining bus. The term *bus* describes any electric conductor to which one or more incoming signals may be routed. After the signals are combined on the bus, its output is assigned to a single destination such as a track on a tape recorder. Other buses are used to route signals to a variety of destinations, some of which are listed in Table 12-1. Additional details about each of these buses will be given later in the chapter.

Table 12-1. Recording Console Buses

Bus Nomenclature	Bus Output Is the Send Line to
Bus, channel, track summing	a single track on a multitrack tape recorder
Cue	the studio headphone system
Echo, Effects, Send	an echo/reverberation system or other external signal processing device
Mixing, 2-channel*	a two-track tape recorder
Monitor*	the control room and studio monitor systems
Slate	all active track-summing and mixdown buses (for spoken identification of takes, etc.)
Solo	solo system (temporarily replaces regular monitor signal)

*Generally, the same bus pair serves both of these functions.

Console Operating Modes

Table 12-2A lists the various operating modes in which any modern console will be required to function. The console must provide all the controls necessary for each of these modes, and it should be possible for it to function simultaneously in more than one mode.

For convenience, the operating controls may be grouped into separate sections, as listed in Table 12-2B.

Table 12-2. Console Operating Modes and Division of Controls

(A) Console Operating Modes	
Operating Mode	**Purpose**
Record	initial recording of one or more tracks on a fresh reel of tape
Overdub	recording of one or more new tracks while simultaneously playing back previously recorded material
Mixdown	balancing and mixing all previously recorded tracks to a two track master tape
Monitor	monitoring of record, overdub or mixdown modes as required
(B) Division of Controls	
Console Section	**Controls for**
Input	input levels and signal processing, effects sends, routing of all input signals
Output	output levels and signal processing of combined input signals and effects returns
Communication	talkback to studio, announcements to tape
Monitor	control room and studio monitoring of console input and/ or output signals
Meter	visual indication of signal level

Console Design Styles

Needless to say, there is no standard size, shape, or location for any console control, so it does little good to remember that such and such a setting is, say, a quarter-turn clockwise on a little red knob ten inches up from the bottom of the module. The same function (if it exists) on another console will be elsewhere, and surely its knob will be blue. Therefore, the user will have to become familiar with the finer points of signal flow that apply to all consoles, and then learn where to find the desired controls on the specific console at hand.

The physical layout of console controls has changed considerably over the years, to the point where there is almost no resemblance between the two consoles shown in Figure 12-1, even though they are separated by scarcely thirty years—merely a moment in history, but an eternity in the recording industry. And although this chapter will make no attempt to catalog every knob, switch, and button change between the oldest and newest designs, we can nevertheless describe three important variations in basic console design. These comprise the rotary knob, the split-section, and the inline console that now enjoys such widespread popularity. Each of these design styles is described separately.

Rotary Knob Console

As its name suggests, the distinguishing feature of the rotary knob console is its use of a rotary potentiometer as a level control. Although the ubiquitous slide fader has long since replaced the large round knob on most recording consoles, the rotary potentiometer is still preferred by some broadcast facilities, and is also found on very small consoles, usually identified as *mixers*. A few representative examples are shown in Figure 12-2.

Split-Section Console

As console design progressed during the early days of multitrack recording, the rotary potentiometer found in each input line was eventually replaced by the slide fader now seen on all multitrack recording studio consoles. And as control of even more inputs and more outputs became necessary, the most efficient arrangement was to divide these controls into three separate sections according to function. The three sections are input, output, and monitor, and a console so designed is designated as a *split-section console*.

Figure 12-3 (pages 468–469) shows a signal flow chart and the physical layout of a very simple 8 input/2 output split-section recording console, in which the three sections are clearly identified. The letters in parentheses in both parts of the figure are cross-references to the equivalent controls in the inline console described later in this chapter and illustrated with a signal flow chart in Figure 12-5 (pages 474–476). Bracketed letters are cross-references to Figure 12-19, also a signal flow chart (pages 500–501).

Signal Flow

In Figure 12-3A, the split-section console's input section consists of a microphone preamplifier, followed by an equalizer (c) and the channel input fader (e), after which the bus selector switch (h) routes the signal to the desired track-summing bus. On some split-section consoles, an additional equalizer (c) in the output section precedes the bus fader (i) and master fader [v]. In the monitor section, a bus/tape switch (r) routes either the bus output (bus) or return from the tape recorder (tape) to the monitor system, where a ganged potentiometer [w] adjusts the control room listening level.

As multitrack recording came into widespread use, the outputs of the multitrack tape recorder were also returned to the input section, as shown by the inset in the figure.

Although Figure 12-3A leaves out more than it shows (for example, pan pots, auxiliary sends, and the communication and meter sections are all missing), it is nevertheless sufficient to show the basic signal paths that exist in any console, to

(A) The early and still popular Shure M67 Microphone Mixer.
(Courtesy Shure Brothers, Inc.)

(B) Audio-Technica AT 4462 Stereo Portable Field Mixer.
(Courtesy Audio-Technica U.S., Inc.)

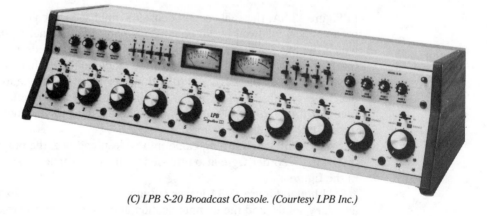

(C) LPB S-20 Broadcast Console. (Courtesy LPB Inc.)

Figure 12-2. Rotary-knob consoles.

illustrate a simple track-summing bus system, and to help introduce an important aspect of console design: redundancy.

Note that much of the console (Figure 12-3B) is taken up by a series of identical subsections, and to be familiar with one of these is therefore to be familiar with all of them. With luck, the outsider will be sufficiently intimidated by the mass of buttons, knobs, faders, and switches comprising the total system, while the insider will realize the system is simply (and sometimes not so simply) the sum of many redundant parts.

The split-section console design layout shown in Figure 12-3B was the basis of most multitrack consoles manufactured during the first ten years or so of multitrack recording. Although such consoles were vast improvements over their early mono and stereo ancestors, the basic design approach was simply an expansion of what had gone before. The number of console inputs generally exceeded the number of outputs and the physical arrangement made ergonomic sense; the large input section was directly in front of the engineer, with the smaller output and monitor sections off to the side, but usually within arm's reach. Assuming expansion space was available within the console, additional input modules could be added as required, although the output section capacity was usually fixed during manufacture.

The split-section design continues to work very well in consoles with comparatively few output lines and continues to be found in a few consoles with 24-track output capacity. Examples of both are shown in Figure 12-4. However, as the number of output tracks expanded to 16 and then beyond, the input/output dimensions approached a 1:1 ratio, as may be seen by comparing the consoles in the illustration. In other words, the output section soon became just about as big as the input section, and the console began to look—and function—like two consoles in one. Meanwhile, evolution had done nothing to increase the arm length of the recording engineer. Chairs with wheels were a partial solution, but something else was obviously required.

Inline Console

Part of the eventual solution to the expanding-size problem was to rethink the roles of various components in the signal path. In an effort to redesign the recording console to better meet the new demands of contemporary multitrack recording, the inline console was introduced in the early 1970s by MCI (subsequently purchased by and absorbed into the Sony Corp.). As the term suggests, the *inline console* places all input, output, and monitor controls for a single audio channel within a single inline console module.

Inline Console Modules

Of course not all functions lend themselves to placement in the same module. For example, there must be a convenient single location for certain master controls, for communication with the studio, and for the adjustment of control room and studio monitoring levels, etc. Accordingly, the inline console usually contains the following types of module.

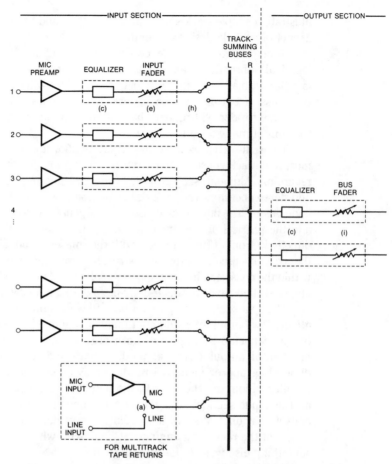

(A) Simplified flow chart for an 8 in/2 out console. Note the presence of the two track-summing buses.

Figure 12-3. Split-section recording studio console. Letters in parentheses are cross-references to Figure 12-5A, letters in brackets to Figure 12-19.

Module	Includes Controls for
I/O (Input/Output)	Level, equalization, dynamics, monitoring for a single input and output line; for example, microphone line 12 and tape recorder track 12
Echo	Master echo sends and returns
Communications	Talkback to the studio, tape slating, signal generator
Monitor	Master fader, studio and control room monitor levels, speaker selection
Auxiliary	Various accessory functions, group faders, user options, computer controls, controls for an additional input, not associated with a dedicated output line (for example, a 25th microphone line on a 24-track console)

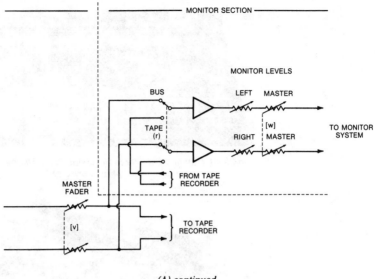

(A) continued

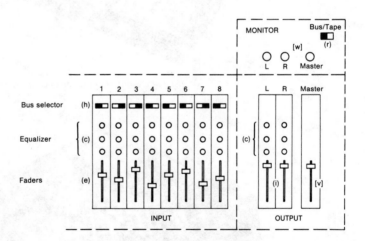

(B) Layout of console controls.

Figure 12-3 *(continued)*

(A) 32-in/8-out. (Yamaha PM3000 Professional Audio Mixing Console Courtesy Yamaha Music Corp., USA)

(B) 24-in/8-out. (DDA Q series courtesy DDA)

(C) 8-in/4-out. (Soundcraft Series 200BVE courtesy Soundcraft USA/JBL Professional)

Figure 12-4. Split-section multitrack consoles.

The console must have at least as many I/O modules as there are tracks on the control room multitrack tape recorder. Thus a console with n such modules has by default n input lines and n output lines. As more modules are installed, the input and output capacities of the console increase simultaneously (up to a point, beyond which the output capacity remains fixed).

There is, however, no point to having any more than one each of the other types of modules listed above. And as noted previously, there is no point in providing a complete set of bus faders, most of which will not be required. Instead, a means for providing such faders as needed is built into the console, and will be described later in the chapter, in the section on group faders (page 492).

Other Variations from Split-Section Design

In addition to the I/O module itself, the inline console introduces a few other significant variations to the older split-section console design. Some of these changes are briefly introduced here, with further details given later in the chapter.

Output Section

The output section itself requires considerably less space than it occupied on the earlier style console. For example, in a typical split-section console with many inputs and comparatively few outputs, the track-summing faders seen in Figure 12-3 at (i) were important; chances are several input signals would be combined to a single bus, so it was necessary to control the level of the combined signal by a convenient single slide fader.

However, if a console has an equal number of inputs and outputs (24/24, for example), it's likely that on many sessions a single input line feeds a single console output; that is, one microphone feeds one tape track. In this case the input fader itself is sufficient for level control and the track-summing fader is redundant. Considerable space might be saved by replacing it with a small rotary potentiometer located on the I/O module, for use as required.

Furthermore, every time multiple inputs are combined to a single bus, the need for additional buses diminishes. For example, the minimum number of inputs that can be combined is of course, two. In the unlikely event that each output signal is a combination of two inputs, the 24-input console could only feed 12 outputs at a time, and even less if one or more outputs contained signals from more than two inputs.

Signal Processing Requirements

As another important design consideration, synchronous recording has changed the nature of most pop-music recording sessions, which are now recorded sequentially; that is, a few basic tracks are recorded first, followed by multiple overdubs until all tracks on the multitrack tape are filled. As a practical consequence, it is often necessary to postpone equalization and other signal processing decisions until after all the tracks are completed. For example, at the time the basic tracks are recorded, certain equalization, compression, and echo/reverberation settings might seem to be ideal. But after the last of the overdubbed tracks is eventually added days, weeks, or months later, the same settings no longer produce the desired effect. In some cases the engineer may have to attempt to undo settings recorded along with the basic tracks and then try something else more appropriate in the context of the completed multitrack master tape.

To avoid this problem, the inline console may provide the option of assigning equalization and other signal processing to the monitor path for each track, while the track itself is recorded without processing. By so doing, the effects may be heard during the recording session, but do not become permanent until later on, when the completed multitrack master tape is mixed down to two tracks.

Wet and Dry Recording

A track recorded in an acoustically dead environment is often referred to as sounding a bit "dry." Artificial echo and reverberation are of course the obvious solution, and when lots of the latter is applied the track is often referred to as sounding "wet." By extension, the terms are often used as follows:

Dry   Recorded with no signal processing
Wet   Recorded with signal processing added, especially echo and/or reverberation

The terms are often used to describe the method in which signal processing (especially echo and reverberation) is used during recording. In the *dry* mode, the processing is applied in the monitor section only; in the *wet* mode, what you hear is what you get—the processing is applied to the incoming signal and recorded on tape. Most modern consoles provide the means to record in either mode.

Line Level and Line Inputs

In addition to its appearance in "inline," the word *line* may have one of the following two meanings in this chapter, and in audio technology in general.

1. Pertaining to a signal that is at a specified transmission-*line* level; or simply, at *line level*. A line level signal is understood to be at or near 0 dB (0.775 volt).

2. Any signal path; for example, a microphone line, cue line, power line, etc. In this context, the word *line* itself does not define the level of the signal.

With luck, the meaning of *line* should be clear from the context in which the word appears. Thus, the signal level on a microphone line is not a line-level signal, and a mic/line switch is one that switches between a microphone line and some other signal that is (or should be) at line level. In most cases, a line-level signal is routed to or from the tape recorder.

Inline Console Module Descriptions

As noted earlier in the chapter, the modern recording console is largely composed of redundant controls. However, the number of such controls on a single I/O module probably far exceeds the total knob count on a complete console from an earlier day. (For example, compare the two consoles in Figure 12-1.) Therefore, to introduce the fundamental design concepts of the inline console, we begin by describing the basic controls found on a console of reasonable proportions. This is supplemented by a look at some of the additional control functions that may be encountered on larger consoles, accompanied by detail drawings that show the additional signal flow details. At the conclusion of the chapter, a set of signal flow block diagrams from a currently available inline console will be shown (Figures 12-25 and 12-26, pages 514–517). The drawings were selected to show the way some of the various components and signal flow details described here may actually appear in a recording studio console.

I/O (Input/Output) Module

Figure 12-5A shows the basic signal flow chart and Figure 12-5B the physical layout for an I/O module in an inline console. The flow chart shows the signal paths to the track-summing, effects send, cue send, and stereo monitor buses. Although most inline consoles will have many more buses than are illustrated here, the additional capacity usually consists of multiple copies of the various basic elements shown in the illustration. This chart will serve as the basis for most of the following section on the I/O module. A letter in parentheses serves as a cross-reference between the indicated component and its text description. The same lettering system was also used in Figure 12-3.

Channel and Monitor Paths

Within the I/O module, the incoming signal travels along two paths, which are separately identified as the *channel path* and the *monitor path*.

The channel path is the path from the mic/line switch (a) to the bus-selector matrix (h). At various stages in the channel path, the characteristics of the incoming signal (e.g., equalization, dynamics, level) may be modified prior to recording the signal on a multitrack tape recorder.

The monitor path is the path from the bus/tape switch (r) through the various controls associated with the monitor and two-channel mixdown system.

The distinction between channel and monitor paths becomes important when various signal processing devices are switched between one path and another, as described later in the chapter. In the discussion that follows, the level control in the channel path will be referred to as the *channel fader*, the one in the monitor path as the *monitor potentiometer*. However, the latter may be a slide fader too, although slightly smaller than the channel fader.

Microphone Input
The typical mic operating level is considerably below that of a tape recorder. Therefore, a mic preamplifier in the console (not in the microphone) provides the gain required to bring the signal up to typical line level. The preamp gain is usually adjustable via a rotary trim potentiometer, as shown in the detail drawing in Figure 12-6 (page 477). To prevent high-level microphone signals from overloading the preamp, an attenuation pad is usually found in the mic input line, as also shown in the illustration.

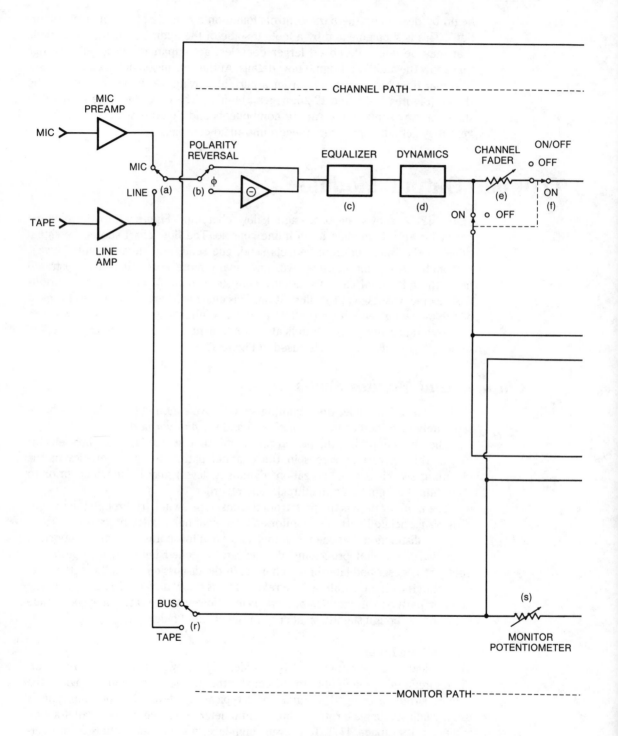

(A) Signal flow chart.

Figure 12-5. The basic inline console design.

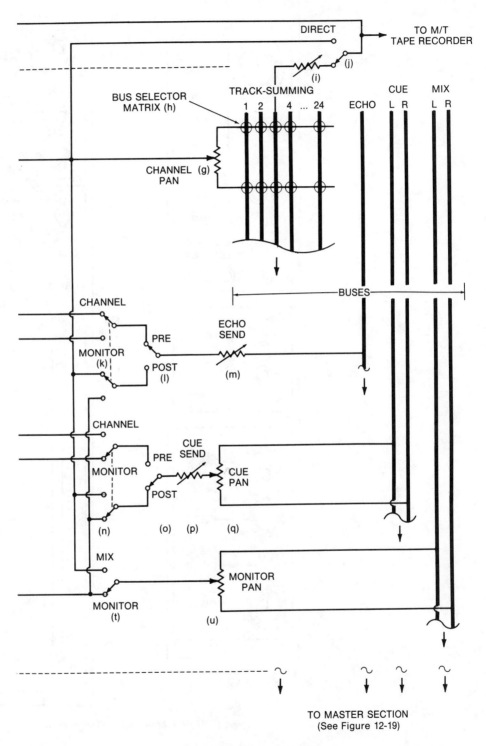

Figure 12-5A *(continued)*

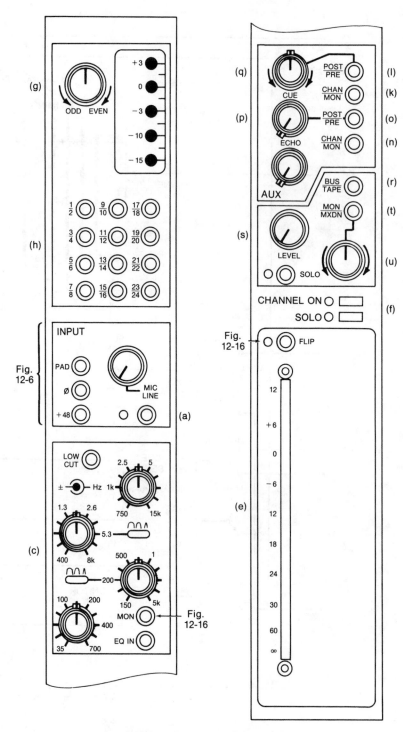

(B) Physical layout of the I/O module.

Figure 12-5. The basic inline console design. *(continued)*

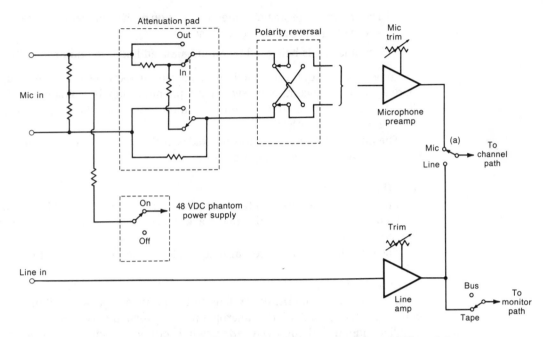

Figure 12-6. Microphone/line input section of I/O module.

There are therefore three level controls in the input section that affect the signal level from a microphone: the input pad, the mic preamp, and finally the channel fader, at (e) in Figure 12-5A. Since the latter control comes after the mic preamp and the equalizer, the physical position of its slider is a good indication of the incoming signal level. Ideally, the slider should be somewhere near the top of its range, in a position typically marked with a distinctive color band or a 0-dB legend, as shown later on (Figure 12-10, page 483). A slider placed very low down is a visual warning that the level through the equalizer is too high, possibly resulting in some overload distortion. With the attenuation pad switched out of the circuit, the preamp gain should be adjusted until the fader can be moved up to its ideal position. If the gain cannot be reduced sufficiently, the pad may be used to attenuate the incoming signal before it reaches the preamp. The pad should also be used if the signal on the mic line is from a line-level source (the output of a guitar amp, for example).

The microphone input section also provides a switch for routing the phantom power supply voltage to the mic line. Assuming the applied voltage on each conductor is identical, there is no need to switch it off when a nonphantom-powered mic is on the line since (in theory) such microphones simply "ignore" the phantom voltage which reaches them. However, there is always the possibility that something will go wrong. For example,

- When a mic is plugged in or out, both its signal pins do not make simultaneous contact with their conductors.
- There is a slight imbalance in the precision resistors seen in Figure 12-6.
- The microphone output is unbalanced (one side grounded).

- The microphone was designed to work on a phantom supply other than + 48 volts (supplied by most consoles).
- The mic line is being fed by an unbalanced line-level guitar amplifier.

To prevent any of these conditions from causing damage to a microphone, it's good operating procedure to switch all phantom supply voltages off before plugging in any microphones. Then, switch on those lines that require phantom power and leave the others off.

The microphone input section concludes at the mic/line switch, seen at (a) in Figures 12-5A and B and in Figure 12-6.

Tape (Line) Input
Each I/O module may also contain a separate line-level trim control for adjusting the incoming signal level from one track on the multitrack tape recorder, as shown in Figure 12-6.

The tape (line) input section also concludes at the mic/line selector switch.

Mic/Line Selector
Returning to Figure 12-5A, depending on the position of a two-position *mic/line* switch (a), the output of the microphone- or tape-input section is fed to the equalizer input. Although the latter switch position might have been labeled "tape," the "line" designation is generally used in this context as a reference to the operating level of the incoming signal.

Given the current popularity of directly recording the output of various electronic devices, the line-level output of a synthesizer or instrument amp is often inserted in the tape-in line, and this signal is applied to the equalizer in place of the usual microphone-line input. Therefore, in the following discussions of incoming microphone signals, the same comments usually apply to the signal from any other device used in place of a microphone.

To help keep things confusing, the tape-in line is also routed to the *tape* position on the *bus/tape* switch (r) described later in the chapter (page 491).

Channel Path Controls

The controls described in this section are those normally found in the channel-path between the mic/line switch and the bus-selector matrix.

Polarity (Phase) Reversal
Given the vagaries of multimic recording, it's sometimes necessary to reverse the polarity of one or more microphone signals to prevent acoustic phase cancellations (and sometimes, as a quick fix for a miswired cable). Therefore, most consoles provide a module switch for this purpose. Depending on design details, the switch may insert an inverting stage in the circuit, or actually flip the signal conductors.

The polarity-reversal switch (b) is usually referred to as a *phase* reversal switch, and is invariably labeled with a $\emptyset$ symbol or a θ. In Figure 12-5A the switch inserts an inverting amp immediately before the equalizer, while in the detail drawing in Figure 12-6, there is a mechanical switch in the microphone input section. In either case, the polarity of the signal from the microphone is reversed throughout the console. Although the former position allows the reversal to affect any signal applied to the equalizer, it should be noted that the polarity of the same signal applied elsewhere is *not* affected by this reversal. This point should be kept in mind later on, when more-complex switching systems are in use. As a further consideration, if a polarity reversal is required elsewhere than in a microphone line, the condition may indicate a wiring problem that should be corrected before the next session. In the meantime, a temporary reversal can probably be effected at the patch bay (described later in the chapter).

Equalizer Section

Many early consoles provided little onboard equalization beyond a rudimentary lowpass and highpass filter network. By contrast, the equalizer, at (c) in Figure 12-5A, on the modern inline console may offer facilities to rival or surpass those found on a considerably larger dedicated rack-mount system.

Figure 12-7 shows some of the equalizer sections that are to be found on a representative sampling of recording studio consoles, and gives brief descriptions of their various controls. The equalizer itself was covered in greater detail in Chapter 7.

Not to be overlooked on any console equalizer is the in/out switch. Given the knob factor on a multiband equalizer in a sophisticated inline module, it's no trouble at all to apply the wrong settings, usually because an engineer on a previous session (or you on this one) forgot to restore all previous controls to their zero position. Therefore it's not a bad idea to routinely switch off all equalizers until such time as one is needed. That way there will be no little accidents (at least in equalization) that need to be fixed later on.

Dynamics Section

A comparatively recent addition to the recording console is a dynamics section at (d) in Figure 12-5A, within each I/O module. The section contains the controls required for compression, limiting, and expansion of a signal. In the split-section console, and even in the early generations of inline consoles, a dynamics section was a luxury not to be found in each module and in fact not even elsewhere on the console at all. Such signal processing required the use of an external device, usually found just out of reach in an equipment rack. However, given modern electronic design capabilities, the signal processing facilities to be found on any module are usually limited only by the physical space required for the controls needed to operate them.

Figure 12-8 shows the dynamics section on an I/O module. The modification of dynamic range itself was covered in detail in Chapter 8.

Equalizer/Dynamics Routing Sequence

The nature of a signal output can vary considerably depending on the sequence in which an equalizer and a dynamics processor are placed in the signal path. For example, if a compressed signal seems to need, say, a little high-frequency equalization, the equalizer should be inserted after the compressor. Otherwise, the equalizer will affect the performance of the compressor. For example, a high-frequency precompression boost will cause the equalized band to be compressed

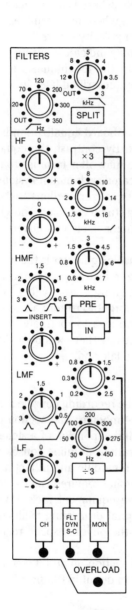

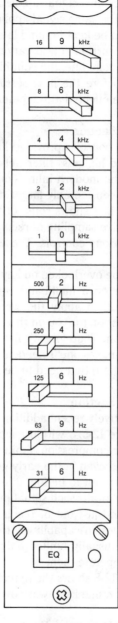

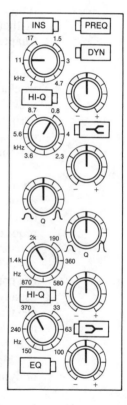

(A) Highpass and lowpass filters (top of module) and four-band parametric equalizer (Solid State Logic SL611G).

(B) Ten-band graphic equalizer at one-octave center frequencies (Sony MXBK-EQ35 option for MXP-3000 series console).

(C) Four-band Formant Spectrum Equalizer (Neve V series console).

Figure 12-7. I/O module equalizers.

even more, and this may work against the desired effect. However, if this is the desired effect, then the equalizer should of course come first.

If both devices are in an external rack, then they can be patched into the signal path in the desired sequence. Or if one or both are internal, the console patch bay may provide the facility to reverse their default sequence. As an alternative, some I/O modules provide a switching facility for this purpose. Figure 12-9 shows how the positions of the equalizer and dynamics processor may be reversed by a switching system such as the one seen at the bottom of the dynamics section module in Figure 12-8B.

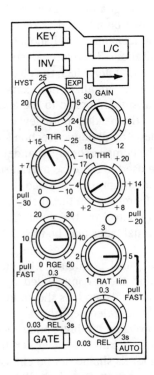

(A) Neve V series I/O module, with expander on left, compressor on right. (Courtesy Rupert Neve Inc.)

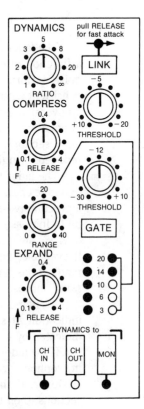

(B) Solid State Logic SL611G I/O module with compressor above expander. The three pushbuttons at the bottom of the module determine the location of the dynamics section in the signal path. (Courtesy Solid State Logic Inc.)

Figure 12-8. The dynamics section on an I/O module, showing compressor and expander functions.

Channel Fader

The channel fader is the primary level-controlling device in the signal path, and its usual position in the signal path is immediately after the equalizer and dynamics section as shown at (e) in Figure 12-5A.

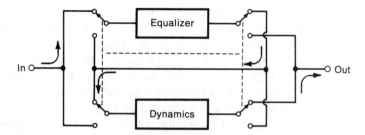

Figure 12-9. Switching detail for reversing the sequence of two signal processors in a signal path.

The fader follows the equalizer and dynamics section so that level changes as a function of either device may be adjusted as required. For optimum signal-to-noise performance, the equalizer input level should be kept as high as possible, consistent with overload limitations. Therefore, an equalization boost may require an overall attenuation of its output, for which the channel fader can be used. If the attenuation took place before the equalizer (for example, within the microphone input section), then the input signal applied to the equalizer would of course be reduced, bringing it closer to the residual noise level.

The fader must also follow the dynamics section so that it does not affect the dynamic characteristics of the compressor or expander. As an obvious example, if a precompressor fader were used to increase overall signal level, its effect would be to increase the amount of compression instead. If this is indeed required, the device's own input controls (compression threshold, for example) should be used. If available, an output level control on the dynamic processor may be used to readjust the gain, or the channel fader may be raised/lowered as required for the same purpose.

As noted earlier, the physical position of the fader knob is a good visual indication of signal level, and the recommended operating position is usually indicated by a shaded area or "0" legend, as shown in Figure 12-10.

If the fader is consistently operated near the bottom of its range, the incoming microphone or line level is probably too high, and should be adjusted as required. However, if the high level is a function of either the equalizer or dynamics sections, then the incoming levels should not be changed. Instead, use an output gain adjust in the appropriate section if one is available. If not, then the fader may be left in a lower-than-customary position.

Channel On/Off

From time to time it may be necessary to temporarily turn an input channel off completely, but without disturbing any of the level setting controls in the signal path. The *channel on/off switch* (f) in Figure 12-5A accomplishes this. The switch also disables the cue- and echo-send lines, as will be described later in the chapter.

Channel Path Feeds

At the output of the fader, the channel signal may be routed to one or more of the following destinations:

- Multitrack tape recorder
    - via track-summing buses
    - via direct output
- Echo/reverberation system, or other auxiliary device
- Cue system
- Monitor system and two-track tape recorder
- Solo bus

The echo/reverberation and cue signals may also originate from a point ahead of the channel fader, as will be described later.

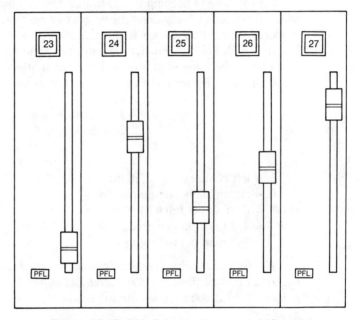

Figure 12-10. Slide faders in the console I/O section.

Multitrack Tape Recorder Lines

The primary destination of any incoming microphone signal is of course one or more tracks on a multitrack tape recorder. For this purpose, the channel signal is routed either through a pan pot and track-summing matrix system, or directly to a single track. Both options are described here.

Stereo Image Control

In Figure 12-3A, a simple two-position switch (h) permits the input signal to be routed to either the left or the right track-summing bus. Although this is not a very flexible arrangement, some early stereo consoles, such as the one seen in Figure 12-1A, lacked even this simple control. A few microphone input lines were hard-wired to track 1, a few others to track 2; a center signal was derived by hanging two microphones (!) and feeding their identical (with luck) outputs to separate input lines. Off-center panning was pretty much a matter of having the musicians properly seated between the microphones (RCA 1954, 1956).

Today most consoles provide the means to route every incoming signal to one or more track summing buses, and to vary the balance of a signal sent to two destinations. In addition, a few I/O modules may accept dual inputs, as for example from a stereo microphone, and offer the same type of control.

Pan Pot   On each I/O module, a *pan pot* (panoramic potentiometer) (g) allows the incoming signal to be routed in varying proportions to a pair of track-summing buses. With one bus subsequently routed to the left speaker and the other to the right, the pan pot allows the signal to be moved, or panned, from left to center to right, as desired. Actual selection of the two buses is via the bus-selection matrix (h) discussed later.

For the sake of keeping things simple, the pan pot may be drawn as a single wiper arm which travels along the length of a resistor, as shown in Figure 12-11A. However, the actual device is more often a dual-ganged control as shown in Figure 12-11B. The two resistive elements are required so that the resistance value of each may be tapered to provide the desired attenuation characteristics. In the graph shown in Figure 12-11C, the attenuation is calculated from the equations

$$L = 20 \log(\cos \theta)$$
$$R = 20 \log(\sin \theta)$$

where
   L = left channel output, in dB
   R = right channel output, in dB
   θ = 0° (pan pot full left)
      = 45° (pan pot centered)
      = 90° (pan pot full right)

The sine and cosine functions provide outputs varying between 1 and 0, and the logarithms of these functions give the output levels in dB. Therefore, as the pan pot is rotated from one extreme position to the other, the output levels vary as follows:

	Potentiometer Rotated to		
Attenuation	*Full Left*	*Center*	*Full Right*
Left channel	0 dB	− 3 dB	∞ dB
Right channel	∞ dB	− 3 dB	0 dB

Note that in either output, the attenuation is gradual at first, then falls off rapidly beyond the center position. Furthermore, at all positions of the pan pot the combined acoustic output level remains constant, as indicated by the dashed line at 0 dB in the graph. In other words, the signal appears to move from extreme left to center to extreme right with no change in level due to the panning motion.

However, if the two outputs are summed later on (as in a mono broadcast), there will be a 3 dB center-channel build-up, as also shown in the graph. As compensation, a pan pot may be designed to provide more than 3 dB attenuation in its center position. For example, at 6 dB attenuation in both lines, the summed (mono) output will be 0 dB. Some pan pots "split the difference" with 4.5 dB center attenuation, and a few console modules have provided a switch-selectable center attenuation value. Verification of the actual taper is easy enough: pan something from left to right and watch the meters.

For applications that do not require the use of a pan pot, a pan in/out switch is sometimes provided (Figure 12-11B, for example). In the released (out) position, the signal is routed directly to the bus selector matrix and the pan pot has no effect.

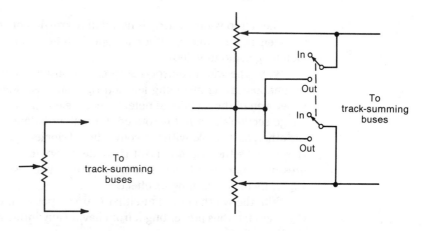

(A) As often drawn on console signal flow charts.

(B) Actual circuit design, also showing pan in/out switch.

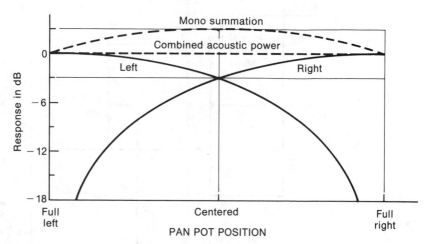

(C) Graph of attenuation in either output line as a function of the rotary position of a true sine/cosine potentiometer.

Figure 12-11. Pan pot details.

Stereo Width Control   Figure 12-12A shows the signal flow paths through the image control section of a stereo I/O module. The first potentiometer functions as an *image width* or *blend* control of the incoming stereo (left and right) signals. As the potentiometer is rotated from one extreme position to the other, the two-channel output of the module varies as follows.

Potentiometer	Output 1	Output 2	Image Width
fully ccw	left	right	normal stereo
centered	left + right	left + right	mono
fully cw	right	left	reverse stereo

The stereo width control is useful in narrowing or reversing the stereo spread between two speakers, either for special effects or as may be required when matching audio to video.

When the width control is at its center position, both outputs contain a mono summation of the incoming left and right signals. Note that in this position, the wiper arm of the additional potentiometer element is grounded. Therefore, as the image section's *pan pot* is rotated, the output balance shifts from one output to the other, as it would with the conventional single-input pan pot described before. However, as the width control is rotated towards either extreme position, progressively more resistance is inserted in the line between ground and the pan pot wiper, thereby lessening its effect.

With the width control at either extreme position, the pan pot is in effect out of the circuit, thus preventing it from having any influence on a normal or reverse stereo output.

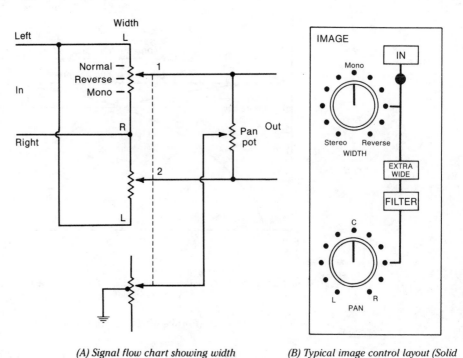

(A) Signal flow chart showing width control and pan pot.

(B) Typical image control layout (Solid State Logic SL 611S Stereo Channel Module).

Figure 12-12. The image control section of a stereo I/O module.

Width Enhancement In the stereo I/O module detail also shown in Figure 12-12B, the *extra wide* push button enables a phase-shift network that may be used to create the illusion that the stereo image spreads beyond the limits of a pair of speakers. A highpass *filter* network may be used to compensate for low-frequency response shifts caused by the phase-shift network.

Bus Selector Matrix

As Figure 12-5A shows, the outputs of the pan pot feed the bus-selector matrix (h), a set of switches such as those seen in Figure 12-13. Note that switch configurations vary; a single switch may select an odd/even bus pair, or a dual set of switches may allow the user to select any combination of odd- and even-numbered buses. The latter option is usually included on consoles where the pan pot may be disabled, so that a signal may be routed to a single bus, as well as to various bus pairs.

Track-Summing Buses

A track summing bus is the conductor to which all signals assigned to a certain track are routed. For example, if the incoming signals on I/O modules 3, 4, and 7 are to be routed to track 2, then bus 2 must be selected at the bus selector matrix on modules 3, 4, and 7. Assuming bus pair 1 & 2 are enabled by a single switch (Figure 12-13A for example), then the module pan pot must be turned to the extreme right to route the signal to bus 2 only.

Bus Output Master

In the split-section console described earlier in the chapter, the bus output master control (i) was a slide fader in the console's output section, as was shown in Figure 12-3. The equivalent control on the inline console may be a rotary potentiometer used as a simple bus level trim control, or it may be omitted entirely.

When more than one input is routed to a single bus and a slide fader to control the combined group would be convenient, a group fader function may be enabled, as will be described later in this chapter (page 492).

Direct Output Select

As noted earlier, the output of only one microphone or other source is often the only signal to be routed to a single track on the multitrack tape recorder. In this case, there is no need for a pan pot, for track-summing buses, or for combining amplifiers; the signal might just as well be routed directly from the channel fader to the tape recorder, bypassing the unnecessary components just mentioned.

The *direct* switch (j) accomplishes this by providing a direct path from the channel fader to a single track output. The destination fed by the direct switch may be either

- The track with the same number as the I/O module, or
- A patch point, for routing to any tape track input.

In Figure 12-5A the direct output on the I/O module feeds the track associated with that module. In the absence of a direct switch, the module pan pot and bus selector matrix are instead used to route the signal to the desired single bus.

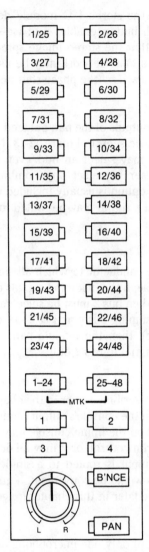

(A) Each button selects an odd/even bus pair.

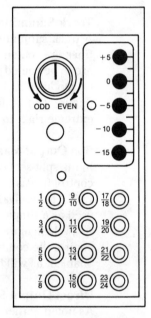

(B) A separate button for each track-summing bus allows any track combination to be selected.

Figure 12-13. Bus selector matrix section of an I/O module. In either case, the pan pot pans between the selected odd and even buses.

Echo (or Auxiliary) Path Controls

In addition to routing an incoming signal to the desired track, each signal may also be sent to one or more external signal processing devices. The most-often used device is an echo/reverberation system, so the appropriate I/O module controls are frequently labeled *echo*. However, since the same controls may be— and often are—used for other purposes, the module label may instead be *effects, aux, send,* etc. For purposes of the present discussion, it will be assumed that the signal is to be sent to an echo/reverberation system, and that the system return controls (described later in the chapter) are appropriately set.

The channel/monitor select and pre/post fader send switches are used to select the point at which the echo send signal originates, as described here.

Channel/Monitor Select

The signal to be sent to the external echo/reverberation system may be taken from the channel or monitor path, as determined by the position of the *channel/ monitor select switch* at (k) in Figure 12-5A. In the *channel* position, the echo send signal may be from either an incoming microphone or a previously recorded tape track, as determined by the mic/line switch (a) at the beginning of the channel path. In the *monitor* position, the send signal is determined by the bus/tape switch (r).

Pre/Post Selector

In either case, the immediately following *pre/post* switch (l) determines whether the signal is picked up before or after the channel fader or monitor potentiometer. Thus the combination of the two switches selects the echo send point as listed here.

Pre/Post	Channel Selected	Monitor Selected
Pre	before channel fader	before monitor potentiometer
Post	after channel fader	after monitor potentiometer

With the pre/post switch in its post position, the send level follows either the fader or potentiometer position; as the selected control is moved, the send level varies accordingly. For most applications, this is the preferred position, so that the echo-send signal bears a direct relationship to the direct signal level.

Send Level and On/Off Switch

The send level is further adjusted by a *send level* potentiometer (m) immediately after the pre/post switch. If the switch is in the *pre* position, the send level is not affected by movement of the channel fader (or monitor potentiometer). When feeding an echo/reverberation system, this position is often used to simulate the effect of a sound source moving towards, or away from, the listener. With the fader/potentiometer at some convenient reference position, the send-level potentiometer is adjusted for the desired send level, which now remains fixed. Therefore, the ratio of direct sound to echo/reverberation varies as the fader is moved up and down. At low fader settings, the direct signal level is much lower than the echo-send level; at higher settings the direct signal is greater than the send level. As a result, the direct signal appears to recede or move forward, depending on which way the fader is moved.

The use of the pre/post switch and send level potentiometer for echo-send applications was discussed in greater detail in Chapter 6 (page 233).

When the *channel on/off* switch (f) is in its *off* position, the channel feeds to both sides of the *pre/post* switch are disabled, thus ensuring that an incoming channel-path signal does not feed an auxiliary device when the channel itself is disabled.

Cue Path Controls

When adding tracks to a tape that already contains one or more recorded tracks, it is of course necessary for the musicians to hear whatever was recorded earlier. When recording the electronic output of an instrument only, it's possible to monitor the previously recorded tracks via a studio speaker, since there is no open microphone to pick up, and thereby rerecord, the reproduced tracks.

However, if a microphone is currently in use, then the musicians must listen over headphones to whatever it is that they are to accompany. In this case it may be difficult for them to hear themselves unless the engineer can also feed a little of the microphone signal into the headphone system along with the previously recorded tracks.

The console cue system is used for both purposes, as may also be seen in the signal flow chart in Figure 12-5A. Signals from incoming microphone lines and from previously recorded tape tracks are routed to the cue bus, balanced, and sent to the cue system amplifier, which in turn feeds the headphones in the studio.

Channel/Monitor Select

The *channel/monitor select switch* (n) in the cue send lines performs the same function as the same switch (k) in the echo send line.

Pre/Post Selector

The cue send *pre/post* switch (o) also performs the same function as the same switch (l) in the echo send line.

Send Level and On/Off Switch

Finally, the *cue send level* potentiometer (p) performs the same function as the echo send level potentiometer (m) described above.

The choice of send levels to the cue system often bears little resemblance to the monitor mix heard in the control room, usually because the studio musicians want to hear more, or less, of themselves in the headphones in order to sing/play along with whatever was previously recorded. Therefore, the pre/postfader switch is often placed in its prefader position and a separate cue mix prepared using the cue send level potentiometers. By utilizing the prefader side of the switch, the studio musicians will not be distracted by whatever gain riding is taking place at the channel faders.

Pan Pot

Many consoles provide a pair of cue buses, generally used for a stereo cue feed to the studio. In this case, a *cue pan pot* (q) allows the cue send signal to be panned between the buses as desired.

Monitor Path Controls

The console must provide the means to simultaneously monitor the material currently being recorded and anything already on tape from an earlier session. And while one is punching in and out on a previously recorded track it is necessary to hear first the old program, then the punch-in, then the original track immediately after the punch-out. During a multitrack mixdown session it is of course necessary to monitor either the incoming 24 (or whatever) tracks, or the finished two-track master tape.

The console controls described in the following material, as well as others on the master module, are used to set up the desired monitor conditions.

Mixdown/Monitor Buses

Each of the track-summing buses described earlier in the chapter is associated with a specific track on the multitrack tape recorder. It is not however associated with a specific left-to-right position within the monitoring environment. Thus track-summing bus 1 might be monitored on the right speaker, bus 2 on the left, bus 3 in the center, and so on. Assuming that someone in the control room has at least a vague idea of what's being recorded, the monitoring location for each bus may be assigned as desired, without the assignment having any effect on the multitrack recording itself.

The first step is to select the signal to be monitored, then adjust its monitor level, and, finally, pan the signal to the location desired for monitoring. As before, the output of the pan pot feeds two summing buses, generally identified as *mixdown buses*, since in addition to feeding the monitor system, these bus outputs are also routed to the two-track tape recorder which will be used for recording the stereo mixdown of the multitrack tape.

Bus/Tape Select

If several microphones are routed to, say, track-summing bus 3, then that bus must be monitored in order to hear the resultant combination. However, if tape track 3 has already been recorded, then it will be necessary to monitor this tape output instead.

The *bus/tape* switch (r) selects either of these points and routes the appropriate signal to the immediately following monitor level potentiometer, shown at (s).

Note that the tape-in line is identified as *line* at the *mic/line* switch (a) and as *tape* at the *bus/tape* switch (r). The latter switch nomenclature is used because the *tape* position is invariably used only when monitoring a multitrack tape output.

Monitor Level

The *monitor level potentiometer* at (s) allows the monitor level to be varied independently of the signal level being recorded. Thus, while recording a signal at a rather high level (for signal-to-noise considerations), it may be monitored at a level closer to that desired in the final mixdown.

Monitor Select

During a recording session, the signal selected previously by the bus/tape switch is sent to the monitor system via the pan pot to be described later. For this purpose, the *mixdown/monitor* switch (t) immediately before the pan pot must be in the *monitor* position.

Two-Channel Mixdown Select

When a multitrack tape is ready for mixdown to a two-track master tape, the track-summing buses are not required. Instead, each of the mic/line switches (a) is placed in its *line* position, the level and equalization of each track are adjusted as required, and each channel signal is routed to the monitor system, via the mixdown buses. Therefore, each mixdown/monitor switch should be in its *mix-down* position.

Note that the feed to the monitor system is now taken from a point immediately beyond the channel fader, and that the monitor level potentiometer has no effect on the applied signal. This means that all balancing is done at the channel faders, with no further level controls in each signal path.

Monitor Pan Pot

As before, the *monitor pan pot* (u) is used to route the incoming signal to the desired position between two buses. However, since the mixdown buses are permanently associated with the left and right signals of a two-channel stereo image, the monitor pan pot is usually not followed by a bus-selector matrix.

Additional I/O Module Functions

The following section describes some of the additional controls that may be found on the I/O module, but which are not permanently assigned to one of the signal paths described earlier.

Group Faders

On the split-section console described earlier in this chapter, a slide fader is located in each track-summing bus output to control the level of the combined signal on that bus. This fader is usually replaced by a rotary potentiometer (or a smaller fader) on the inline console, and this function is located on the I/O module as was shown in Figure 12-5B.

In either case, a single level control of a track-summing bus output is useful when the engineer needs to ride gain on a group of inputs assigned to one bus. As just described however, the control cannot be used to adjust the gain of a group of incoming signals assigned to more than one bus as, for example, a multi-microphone drum pickup routed to, say, three tracks. Nor is it needed at all when only one input is routed to a tape track.

The inline console often provides a group function mode, in which the level of any group of incoming signals may be adjusted by a single slide fader, which is designated as the *group fader*. A typical implementation of a group fader is shown in Figure 12-14. Note that the traditional slide fader in the signal path in (A) has been removed and replaced by a VCA (voltage-controlled amplifier), seen in (B), whose gain is controlled by an external DC voltage. The slide fader is now used to vary the control voltage and this in turn varies the gain in the audio signal path.

Once the fader is isolated from the audio signal path, its DC output may now be routed not only to its own VCA, but to the control-voltage inputs on other VCAs in other signal paths as well as in (c). Thus, given the necessary switching facility, a single fader may be assigned as a group fader whenever the need arises.

Some inline consoles provide a separate set of group faders, while on others any fader may be temporarily designated as a group fader. For example, the dump mode described immediately below may be used to establish a temporary group fader function.

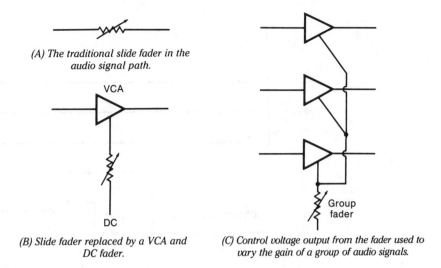

(A) The traditional slide fader in the audio signal path.

(B) Slide fader replaced by a VCA and DC fader.

(C) Control voltage output from the fader used to vary the gain of a group of audio signals.

Figure 12-14. The group fader mode.

Dump Mode

The output of the monitor pan pot may also be "dumped" onto a pair of track-summing buses by depressing a *dump* switch, usually located near the track-summing bus selector matrix, as shown by the detail drawing in Figure 12-15. For example, the monitor path signal in, say, I/O module 5 may be a mix of several incoming signals. By pressing the dump switch on I/O module 5, the panned monitor signal is also routed to the bus pair designated by the bus selector matrix, where it is combined with any other signals also routed to the same buses. To avoid feedback, the track-summing bus selector matrix should not be used to select the same bus as that of its own module (bus 5 in this example).

The incoming channel-path signal on module 5 no longer feeds its bus selector matrix, but it is still available as a direct feed to bus 5, as shown in the illustration.

Note also that the monitor path potentiometer now functions as a group fader for bus 5. In this case, the swap mode described immediately below may be used to insert a slide fader in the monitor path.

Swap Mode

In the I/O module as so far described, the equalizer, dynamics section, and slide fader were shown in the channel path, where each device may be used prior to recording the incoming signal on the multitrack tape. In the monitor path, a simple rotary potentiometer—or sometimes, a smaller slide fader—is used to adjust the monitor level.

However, in some applications it may be desirable to record a signal with no equalization, but nevertheless to monitor that signal with some equalization applied. By so doing, the engineer can experiment with various settings without affecting the actual recording. It may also be desirable to insert a large slide fader in the monitor path, as for example during a dump mode operation as described previously.

Many consoles provide a *swap* switch, whose purpose is to move a signal processing device from the channel path to the monitor path, or to swap the slide

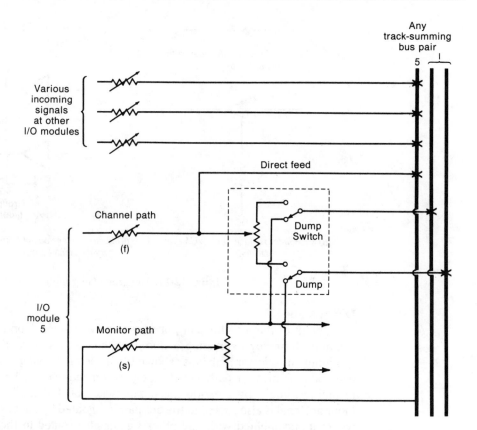

Figure 12-15. The dump mode. The potentiometer in the monitor path at (s)
may be used to adjust the gain of the group of signals routed
to a track-summing bus pair.

fader and rotary potentiometer. The basic switching system for enabling the swap mode is shown in Figure 12-16.

Solo Modes

During a multitrack recording session it is often helpful to briefly check a single channel to verify that no extraneous signals are being recorded along with the desired input. For example, low-level background noise, headphone leakage, and/or a forgotten console switch can all contribute to recording the unexpected on tape. In other words, are you *sure* the equalization or compression is in the monitor system only?

To verify what is actually taking place on a channel, most consoles provide a *channel solo* switch. When the switch is depressed, the channel signal is routed to the solo bus, and the bus output is routed to the monitor system, where it temporarily takes the place of the regular monitor mix. Thus, the solo channel alone is heard, although the actual recording is not affected.

Some consoles provide a stereo solo system, in which case the solo feeds originate after the channel pan pot. Therefore, the solo signal is heard at the

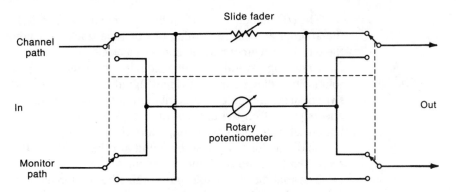

Figure 12-16. I/O module circuit detail, showing swap-mode switches for exchanging the positions of the slide fader and rotary potentiometer. Similar switching may be provided for moving an equalizer or dynamics processor from the channel to the monitor path.

same left/right position as the channel feed to the track-summing buses. The function is sometimes identified as *solo-in-place.* Both types of solo functions are illustrated in the detail drawing in Figure 12-17. Note that the mono solo mode is not disabled by the channel on/off switch, but a stereo solo is.

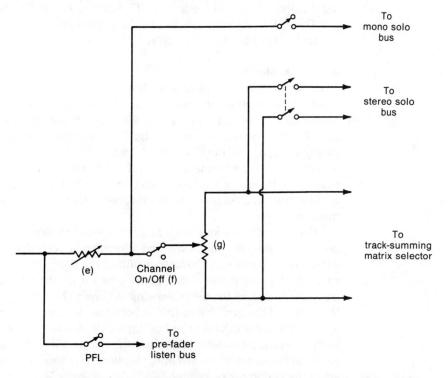

Figure 12-17. Solo mode detail drawing. The solo mode routes either an individual channel or a monitor path signal to the solo bus, the output of which temporarily replaces the normal program heard in the control room without affecting the recording. Mono and stereo solo functions are both shown.

The I/O module may also provide a *monitor solo* switch, so that the output of the appropriate track-summing bus or tape track (depending on the position of the bus/tape switch) may be checked as well.

Assuming several incoming signals are routed to the same bus, the channel solo switch allows each individual signal to be checked, while the monitor solo switch auditions the entire combination, plus any echo/reverberation or other effects present on the bus. On most consoles, it is possible to press several solo buttons at once, thereby routing more than one signal to the solo bus.

Solo functions may also be found at other points in the console signal path, such as in the echo send and return lines.

The routing of the solo bus within the master monitor system is described below in the section on monitor override modes (page 509).

Prefader Listen

As a variation on the solo function, many consoles provide a *prefader listen* (PFL) button, usually placed near the I/O module slide fader. When the PFL button is depressed, the signal at the input side of the fader is routed to the PFL bus, which may in turn feed the solo bus or be sent to a separate PFL monitor, for example, a small speaker located in or near the console. The latter option allows the engineer to make a quick check of the prefader channel signal without interrupting the normal monitor feeds. The PFL function is also illustrated in Figure 12-17.

The PFL feed to the selected monitor system also is described in the Monitor Override Modes section (page 509).

Broadcast Mode

To quickly review the typical recording procedure, each incoming signal is routed to one or more track-summing buses, the outputs of which are routed to the multitrack tape recorder and at the same time to the monitor system. Since each track is recorded at a reasonably high level, consistent with the limitations of the magnetic tape, the monitor level of each bus may be separately adjusted to provide a close approximation of the final mixdown. Thus, changes made in the channel path to the track-summing buses affect the multitrack tape and the monitor system; changes in the monitor path affect the monitor system but not the multitrack tape.

For some applications, such as a live stereo broadcast, it may be necessary to produce a two-track mixdown and a multitrack recording simultaneously. The former is of course sent to the transmitter, the latter saved for future use. In this case, the *broadcast mode* may be used to isolate the channel and the monitor paths. As shown by the detail drawing in Figure 12-18, the broadcast mode routes the output of the mic/line switch to both the channel and the monitor paths and at the same time disables the bus/tape output. Thus, the console provides two independently functioning signal paths; changes in the channel path have no effect on the stereo mixdown and, as before, changes in the monitor path do not affect the multitrack recording.

The broadcast mode allows the engineer to make changes to the multitrack recording while the broadcast is in progress, without having those changes affect the broadcast signal. The swap mode described previously will have been used to place the equalizer and the slide fader in the monitor path and, since the

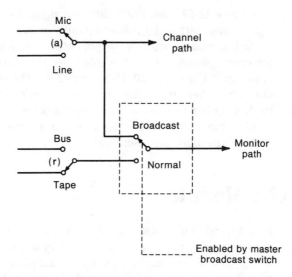

Figure 12-18. Broadcast mode switching system. A single broadcast mode switch in the master module section (Figure 12-22) enables the broadcast mode on all I/O modules.

broadcast signal will no doubt be monitored exclusively, changes to the track-summing buses will probably be limited to whatever it takes to keep the meters on scale.

A single *broadcast* switch (Figure 12-22A) in the master module section switches all I/O modules to the broadcast mode as shown by the detail drawing in Figure 12-18.

Master Module Section

The master module section provides space for those controls that are not associated with each I/O channel. For example, when the outputs of several channel paths are to be sent to some external signal-processing device (e.g., an echo/reverberation system), some control must be provided for the regulation of the signals sent to, and returned from, that device. Other master functions include cue-system routing, communication facilities, monitor functions, and so on.

On most inline consoles the master section controls are split among two or more modules, according to function. As a typical example, the controls may be divided among the three modules listed here.

Module	See Figure	Controls
Echo	12-20B	Master echo send and echo return controls
Communication	12-21	Master cue sends, talkback, test oscillator
Monitor	12-22	Control room and studio monitor level controls, monitor modes, mixdown recording/monitor level

Figure 12-19 (pages 500–501) is a signal flow chart that illustrates the basic signal paths within the master module, or modules. As in the earlier description of the I/O module, various components in the signal path are identified by a letter for cross reference with the following text explanation and with the module drawings in Figures 12-20, 12-21, and 12-22. The letters are enclosed in brackets to distinguish them from those in parentheses previously used to describe the I/O module. Other illustrations are also included to help illustrate various extended monitor functions that are not shown in Figure 12-19. This chart is the basis for much of the following discussion.

Master Echo Module

In a typical multitrack recording session, the incoming signals from several channels may be sent to a single auxiliary signal processing system, in addition to being routed to the desired track-summing buses. Again using an echo/reverberation system as our example, it may be desirable to add a little reverberation to, say, tracks 3, 5, and 11. Therefore, the echo-send controls on these I/O modules are adjusted as required to send the proper mix to the echo/reverberation system, as shown by the signal flow chart in Figure 12-19 and the module drawing in Figure 12-20B (page 503).

Echo Send Section

Within the master echo module, the master echo send path description is quite brief, since only one master control is required.

Master Echo Send Level
As noted before, more than one channel signal is often sent to a single echo send bus. Therefore, the inline console provides a master send-level potentiometer [a] to vary the combined send level as required.

Echo Return Section

Note that the external echo/reverberation system shown in Figure 12-20A has two outputs, one or both of which must now be returned to the console for monitoring purposes. However, it is unlikely that either return signal should be mixed into one or more of the track-summing buses just mentioned. To do so would be to record the combined echo/reverberation signal from the three instruments along with the recorded signal from only one of them. During mixdown later on, there would be no means to separate the echo/reverberation from the track it was recorded on.

In this case it would be better to route the echo returns to the monitor system only, thus recording the tracks dry, with permanent echo/reverberation settings deferred until the mixdown session later on.

However, when recording multiple instruments to a single track, if one or more need echo/reverberation, it will be necessary to add it during the initial recording.

As a typical example, a multimicrophone drum pickup may require a little reverberation (*very* little) applied to the snare drum only. If the rest of the drum set is recorded on the same track, the reverberation must be mixed in during recording.

Echo Return Level

Regardless of the eventual routing of an output signal from an echo/reverberation system, the first console control after the system output is usually a *return level potentiometer* [b]. This additional control is necessary due to the nature of a reverberation system's output signal, which may vary considerably as a function of the applied input signal level. Therefore, as the echo send level is varied to produce the desired effect, the echo return level is used to adjust the return-line gain prior to routing the signal to one of the system buses.

Echo Return Pan Pot

An *echo return pan pot* [c] is often provided in each return line for use when it is necessary to pan the echo return signal between two buses. For normal stereo reverberation, the pan pot in one of the two return lines from a stereo reverberation system should be panned extreme left, the other extreme right.

Echo-to-Tracks, Echo-to-Mix/Monitor

If the echo/reverberation is indeed going to be recorded on the same track as the channel signal from which it was derived, then of course the same bus assignment must be made, using the echo return selector matrix described below.

However, during multitrack recording the returns are perhaps more often routed to the monitor system. During mixdown, the echo returns are also routed to the monitor system and to the two-track tape recorder. Therefore, *echo-to-tracks* [d] (i.e., to the track-summing buses) and *echo-to-mix* [e] switches are often provided to select either option.

Although turning the echo return level potentiometers down would accomplish the same thing, the echo-to-tracks switch [d] is provided so that the echo may be disabled in the mixdown/monitor system without affecting the feed to the cue system (see the section on echo return to cue, which follows).

Echo Return Solo

The *echo return solo* switch [f] performs the same function as the other solo buttons described previously. Examples of both mono and stereo echo return solo functions are shown in Figure 12-19.

Note that it is not possible to solo the echo return for a single channel feed, since to do so would require that all other send signals to the same system be cut off, thus affecting the recorded echo signal.

Echo Return Selector Matrix

Assuming the echo returns are to be routed to the track-summing buses, the function of the *echo return selector matrix* [g] is similar to the track-summing bus selector matrix described earlier in the chapter. In some cases however, an echo-return pair is permanently assigned to the stereo mixdown buses. In this case there

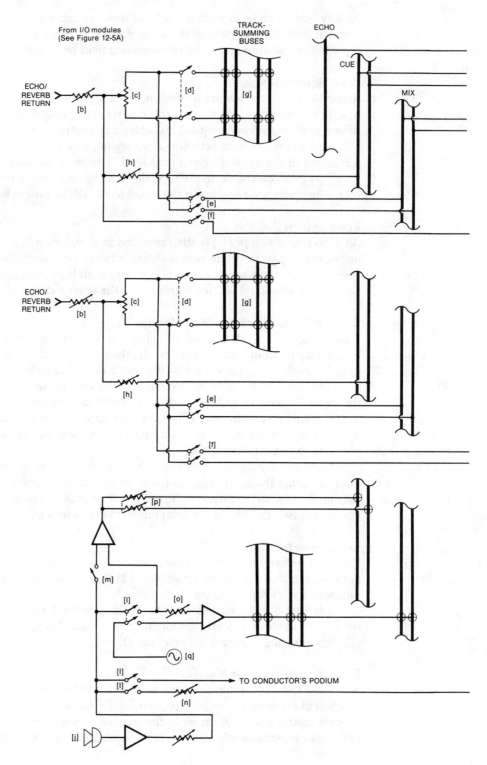

Figure 12-19. Signal flow in the master

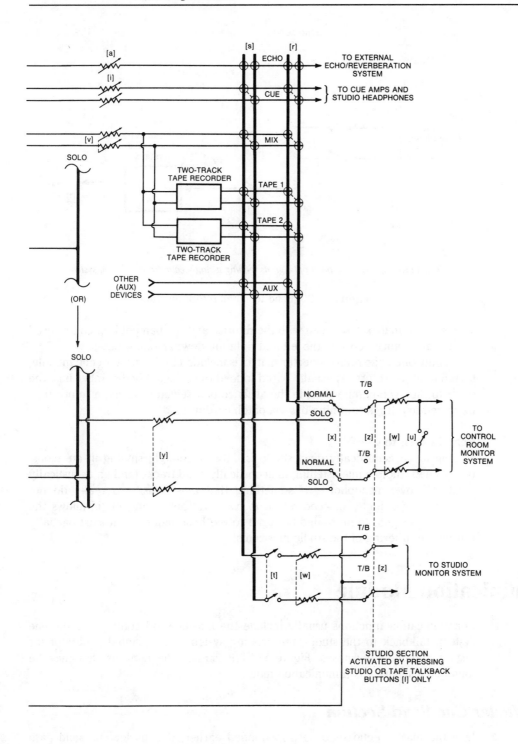

module section of an inline console.

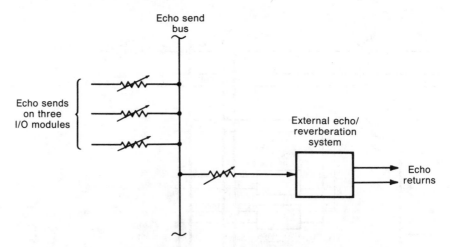

(A) An example of multiple input signals feeding a single echo/reverberation system.

Figure 12-20. Echo send and return functions.

is no selector matrix associated with the returns, and the pan pot is of course used to pan each return between the left and right mixdown/monitor buses.

If only one echo return selector matrix is included in the master echo module, then one of the returns is usually wired to feed the selected odd-number bus, the other to the even-number bus. In the absence of a selector matrix, a return may be routed to a track-summing bus via patch cord instead.

Echo Return to Cue

Singing in an acoustically dead studio is difficult enough; singing in an acoustically dead studio while listening to acoustically dead tracks (and an acoustically dead self) over headphones is something that most musicians really do not deserve. Accordingly, an *echo return to cue* level potentiometer [h] allows the echo return signal to be routed back out to the headphones to at least partially relieve the suffering of the studio musicians.

Communication Module

Communication functions usually include the master send controls for the cue system, talkback to the studio, tape slating system, and a signal generator for testing/alignment purposes. Figure 12-21 illustrates the controls that may be found on a separate communication module.

Master Cue Send Section

Like the master echo send path mentioned earlier, the master cue send path requires but one master control.

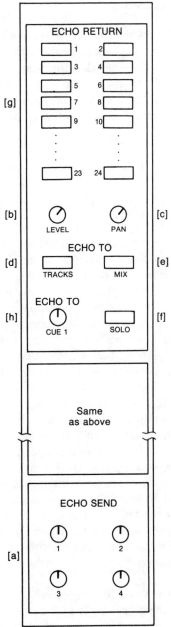

(B) Master echo send and return controls on the master echo module.

Figure 12-20 *(continued)*

Master Cue Send Level

Once the various cue feeds from the console I/O modules are combined to the cue bus, the *master cue send level* potentiometers [i] are used to vary the combined cue level signals as required.

Talkback System

A talkback microphone [j] is usually built into the console so that the engineer or producer can communicate with the studio musicians or record announcements on tape, as required. A *microphone level* potentiometer [k] may be found near the microphone to compensate for varying voice levels in the control room. Generally, a set of push buttons allows the microphone output to be routed to one or more destinations, as indicated here.

Push Button		Destination
Podium	[l]	Conductor's podium in studio
Studio	[l]	Studio monitor speakers and cue system
Tape	[l]	All tracks currently in the record mode
Cue	[m]	Cue system alone

The talkback switching logic may be set up so that each push button [l] routes the signal to the indicated destination, *and* to all destinations listed above it. Thus an announcement to the studio is also sent to the podium speaker and to the cue system for the possible enlightenment of musicians wearing headphones, and tape announcements go to the tape recorder and out to the other systems in the studio as well. However, the *cue* button [m] lets the control room staff talk into the cue system alone while a recording is in progress, without interrupting the recording.

The push buttons are momentary contact devices, so that the talkback microphone is active only for as long as one of the buttons is depressed.

Slating Function and Slating Tone

The term *slating* had its origins in the film industry where a chalkboard (slate) was used to visually identify the scene about to be shot. Closing a hinged clapstick at the top of the slate to produce a percussive sound for later synchronization use came to be known as "slating" the scene. Today's magnetic audio tapes are often slated with a spoken announcement of the take number, accompanied by a low-frequency tone mixed into the talkback signal when the *tape* or *slate* push button [l] is depressed. When the tape is rewound at high speed later on, the tone is heard at a higher frequency, making it reasonably easy to hear the point at which each take begins.

For tapes on which the time code of the desired location is known, the slating tone serves no practical purpose.

Talkback and Slating Level

Depending on who is in the studio (large noisy group, solo performer, etc.) the *studio talkback level* potentiometer [n] will need to be adjusted so that announcements can be heard over the prevailing prerecord noise level. Separate *slate level* [o] and *cue level* [p] potentiometers may be provided to control the level of announcements sent to the tape recorder and to the cue system.

Signal Generator

Most consoles provide a built-in signal generator [q] whose output may be either a sine wave, or white or pink noise.

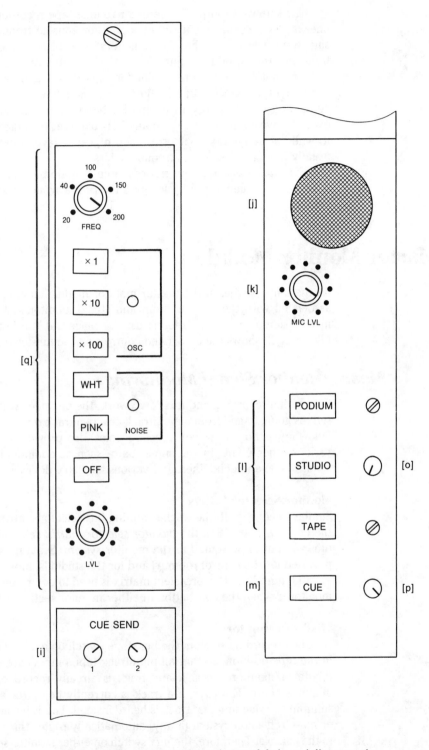

Figure 12-21. The communication module in an inline console.

The sine wave output is useful for routine tape recorder level and alignment checks or as a convenient signal source for console troubleshooting work. The sine wave section of the signal generator is usually the source of the low-frequency tone used in conjunction with the slating function described before.

The noise sources are useful for checking the broadband response of a component in the signal path. *White noise* is defined as a random noise source containing equal energy in each 1-Hz band within the audio spectrum. Since every octave contains twice as many 1-Hz bands as the octave immediately below it, white noise energy doubles at each higher octave, and the noise is therefore usually thought of as a high-frequency hiss.

Pink noise is a random noise source containing equal energy per octave, which may be generated by lowpass filtering a white noise source at 3 dB per octave.

Master Monitor Module

As the name suggests, the master monitor module contains the master controls associated with the control room and studio monitor systems. In addition, the master stereo mixdown fader is usually placed at the bottom of this module. Figure 12-22 shows the associated controls on the master monitor module.

Master Monitor Signal Monitoring

For routine recording and mixdown work, the engineer will need to monitor the signals going to and from a multitrack or a two-track recorder, as described in the following section. However, most consoles also provide facilities for monitoring various other points in the signal path, such as additional tape recorders, the sends to cue and echo lines, and various auxiliary devices.

Monitor Selector Matrix

Similar in concept to the track-summing bus selector matrix described earlier in the chapter (page 487), the *monitor selector matrix* selects the tape recorder or other output to be routed to the monitor system. Separate selector matrixes are provided for the control room [r] and for the studio [s] monitor system.

In Figure 12-22B, a preselect matrix is used to determine which signal will be monitored when the *aux* button in either monitor section is pressed.

Mixdown Monitor

During a recording session, the bus/tape switch on each I/O module is generally in the *tape* position, so that all multitrack tape outputs are routed to the 2-track mixdown/monitor buses. If any track is already recorded, then its sync-head output is heard. However, if a track is currently being recorded, then the track-summing bus feeding that track is heard instead. This is because the tape recorder or noise reduction system (if any) automatically routes this incoming signal back to the console. Therefore, the *mix* switch on either monitor selector matrix—[r] or [s]—routes any active recording buses and all tape tracks previously recorded to

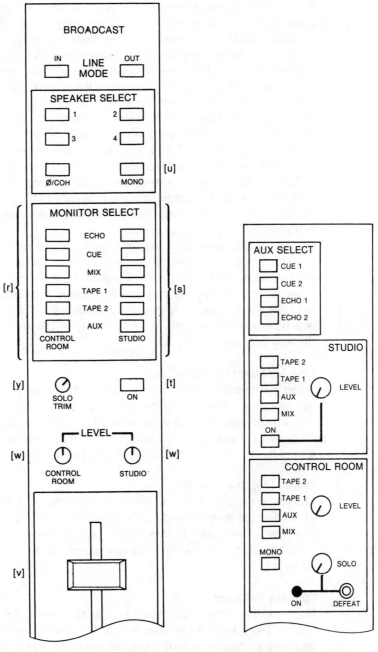

(A) Dual monitor selector matrixes for
the control room and studio monitor
systems.

(B) The auxiliary select matrix preselects
the signal that will be monitored when
the aux button in the studio or control
room matrix section is pressed.

Figure 12-22. Master monitor module in an inline console.

the monitor system. During playback only, the same switch position by default routes all tape track outputs and no summing buses to the monitor.

Although the switch positions just described work well for routine recording work, it should be noted that a track-summing bus output is *not* heard unless the equivalent track is in the record mode. This is convenient when punching in and out of a previously recorded track, since it lets the engineer hear the old, then the new, program as the recorder goes in and out of record. However, the arrangement is not very helpful at the start of a completely new recording on a fresh roll of blank tape. Since there are no previously recorded tracks, the engineer now hears nothing at all until the record button is pressed.

There are two means available to avoid this problem. The first is to select the all-input mode on the tape recorder itself. This simply routes all tape recorder inputs (that is, track-summing bus outputs) back to the console monitor system via the tape output lines. The all-input mode switch on a multitrack tape recorder was described in Chapter 10 (page 401).

As another alternative, the bus/tape switch on the appropriate I/O module(s) may be placed in the *bus* position instead. Now the monitor system is fed by the track-summing bus, regardless of the mode of the tape recorder. This means, however, that the monitor system will continue to be fed from the track-summing bus even during a playback of the multitrack tape. Therefore the equivalent track, now recorded on tape, will not be heard unless the bus/tape switch is returned to the *tape* position.

Line In/Line Out Select

As an additional monitor control, some console monitor sections provide a *line in/line out* function, whose purpose is to switch all I/O modules between tape (line in) and bus (line out) monitoring. On consoles so equipped, a *reverse* switch on each I/O module may be enabled, in which case the mode of that module is always the reverse of the one selected by the line in/out switch.

Studio Monitor On/Off

The studio section of the master monitor module also includes an *on/off* switch [t], so that the monitor feed can be disabled to prevent acoustic feedback during recording. The talkback feed to the studio monitor system is after the on/off switch, so that control-room-to-studio communication is not disabled by the on/off switch.

Speaker Selectors

Most modern control rooms provide at least two sets of monitor speakers, usually a large pair permanently mounted at some distance from the console, and a smaller pair placed near the console for close-field monitoring (see Chapter 6, page 244). The console monitor module may contain a set of two or more switches to select the desired speaker pair, as shown on the monitor module in Figure 12-21A.

Mono Monitor Mode

The control room section provides a *mono* switch [u] which combines the left and right monitor outputs and feeds the resultant mono signal to the monitor system.

This allows the engineer to check the stereo output for general mono compatibility and, if necessary, to compensate for any mono-related problems, such as center-channel build-ups, phase cancellations, etc.

Phase/Coherence Check

To quickly double-check mono compatibility, some consoles provide an additional control, such as the *phase/coherence* switch seen in the Speaker Select section at [u] in Figure 12-22A. When the switch is depressed, the polarity of the left monitor feed is reversed prior to combination with the right monitor feed. As a result, center channel images should be severely attenuated and the overall sound quality should suffer by comparison to the normal mono mode described before. However, if the phase/coherence check reveals an improved mono signal, then there is a mono-compatibility problem elsewhere in the signal path which should be traced and corrected.

Speaker Muting

A pair of *mute* switches may be provided to mute either the left or right speaker.

Monitor and Mixdown Level

The *stereo master fader* [v] is a single slide fader used to adjust the output levels from the mixdown/monitor buses before these signals are sent to the two-track tape recorder and to the monitor system.

The final step in the signal path to the control room and studio monitor amplifiers is the *monitor level* potentiometer [w], one each for the studio and the control room. (At this late stage, the reader who requires an explanation of either should perhaps consider some other line of work.)

Monitor Override Modes

As described earlier in the chapter, various functions may temporarily override the monitor system for various purposes, for example, channel or other solo modes, pre-fade listen, and talkback-to-studio. In each case, pressing a console control button routes a signal to the appropriate destination, and simultaneously mutes the normal signal at that location.

Solo Mode and Level Control

When any solo button (Figure 12-17) is depressed, the appropriate signal is routed to the solo bus, as described earlier in this chapter (page 494). At the same time, the normal feed to the monitor systems is replaced by the solo bus feeds, as shown by the solo mode switch [x] in Figure 12-19. Note that a separate *solo level* potentiometer [y] is used to adjust the solo level as required.

Prefader Listen

The PFL bus (also in Figure 12-17) may be routed directly to the solo bus, in which case the two functions are identical and the PFL signal is treated as any other solo signal. However, if the PFL system is routed to a separate monitor device, then depressing the PFL button has no effect on the normal monitor system.

Optional press-to-talk microphones in the studio are sometimes incorporated into the PFL system. In this case, the button on the microphone activates the PFL monitor in the control room so that someone in the studio can talk to the control room independently of the recording microphone setup. By sending this signal to the PFL monitor, a comment from, say, the conductor out in the studio may be heard without disrupting the normal monitor system.

Talkback

The talkback system described earlier in the chapter (page 504) must also interrupt the normal monitor signal paths, as shown by the talkback mode switch [z] in Figure 12-19. Note that the talkback signal simultaneously replaces the studio speaker feed when the studio or tape buttons are pressed, but does not do so when the podium button is used instead. To prevent acoustic feedback, the control room monitor system is also muted while the talkback microphone is active.

Console Patch Points

A *patch point* is a location in the signal path at which normal signal flow may be modified via a set of input and output jacks. The output jack occurs first in the signal path, and at this point the signal may be routed to another destination by inserting a patch cord into the jack. Depending on the way the output jack is wired, the insertion may or may not interrupt the normal signal flow, as shown by the detail drawing in Figure 12-23. In most cases, the output jack is wired so that normal signal flow is maintained; thus the output patch point becomes a junction rather than a switch.

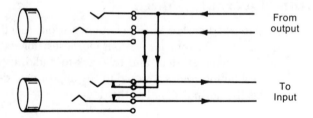

(A) An output jack wired so that insertion of a patch cord does not interrupt the normal signal flow.

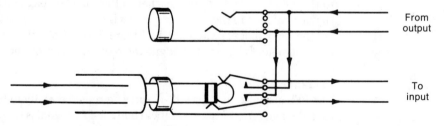

(B) An output jack wired so that insertion of a patch cord does interrupt the normal signal flow.

Figure 12-23. Patch points and patch cords.

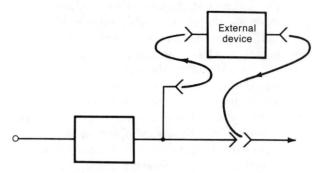

(C) An external device inserted in the signal path via patch cords.

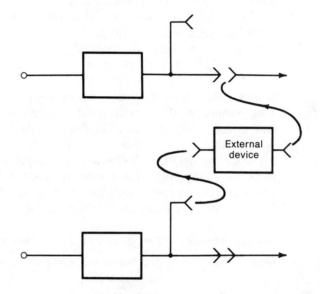

(D) The output of the external device is routed to a different signal path.

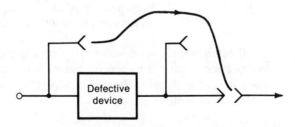

(E) Use of a patch cord to route a signal around a defective device in the signal path.

Figure 12-23 *(continued)*

By contrast, the immediately following input jack is wired so that an insertion does interrupt the normal signal flow through the patch point. Thus when a patch cord is inserted in an input jack, the new signal takes the place of the normal signal, which is interrupted by the insertion of the patch cord.

In addition to the patch points just described, additional jack pairs are assigned to each external signal processing device. To insert any such device in the desired signal path, a pair of patch cords is used to connect the signal path output jack to the device input, and the device output back to the signal path input, as also shown in Figure 12-23. As an alternative, the signal processor output might be returned to an input patch point located elsewhere in the console signal path, as also shown in the figure.

For convenience, all patch points are physically brought to a central *patch bay* such as that shown in Figure 12-24.

The patch bay is also helpful in troubleshooting work. For example, if an incoming signal seems to be getting lost somewhere within the depths of the console, there's always the possibility that some device in the signal path is defective. As a quick check, reroute the signal to some other channel, using a patch cord inserted at the first set of patch points in the signal path. If the signal is now heard, then the faulty device (or perhaps an overlooked switch) lies somewhere beyond the patch point. Repeat the procedure at succeeding points until doing so has no effect. The defective device is now somewhere before the patch point.

Once the defective device has been isolated, a patch cord can be used to route the signal around the device, as shown in Figure 12-23, or a replacement device can be inserted in the signal path, again via the patch bay.

The patch bay may also provide jacks for the following purposes.

Polarity reversal	Two jacks with a wired polarity reversal between them
Mult	A group of three or more jacks wired in common so that one signal may be routed to the mult for splitting to two or more destinations
Tie lines	Jacks connected by lines to another jack bay located elsewhere, used for sending and receiving signals from another studio or other location

If patch points are provided in the microphone input lines, make sure that the microphone section is turned off before inserting a patch cord. Due to the very low level of the signal in the microphone line, the noise of patching in or out will otherwise be quite loud.

Summary

As a final review of the components of the inline console described in this chapter, Figures 12-25 and 12-26 (pages 514–517) show the signal flow block diagrams for a currently available recording studio console. The console itself is shown in Figures 12-27 and 12-28 (pages 518–519).

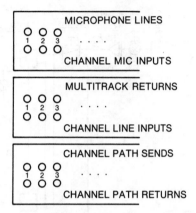

Figure 12-24. The patch bay.

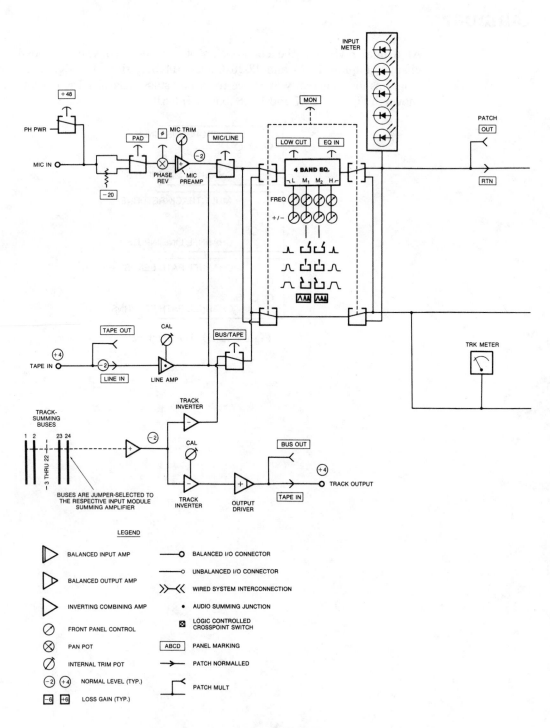

Figure 12-25. Signal flow block diagram for the Input/Output module
in an inline console. *(Series 34C Audio Console courtesy
Sound Workshop Professional Audio Products, Inc.)*

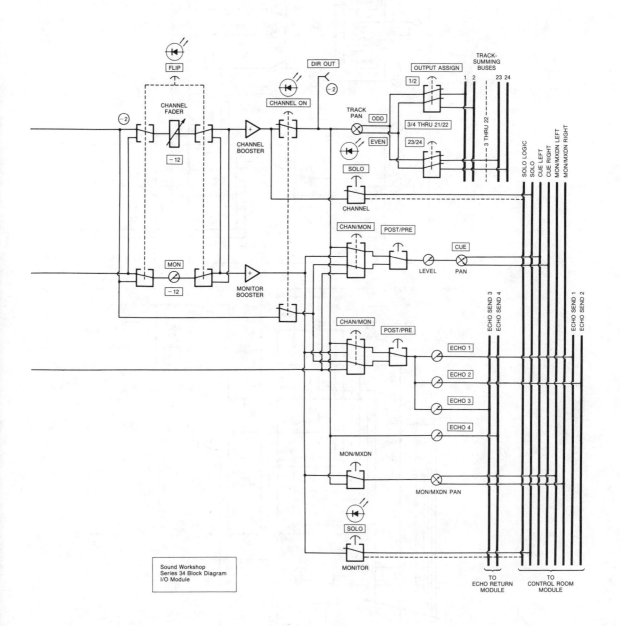

Figure 12-25 *(continued)*

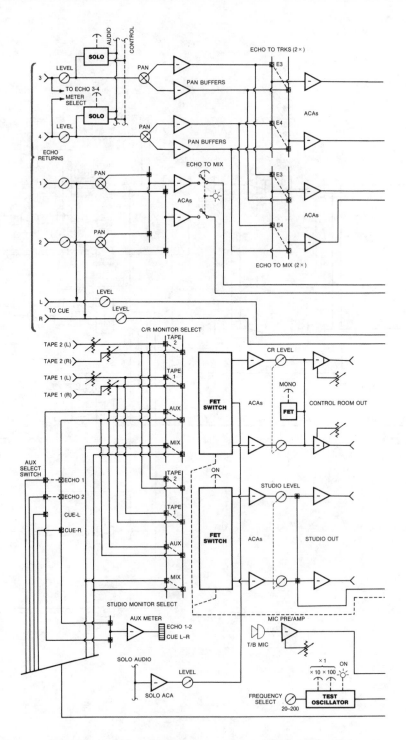

Figure 12-26. Signal flow block diagram for the Master Module section of a representative inline console. *(Series 34C Audio Console courtesy Sound Workshop Professional Audio Products, Inc.)*

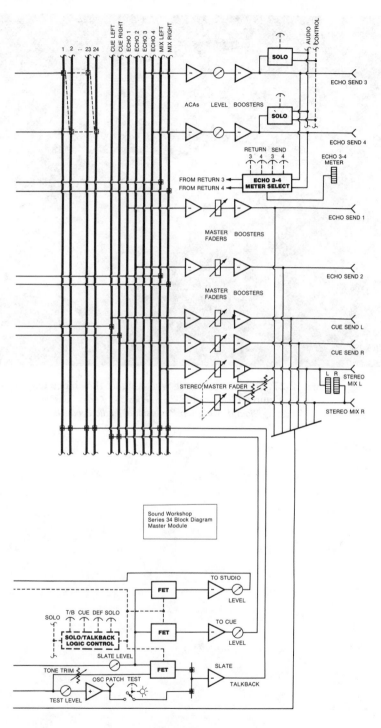

Figure 12-26 *(continued)*

Figure 12-27. The inline console whose signal flow block diagrams are seen in Figures 12-25 and 12-26. *(Series 34C Audio Console courtesy Sound Workshop Professional Audio Products, Inc.)*

Figure 12-28. Detail view of inline console, showing I/O modules 19-24 and master section followed by additional I/O modules 25-26. The detail drawings shown in Figures 12-5B, 12-13B, and 12-22B are based on the I/O module and master section seen here. *(Series 34C Audio Console courtesy Sound Workshop Professional Audio Products, Inc.)*

A SMPTE Time Code

American National Standard for Television—Time and Control Code—Video and Audio Tape for 525-line/60-field Systems[1]

CAUTION NOTICE: This American National Standard may be revised or withdrawn at any time. The procedures of the American National Standards Institute require that action be taken to reaffirm, or withdraw this standard no later than five years from the date of publication. Purchasers of American National Standards may receive current information on all standards by calling or writing the American National Standards Institute.

1. Scope

1.1 The first part of this standard specifies a format and modulation method for a digital code to be recorded on a longitudinal track of video and audio magnetic tape recorders. The code is to be used for timing and control purposes.

1.2 The second part specifies the digital format to be inserted into the television signal vertical interval to be used for timing and control purposes in video magnetic tape recorders. This part also specifies the location of the code within the television baseband signal and its relationship to other components of the television signal and to the longitudinal track code described in the first part of this standard.

---

[1]Approved January 29, 1986. Sponsor: Society of Motion Picture and Television Engineers. Copyright 1986 by the Society of Motion Picture and Television Engineers. Reprinted by permission.

2. Referenced Standards

This standard is intended for use in conjunction with the following standards:

EIA Industrial Electronics Tentative Standard No. 1, Color Television Studio Picture Line Amplifier Output Drawing

International Standard ISO 646-1983, Information Processing—ISO 7-Bit Coded Character Set for Information Interchange

International Standard ISO 2022-1982, Information Processing—ISO 7-Bit and 8-Bit Coded Character Sets—Code Extension Techniques

3. Longitudinal Track Application

3.1 Modulation Method. The modulation method shall be such that a transition occurs at the beginning of every bit period. "One" is represented by a second transition one-half a bit period from the start of the bit. "Zero" is represented when there is no transition within the bit period (See Figure A-1).

3.2 Code Format

3.2.1 Frame Make-up. Each television frame shall be identified by a unique and complete address. A frame consists of two television fields or 525 horizontal lines. The frames shall be numbered successively 0 through 29, except as noted in 5.2.2 (Drop Frame). If color frame identification in the code is required, the even units of frame numbers shall identify Frame A and odd units of frame numbers shall identify Frame B, as defined by EIA Tentative Standard No. 1.

3.2.2 Frame Address. Each address shall consist of 80 bits numbered 0 through 79.

3.2.2.1 Boundaries of Address. The address shall start at the clock edge before the first address bit (bit 0). The bits shall be evenly spaced throughout the address period, and shall occupy fully the address period which is one frame. Consequently, the bit rate shall be 80 times the frame rate in frames per second. (See 3.2.1 for definition of a television frame.)

3.2.2.2 Start of Address. The start of the address shall occur at the beginning of line 5 in fields I and III, as defined in EIA Tentative Standard No. 1. The tolerance shall be ±1 line.

3.3 Longitudinal Recorder Input Waveform Characteristics (See Figure A-1)

3.3.1 Rise Time. The rise and fall times of the clock and "one" transitions of the code pulse train shall be 25 ±5 microseconds, measured between the 10 and 90 percent amplitude points on the waveform.

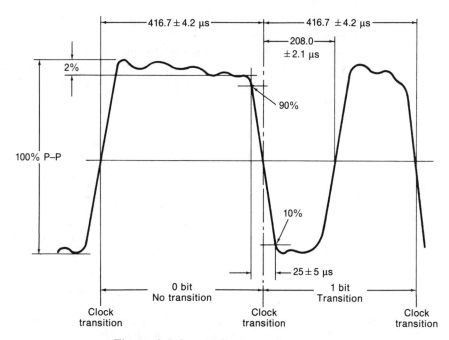

Figure A-1. Longitudinal recorder waveform.

3.3.2 Amplitude Distortion. Amplitude distortion, such as overshoot, undershoot, and tilt, shall be limited to 2 percent of the peak-to-peak amplitude of the code waveform.

3.3.3 Time of Transitions. The time between clock transitions shall not vary more than 1 percent of the average clock period measured over at least one frame. The "one" transition shall occur halfway between two clock transitions within 0.5 percent of one clock period. Measurements of these timings shall be made at half-amplitude points on the waveform.

3.4 Use of Binary Groups

The binary groups are intended for storage of data by the users, and the 32 bits within the 8 groups may be assigned in any manner without restriction if the character set used for the data insertion is not specified and the binary group flag bits 43 and 59 are both zero.

If an 8-bit character set is used, the binary group flag bits 43 and 59 shall be set according to the following truth table:

	Bit 43	Bit 59
Character set not specified	0	0
Eight-bit character set	1	0
Unassigned	0	1
Unassigned	1	1

Unassigned states of the truth table cannot be used and their assignment is reserved to the SMPTE.

3.4.1 If an 8-bit character set conforming to ISO 646-1983 and ISO 2022-1982 is signaled by the binary group flag bits 43 and 59, the characters should be inserted in accordance with Figure A-2. Information carried by the user-bits is not specified.

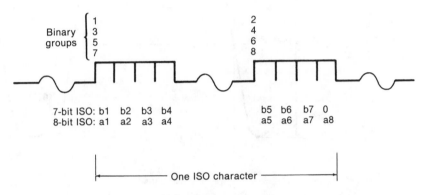

Figure A-2. Use of binary groups to describe ISO characters coded with 7 or 8 bits.

3.5 Assigned and Unassigned Address Bits

Six bits are reserved within the address groups: 4 for identifying operational modes, 1 for biphase correction, and 1 unassigned bit reserved for future assignment and defined as zero until further specified by the SMPTE.

Bit 10—Drop Frame Flag. If certain numbers are being dropped to resolve the difference between real time and color time, as defined in 5.2.2, a "1" shall be recorded.

Bit 11—Color Frame Flag. If color frame identification has been intentionally applied, as defined in 3.2.1, a "1" shall be recorded.

Bit 27—"Bi-phase Mark" Phase Correction. This bit shall be put in a state so that every 80-bit word will contain an even number of logical zeroes. This requirement results in the following truth table for bit 27:

Number of Logical Zeroes in Bits 0 to 63 (27 exclusive)	Bit 27
Odd	1
Even	0

Bits 43 and 59—Binary Group Flag Bits. These two bits shall be set in accordance with the truth table as specified in 3.4.

Bit 58—Unassigned Address. "0" until assigned by SMPTE.

The bits shall be assigned as shown in Figure A-3 and described below:

0–3	Units of frames
4–7	First binary group
8–9	Tens of frames
10	Drop frame flag (see 3.5)
11	Color frame flag (see 3.5)
12–15	Second binary group
16–19	Units of seconds
20–23	Third binary group
24–26	Tens of seconds
27	Bi-phase mark phase correction bit (see 3.5)
28–31	Fourth binary group
32–35	Units of minutes
36–39	Fifth binary group
40–42	Tens of minutes
43	Binary group flag bit (see 3.4)
44–47	Sixth binary group
48–51	Units of hours
52–55	Seventh binary group
56–57	Tens of hours
58	Unassigned address bit (0 until assigned by the SMPTE)
59	Binary group flag bit (see 3.4)
60–63	Eighth binary group
64–79	Synchronizing word
64–65	Fixed zero
66–77	Fixed one
78	Fixed zero
79	Fixed one

4. Vertical Interval Application

4.1 Modulation Method. The modulation method shall be such that each state of the signal corresponds to a binary state and a transition occurs only when there is a change in the data contained in adjacent bit cells from a "1" to "0" or "0" to "1." No transitions shall occur when adjacent bits contain the same data. Synchronization bit pairs shall be inserted as required in 4.2.3 (modified NRZ).

4.2 Code Format

4.2.1 Make-up. The frames shall be numbered successively 0 through 29, except as noted in 5.2.2 (Drop Frame), with field identification as specified in 4.4.

The address recorded in each field shall relate directly to the field/frame identification as set forth in EIA Tentative Standard No. 1, and shall be related to the longitudinal code as shown in Figure A-4.

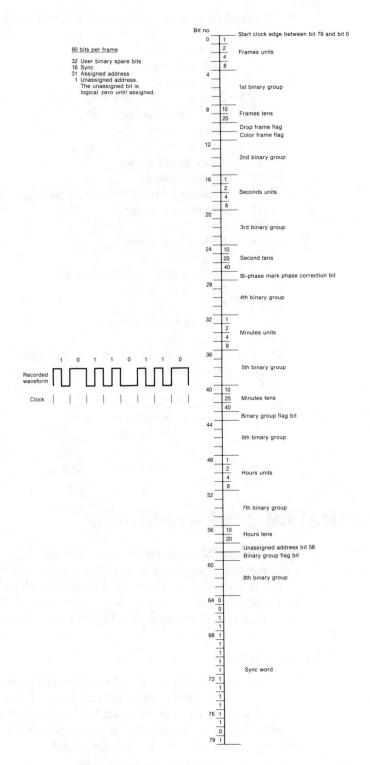

Figure A-3. Longitudinal bit assignment.

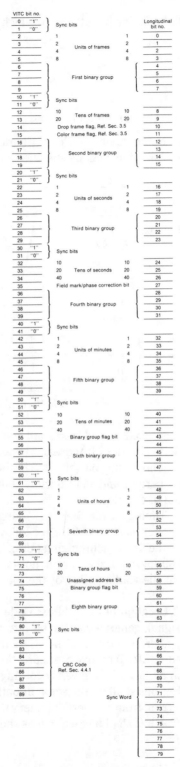

Figure A-4. Relationship of vertical interval code to longitudinal code.

Bit Rate. The bit rate, F_e, at which the address is generated shall be as follows:

$$F_e = F_h \times \frac{455}{4} \pm 200 \text{ Hz}$$

where

F_h is the horizontal line rate.

Recorder Input Waveform Characteristics. The baseband video signal after address insertion shall be specified as shown in Figure A-5.

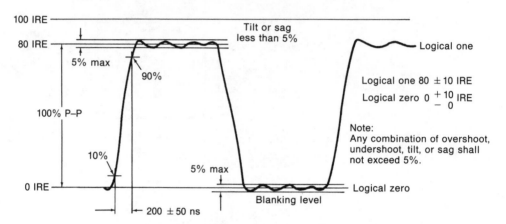

Figure A-5. Vertical interval recorder waveform.

4.2.2 Address. Each address shall consist of 90 bits numbered 0 through 89.

4.2.2.1 Boundaries of Address. The address shall start at the leading edge of the first synchronizing bit (bit 0). The bits shall be evenly spaced throughout the address period, and shall occupy fully the address period which is 50.286 μsec nominal in duration.

4.2.2.2 Timing of the Start of Address. The half-amplitude point of bit 0 shall occur not earlier than 10.0 μsec following the half-amplitude point of the leading edge of the line synchronizing pulse. The half-amplitude point of the trailing edge of bit 89 logical 1 shall occur not later than 2.1 μsec before the half-amplitude point of the leading edge of the following line synchronizing pulse (see Figure A-6).

4.2.2.3 Location of the Address Code Signal in the Vertical Interval. The address code signal, generated at the bit rate F_e, shall be inserted in both fields. Insertion of the address code shall not be earlier than line 10 or later than line 20, as defined in EIA Tentative Standard No. 1. The address code shall be on the same lines in all fields for a given recording.

User bits shall be the same in both fields of a frame to avoid confusion when transferring from the vertical interval to the longitudinal code.

4.2.3 The bits shall be assigned as shown in Figure A-6.

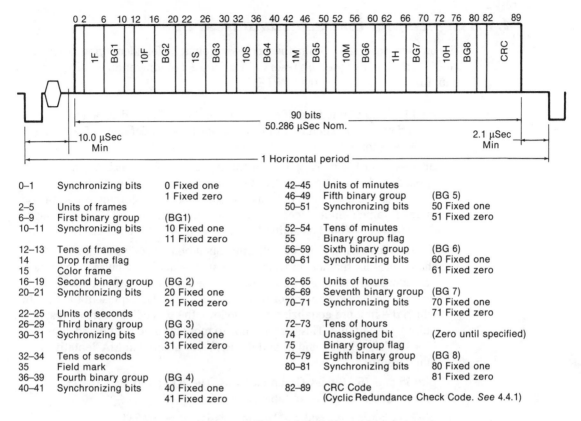

0–1	Synchronizing bits	0 Fixed one
		1 Fixed zero
2–5	Units of frames	
6–9	First binary group	(BG1)
10–11	Synchronizing bits	10 Fixed one
		11 Fixed zero
12–13	Tens of frames	
14	Drop frame flag	
15	Color frame	
16–19	Second binary group	(BG 2)
20–21	Synchronizing bits	20 Fixed one
		21 Fixed zero
22–25	Units of seconds	
26–29	Third binary group	(BG 3)
30–31	Sychronizing bits	30 Fixed one
		31 Fixed zero
32–34	Tens of seconds	
35	Field mark	
36–39	Fourth binary group	(BG 4)
40–41	Synchronizing bits	40 Fixed one
		41 Fixed zero
42–45	Units of minutes	
46–49	Fifth binary group	(BG 5)
50–51	Synchronizing bits	50 Fixed one
		51 Fixed zero
52–54	Tens of minutes	
55	Binary group flag	
56–59	Sixth binary group	(BG 6)
60–61	Synchronizing bits	60 Fixed one
		61 Fixed zero
62–65	Units of hours	
66–69	Seventh binary group	(BG 7)
70–71	Synchronizing bits	70 Fixed one
		71 Fixed zero
72–73	Tens of hours	
74	Unassigned bit	(Zero until specified)
75	Binary group flag	
76–79	Eighth binary group	(BG 8)
80–81	Synchronizing bits	80 Fixed one
		81 Fixed zero
82–89	CRC Code	
	(Cyclic Redundancy Check Code. See 4.4.1)	

Figure A-6. Address bit assignment.

4.3 Use of Binary Groups

The binary groups are intended for storage of data by the users, and the 32 bits within the 8 groups may be assigned in any manner without restriction if the character set used for the data insertion is not specified and the binary group flag bits 55 and 75 are both zero.

If an 8-bit character set is used, the binary group flag bits 55 and 75 shall be set according to the following truth table.

	Bit 55	Bit 75
Character set not specified	0	0
Eight-bit character set	1	0
Unassigned	0	1
Unassigned	1	1

Unassigned states of the truth table cannot be used and their assignment is reserved to the SMPTE.

4.3.1 If an 8-bit character set conforming to ISO 646-1983 and ISO 2022-1982 is signalled by the binary group flag bits 55 and 75, the characters should be inserted in accordance with Figure A-2. Information carried by the user-bits is not specified.

4.4 Assigned and Unassigned Address Bits

Six bits are reserved within the address groups: 5 for identifying operational modes, and 1 unassigned bit reserved for future assignment and defined as zero until further specified by the SMPTE.

Bit 14—Drop Frame Flag. If certain numbers are being dropped to resolve the difference between real time and color time, as defined in 5.2.2, a "1" shall be recorded.

Bit 15—Color Frame Flag. If color frame identification has been intentionally applied, a "1" shall be recorded. Color frame identification of the code is defined as the even units of frame numbers identifying frame A and the odd units of frame numbers identifying frame B. Frames A and B correspond to color frames A and B as defined by EIA Tentative Standard No. 1.

Bit 35—Field Mark. Field identification shall be recorded as follows: A "0" shall represent the field in which the first pre-equalizing pulse follows the preceding horizontal sync pulse by a whole line. This corresponds to monochrome field I and color field I or III. A "1" shall represent the field in which the first pre-equalizing pulse follows the preceding horizontal sync pulse by a half line. This corresponds to monochrome field II and color field II or IV. Color fields I and III and II and IV are defined in EIA Tentative Standard No. 1.

Bits 55 and 75—Binary Group Flag Bits. These two bits shall be set in accordance with the truth table as specified in 4.3.

Bit 74—Unassigned Address. "0" until assigned by SMPTE.

4.4.1 Cyclic Redundancy Check Code. Eight bits, 82 to 89, are set aside at the end of the code to provide for error detection by checking for cyclic redundancy. The generating polynomial of the cyclic redundancy check, $G(X)$, will be applied to all bits from 0 to 81 inclusive and shall be as follows:

$$G(X) = X^8 + 1$$

The received data divided by the generating polynomial shall result in a remainder of "all zeroes" when no error exists in the received data.

5. Time Discrepancies

5.1 Definitions of Real Time and Color Time

5.1.1 One-second real time is defined as the time elapsed during the scanning of 60 fields (or any multiple thereof) in an ideal television system at a vertical field rate of exactly 60 fields per second.

5.1.2 One-second color time is defined as the time elapsed during the scanning of 60 fields per second.

5.2. Because the vertical field rate of a color signal is approximately 59.94 fields per second, straightforward counting at 30 frames per second (60 fields per second) will yield an error of $+108$ frames ($+216$ fields), approximately equivalent to $+3.6$ seconds timing error, in one hour of running time. For correction of this time discrepancy, two methods of operation are allowed:

5.2.1 Nondrop Frame—Uncompensated Mode. During a continuous recording, no numbers shall be omitted from the chain of addresses. Each address shall be increased by 1 frame over the frame number immediately preceding it. When this mode is used, the drop-frame flag of each address shall be a "0" as specified in 3.5 and 4.4.

5.2.2 Drop Frame—Compensated Mode. To resolve the color time error, the first two frame numbers (0, 1) at the start of each minute, except minutes 0, 10, 20, 30, 40, and 50, shall be omitted from the count. When this mode is used, the drop-frame flag of each address shall be a "1" as specified in 3.5 and 4.4.

6. Structure of the Address Bits

6.1 The basic structure of the address is based upon the Binary Coded Decimal (BCD) system. Because the count in some cases does not rise to 9, conservation of bits is achieved because 4 bits are not needed as in an ordinary BCD code. (The 24-hour clock system is used; 2:00 PM is 1400 hours.)

6.2 Longitudinal Track and Vertical Interval Applications

Assignment of bits and binary coded decimal arrangements for both applications are shown in the following table:

Longitudinal Track and Vertical Interval Structure

Structural Member	Assignment of Bits		Binary Coded Decimal (BCD)		
	Longitudinal	VIT	No. of Bits	Arrangement	Count
Units frames	0–3	2–5	4	1 2 4 8	0–9
Tens frames	8–9	12–13	2	1 2	0–2
Units seconds	16–19	22–25	4	1 2 4 8	0–9
Tens seconds	24–26	32–34	3	1 2 4	0–5
Units minutes	32–35	42–45	4	1 2 4 8	0–9
Tens minutes	40–42	52–54	3	1 2 4	0–5
Units hours	48–51	62–65	4	1 2 4 8	0–9
Tens hours	56–57	72–73	2	1 2	0–2

B Glossary

The glossary contains concise definitions of various terms found in the text. In addition, a few terms not discussed in the book are given brief definitions here. SMPTE references in parentheses refer to the appropriate section of the SMPTE Time Code, which appears in Appendix A.

A-B microphone pair A pair of spaced microphones used for a stereo pickup.

Absorption coefficient At any surface, the ratio of absorbed to incident sound energy (0 = a perfect reflector, 1 = a perfect absorber).

Acicular Needle-shaped, as in magnetic tape oxide particles.

Acoustic center In a loudspeaker, that point from which its spherical output waveform appears to originate.

Acoustic suspension system A sealed speaker enclosure, in which the air trapped inside acts as an acoustic stiffness against the speaker cone.

Active bias *See* Bias, active.

Active network Any network whose circuit elements include active components; transistors, vacuum tubes, etc.

AES recommended practice The recommendation of the AES (Audio Engineering Society) for tape recorder equalization at 30 in/s (76 cm/s).

A-format outputs The four subcardioid outputs of the Soundfield microphone (q.v.).

Alignment Any mechanical or electronic adjustment to a system to bring it into conformance with some standard set of values.

Ambient noise The prevailing sound field in a room in the absence of an applied signal from a loudspeaker, musical instrument, or other sound source.

Ambisonic surround sound system A surround sound system developed in conjunction with the Soundfield microphone (q.v.).

Anechoic chamber A room with highly absorptive surface treatments, such that the sound field contains no reflected energy (an·echoic = without echoes).

Angle of incidence At a reflective surface, the angle between an arriving wave and a line drawn perpendicular to the surface.

Attack time In a compressor or expander, the interval during which the output level moves from its prethreshold level to whatever gain is dictated by the compression/expansion ratio.

Azimuth Pertaining to the angular alignment of the gap width of a tape head along the vertical axis; that is, along a line parallel to the width of the tape.

Back coating On magnetic recording tape, a special coating applied to the side opposite the magnetic oxide, to improve the tape's winding characteristics and reduce static electricity.

Back-electret An electret capacitor microphone in which the electret substance is applied to the backplate of the capacitor diaphragm assembly.

Baffle A panel or other surface whose purpose is to prevent the transmission of sound.

Bandpass filter A filter designed to pass a band of frequencies with little or no attenuation. Frequencies below and above the band are attenuated.

Bandstop filter A filter designed to attenuate a band of frequencies, while passing frequencies on either side of the band.

Bandwidth The difference between the lower, f_1, and the upper, f_2, cutoff frequencies. Thus, an equalizer with cutoff frequencies of 200 and 2,000 Hz has a bandwidth of 1,800 Hz.

Base, magnetic tape A flexible surface (usually polyester) upon which a magnetic coating is applied to form magnetic recording tape.

B-format outputs The four matrixed signals (one omnidirectional, three bidirectional) derived from the Soundfield microphone A-format outputs and used to create the desired sound field.

B-H curve The magnetic transfer characteristic of magnetic recording tape or any other magnetic substance.

Bias A constant AC (formerly, DC) voltage applied to a system to shift the transfer characteristic into a linear operating range. Also called *static bias*, to distinguish it from active bias. *See* Bias, active.

Bias, active The actual momentary bias level that is a function of both the applied (static) bias and the biasing effects of the high-frequency program content.

Bidirectional microphone A microphone that is equally sensitive to sounds arriving from the front and back, and insensitive to sounds arriving from the sides. A figure-8 microphone.

Bilinear characteristic A system with constant gain characteristics both below and above a compression or expansion range.

Bilinear compander A compressor/expander system in which linear gain segments appear on either side of the input range segment which is subject to compression/expansion.

Binary group flag bits SMPTE Time Code bits 43 and 59, set to define usage of binary groups (SMPTE 3.4).

Binaural Pertaining to two ears, or to a recording system in which a dummy head is used with a microphone placed at each ear position.

Binder The nonmagnetic substance in which magnetic tape oxide particles are suspended to form the magnetic coating that is applied to the tape base. *See also* Base.

Bi-phase mark phase correction bit SMPTE Time Code bit 27, set to 1 or 0 as required so that every 80-bit word will have an even number of logical zeros (SMPTE 3.5).

Bi-phase modulation A rectangular waveform whose polarity alternates between positive and negative maxima, as in a digital bit stream of 1s and 0s. Used to describe the waveshape of SMPTE Time Code.

Bi-Radial horn A horn in which both the vertical and horizontal surfaces flare outward, though usually at different rates. *See also* Radial horn.

Blend control *See* Width control.

Blumlein microphone (or Blumlein pair) A coincident pair of bidirectional capsules with an included angle of 90 degrees. So called after Alan Dower Blumlein.

Bounce mode *See* Dump mode.

Bouncing tracks On a multitrack tape recorder, the technique of transferring one or more previously recorded tracks onto a new track. Usually, several old tracks are combined and then recorded on a single new track.

Boundary layer The region in the immediate vicinity of a surface in which the phase shift between a direct and a reflected-path wave is negligible within the audio frequency spectrum of interest. The Pressure Zone.

Boundary layer microphone A microphone designed or placed so that its diaphragm is very close to a large surface boundary (the floor, for example).

"Breathing" The characteristic sound of a system in which sudden gain changes produce a rising/falling background noise level. Also called "pumping."

Broadcast mode In a console, the mode in which an incoming signal is routed to both the channel and monitor paths, so that controls in either path have no effect on the other path.

Bus Any conductor or terminal to which multiple input signals may be routed and combined to form a single output signal. Often misspelled as "buss."

Bus selector matrix In any console, a group of push buttons used to select the track-summing bus, or buses, to which the incoming signal is to be routed.

Calibration tape A tape recorded under laboratory conditions which contains a series of test tones recorded at a known level.

Capacitor loudspeaker *See* Electrostatic loudspeaker.

Capacitor microphone A microphone whose diaphragm is one plate of a capacitor. Formerly referred to as a condenser microphone.

Capstan On a tape recorder, the rotating shaft used in conjunction with a pressure roller (q.v.) to pull tape across the heads.

Capstan idler A pressure roller.

Cardioid microphone   A unidirectional microphone with 6 dB of attenuation at the sides ($\pm 90°$) and a null at 180 degrees. So called due to the cardioid-like shape of its polar pattern.

Cartesian coordinate system   A two-dimensional graphing system in which one variable is plotted along the horizontal (x) axis, and the other along the vertical (y) axis. *See also* Polar coordinate system.

Center frequency   The geometric mean between cutoff frequencies. Thus, the center frequency, f_c, in the bandwidth between 100 and 1,000 Hz is given as

$$f_c = [f_1(f_2)]^{1/2} = [100(1,000)]^{1/2} = 316.23 \text{ Hz}$$

cgs (centimeter-gram-second) system   The metric system of measurement in which the indicated quantities are the fundamental units.

Channel fader   The level control (usually, a slide fader) normally found in the channel path.

Channel path   In an inline console, the signal path from the mic or line input to the point at which the signal is combined with other incoming signals. *See also* Monitor path.

Chase mode   On a tape recorder, the mode in which the transport tracks the motion of another tape recorder.

Chorus effect   The combination of a direct sound and several delayed replicas to simulate the effect of a chorus.

Closed-back cabinet   A loudspeaker enclosure in which the speaker is mounted in the surface of an otherwise sealed enclosure; therefore, a sealed enclosure.

Closed-loop tape drive   In a tape recorder, a drive system in which the tape is mechanically isolated from both the supply and takeup reels by a dual capstan/pressure roller system.

Close-field monitor system   A pair of loudspeakers mounted close to the engineer's position in order to minimize the influence of the control room acoustics on the sound field at that position.

Coercivity (*H*)   A measure of the magnetic field strength required to return a magnetic material to a state of zero magnetization.

Coherence   The polarity relationship between two complex waveforms. If the waveforms are identical, coherence is 100%. With a polarity reversal in one line, coherence is zero. An "ideal" stereo signal will exhibit random coherence over time.

Coincident pair   A pair of microphones whose diaphragms lie on the same vertical axis, but are angled in different directions (0° and 90° for *M-S*, $\pm\theta$ for *X-Y*, where $\pm\theta$ is about 90–135°). *See also* Near-coincident pair.

Color frame flag   SMPTE Time Code address bit 11, used to indicate color-frame mode status (SMPTE 3.5).

Coloration   A distortion of the normal frequency response. *See also* Off-axis coloration.

Comb filter   Any device that produces a series of sharp attenuation notches in the output response that resemble the teeth of a comb.

Communications module   In some inline consoles, a module containing all controls related to communication (talkback, cue send, etc.).

Compander   A *com*pressor/*expand*er. A signal processing device that may be used for either compression or expansion. Generally used in reference to compression followed later in the signal chain by expansion, as in a studio noise reduction system.

Complementary signal processing Any signal processing in which the applied signal modification is followed by complementary (i.e., equal and opposite) processing later in the signal chain, as, for example, in tape pre/postemphasis and studio noise reduction systems. Double-ended signal processing. *See also* Single-ended signal processing.

Compression chamber The air cavity within a compression driver, bounded on one side by the driver diaphragm and on the other by a small opening to which a horn is attached.

Compression driver A loudspeaker driver in which the diaphragm radiates into a confined space (the compression chamber) with an opening smaller than the surface area of the diaphragm.

Compression ratio The ratio of the input to output dynamic range of a compressor or limiter.

Compressor A variable-gain amplifier in which the dynamic range of the output signal is less than that of the input signal. The compression range may vary from 1:1 to 10:1. *See also* Expander, Limiter.

Compressor, broadcast A high-frequency compressor designed to compensate for the high-frequency boost used in broadcast transmission.

Condenser microphone *See* Capacitor microphone.

Conical horn A horn whose cross-sectional area A_m, increases according to the equation $A_t(1 + mx/2)^2$, where A_t is the throat area, m is the

flaring constant, and x is the horn length. So called because the horn is cone-shaped.

Console The central system to which multiple input signals are routed for level control and signal processing, and for combination with other input signals and subsequent routing to a tape recorder, broadcast transmitter, or sound reinforcement system. A Mixer.

Consonance The degree of blending and fusion between two musical notes. *See also* Dissonance.

Continuous jam sync Procedure in which a time code generator is continuously jam-synced against an external time code signal.

Cosine (cos) For either acute angle in a right triangle, the ratio of the adjacent side to the hypotenuse.

Coverage angle The included angle between the points on either side of a loudspeaker axis at which the response is attenuated by 6 dB, with respect to the on-axis level.

Critical distance The distance from a sound source at which the direct and reverberant energy are equal.

Crossover frequency In a crossover network, the frequency at which the outputs of two adjacent filter networks are both attenuated by 3 dB.

Crossover network A filter network which divides the audio bandwidth into two or more frequency bands.

Cue system In a console, the controls used to route an incoming signal out to the studio headphone system. A foldback system.

Cutoff frequency 1. The frequency at which the output of a filter, loudspeaker, or other system is 3 dB below its maximum output. In the case of a bandpass or band-reject filter there are two cutoff frequencies, one at either end of the passband. Sometimes called the *cutoff point*. 2. The lower frequency limit of a loudspeaker.

Damping An absorption of energy, as for example in the leveling off of a response peak.

Decay At the cessation of a sound, the gradual attenuation of the sound field over time.

Decibel (dB) The unit used to express the ratio of a measured power, p, to a specified reference power, p_r. Thus, $L = 10 \log (p/p_r)$, where L = level, in dB. When the two powers are dissipated within the same resistance, $L = 20 \log (e/e_r)$, where e and e_r are voltages.

Decibel notation The decibel abbreviation (dB) is frequently followed by a letter to indicate the reference power or voltage. *dBm*: 1 mW; *dBu*: 0.775 volt; *dBv*: formerly used to define a zero reference level of 0.775 volt; *dBV*: 1 volt.

Decoding Any signal processing applied during playback as a complement to signal processing applied during recording (*See* Encoding). Noise reduction expansion.

Deemphasis *See* Postemphasis.

De-Esser A compressor with an equalizer in the side chain. The equalizer is set to boost frequencies in the sibilant range, thus causing additional compression in the presence of sibilant sounds.

Delay The time between the arrival of a direct sound and a discrete echo of that sound.

Difference pattern The resultant microphone polar pattern when the two outputs of an *M-S* microphone are subtracted. *See also* Sum pattern.

Diffraction A change in the direction of a sound wave as it passes over an obstacle in its path.

Diffraction horn A horn design in which sound waves leaving the horn mouth are diffracted around the mouth edges.

Diffuse sound field An environment in which sounds arrive at a fixed point, such as a microphone diaphragm, from every direction.

Digital equalizer An equalizer whose frequency-modification circuits operate in the digital domain.

Dipole, doublet In loudspeaker terminology, a device that exhibits opposite polarities at two points (e.g., the front and back of the diaphragm).

Direct output In a console, a direct line from a channel path to an output line, so that the channel signal may be routed directly to a track on the multitrack tape recorder.

Direct path The single straight-line path between a sound source and a listener or microphone.

Direct radiator A loudspeaker whose diaphragm is in direct contact with the surrounding air mass of the listening room.

Direct sound The sound that reaches the listener via a straight-line path from the sound source.

Directional characteristic A description of a microphone's output level as a function of the angle of the arriving sound.

Directional microphone Any microphone whose output level varies as a function of the angle of the arriving sound. Generally, a unidirectional microphone.

Directivity factor (DRF)—loudspeaker *See* Q, loudspeaker.

Directivity factor (DRF)—microphone The ratio of a microphone's response to two identical intensity levels, p_1 and p_2, where p_1 is a diffuse sound field of reference intensity and p_2 is the response created by an on-axis source of the same average intensity. DRF = 1/REE (random energy efficiency).

Directivity index (DI) In a loudspeaker, the ratio of its sound pressure level at a given angle to that of an omnidirectional loudspeaker.

Dissonance The degree of discord between two musical notes. *See also* Consonance.

Distance factor (DSF) Compared to an omnidirectional microphone, the relative distance at which a microphone maintains the same ratio of direct-to-diffuse sound pickup. DSF = (DRF)$^{1/2}$ (directivity factor).

Dolby tone, Dolby noise A distinctive tone or noise signal used as an identification/calibration signal by various Dolby noise reduction systems.

Domain, magnetic The smallest particle that can sustain permanent magnetization.

Double-ended noise reduction system Any noise reduction system in which a compressor is followed later in the signal chain by a complementary expander.

Double-ended signal processing *See* Complementary signal processing.

Doubling The combination of a single direct sound and one delayed replica to simulate the effect of two voices or instruments.

Driver In a loudspeaker, the voice coil to which a speaker diaphragm is attached, and the related magnetic assembly.

Drop-frame flag SMPTE Time Code address bit 10, used to indicate drop-frame status (SMPTE 3.5).

Drop-frame time code The elimination of two frame counts within each minute, except during the minutes beginning at 00, 10, 20, 30, 40 and 50. The resultant 108-frame loss compensates for the differing monochrome and color frame rates.

Dropout Any momentary signal attenuation that is a function of a disturbance in tape-to-head spacing.

"Dry" recording Any recording in which signal processing, especially echo and reverberation, is not applied to the recorded signal. The processing may, however, be heard over the studio monitor system. *See also* "Wet" Recording.

"Ducker" A voice-over compressor, used to "duck" the level of the background program. *See* Voice-over compression.

Dump mode In a console, the mode in which the outputs of a pan pot in the monitor path are routed to a track-summing bus pair. The bounce mode.

Dynamic complementary signal processor Any dynamic signal processor whose parameter settings are followed by a complementary (i.e., equal and opposite) processor later in the signal path, as, for example, a studio noise reduction system.

Dynamic loudspeaker or microphone Any loudspeaker or microphone whose output is a function of magnetic induction in a voice coil, ribbon, or other conductor moving within a permanent magnetic field.

Dynamic noise filter, Dynamic noise suppressor A lowpass and/or highpass filter set in which each cutoff frequency varies dynamically, in response to the frequency spectrum of the applied audio signal.

Dynamic pressure The rapid fluctuations in air pressure that occur as a function of a sound pressure wave. *See also* Static pressure.

Dynamic range The difference, in dB, between the lowest and highest level a system is capable of handling.

Dynamic signal processor Any signal processor whose parameter settings vary in response to the signal passing through the device, as for example, a compressor. *See also* Static signal processor.

Early reflections The first few reflected-path sounds that arrive at the listening position, usually containing a single reflection in each path.

Echo A single repetition of a sound, which arrives at the listener's location some time after the direct sound is heard.

Echo chamber A reverberation chamber (q.v.).

Echo cluster A sequence of closely spaced echoes, usually preceded and followed by a delay longer than that between the echoes in the cluster.

Echo module In some inline consoles, a separate module containing the master echo send and echo return controls.

Echo send, Effects send In a console, the controls used to route an incoming signal to an echo/reverberation system or to any other external signal processing system.

Efficiency The ratio of output energy to applied input energy.

Electret A dielectric substance that exhibits a continuing polarization after an electric field is applied and

then withdrawn. *See also* Back electret.

Electret microphone A capacitor microphone in which one plate is covered with an electret material.

Electrostatic loudspeaker A loudspeaker in which the diaphragm is one of the plates of a very large capacitor.

Elevated level calibration tape A calibration tape whose operating level is several dB above 185 nWb/m.

Encoding Any signal processing applied during recording which is to be followed by complementary processing during playback (*See* Decoding). Noise reduction compression.

Epsilon (ε) The numeric constant, 2.71828 ..., which is the base of the system of natural logarithms.

Equal loudness contour A curve which shows the actual sound pressure level versus frequency for all tones which the listener perceives to be reproduced at the same level as a 1,000 Hz reference level tone.

Equalization The process of modifying the frequency response of an audio signal.

Equalization, record and playback The equalization applied at the input and output of a magnetic tape recorder to compensate for the nonlinear transfer frequency characteristic of the magnetic tape. Pre- and postemphasis.

Equalizer The signal processing device used to modify the frequency response of an audio signal. So called because the first such devices were used to correct, or "equalize," the losses in a transmission line.

Equal-tempered scale The division of the octave into 12 semitones, each of which is $2^{1/12}$ times higher than the preceding tone.

Expander A variable-gain amplifier in which the dynamic range of the output signal is greater than that of the input signal. The expansion range may vary from 1:1 to 1:10 or more. *See also* Compressor, Limiter.

Expansion ratio The ratio of the input to output dynamic range of an expander.

Exponential horn A horn whose cross-sectional area increases at an exponential rate.

Far field The area beyond the near field (q.v.) boundary.

Figure-8 microphone A bidirectional microphone, so called because of the figure-8 shape of its polar pattern.

Filter Any network that attenuates a portion of the audio frequency spectrum.

Filter, *n*-order A filter whose circuit contains *n* reactive components.

Finishing point In a compressor, the above-threshold point at which compression action ceases.

Flanging The effect created when a signal is combined with a delayed replica of itself with the delay time varied continuously. So called because the effect was first created by applying holdback pressure to the flange of a tape recorder supply reel.

Flaring constant A constant ($m = 4\pi f_c/c$) used in various loudspeaker horn equations, where f_c is the horn cutoff frequency, c is the speed of sound.

Flat baffle A flat panel of finite dimension with a cutout into which a loudspeaker is placed.

Fletcher-Munson curve *See* Equal loudness contour.

Flow chart A diagram showing the signal flow paths through a console or other device, but not the specific electronic components (resistors, capacitors, etc.) within each path.

Flutter On a tape recorder, the high-frequency modulation of an audio signal due to speed irregularities in the transport system. *See also* Scrape flutter.

Flux (ϕ) The lines of force within a magnetic field. Magnetic flux.

Flux density (B) A measure of the number of lines of force per unit of area. An indication of a material's magnetic field strength.

Foldback system A cue system (q.v.)

Folded baffle A flat baffle in which the sides have been folded back to form an open-back cabinet for a loudspeaker.

Frame address bits The 80-bit word used by the SMPTE Time Code to define the address and other data for each frame (SMPTE 3.2).

Free field The field in which the inverse square law applies. It begins at the near field boundary and ends wherever the sound pressure level no longer falls off at 6 dB per doubling of distance.

Free field, Free space A space surrounding a sound source in which there are no physical obstructions in the path of the pressure wave radiating from the sound source.

Frequency (Hz) The number of repetitions of a periodic waveform per unit of time. Formerly expressed as cycles per second, now given in hertz (Hz).

Frequency response A graph of output level or sensitivity versus frequency.

Fringing   In a playback head, a low-frequency response boost, caused by picking up additional flux from the fringe areas on either side of the gap.

Front-to-total ratio (FTR)   A measurement of a microphone's ability to favor sounds originating in front of it, calculated by dividing its random energy in front (REF) by the total random energy efficiency (REE).

Full space, Free space   An obstruction-free environment in which a sound source can radiate into the full sphere surrounding it.

Function   The mathematical relationship between any two variables, in which the value of one depends on (is a *function* of) the other. Thus, if $y = 2x$, then y is a function of x. In general terms, such an equation may be symbolized as $y = f(x)$, where f = "a function of."

Function, trigonometric   A function in which the dependent variable is the sine, cosine, tangent, etc., of an angle.

Fundamental frequency   The lowest frequency at which a complex system vibrates. The lowest audible frequency in a complex tone.

Gain   An increase in signal level between the input and output of a device, usually expressed in decibels.

Gain before threshold   In a compressor, the amount that low-level signals are boosted before compression begins.

Gain, constant   In any signal processing device, a system gain that does not change as a function of input level or frequency, for example, a power amplifier.

Gain riding   The process of making continuous level adjustments ("riding

the gain") during the recording or mixing of a program.

Gain, unity   In any signal processing device, a condition in which the output level is equal to the input level. A gain of 0 dB.

Gap length   The dimension of a head gap measured in the direction of tape travel. (Note that gap length is less than gap width.)

Gap loss   In a magnetic tape playback head, an attenuation of output level as a function of gap length.

Gap scatter   A physical misalignment of the gaps within a multitrack tape head.

Gap width   The dimension of a head gap measured in the same direction across the head as tape width.

gauss (G)   The cgs unit for flux density.

Gobo   An acoustic barrier placed between a sound source and a microphone, or between two sound sources. Derivation uncertain (gobo = go-between?).

Golden section   A ratio of length:width:height of $(\sqrt{5} + 1):2:(\sqrt{5} - 1)$.

Graphic equalizer   A multiband equalizer whose level controls are a series of side-by-side vertical-motion slide faders, whose positions give a graphic visual indication of the device's frequency response.

Group fader   Any fader used to vary the level of a group of incoming signals.

Gyrator filter   An RC network that simulates the effect of an inductor.

Haas effect   The phenomenon noted when a sound source arrives from two locations, in which one sound is slightly delayed. Localization is toward the direction of the source that arrives first, but is biased by level difference and actual time delay. Named after Helmut Haas.

Half space The hemisphere into which an ideal sound source radiates when the source is placed against a flat surface.

Harmonic distortion The presence of a spurious harmonic of an applied fundamental frequency.

Harmonic series A frequency series consisting of a fundamental frequency, f, and a series of integer multiples, $2f$, $3f$, $4f$, ...

Harmonic structure The frequency and amplitude components of any complex waveform.

Head block On a tape recorder, the assembly containing the erase, record, and playback heads.

Head gap In a magnetic recording head, the space between the head's pole pieces.

Head, magnetic tape On a magnetic tape recorder, any of the transducers used to convert energy from electric to magnetic form, or vice versa. An erase, record, or playback head.

hertz (Hz) The unit for measuring frequency. Formerly, cycles-per-second.

Highpass filter A filter designed to pass high frequencies with little or no attenuation. A low-frequency filter.

Horn, indirect radiator An acoustic impedance-matching device inserted between a compression driver and the surrounding air mass in the listening room, so called because of its characteristic shape.

***HX, HX Pro* (Headroom Extension) system** A signal processing system in which the recordable dynamic range is increased through the use of a dynamic biasing system, in which

bias level varies according to program content. Dolby introduced the HX and Dolby/Bang & Olufsen introduced the HX Pro.

Hyperbolic horn A horn whose cross-sectional area, A_m, increases according to the equation $A_t(\cosh mx/2 + T \sinh mx/2)^2$, where A_t is the throat area, T and m are the shape and flaring constants, and x is the horn length.

Hypercardioid microphone A directional microphone with greater attenuation at the sides than a pure cardioid pattern, but with less attenuation at the rear (-12.04 dB at 90°, -6.02 dB at 180°). So called because its cosine (pressure gradient) component is above both the cardioid and the supercardioid.

Hysteresis loop A graph of retentivity versus coercivity.

Hysteresis synchronous motor A motor operating at a fixed speed determined by the line frequency and the number of poles in the motor.

Ideal sound source A dimensionless point suspended in space, from which sound energy may radiate spherically.

IEC recording characteristic A standard specifying the IEC (International Electrotechnical Commission) equivalent of the NAB Standard Reproducing Characteristic (q.v.).

Incidence, angle of At any surface, the angle between an arriving sound wave and a line drawn perpendicular to the surface.

Indirect radiator A speaker system in which the driver is indirectly coupled to the surrounding air mass, usually by a tapered horn assembly.

Infinite baffle A barrier with a path length around it of infinity. For example, a wall in which a loudspeaker is mounted.

Inline console A console in which all input, output, and monitor controls pertaining to a single track or channel are located in a single I/O module (q.v.).

Intensity *See* Sound intensity.

Interaural Pertaining to any comparison between an audio signal measured at one ear and the same signal measured at the other ear.

Inverse-square law Pertaining to any condition in which the magnitude of a physical quantity follows an *inverse* relationship to the *square* of distance.

I/O (Input/output) module In an inline console, the module in which all input, output, and monitor controls for a single track or channel are located.

Jam sync The mode in which a time code reader/generator is set, or "jammed," against an external time code, so that its output code is identical to that of the external generator. *See also* Continuous jam sync, One-time jam sync.

Just diatonic scale A musical scale based on natural harmonics. Each frequency is related to the fundamental through a ratio of two integers; the numerator is a harmonic and the denominator is the integer required to place the frequency within the octave beginning at the fundamental.

Keyable signal processor A signal processor, especially an expander, whose gain-sensing circuit may be varied (or "keyed") as a function of some external audio signal. The keying signal is usually applied via an auxiliary input in the side-chain path.

Leakage Any unwanted sound picked up by—or "leaking" into—a microphone, generally from instruments other than the one(s) in front of the microphone.

LEDE (Live End, Dead End) An acoustic design which specifies that the front surfaces are acoustically absorbent, while the rear surfaces are reflective.

Level The difference between some measured quantity and a specified reference quantity, usually expressed as the logarithm of the ratio of the quantities.

Library winding On a tape recorder, a winding mode that is faster than normal play speed but generally slower than fast-forward, used to quickly wind tape prior to storage.

Limiter A variable-gain amplifier in which the output signal level remains constant (or nearly so) regardless of the input signal level. A compressor with a compression ratio of 10:1 or more. *See also* Compressor, Expander.

Line input Any input designed to accept a line-level input signal.

Line level Pertaining to an audio signal that is at or near a 0 dB (0.775 V) operating level.

Linear compander A compressor/expander system in which the compression/expansion ratios are constant across the entire input range of the system. *See also* Nonlinear compander.

Linear phase Pertaining to a multispeaker system in which the speakers are physically and/or electronically aligned to provide a linear phase response, that is, a phase shift which varies as a linear function of frequency.

Localization Pertaining to the listener's ability to perceive the distance and/or angular location from which a sound source seems to arrive.

Logarithm, common (log) The power to which 10 must be raised to equal a certain number. Thus, if $3 = 10^{0.47712}$, then 0.47712 is the common logarithm of 3.

Logarithm, natural (ln) The power to which ϵ (*epsilon*, $= 2.71828$) must be raised to equal a certain number. Thus, if $3 = 2.71828^{1.09861}$, then 1.09861 is the natural logarithm of 3.

Lowpass filter A filter designed to pass low frequencies with little or no attenuation. A high-frequency filter.

Low-print tape A magnetic recording tape designed to minimize the print-through phenomenon. *See also* Print-through.

Masking A process by which the threshold of audibility for one sound is raised by the presence of another sound.

Master In a multiple tape recorder operation, the tape transport system to which all other transports (slaves) are run in synchronization.

Master module, Master module section In an inline console, the module or modules containing all controls that are not related to a single track or channel (master sends and returns, monitor and communication controls, etc.).

Matrix 1. Any system in which two or more inputs may be routed to two or more outputs. 2. A combining network whose inputs are M and S microphone signals and whose outputs are sum $(M + S)$ and difference $(M - S)$ signals, or vice versa. 3. A bus-selector matrix (q.v.).

Maximum output level (MOL) The magnetization level at which a recorded 1 kHz sine wave reaches 3 percent third-harmonic distortion.

maxwell (Mx) The cgs unit for flux.

Mic (microphone) level Pertaining to the audio signal level at the output of a microphone.

Microphone, nth-order A microphone whose polar response may be plotted from the equation $A + B \cos^n \theta$, where $n = $ any integer (generally, 1–3). The microphones desribed in Chapters 3 and 4 are all first-order.

Minimum audible field (MAF) For a pure tone or narrow-band noise, the minimum sound pressure level that a person with normal hearing can detect.

Mixdown bus(es) The bus, or bus pair, to which all incoming signals are routed to form a mono or stereo program. Usually, the same as the monitor bus(es) (q.v.).

Mixdown, Mixing The process of combining two or more input signals and routing the combined signal to a tape recorder or other destination.

Mixer A Console. Generally used to denote a small console.

mks (meter-kilogram-second) system The metric system in which the indicated quantities are the fundamental units.

Modal frequency An acoustic resonance frequency in a room.

Modulation lead powering A powering system for capacitor microphones in which the required voltage is routed to the microphone from the console, using one of the normal audio signal conductors. The return path is via the other signal conductor (not the shield). Also called *T*-system powering (from the German *Tonader Speisung*, literally, "sound artery powering"). *See also* Phantom powering.

Modulation noise A low-level noise signal occurring on either side of a recorded tone.

Monitor bus(es) The bus, or bus pair, to which all incoming signals are routed to form a mono or stereo program for monitoring purposes. Usually, the same as the mixdown bus(es) (q.v.).

Monitor module In some inline consoles, a module containing all controls related to the monitor system.

Monitor path In an inline console, the signal path from the bus output or tape input to the monitor system. *See also* Channel path.

Moving-coil loudspeaker A dynamic loudspeaker in which the speaker diaphragm is attached to a voice coil which moves within a permanent magnetic field.

Moving-coil microphone A dynamic microphone whose output voltage originates in a coil attached to the diaphragm, which moves within a permanent magnetic field.

M-S (Middle-sides, or Mono-stereo) microphone A stereo microphone in which one output is from a forward-oriented uni- or bidirectional capsule and the other is from a side-oriented bidirectional capsule.

Mult In a patch bay, three or more jacks wired together so that one signal may be patched into the mult to provide two or more outputs.

Multicell horn A horn system comprised of two or more horns coupled to a single compression driver.

Multiflare horn A horn whose outward flare makes a transition from one contour type to another at a specified distance from the throat.

Multitrack tape recorder Any tape recorder with two or more (but usually, eight or more) separate tracks.

NAB standard reproducing characteristic A standard specifying the output of a reproducing amplifier when responding to a constant-flux signal in the core of an ideal reproducing (playback) head (NAB = National Association of Broadcasters).

Near-coincident pair A pair of spaced microphones used for a stereo pickup, in which the distance between the microphones is slight; however, the microphone diaphragms are not on the same vertical axis. *See also* Coincident pair.

Near field The area quite close to a transducer. For a speaker this is probably within a few feet of the diaphragm; for a microphone, it is whatever it takes to eliminate the effects of the sound field—perhaps just a few inches.

NoiseEx recording system An early (c. 1960) dynamic complementary noise reduction system introduced by EMT.

Noise gate An expander whose parameters are set to sharply reduce system gain when the applied input level falls below threshold, thereby attenuating noise in the absence of a signal.

Nonlinear compander A compressor/expander system in which the compression/expansion ratios vary across the input range of the system. *See also* Linear compander.

Nonsymmetric filter A filter whose bandpass and bandstop responses are not mirror images. The bandstop response is usually that of a notch filter.

NOS microphone pair A pair of cardioid microphones separated by 30 cm and angled 45 degrees left and right of the center axis (NOS = *Nederlandsche Omroep Stichting*, Dutch Broadcasting Organization). *See also* ORTF microphone pair.

Notch filter A bandstop filter in which a narrow frequency band is sharply attenuated. So called because of the distinctive "notch" in the frequency response.

Octave (8va) The interval between any two frequencies f_1 and f_2, when $f_2 = 2f_1$.

Octave, one-half The interval between any two frequencies f_1 and f_2, when $f_2 = f_1 \times 2^{1/2}$.

Octave, one-third The interval between any two frequencies f_1 and f_2, when $f_2 = f_1 \times 2^{1/3}$.

oersted (Oe) The cgs unit for coercivity.

Off-axis Pertaining to a sound source received from, or transmitted to, a location other than directly in front of a tranducer.

Off-axis coloration A distortion in frequency response that occurs when a signal arrives off-axis at, or from, a transducer. *See also* On-axis.

Omnidirectional microphone A microphone that is insensitive to the angle at which a sound arrives.

On-axis Pertaining to a sound source received from, or transmitted to, a location directly in front of a transducer.

One-eighth space The available radiation space when an ideal sound source is placed at the intersection of three adjoining surfaces (e.g., two walls and a floor).

One-quarter space The available radiation space when an ideal sound source is placed at the intersection of two adjoining surfaces (e.g., two walls).

One-time jam sync Procedure in which a time code generator is momentarily jammed against an external generator, after which it operates independently.

Operating level An indication of the recorded flux required to deflect a meter to its zero reference mark. Reference fluxivity or Reference level.

ORTF microphone pair A pair of cardioid microphones separated by 17 cm and angled 55 degrees left and right of the center axis (ORTF = *Office de Radiodiffusion Télévision Française*, French National Broadcasting Organization). *See also* NOS microphone pair.

Overdub On a multitrack tape recorder, the technique of recording new tracks while simultaneously monitoring previously recorded tracks via a single head. Also called synchronous recording. Originally, the process of adding new program material to a previously recorded program by recording both new and old onto a new tape.

Oxide, magnetic The magnetic coating applied to a base material to form magnetic recording tape.

Pan pot A potentiometer used to vary the balance of a sound source routed to two tracks, either to create the illusion that the source is actually moving between two locations, or to place the source at some fixed location between the two sound sources.

Panning Continuously moving the apparent location of a sound source from left to right, usually via a pan pot (q.v.) on the console.

Parabolic horn A horn whose cross-sectional area A_m, increases according to the equation $A_t x$, where A_t is the throat area and x is the horn length. So called because the equation (not the horn shape) is that of a parabola.

Paragraphic equalizer A parametric equalizer with slide-fader control of boost/cut at each selected frequency (from *parametric/graphic*).

Parametric equalizer An equalizer with separate controls for all center frequency, bandwidth, and boost/cut parameters.

Pass band The range of frequencies that are attenuated by less than 3 dB.

Passive network Any network whose circuit elements are limited to passive components: inductors, capacitors, and resistors.

Patch bay In a console or equipment rack, a central location containing a jack field—a grouping of jacks wired to various input and output points within the console or to the input and output of various signal processing devices.

Patch cord A short length of cable with a plug at either end, for use in connecting one patch bay jack to another.

Patch point Any point in the audio signal path at which the signal flow may be diverted or interrupted by the insertion of a patch cord.

Period The time it takes for a periodic waveform to make one complete alternation.

Periodic waveform Any waveform comprised of identical repetitions. Thus, a mixture of two or more fixed-frequency signals is a periodic waveform, while a music or voice waveform is not.

Permeability (μ) The ratio of magnetic flux density, B, to magnetic field strength, H.

Permeability, relative The ratio of a material's own permeability to that of air.

Phantom power A powering system for capacitor microphones in which the required voltage is routed to the microphone from the console, using the normal audio signal lines. The return path is usually via the microphone cable shield. *See also* Modulation lead powering.

Phase At any point in a pure sinusoidal waveform, a measure of that point's distance from the most recent positive-going zero crossing of the waveform.

Phase, absolute *See* Polarity, absolute.

Phase plug In a compression driver, a barrier inserted between the diaphragm and the driver mouth. The multiple holes bored through the phase plug are all the same length, so that the length of all sound paths from diaphragm to driver mouth are equal.

Phase response A graph of phase shift versus frequency.

Phase shift The distance, in degrees, between the same point on two identical sinusoidal waveforms.

Phasing The use of a phase-shift network to create the comb-filter effect of flanging.

Phon The sound pressure level of the 1,000 Hz tone used as a reference level in an equal-loudness contour (q.v.).

pi (π) The numeric constant, 3.14159 ..., which is the ratio of the circumference of a circle to its radius.

Pinch roller *See* Pressure roller.

Pink noise A random noise containing equal energy per octave. *See also* White noise.

Piston band The frequency range in which a loudspeaker (the piston) is designed to operate.

Plane wave The surface of a spherical waveform when its distance from the sound source is so great that the surface area of interest can be considered to be a flat (plane) surface in comparison to the dimension of a microphone or other object in the waveform path.

Polar coordinate system A graphing system in which one variable (amplitude) is represented by the distance of a point from the origin of a circle and the other variable (direction) is represented by the angle at which the point is placed with respect to the origin. Used to plot the familiar microphone polar pattern.

Polar equation An equation in the form $A + B \cos \theta$ that describes a microphone's output sensitivity versus the angle of an arriving constant-level sound source. For all microphones, $A + B = 1$.

Polar pattern, Polar response A graph of microphone output level or sensitivity versus angular direction of the arriving constant-level sound source; a graph of speaker output level versus angular direction around the speaker in the presence of an applied constant-level signal.

Polarity Pertaining to an electric or electronic system in which two points have opposite electric potentials.

Polarity, absolute Pertaining to a signal chain in which the instantaneous polarity of the output waveform is identical to that of the original acoustic source.

Polyester (polyethylene terephthalate) The material commonly used as a base for magnetic recording tape.

Postecho An echo of a recording signal heard slightly after the actual signal itself. Generally an artifact of print-through (q.v.).

Postemphasis Equalization applied at the output of a tape recorder or other device to compensate for pre-emphasis (q.v.) equalization applied at the input of the same device or system.

Postroll Pertaining to the interval in which the tape continues to play after a punch-out.

Power *See* Sound power.

Preecho An echo of a recorded signal heard slightly before the actual signal itself. Generally an artifact of print-through (q.v.).

Preemphasis Frequency-selective equalization applied at the input of a tape recorder or other device, to be removed by a complementary postemphasis (q.v.) at the output of the same device or system.

Prefader listen mode In a console, the mode in which a signal is temporarily routed to the monitor system from a point before the fader.

Pre/post switch In a console, any switch whose purpose is to route a signal to a send line from a point before (pre) or after (post) a level control, such as the channel fader or monitor potentiometer.

Preroll Pertaining to the short interval of tape played just before a punch-in point.

Pressure *See* Dynamic, sound, static pressure.

Pressure antinode   A point at which the sound pressure is maximum. *See also* Pressure node.

Pressure gradient microphone   A microphone whose output level is a function of the pressure difference, or pressure *gradient*, between the front and back of its diaphragm.

Pressure microphone   A microphone whose output level is a function of the air pressure at the front of its diaphragm.

Pressure node   A point at which the sound pressure is zero. *See also* Pressure antinode.

Pressure roller   On a tape recorder, a large rubber wheel held under pressure against the capstan (q.v.). A capstan idler, pinch roller.

Pressure Zone   *See* Boundary layer.

Pressure Zone Microphone (PZM)   A surface-mounted microphone in which the diaphragm is located within the boundary layer (q.v.)

Preview mode   *See* Rehearse mode.

Print-through   A magnetic imprinting of a signal from one layer of tape onto the layers immediately above and below it.

Program compression, Program expansion   Compression or expansion applied to a composite mono or stereo program, rather than to a single instrument or track.

Proximity effect   In a pressure-gradient microphone, a low-frequency response boost when the microphone is placed at a very close working distance to a sound source.

Psychoacoustics   The study of the complex reactions of the listener to the surrounding sound field.

"Pumping"   *See* "Breathing."

Punch-in, Punch-out   The technique of entering and exiting the record mode while the tape is in motion, usually for the purpose of recording over a previously recorded tape segment without erasing the program on either side of that segment.

Q—equalizer quality factor   The ratio of the center frequency to the bandwidth. Thus,

$$Q = f_c/(f_2 - f_1)$$

Q—loudspeaker directivity factor   The ratio of sound pressure squared, at some fixed distance and specified direction, to the mean-squared pressure at the same distance, but averaged over all directions from the speaker. Q = 1/REE (random energy efficiency).

Quality factor   *See* Q—equalizer quality factor.

q.v.   Abbreviation meaning, literally, "which see." Refers the reader to another item in a glossary, book, etc.

Radial horn   A horn with straight vertical sides whose top and bottom surfaces flare outwards at whatever rate is required to achieve the desired mouth area. *See also* Biradial horn.

Radian   At the origin of a circle, the angle between two radii joined by an arc of circumference whose length is equal to the radius. 1 radian = 0.01745 degrees, 2π radians = 360 degrees.

Random energy efficiency (REE)   The ratio of a microphone's random energy response to that of an omnidirectional microphone placed at the same location in a diffuse sound field.

Random energy response (RER)   The response of a microphone to a diffuse sound field. *See* Random energy efficiency.

Ready mode On a tape recorder, the mode in which a track will go into the record mode when the record button is pressed.

Rear-entry port On a directional microphone, an opening (port) that allows a sound wave to reach the rear of the diaphragm.

Reciprocal filter *See* Symmetric filter.

Recording field The magnetic field set up at the record head by an applied input signal.

Reference fluxivity, Reference level *See* Operating level.

Reflected path Any path between a sound source and a listener or microphone in which the arriving sound wave has been reflected from one or more surfaces before reaching its destination.

Reflection The return of a waveform from an obstruction in its path.

Refraction The bending of a waveform as it passes from one medium to another, or as it experiences a change (e.g., in temperature) within the medium.

Rehearse mode On a tape recorder, the mode in which the effect of entering the record mode is simulated without actually doing so, thus protecting previously recorded material from being erased. The preview mode.

Release time At the cessation of compression or expansion, the interval required for the system to return to normal gain.

Remanent saturation flux A measure of the fluxivity per unit of track width after a saturating magnetic field has been withdrawn.

Remanent tape magnetization The magnetic field permanently stored on a magnetic recording tape.

Repro (reproduce) head A playback head, so-called to differentiate it from the sync (record) head, which is also used for playback during synchronous recording. *See also* Sync head.

Repro mode On a tape recorder, the playback mode in which all tracks are monitored from the repro (playback) head.

Resonance frequency The natural frequency at which a loudspeaker or other mechanical device freely oscillates when a disturbing force is momentarily applied.

Retentivity (B) A measure of the flux density remaining after an external magnetic force has been removed.

Reverberant field The sound field in an area in which the sound source itself is no longer the strongest component.

Reverberation A sequence of echoes that are so closely spaced in time that it is impossible to distinguish one from another.

Reverberation chamber A specially treated room in which all surfaces are highly reflective, or an electronic device designed to simulate the sound of a reverberant room.

Reverberation plate A steel plate in which bending waves are created by a driver element and picked up by contact transducers attached to the plate. The resultant output signal simulates the reverberation characteristics of an actual room.

Reverberation time When a steady-state sound source is stopped, the time it takes for the sound pressure level to decrease by 60 dB.

Ribbon loudspeaker A dynamic loudspeaker in which the diaphragm is a ribbon suspended within a permanent magnetic field.

Ribbon microphone A dynamic microphone whose moving element is a ribbon suspended within a permanent magnetic field.

Room mode A modal frequency (q.v.)

Room sound The prevailing background noise level in a concert hall or other room during silent intervals, for example during a pause in a performance.

Rotary knob console A console in which the channel faders are rotary potentiometers.

Rotation point In a compressor, expander, or limiter, the point at which the device's transfer characteristic passes through the unity gain characteristic.

Safe mode On a tape recorder, a protective mode which prevents a track from being recorded when the record button is pressed.

Saturation The condition in which further increase in applied magnetic force has no additional effect on the magnetic domains on a recording tape.

Saturation recording Magnetic recording process in which a digital bit stream is recorded by driving the tape into positive or negative saturation, with the magnetic saturation directions representing the digital bits 0 and 1.

Scrape flutter On a tape recorder, flutter caused by high-frequency vibrations of the tape as it passes

between two support surfaces, usually a function of excessive friction.

Sealed enclosure A closed-back cabinet (q.v.) for a loudspeaker.

Sel-rep (Selective reproduction) A term used by the Otari Corporation to describe the synchronous recording (q.v.) technique.

Sel-Sync Selective Synchronization. A trademark of the Ampex Corporation to describe the synchronous recording (q.v). technique.

Semitone In the well-tempered scale, the interval between any two frequencies, f_1 and f_2, when $f_2 = f_1 \times 2^{1/12}$ ($f_2 = 1.059 f_1$).

Sensitivity A dimensionless ratio of output to input amplitude, generally used to express the gain range between unity gain (1) and infinite attenuation (0).

Servo-control drive system A DC motor whose rotational speed is regulated by a control voltage derived from a tachometer-generated reference signal.

Shape constant A design constant used in horn design to adjust the length of the horn.

Shelving filter A filter in which a rising or falling response eventually levels off at a fixed gain or attenuation shelf.

SI Units (*Système International d'Unités*) The International System of Units, incorporating mks (q.v.) and other units of measurement.

Sibilance A hiss-like effect occurring when 's' sounds (as in the word "this") are excessive.

Side chain A secondary path used to route an audio signal to the gain-control section of a compressor or other signal processing device. Any secondary path along which a signal is routed for processing prior to combination with the same signal in the primary path.

Side chain signal processor Any signal processor inserted in a side chain, as, for example, an equalizer in a compressor side chain. The equalizer affects the compressor's gain sensing mechanism, but does not equalize the signal passing through the compressor's primary signal path.

Signal-to-noise ratio The ratio of the amplitude of a signal to the amplitude of the noise measured at the same point in the system.

Sine (sin) For either acute angle in a right triangle, the ratio of the opposite side to the hypotenuse.

Sine wave The graph of $y = \sin \theta$ for all values of θ from $0°$ to $360°$.

Single-ended noise reduction Any noise reduction system in which the signal processing is applied at only one point in the signal chain, as for example, a low- or highpass filter.

Single-ended signal processing Any signal processing in which the applied signal modification is permanent, for example, equalization or compression. *See also* Complementary signal processing.

Sinusoidal waveform A sine wave or any other waveform (e.g., cosine) exhibiting the same periodic shape.

Slap echo A series of regularly spaced echoes.

Slate, Slating Pertaining to a spoken announcement recorded on tape to identify the recording immediately following.

Slating tone A low-frequency tone recorded on tape along with a spoken announcement.

Slave In a multiple tape recorder system, any transport whose motion is controlled by another tape recorder, designated as the master.

Slope The rate at which a quantity falls within a specified interval: dB per octave, dB per decade, etc.

Slurry The mixture of magnetic particles and the nonmagnetic liquid binder in which they are suspended. The slurry dries to form the oxide coating on a magnetic tape.

SMPTE Time Code A time code standard published by the Society of Motion Picture and Television Engineers (*See* Appendix A). *See also* Vertical Interval Time Code.

Soft key Any control whose function varies according to a software instruction. For example, a single control used to adjust the same parameter on all tracks of a multitrack tape recorder. The designated track may be selected by another soft key.

Solo mode The monitor mode in which an individual signal, or a few such signals, is heard over the monitor system in place of the regular stereo program.

Sound field The complex combination of direct and reflected energy that exists in, or at a certain point in, a listening environment.

Sound intensity A measure of the rate at which acoustic energy radiates through an area of known dimension. The SI unit is watts per square meter (W/m^2).

Sound power The total sound energy radiated by a sound source per unit of time. The SI unit is watts (W).

Sound pressure In the presence of a sound wave, the measured air pressure less the static pressure at the point of measurement.

Sound pressure level The ratio between the sound pressure at a point, p, and a reference pressure, p_r. SPL = 20 log (p/p_r), where SPL = sound pressure level, in dB.

Soundfield microphone A microphone containing four subcardioid capsules oriented on the four surfaces of a regular tetrahedron (four-sided pyramid). Via matrixing of the four output signals, two outputs at any orientation and polar pattern may be created.

Spacing loss A signal attenuation caused by the space between a magnetic tape head gap and the tape oxide.

Spectral program filter A low- and/or highpass filter set in which each cutoff frequency dynamically varies according to the music spectrum of the applied audio signal.

Spectral recording process A complementary encoding/decoding format introduced by Dolby Laboratories, in which the processing parameters vary according to the spectral content of the applied audio signal.

Speed The rate, per unit of time, at which an object moves, without regard to the direction of that movement. The speed of sound is 331.45 meters/second (1087.42 feet/second) at 0 degrees Celsius (about 32 degrees Fahrenheit). *See also* Velocity.

Spherical wave A sound pressure wave whose pattern of condensations and rarefactions forms an expanding spherical surface radiating away from the sound source.

Split-section console A console in which the input, output, and monitor functions are grouped in three separate sections.

Square wave A waveform with a periodic discontinuity between two constant amplitudes. A perfect square wave is comprised of a sine wave and a series of odd harmonics such that

$$y = (4/\pi) [\sin (x) + \tfrac{1}{3} \sin(3x) + \tfrac{1}{5} \sin (5x) + ...]$$

where
$$x = 2\pi f t$$

Squawker A midrange speaker (occasionally used in discussions of tweeters and woofers to describe the speaker in between).

Standing wave A series of stationary pressure nodes and antinodes created by the interaction between an incident and a reflected waveform.

Static pressure The prevailing atmospheric (barometric) pressure in the absence of a disturbing sound pressure wave.

Static signal processor Any signal processor whose parameter settings do not vary in response to the signal passing through the device, for example, an equalizer. *See also* Dynamic signal processor.

Steradian In a sphere, the solid angle contained by a surface whose area equals the square of the sphere's radius.

Stereo microphone Any microphone or microphone pair with two discrete outputs, intended for use in stereophonic recording.

Stereosonic microphone pair A Blumlein pair of bidirectional microphones with an included angle of 90 degrees, ±45 degrees from the center axis.

Stop band The range of frequencies that are attenuated by a specified amount. For example, a 6 dB stop band is the range that is attenuated by 6 dB or more.

Subcardioid microphone Any microphone whose polar pattern places it somewhere between an omnidirectional and a pure cardioid pattern. In the polar equation $A + B \cos \theta$, $A < 1$ and $A > B$.

Sum pattern The resultant microphone polar pattern when the two outputs of an *M-S* microphone are added. *See also* Difference pattern.

Supercardioid microphone A directional microphone with greater attenuation at the sides than a pure cardioid pattern, but with less attenuation at the rear (-8.7 dB at $90°$, 11.44 dB at $180°$). So-called because its cosine (pressure gradient) component is above the cardioid.

Swap mode In a console, the mode in which the positions of the channel fader and the monitor path potentiometer are exchanged, or in which a signal processor in either path is moved to the other path.

Symmetric filter A filter whose bandpass and bandstop responses are mirror images. A reciprocal filter.

Sync head A record head, so called in reference to its ability to alternately function as a normal record head or as a reproduce head in the sync mode.

Sync mode On a tape recorder, the mode in which previously recorded tracks are monitored via the sync (record) head while new material is being recorded on other tracks.

Sync word In SMPTE Time Code, the 16-bit word (bits 64–79) containing a unique bit sequence used to define the end of each 80-bit word (SMPTE 3.5).

Synchronous recording On a multitrack tape recorder, the technique of recording new tracks while simultaneously monitoring previously recorded tracks via a single head. Thus, the same head functions simultaneously in the record and playback, or sync, mode.

Tangent (tan) For either acute angle in a right triangle, the ratio of the opposite side to the adjacent side. Also for the same angle, the ratio of its sine to cosine.

tesla (T) The SI unit for flux density or retentivity.

Thickness loss, tape The attenuation in recorded signal level in magnetic tape oxide layers that are separated from the head by other layers of oxide.

Threshold The applied input level above which a compressor begins to function, or below which an expander begins to function.

Threshold of feeling The minimum sound pressure level of a pure tone which creates the physical sensation of feeling in the ear. About 120 dB SPL.

Threshold of hearing The minimum sound pressure level of a pure tone that can be perceived by a person with good hearing. A sound pressure of 20×10^{-6} pascals (20 μPa) is defined as 0 dB SPL.

Threshold of pain The minimum sound pressure level of a pure tone which causes a sensation of pain in the ear. About 140 dB SPL.

Tie line A signal line from one point to another, as for example from one patch bay to another patch bay at a different location, and terminated at an input/output jack at each location.

Time alignment A multispeaker system design method in which the physical and electric components are adjusted so that the fundamental and overtones of a complex signal arrive at the listener's ears with the same time relationship they had in the electronic signal.

Time code A coded signal used to display tape running time in hours, minutes, seconds, and frames. *See* SMPTE Time Code, Vertical Interval Time Code.

Time constant In a filter, the product of circuit resistance and capacitance, measured in ohms and farads respectively.

Tone In the equal-tempered scale, the interval between any two frequencies, f_1 and f_2, when $f_2 = f_1 \times 2^{2/12}$ ($f_2 = 1.122f_1$, that is, two semitones).

Track-summing bus A bus to which the outputs of two or more input signals are routed for combination into a single output signal.

Transaural stereo A stereo system in which the listener's ears, not the loudspeakers, are considered as the end point of the recording/reproduction chain.

Transducer Any device which converts an input signal into an output signal of a different energy form (e.g., acoustic to electric). A microphone, loudspeaker, phonograph cartridge, etc.

Transfer characteristic An equation or graph that plots the output amplitude or level of a device with respect to its input amplitude or level.

Transition frequency For a baffle-mounted loudspeaker, the frequency whose wavelength is twice the effective path length around the baffle, and at which the response level is maximum.

Trigonometric function *See* Function, trigonometric.

T-system powering *See* Modulation lead powering.

Tweeter A high-frequency speaker.

Unassigned address bit SMPTE Time Code Bit 58, set at zero until otherwise assigned (SMPTE 3.5).

Unidirectional index (UDI) An indication of a microphone's relative ability to accept sounds arriving from the front hemisphere while rejecting those arriving from the back hemisphere. UDI = REF/REB (random energy efficiency, front-to-back hemispheres).

Unidirectional microphone A microphone that is most sensitive to sounds arriving from the front.

User-assigned bits In SMPTE Time Code, eight groups of four bits each available for user storage of data (SMPTE 3.4).

Variable, dependent and independent In any equation, a dependent variable is one whose value depends on some other (the independent) variable. Thus, if $y = 2x$, y is the dependent variable, x the independent variable.

VCA A voltage-controlled amplifier (q.v.).

Velocity The speed of an object, when measured with respect to its direction (which should be stated).

Vented cabinet An otherwise closed-back cabinet in which a vent or port has been cut in the face of the enclosure, usually below the speaker cutout.

Vertical Interval Time Code (VITC) Time code recorded within the vertical blanking interval on videotape.

Voice-over compression Signal processing technique in which the voice signal is fed by a side chain to compressors in the background program line, but not to the vocal line itself. Thus, compression action attenuates the background signal but not the voice itself.

Voltage-controlled amplifier (VCA) An amplifier whose gain is varied by a DC control voltage.

Wavelength (λ) The length of one complete cycle of a sound wave. Wavelength is equal to c/f, where c is the speed of sound in air (or tape speed) and f is the frequency, in hertz.

weber (Wb) The SI unit for flux or retentivity.

Well-tempered scale *See* Equal-tempered scale.

"Wet" recording Any recording in which signal processing, especially echo and reverberation, is applied to the recorded signal. *See also* "Dry" recording.

White noise A random noise containing equal energy in each 1-Hz band within the audio spectrum. Analogous to white light. *See also* Pink noise.

Width control In a stereo (dual-channel) line, a control used to blend the two signals in varying proportions from mono to stereo. A Blend control.

Width enhancement In a stereo (dual-channel) line, a phase-shift network used to create the illusion that the stereo field extends beyond the range between the two monitor speakers.

Woofer A low-frequency speaker.

Wow On a tape recorder, the low-frequency modulation of an audio signal caused by uneven motion of the tape during recording, playback, or both.

***X-Y* microphone pair** 1. A pair of coincident microphones oriented at equal and opposite angles with respect to zero degrees. The included angle is generally between 90 and 135 degrees. 2. The resultant patterns when the outputs of an *M-S* microphone pair are matrixed.

Zenith Pertaining to the angular alignment of a tape head along its vertical axis and at right angles to its azimuth; a forward/backward tilt of the head, when viewed from the front.

C Abbreviations, Acronyms, and Symbols

This appendix is divided into four sections:

1. Abbreviations and acronyms
2. Frequently encountered Greek letters
3. Mathematical symbols
4. Mathematical prefixes

Abbreviations and Acronyms

A	ampere, amp
ACN	active combining network
AES	Audio Engineering Society
AME	Ampex master equalization
ASA	Acoustical Society of America
atn	arc tangent
c	speed of sound in air
CCIR	*Comité Consultatif International des Radiocommunications* (International Telecommunications Consultative Committee)
CCITT	*Comité Consultatif International Télégraphique et Téléphonique* (International Telegraph and Telephone Consultative Committee)
cgs	centimeter-gram-second system
cm/s	centimeters per second
cos	cosine

cm/s	centimeters per second
cps	cycles per second (now Hz, hertz)
dB	decibel
dBm	decibel, 1 mW reference level
dBu	decibel, 0.775 V reference (current usage)
dBv	decibel, 0.775 V reference (former usage)
dBV	decibel, 1.0 V reference
DI	directivity index
DIN	Deutsche Industrie-Norm (German Industrial Standard)
DRF	directivity factor
DSF	distance factor
E	electromotive force
EBU	European Broadcasting Union
EIA	Electronic Industries Association
FTR	front-to-total ratio
G	gauss
Hz	hertz (formerly cycles per second)
I	current
IBEW	International Brotherhood of Electrical Workers
IEC	International Electrotechnical Commission
IEEE	Institute of Electrical and Electronics Engineers, Inc.
in/s, ips	inches per second
IRE	Institute of Radio Engineers (now IEEE)
ISO	International Organization for Standards*
LCD	liquid crystal display
LED	light-emitting diode
MAF	minimum audible field
MIDI	musical instrument digital interface
mks	meter-kilogram-second system
MOL	maximum output level
NAB	National Association of Broadcasters
NABET	National Association of Broadcast Engineers and Technicians
NARTB	National Association of Radio and Television Broadcasters (now NAB)

---

*"ISO" is not an acronym; it is an abbreviation of the Greek *isos* (equal), to suggest "uniform" or "standard." The acronym "IOS" is not used by the organization.

NOS	*Nederlandsche Omroep Stichting* (Dutch Broadcasting Organization)
NRBA	National Radio Broadcasters Association (merged with NAB, 1986)
NRDC	National Research Development Corporation
nWb	nanowebers
nWb/m	nanowebers per meter
Oe	oersted
ORTF	*Office de Radiodiffusion Télévision Française* (French National Broadcasting Organization)
P	power
Pa	pascals
PAL	phase-alternation line
PCM	pulse code modulation
PZM	pressure zone microphone
Q	directivity factor, quality factor
R	resistance
REE	random energy efficiency
RER	random energy response
RGB	red-green-blue
RIAA	Recording Industry Association of America
SBE	Society of Broadcast Engineers
SCSI	Small Computer Standard Interface
SECAM	*Séquential couleur à memoire* (sequential color with memory)
SI	*Système International d'Unités* (International System of Units)
sin	sine
SMPE	Society of Motion Picture Engineers (now SMPTE)
SMPTE	Society of Motion Picture and Television Engineers
SPARS	Society of Professional Audio Recording Studios
SPL	sound pressure level
T	tesla
tan	tangent
UDI	unidirectional index
V	volt
VCA	voltage-controlled amplifier
VITC	vertical interval time code
W	watt

Frequently Encountered Greek Letters

Greek Letter	Name of Letter	Used to Denote
α	alpha	
β	beta	
Γ	gamma	
δ & Δ	delta	a change in
ϵ	epsilon	2.71828, natural logarithm base
θ	theta	an angle
λ	lambda	wavelength
μ	mu	micro, 10^{-6}, permeability
π	pi	3.14159
ρ	rho	
Σ	sigma	summation
ϕ	phi	flux
Ω	omega	ohms
ω	omega	$2\pi f$ (f = frequency)

Mathematical Symbols

∞	infinity
$>$	greater than
$<$	less than
$\geq$	equal to or greater than
$\leq$	equal to or less than
$\approx$	approximately equal to
$\pm$	plus or minus
$f(x)$	a function of x

Mathematical Prefixes

p	pico	10^{-12}
n	nano	10^{-9}
μ	micro	10^{-6}
m	milli	10^{-3}
k	kilo	10^{3}
K		$2^{10} = 1{,}024$
M	mega	10^{6}

D Bibliography and References

AES (Audio Engineering Society). 1971. Audio Standards, Work in Progress: AES Standards Committee; Engineering Committees and Related Groups. *Journal of the Audio Engineering Society* 19:1 (January), 68.

Ampex Corporation. 1953. *Model 350-2 Operation and Maintenance Manual.* Redwood City, CA: Ampex Corp.

Bauer, B. B. 1940. [Benjamin Baumzweiger]. Graphical Determination of the Random Efficiency of Microphones. *Journal of the Acoustical Society of America* 11 (April), 477–479.

Bauer, B. B., and J. W. Medill. 1954. A Miniature Unidirectional Microphone. *I. R. E. Convention Record,* 12–15.

Bauer, Marion. 1956. *Consonance.* In *International Cyclopedia of Music and Musicians.* Edited by N. Slonimsky. 7th Ed. New York: Dodd, Mead & Company.

Bertram, H. Neal. 1974. Long-Wavelength AC Bias Recording Theory. *IEEE Transactions on Magnetics* MAG-10:4 (December), 1039–1048.

———. 1975. Wavelength Response in AC-Biased Recording. *IEEE Transactions on Magnetics* MAG-11:5 (September), 1176–1178.

Bertram, H. Neal, and Michael K. Stafford, David R. Mills. 1980. The Print-Through Phenomenon. *Journal of the Audio Engineering Society* 28:10 (October), 690–705.

Bevan, William E., and Robert B. Schulein, Charles E. Seeler. 1978. Design of a Studio-Quality Condenser Microphone Using Electret Technology. *Journal of the Audio Engineering Society* 26:12 (December), 947–957.

Blesser, Barry, and Fred Ives. 1972. A Reexamination of the S/N Question for Systems with Time-Varying Gain or Frequency Response. *Journal of the Audio Engineering Society* 20:8 (October), 638–641.

Blumlein, Alan Dower. 1931. *Improvements in and Relating to Sound-transmission, Sound-recording and Sound-reproducing Systems.* British Patent Specification 394,325. Abridged version printed in *Stereophonic Techniques Anthology*, 1986. New York: Audio Engineering Society, Inc.

Bode, H. W. 1945. *Network Analysis and Feedback Amplifier Design.* New York: Van Nostrand Co.

Bohn, Dennis. 1983. Bandpass Filter Design. *Studio Sound* 25:1 (January), 36–37.

———. 1985. *Constant-Q Graphic Equalizers.* Audio Engineering Society Preprint 2265 (D-15).

———. 1988. Operator-Adjustable Equalizers: An Overview. *Proceedings of the Audio Engineering Society 6th International Conference: Sound Reinforcement.* New York: Audio Engineering Society.

Bruck, Jerry. 1987. *MK-21 Sub-cardioid Capsule.* New York: Posthorn Recordings: Schoeps New Product Release.

Brüel & Kjaer. 1984. *Measuring Sound.* Nærum, Denmark: Brüel & Kjaer.

———. 1986. *Sound Intensity.* Nærum, Denmark: Brüel & Kjaer.

Burroughs, Lou. 1973. The Mighty Mike Mouse. *Sound Technique* 3:1 (June). Buchanan, MI: Electro-Voice, Inc.

Burwen, Richard. 1971a. A Dynamic Noise Filter. *Journal of the Audio Engineering Society* 19:2 (February), 115–120.

———. 1971b. Design of a Noise Eliminator System. *Journal of the Audio Engineering Society* 19:11 (December), 906–911.

Camras, Marvin. 1941. Patent 2,351,004 (granted June 13, 1944).

———. 1988. *Magnetic Recording Handbook.* New York: Van Nostrand Reinhold Co.

Canby, Edward Tatnall. 1967. Audio ETC.—The Dolby. *Audio Magazine* 51:3 (March), 8.

Carlson, Wendell L., and Glenn W. Carpenter. 1927. *Radio Telegraph System.* Patent 1,640,881. U. S. Patent Office. Reprinted in Tall 1958, pp. 10–11.

Ceoen, Carl. 1972. Comparative Stereophonic Listening Tests. *Journal of the Audio Engineering Society* 20:1 (January/February), 19–27.

Cipher Digital, Inc. 1987. *Time Code Handbook: A Guide for the User from Fundamentals to Technical Specifications.* Frederick, MD: Cipher Digital, Inc.

Cooper, Duane H., and Jerald L. Bauck. 1989. Prospects for Transural Recording. *Journal of the Audio Engineering Society* 37:1/2 (January/February), 3–19.

Crane, G. R., and G. A. Brookes. 1961. Artificial Reverberation Facilities for Auditoriums and Audio Systems. *Journal of the Audio Engineering Society* 9:3 (July), 198–204.

Crown International, Inc. 1983. *Pressure Zone Microphone: Theory and Applications Guide.* Elkhart, IN: Crown International, Inc.

Davis, Chips. 1979. (LEDE) Live End-Dead End Control Room Acoustics ... (TDS) Time Delay Spectrometry ... (PZM) Pressure Zone Microphones. *Recording engineer/producer* 10:1 (February), 41.

Davis, Don. 1980. *Engineering an LEDE™ Control Room for a Broadcasting Facility.* Audio Engineering Society Preprint 1688 (I-1).

Davis, Don and Carolyn. 1987. *Sound System Engineering.* 2nd ed. Indianapolis: Howard W. Sams & Co.

Dolby, Ray M. 1967. An Audio Noise Reduction System. *Journal of the Audio Engineering Society* 15:4 (October), 383–388.

———. 1971. A Noise Reduction System for Consumer Tape Recording. (Paper presented at the Audio Engineering Society Central Europe Section Convention, 16–18 March, at Cologne, Germany.)

———. 1983. A 20 dB Audio Noise Reduction System for Consumer Applications. *Journal of the Audio Engineering Society* 31:3 (March), 98–113.

———. 1987. The Spectral Recording Process. *Journal of the Audio Engineering Society* 35:3 (March), 99–118.

Dolby Laboratories. 1987. *Dolby Spectral Recording: What It Is and What It Does.* San Francisco: Dolby Laboratories Technical Paper. Reprinted in *Studio Sound* 29:7 (July 1987), 68.

Dow, Harrison E., and Maurice E. Swift. 1961. Reverberation System for Home Entertainment Equipment. *Journal of the Audio Engineering Society* 9:3 (July), 187–191.

Dyer, Robert B. 1976. An Anecdotal Review of Head Design Problems: Part I. *Journal of the Audio Engineering Society* 24:4 (May), 322–327.

Eargle, John. 1986. *Handbook of Recording Engineering.* New York: Van Nostrand Reinhold Co.

Eilers, Delos A. 1969. Polyester and Acetate as Magnetic Tape Backings. *Journal of the Audio Engineering Society* 17:3 (June), 303–308.

EMT. 1972. EMT 258: Program Controlled Dynamic Noise Filter. *EMT Courier.* Vol. 22 (November), 3–6. Lahr, West Germany: EMT-Franz GmbH.

———. 1985. The First Epoch of Artificial Reverberation. *EMT Courier,* Special Issue No. 1. Lahr, West Germany: EMT-Franz GmbH.

Eyring, Carl F. 1930. Reverberation Time in "Dead" Rooms. *Journal of the Acoustical Society of America,* 1 (January), 217–235. Reprinted in 1977 in *Architectural Acoustics,* edited by T. D. Northwood, Stroudsburg, PA: Dowden Hutchinson & Ross, Inc., Benchmark Papers in Acoustics, Vol. 10.

Farrar, Kenneth. 1977. *Soundfield Microphone.* AMS Calrec technical paper.

Fidi, W. c. 1973. *AKG Reverberation Unit BX 20E.* New York: North American Philips Corp.

Ford, Hugh. 1978. Telefunken Telcom c4 Noise Reduction System. *Studio Sound* 20:3 (March), 74.

Gardner, Mark B. 1968. Proximity Image Effect in Sound Localization. *Journal of the Acoustical Society of America* 43:1 (January), 43.

Geffe, Philip R. 1966. *Simplified Modern Filter Design.* New York: Hayden Book Company, Inc.

Glover, Ralph P. 1940. A Review of Cardioid Type Unidirectional Microphones. *Journal of the Acoustical Society of America* 11, 296–302.

Griesinger, David. 1985. *Griesinger's Coincident Microphone Primer.* (Manuscript).

———. 1989a. Theory and Design of a Digital Audio Signal Processor for Home Use. *Journal of the Audio Engineering Society* 37:1/2 (January/February), 40–50.

———. 1989b. Equalization and Spatial Equalization of Dummy-Head Recordings for Loudspeaker Reproduction. *Journal of the Audio Engineering Society* 37:1/2 (January, February), 20–29.

Gundry, Ken. 1979. *Headroom Extension for Slow-Speed Magnetic Recording of Audio.* Audio Engineering Society Preprint 1534 (G-2).

Haas, Helmut. 1949 [1972]. The Influence of a Single Echo on the Audibility of Speech. Reprint, translated by K. P. R. Ehrenberg. *Journal of the Audio Engineering Society*, 20:2 (March), 146–159. Originally published in German as Über den Einfluss des Einfachechos auf die Horsamkeit von Sprache. Ph.D. diss., University of Gottingen, Gottingen, Germany.

Henricksen, Clifford A. 1987. *Loudspeakers, Enclosures, and Headphones.* In *Handbook For Sound Engineers: The New Audio Cyclopedia.* Edited by Glen Ballou. Indianapolis: Howard W. Sams & Co.

Ives, Fred H. 1972. A Noise-Reduction System: Dynamic Spectral Filtering. *Journal of the Audio Engineering Society* 20:7 (September), 558–561.

Jensen, Jorgen Selmer. 1983. Recording with Feedback-Controlled Effective Bias. *Journal of the Audio Engineering Society* 31:10 (October), 729–736.

Keele, Jr., D. B. 1975. *What's So Sacred About Exponential Horns?* Audio Engineering Society Preprint 1038 (F-3).

Kinsler, Lawrence E., and Austin R. Frey, Alan B. Coppens, James V. Sanders. 1982. *Fundamentals of Acoustics.* 3rd ed. New York: John Wiley & Sons.

Klepper, David L. 1975. *Application of Digital Delay Units to Sound Reinforcement Systems.* Lexicon Application Note AN-2. Waltham, MA: Lexicon, Inc.

Knowles, Hugh S. 1977. *Loudspeakers.* In *McGraw-Hill Encyclopedia of Science and Technology.* Edited by Daniel N. Lapedes. 4th ed. New York: McGraw-Hill Book Co.

Lewis, Len. 1978. Doing It For Effect ... Time Delay. *Studio Sound* 20:6 (June), 56–60.

Lipshitz, Stanley P., and Mark Pocock, John Vanderkooy. 1982. On the Audibility of Midrange Phase Distortion in Audio Systems. *Journal of the Audio Engineering Society* 30:9 (September), 580–595.

———. 1983. Authors' Reply (to Comments on "On the Audibility of Midrange Phase Distortion in Audio Systems"). *Journal of the Audio Engineering Society* 31:6 (June), 447.

———. 1986. Stereo Microphones Techniques: Are the Purists Wrong? *Journal of the Audio Engineering Society* 34:9 (September), 716–744.

Long, Edward M. 1977. Time Alignment in Loudspeakers. *Audio* 61:8 (August), 58.

Manquen, Dale. 1987. *Magnetic Recording and Playback.* In *Handbook for Sound Engineers: The New Audio Cyclopedia.* Edited by Glen Ballou. Indianapolis: Howard W. Sams & Co.

McKnight, John G. 1960. The Frequency Response of Magnetic Recorders for Audio. *Journal of the Audio Engineering Society* 8:3 (July), 146–153.

———. 1962. The Case Against Low-Frequency Pre-Emphasis in Magnetic Recording. *Journal of the Audio Engineering Society* 10:2 (April), 106–107.

———. 1967a. Tape Reproducer Response Measurements with a Reproducer Test Tape. *Journal of the Audio Engineering Society* 15:2 (April), 152–156.

———. 1967b. Biasing in Magnetic Tape Recording. *Electronics World* (August), 34.

Mee, C. Denis, and Eric D. Daniel. 1987. *Magnetic Recording.* Vol. 1: *Technology.* New York: McGraw-Hill Book Co.

Minnix, Richard B. 1978. *The Nature of Sound.* In *Noise Control: Handbook of Principles and Practices.* Edited by David M. Lipscomb and Arthur C. Taylor, Jr. New York: Van Nostrand Reinhold Co.

Møller, Henning. 1974. *How to Measure Phase Response on Loudspeakers Using a Digital Delay Line.* Audio Engineering Society Preprint 962 (N-5). Expanded version reprinted as *Loudspeaker Phase Measurements, Transient Response and Audible Quality.* Nærum, Denmark: Brüel & Kjaer Application Note 17–198 (n. d.).

Møller, Henrik. 1989. Reproduction of Artificial-Head Recordings through Loudspeakers. *Journal of the Audio Engineering Society* 37:1/2 (January/February) 30–33.

Morrison, Bill. 1988. A Look at Control Room Design and Geometry. *Mix: The Recording Industry Magazine* 12:8 (August), 52.

Müller, Rudolf. 1988. On Improvements of Magnetic Tape Shown by Measurements on Early and Newer Tapes. *Journal of the Audio Engineering Society* 36:10 (October), 802–820.

Nagai, K., and S. Sasaki, J. Endo. 1938. Experimental Consideration Upon the A-C Erasing on the Magnetic Recording and Proposition of the New Recording Method. *Journal of the Institute of Electrical Engineers of Japan* 180, 445–447.

Neve Electronics International, Ltd. 1986. *V Series 3 Operator Handbook.* Bethel, CT: Rupert Neve, Inc.

Noble, James J. 1967. Design Evolution of a FET Condenser Microphone System. *Journal of the Audio Engineering Society* 15:3 (July), 273–278.

Olson, Harry F. 1967 [1952]. *Music, Physics and Engineering.* New York: Dover Publications, Inc. Revised, enlarged version of *Musical Engineering.* New York: McGraw-Hill Book Co.

Otari Corporation. 1988. *MTR-100A Operation and Maintenance Manual.* Foster City, CA: Otari Corp.

Peus, Stephan. 1988. *The MS Recording Technique for the Stereophonic TV and Movie Sound.* Audio Engineering Society Preprint 2674 (G-2).

Plach, Daniel J. 1953. Design Factors in Horn-Type Speakers. *Journal of the Audio Engineering Society* 1:4 (October), 276–281. Reprinted in *JAES* anthology *Loudspeakers: Vol. 1,* 1978.

RCA (Digitally remastered compact discs). 1954. Brahms, Johannes. *Concerto No. 1 in D Minor, Op. 15.* Chicago Symphony Orchestra, Artur Rubinstein. RCA 5668-2-RC.

———. 1956. Rachmaninoff, Sergei. *Concerto No. 2 in C Minor, Op. 18; Rhapsody on a Theme of Paganini, Op. 43.* Chicago Symphony Orchestra, Artur Rubinstein. RCA RCD14934.

Rettinger, Michael. 1977a. *Acoustic Design.* Vol. 1 of *Acoustic Design and Noise Control.* New York: Chemical Publishing Co.

———. 1977b. *Noise Control.* Vol. 2 of *Acoustic Design and Noise Control.* New York: Chemical Publishing Co.

Robertson, A. E. 1963. *Microphones.* 2nd ed. New York: Hayden Book Co. Inc.

Robinson, D. W., and R. S. Dadson. 1956. A Re-Determination of the Equal-Loudness Relationships for Pure Tones. *British Journal of Applied Physics* 7, 166–181.

Schneider, Wolfgang. 1988. An Analogue Alternative to Digital Recordings. *Swiss Sound* 24 (October), 7–10. Regensdorf, Switzerland: Studer International AG.

Schomer, Paul A. 1985. *Electroacoustics.* In *Reference Data for Engineers: Radio, Electronics, Computer, and Communications.* Edited by E. C. Jordan. 7th ed. Indianapolis: Howard W. Sams & Co.

Shepherd, W. Ford. 1985. *Filters, Modern-Network-Theory Design.* In *Reference Data for Engineers: Radio, Electronics, Computer, and Communications.* 7th ed. Indianapolis: Howard W. Sams & Co.

Simmons, Warren. 1979a. Tape Talk: Part One. *Mix: The Recording Industry Magazine* 3:5 (September).

———. 1979b. Tape Talk: Part Two. *Mix: The Recording Industry Magazine* 3:7 (November).

Small, Richard H. 1972. Direct-Radiator Loudspeaker System Analysis. *Journal of the Audio Engineering Society* 20:5 (June), 383–395.

Solid State Logic. 1988. *G Series Master Studio System: Console Operator's Manual.* Oxford, England: Solid Stage Logic, Ltd.

Sony Corporation. 1988. *Audio Recorder APR-24 Operation and Maintenance Manual.* Ft. Lauderdale, FL: Sony Corp.

———. n.d. *MXP-3000 Series Professional Mixing Console.* Ft. Lauderdale, FL: Sony Corp.

Sound Workshop. 1985. *Series 34 Record/Mix Audio Console Owner's Manual.* Hicksville, NY: Sound Workshop Professional Audio Products, Inc.

Studer Corporation. 1988. *A820MCH Operating and Service Instructions.* Regensdorf, Switzerland: Studer International AG.

Tall, Joel. 1958. *Techniques of Magnetic Recording.* 5th ed. New York: Macmillan Co.

Tedeschi, Frank P. 1979. *The Active Filter Handbook.* Blue Ridge Summit, PA: Tab Books.

Thiele, Heinz H. K. 1988. Magnetic Sound Recording in Europe Up to 1945. *Journal of the Audio Engineering Society* 36:5 (May), 396–408.

3M Company. 1972. *3M Series 79 Recorder Instruction Manual.* Camarillo, CA: Mincom Division, 3M Company.

Tyler, Leslie B. n.d. *Broadcast Signal Processing: The View from dbx.* Newton, MA: dbx, Inc. White Paper.

Uzzle, Ted. n.d. *Polarity and Phase.* Altec Lansing Application Note AN-9.

von Braunmühl, Hans Joachim, and Walter Weber. 1943. *Method of Magnetic Sound Recording.* Patent 413,380. U. S. Patent Office.

Waldman, Witold. 1988. Simulation and Optimization of Multiway Loudspeaker Systems Using a Personal Computer. *Journal of the Audio Engineering Society,* 36:9 (September), 651–663.

Weinberger, Julius, and Harry F. Olson, Frank Massa. 1933. A Uni-Directional Ribbon Microphone. *Journal of the Acoustical Society of America* 5, 139–147.

Wermuth, Jürgen. 1975. Telcom c4: Increased Dynamic Range Using a New Studio Quality Compander. *ELA Studiotechnik* Nr. STSB-7607, with English translation by S. F. Temmer. Wolfenbüttel, Germany: AEG—Telefunken.

Wood, Alexander. 1975. *The Physics of Music.* Revised by J. M. Bowsher. 7th ed. New York: John Wiley & Sons, Halsted Press.

Standards

ANSI (American National Standards Institute)
  S1.1-1960 (R1976). *USA Standard: Acoustical Technology.* (Revision of Z24.1-1951 and including Z24.1A.)

  S1.6-1984. *American National Standard: Preferred Frequencies, Frequency Levels, and Band Numbers for Acoustical Measurements.*

DIN (*Deutsche Industrie-Norm*: German Industrial Standard)
  DN 45 595. *Connection of Transistor Equipped Microphones with Modulation Lead Powering.*

  DN 45 596. *Connection of Transistor Equipped Condenser Microphones using Multiplex Powering.*

IEC (International Electrotechnical Commission)
IEC 94-1. *Magnetic Tape Sound Recording and Reproducing Systems, Part 1: General Conditions and Requirements.* 4th ed., 1981.

ISO (International Organization for Standardization)
ISO 266-1975. *Acoustics—Preferred Frequencies for Measurements*

ISO 226: 1987 (E). *Acoustics—Normal Equal-Loudness Level Contours.*

NAB (National Association of Broadcasters)
1965. *NAB Magnetic Tape Recording and Reproducing Standards: Reel-to-Reel.*

SMPTE (Society of Motion Picture and Television Engineers)
ANSI/SMPTE 12M-1986. *American National Standard for Television: Time and Control Code—Video and Audio Tape for 525-line/60-field Systems* (Reprinted in Appendix A).

Index

A

A-B microphone pair, 133, 134
Absorption coefficient, 28, 29
Acetate, cellulose, tape base, 333
Acicular particles
  described, 333
Acoustic
  center of loudspeaker, 199–201
  reverberation chamber, 226–228
  suspension system, 175
  waveform, 14–18
Acoustics
  control room, and echo and
     reverberation, 242–245
Action substitution, Dolby *SR* System, 444,
  446
Active
  bias, 441
  equalizer, defined, 247–248
  filter, 270–272
  network in loudspeaker crossover, 195
Address bits (SMPTE),
  longitudinal code, 524–525
  structure of, 531
  vertical interval code, 529–530
Adjacent side in right triangle, 5
ADT, 239
AES recommended practice, 369
A-format outputs, Soundfield microphone,
  144–145, 148

Alignment, tape recorder, 409–417
  automatic, 417–418
  digitally-controlled, 414–418
  electronic system, 412–418
  See also Calibration
Alternate key, tape transport
     use of, 396
Ambisonic Surround Sound System, 143
Amplitude, sine wave, 9
Angle
  of arrival
    cues, 55–59
    defined, 54
  of incidence defined, 28
Antinode, pressure, 34, 36
Artificial double tracking, 239
Attack time
  compressor, 307–308
  expander, 313
Attenuation, high-frequency
  as a distance cue, 55
Audio theory, basic, **1–38**
Auxiliary path controls
  on I/O module, 488–489
Axial mode, 36, 38–39
Azimuth
  adjustment and calibration tape,
    372–374
  alignment, 411
  angle, 372
  correction of, 373–374

Boldface page numbers indicate a chapter devoted to the topic.

B

Back coating, magnetic tape, 334, 336–337
Back-electret microphone, 66, 69
Back-to-back microphones, 139–140
Baffle
  flat, 173–175
  folded, 175
  infinite, 172–173
  loudspeaker, 172–178
  open-back, 175
Bandpass filter, 259–261
  defined, 248
  parallel, 275, 277
  phase response, 276–277, 280
  series, 275, 276
Bandstop filter, 261, 262
  defined, 248
  parallel, 276, 279
  phase response, 277–278, 281
  series, 275, 278
Bandwidth
  defined, 249
  expressed in octaves, 251
Base
  logarithmic, 1–2
  magnetic tape, 332–333, 336–337
Bass rolloff switch
  microphone, 103
Battery power
  for capacitor microphones, 72–74
Bessel functions
  and speaker directional characteristics, 168
B-format outputs, Soundfield microphone, 144–145, 148
Bias
  AC, 344–350
  active, 441
  DC, 343, 348
  and distortion, 345
  and erase frequencies, 353, 354
  and gap scatter, 374
  level and gap length, 360
  optimum setting, 347–348
  and recorded performance
    specifications, 345–347
  and sensitivity, 345
Bidirectional
  microphone, 80–83, 84
    characteristics of, 101–102
    polar equation, 82–83
    polar pattern, 83, 84

operation of tape transport, 384–385, 386
Bilinear characteristic,
  compressor, 305
  of Dolby Noise Reduction System, 454
Binary groups, use of (SMPTE)
  longitudinal code, 523–524
  vertical interval code, 528–529
Binaural
  defined, 133
  microphone system, 133–135, 136
Binder, magnetic tape, 333
Bi-Phase mark (SMPTE)
  longitudinal track, 524
BiRadial horn, 189
Blend control, 485–486
Blumlein microphone pair, 132
"Boing box," 228
Bounce mode. *See* Dump mode.
Bouncing tracks, 421–422
Boundary layer
  defined, 149
  microphone, 149–155
  recording theory, 145–149
Braking system
  tape transport reel, 392
"Breathing," compressor, 306–307
Broadcast
  compression, 327–328
  mode in console I/O module, 496–497
Burwen
  Dynamic Noise Filter, 429–430
  Noise Eliminator System, 451
Bus
  defined, 463
  mixdown/monitor, 491
  output master on I/O module, 487
  selector matrix on I/O module, 487, 488
  /tape select on I/O module, 491
  track-summing, 487, 488

C

Calibration
  playback, procedure, 375
  record, procedure, 375–376
  tape, 371–375
    elevated level, 376–378
    frequency response section, 374–375
    reference fluxivity section, 372
  tape recorder, 370–375
  See also Alignment
Capacitor
  loudspeaker, 160–161

Boldface page numbers indicate a chapter devoted to the topic.

microphone, 64–67
  battery power for, 72–74
  electret, 66–67, 69
  power supply for, 67–74
Capstan
  described, 380
  drive systems, 382–385
  idler. *See* Pressure roller
Cardioid microphone
  characteristics of, 100
  described, 84
  polar equation, 84
  polar pattern from two microphones,
      137–140, 141–143
  See also Unidirectional microphone
Cartesian coordinate system, 110–112
CCIR equalization, 369
Cellulose acetate tape base, 333
Center
  blend microphone, 133
  frequency
    filter, defined, 248
    graphic equalizer, 290, 292–293
  image by panning, 239
Channel
  fader, 481–482
  /monitor select, 489
  on/off switch I/O module, 474, 482
  path
    controls in, 478–482
    described, 218, 473
    feeds in I/O module, 482–483
Chase mode
  on tape transport system, 409
Chorus effect, 238–239
Cleaning procedures
  tape transport, 410
Closed loop tape drive system, 389, 390
Closed-back speaker cabinet, 175–177
Close-field monitoring, 244–245
Coating, magnetic tape, 333–334,
      336–337
Coercivity defined, 339
Coherence
  described, 13
  /phase check on console, 509
Coincident pair. *See* X-Y microphone pair
Color (SMPTE)
  frame flag
    longitudinal track, 524
    vertical interval, 530
  time, 530
Coloration, off-axis, 103
Comb filter effects
  of flanging, 236–237

at listening position, 244
Common logarithms, 2
Communication module
  in inline console, 502–506
Compander described, 427–428
Companding
  linear and nonlinear, 454
  systems, gain errors in, 454–456
Complementary signal processing, 426,
      427–428
Compression
  broadcast, 327–328
  chamber, 179
  combined with limiting and expansion,
      316
  delay-line, 325
  drivers, 179–180
  frequency-dependent, 326–329
  and loudness perception, 325–326
  low-frequency, 328–329
  and noise reduction, 425
  program, 324–326
  ratio
    dbx, Dolby, Telcom, compared, 452
    defined, 303
    of limiter, 310
  voice-over, 326
Compressor defined, 303
Condensations, 17–18
Condenser microphone, 65
  See also Capacitor microphone
Conical horn, 185–186
Consoles, recording, **461–519**
  design styles, 464–465
  inline, 467–468, 471–473
  rotary knob, 465, 466
  split-section, 465, 467, 468–470
Consonance, 41
Contours, horn, 182–183
Control systems, tape transport,
      392–399
Cosh. *See* Hyperbolic cosine
Cosine
  function, 6, 7, 8
    in loudspeaker theory, 163
    in microphone polar equation, 75
    in pan pot design, 484–485
    and stereo microphone theory, 113
  hyperbolic, horn, 185
  microphone defined, 83
Coverage angle, loudspeaker, 164–165
Crossover
  frequency, of loudspeaker network,
      195–196
  networks, loudspeaker, 192–198

Boldface page numbers indicate a chapter devoted to the topic.

Cue
path controls on I/O module, 490
send level, master, 503
system
echo return to, in inline console, 502
master, send section in inline console, 502–503
wheel on tape transport system, 395, 417
Cutoff frequency
filter
calculation of, 250
defined, 249
horn, 182
loudspeaker, 162
network, 195–196
Cyclic redundancy check code (SMPTE), 530

D

Damping, filter, 286–287
dbx noise reduction systems, 446–451
Decay
defined, 216
Decibel
defined, 4
notation, 3
dBm, 5
dBu, 4
dBV, 4
on polar pattern, 106–108
sound pressure level in, 27
Decoding
noise reduction, defined, 433
Deemphasis. *See* Postemphasis
De-Esser, use of, 327
Delay
chorus and doubling effects, 238–239
defined, 216
echo-related, applications, 225
and equalization, 218
and flanging, 236–239
of microphone output, 235–236
and phasing, 238
and reverberation, with time delay system, 225
and reverberation systems, **205–246**
and sound reinforcement, 241–242
systems, 221–223
digital, 222–223
magnetic, 221–222
use of tape recorder as, 221

Delay-line compression, 325
Demagnetization of tape head, 410
Difference pattern, 113
Differentiating head, 360
Diffraction, 29–31
horn, 189–191
Diffuse field response, microphone, 88–89
Digital
delay systems, 222–223
equalizer, 290–291, 293, 294–296
Dimensions, physical, of magnetic tape, 336–337
Dipole
defined, 171
effect, 172
Direct
box, 153–154
output
console, 487
select, on I/O module, 474, 489
path in a room 210, 211, 212, 213, 214
sound defined, 215
radiator, 170–171
enclosures, 171–178
-to-reflected
energy ratio in the sound field, 207–208
sound as a distance cue, 55
Directional characteristics
loudspeaker, 168–170
microphone, 74–88
Directivity
factor
loudspeaker (Q), 163–164
microphone (DRF), 92–93
index (DI)
loudspeaker, 162–163
loudspeaker, 162–165
Dissonance, 41
Distance
cues, 54–55
factor (DSF), microphone, 92, 93
Distortion
and bias, 345
harmonic, 51–52
high-level, vs. noise floor, 424
Dolby
A-type noise reduction system, 434–438, 439
B-type noise reduction system, 437, 440
C-type Noise Reduction System, 442–443
HX Pro System, 441–442
HX System, 438, 440–441
noise (*SR* System identification signal), 446

Spectral Recording (*SR*) process, 443–446
Stereo, 446
Surround, 446
tone (identification signal)
  A-type, 437
  B-type, 437
  C-type, 443
Domain theory, 335
Double-ended noise reduction systems, 433–452
Doublet
  action, 172
    elimination of, 175
  defined, 171
Doubling, 238–239
Driver, loudspeaker, 159
Drop frame (SMPTE)
  compensated mode, 531
  flag
    longitudinal track, 524
    vertical interval, 530
Dropouts, 361–362
Dry
  sound, 233
  and wet recording, 472
Dual-capstan tape drive system, 387–388
"Ducker," 326
Dump mode on I/O module, 493–494
Dynamic
  complementary signal processing, 427–428
  loudspeaker, 159–160
  microphone, 62–64
    moving-coil, 62, 63, 64
    ribbon, 62–64
  Noise Suppressor, Scott, 429
  pressure, 27
  range, **299–329**
    defined, 299–300
  signal processing
    complementary, 427–428
    defined, 426
Dynamics section
  described, 299
  and equalizer sections, sequence of, 479, 481, 482
  in I/O module, 479, 481

E

Early reflections, 216
  with time delay system, 225

Echo
  chamber. *See* Reverberation chamber
  cluster, 215
    defined, 216
  console control of, 233–235
  and control room acoustics, 232–245
  and echoes, defined, 216
  master, module in inline console, 498–502
  path controls on I/O module, 488–489
  return
    controls, use of, 235
    level in inline console, 499
    pan pot, 499
    section in inline console, 498–499, 502
    selector matrix in inline console, 499, 502
    solo in inline console, 502
    to cue in inline console, 502
  send
    controls, use of, 233–235
    section in inline console, master, 498
  slap, with time delay system, 225
  -to-tracks, -to mix/monitor
    in inline console, 499
Edit button, functions of, 395
Editing control on tape transport, 394–395
Effects send. *See* Echo send
Electret capacitor microphone, 66–67, 69
Electrostatic loudspeaker, 160–161
Elevated level
  calibration tape, 376–378
Enclosure, direct radiator, 171–178
Encoding, noise reduction, defined, 433
Energy conversion in a transducer, 158
Epsilon
  natural log base, 2
  use of, in horn design, 182, 184
Equal loudness contours, 52–53
Equalization, **247–297**
  and delay, 218
  and noise reduction, 425
  playback, high-frequency, 366
  record and playback, 365–370
  tape recorder, with first-order filters, 264, 265–267
  while recording, 297
Equalizer
  applications
    signal correction, 296
    signal enhancement, 297
  described, 247

Boldface page numbers indicate a chapter devoted to the topic.

Equalizer—*continued*
  and dynamics sections, sequence of,
      479, 481, 482
  recording studio, phase response,
      278–283
  section in I/O module, 479–480
Equal-tempered scale, 43–45
Erase
  and bias frequencies, 353, 354
  head, 359
  spot, mode on tape transport system,
      398
Erasure
  magnetic tape, 350–354
Error signal, tachometer, 383
Expander, 311–313
  defined, 311
  keyable, 322–324
Expansion
  combined with compression, limiting,
      316
  and noise reduction, 425
  ratio, of expander, 312
Exponential horn, 183–185

F

Fader
  channel, 481–482
  group, 492–493
Far field defined, 33
Figure-8 microphone defined, 83
  See also Bidirectional microphone
Film
  and noise reduction, 446, 447
  matching sound to picture, 127–128
Filter
  defined, 248
  design, 252–254
  first-order, 254–264
    applications, 264–267
  spectral program, 431–432
  static, as noise reduction system,
      428–429
Finishing point
  compressor, defined, 305
First-order filter, 254–264
  applications, 264–267
  defined, 248
Flanging, 236–239
  electronic, 238
  first use of the term, 239
Flaring constant, 181
Flat baffle, 173–175

Fletcher-Munson curves, 52
Flutter, 399
Flux, magnetic
  defined, 338
  density, defined, 338–339
Fluxivity
  reference, on calibration tape, 372, 378
  remanent saturation, 340
Foldback. *See* Cue system
Folded baffle, 175
Forward-biased omnidirectional
      microphone, 95
Fourier series, 47
Free field
  defined, 18
  and inverse-square law, 34
Free space
  defined, 18
  loudspeaker in, 165–166
Frequency
  defined, 10–11
  -dependent compression, 326–329
  fundamental, 40
  linear, graphs of, 14–15
  logarithmic, graphs of, 14–15
  perception, 40
  preferred, 45–47
Frequency response
  as angle-of-arrival cue, 56–57
  section on calibration tape, 374–375
  in sound field, 207, 208–209
  of speaker in
    closed-back cabinet, 175–177
    flat baffle, 173–175
    infinite baffle, 172–173
    open-back cabinet, 175
    vented cabinet 178
Fresnel integrals
  and diffraction effects, 30
Fringing, 374–375
Front-to-total ratio (FTR)
  microphone, 92, 94
Full space, loudspeaker in, 165–166
Function, trigonometric, 5
Fundamental frequency, 40

G

Gain
  before threshold defined, 305
  compressor, calculation of, 317–319
  errors in companding systems, 454–456
  riding, 301–302

Boldface page numbers indicate a chapter devoted to the topic.

electronic, 302
    at head block cover, 396
    to reduce noise, 428
Gap
    dimensions, 356–358
    effective, length, 359–360
    loss, 364
    scatter, 374
gauss, cgs unit, 339
Gobo, 31
Golden section
    room dimension ratio of, 37–38, 40
Graphic equalizer, 289–290, 291, 292–293
    center frequencies, 290, 292–293
Group faders, 492–493
Gyrator filter, 251

H

Haas Effect, 223–225
Half space
    loudspeaker in, 166–167
Harmonic
    distortion, 51–52
    series, 40
    structure, 40–41
Harmonics
    in music and electronics, 47–52
Head
    block, 359
    demagnetization, 410
    design details, 358–359
    differentiating, 360
    erase, 359
    gap dimensions, 356–357
    playback, 360–365
        losses, 361–364
        response of, 364–365
    record, 359–360
        response of, 360
Hearing
    range and threshold of, 26–27
henry, SI unit, 339
hertz defined, 11
High output tapes, 376
Highpass filter, 258–259
    defined, 248
    shelving, 258–259
"Hole in the middle" effect, 133
Horn
    BiRadial, 189, 190
    conical, 185–186
    contours, 182–183

cutoff frequency, 182
diffraction, 189–191
exponential, 183–185
flaring constant, 181
hyperbolic, 185
indirect radiator, 180–191
mouth, 182
multicell, 189, 192
multiflare, 189, 191
parabolic, 186–187
practical designs, 188–191
radial, 188, 190
selection criteria, 187–188
shape constant, 182
HX Pro System, Dolby, 441–442
HX System, Dolby, 438, 440–441
Hyperbolic
    horn, 185
    sine, cosine functions
        use of, in horn design, 182–183
Hypercardioid microphone, 3–38
    characteristics of, 100–101
    polar equation, 97
    polar pattern, 96, 97
Hypotenuse
    defined, 5
    as path length, 210
Hysteresis
    loop, 341, 343
    synchronous motor for capstan, 382–383

I

Ideal sound source
    defined, 18
    and room boundaries, 165–167
Identification signal
    Dolby
        A-type noise reduction system, 437
        B-type noise reduction system, 437
        C-type, 443
        SR, 445–446
    Telcom *c4*, 452
IEC
    /NAB comparisons, 369
    recording characteristic, 368–369
Image
    center, by panning, 239
    localization parameters, 54–59
    stereo, control on I/O module, 483–487
Incidence
    angle of, defined, 28
Incident sound, 28

Boldface page numbers indicate a chapter devoted to the topic.

Indirect radiator, 178–179
  horn, 180–191
Infinite baffle, 172–173
Inline console, 467–468, 471–473
  I/O module. *See* I/O module
  output section, 471
  signal processing requirements, 471
Input/Output module. *See* I/O module
Intensity of sound defined, 25
Interaural defined, 54
Inverse-square law
  defined, 18
  and free field, 34
  as sound field component, 207
I/O module
  inline console, 473–497
  signal flow chart, inline console,
    514–515
Isoloop tape drive system, 389, 390

J

Jog mode
  on tape transport system, 395
Just diatonic scale, 42–43, 44

K

KEPEX, 322
Keyable expander, 322–324

L

LEDE control room design, 244
Les Paul and Mary Ford, 419
Library winding, 398
Limiter, 310–311
  defined, 310
Limiting
  combined with compression, expansion,
    316
Line
  in/line out monitor select, 508
  input, 477, 478
  level defined, 472
Linear phase loudspeakers, 201–202
Localization
  distance, and echo and reverberation,
    218–219

image, parameters, 54–59
  by panning, 239–241, 484–485
Locate function, 407
Logarithms, 1–2
  applications of, 2–5
    in compressor gain calculation,
      317–318
    in crossover network design, 195
    in decibel notation, 3–5
    in directivity index, 162–163
    in loudspeaker system design, 162–163
    in pan pot design, 484
  common, 2
  natural, 2
Longitudinal
  code format, SMPTE, 522
  recorder input waveform characteristics,
    522
Loudness
  control, 54
  as distance cue, 55
  perception of, and compression,
    325–326
  relative, as angle-of-arrival cue, 56
Loudspeaker
  baffles, 172–178
  capacitor, 160–161
  crossover networks, 192–198
  directional characteristics, 168–170
  dynamic, 159–160
  electrostatic, 160–161
  moving-coil, 159
  parameters, 161–165
  ribbon, 159
  See also Monitor Systems
Low-frequency compression, 328–329
Lowpass filter, 254–258
  circuit analysis, 256–258
  defined, 248
  shelving, 255–256
Low-print tapes, 355, 357

M

MAF, 52–53
Magnetic tape
  noise characteristics of, 423–425
  and tape heads, **331–378**
Magnetization
  vs. recording field, 340–343
  remanent tape, defined, 338
Major
  scale, 41

Boldface page numbers indicate a chapter devoted to the topic.

triad, 41
Marconi-Stille tape recorder, 331
Masking, noise, 424–425
Master
    echo module in inline console, 498–502
    module section in inline console,
        497–502
        signal flow chart, 516–517
Matrix
    bus selector, on I/O module, 487, 488
    echo return selector, in inline console,
        499, 502
    monitor selector, in inline console, 506
    system for *M-S* microphone, 117–119
Maximum output level (MOL), 346
maxwell, cgs unit, 338
Memory registers on tape recorder,
        407–408
M-H curve, 341–342
Mic/line selector, console, 478
Microphone input, console, 473, 477–478
Microphones, **61–108**
    back-electret, 66
    bidirectional, 80–83, 84
    binaural, 133–135, 136
    capacitor, 64–67
    cardioid, 84, 100
    center blend, use of, 133
    coincident pair. *See X-Y* pair
    combined outputs of, 109–110,
        112–113
    condenser, 65
    directional characteristics, 74–88
    dynamic, 62–64
    electret, 66–67, 69
    hypercardioid, 3–38
    M-S, 115–130
    multipattern, 140–141
    omnidirectional, 78–80
    polar equation, 74–76
    polar pattern, 76–78
    pressure, 78
    Pressure Zone, 152–153
    pressure-gradient operation, 80, 82,
        102, 104
    PZM, 152–153
    response parameters, 88–94
    ribbon, 62–64, 65
    Soundfield, 143–145, 147, 148
    special purpose, **109–156**
    stereo, theory, 113–137
    subcardioid, 94–95, 96
    supercardioid, 95–97
    unidirectional, 83–87
    X-Y pair, 131–132

Middle-Side microphone. *See M-S*
        microphone
"Mike mouse," 153
Minimum audible field, 52–53
Mixdown
    level on inline console, 509
    /monitor buses, 491
    monitoring of, on inline console, 506,
        508
    select on I/O module, 491–492
Mixer, 465
Modal frequency, 36, 38–39
Modulation
    lead power supply, 71
    noise, 346–347
MOL, 346
Monitor
    /channel select
        in cue path, I/O module, 490
        in echo/aux path, I/O module, 489
    level control
        on I/O module, 491
        on inline console, 509
    /mixdown buses, 491
    mode
        with noise reduction system, 402–404,
            457
        of tape recorder, 401–404
    module
        master in inline console, 506–511
    mono mode, on inline console, 508–509
    override modes
        on inline console, 509–511
    pan pot, on I/O module, 492
    path
        controls on I/O module, 490–492
        defined, 473
    select on I/O module, 491
    selector matrix in inline console, 506
    systems, **157–204**
Monitoring, close-field, 244–245
Mono
    mode monitoring on inline console,
        508–509
    pickup angle
        defined, 123
        matched to stereo pickup angle,
            128–129
        of *M-S* microphone, 123–124, 125
Mono-Stereo microphone. *See M-S*
        microphone
Mouth
    of horn, 182
Moving-coil
    loudspeaker, 159

Boldface page numbers indicate a chapter devoted to the topic.

Moving-coil—*continued*
microphone, 62, 63, 64
M-S microphone, 115–130
matrix system for, 117–119
using console faders, 117, 118
mono pickup angle, 123–124, 125,
128–129
sample problems, 121–123
stereo pickup angle, 124–127
summary, 129–130
Mult on console patch bay, 512
Multicell horn, 189, 192
Multiflare horn, 189, 191
Multimicrophone system
for stereo recording, 135–137
Multipattern microphone, 140–141
Multiplex phantom power, 71
"Multitrack mono," 135
Music, electronics, and psychoacoustics,
39–59
Mute
switch (channel on/off), console, 482
used to reduce noise, 428
system on tape transport system, 396

N

NAB
/IEC comparisons, 369
standard reproducing characteristic,
366–368
Natural logarithms, 2
Near field described, 34–35
Near-coincident microphone pair, 133
Node, pressure, 34, 36
Noise
characteristics of magnetic tape,
423–425
filter, 428–429
Burwen Dynamic, 429–431
gate, 313–316
defined, 314
as noise reduction system, 428
level, and number of tape tracks, 424
low-level tape, 423–424
masking, 424–425
modulation and bias, 346–347
reduction, **423–460**
suppressor, dynamic, 429
Noise reduction systems
basic, 425–428
Burwen
Dynamic Noise Filter, 429–430

Noise Eliminator, 451
comparisons, 452, 454–457
compatibility, 457
cross-reference guide, 459–460
dbx, 446–451
Types *I* and *II*, 448–451
Dolby, 434–446, 447
A-type, 434–438, 439
B-type, 437, 440
C-Type, 442–443
on film and videotape, 446, 447
HX, 438, 440–441
HX Pro, 441–442
Spectral Recording, 443–446
double-ended, 433–452
Dynamic Noise Suppressor, Scott, 429
film, 446, 447
multitrack, 457–458
noise gate, 428
NoisEx Recording System, 434
single-ended, 428–433
static filtering in, 428–429
and tape recorder interface, 402–404,
457
Telcom *c4*, 451–452, 453–454
tick and pop removers, 432–433
Ultra Stereo System, 446
NoisEx Recording System, 434
Nondrop Frame (SMPTE), 531
Nonsymmetric filter, 268
Normal
frequency, 34
mode, 34
frequencies, computing, 36
NOS microphone pair, 133
Notch filter, 261, 262

O

Oblique mode, 36, 38–39
Octave
defined, 41
one-half and one-third, 45
oersted, cgs unit, 338
Off-axis coloration
microphone, 103
Omnidirectional microphone, 78–80
characteristics of, 99
forward-biased, 95
polar equation, 78
polar pattern, 78, 80
One-eighth space, loudspeaker in, 166–167

Boldface page numbers indicate a chapter devoted to the topic.

One-quarter space, loudspeaker in, 166–167
Open-back baffle, 175
Operating level defined, 340
Operating modes, console, 463–464
Opposite side in right triangle, 5
Orientation angle
  of sum and difference patterns, 119–120
Original source defined, 54
ORTF microphone pair, 133, 134
Output level of compressor, calculation of, 317–319
Overdubbing, original method of, 418–419

P

Packing density
  of magnetic particles, 334
Pain
  threshold of, 27
Pan pot
  and cue buses, 490
  echo return, in inline console, 499
  I/O module, 484–486
  monitor, on I/O module, 492
Panning and localization, 239–241, 484–485
Parabolic horn, 186–187
Paragraphic equalizer, 290, 292
Parallel filter
  bandpass, 275, 277
  bandstop, 276, 279
Parametric equalizer, 289, 290
Pass band
  filter, defined, 248
Passive
  equalizer defined, 247
  filter, 269
  network in loudspeaker crossover, 192–195
Patch bay and patch points, console, 511–513
Period defined, 11
Permeability
  defined, 339
  relative, defined, 339–340
Pfleumer, Fritz, 331
Phantom power
  multiplex, 71
  supply, 70–72
Phase
  adjustment and calibration tape, 372–374

angle, and tape heads, 372–374
cancellations, 13
/coherence check on inline console, 509
defined, 11
plug in compression chamber, 179–180
response
  bandpass filter, 276–277, 280
  bandstop filter, 277–278, 281
  recording-studio equalizer, 278–283
reversal switch, console, 474, 478–479
shift
  as angle-of-arrival cue, 59
  defined, 12
  filter, perception of, 283–286
  in loudspeaker crossover network, 196–197
  in second-order filter, 276–283
Phasing, 238
Phon, 53
Photoelectric cell as tape sensor, 391
Pinch roller
  described, 380
Pink noise
  defined, 506
Piston band, loudspeaker, 173
Plane wave, 20–23
Plate reverberation system, 228, 230
Playback head losses, 361–364
Point source defined, 18
Polar coordinate system, 110
Polar equation, microphone, 74–76
  bidirectional, 82–83
  cardioid, 84
  hypercardioid, 97
  omnidirectional, 78
  subcardioid, 95
  of sum or difference pattern, 121
  supercardioid, 95
  unidirectional, 84
Polar pattern, microphone, 76–78
  bidirectional, 83, 84
  cardioid, 84–85
  from combining microphones, 109–110, 112–113
    in *M-S* configuration, 117, 119–123
  using decibel notation, 106–108
  hypercardioid, 96, 97
  and microphone selection, 98–102
  omnidirectional, 78–80
  response comparisons, microphone, 87–88, 97–102
  review of, 97–98
  subcardioid, 95, 96
  sum and difference patterns, 115–123
  supercardioid, 96, 97

Boldface page numbers indicate a chapter devoted to the topic.

Polar pattern, microphone—*continued*
three-dimensional, 88, 89
tradeoff considerations, 104–106
unidirectional, 84–85
See also Cartesian coordinate system
Polarity
absolute, loudspeaker system, 202–203
described, 13
reversal
in *M-S* matrix, 117–118
via patch points, 512
switch, console, 474, 477, 478–479
speaker terminal, 198
Polyester tape base, 333
Postecho in print-through, 354
Postemphasis
equalization, 296
network, playback, 360
in noise reduction system, 425, 426
Post-roll defined, 408
Poulsen, Valdemar, 331
Power
sound, defined, 25
supply
for capacitor microphone, 67–74
phantom, 70–72
Predelay in compressor, 325
Preecho in print-through, 354
Preemphasis
equalization, 296
network, record, 360
in noise reduction system, 425, 426
Prefader listen
control, on inline console master
module, 509–510
on I/O module, 496
Pre/post selector, I/O module
in cue path, 490
in echo/aux path, 489
Pre-roll defined, 408
Pressure
antinode, 34, 36
dynamic, 27
gradient microphone, 80, 82, 83, 102,
104
microphone, 78
node, 34, 36
roller described, 380
rollerless tape drive system,
388, 389
sound, 26–28
static, 27
wave, sound, 16–18
zone. *See* Boundary layer microphone,
152–153

Preview mode on tape transport system,
409
Print-through, 354–355
low-print tapes, 355, 357
reduction, 355
Program compression, 324–326
Proximity effect, microphone, 102–103,
104
Psychoacoustics, 52–59
music, electronics, and, **39–59**
Pumping
compressor, 306–307
and low-frequency compression, 328
Punch-in/out
described, 408
data entry, 409
PVC tape base, 333
PZM, 152–153

Q

Q
effect of, on output response, 268
equalizer, defined, 249
filter, actual and apparent, 271–272
loudspeaker directivity factor, 163–164
Quality factor (*Q*), equalizer, defined, 249

R

Radial horn, 188, 190
Radian measure, 22
Radiator
direct, 170–171
indirect, 178–179
RAM, use of in digital delay system, 223
Random-energy
efficiency
and loudspeaker Q, 164
of microphone (REE), 91–92
response (RER), 90–91
Rarefactions, 17–18
Ready/Safe mode, tape recorder, 400–401
Real time (SMPTE), 530
Rear-entry port, microphone, 85–87
Reciprocal filter, 268
Recording
consoles, **461–519**
field
magnetic, defined, 338
vs. magnetization, 340–343

Boldface page numbers indicate a chapter devoted to the topic.

Reel
  braking system, 392
  motors, tape transport, 390–392
Reference fluxivity or level, 340
Reflected paths in a room, 211, 212, 213, 214
Reflection, 28, 31
  early, 216
    with time delay system, 225
Refraction, 28–29, 31
Rehearse mode
  programmed, 408–409
  tape transport system, 408–409
Release time
  compressor, 309
  expander, 313
Remanent
  saturation fluxivity, 340
  tape magnetization defined, 338
Remote control of tape recorder, 400–409
Repeat mode on tape transport system, 409
Repro head, function of, 401
Reproduced source
  defined, 54
Resonance
  frequency
    defined, 272
    loudspeaker, 161–162
  series and parallel, 272–275
Retentivity defined, 339
Reverberant field defined, 34
Reverberation
  chamber, acoustic, 226–228
  console control of, 233–235
  control room acoustics and, 242–245
  defined, 216
  delay, with time delay system, 225
  plate, 228, 230
  recording and mixdown with, 233
  stereo, 231–233
  systems, 228–231
    digital, 230–231
    gold foil, 230
    spring, 228, 229
    steel plate, 228, 230
  time defined, 216–217
Reverse play/record modes
  on tape transport system, 396, 398
Review mode on tape transport system, 409
Ribbon
  loudspeaker, 159
  microphone, 62–64, 65
Right triangle

and path length, 210
and plane wave, 21
and trigonometric functions, 6
Room
  boundaries
    and ideal sound source, 165–167
    and practical loudspeaker system, 167–170
  modes, 36–40
Rotary knob
  console, 465, 466
  equalizer, 287, 289
Rotation point
  compressor, 303, 304
  defined, 303
  expander, 312

S

Safe mode on tape recorder, 400–401
Saturation
  magnetic tape, 335, 337
  recording (digital), 337
  remanent, fluxivity, 340
Scale
  equal-tempered, 43–45
  just diatonic, 42–43, 44
  major, 41
Scrape flutter defined, 399
Sealed enclosure. *See* Closed-back enclosure
Second-order filter, 267–268
  amplitude response, 267–268
  defined, 248
  phase shift in, 276–283
Sel-Sync, introduction of, 419
Semitone interval, 43
Send level and on/off switch, I/O module
  in cue path, 490
  in echo/aux path, 489
Sensing systems, tape, 389, 391
Sensitivity
  and bias, 345
  microphone, 75–76
  of sum or difference pattern, 121
Series filter
  bandpass, 275, 276
  bandstop, 275, 278
Servo control drive systems, 383–385
Shape constant, 182
Shelving filter
  boost/cut, 261, 263–264

Boldface page numbers indicate a chapter devoted to the topic.

Shelving filter—*continued*
   defined, 248
   highpass, 258–259
   lowpass, 255–256
Shuttle mode
   on tape transport system, 395
Side chain
   in Dolby noise reduction system,
      435–436
   signal processing, 319–324
      compressor, 319–320
      for compressor/expander gain
         control, 321–322
      expander, 320–321
Signal
   generator in inline console, 504, 506
   processing
      complementary, 426–428
      dynamic and static, 426
      dynamic complementary, 427–428
      single-ended, 426
   -to-noise ratio defined, 300
Sine
   function, 6, 7, 8
      in pan pot design, 484, 485
      and stereo microphone theory, 113
   hyperbolic, horn, 185
   wave application, 8
Single-ended signal processing, 426
Sinh. *See* Hyperbolic sine
Sinusoidal waveforms, 7
Slap echo with time delay system, 225
Slating, 504
Slitting, tape, 334
Slope, filter, defined, 249–250
Slurry described, 333
Smith, Oberlin, 331
SMPTE Time Code, **521–531**
Soft key
   example of, 393–394
   tape recorder alignment using, 414,
      416–418
Solo
   echo return, in inline console, 499
   mode
      on I/O module, 494–496
      on master module, 509
Sound
   field 33–35
      components of, 207–210
      defined, 33, 206
      echo in, 220–225
      reverberation in, 225–233
      signal paths in, 206–207, 211–213, 214
      in typical room, 210–214

intensity defined, 25
   level in the sound field, 207, 208
   power defined, 25
   pressure, 26, 27
      level in dB, 27
      wave, 16–18
   reinforcement, use of delay line in,
      241–242
   source, ideal, defined, 18
   speed and velocity of, 22
Soundfield microphone, 143–145, 147, 148
   A-format outputs, 144, 148
   B-format outputs, 144–145, 148
Spaced microphone pair, 133, 134
Spacing loss, 361–362
Speaker
   muting on inline console, 509
   selectors on inline console, 508
   See also Loudspeakers, Monitor systems
Spectral
   program filter, 431–432
   Recording, Dolby, 443–444, 446
Speed
   defined, 22
   of sound, 22
      and time delay, 57–58
      and velocity, 23–25
Spherical wave, description of, 19–20
Split-section console, 465, 467, 468–470
Spot erase mode on tape transport system,
   398
Spring reverberation system, 228, 229
Square wave analysis, 47–51
Squawker, 192
SR (Spectral Recording) Process, Dolby,
   443–446
Staggered action
   in Dolby *C*-type Noise Reduction System,
      443
   in Dolby *SR* Spectral Recording System,
      444
Standing waves, 35–36
Static
   pressure, 27
   signal processing defined, 426
Status light, tape recorder mode, 401
Steradian measure, 22
   and sound source radiation, 165–167
Stereo
   image control on I/O module, 483–487
   microphone system
      A-B pair, 133, 134
      Blumlein pair, 132
      cable requirements, 137
      coincident pair. *See X-Y* pair

Boldface page numbers indicate a chapter devoted to the topic.

multimicrophone, 135–137
near-coincident pair, 133
M-S. See M-S microphone
NOS, 133
ORTF, 133, 134
spaced pair, 133, 134
stereosonic, 132
X-Y pair, 131–132
microphone theory, 113–137
pickup angle, 124–129
matched to mono pickup angle,
128–129
of *M-S* microphone, 124–129
reverberation, 231–233
transaural, 135
width control on I/O module,
485–487
Stereosonic microphone pair, 132
Stop band, filter, defined, 248
Studio monitor on/off
on inline console, 508
Subcardioid microphone, 94–95, 96
characteristics of, 100
polar equation, 95
polar pattern, 95, 96
Sum
-and-difference patterns
conversion to *M-S* patterns, 122–123
pattern, 113
Supercardioid microphone, 95–97
characteristics of, 100
polar equation, 95
polar pattern, 96, 97
Swap mode on I/O module, 493–494, 495
Sync head, function of, 401
Synchronous
recording, 419–421
speed of capstan motor, 383
System gain
compressor, 305–307

T

T-system power supply, 71
Tachometer on capstan motor, 383–384,
386
Talkback
monitor override on master module,
510–511
and slating level, 504
system in inline console, 504
Tangent function, 6, 7, 8
Tangential mode, 36, 38–39

Tape
/bus select on I/O module, 491
drive system, 380–382
alternate, 385–389
closed loop, 389, 390
dual-capstan, 387–388
Isoloop, 389, 390
pressure rollerless capstan, 388, 389
servo-controlled, 383–385
vacuum bin, 386, 387
editing control, 394–395
head adjustments, 410–412, 413
azimuth alignment, 411
zenith and other adjustments,
411–412, 413
heads and magnetic tape, **331–378**
input, console, 477, 478
lift systems, 396
search functions, 407–408
sensing system on transport, 389, 391
speed
and capstan diameter, 383
of representative tape recorders, 385
varying, 383–384
thickness loss, 362–363
transport control systems, 392–399
transport systems, **379–422**
subsystems, 379
Telcom *c4* noise reduction system,
451–452, 453–454
Telegraphone briefly described, 331
tesla, SI unit, 339
Thickness loss, 362–363
Threshold
compression
defined, 304
gain before, 305
expander, 313
of hearing, 26
of pain, 27
Tick and pop removers, 432–433
Tie lines, use of, 512
Time
alignment in loudspeaker system, 201
Code, SMPTE, **521–531**
constant, 264, 266–267
delay
as distance cue, 55
and Haas effect, 223–224
and monitor systems, 198–201
in sound field, 207
and speed of sound, 57–58
discrepancies (SMPTE), 530–531
reading functions, tape recorder,
404–406

Boldface page numbers indicate a chapter devoted to the topic.

Time of arrival difference
  as angle-of-arrival cue, 57–58
Tracking, artificial double, 239
Track-summing buses, 487, 488
Transaural stereo, 135
Transducer
  defined, 61
  energy conversion in a, 158
Transfer characteristic
  compressor, 303
  expander, 312
  introduced, 301
  magnetic tape 341, 346
  unity gain, 302
Transformer in direct box, 153–154
Transition frequency
  loudspeaker system, 174
  microphone response, 82
Transport system, basic controls, 393, 394
Triad, major, 41
Triangle, right
  described, 5
  similar, 210
Trigonometric functions, 5
  graph of, 7, 8
Tuning fork, effect on air particles, 16–17
Tweeter, 192

U

Unidirectional microphone
  index (UDI), 92, 93–94
  polar equation, 84
  polar pattern, 84–85
  single element, 85–87
  two
    back-to-back, 139–140
    at less than 180 degrees, 141–143

V

Vacuum bin transport system, 386, 387
Velocity
  defined, 22

and speed, 22–24
Vented cabinet
  loudspeaker, 178
Vertical interval code format (SMPTE),
    525–528
Visual cues, 207, 209–210
Voice-over compression, 326
Von-Braunmühl-Weber AC-bias theory, 344

W

Wave
  motion, 17–18
  plane, 20–23
  spherical, 18
Waveform
  acoustic, 14–18
  periodic, construction of, 47
  sinusoidal, 7
Wavelength
  defined, 24
  in air, 24–25
  on magnetic tape, 25
weber, SI unit, 339
Wet
  and dry recording, 472
  sound, 233
White noise defined, 506
Width
  enhancement control, 487
  stereo, control, 485–487
Woofer, 192
Wow, 399

X

X-Y microphone pair, 131–132

Z

Zenith adjustment, 411–412, 413

Boldface page numbers indicate a chapter devoted to the topic.

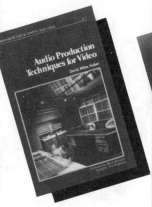
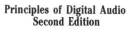

How to Build Speaker Enclosures
Badmaieff and Davis

A practical guide to the whys and hows of constructing high quality, top performance speaker enclosures. A wooden box alone is not a speaker enclosure—size, baffling, sound insulation, speaker characteristics, and crossover points must all be carefully considered.

The book contains many detailed drawings and instructions for building the various basic types of enclosures, including the infinite-baffle, the bass-reflex, and the horn-projector types, as well as different combinations of these. This practical book covers both the advantages and disadvantages of each enclosure type and includes a discussion of speaker drivers, crossover networks, and hints on the techniques of construction and testing.

Topics covered include:

- Speaker Enclosures
- Drivers for Enclosures
- Infinite Baffles
- Bass-Reflex or Phase-Inversion Enclosures
- Horn Enclosures
- Combination Enclosures
- Crossover Networks
- Construction and Testing Techniques

144 Pages, 5½ x 8½, Softbound
ISBN: 0-672-20520-3
No. 20520, $6.95

Introduction to Professional Recording Techniques
Bruce Bartlett,
The John Woram Audio Series

This all-inclusive introduction to the equipment and techniques for state-of-the-art recording—whether in residences or professional studios or on location—offers a wealth of valuable information on topics not found in other books on audio recording.

Geared primarily for the audio hobbyist or aspiring professional, this book delivers a comprehensive discussion of recording engineering and production techniques, including special coverage of microphones and microphone techniques, sampling, sequencing, and MIDI. It provides up-to-date coverage of monitoring, special effects, hum prevention, and spoken-word recording, as well as special sections on recognizing good sound and troubleshooting bad sound.

Topics covered include:

- The Recording and Reproduction Chain
- Simple Home Recording
- Setting Up the Studio
- Microphones and Microphone Techniques
- Control-Room Techniques
- On-Location Recording
- Judging the Recording
- Appendices: dB or not dB, Introduction to SMPTE Time Code, and Further Education

416 Pages, 7½ x 9¾, Softbound
ISBN: 0-672-22574-3
No. 22574, $24.95

John D. Lenk's Troubleshooting & Repair of Audio Equipment
John D. Lenk

This manual provides the most up-to-date data available and a simplified approach to practical troubleshooting and repair of major audio devices. It will enable both the beginning and the intermediate level technician or hobbyist to apply tips and tricks to any specific equipment.

This book also includes such time-saving hints as circuit-by-circuit troubleshooting based on failure or trouble symptoms, universal step-by-step procedures, and actual procedures recommended by manufacturers' service personnel.

Topics covered include:

- Introduction to Modern Audio Equipment Troubleshooting
- Troubleshooting and Repair of Amplifiers and Loudspeakers
- Troubleshooting and Repair of Linear-Tracking Turntables
- Troubleshooting and Repair of Audio Cassette Decks
- Troubleshooting and Repair of AM/FM Stereo Tuners
- Troubleshooting and Repair of CD Players

208 Pages, 8½ x 11, Softbound
ISBN: 0-672-22517-4
No. 22517, $21.95

Recording Demo Tapes at Home
Bruce Bartlett

This easy-to-follow guide details how to create a professional-quality demo tape without the expense of a recording studio. It describes what equipment is needed, how it works, and how to use it, then explains how to use the newly created tapes to get engagements and recording contracts. Clearly organized and thorough, its extensive coverage includes judging sound quality, troubleshooting bad sound, promoting the demo tape, on-location recording, and sampling/sequencing/MIDI.

Topics covered include:

- The Recording and Reproduction Chain
- Equipping Your Home Recording System
- Setting Up the System
- Recording a Soloist or Small Acoustic Group
- Recorder/Mixer Features
- Signal Processors
- Microphone Techniques
- Tape Recording
- Session Procedures
- On-Location Recording of Popular Music
- Judging Sound Quality
- Sampling, Sequencing, and MIDI
- Uses for Your Demo Tape
- Appendices: Training Your Hearing, Basics of Sound, Reference Sources

256 Pages, 7½ x 9¾, Softbound
ISBN: 0-672-22644-8
No. 22644, $19.95

Visit your local book retailer or call
800-428-SAMS.